MW01104265

# The Urban Climatic Map

Rapid urbanization and increasingly compact cities with a higher population density have brought about a new science of urban climatology. Understanding the mapping for this phenomenon is crucial for city planners. This book brings together experts in the field of urban climatic mapping to provide state-of-the-art understanding on how urban climatic knowledge can be made available and utilized by city planners. It contains information on the technology, methodology and a range of different approaches to urban climatic map-making and illustrates this with examples and case studies from around the world.

The book attempts to bridge the gap between the science of urban climatology and the practice of urban planning by explaining how urban climatic information can be analysed, interpreted and applied in urban planning. It provides a useful one-stop reference for postgraduates, academics and urban climatologists wishing to better understand the need for urban climatic knowledge in city planning. Urban planners and policymakers will also find the book indispensable for applying this knowledge to design future sustainable cities and quality urban spaces.

**Edward Ng** is an architect and Yao Ling Sun Professor of Architecture in the School of Architecture at the Chinese University of Hong Kong (CUHK). He specializes in Green Building, Environmental and Sustainable Design, and Urban Climatology for City Planning. Professor Ng is also Director of the MSc Sustainable and Environmental Design Programme. As an environmental consultant to the government of Hong Kong Special Administrative Region, Professor Ng developed the 'Performance-based Daylight Design Practice Note', the 'Air Ventilation Assessment Technical Guidelines' and the urban climatic maps for Hong Kong city planning. He is now working with governments and agencies in Singapore and Macau, as well as a number of Chinese cities, on urban climatic maps. Professor Ng has published over 400 papers and three books. He has twice received the International Award from the Royal Institute of British Architects (RIBA).

**Chao Ren** is an Assistant Professor in the School of Architecture, the Chinese University of Hong Kong (CUHK). Her research interests are sustainable urban and environmental design and urban climatic application in urban planning. She has been involved in several government research projects, such as (in Hong Kong) the 'Urban Climatic Map and Standards for Wind Environment – Feasibility Study', 'Eco-Planning for Kaohsiung, Taiwan by Using Urban Climatic Map', 'Macau Urban Climatic Map Study', 'Arnhem Urban Climatic Map' and 'The Study of Plan and Management of Wuhan Urban Air Path'. She is the Deputy Director of the MSc Sustainable and Environmental Design Programme, and a research fellow of the Institute of Future Cities (IOFC) and the Institute of Energy, Environment and Sustainability (IEES) at CUHK. She is a registered BEAM professional and has recently joined the working group of the BEAM Society.

# The Urban Climatic Map

## A Methodology for Sustainable Urban Planning

Edited by Edward Ng and Chao Ren

LONDON AND NEW YORK

First published 2015
by Routledge
2 Park Square, Milton Park, Abingdon, Oxon OX14 4RN

and by Routledge
711 Third Avenue, New York, NY 10017

Routledge is an imprint of the Taylor & Francis Group, an informa business



*British Library Cataloguing-in-Publication Data*
A catalogue record for this book is available from the British Library

*Library of Congress Cataloging in Publication Data*
The urban climatic map : a methodology for sustainable urban planning / edited by Edward Ng and Chao Ren.
pages cm
Includes bibliographical references and index.
ISBN 978-1-84971-376-4 (hardback : alk. paper) -- ISBN 978-1-315-71761-6 (ebook : alk. paper) 1. Sustainable urban development. 2. City planning--Climatic factors. 3. City planning--Environmental aspects. I. Ng, Edward. II. Ren, Chao.
HT166.U71256 2015
307.1'16--dc23
2014038307

ISBN: [978-1-84971-376-4] (hbk)
ISBN: [978-1-315-71761-6] (ebk)

Typeset in Bembo by
Servis Filmsetting Ltd, Stockport, Cheshire

Printed and bound in the United States of America by Publishers Graphics, LLC on sustainably sourced paper.

# Contents

# Plates

# Figures

# Tables

# Contributors

## Editors

**Professor Edward Ng** is an architect and Yao Ling Sun Professor of Architecture in the School of Architecture, the Chinese University of Hong Kong (CUHK). His specialty is environmental and sustainable design, and urban climatology for city planning. At CUHK, he is the Programme Director of the MSc in Environment and Sustainable Design; he is an Associate Director of the Institute of Future Cities and the team leader of Urban Sustainability and Public Health at the Institute of Energy, Environment and Sustainability. As an environmental consultant to the Hong Kong SAR Government, Professor Ng developed the performance-based daylight design building codes, the Air Ventilation Assessment (AVA) Technical Guidelines, and the solar access best practice. He was team leader of the Hong Kong Urban Climatic Map study (2006–2012). As a designer, he has twice been a recipient of the International Awards of the Royal Institute of British Architects (RIBA), in 2006 and 2009; and he has twice been awarded the UNESCO Innovation Awards, in 2009 and 2011.

**Dr Chao Ren** is Assistant Professor in the School of Architecture, The Chinese University of Hong Kong (CUHK). Her research interest is sustainable environmental design and urban climatic application in urban planning. She has been involved in several governmental research projects, such as '(Hong Kong) Urban Climatic Map and Standards for Wind Environment – Feasibility Study', 'Eco-Planning for Kaohsiung, Taiwan by Using Urban Climatic Map', 'Macau Urban Climatic Map Study', 'Arnhem Urban Climatic Map' and 'The Study of Plan and Management of Wuhan Urban Air Path'. She is Deputy Director of the M.Sc. in Sustainable and Environmental Design Programme at CUHK and a registered BEAM Pro.

## Contributors

**Dr Juan A. Acero** is Senior Researcher at Tecnalia R&D (Spain). He is focused on urban climate including atmospheric pollution and thermal comfort, having taken part in a great number of studies in these fields. Starting in 1999 with atmospheric pollution diagnosis, studying the impacts of urban traffic, and modelling pollutant dispersion, he has been working on urban climate and thermal comfort at different spatial scales, analysing the effects of vegetation, urban morphology and typology since 2007. He has worked with both measurement and modelling techniques. In this way he has developed the first Urban Climate Map for planning purposes in Spain.

**Professor Maria João Alcoforado** is Senior Researcher of the Zephyrus Group at the Centre of Geographical Studies (CEG) of the University of Lisbon (ULisboa) and former Full Geography Professor at the Institute of Geography and Spatial Planning (IGOT-ULisboa). Since 2000, she has been the Editor of Finisterra (http://revistas.rcaap.pt/finisterra), the main Geography Journal in Portugal. Her key research areas are Physical Geography, Applied Climatology, Urban Climatology and its application to planning, Bioclimatology, and lately, Historical Climatology. She was team leader of the urban climate map of Lisbon (2004–2006), where she collaborated with the co-authors of this chapter. She was a member of the Expert Team 9 on Urban Climatology and Training, OPAG 3 of the WMO (2002–2006) and she is a member of the jury of the Vautrin Lud Prize (the highest award in geography). She has coordinated numerous research projects, been published in peer-reviewed international journals (http://clima.ul.pt) and supervised numerous students.

**Dr Telma Andrade** was licensed and received her bachelor degree in Physics from the Federal University of Bahia - UFBA (1980), and received her Masters Degree and PhD in Geophysics (UFBA, 1985; USP, 1998). She is a researcher at UFBA and a leader of the research group Laboratory of Environmental Comfort - Lattes / CNPq / UFBA. She has conducted research and activities related to energy, thermal comfort and urban climate. In 2007 she was awarded first place by the Scholarship Program to Support the Development of Technological Initiation (BITEC -IEL/Sebrae and CNPq). From 2007 until now she has held the position of Director of the Department of Science, Technology and Innovation – SECTI.

**Professor Yasunobu Ashie** is the head of the Environmental and Equipment Standards Division at the National Institute for Land and Infrastructure Management, Government of Japan. His specialty is in urban thermal environments and low-carbon buildings. He contributed in technical terms in the decision of the guideline of heat island countermeasures by the Tokyo government in 2007. He was a representative of the earth simulator research project from 2004–2012, and made the Heat Map of Tokyo, and the Heat Map of Hong Kong by means of large-scaled CFD simulations. He was awarded the Commendation for Science and Technology by the Minister of Education, Culture, Sports, Science and Technology, in 2012.

**Mr Richard Bassett** is a Doctoral Researcher in the School of Geography, Earth and Environmental Sciences at the University of Birmingham. Richard's interests are in the formation and characteristics of urban heat islands, particularly during heat waves, and how this knowledge can be combined with social-environmental risks. Current research includes quantifying the influence of wind advection on heat in urban areas through numerical modelling. Richard was awarded the Lord Stafford Award for Environmental Sustainability in 2013 for his work as a knowledge transfer associate on the BUCCANEER partnership between the University and Birmingham City Council.

**Professor Dr Jürgen Baumüller** is a meteorologist and urban climatologist and was the director of the Department of Urban Climatology in the Office of Environmental Protection of the State Capital Stuttgart (1978–2008) in the south of Germany. He was the Chairman of the German Meteorological Society (DMG) expert committee 'Environmental Meteorology' (AKUMET) (1981–1986). Since 1982 he has been a lecturer at the University of Stuttgart, Institute of Landscape Planning and Ecology for the topic 'Urban climate and planning'. As a member in a working group of the Verein Deutscher Ingenieure (VDI, The Association of German Engineers) committee 'Urban climate and air pollution', he took part in the VDI-Standard:

VDI 3787 Part 1 Environmental Meteorology – Climate and Air Pollution Maps for Cities and Regions. Since 1993 he has been an Honorary Professor at the University of Stuttgart at the faculty of architecture. He was the project manager for the urban climate information system of Stuttgart 'Urban Climate 21' (DVD, 2008) and the climate atlas of the Region of Stuttgart (2008).

**Mr René Burghardt** is a landscape planner and landscape ecologist. Since 2009 he has been working at the Department of Environmental Meteorology, which is dedicated to the Institute for Architecture, Urban Planning and Landscape Design at the University of Kassel, Germany. He is also a managing partner of the engineering Office 'Burghardt and Partner', established in 2013. Mr Burghardt is well trained in the use of Geographic Information Systems (GIS). His main objectives at the Department of Environmental Meteorology are the development and elaboration of urban climate analysis and recommendation maps, next to geo-statistical analyses and development of GIS-based solutions. In cooperation with Professor Katzschner, Mr Burghardt holds national and international teaching sessions at the Technical University Munich (TU München) and at the Vietnamese-German-University (VGU) in Ho-Chi-Minh City, Vietnam.

**Dr Xiaoming Cai** is a Senior Lecturer in the School of Geography, Earth and Environmental Science at the University of Birmingham. His research interests are in the areas of meso- and micro-scale numerical modelling, large-eddy simulation (LES) of turbulence in the atmospheric boundary layer and urban street canyons (including the dispersion of air pollutants in urban environments). In particular, he developed a street-canyon LES model capable of coupling turbulence with photochemical reactions. He has supervised the studies of modelling urban heat islands in London and Birmingham using meso-scale models. He also supervised the BUCCANEER project, which has won the Lord Stafford Award for Environmental Sustainability, November 2012. He has published more than 40 refereed journal papers and more than half of these are related to urban environment.

**Ms Sabrina Campe** is a landscape architect and an assistant of Professor Lutz Katzschner at the University of Kassel, Germany, Department of Architecture, Urban Planning and Landscape Design in the subject area Environmental Meteorology. Her main research interests lie in climatic research of inner-city public open space and green infrastructure at the microclimatic level. In various different national and international projects, she worked on sensitive urban open space planning and urban development concerning climate adaption.

**Dr Gina Cavan** is a Lecturer in Geographical Information Science and Climate in the School of Science and the Environment at Manchester Metropolitan University and Honorary Research Fellow in Geography, School of Environment, Education and Development at The University of Manchester. Her research interests include applying Geographical Information Science to assess climate change exposure, risk and vulnerability, in order to aid cities across the UK, Europe and Africa, in adapting to the impacts of climate change. Additionally, she focuses upon spatial characterisation of urban environments and mapping and quantification of urban ecosystem services. Gina has worked with the public and private sectors in a range of initiatives and projects. Her research is strongly applied and therefore bridges the gap between policy and implementation.

**Mr Ezequiel Correia** is a geographer and researcher at the Climate and Environmental Changes Research Group in the Institute of Geography and Spatial Planning, University of Lisbon.

Climate variability, extreme weather events, and its spatial patterns are their main scientific interests. Professionally involved for some years in the development of applications to structure and analyse geographic information, he now belongs to a team that is developing a new generation of UCMaps in a GIS environment.

**Dr Lee Chapman** is a Reader in Climate Resilience in the School of Geography, Earth and Environmental Sciences at the University of Birmingham. His research interests lie at the interface of climatology and civil engineering and focus on the impact of weather and climate on the built environment, capturing a range of topics from the development of climate-response models under the baseline climate to assessing the future impact of climate change on hard infrastructure and urban heat islands and associated impacts. In 2013, he won the RGS Cuthbert Peek Award for advancing urban climatology through the use of GIS and remote sensing. He has over 50 refereed journal articles published or in press in international peer-reviewed journals and has been invited to speak and chair sessions at numerous conferences and events across the world.

**Dr Xiaoyi Fang** obtained her Doctor of Science and graduated from the Department of Atmospheric Sciences, Nanjing University in June 2004. At present, she serves as the Deputy Director of the Beijing Municipal Climate Center, Director of Application Climate Department, and is senior engineer, specialising in urban climate research and applied work. She has presided over and completed more than ten research projects of the China Meteorological Bureau, Ministry of Environmental Protection; published nearly ten papers; and compiled some chapters of three books. She also directed and completed more than ten climatic feasibility projects of urban planning and completed more than ten important reports.

**Mr Wenli Guo** is the Director of the Beijing Municipal Climate Center. He has done profound research in climate resources development and utilisation, climate and environment assessment in urban planning, and ecological environment meteorology. In recent years, he has presided over more than ten examples of provincial and ministerial-level scientific research projects, won a first prize at the Beijing Municipal Science and Technology and another first prize for outcome application at the China Meteorological Administration in the field of climate and environment assessment in urban planning. He has published more than 30 articles.

**Professor Bo Huang** is a Professor with the Department of Geography and Resource Management at the Chinese University of Hong Kong, Shatin, Hong Kong, where he is also the Associate Director of the Institute of Space and Earth Information Science and Director of the MSc Program in Geoinformation Science. He serves as the Executive Editor of Annals of GIS (Taylor & Francis) and Asia-Pacific Regional Editor of International Journal of Geographical Information Science (Taylor & Francis), and on the editorial boards of several international journals. His research interests are broad, covering most aspects of Geoinformation science, specifically spatiotemporal image fusion for environmental monitoring, spatial/spatiotemporal statistics for land-cover/land-use change modelling, and multi-objective spatial optimisation for sustainable land-use planning. He is currently leading a comprehensive research project on Urban Resilience Planning for Nansha District, Guangzhou using revolutionary Geoinformation Technologies.

**Professor Björn Holmer** is a geographer at the Department of Earth Sciences, University of Gothenburg, Sweden. His speciality is urban climatology and he works with thermal comfort, the physics of urban cooling and air pollutants as well as the development of the SOLWEIG model in the Urban Climate Group at the University of Gothenburg. For seven years he worked as a climate consultant with energy savings due to the adaption of built-up areas to the surrounding terrain as an important issue.

**Professor Shusuke Inachi** is the Associate Professor of Architecture in the Faculty of Science and Engineering at the Setsunan University. He received his PhD in Engineering from Kobe University. He worked in an architectural firm before moving to the Setsunan University. His specialty is in regional planning and design, as well as architectural planning and design. His recent studies are focused on developing a land-use prediction system for regional planning in an age of depopulation.

**Professor Weimei Jiang** is a meteorologist and a teacher in atmospheric sciences. He is a supervisor for the Doctorate of Philosophy in Nanjing University, China. His speciality is atmospheric physics, atmospheric environment and atmospheric turbulence and diffusion, air pollution meteorology, and urban meteorology. He is now a retired teacher. He has published several books: *Physical Simulation for Atmospheric Environment* (1991), *Basic Boundary Layer Meteorology* (1994), *Course of Air Pollution Meteorology* (1st edition in 1993 2nd edition in 2004; 3rd edition in 2007), and *Air Pollution Meteorology* (2003). He has published over one hundred academic theses, 50 in the aforementioned study fields. As a researcher he has been the recipient of the scientific and technological awards from the Minister of Education, China; China Meteorological Bureau; and Jiangsu province, Shanghai city, etc.

**Dr Steve Kardinal Jusuf** is a Senior Research Fellow in the NUS Environmental Research Institute (NERI), Singapore. He has a PhD degree in Building Science from the Department of Building, National University of Singapore. He received the World Future Foundation PhD Prize in Environmental and Sustainability Research for his work on air temperature prediction models within the urban climatic mapping method. His research interests are in the area of urban microclimate and urban climatic mapping with Geographical Information System (GIS). He has worked on a number of research projects with various Singaporean government agencies, mainly in the topic of urban climatic mapping for sustainable urban development.

**Professor Lutz Katzschner** is a meteorologist and professor for environmental meteorology at the University of Kassel, Germany, in the Faculty of Architecture and Urban Planning. His main science interest is urban climatic mapping from meso- to micro-scales and their implementation in an urban planning perspective and the impact of global climate change in cities. He is the chairman of the guideline committee for urban climate and planning Verein Deutscher Ingenieure (The Association of German Engineers) in Germany. He is currently carrying out projects on global warming and its effects on urban climate in different cities and countries. He also does courses on the fundamentals of urban climate at the Technical University München, the Chinese University Hong Kong, and Vietnamese German University.

**Mr Sebastian Kupski** is a research assistant at the University of Kassel (Germany) in the Department of Environmental Meteorology. He studied urban planning with a main focus on urban development. Now, his speciality is urban climate in all mentioned planning scales. His research aim is to develop adaptation tools for cities based on urban climatic maps. Sebastian Kupski worked on a regional research project called KLIMZUG (2008–2013) and developed a regional climate zone map with recommendation on the meso-scale, based on the fact that more detailed investigations could follow, such as city-wide or microclimate analyses.

**Dr Kevin Ka-Lun Lau** is a researcher in the Department of Earth Sciences, University of Gothenburg, Sweden. He specialises in the effect of climate change on urban climate and outdoor thermal comfort. His research interests include the role of urban geometry in urban thermal environments and their implications for urban planning and design practices. He is currently working on the spatial modelling of mean radiant temperature in complex urban settings.

**Dr Marcus Oliver Letzel** is a meteorologist and senior scientist at Lohmeyer Consulting Engineers. His responsibility there is for the exploration of innovative computational fluid dynamics methods in environmental consulting, focusing on urban large-eddy simulation (LES). He has been a co-developer of the German LES model PALM since its early days. His specialties are urban meteorology, boundary layer meteorology, computational wind engineering, and environmental aerodynamics. He gained his research experience with academia and industry in Germany and Japan, and actively collaborates with academic and industry partners at national and international levels to further foster urban LES. His collaborative LES research with Japanese colleagues received awards from the Japan Society of Civil Engineers (JSCE) in 2002 and the International Association for Urban Climate (IAUC) in 2009. His pioneering animations of turbulent flow in Tokyo (2005) and Hong Kong (2006) demonstrated his commitment to an intuitive visualisation of urban LES results for interdisciplinary decision-making.

**Professor Victor O. K. Li** received SB, SM, EE and ScD degrees in Electrical Engineering and Computer Science from MIT in 1977, 1979, 1980, and 1981, respectively. He is Chair Professor of Information Engineering and Head of the Department of Electrical and Electronic Engineering at the University of Hong Kong (HKU). He served as Managing Director of Versitech Ltd, the technology transfer and commercial arm of HKU, and Associate Dean of Engineering. Previously, he was a Professor of Electrical Engineering at the University of Southern California (USC), Los Angeles, California, USA, and Director of the USC Communication Sciences Institute. He has received numerous awards, including the Senior Visiting Fellowship, UK Royal Academy of Engineering, the Croucher Foundation Senior Research Fellowship, the Chang Jiang Chair Professorship at Tsinghua University, and the Bronze Bauhinia Star, Hong Kong. He is a Fellow of the Hong Kong Academy of Engineering Sciences, the IEEE, the IAE, and the HKIE.

**Dr Fredrik Lindberg** is an urban climatologist in the Urban Climate Group at the University of Gothenburg, Sweden. His main research areas include the spatial modelling of urban climates focusing on the influence of buildings, vegetation, and green spaces on human thermal comfort in urban areas as well as modelling of the mean radiant temperature in complex urban settings. Fredrik is the main developer of the SOLWEIG-model which estimates 3D-radiant fluxes and mean radiant temperature in urban environments and the SEES-model which simulates potential solar energy production on building roof structures. Currently, Fredrik is developing a fast responsive modelling system for urban climatology and climate-sensitive planning applications.

**Dr Sarah Lindley** is a Senior Lecturer in GIS in the School of Environment, Education and Development at the University of Manchester, UK. Her research interests include air pollution, and her work has focused particularly on understanding spatial patterns in emissions and pollutant concentrations. She was a member of the UK government's Air Quality Expert Group 2002–2009 and has worked on the UK Research Council- and EU-funded projects concerned with air pollution exposure assessment. Over the last decade she has developed a second research strand focusing on climate change adaptation, particularly to urban heat. Themes within this work include the geospatial analysis of risk and vulnerability and research into urban ecosystem services, e.g. as part of the EU CLUVA project – a collaboration between 13 partners across Europe and Africa.

**Professor António Saraiva Lopes** is a Physical Geographer and Professor at the Institute of Geography and Spatial Planning (IGOT) of the University of Lisbon (ULisboa), Portugal. He is the head of the research group ZEPHYRUS (Climate Change and Environmental Systems) of the Centre of Geographical Studies (CEG). His main research interests are: Urban and Local Climatology, Remote Sensing and GIS. Until now he has participated in several Portuguese and international projects about urban climate and applications in Portuguese and Brazilian cities, environmental problems in coastal areas, thermal comfort and tourism, natural hazards and historical climatology. He supervised more than 20 research students, including PhD, MSc and international internships.

**Professor Andreas Matzarakis** received a degree in meteorology in 1989 from the physics department, Ludwig Maximilian University of Munich in 1989 and a PhD degree in Meteorology and Climatology from the Aristotle University of Thessaloniki. From 1995 to 2001 he was a scientific assistant at the Meteorological Institute of the Albert Ludwigs University of Freiburg and earned his habilitation about the 'thermal component of the urban climate' in 2001. He was appointed Professor at the University of Freiburg in October 2006. His research mainly focuses on urban climatology, human-biometeorology, tourism climatology, regional climatology, forest meteorology, and climate impact research. He is founder and editor of the urban climate website. Since 1996 he has chaired the commission on climate, tourism and recreation of the International Society of Biometeorology. He is the developer of several models and tools in applied climatology and biometeorology, such as the RayMan Model, the SkyHelios Model, the Climate Mapping Tool and CTIS (Climate-Tourism-Information-Scheme).

**Professor Helmut Mayer** is a meteorologist. He is the head of the Chair of Meteorology and Climatology, Albert Ludwigs University of Freiburg (Germany). His specialty in research and teaching is in urban meteorology, especially urban human-biometeorology. His research focuses on assessment of the urban atmosphere in a way that is significant for citizens. This implies that suitable assessment indices have to be developed for both the thermal and air pollution component of the urban atmosphere as well as having to be applied in urban planning. His research is based on a well-matched investigation design combining experiments with numerical simulations, statistical analyses, questionnaires and applications in Central European cities. This research becomes more important for urban planning due to climate change, which will show an intensification of severe heat waves for many regions worldwide. From 2011 to 2013, Professor Mayer was chairman of the German Meteorological Society.

**Dr Gerald Mills** is a Senior Lecturer in the School of Geography, Planning and Environmental Policy at University College Dublin (UCD) Ireland. He is a physical geographer with a particular interest in climates near the ground and especially those of cities. He has published on aspects of urban energy budget modelling, the global effect of cities and the history of the study of urban climates. He has been involved in the development of the International Association for Urban Climates (IAUC), and served as its President between 2010 and 2014. He was the lead organiser of the 8th International Conference on Urban Climate, held in Dublin in 2012.

**Professor Akashi Mochida** is Professor in the Department of Architecture and Building Science at the Tohoku University. Since the 1980s, Mochida has been actively involved in enormous studies in the field of Computational Wind Engineering. Since 1998, Mochida has been the chairman of the working group of CFD prediction of pedestrian wind environments organised in the Architectural Institute of Japan (AIJ). Recently, his working group issued the AIJ guidelines for the practical application of CFD to the pedestrian wind environment around buildings.

He was also chairman of the committee on countermeasures to urban heat island, organised by the AIJ from 2001 to 2004, and since 2007 he has chaired the technical committee on the development of CASBEE-HI (Comprehensive Assessment System for Built Environmental Efficiency on Heat Island Relaxation). He received the best paper award of the *International Journal of Asian Architecture and Building Engineering* in 2003. He also received the best paper award of the Society of Heating, Air-conditioning and Sanitary Engineering of Japan and the Architectural Institute of Japan Prize in 2005.

**Professor Masakazu Moriyama** is a Professor of urban and architectural environmental planning in the Setsunan University located in Osaka Prefecture, Japan. His specialty is environmental and sustainable planning, and urban climatology for city planning. He is a director of the Osaka Heat Island Technology Consortium.

**Ms Tereza Moura**, an architect graduate of the Federal University of Bahia (UFBA) in 1983, became a faculty member at the same university in 1992, following some years of working experience in architecture and after having received her MSc in Environmental Principles and Engineering from the Bartlett School of Architecture, University College London in 1986. Her research focused on natural ventilation in buildings aimed at saving energy by natural means. In 1997 she also coordinated the 'IV National Meeting on Comfort in the Constructed Environment', and organised its proceedings. She has been studying and researching environmental comfort and energy efficiency in buildings since 1985 and urban climate in Salvador since 1995. Broadening the scope of her studies, she is currently taking her PhD in City and Regional Planning at The Ohio State University, USA.

**Mr Keisuke Mouri** is a facility designer of Shimizu Corporation in Japan. Until 2010, Mouri was a member of the Regional Environment Planning Lab, Department of Architecture and Building Science, Graduate School of Engineering, Tohoku University in Japan. At that time, he developed the method of zoning for selecting appropriate countermeasures against urban warming based on heat balance analysis with Professor Mochida. He received the award for excellence for the proposal of the reconstruction plan for housing located in the area damaged by the Great East Japan Earthquake in 2013.

**Professor Jussana Nery** is an architect and graduate of the Federal University of Bahia (UFBA) where she was Professor of Architecture for 30 years. She is an Environmental Comfort Specialist accredited by the Ministry of Culture and Education (1983), and received her Masters Degree in Architecture – Urban Design from the UFBA. The focus of her research was the ecological approach to the urban planning (1992). In 1997 she coordinated the 'IV National Meeting on Comfort in the Constructed Environment', editing its annals. She has been studying environmental comfort since 1983, urban climate since 1995, and coordinated the Environmental Comfort Laboratory (LACAM/UFBA) from 1986 until 2007.

**Professor Timothy R. Oke** is an Emeritus Professor of Geography at the University of British Columbia in Vancouver, Canada. He is a former Head of Geography and founder of the Atmospheric Science Programme. He conducts research and writes about micro- and urban climates and boundary layer meteorology. He is author or co-author of almost two hundred publications including nine books (including the widely used text *Boundary Layer Climates*), six monographs and more than one hundred refereed scientific papers. He was the first to receive both the Helmut Landsberg and Luke Howard Awards for his pioneering studies in urban meteorology. He received both the Patterson and Massey Medals (Canada's highest honours in meteorology and geography). He is a Fellow of the Guggenheim Foundation, the Canadian and American Meteorological Societies, the Royal Canadian Geographical Society and the Royal Society of Canada. He founded the International Association for Urban Climate, holds an honorary doctorate of the University of Łódź and is an Officer of the Order of Canada.

**Mr Richard Rees** is a Strategic Energy Officer for Birmingham City Council, UK. He specialises in strategy development and project management relating to sustainability and energy for the City of Birmingham, most recently co-authoring the Green Commission's Vision Statement (March 2012) and Carbon Roadmap (November 2013). Richard was the Lead Officer for Birmingham's Green Infrastructure and Adaptation Delivery Group (2010–2012), leading the production of the Climate Change Adaptation Action Plan (January 2012) and Places for the Future Supplementary Planning Document. He was Lead Supervisor and Chair of the BUCCANEER project, which won the Lord Stafford Award for Innovation in Environment and Sustainability (2012). Richard completed his undergraduate studies in History and Politics at Keele University (2008) and postgraduate studies in Public Management at the University of Birmingham (2013).

**Dr Ulrich Reuter** since 1980 has been a meteorologist in the Department for Urban Climatology at the Office for Environmental Protection of the municipality of Stuttgart, Germany. Since 2008 Dr Reuter has been the head of this department. His specialities are urban climatology for city planning, adaptation to global climate change by planning measures and air pollution control. Since 1994 he has been a lecturer in Urban Climatology at the University of Applied Sciences Stuttgart. From 1999 to 2002 Dr Reuter was the Chairman of the German Meteorological Society (DMG) expert committee 'Environmental Meteorology (FA UMET)'. Since 2002 he has been a member of the committees 'Climate' and 'Environmental Meteorology' of Verein Deutscher Ingenieure (VDI, The Association of German Engineers). Dr Reuter is the author of a number of books and many publications.

**Dr Rainer Röckle** received a degree in meteorology in 1990 from the Meteorological Department of the Technical University of Darmstadt. From 1991 to 1995 he worked as an expert for atmospheric dispersion calculation and urban climatology at the TUEV Suedwest. In 1995 he was co-founder of an engineering office in Freiburg in which he is still working. The focus is on dispersion studies and questions of micro- and mesoscale meteorology. He developed models in the field of applied meteorology, i.e. ABC and GAK. ABC is a diagnostic micro-scale flow model. GAK is a cold air drainage flow model for screening purposes, which covers whole states.

**Professor Satoru Sadohara** is a Professor of Graduate School of Urban Innovation, Yokohama National University. He also teaches at the Department of Architecture in the School of Engineering and Science (undergraduate course). His research interests include urban environmental planning on the basis of low-carbon society and biodiversity, and environmental information infrastructure for supporting stakeholders' collaboration to solve complicated environmental problems. At present, he is a member of the Management Advisory Committee of Yokohama City and vice-chairman of Advisory Bodies of Environment Creation in Yokohama City. His publications include *Establishing a Common Platform for Geospatial-temporal Information* (2010, editor) and *Urban and District Energy Systems* (2012, Co-author). In 2013 the Architectural Institute of Japan awarded him the Research Theses Division prize.

**Dr Alessandra R. Prata Shimomura** is a Lecturer at Universidade de São Paulo at School of Architecture and Urbanism (FAUUSP)/Brazil. She is an architect with a Ph.D. in Architecture and Urbanism from Universidade de São Paulo, with work developed at Laboratório Nacional de Engenharia Civil (LNEC)/Lisbon/Portugal. She was a Researcher with an Auxílio à Pesquisa/JP grant from Fundação de Amparo à Pesquisa do Estado de São Paulo (FAPESP) at School of Civil Engineering, Architecture and Urbanism – University of Campinas (FEC/UNICAMP)/Brazil, in urban dynamics and territorial planning: urban climatic map and its use in master-plan. Her Post-doctorate was in building and urban design with density and environmental quality, and urban densification. She has experience in Architecture and Urban Planning, having acted on: environmental comfort, natural ventilation, urban climatic map, wind tunnel, CFD simulation and SIG. Her paper "Physiological Equivalent Temperature index applied to wind tunnel erosion technique pictures" was awarded a prize by the IAUC Awards Committee at the 7th International Conference for Urban Climate (ICUC-7) Japan/2009.

**Dr Claire Smith** is a New Blood Lecturer in Climate Change Adaptation in the Department of Geography at the University of Leicester, where she is a member of both the Adapting to Changing Environments research group and the Centre for Landscape and Climate Research. She has over seven years' experience in the field of urban meteorology and climatology, which is complemented by expertise in GIS and spatial analysis. She also has significant experience in monitoring urban meteorology and additional interests in the development of spatial decision-support tools related to climate change adaptation. She has published over 20 peer-reviewed publications in international journals and her research outputs have been used directly to inform policy.

**Professor Tejo Spit** (1955) is a full professor in Urban and Regional Planning at the Department of Human Geography and Planning (Faculty of Geosciences, Utrecht University) in the Netherlands. He is specialised in sustainable spatial development, more specifically focused on land policy, planning methodology, infrastructure planning and administrative aspects of spatial planning. Until now he has published more than 200 papers, books, book chapters and research reports. In the administrative circles of which he has been a member, he has chaired many committees on specific items in public administration. He is well known in the world of consultancy firms; witness his commissionerships with a number of them. Since 1998, he has been a frequent member of the Council of Representatives (CoRep) of the Association of European Schools of Planning (AESOP), representing the Netherlands.

**Dr Iain D. Stewart** is a postdoctoral fellow in the Department of Civil Engineering, University of Toronto. He is a specialist in the urban heat island effect and the metabolism of cities. Iain obtained his PhD in geography from the University of British Columbia (Vancouver), where his research has helped to establish scientific guidelines and standardised methods for urban climatologists. Iain is twice recipient of the William P. Lowry Memorial Award, given for his advances in climate methodology by the International Association for Urban Climate.

**Professor Takahiro Tanaka** is the Associate Professor of Architecture in the Graduate School of Engineering at the Hiroshima University. He received his PhD in engineering from the Yokohama National University. He worked in a private firm and at Kobe University before coming to Hiroshima University. His specialty is urban environmental planning and design, urban climatology and urban ecology for urban planning. He is a member of the Practical Use of Urban Environmental Climate Map Sub Committee in the Architectural Institute of Japan

(2009–present). From 2008 to 2010 he was also a member of the Yokohama Urban Climatic Map study.

**Professor John E. Thornes** is currently a Principal Climate Change Scientist at Public Health England. He was formally Professor of Applied Meteorology at the University of Birmingham. He was the lead author on the recent UK Climate Change Risk Assessment on Transport and was recently Managing Director of two University spin-out companies developing improved weather forecasts for Transport Authorities. He is the author of nearly 100 academic articles on the impact of weather, climate and climate change on society as well as being the author of a book on 'John Constable's Skies'. Current research projects include improving Ambulance Response Times (working with West Midlands Ambulance Service and London Ambulance Service), monitoring air quality at railway stations (working with Network rail) and BUCCANEER (Birmingham Urban Climate Change Adaptation with Neighbourhood Estimates of Environmental Risk) working with Birmingham City Council and Birmingham PCT.

**Professor Sofia Thorsson** is Associate Professor in Physical Geography at the Department of Earth Sciences, University of Gothenburg. Prof. Thorsson has expertise in urban climatology/meteorology and biometeorology as well as its impact on urban daily lives, i.e. outdoor activities, daily mobility patterns, place perception and emotions, well-being and health. The effectiveness of different measures (e.g. vegetation, building geometry) to reduce heat stress in urban areas and integrating climate knowledge in urban design/planning are other important research topics. She also coordinates several multi-, inter- and transdisciplinary research projects and cooperates with scientists from different disciplines such as climatology, atmospheric science, architecture, environmental psychology, sustainable development, biology and health as well as with people outside academia.

**Ms Juan Wang** is a PhD student specialising in urban heat island monitoring and analysis. She received her Bachelor degree in geography from the East China Normal University and her Masters degree in GIS and Remote Sensing from the Chinese Academy of Sciences.

**Mr Jörn Welsch** is a landscape planner working at the Information System Urban and Environment, Environmental Atlas unit of the Department of Urban Development and Environment of the Senate of Berlin. Since 1987 he has been responsible for all aspects concerning 'Urban Climate' at city level, database development as well as consulting services in the context of project planning. Several overseas invitations have enabled him to exchange knowledge professionally at an international level. Most recently he has contributed to the Megacity Research Project TP. Ho Chi Minh. He has also been involved with developing guidelines for environmental mapping in a working group of the Association of German Engineers (VDI).

**Professor Nyuk-Hien Wong** is a Professor in the Department of Building, National University of Singapore. Prof. Wong is the principal investigator of a number of research projects related to Urban Heat Island, urban climatic mapping and greenery, in collaboration with the various government agencies, such as the National Parks Board (NParks), Housing Development Board (HDB), National Environmental Agency (NEA) and Building Construction Authority (BCA). Prof. Wong has published more than 150 internationally refereed journals and conference papers and was co-author of three books on rooftop and urban greenery. He has been invited to deliver keynote papers and research findings at various conferences and symposiums. He has also been invited to serve on various advisory committees both locally and internationally.

**Professor Steve H. L. Yim** is Assistant Professor in the Department of Geography and Resource Management at the Chinese University of Hong Kong (CUHK). His research focuses on urban climatology and urban air quality, with particular attention to local air ventilation and pollutant dispersion, and the future projection of environmental impacts in urban areas. With expertise in multi-scale atmospheric modelling, Dr Yim has previously studied wind availability in Hong Kong (HK), the Pearl River Delta (PRD) and Guangdong, providing wind information for the development of the Hong Kong Urban Climatic Map. Dr Yim also investigated air quality impacts due to various combustion sources in different regions worldwide, including the PRD, the United Kingdom and the United States.

**Dr Chao Yuan** is a SUTD-MIT Postdoctoral fellow. He obtained his doctoral degree from the Chinese University of Hong Kong, and worked as an architect prior to his PhD study. He has a broad academic background in urban climatic research, and has mastered scientific modelling as well as urban design and planning technique. Dr Yuan has participated in several key policy-level research projects commissioned by Hong Kong Government, as well as actively involved in a few Chinese (e.g. Wuhan and Macau) projects. He has published several manuscripts in high impact factor journals. He developed the Frontal Area Density understanding, which provides an important knowledge linking the built morphology and the city's aerodynamic potentials. This work is now incorporated into Hong Kong and Wuhan's urban climatic research for city planners' references.

# Foreword

*Professor Lord Julian Hunt, University College London, Visiting Professor, Hong Kong University, UK House of Lords*

City climates and environments have been planned and controlled since civilization began, with the irrigated hanging gardens of Babylon in Eurasia modifying the harsh desert climate, or walled cities in central China sheltering people from the cold winds and sandstorms. Cities are mostly long-lasting social organisations which will continue into the future. But some cities have disappeared, e.g. by geologically caused sinking of coast-lines in Europe, or by flooding in the Indus valley, or from war as in the fabled Xanadu. But from the middle ages to the present time as cities grew in population and wealth, their climates and environments began to deteriorate as they began to rely for their energy on coal and later oil, and to rely on rivers and coastal waters to deal with sewage. Kings, governments, scientists and communities had to understand the problem and began to take action. John Evelyn wrote one of the first scientific reports about smoggy London in 1661. By 1800 many cities' measurements demonstrated some of the special features of urban climates. But it was not until the last 20 years that the World Meteorological Organisation had urged its member countries to measure and study urban climates with the same rigour as in open terrain; after all most people now live in towns and cities.

This excellent and timely book with contributions by international experts is about what science can do today to assist cities with the analysis of their climates, to suggest what policies and actions are needed now and in the future as cities keep growing, which in Asia and Latin America is on ten-year time scales comparable to the growth of vegetation! The authors rightly echo the call of previous writers that the many factors in addressing these urban problems should be considered holistically (Smuts, 1925) and sustainably (Brundtland, 1987), concepts now accepted in legislation across the world. In many countries, the radical solution has been tried of limiting the growth of megacities by moving some their populations to newly constructed 'garden' or 'government' cities with improved environments. Although policy like this has been generally successful, from Washington DC to Brasilia and most recently to Putra Jaya, there have been some disappointments, as in Africa.

The overarching problem in planning the future climate in all types of city is to take into account the worsening of natural hazards associated with changing global climate and their impacts on the safety and well-being of urban communities and economic activities. The leaders of the world's major cities have accepted that the high energy use of their citizens is the cause of the emissions of greenhouse gases produced by coal or oil combustion in power plant and transport systems. If cities can be planned and operate with reduced carbon emissions, they will help themselves by helping the world to reduce the likely rise of global temperature and other climatic hazards, such as extreme rainfall events. Methodologies are presented here for designing and planning buildings, infrastructure, natural habitats and landscapes to improve the climates and environments of cities. Some parts of these policies and measures are aimed at reducing directly or indirectly carbon emissions and energy use, and the many contributors show how new technologies are being deployed effectively in the scientific studies to assist in these strategies. Perhaps there should be more emphasis on psychological and social studies and community projects to ensure participation in planning procedures and also that neighbourhoods benefit from new developments.

The key development has been mapping with Geographical Information Systems; these enable measured data from all sources, including satellite data, social data and modelling outputs to be displayed separately or together, which is what decision makers need.

Each of the contributing chapters shows particular design and planning initiatives, and research results, such as how to control the surface wind in inner cities – not too much and not too little! The value of new software tools is explained, some of which require considerable expertise and computer facilities, while there are also simpler and faster methods, based on modelling experience for typical situations. These kinds of tools have enabled large planning projects to be designed, discussed and then completed in a few years at the same time as planning for the future of the site when the first stage of uses are completed, as was done in Beijing and London for their Olympic Games. In other words climate planning technology is actually hastening the change in urban environments, and even the local climate.

*Julian Hunt*
*5 May, 2014*

## References

Brundtland, G. H. (1987). *Report of the World Commission on Environment and Development: Our Common Future.* New York: United Nations.

Smuts, J. C. (1925). *Holism and Evolution.* New York: J. J. Little and Ives Co.

# Foreword

*Professor Robert Bornstein, Professor Emeritus, Department of Meteorology and Climate Science, San Jose State University*

Over half the world's population now lives in urban areas, and by 2050 this percentage is estimated to increase to over 67 per cent (i.e. to over 6 billion people). Over 20 global megacities now exist, each with a population of at least 10 million. Rapid urban development, increasingly burdened ecosystems, aging infrastructure, and changing demographics all have contributed to increases in human exposure and vulnerability to climate and weather stresses.

As a now rapidly changing climate will modify the frequency, intensity, spatial pattern, timing, and duration of such stresses, urban areas will face ever increasing and unprecedented risks. For urban areas to maintain sustainable growth under these projected increases in urban population makes it imperative to plan cities for reduced exposures, increased resiliency, and increased adaptive capacity to climate and weather stressors.

These goals can be achieved by: (1) assessing impacts from climate and weather stresses at the varying scales in the urban system and evaluating the related uncertainties of such impacts in the future, (2) devising measures for increased resiliency, increased adaptive capacity, and reduced exposure to these perturbations, and (3) risk, cost-benefit, and policy analyses in evaluating the feasibility of these measures, and investigating suitable financing strategies for needed investments in such measures.

Given this current era of both unprecedented global urbanization and rapid climate change, this volume is thus a welcome addition to the important field of sustainable urban planning for cities of all sizes in a wide variety of climate regimes. The text is a collection of 33 papers by leading international engineers, climatologists, and planners on the application of the unique Urban Climatic Map Study technique for the development of sustainable urban planning in a variety of cities around the world.

The volume first includes a description of the historical development of the technique and of its methodology, while most of the volume comprises case study applications of the methodology to select cities of all sizes in a variety of climate regimes. The volume finishes with a discussion of possible future directions in the use of the Urban Climatic Map Study technique for technological solutions to problems associated with the variety of urban scales (ranging from building to city-wide), image fusion techniques, use of meteorological data, urban-scale computer modelling, and building-scale computational fluid dynamics modelling.

The timeliness, completeness, and organisation of the volume makes it indispensable for providing both professionals and students with an understanding of the formulation, solution techniques, applications, and limitations of the urban climatic map study technique. This unique volume is enriched by the experiences, knowledge, and deep insights of the authors, who bring together a vast range of engineering, climatological and planning backgrounds. I am certain that working professionals, instructors, and students alike will find this volume an indispensable resource for their libraries.

*Robert Bornstein*
*April 2014*

# Foreword

## *Mr Kam-Sing Wong, Secretary for the Environment, Hong Kong SAR Government*

The subject of a sustainable built environment has been close to my heart since I practised as an architect some 20 years ago. It has been an area in which I have laboured not only in my professional practice but also in public service. It is not only about individual buildings or estates but also urban design and the integration of relevant factors such as urban climate consideration in the design and planning decision.

Before joining the Government, I took part in the consultant team for the research and development of Hong Kong's first Air Ventilation Assessment method as well as the subsequent Urban Climatic Map. I am delighted to return to this subject in my current capacity, with a bigger responsibility for the environment of Hong Kong. As a policymaker in charge of the subjects of climate change, energy, air quality and green building, I am in a privileged position to appreciate the significance and impact of this book, more so from the perspective of the environmental conditions of a city. The book is comprehensive both in its timing dimension, with its account from past to future, and in the geographical dimension, with the variety of localities covered. It is an important reference for policymakers, architects, engineers, town planners, academics and those with an aspiration towards sustainable urban environment. I wholeheartedly commend the efforts made for this meaningful project and look forward to seeing the wise application of urban climatic maps in shaping our cities, especially those building on the approach of urban densification.

Personally my family has been demonstrating a low carbon lifestyle for more than two decades. For instance, our living-cum-dining room capitalizes on natural ventilation for thermal comfort even during the hot and humid summer days in Hong Kong. The air conditioner is avoided although an electric fan is occasionally needed during the hottest period. Such a lifestyle, which is low carbon yet healthy, relies not only on personal attitude but also on environmentally benign architectural design and urban climate. I hope that our children and grandchildren in future will continue to have the opportunity to adopt a low carbon, healthy lifestyle in our cities. *The Urban Climatic Map* will be a valuable tool for shaping a more adaptable and sustainable future for all of us.

*Kam-Sing Wong*
*Secretary for the Environment*
*Hong Kong SAR Government*

# Preface

Without a doubt, the most important scientific publication in 2013 was the IPCC AR5 Report. The 'Summary for Policymakers' bluntly stated this:

> Warming of the climate system is unequivocal, and since the 1950s, many of the observed changes are unprecedented over decades to millennia. The atmosphere and ocean have warmed, the amounts of snow and ice have diminished, sea level has risen, and the concentrations of greenhouse gases have increased.
>
> Each of the last three decades has been successively warmer at the Earth's surface than any preceding decade since 1850 (see Figure SPM.1). In the Northern Hemisphere, 1983–2012 was likely the warmest 30-year period of the last 1400 years.
>
> Global surface temperature change for the end of the 21st century is *likely* to exceed 1.5°C relative to 1850 to 1900 for all RCP scenarios except RCP2.6. It is *likely* to exceed 2°C for RCP6.0 and RCP8.5, and more *likely* than not to exceed 2°C for RCP4.5. Warming will continue beyond 2100 under all RCP scenarios except RCP2.6. Warming will continue to exhibit interannual-to-decadal variability and will not be regionally uniform.
>
> (IPCC, 2013)

Our cities' urban climates will change. We know it is likely that we will suffer more heat waves. They will last longer and they will be more intense. Lives will be lost. The problem will only be compounded by our aging population and our increased urban population. There is therefore a need to know more about our urban thermal environment (The World Bank, 2010). More importantly, planners and policymakers now need better and easier to understand tools for them to devise mitigation measures that are effective.

Geographic Information System-based (GIS) Urban Climatic Maps (UCMaps) offer a solution. Fundamentally, this is a way for planners to spatially visualise the problems that are 'critical and prevailing' and their solutions. Based on human physiological heat balance models, the different colours of the UCMap indicate different 'climatopes' and thus the different characteristics of the urban thermal environment. The embedded calculations allow one to discern the likely causes of the problems. Hence, it is possible to develop corresponding mitigation methods for planners.

The idea of a UCMap started in Germany (VDI, 1997). Since then, scholars and planners in other countries in Europe and Asia have made attempts to employ the methodology for their respective cities. Some of the studies were limited to the academic circle, but some studies, for example, the Hong Kong Urban Climatic Map, have found their way to policymakers.

This edited volume represents the state of the art in creating and using UCMaps. The book is arranged in five parts. Part 1 has four chapters. The Introductory chapter by Mills summarises the historical developments of looking at the city's urban climate. It starts with Luke Howard's first quantification of the urban heat island (UHI) phenomenon. Gerald reckons that the recent urbanisation process, especially in developing countries, is worsening the impact of the problem, and planners might still not be aware of the issue. He advises therefore that planners of emerging cities, especially those in Less Developed Regions (LDR) pay more attention and employ better and more advanced methods in order to design their cities properly for the future.

The second chapter in Part 1 is by Ren. It is basically a thorough and critical review of the development of UCMaps since 1970s. The chapter finishes by stating the advantages and limitations of UCMap-making at this point in time. It hints at the need for future development that is more planning orientated. Appendix 1 at the end of this book contains the chronology of UCMap studies in the world.

The third chapter of Part 1 by Jürgen Baumüller tries to summarise the key methodologies for making UCMaps. The need for data and the need for collating the data spatially and hierarchically is clearly explained. The concept of Climatopes is defined. The need for analysis maps and planning recommendation maps is explained. A few examples of how urban climate information may be interpreted by planners are illustrated.

The fourth and final chapter of Part 1 by Katzschner further discusses the importance of understanding the concept of scale when making UCMaps. Different map scales are used for different scales of planning. From the urban master plan to the zoning plan and further down to the site plans, the need for information is different. Therefore UCMap makers need to make sure that the right information is presented to planners.

Parts 2 to 4 consist of case studies, covering large, medium-sized and small cities. The scales and issues, as well as the possible solution for different city sizes can vary. The differences are elaborated further by the authors of their respective chapters. Part 2 has nine cities: Tokyo and Yokohama in Japan, Beijing in China, Osaka in Japan, Ho Chi Minh City in Vietnam, Wuhan in China, Hong Kong, Hesse in Germany (it is not exactly a city, but a region) and Singapore.

Tokyo is one of the world's largest metropolises. Some 35 million people live on a land area of around 2,200km$^2$. Recently, the increasing number of hot days and hot nights are worrying signs. Hotter urban living not only impacts healthy living, but causes electricity consumption of the city to rise rapidly. The Tokyo Metropolitan Government (TMG) was serious about the problem and has, since 1999, conducted studies to look into the situation in the hope of finding good practice. Scientists Ashie *et al.* employed their Urban Climate Simulation System (UCSS) to generate the Heat Environment Map of Tokyo. Countermeasures have been recommended. The area in front of the Tokyo Station was further studied and a wind passage plan has been proposed. Similar studies were also conducted in the nearby Yokohama, and a number of guidelines have also been stated there.

Across the East China Sea, Beijing has a more serious problem as it does not enjoy the kind of relieving sea breezes that Tokyo enjoys. Beijing thus suffers more frequent and more intense urban heat island problems. The urban wind environment is poor, which does not help the city's pollution problem either. After conducting their studies, Fang *et al.* recommended that the city needs to intensify its greening programme. More importantly, it needs to develop plans to become a low-carbon city.

Back to Japan, this time focusing on its second largest city, Osaka. Tanaka and Moriyama drafted an Urban Climatic Analysis Map (UC-AnMap) and an Urban Climatic Recommendation Map (UC-ReMap) for the city government. The authors have been very careful to ask what kind of data planners and policymakers need. They identify that to be effective it is necessary to focus on the work span of each government department when making recommendations.

The fourth chapter in Part 2 goes south to Ho Chi Minh City. The city has been urbanising rapidly. Katzschner and Burghardt consider the city's wind environment. Using the land use characteristics of the City, they developed the city's UCMap. They also propose a number of urban climate planning zones for the city planners' easy reference.

Wuhan is an inland megacity in China. The Yangtze River flows through it and bisects the city. In the past, it enjoyed the benefits of a number of large lakes within its vicinity. Unfortunately, recently the water surface areas of the lakes are shrinking due to reclamation and urbanisation. Wuhan has now become China's well-known 'hot spot city'. There is a need to spatially map out the wind environment so that the city may be more effectively cooled. Yuan employed a morphological method to calculate the city's roughness in order to estimate its ground level wind speeds. The city's existing urban air paths are mapped and the poorly ventilated city areas are identified. City planners have been requested to look into these areas more carefully.

Hong Kong is located in the sub-tropical climate zone with cool winters and hot and humid summers. Rapid urbanisation since the 1980s has meant that the urban living environment is deteriorating. From 2003 to 2006, scientist and architect Ng has led his team studying Hong Kong's urban wind environment. Since 2006, he has further worked on the city's UCMap. The Physiological Equivalent Temperature (PET) model has been useful to calibrate and to categorise the Map. Based on the understanding, mitigating measures providing 'green' and 'wind' have been proposed. More importantly for planners, Hong Kong is divided into five Urban Climatic Planning Zones, each with its own set of characteristics and recommendations. The government of Hong Kong has taken note of the findings and has implemented its recommendations in the planning and development of a number of urban sites.

Hesse is not a city but a region in Germany. Urban climatologists Katzschner and Kupski utilise the UCMap methodology to advise the regional government on the importance of adaptation to climate change. The study focuses more on the future, demonstrating the capability of the UCMap in downscaling the global and regional climate signs to the urban environment.

The last chapter of Part 2 is on the city of Singapore. Singapore is located on the equator. It is hot and humid throughout the year. Designing for urban thermal comfort to alleviate the problem of heat stress and thermal discomfort is the task of designers and planners. Like Hong Kong, Singapore is also a high-density compact city. It is therefore paramount for map makers to carefully consider the urban morphology of the city in order to optimise it for thermal comfort. It is worth noting that Singapore is perhaps the greenest city on the planet. As such, the urban climatic environment of the city state has already benefited. Greening, more than anything else, contributes to the uniqueness of the city in the tropical region.

The problem with larger cities is that the core is very far away from the boundaries. Therefore it is difficult to bring in help from surrounding rural areas; the city must find its own solutions. On the other hand, large cities can accommodate more diverse urban interventions. It is possible for the city government to pull resources together to create larger and more effective areas and networks of solutions.

Part 3 looks at eight medium-sized cities: Salvador in Brazil, Berlin in Germany, Kaohsiung in Taiwan, Lisbon in Portugal, Campinas SP in Brazil, Frankfurt in Germany, Birmingham in the UK, and Manchester in the UK. Salvador is a tropical city with hot and humid summer months. Andrade *et al.* generated the city's UCMap. The urban climates of the city's various districts are described and this forms the basis for planning recommendations. Such a strategy for the planners is very important for the city's continued development.

Since unification, Berlin has experienced rapid growth, though not as rapid as many cities in Asia. Coordinated by Welsch, the UCMap of Berlin is the most comprehensive set of map-based and layered information sources on the city's urban climate anywhere on earth. It is under the charge of the Senate Department of Urban Development and the Environment (SDUDE). As such, it easily finds its way into the city government's daily operation for the city's planning decision-making process. The redevelopment of Tempelhofer Freiheit provides an interesting example of how urban climatic consideration is used by planners.

Kaohsiung, the second largest city in Taiwan, used to be an industrial shipping city. Ren has analysed the city's urban climate and drafted its UCMap. Apart from the wind environment, the city's greenery areas and its water bodies were carefully studied in order to synergise the findings into a comprehensive set of planning guidelines for the future. This is visualised using planner-friendly pictures and diagrams.

Like Berlin in Germany, Lisbon is a capital city and has also grown significantly in recent years. Alcoforado *et al.* try very hard to bridge the gap between urban climatologists and city planners. They employed UCMaps, and studied the city from the meso- down to the micro-scale. Different planning recommendations were then made for different homogeneous climate-response units (HCR Units). While on this subject, I must say that it is unfortunate that Henrique Andrade died halfway through the book's preparation stage. He will be remembered.

The city of Campinas in Brazil is just north of the megacity São Paulo in the sub-tropical climate region. As an inland city, the wind environment can be an issue. Following the typical UCMap-making process, Prata-Shimomura *et al.* studied the wind fields of the city, and defined its climatopes.

Frankfurt's city planning officials approached Katzschner and Campe for their UCMap. Further densification was expected and it was deemed important to better understand the city's urban climate and identify the important features, like wind paths, of the city. The result indicates that finger-like green paths for the city's cool air exchange are useful to respect.

For the city of Birmingham it suffers up to 5°C of UHI intensity. The city planners are also interested in climate change problems. The study was conducted by Bassett *et al.* Like many others drafting UCMaps, meso-scale data was combined with urban data using Geographical Information Systems (GIS). The study results are visualised for easy reference by the planners. The study team also emphasised the importance of the relationship between urban climate and public health. The last chapter of Part 3 concerns the city of Manchester, Smith *et al.* build their study on the basis of previous climate change action plan studies. The city's UCMap was drafted and its various risk areas were defined.

Part 4 examines six small cities: Sendai in Japan, Stuttgart in Germany, Bilbao in Spain, Gothenburg in Sweden, Arnhem in the Netherlands, and Freiburg in Germany. By the way, the use of the term 'small city' has more to do with the city's physical size and population size when it is compared to other larger cities.

Sendai is the first 'small city' of this sub-section. Mochida and Mouri drafted its UCMap using computational simulations to better understand the city's wind fields. Very careful cross comparison studies between simulated and measured data were made, and an understanding of the heat budget of the city was arrived at together with the city's potential wind benefits.

Stuttgart in Germany is in a basin surrounded by hills. The city has weak winds and often suffers from air pollution problems. It is unique in being one of the few cities on earth in which urban climatology has been integrated into its city planning since 1993. As such, the city can perhaps be regarded as the Mecca of UCMap makers. Reuter is the Head of its Department of Urban Climatology, Office for Environmental Protection in the city of Stuttgart. Apart from making and using UCMaps, his department also produces booklets on guides to good planning.

The city of Bilbao is located in northern Spain. Acero and Katzschner made an initial study of the city's UCMap. A few generic planning recommendations have been suggested. Likewise, Gothenburg in Sweden was studied by Holmer *et al.* Two scales of UCMap were made; one for building design and the other for urban planning. The radiative energy flux of the city was studied, as shading was deemed an important parameter.

In the Netherlands, Arnhem's UCMap was made by Ren *et al.* It was suggested that the recommendations be incorporated into the city's zoning schemes. Ren's suggestions are further conceptualised by Spit and Kokx in their part on 'Tracing Climate Adaptation in a Hard Planning Process, the Dutch experience'.

The last chapter of Part 4 is Freiburg, which is located in the foothills of the Black Forest. Matzarakis *et al.* employed measurement and imaging techniques to understand the city's thermal environment. They also used model simulation tests for the city's wind environment. They drafted the city's UCMap and classified the city's urban areas into 'areas of low, medium, and high sensibility in relation to urban development or extension based on the effect value' (p.376).

Part 5 is about the future. Relatively speaking, the UCMap is still a young methodology needing further development. This Part outlines a few of them. Suffice it to say that what this part does not include might turn out to be more important. We should therefore be open-minded about UCMap's further developments.

To appropriate and evaluate the urban environment better, the global, regional and meso scales of the climate need to be better understood. Yim delineates a future based on meteorological modelling using the Weather Research and Forecasting Model (WRF) for example. In future, this would be the first step for any UCMap-making process. Downscaling techniques are needed to improve the grid resolution of the results of meteorological models. Lau outlines some of the techniques that UCMap makers might use.

To better harmonise results of UCMaps, it is necessary to develop a descriptive schema. Stewart and Oke offer an attractive possibility. Local Climate Zones (LCZs) attempt to describe the surface characteristics of the city based on a number of physical parameters. Since the urban areas of the city are highly diverse, high-resolution field data is needed to calibrate and validate UCMaps. Currently, only case-based studies may be used. However, in future, ubiquitous sensing and big data techniques might provide a solution. Li explains how this might work.

The chapter by Wang and Huang describes the use of remote sensing images to better inform the urban climatic map-making process. High-resolution images using spatiotemporal image fusion techniques can provide UCMap makers with tools to better appreciate the dynamic quality of the urban climatic environment. In future, not only can summer conditions can be captured, but winter seasons, thus providing a more comprehensive information reference for better decision-making.

Whereas Wang and Huang's efforts in Chapter 31 consider the city's thermal environment, Letzel's chapter describes how UCMap makers might benefit from the more advanced tools to assess the dynamic, or wind, environment of the city. Better Computational Fluid Dynamics (CFD) techniques together with the development of fast and reliable computers have now made the CFD useful for urban climatic map makers. Letzel talks a lot on the importance of using the right turbulence model. He also demonstrates using a case study on how the model simulated results could be appropriately interpreted for guiding actions.

Last but not least, the Holy Grail of UCMap-making is that the maps are used, and that they are used appropriately by planners in an evidence-based manner. Currently, there is still a gulf between urban climatologists and city planners. Ng explains how this might be overcome. Providing the planners with 'critical' and 'prevailing' information, no more and no less, is the suggestion.

We now come to consider the book as a whole. The question must surely be: why the city? Is city living the only future? When I was young, I slept without the need for air conditioning. We just needed to open a window and sleep very close to it. It is impossible to do this now, since according to the Hong Kong Observatory's data, the city's wind availability has reduced by two-thirds and, at the same time, the city's temperature has increased by one to two degrees. All this is due to our relentless pursuit of urbanisation and human development.

A couple of years ago, I edited another book, *Designing High-Density Cities* (Ng, 2009). The thesis was that cities will become denser and more compact. It seemed to be then, and still is, the inevitable trend. After editing this book on *The Urban Climatic Map*, I have somehow altered my beliefs. I now reckon that there is an optimal point that mankind must not overshoot and sin against. One must also respect the forces of nature. There is only so much wind available to a city. The areas for water bodies and vegetation are limited. The topographies of a city are fixed. And the climate of the city is more or less given.

I am sure that if the urban climates of cities are considered more carefully, cities will not be like what we have today. We city dwellers are now basically relying on the use of a lot of energy in order to sustain our city way of living. The relentless popularisation of the use of air conditioners is an obvious symptom. I believe that many cities have now come to their respective threshold beyond which quality urban living may no longer be feasible.

Let's start to rethink our city-making process and more carefully evaluate the importance of the urban climate.

*Edward Ng*
*February 2014*

## References

IPCC (2013). Summary for policymakers. In: *Climate Change 2013: The Physical Science Basis*. Contribution of Working Group I to the Fifth Assessment Report of the Intergovernmental Panel on Climate Change [Stocker, T. F., D. Qin, G.-K. Plattner, M. Tignor, S. K. Allen, J. Boschung, A. Nauels, Y. Xia, V. Bex and P. M. Midgley (eds.)]. Cambridge and New York: Cambridge University Press.

Ng, E. (ed.) (2009). *Designing High-Density Cities – For Social and Environmental Sustainability*. London: Earthscan Publications Ltd.

The World Bank (2010). *Cities and Climate Change: An Urgent Agenda*. Urban Development Series Knowledge Papers, Dec 2010, vol. 10. Washington: The World Bank.

VDI (1997). *VDI-Standard: VDI 3787 Part 1 Environmental Meteorology – Climate and Air Pollution Maps for Cities and Regions*. Berlin: Beuth Verlag.

# Acknowledgement

I used to be able to remember dates, but I must be getting old. I believe it was in 2005 that I first shared the idea of visualising the urban environment using maps with my planner colleagues. I realised then that since their working tools were maps, it was obvious that we urban climatologists should give them tools in map form.

In 2006, at the Passive Low Energy Conference in Eindhoven in the Netherlands, I met Professor Lutz Katzschner for the first time. I was deeply impressed with his urban climatic map for the City of Kassel. I realised then that the idea of using maps to represent the urban environment was not new.

In late 2006, I brought the idea back to Hong Kong and shared it with the Planning Department of the Hong Kong SAR Government. Surprisingly, they were not as bureaucratic as I had originally believed. In December 2006, they commissioned me to draft the Hong Kong Urban Climatic Map (HK-UCMap) for Planning. It was a tough task for a novice like me, but I was lucky. I started knocking on the doors of scientists and experts around the world; they were all very kind and taught me well, starting with Urban Climate Map 101. By 2012, we finished the HK-UCMap. While I was busy finishing off the report for the Hong Kong SAR Government, I thought that an edited book to thank everybody who had helped me would not be a bad idea. With that thought, I contacted Earthscan (now part of Taylor & Francis). We signed the book contact in February 2011. It has been a long three years – 'long' means I have not been paying attention. In July 2013, I decided to bite the bullet, took my sabbatical leave, locked myself in a college room in Cambridge University and concentrated on finishing the manuscript.

I have to thank all of the contributors. Without your support and scholarship, I am sure this book would still be a dream. I have to thank Sze Wai Wong, my assistant, who did most of the editing chores. I have to thank Simon Ng, my son, who proofread the English in the manuscript for me.

I would like to take this opportunity to pay my tribute to the late Ms S. C. Lau, Chief Planner of Planning Department of the HKSAR Government. She was the project coordinator of the HK-UCMap study. It is sad that she left us in October 2009, before she could see the fruit of her efforts. Sadly, two of the contributors to this book, Henrique Andrade (Lisbon) and Anita Kokx (Arnhem) have also parted us. They will all be missed.

The future belongs to the next generations; they will have to make good a lot of the mistakes that we are leaving them. I dedicate this book to them and to my two sons Michael and Simon.

*Edward Ng*
*February 2014*

# Acknowledgement

I was trained to be an architect. 'Urban heat island' was the first urban climatic term I learned from my architectural physics class when I was a third-year undergraduate. I still remember that there were only two sentences to describe this phenomenon. At that time, I had never thought that my research interests would be urban climatic applications. Given the rise in public concern towards the environmental problem in mainland China, I decided to put my interest in the field of sustainable urban and environmental design.

In 2006, I came to the Chinese University of Hong Kong to pursue my PhD degree and was very lucky to participate in 'Urban Climatic Map and Standards for Wind Environment – Feasibility Study' funded by the Hong Kong Government. This special experience had a great influence on my current research work and even changed my whole life path. Through this important governmental project, I had the opportunity to work with many worldwide famous researchers and professors. In particular, I would like to thank Professor Akashi Mochida, Professor Lutz Katzschner, Professor Helmut Mayer, Professor Jimmy Fung, Dr Raymond Yau, Dr Tsz-Cheung Lee, Dr Yasunobu Ashie, Professor Nyuk-Hien Wong and Mr Kam-Sing Wong. They selflessly shared a lot of their advanced knowledge and recent research findings with me, but more importantly, through communication and discussions with them, I was inspired by their passion for the research and their care towards the society and people's lives.

In 2009, I went to Yokohama to attend the 7th International Conference on Urban Climate, and many of the presentations provided much of the inspiration for this book. I especially thank Professor Masakazu Moriyama and Professor Takahiro Tanaka who helped introduce a few Japanese researchers to me during that conference and fully supported this book.

I would like to acknowledge Miss Sze Wai Wong, my assistant, who contributed many hours of hard work towards the editing of this book. Although not directly involved in this book, I would like to thank Dr Justin Ho, Dr Kevin Lau, Dr Chao Yuan, Ms Cecilia Chan, Mr Max Lee and Ms Una Wang for their support to my work.

Last, but not least, I would like to dedicate this book to my parents Xiyong Ren and Jine Zhao who instilled in me a love for architecture and urban planning.

*Chao Ren*
*February 2014*

# Acronyms and Abbreviations

| | |
|---|---|
| AMeDAS | Automated Meteorological Data Acquisition System |
| API | Application Programming Interface |
| AR5 | Fifth Assessment Report |
| AVA | Air Ventilation Assessment |
| BCC | Birmingham City Council |
| BEP | Building Effect Parameterization |
| BHWP | Birmingham Health and Wellbeing Partnership |
| BUCCANEER | Birmingham Urban Climate Change with Neighbourhood Estimates of Environmental Risk |
| BV | building volume |
| CAS | The Chinese Academy of Sciences |
| CASBEE-HI | Comprehensive Assessment System for Building Environmental Efficiency for Heat Island Relaxation |
| CBD | Central Business District |
| CDF | cumulative distribution functions |
| CET | Central European Time |
| CEST | Central European Summer Time |
| CFD | computational fluid dynamics |
| CML | Câmara Municipal de Lisboa (Lisbon) |
| $CO_2$ | Carbon dioxide |
| COST | European Cooperation in Science and Technology |
| CV | Control Volume |
| DEM | digital elevation model |
| DGOTDU | Directorate General for Spatial Planning and Urban Development (Portugal) |
| DNS | Direct Numerical Simulation |
| DSM | Digital Surface Model |
| DTM | Digital Terrain Model |
| DWD | Deutscher Wetterdienst |
| EA | Environmental Atlas (Berlin) |
| EIA | Environmental Impact Assessment |
| ETM+ | Enhanced Thematic Mapper Plus |
| FITNAH | Flow over Irregular Terrain with Natural and Anthropogenic Heat Sources |
| FLAASH | Fast Line-of-sight Atmospheric Analysis of Spectral Hypercubes |
| GCM | General Circulation Model |
| GCP | ground control point |

GFA Gross Floor Area
GHG greenhouse gases
GIC Government, Institution or Community (sites)
GIS Geographic Information System
GPS Global Positioning System
H/W height to width ratio
HCR Unit homogeneous climate-response unit
HKPSG Hong Kong Planning Standards and Guidelines
HLUG Hessisches Landesamt für Umwelt und Geologie
IAUC The International Association of Urban Climate
IBEC Institute for Building Environment and Energy Conservation
IPCC Intergovernmental Panel on Climate Change
JULES Joint UK Land Environment Simulator
KTP Knowledge Transfer Partnership
kW kilowatt
LCZ local climate zone
LDR Less Developed Regions
LEED Leadership in Energy and Environmental Design
LES Large-Eddy Simulation
LST land surface temperature
MASON Metropolitan Area Sensing and Operation Network
MBC Metropolitan Borough Council
MDR More Developed Regions
MLIT Ministry of Land, Infrastructure, and Transport (Japan)
MMP Municipal Master Plan (Portugal)
MODIS Moderate Resolution Imaging Spectroradiometer
MOE Ministry of the Environment (Japan)
MOSES Met Office Surface Exchange Scheme
NASA National Aeronautics and Space Administration
NDVI Normalized Difference Vegetation Index
NMHS National Meteorological and Hydrological Service
$NO_2$ nitrogen dioxide
OZP Outline Zoning Plan
Pa vapour pressure
PALM Parallelized Large-Eddy Simulation Model
PET physiological equivalent temperature
$PM_{10}$ particulate matter
RANS Reynolds-averaged Navier-Stokes
RH relative humidity
RMSE root mean square error
RS remote sensing
SARS Severe Acute Respiratory Syndrome
SD statistical downscaling
SDUDE Senate Department of Urban Development and the Environment (Berlin, Germany)
SEA Strategic Environmental Assessment
$SF_6$ sulfur hexafluoride
$SO_2$ sulphur dioxide
SOLWEIG Solar and Longwave Environmental and Irradiance Geometry

| | |
|---|---|
| STARFM | spatial and temporal adaptive reflectance fusion model |
| STEA | spatial-temporal-entangled analysis |
| StEP | Stadtentwicklungsplan (Germany) |
| SUHI | Surface urban heat island |
| SUHII | Surface urban heat island idensity |
| SVF | sky view factor |
| $T_a$ | air temperature |
| TEMap | Thermal Environment Map |
| TI | thermal inertia |
| TJ | terajoule |
| TM | Thematic Mapper |
| TMG | Tokyo Metropolitan Government |
| $T_{mrt}$ | mean radiant temperature |
| TMY | Typical Meteorological Year |
| TRY | Test Reference Year |
| TVX | temperature vegetation index |
| UC-AnMap | Urban Climatic Analysis Map |
| UCG | Urban Climate Group (Gothenburg, Sweden) |
| UCI | urban cold island |
| UCL | urban canopy layer |
| UCM | urban canopy model |
| UCMap | Urban Climatic Map |
| UCPZ | Urban Climatic Planning Zone (Hong Kong) |
| UC-ReMap | Urban Climatic Recommendation Map |
| UCSS | Urban Climate Simulation System |
| UCZ | urban climate zone |
| UEIS | Urban and Environmental Information System (Berlin, Germany) |
| UHI | urban heat island |
| UKCP09 | UK Climate Projections |
| UN | United Nations |
| URANS | unsteady RANS |
| USGS | United States Geological Survey |
| v | wind speed |
| VDI | Verein Deutscher Ingenieure (The Association of German Engineers) |
| $VR_w$ | Wind Velocity Ratio |
| WAsP | Wind Atlas Analysis and Application Program |
| WHO | World Health Organization |
| WRF | Weather Research and Forecasting Model |

# Part 1

# Introduction, Historical Development and Methodology

## Chapter 1

# Introduction

*Gerald Mills*

That cities alter the climate experienced by inhabitants, often creating uncomfortable and/or unhealthy conditions is indisputable. As early as 1818, Luke Howard wrote on London's impact on air temperature, concluding that the Mean Temperature of the Climate, 'is strictly about 48.50°Fahr.: but in the denser parts of the metropolis, the heat is raised, by the effect of the population and fires, to 50.50°; and it must be proportionately affected in the suburban parts.'[1] This is the first account of what is known as the urban heat island, a phenomenon that has been detected in innumerable subsequent studies. Urban areas also have effects on wind, humidity, precipitation and, of course, air quality. While the effects are greatest in cities themselves, the impact on the overlying atmosphere extends downwind so that the urban 'signature' is present in places distant from cities. In fact, the urban plumes extending from the largest cities are now detectable many thousands of miles away, albeit in a diluted form. Taken together, the cities of the world, as the foci of human activity, of resource consumption and of waste generation (including greenhouse gas emissions), have a global impact. As urban living becomes the norm on the planet, managing cities is a key to achieving global sustainability.[2]

During Howard's time, London was perhaps among the largest cities in the world, rivalled only by Beijng, Guangzhou, Tokyo, Constantinople and Paris, each of which had more than 500,000 inhabitants. At that time, the total population of the planet was about 1 billion, of which just 3 per cent lived in urban areas. Now the planet's population is estimated at close to 7 billion, of which more than half live in cities. Broadly, this transformation describes two 'waves' of demographic transition, one of which is now substantially over. The first wave was initiated with the Industrial Revolution in the mid-eighteenth century and sparked hitherto unprecedented growth in the urban populations of Europe, North America and Japan as displaced agricultural workers moved to cities. This wave peaked in 1950 when 50 per cent of those in living in the More Developed Regions (MDR)[3] lived in urban areas. At this time the population of the planet exceeded 2.5 billion and 800 million lived in the MDR. It is in the Less Developed Regions (LDR) that the second wave of urbanisation is now occurring and its peak will take place in about a decade. By 2025, the planet's population will be over 8 billion, 56 per cent of whom will live in urban areas, and 75 per cent of these urban dwellers will live in the LDR. Whereas the MDR had over 200 years to cope with implications of urban growth, the LDR have to cope with far greater numbers in less than half of the time.

This transition is occurring at different paces in different countries. For example, the growth of China's urban population is dramatic (see Figure 1.1). In 1950 the population of China was 545 million, of which just 12 per cent lived in urban areas. Both urban and rural population growth continued until the end of the twentieth century, when the population exceeded 1.2 billion and nearly 36 per cent lived in urban areas. In 2000, 453 million lived in urban areas, mostly in places

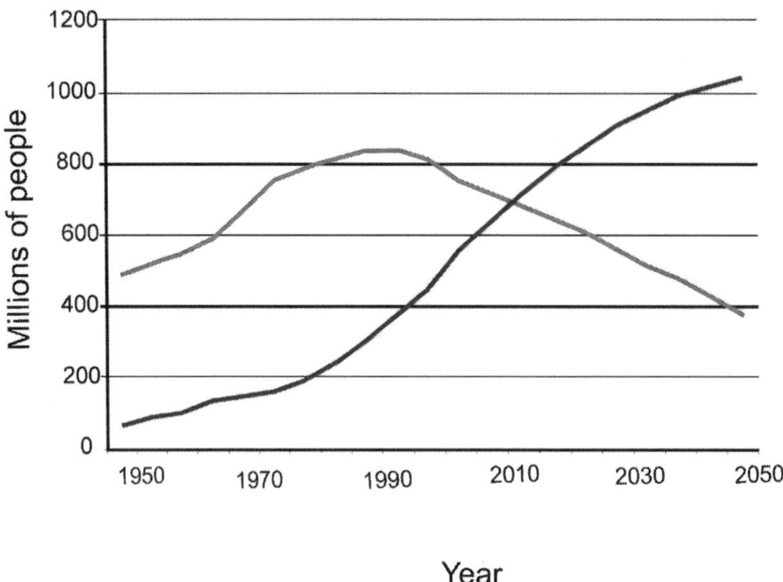


*Figure 1.1* The rural (light grey) and urban (dark grey) populations of China. Note that from the late 1990s onward the rural population has started to decline even as the overall population and that of the urban areas continues to rise.

Source: World Urbanization Prospects: The 2009 Revision Population Database available at http://esa.un.org/unpd/wup/doc_highlights.htm.

with populations of less than 500,000. In the last decade the rural population of China has begun to decline, while overall population growth continues. The United Nations (UN) predicts that by 2025, the population of China will exceed 1.4 billion, of which 851 million will live in urban areas. Although the number of large cities will continue to grow, the bulk of this urban population (40 per cent) will continue to reside in urban areas of less than 500,000 inhabitants. To put this change in context, China's urban population grew from 64 to 453 million in just 50 years (1950–2000) and is estimated to grow to 851 million by 2025. By comparison, the urban population of Europe continues to grow, but at a very slow rate. In 2000, the urban population of Europe was estimated at about 514 million and this comprised 71 per cent of the population. By 2050 it is predicted that 84 per cent of Europe's population will be urban dwellers and this will amount to 582 million.

To summarize, the transition from rural to urban living has occurred substantially in the countries of the MDR, such as those of Europe and North America. Much of the attendant investment in housing, infrastructure and city building has already taken place over a lengthy period and there is both an institutional and financial capacity for addressing urban issues. For most urban dwellers in these cities, the last century has seen a steady improvement in living conditions as the supply of drinking water, the removal of waste, and air quality have been addressed. While the rate of global urbanisation (and the degree of associated landscape change) that is now occurring is unprecedented in scale and intensity, we already know the problematic issues that are likely to arise in these growing cities. Experience has shown that, once established, urban built form is difficult and expensive to change. The current rate of urbanisation in the LDR poses enormous challenges but it also provides an opportunity to construct cities that provide healthy environments and do not place excessive burdens on the environment.

Before continuing further we should clarify what we mean by 'urban' and 'urbanisation'. Here, 'urban' is used to refer to densely populated areas where the landscape is substantially covered by manufactured materials and dwellers engage primarily in non-agricultural activities. Critically, this definition refers to both a particular land cover (form) and land use (function). It is the correspondence of cover and use that makes a place 'urban'. The term 'city' is used interchangeably and does not refer to either a specific administrative area or size of settlement (whether area or population). The term 'urbanisation' is used to convey two distinct processes: the growth in the number of urban dwellers (and their proportion of the overall population) most of whom are engaged in non-agricultural activities, and the transformation of land cover from natural to manufactured materials. From an environmental planning perspective then, managing urban areas requires consideration of both urban form and functions together.

Urban form includes both the two- and three-dimensional character of the city and its material composition. It is the product of an investment of materials and energy and could be referred to as the urban stock. As a consequence, the exchanges of momentum and energy between the surface and the overlying atmosphere are profoundly changed. Ignore the three-dimensional nature of the city for a moment and consider the impact of a flat, smooth impervious surface. Such a surface is most often dry and quickly sheds water after a rain shower, often resulting in excess water entering stream courses, and flooding. In the absence of water or vegetation (which allows for evaporation), surfaces will transfer energy to the atmosphere in the form of direct heat. As a result, the temperature of the adjacent air changes quickly in response to that of the underlying surface. If the surface is dark (like asphalt) the temperature changes can be extreme; anyone who has placed their hand on an asphalt surface on a sunny day will attest to this. Now consider the impact of urban geometry that retards and channels the flow of air, casts shadows and obstructs access to the sky. Suddenly the climate near the ground becomes a great deal more complex. The environment that one experiences when walking alters constantly as your body experiences gusts and lulls, alternating sunshine and shadow and pools of warm and cool air. In a very tangible sense, one can encounter many distinctive microclimates over very short distances.

Urban functions refer to the activities in the city, which require a constant throughput of energy and materials (an urban flux) to continue. This flux includes the energies used to heat, cool and light buildings, to drive industry and to enable transportation of people, goods and materials. Inevitably, this generates wastes in the form of materials and/or energy that are deposited into the environment. In the atmosphere, these wastes alter the thermal structure of the urban atmosphere and change its gaseous and material composition. This has effects on other aspects of climate and, most significantly, the air quality experienced by citizens. Of course, the form and functions of a city are closely related and it is the combination of these two properties that produce distinctive urban microclimates (see Figure 1.2). While many aspects of form and function are common to cities worldwide, their particular manifestation at a place will depend upon its historical development and cultural context. For example, a city that is designed for private vehicle use will have a different character (e.g. layout and air quality) to one that is designed for mass transit systems and one that has an industrial base will be different from one that is primarily administrative.

The local impact of decisions on form and function depends partly on the geographical and topographical location of the city. The former will place the city within a regional climate regime that will determine access to sunshine and regulate diurnal and seasonal oscillations of wind, temperature, rainfall, etc. It will also determine the exposure of the city to extreme events, such as storms. Topographical variations will modify the regional climate by, for example, sheltering the urban location when the airflow is from a certain direction or, when regional influences are weak,

*Figure 1.2* A busy street in Hong Kong illustrates the extent of modification in urban environments. Take note of: the vertical extent of the buildings that restrict access to sunshine, light and ventilation at street level; the pervasive use of hard, manufactured materials and the absence of vegetation; and the air conditioning units on the walls, which maintain indoor climates while disposing of waste heat and moisture into the outdoors where cars and buses emit a cocktail of particulates, gases and heat.

Source: Author

by promoting local circulation systems, such as sea breezes. Taken together, urban development should be cognizant of this local context and the concomitant (dis)advantages.

Consider, for example, the climate context of Los Angeles, which is located in the subtropics (34° N) alongside the Pacific Ocean. The urbanized area extends across several basins that are separated by tall mountains. Its geographical location places it under a near permanent high pressure cell that produces an inversion over the city. Clear sunny days, with light winds, are the norm during the summer months. Its topographic context allows for the formation of land–sea breezes that transfer a shallow pool of air between land and water on a daily basis. The inversion and the sea breeze act to limit the vertical dilution of pollutants emitted at the urban surface and the near surface wind sea breeze accumulates contaminants as it progresses inland during the daytime. The warm temperatures and intense sunshine provide conditions for the transformation of primary pollutants (those emitted at the surface) into secondary pollutants (such as ozone) in the urban atmosphere. As a consequence the city has poor air quality that can only be resolved by limiting emissions. In another climate setting where regional winds were strong, emissions would be advected downwind away from the city sources and urban dwellers. Still further, in another set of circumstances, a sea breeze could be employed as a valuable natural resource that provides a flow of cool and clean air into the urban area to relieve heat stress on warm days. This would promote the use of outdoor space and obviate the need for mechanical air conditioning.

It is the awareness of the natural climate within which we build cities that is at the heart of climate-conscious design and the subject of this book. However, with the exception of internal building climate, urban planning has not considered the climate context within which urbanisation occurs and how this impacts climate in the city and beyond. Where actions have had unintended consequences, responses have been focused on solving the immediate problem rather than assessing how the planning process generated that outcome. Thus, trees may be planted to provide shelter from winds that have been generated as a result of poor building design, or building envelopes may be redesigned to allow solar access to streets. Generally, the only examples where urban form has been modified to address climatic issues has been where cities are subject to extreme weather, such as the winds and high seas associated with hurricanes. Our understanding of cities and their role as drivers of significant environmental change at all scales demands a different approach to the building of cities.

The reasons for the failure to integrate climate issues into planning practice are manifold. Among these is the low priority given to climatic factors in the urban planning process. Another has been the difficulty in translating our scientific understanding of urban effects into methods that can be readily employed by decision makers to formulate and implement urban plans. This is not a trivial problem as it requires both integrating different types of knowledge and practices and reaching a decision through a deliberative process that involves many actors, each representing particular viewpoints. Moreover, as cities are distinctive places that occupy particular landscapes, it is unlikely that the solutions for one place can be transferred naively to another. However, the rationale underlying each of these reasons is changing.

First, it is clear that issues of global environmental sustainability will have to be addressed through actions at a scale that matters. Although international agreements on global climate change are made between national governments, actions will take place where resource use and waste generation are concentrated; that is, in the cities of the MDR. Thus, reducing the global impact of these cities and ensuring that the emerging cities of less developed regions do not take the same pathway to economic development is a political imperative. This presents a big challenge as cities in the LDR begin to take shape. It will almost certainly require a different approach to planning and building that produces new urban forms that are fitted to the geographical/topographical context of the place. While cities are the drivers of global environmental change, they are also especially vulnerable to any changes that will occur. As an example, most urban areas are located at low altitudes, often in river valleys adjacent to coasts; in other words, places that will have to adapt to the sea-level rises expected as a result of anthropogenic climate change.[4]

Second, there has been significant progress in our understanding of the climates of urban areas and how best to transfer this knowledge into practice. One of the major outcomes as a result of urban climate research has been the identification of climate effects that are associated with common urban forms, such as streets and types of neighbourhood. This has allowed climatologists to establish links between urban place-making decisions and environmental outcomes. Urban Climatic Mapping, which is discussed in considerable detail in this book, takes as its starting point a graphical description of the background climate of an urban place and examines how urban developments may modify this climate to worsen or improve the climatic environment. It achieves this by structuring a dialogue between urban climatologists and urban planners/designers, using maps of urban characteristics (including urban form, urban functions and climate parameters) as a common platform. Its advantage is that it is not prescriptive in nature and can be adjusted to the geographical/topographical context of an urban place. It recognises the deliberative process that underpins planning in many cities and provides a framework for the routine inclusion of urban climate knowledge into that process.

Finally, it must be stressed that our understanding of cities and their climate impact is still developing. Our current knowledge base has been derived for the cities of the MDR, which are largely complete and are located primarily in the climates of the middle-latitudes. Future building here will mostly take the form of reconstruction. There is a dearth of information on the character and impact of the cities of the LDR, which are being built and are located primarily in the tropics. There is an unimpeachable need for the scientific study of these emerging cities that will house the great proportion of the population of the planet. Nevertheless, there is sufficient expertise that has been garnered elsewhere that can be judiciously applied to plan and build settlements that do not produce wasteful and unhealthy outcomes.

## Notes

1 The second edition of Howard's *The Climate of London* was published in 1833. It consisted of three volumes, the first of which contains his analysis of daily observations that he made at locations outside London over a period of 26 years. When comparing his observations against those made in London, he discovered significant discrepancies that were not attributable to errors. Although others had drawn attention to urban climatic effects before Howard, he was the first to measure this effect. This edition has been republished by the International Association for Urban Climate (IAUC) and is available at www.urban-climate.org.

2 Ree, W. and Wackernagel, M. (2008). Urban Ecological Footprints: Why Cities Cannot be Sustainable—and Why They are a Key to Sustainability. *Urban Ecology*, Section V, 537–555, DOI: 10.1007/978-0-387-73412-5_35.

3 The terms 'More Developed Regions' (MDR) and 'Less Developed Regions' (LDR) are taken from the UN *World Urbanization Prospects: The 2009 Edition* (http://esa.un.org/unpd/wup/index.htm). According to their definitions,

> The designations "more developed regions" and "less developed regions" are used for statistical convenience and do not necessarily express a judgment about the stage reached by a particular country or area in the development process. The term "country" as used in this publication also refers, as appropriate, to territories or areas. The more developed regions comprise all regions of Europe plus Northern America, Australia/New Zealand and Japan. The term "developed countries" is used to designate countries in the more developed

regions. The less developed regions comprise all regions of Africa, Asia (excluding Japan) and Latin America and the Caribbean, as well as Melanesia, Micronesia and Polynesia. The term "developing countries" is used to designate countries in the less developed regions.

4 See the Intergovernmental Panel on Climate Change (IPCC) Fourth Assessment Report. The report of Working Group 2 on Impacts, Adaptation and Vulnerability is available at http://www.ipcc.ch/.

## Chapter 2

# A review of the historical development of urban climatic map study

*Chao Ren*

## Introduction

More than half of the world population now lives in urban areas (UNFPA, 2007). By 2030, nearly 60 per cent of the earth's population will be urban dwellers (UN, 2008). The rapid urbanisation in the past half a century has not only brought new immigrants into the urban areas, but has also gradually changed the physical urban environment. Both the landscape transformation and the associated activities of urban areas have modified the city's meteorology and urban climate (Esser, 1989; Lambin *et al.*, 1999; Zhou *et al.*, 2004; Lam, 2006; He *et al.*, 2007), especially the climate below the rooftops of buildings or the urban canopy layer (UCL)(Oke, 1987; Mills, 1997; AMS, 2010). In this layer, the climate is dominated by micro-scale processes and exchanges and is highly relevant to human comfort and the environmental health of the city (Leung *et al.*, 2008; Jendritzky *et al.*, 2010). There has been a worldwide vision to design cities that are sustainable, healthy, comfortable, and even enjoyable (UN, 2008). To achieve this goal, it is necessary to understand and apply urban climatic information in the urban planning and design process (Mills *et al.*, 2010). However, urban climatic consideration thus far has had a low impact on planning (de Schiller and Evans, 1991; Eliasson, 2000). There is a need to bridge the gap between urban climatology, town planning, and urban design, and to transfer the climatic knowledge into planning languages (de Schiller and Evans, 1991; Eliasson, 2000; Alcoforado *et al.*, 2009). One important link is to create an information platform for interdisciplinary communication and collaboration.

An urban climatic map (UCMap) is an information and evaluation tool for integrating urban climatic factors and town planning considerations by presenting climatic phenomena and problems in two-dimensional spatial maps (Baumüller *et al.*, 1992; VDI, 1997; Scherer *et al.*, 1999). It has two major components: the urban climatic analysis map (or synthetic climate function map) (UC-AnMap) and the urban climatic planning recommendation map (UC-ReMap). This concept of urban climatic mapping was first developed by German researchers in the late 1970s (Matzarakis, 2005). To date, there are over 15 countries around the world processing their own UCMaps, applying climatic measures and guidelines to local planning practices.

In order to further develop our knowledge and to plan project studies concerning urban climatic planning strategies and application, it is useful to study past UCMap developments and projects. This paper is the first review of the development of the UCMap tool. More than 30 relevant studies in the world are cited, and both significant developments and existing problems are discussed. Selected examples of UCMap studies from different countries are compared and summarised. Second, the structure and the map-making procedure of UCMaps are described by citing key examples. The analytical aspects and consideration parameters, as well as any planning instructions and climatic considerations in planning, are elaborated. Third, the advantages and limitations of

UCMap studies are discussed critically. Finally, the review delineates the opinions of the authors on the future of UCMap research and application. There is still the need to apply and to refine the methodology, and it is important to continue the communication and implementation of results in collaboration with city planners.

## Review of the development of urban climatic map study

In the field of UCMap study, German researcher Professor Kar Knoch (1951, 1963) first proposed a climate-mapping system for planning purposes. He suggested a series of urban climatic maps with different scales in his publication *Die Landesklima-aufanhme*, which should be fitted into the local planning system. Since the 1970s, West Germany has intensified its geoscientific activities in presenting maps relevant to planning (Lüttig, 1972, 1978a, 1978b). Stuttgart climatologists led by Dr Baumüller were the first to conduct UCMap studies for mitigating air pollution problems under weak wind conditions, and to apply the climatic knowledge to land use planning and environmental planning (Baumüller and Reuter, 1999; Baumüller, 2006).

In the 1980s, with the aim to control heavy metal pollution in the old industrial areas of the Ruhr, the Association of Local Authorities of Ruhr Areas (KVR, 1992) implemented clean air management programmes using the urban climatic analysis map to differentiate the areas according to their different climatic functions and characteristics. More than 25 cities in the Ruhr Areas were involved in this project; they included Dortmund (Stock *et al.*, 1986; Littlefair *et al.*, 2000), Essen (Stock and Beckröge, 1985), Bochum (Stock and Beckröge, 1991), Duisburg (Baumüller and Reuter, 1999), Recklinghausen (Beckröge *et al.*, 1988), and so on. With the aim of planning applications, this project was the first to relate urban climatic factors with spatial information and urban structure, and based on the land use information and their climatic characteristics it defined the various climatopes, which present different urban climatic conditions as spatial units of the UCMap. Meanwhile, in the Federal State of Bavaria, a comprehensive research project named 'Stadtklima bayern' (Urban Climate of the State of Bavaria) was carried out in Augsburg, München, and Nürnberg/Fürth/Erlangen/Schwabach. This project aimed to investigate the impact of built-up areas and greenery on the urban climate and air quality of study areas. Analyses of thermal images and the meteorological data were conducted, and car traverse measurement for examining the air temperature profile of urban areas was also carried out. A geographical distribution of topography, aerial views, thermal image, real land use, and urban air paths were synergised and mapped with a grid resolution of 250m × 250m with map drawings done manually (Mayer, 1988; Matzarakis, 2005; Matzarakis and Mayer, 2008).

In the 1990s, after the re-unification of Germany, several cities in the northern part of the country conducted synthetic climate function mapping (VDI, 1988; Helbig *et al.*, 1999; Matzarakis, 2005). Since 1992, the Section of Urban Climatology of the Office for Environmental Protection in Stuttgart has conducted a series of climate analysis studies, consequently providing a set of climatic atlases for Neighborhood Association Stuttgart (Klimaatlas Nachbarschaftsverband Stuttgart), including synoptic maps, thermal maps, emission maps, climatic analysis maps, and urban climatic planning recommendation maps in Geographic Information System (GIS) (Klimaatlas, 1992). Thus, local planners could easily assess various climatic information and evaluation results using the Stuttgart UCMap. The project 'STUTTGART 21' developed over one hundred climatic map layers at diverse scales that could be implemented in regional, city, and district planning level. In Berlin, another project titled 'Berlin Digital Environmental Atlas' has been conducted since 1995. The UCMap, as one of its eight environmental topics, has been produced for planning purposes to assist the design of settlement areas and green and open space, to control traffic-related air pollution, and to improve the air exchange of the urban areas (Berlin Government, 2008). For guiding the practice in Germany, the National Guideline – VDI 3787: Part 1, namely, 'Environmental Meteorology – Climate and Air Pollution Maps for Cities and Regions', was published in 1993 by the of the urban climatic map work groups at the German National Committee of Applied Urban Climatology. It aimed to define the symbols and representations used in UCMap studies, to recommend methods of developing urban climatic and air pollution maps, and to create a standard for their application. Thus, this guideline – VDI 3787 – has become an important reference, not only for German studies, but also for studies worldwide.

From the mid-1980s, countries in Europe, such as Switzerland, Austria, Sweden, Hungary, Czechoslovakia, Poland, Portugal, and the UK, have carried out UCMap studies (Sterten, 1982; Lindqvist and Mattsson, 1989; Lindqvist, 1991; Paszynski, 1991; Parlow *et al.*, 1995; Scherer *et al.*, 1999; Parlow *et al.*, 2001a; Radosz and Kaminski, 2003; Ward, 2003; Unger, 2004; Hsie and Ward, 2006; Hsie, 2007; Gal and Unger, 2009; Smith *et al.*, 2009). Following significant heat wave events in 2003 and 2006, many other European countries have begun climate change-related spatial planning studies based on the UCMap framework. In France, for example, a multidisciplinary study of climate change impacts, namely the EPICEA Project, has been conducted since 2008 to understand the 2003 summer heat wave over Paris by mapping the city's vulnerability (Desplat *et al.*, 2009). In this project, excess mortality data, together with selected environmental parameters, including surfaces of roof material and built, green, and water surfaces, have been considered and mapped as input analysis layers. Similar research programmes have also been carried out recently in the Netherlands (The Knowledge for Climate Research Programme, 2007; ERDF, 2010).

UCMaps have also been adopted and developed in South America (Evans and de Schiller, 1991; Nery *et al.*, 2006) and in Asian countries since the 1990s (Ashie *et al.*, 1998; Gao and Ojima, 2003; Jittawikul *et al.*, 2004; Tan *et al.*, 2005; Nery *et al.*, 2006; Kim, 2007; Ng *et al.*, 2009). Japan, with assistance from German researchers, has pioneered UCMap study in Asia. Major metropolitan areas in Japan such as Osaka, Kobe, Yokohama, Sendai, Fukuoka, and others have conducted UCMap studies and projects (Moriyama and Takebayashi, 1998; Yoda and Katayama, 1998; Ichinose *et al.*, 1999; Moriyama and Takebayashi, 1999; Tanaka and Morlyama, 2004; Murakami and Sakamoto, 2005; Tanaka *et al.*, 2005; TMG, 2005b; Yoda, 2005; Yamamoto, 2006; Mochida *et al.*, 2007; Moriyama and Tanaka, 2008; Tanaka *et al.*, 2009; Yoda, 2009). Japan's Ministry of the Environment (MOE) and the Ministry of Land, Infrastructure, and Transport (MLIT) have worked actively on UCMaps since 2000 (MOE, 2001, 2002, 2003, 2004, 2005, 2006, 2007, 2008). In 2005, the Tokyo Metropolitan Government (TMG) created and published the Thermal Environmental Map for Tokyo's 23 Wards, and developed relevant control measures and mitigation guidelines (TMG, 2005a, 2005b; Sera, 2006; Yamamoto, 2006, 2007). With the aim to mitigate the urban heat island effect, these studies focused on analysing urban thermal environment from the aspects of anthropogenic heat release, surface cover, urban structure, and green space (AIJ, 2008a). In 2000, the Architectural Institute of Japan edited a reference book to introduce the methodology of UCMap, and to share the relevant research experiences based on various local case studies in Japan (AIJ, 2000).

Thus far, most UCMap studies have focused on low- and medium-density cities. Since 2006, the research team led by Professor Ng from the Chinese University of Hong Kong has worked to implement the UCMap studies for high-density urban scenarios. They have constructed a UCMap study for Hong Kong based on thermal load, dynamic potential, and wind information considerations (Ng *et al.*, 2009). Their studies linked urban climatology, urban morphology, and planning parameters together, not only by relying on land use information as typically practiced in low- and medium-density city studies in Germany, but also by using detailed building block

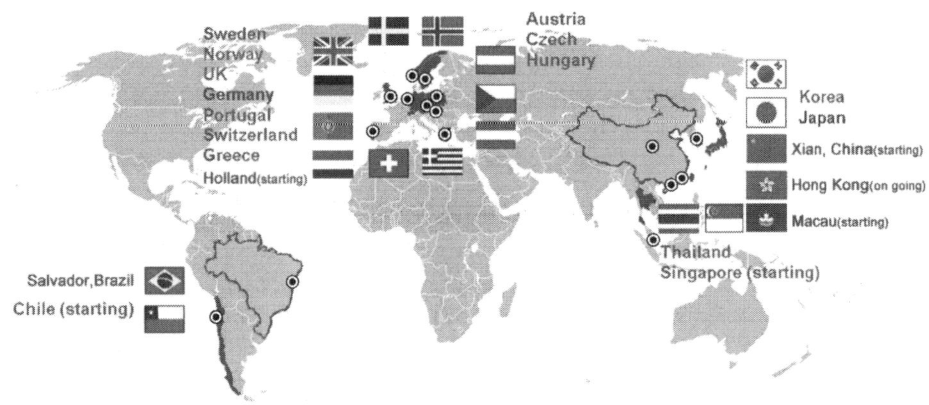


*Figure 2.1* UCMap studies around the world.

Source: Author

and planning information such as building volume (measured by a building's external dimensions) and ground coverage ratio (defined as the buildable area over the total ground area). Both of them are planning parameters and are used to analyse the impact of building density on urban climatic condition. The effort has taken into account biometeorology based on user survey and has used the Physiological Equivalent Temperature (PET) (Höppe, 1993, 1999), a thermal index and a synergetic indication of human thermal comfort, to calibrate the classification of the Hong Kong UCMap.

Based on the chronology of UCMap studies in the world (Appendix 1), more than 15 countries have conducted their own UCMap studies. Recently, UCMap has attracted increasing interest across the world (see Figure 2.1). For example, researchers in China, Chile, Singapore, Macau, France, and the Netherlands are starting relevant projects and studies in pursuit of urban climatic information for good planning and sustainable development (Wong and Jusuf, 2007; Katzschner and Mulder, 2008; Ban *et al.*, 2009).

## The structure of the urban climatic map system

The UCMap system consists of a series of basic input layers and two main UCMap components (see Figure 2.2). The basic input layers contain analytical maps of climatic and meteorological elements, geographic terrain data, greenery information, and planning parameters. There are two main UCMap components: the UC-AnMap, which visualises and spatialises various climatic evaluations and assessments by different climatopes; and the UC-ReMap, which includes planning instructions from the urban climatic point of view.

### *The urban climatic analysis map (UC-AnMap)*

The UC-AnMap provides a platform for climatic information and evaluation. It has also been named 'Synthetic Climatic Function Map', summarising and evaluating the 'scientific' understanding based on the input climatic parameters and land data under annual or specific seasonal scenarios (Stock *et al.*, 1986; Beckröge *et al.*, 1988; Stock and Beckröge, 1991; Lazar *et al.*, 1994; Baumüller and Reuter, 1999; Littlefair *et al.*, 2000). Since planners are used to reading maps and

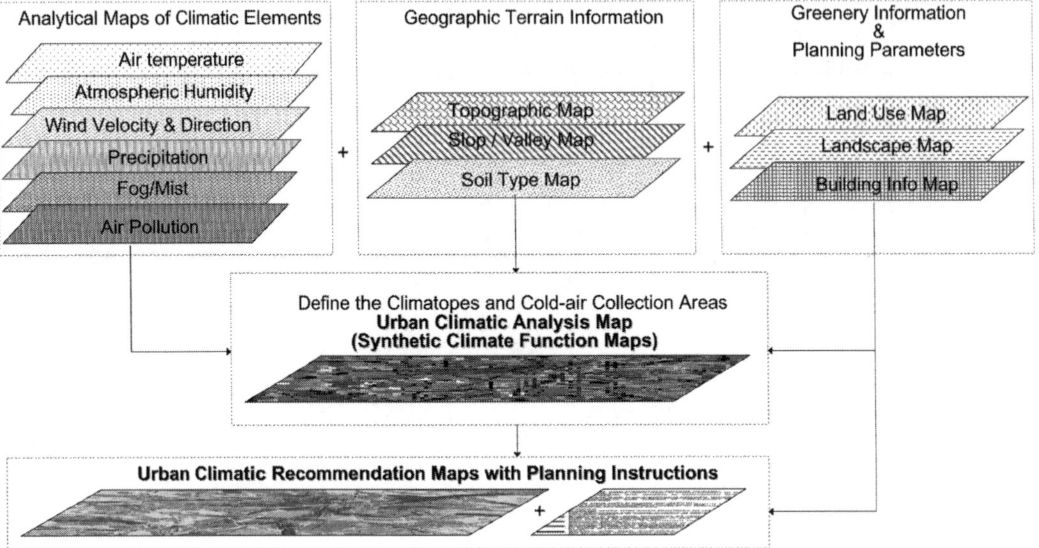


*Figure 2.2* The structure of a UCMap.

Source: Author

working on plans, different coloured graphics, arrows, and symbols with simple explanations in the UC-AnMap present the analysis results of climatic conditions and variations. The UC-AnMap relies on the careful collection and collation of meteorological data (long-term temperature, precipitation, wind, cloud, and solar radiation data), planning, land use, topography, and vegetation information, according to their relationships and effects on the energy balance on the pedestrian level to present local climatic variations at meso- and micro-climatic scale. Thus, technically measured collections of selected climatic and geographic parameters are input as basic analytical maps to present regional and local meteorological conditions. These data and information are collected from the meteorology station and infrared aerial images, and from the simulation results of macro- and meso-scale calculation models, especially on airflow analysis and energy balance. For example, in Freiburg, researchers used the flow simulation model to understand and analyse the cold airflow from the Black Forest to the downtown areas (Röckle *et al.*, 2003). Another type of useful input information is topographic terrain data, mainly derived from the Digital Elevation Model (DEM), which could also help to build up the calculation models and visualise the ground terrain situations.

There are three climatic analytical aspects of UC-AnMap (see Table 2.1). The first, wind environment, focuses on capturing the local air circulation patterns (e.g. channelling wind, land and sea breezes, mountain and valley wind, and local prevailing wind directions), existing and potential air paths, ventilation zones (e.g. cold air production zones), and locations of barrier effects by buildings or plants. The second, thermal environment, focuses on analysing the urban heat island effect and the urban bioclimatic variations, especially the areas with cold or heat stress. The third focuses on exploring the areas of air pollution. Since these analytical aspects are taken as the basic input layers, studies on thermal environment, air ventilation, and air pollution situation within the urban canopy layer play the crucial role in forming the comprehensive understanding of the current urban climatic condition.

*Table 2.1* Climatic analysis and phenomena in a UC-AnMap

| *UCMap component* | *Climatic characteristics and phenomena* | | *Climatic analysis scale* |
|---|---|---|---|
| Urban climatic analysis map | – Analysis of local air circulation pattern (e.g. channelling wind, land, and sea breezes, mountain and valley wind)<br>– Analysis of local prevailing wind direction<br>– Analysis of existing and potential air paths<br>– Analysis of ventilation zones (cold air production zones)<br>– Analysis of the location of barrier effects by buildings or plants | Wind (ventilation) aspect | Meso- (regional) and micro-scale (city and urban) |
| | – Analysis of areas of urban heat island effect<br>– Analysis of urban bioclimatic variations, especially the location of areas with cold or heat stress | Thermal aspect | |
| | – Analysis of air pollution of the area | Air pollution aspect | |

Based on the comprehensive understanding of the basic input information and analysis result, the climatopes as basic units of UC-AnMap could be defined to represent a spatial distribution of urban climate types that are the product of distinct urban land use and cover (Baumüller *et al.*, 1992; VDI, 1997). They vary from place to place depending on what the climate-based issues are at that location. Their spatial scales commonly range from several tens to hundreds of metres (Scherer *et al.*, 1999; Alcoforado *et al.*, 2009). In the early days of UCMap studies, the types of climatopes were commonly classified by urban land use (VDI, 1997). The development process of climatopes mainly relies on expert knowledge and qualitative and subjective assessment. For instance, in the UC-AnMap of Stuttgart city, German climatologists developed 11 categories of climatopes, including water surface, open land, forest, park, country, suburbs, city, city centre, small factory, factory, and railway (see Figure 2.3). Based on the analysis of meteorological data, remote-sensing information, cold airflow simulation, and digital wind field simulation at meso-scale, it was noted that the boundaries of different climatopes are not fixed in reality (Stanhill and Kalma, 1995). Thus, the boundary between two climatopes only shows the possible range of two neighbouring urban climatic conditions.

In some recent cases, calibration and verification studies have been conducted to better understand the distribution pattern of the climatopes of the study areas and to quantitatively define climatopes. For example, in Japan, Moriyama and Takabayashi (1999) used a one-dimensional calculation model of earth surface heat budget to discriminate the minimum temperature of each city area and define the climatopes of the Kobe UCMap. Meanwhile, in the UCMap for Basel, Swiss researchers utilised satellite images to analyse different urban physical surface properties and land use information for understanding the daily thermal variation and surface roughness and for automatically defining the climatopes (Scherer *et al.*, 1999). In the study of the Berlin Digital Environmental Atlas, the prognostic 3D model named FITNAH (Flow over Irregular Terrain with Natural and Anthropogenic Heat Sources) has been used to calculate the detailed wind and temperature conditions in Berlin (Groß, 1993; Richter and Röckle, 2009). The field measurement results were compared with the simulation results of the model application (SDUDB, 2008); they were found to be in good agreement (see Figure 2.4).

Most UCMap studies in the world focus on low-density urban scenarios. There is lack of application of UCMap studies to the urban planning of a high-density city. Since 2006, Professor Ng's research team along with international professionals have attempted to adopt this method into the high-density urban scenario of Hong Kong, to improve the thermal environment and urban

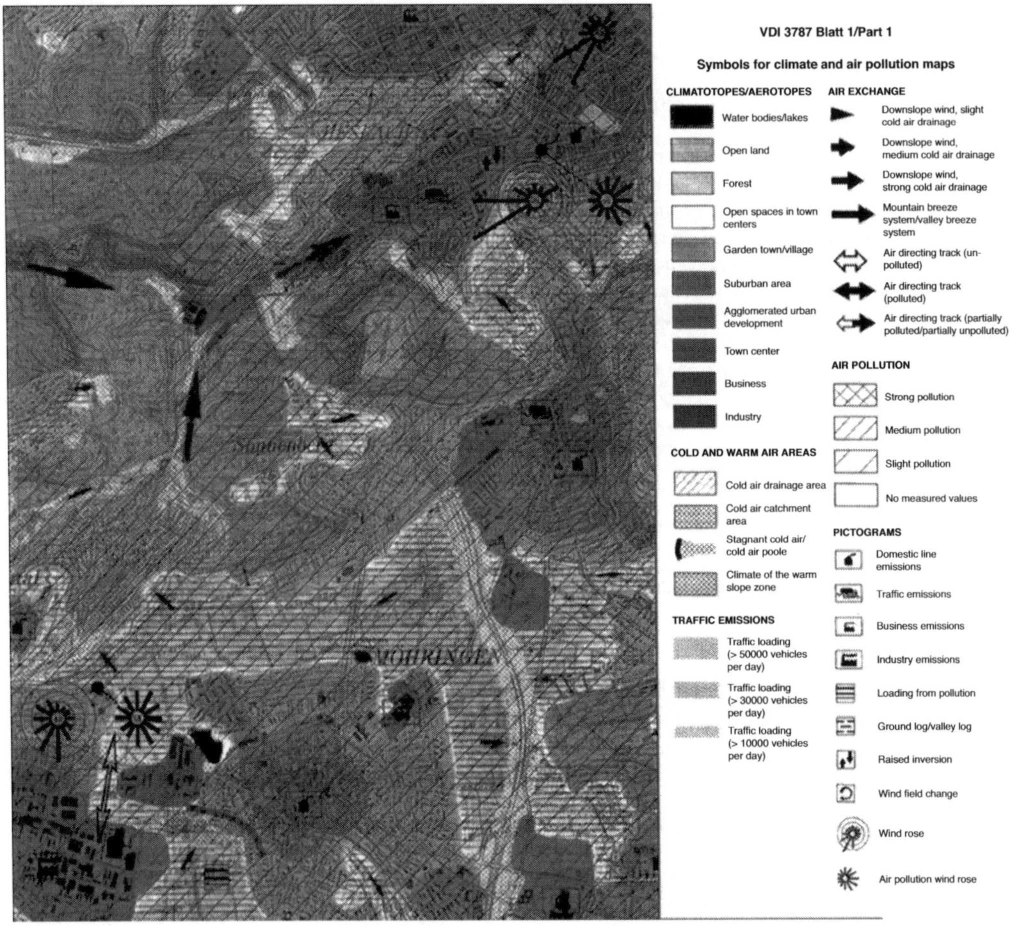

*Figure 2.3* A partial plan of the UC-AnMap and legend for Stuttgart urban areas.

Source: Klimaatlas, 1992; VDI, 1997

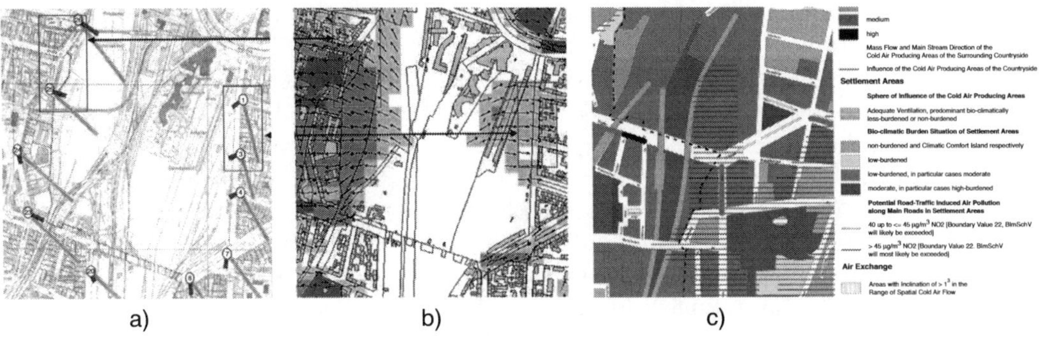


*Figure 2.4* Verification of the climatopes of Gleisdreieck areas: (a) measurement result; (b) FITNAH simulation result; (c) partial plan of UC-AnMap for Berlin.

Source: Vogt, 2002a, 2002b; SDUDB, 2008

ventilation in future development. Given the mixed land-use situation in high-density cities, it noted that the method of defining the climatopes merely based on land use and cover information needs to be improved, and new thoughts and methods are required (Ng, 2009a). Thus, for the UC-AnMap of Hong Kong, not only land use, topography, vegetation, and wind information have been taken into account, but further detailed urban morphology information such as building tower, podium, street, and open space has also been incorporated to calculate the building volume and ground coverage for quantifying the urban density, which affects the urban surface roughness and heat capacity (Ng *et al.*, 2008b). Based on the analysis of these selected planning parameters, three basic analytical input layers (building volume, ground coverage percentage, and the proximity of openness) are generalised with the fine resolution of 100m × 100m per grid. The Hong Kong urban climatic map study efforts follow urban air ventilation studies in 2006 (Ng, 2009b). The climatic condition of a high-density city like Hong Kong is very complicated; therefore, Hong Kong researchers have also conducted spot field measurements, user surveys of thermal comfort, model simulations and wind tunnel studies for calibrating the urban climatic understanding (Ng *et al.*, 2008b). The basic layers of climatic factors and geographical parameters have been synergised to become the Hong Kong UC-AnMap (see Figure 2.5). The Hong Kong UC-AnMap contains eight urban climatic analysis classes as climatopes, categorised by the spatial distribution of PET to illustrate the urban climatic value and inhomogeneous high-density urban context under summer daytime conditions (see Figure 2.6). The map provides the planners with a spatial overview of the urban biometeorological characteristics of the territory of Hong Kong under the conditions of a typical summer daytime. According to the UC-AnMap, clusters of urban climatic analysis Classes 7 and 8 point out the highly built-up urban areas as problem areas from the bio climatic point of view, which creates the need for improvement at the district level of planning implementation (Ng *et al.*, 2008a). That means people in the outdoor environment of those urban areas may suffer from high thermal load (stress) and less wind (low dynamic potential) at the pedestrian level. To calibrate and verify the results of the climatopes of the UC-AnMap for Hong Kong, local researchers conducted some relevant studies, such as spot field measurements, model simulations, and wind tunnel tests (Ng *et al.*, 2008b, 2008c). The results of the field measurement studies in the urban areas of Tsuen Wan and Tsim Sha Tsui have provided useful data as reference for calibrating the classification of the climatopes of the UC-AnMap for Hong Kong. It has been noted that 1 ΔUC-Map Class equals to 1°C of PET value, and that this correlation is strong ($R^2 \approx 0.74$) (Ng *et al.*, 2008b, 2008c). From this study it was found that the classification of the climatopes of the UC-AnMap of Hong Kong and the predicted human comfort pattern in the UC-AnMap in terms of PET are in good agreement with the actual urban climate condition of the city.

### *Urban climatic recommendation map (UC-ReMap) and planning instructions*

The UC-ReMap is an integrated, planning action-oriented assessment base that could be operated at the city or district scale. Based on the analysis obtained from the UC-AnMap, similar climatopes are grouped into zones to present the sensitivity of certain land areas affected by land-use changes. These zones are represented by different colours and symbols, which show different hints for plans of action such as 'Place that requires improvement' or 'Place that should be conserved', from the urban climate point of view (Baumüller *et al.*, 1992) (see Figure 2.7). Detailed principles for developing the UC-ReMap and planning recommendations are presented in Table 2.2.

The development process pays attention to the 'translation' from UC-AnMap to UC-ReMap to ensure that the climatic knowledge and evaluation results are correctly presented in urban planning

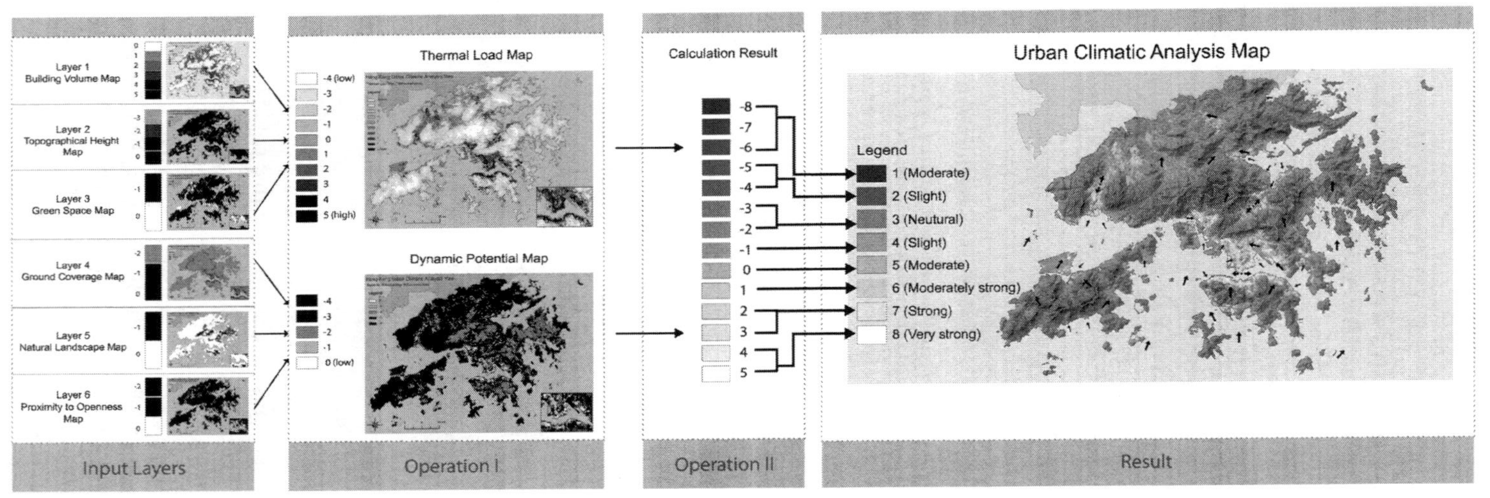


*Figure 2.5* The working process of the UC-AnMap of Hong Kong.

Source: Ng *et al.*, 2008a

| No | Urban Climatic Class | Impact on Thermal Comfort | Urban Climatic Planning Zone | Strategic Action |
|---|---|---|---|---|
| 1 | Moderate negative Thermal Load and Good Dynamics Potentials | •• Moderate | Urban climatically valuable area | Preserve |
| 2 | Some negative Thermal Load and Good Dynamics Potentials | • Slight | | |
| 3 | Low Thermal Load and Good Dynamics Potentials | - Neutral | Neutral urban climatically sensitive area | Preserve & enhance |
| 4 | Some Thermal Load and Some Dynamics Potentials | • Slight | | |
| 5 | Moderate Thermal Load and Some Dynamics Potentials | •• Moderate | Moderate urban climatically sensitive area | Some action encouraged |
| 6 | Moderately High Thermal Load and Low Dynamics Potentials | ••• Moderately strong | Highly urban climatically sensitive area | Action desirable & recommended |
| 7 | High Thermal Load and Low Dynamics Potentials | •••• Strong | | |
| 8 | Very High Thermal Load and Low Dynamics Potentials | ••••• Very strong | Very higly urban climatically sensitive area | Action necessary |

Note:

• 'Cooling' impact

• 'Warming' impact

1 Moderately negative Thermal Load due to higher altitude and adiabatic cooling, and greenery and trans-evaporative cooling

2 Some negative Thermal Load due to vegetated slope and trans-evaporative cooling

3 to 8 Various classes of warming impact due to increasing Thermal Load and decreasing Dynamic Potentials

*Figure 2.6* Description of eight Urban Climatic Classes of the UC-AnMap of Hong Kong.

Source: Ng *et al.*, 2008a

*Table 2.2* Analysis aspects and highlighted zones of a UC-ReMap

| *Type of UCMap* | *Zones with septic land use* | *Climatic impact and function* | | *Planning level and scale* |
|---|---|---|---|---|
| Urban climatic recommendation map | – Forest and woodlands on hill slopes or valleys | Generates and transfers cold/fresh air | Wind aspect | Municipality/City master plan (1:10,000–1:25,000) |
| | – Vegetation on the borders of built-up areas | Contributes to air exchange | | |
| | – Large green belt and interconnected green space or network | Contributes to air exchange and transfers cold/fresh air from rural areas to urban areas | | |
| | – Open space sensitive to the change of land use | Transfers cold/fresh air and improves the air exchange | | Zoning plan (1:5,000–1:10,000) |
| | – Built-up areas | Blocks air exchange | | |
| | – Railway and several wide streets | Contributes to air exchange | | |
| | – Urban greenery and surrounding areas | Mitigates urban heat island effect | Thermal aspect | Landscape/ Land-use plan (1:5,000–1:10,000) |
| | – Open space | Mitigates urban heat island effect | | |
| | – Built-up areas | Contributes to urban heat island effect | | |
| | – Highly built-up areas | Processes heat thermal load | | |
| | – Industrial and commercial areas | Causes air pollution and noise | Air pollution aspect | |
| | – Main traffic roads | Causes air pollution and noise | | |

Source: Baumüller *et al.*, 1992; VDI, 1997

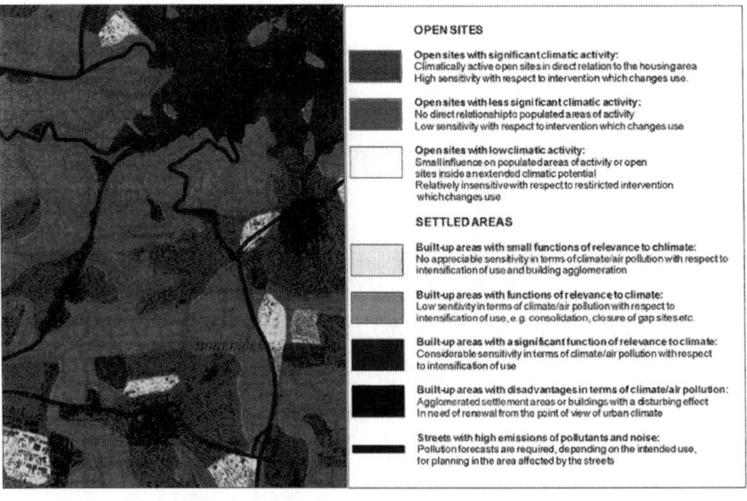


*Figure 2.7* A partial plan of the UC-ReMap of Stuttgart city.

Source: Klimaatlas, 1992; VDI, 1997

language. The UC-ReMap not only presents the evaluation of current climatic characteristics spatially, but also identifies problem and climate-sensitive areas that are in need of strategic attention and further development. Therefore, at this stage, urban climatologists, planners, and policymakers need to work closely together. Planning recommendations and guidelines are developed with the aim of mitigating negative and protecting positive situations. Since different cities have various urban planning systems and urban climatic problems, the implementation of a UC-ReMap and planning recommendations may require emphasis on different aspects.

There are a lot of vegetated hillsides around Stuttgart; katabatic wind can be observed during the night. To protect this kind of cold fresh air, the UC-AnMap of Stuttgart defined the cold air drainage areas. For example, one is located in the Vaihignen area (highlighted with a dark circle in Figure 2.8a). As such, when the UC-ReMap was developed, the further development

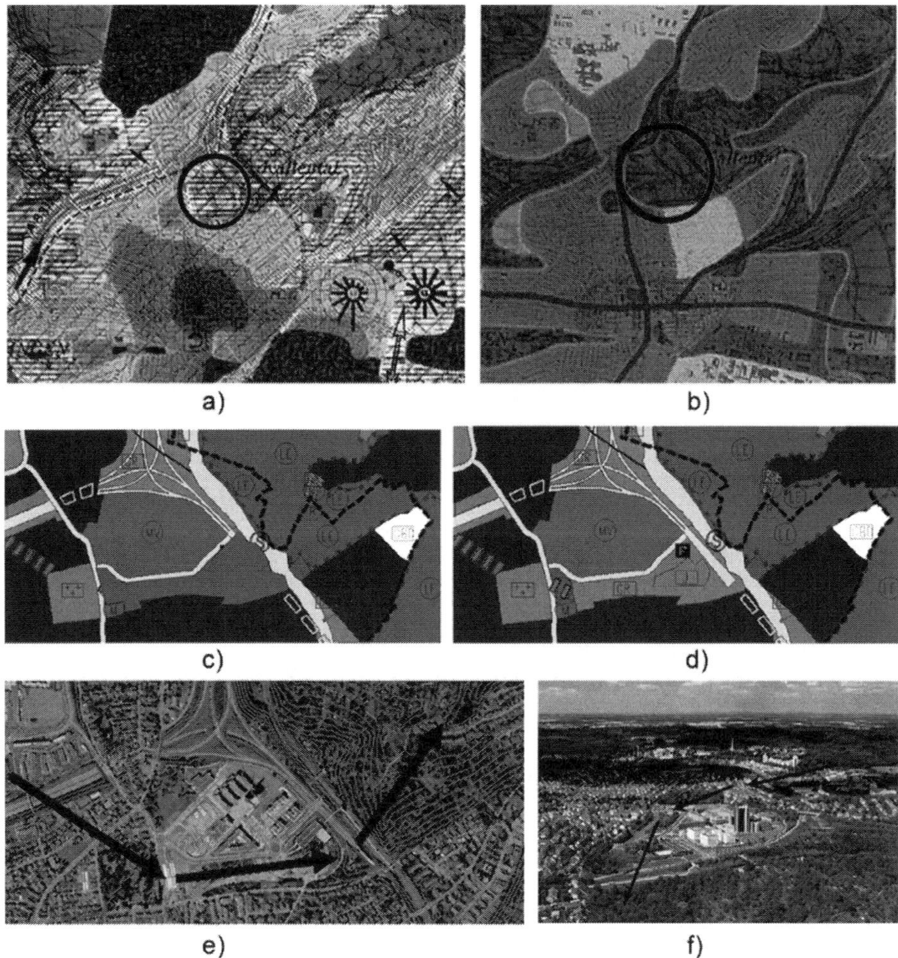


*Figure 2.8* Successful implementation example of Stuttgart UCMap study: (a) UC-AnMap of Stuttgart; (b) UC-ReMap of Stuttgart; (c) original land use plan; (d) revised land use plan; (e) air path; (f) ventilation zone.

Source: Baumüller *et al.*, 1992; Baumüller, 2006

was recommended to respect the local air exchange and to protect this area as an open site with significant climatic activity, while considering intervention changes in land use (see Figure 2.8b). Local planners then revised the original land use plan of this area from buildable land to private and public greenery (see Figures 2.8c and 2.8d). Currently, this area works as an air path (or ventilation corridor) to transfer the cold air mass to the surrounding areas (see Figures 2.8e and 2.8f). The implementation of the UC-ReMap has also been applied to update the master plan of greenery, control building height, and create/protect air paths. The Stuttgart UC-ReMap contains the 'first-cut' nature of the zone boundaries and the general planning recommendations; therefore, it provides a useful reference for local planners in their actual practices. When further details are required, they can refer back to the UC-AnMap together with their urban climatic advisers.

According to the thermal environment map (TEMap) (see Plate 5.1), the TMG designated four focus areas with high urban heat island (UHI) intensity and weak urban ventilation situation: the districts of Shinjuku, Urban Center, Osaki/Meguro, and Shinagawa Station. Based on this TEMap of Tokyo, the local government could invest appropriately in planning improvement actions and research projects, and conduct appropriate action plans to mitigate the UHI and improve poor urban ventilation in the central of Tokyo, such as by increasing greenery converge, controlling frontal areas of building blocks, and decreasing anthropogenic heat release. The Japan Sustainable Building Consortium has worked with the MLIT to develop the national guideline of the Comprehensive Assessment System for Building Environmental Efficiency for Heat Island Relaxation (CASBEE-HI), assessing efforts exerted in buildings to alleviate the heat island effect in the surroundings (IBEC, 2006). Later, the study of 'Kaze-no-michi' was conducted by the MLIT to form a scientific basis for urban air temperature and the wind characteristics at ground level for Tokyo Metropolitan, and to analyse the impact of urban ventilation paths and the cooling effect of sea breeze (AIJ, 2008b; Ashie *et al.*, 2008).

The UC-ReMap of Hong Kong provides information for strategic and district planning applied to an outline zoning plan with the scale of 1:2,000. Given the high-density context of Hong Kong, the useful strategy planning instructions and recommendations focus on reducing ground coverage for improving air ventilation and pedestrian comfort, and on improving greenery coverage in the urban areas.

Based on the above reviewed, it is found that planning instructions and recommendations are elaborated with the UC-ReMap. Since the goals of climate-sensitive planning should be pursued to improve the living conditions and quality relative to bioclimate, UHI, urban air ventilation, and air quality situation, the main planning recommendations focus on the following aspects: reduce urban thermal (heat) load; control building volumes and sealing areas; improve urban dynamic potentials; preserve, maintain, and improve the existing urban ventilation paths and network of the city, chart new air paths if necessary; preserve, maintain, improve, and respect the cold air production and drainage areas of the countryside and vegetated hillsides near to the urban areas; preserve, maintain, improve, and respect the land-sea breezes; preserve, maintain, and improve urban greenery; and reduce the release of air pollutants, greenhouse gases, and anthropogenic waste heat.

Thus, the planning strategies can be taken from four aspects: albedo, vegetation, shading, and ventilation. Detailed plan actions with various operation and climatic impact scales are summarised in Table 2.3. These opportunities for innovation in the face of improving the urban climatic environment contain important lessons for sustainable urban development in the future.

The creation of the UCMap is only the beginning; sustainable efforts are still needed. Planners should consult urban climatologists to interpret UCMap and planning instructions appropriately. Concerns and issues must be balanced and optimised. To improve and update the UCMap, a

*Table 2.3* Lessons on strategies and measures for improving the urban climate environment

| *Objectives* | *Aspects* | *Action plans and strategies* | *Operation and spatial scale* | *Climatic impact scale* |
|---|---|---|---|---|
| bioclimate + urban heat island + urban air ventilation + air quality situation | Albedo | Cooling of building material and pavement<br>Cooling of roof and façade<br>Water retention paving | Material and surface-level intervention | Meso- and micro-scale |
| | Vegetation | Planting greenery | Material and surface-level intervention | Meso- and micro-scale |
| | | Parks and open spaces | Landscape/land use planning-level intervention | |
| | | Green corridors | Landscape/land use planning-level intervention | |
| | Shading | Building geometric design | Building design-level intervention | Micro-scale |
| | | Shelter design | Building design-level intervention | Micro-scale |
| | | Street orientation | Urban planning/zoning-level intervention | Meso- and micro-scale |
| | | Building height/street width ratio | Building design-level intervention | Micro-scale |
| | | Trees along both sides of streets | Landscape/land use planning-level intervention | Micro-scale |
| | Ventilation | Air path | Urban planning/zoning-level intervention | Meso- and micro-scale |
| | | Building ground coverage and building bulks | Urban planning/zoning-level intervention | Meso- and micro-scale |
| | | Building height/street width ratio | Building design-level intervention | Micro-scale |
| | | Street orientation | Urban planning/zoning-level intervention | Meso- and micro-scale |
| | | Layout of building dispositions | Urban planning/zoning-level intervention | Meso- and micro-scale |
| | | Open spaces and greenery areas | Landscape/land use planning-level intervention | Meso- and micro-scale |

Source: Author

professional team is required to monitor the use and the effectiveness of the application, to collect further data as the basis of evaluation, to refine scientific bases as new knowledge develops, and to update the map to cope with the changes in urban morphology.

## Discussion

Based on the available collated information, the UCMap takes into account an expertly balanced evaluation of positive and negative effects of the local climate, topography of the land, vegetation and buildings of the city, and wind patterns. In the planning aspect, this approach provides an evaluation tool that makes use of available spatial data, and proposes solutions for planning use through knowledge-based expert evaluation. The advantages and limitations of UCMaps are elaborated below. Furthermore, the future trend of UCMap study is also discussed from the aspects of the future role of UCMaps in climate change, professional expertise, climatic planning education, and its application in developing countries.

### Advantages

- The UCMap is a cross-disciplinary study and practice bridging urban climatology and urban planning, and focusing on the application of climatic knowledge in planning. The useful climatic understanding and planning recommendations can be implemented into actual physical planning processes such as municipality/city master plans, zoning plans, and land use plans. Since planning-related statements refer to specific areas, the use of a UCMap as an informational basis is recommended. Generated maps are regarded as very significant visual tools for the planner and as meaningful means of communicating information to political leaders and the interested public.
- Climatic phenomena and data are visualised by colours and graphics presented with spatial information in maps. In the planning aspect, this approach provides an evaluation tool that makes use of available spatial data, and proposes solutions for planning use through knowledge-based expert evaluation that is easily understood by planners, developers, and policymakers. These solutions can also be attributed to detailed specific climatic information from the corresponding basic input layers.
- Climatically problematic and sensitive areas are observable using UCMaps. Such areas require the local government to pay close attention and conduct necessary actions to improve the urban living environment in future developments.
- The use of Geographic Information System (GIS) in UCMap studies has become more common since the 1990s. Thus, the framework and database of UCMaps can be managed and updated digitally. It is possible to export maps with different scales and layouts for flexible planning use. Various data and information can be overlaid with accurate spatial information in the GIS platform.
- A UC-ReMap with relevant planning instructions is the result of communication between climatologists, meteorologists, planners, and local governors; thus, it can meet the actual needs of planners, developers, and local governors.

### Limitations

- The UC-AnMap and UC-ReMap are 'synthetic' and 'evaluative' results for planning purposes. The defining of climatopes and the making of climatic assessments and planning recommendations in UCMap studies not only depend on objectively and empirically collected climatic information and evidence, but they also rely on the expert experience and qualitative evaluation of urban climatologists. There may be a need for better and more proper procedures and the standardisation of evaluation and recommendation to ascertain the improvement effect on urban living environment after applying planning recommendations.
- Climatopes are mainly defined by land use; to better understand the distribution pattern of the climatopes of the study areas, researchers have tried to quantitatively calibrate and verify the climatopes. Tracer gas experiments, wind tunnel tests, mobile traverse temperature measurements, computer model simulation tests, and so on, have been conducted to examine the generic climatic variations of urban areas. However, the methods must still be improved with the effort and support of urban climatologists.
- To understand city planning, it is necessary to mention the spatial and landscape planning system, which takes place on different scales, levels, and responsibilities. UCMap and planning instructions with different scales and themes should be generated and adopted to meet different planning uses.

- Urban planning is the result of balancing and weighting many sectors. The study result of UCMaps and planning recommendations should be presented as simply and as clearly as possible. Otherwise, they may not be understood and used by the planners, developers, and policymakers.

### *Future trends*

Currently, more than half of the world's population lives in urban areas. With increasing concern for urban living quality and public health, additional spatial analyses on the bioclimatic condition of urban areas should be conducted in UCMap studies to understand real needs and reveal existing and potential problems.

In facing the global issues of climate change and continuing warming, one of the future roles of UCMaps is to offer assessment and visualise the relevant impact of these phenomena on the urban environment in order to help planners, developers, and policymakers make better decisions on mitigation and adaptation.

Once a UCMap is generated, numerous additional tasks are required, such as updating the map and planning instructions, adding new information and knowledge, offering expert advice on using and reading methods, and so on. Professional expertise on UCMaps in the local government is highly recommended to continue the effort and provide sustainable and up-to-date information to enable better planning and decision-making. For example, in Stuttgart during the 1970s, a section for climatology was set up in the Environmental Department. Thus, communication between climatologists, planners, and governors has become common and frequent.

Planners, developers, and policymakers are accustomed to solving the complex problems from social, environmental, and economic aspects; however, the climatic aspect is generally neglected. Due to limited knowledge on urban climatology, they have less ability to adopt and transfer the climatic knowledge in planning, application, and design. Thus, relevant training and education on urban climatic application and climatic spatial planning is urgently needed.

Today, rapid urbanisation and urban congestion is an urgent concern among developing countries and regions whose climatic environments have been gravely affected, even degraded. Comprehensive climatic assessment and evaluations are seldom incorporated in local urban developments and planning. Thus, it is necessary to conduct international research programmes on UCMap studies in these countries and regions to guide local developments in these areas more sustainably. Likewise, sharing the learned lessons and accumulated experiences on UCMap studies with local researchers, planners, and governors is strongly recommended. Considering the lack of geographic databases, climatic information, and meteorological measurements in these areas, a simplified method of UCMap study is suggested.

## Conclusions

This paper summarised and reviewed the latest concepts, key methodologies, selected parameters, structure and development process, mitigation countermeasures, and relevant planning instructions in UCMap studies. Various climatic phenomena, geographic information, and planning parameters were discussed and described. It was concluded that the thermal environment and air ventilation situation within the UCL play the most important roles in the analytical aspects and climatic-environmental evaluation. Similarly, it was concluded that possible mitigation measures and action plans could be taken by decreasing anthropogenic heat release, improving air ventilation at the pedestrian level, providing shading, increasing greenery, creating air paths, and controlling building construction. Future research should focus on the spatial analysis of the bioclimate in urban outdoor areas and in climate change impacts and adaptation. Sharing the learned lessons and experiences with planners and policymakers in the rapidly expanding cities of developing countries and regions is also important.

## Acknowledgement

This chapter was originally published as Ren, C., Ng, E. Y. Y. and Katzschner, L. (2011). Urban climatic map studies: A review, *International Journal of Climatology*, 31(15): 2213–2233. Kind permission has been obtained from John Wiley and Sons to reproduce it.

## References

AIJ (2000). *Urban Environmental Climatic Atlas: Urban Development Utilizing Climate Information*, Tokyo: Architectural Institute of Japan. (In Japanese).

AIJ (2008a). Anthropogenic heat and urban heat islands: A feedback system. *Newsletter on Urban Heat Island Countermeasures*, Vol. 5. Available at: http://news-sv.aij.or.jp/tkankyo/s3/Newsletter_vol5_081118.pdf (Accessed 10 February 2014).

AIJ (2008b). National research project on kaze-no-michi: Making the best use of the cool sea breeze. *Newsletter on Urban Heat Island Countermeasures*, Vol. 4. Available at: http://news-sv.aij.or.jp/tkankyo/s3/Newsletter_vol4_081118.pdf (Accessed 10 February 2014).

Akasaka, H. (1991). A study on drawing climatic maps related to human thermal sensation. *Energy and Buildings*, 16(3–4): 1011–1023.

Akashi, T. (2008). Creating 'wind paths' in the city to mitigate urban heat island effects - a case study in the central district of Tokyo. Paper presented at *The CIB-W101 (Spatial Planning and Infrastructure Development) Annual Meeting 2008*. Dublin Institute of Technology, Dublin, Ireland, September. Available at: http://okabe.t.u-tokyo.ac.jp/okabelab/yasami/CIB/08-Dublin/Akashi3.pdf (Accessed July 2009).

Alcoforado, M. J. (2006). Planning procedures towards high climatic quality cities: Example referring to Lisbon. *Finisterra*, 41(82): 49–64.

Alcoforado, M. J., Lopes, A., Andrade, H. and Vasconcelos, J. (2006a). *Orientações climáticas para o ordenamento em Lisboa*. Lisboa: Centro de Estudos Geográficos da Universidade de Lisboa. Available at: http://www.proclira.uevora.pt/pdf/RPDMLisboa_avaliacao_climatica.pdf (Accessed 10 February 2014).

Alcoforado, M. J., Lopes, A., Andrade, H. and Vasconcelos, J. (2006b). *Report: Climatic Evaluation for Urban Planning in Lisbon*. Lisbon: Universidade de Lisboa.

Alcoforado, M. J., Andrade, H., Lopes, A. and Vasconcelos, J. (2009). Application of climatic guidelines to urban planning: The example of Lisbon (Portugal). *Landscape and Urban Planning*, 90(1–2): 56–65.

AMS (ed.) (2010). *The Definition of Urban Canopy Layer, Glossary of Meteorology*, American Meteorological Society US. Available at: http://amsglossary.allenpress.com/glossary/search?id=urban-canopy-layer1 (Accessed January 2010).

Ashie, Y., Kodama, Y., Asaeda, T. and Ca, V. T. (1998). Climate analysis for urban planning in Tokyo. *Report of Research Center for Urban Safety and Security, Kobe University*, Special Report Vol. 1: 86–94. Available at: http://www.lib.kobe-u.ac.jp/repository/00044720.pdf (Accessed 10 February 2014).

Ashie, Y., Cho, K. and Kono, T. (2008). Large-scale CFD simulation of heat island phenomenon in Tokyo's 23 wards using the earth simulator. In: Mayer, H and Matzarakis, A. (eds.), *Proceedings of the 5th Japanese-German Meeting on Urban Climatology*. Berichte des Meteorologischen Instituts der Albert-Ludwigs-Universität Freiburg, No. 18. The Albert-Ludwigs-University of Freiburg, Freiburg, Germany, 6–11 October. Freiburg: the Meteorological Institute, Albert-Ludwigs-University of Freiburg, 147–150. Available at: http://www.meteo.uni-freiburg.de/forschung/publikationen/berichte/report18.pdf (Accessed 10 February 2014).

Ban, J., Zhang, F., Liu, Y., Xiao, L., Guo, X., Zhang, T., Liu, B., Wang, X., Lu, Q., Zhao, T., Jin, X. and Ng, E. (2009). A pilot study of urban climatic mapping of the city of Xi'an, China. In: *Proceedings of The 7th International Conference on Urban Climate.*Yokohama, Japan, 29 June–3 July. Available at: http://www.ide.titech.ac.jp/~icuc7/extended_abstracts/pdf/379878-1-090513093132-004.pdf (Accessed 10 February 2014).

Baumüller, J. (2006). Implementation of climatic aspects in urban development: The example Stuttgart. In: *Proceedings of PGBC Symposium 2006: Urban Climate + Urban Greenery.* Hong Kong, 2 December. Hong Kong: The Professional Green Building Council, 42–52.

Baumüller, J. and Reuter, U. (1999). *Demands and Requirements on a Climate Atlas for Urban Planning and Design.* Stuttgart: Office of Environmental Protection.

Baumüller, J., Hoffmann, U. and Reuter, U. (1992). *Climate Booklet for Urban Development.* Stuttgart: Ministry of Economy Baden-Wuerttemberg (Wirschaftsministerium). Environmental Protection Department (Amt für Umweitschutz).

Baumüller, J., Flassak, T., Schädler, G., Keim, M. and Lohmeyer, A. (1998). 'Urban climate 21' – Climatological basics and design features for 'Stuttgart 21'on CD-ROM. *Report of Research Center for Urban Safety and Security, Kobe University*, Special Report Vol. 1 : 42– 52. Available at: http://www.lib.kobe-u.ac.jp/repository/00044716.pdf (Accessed 10 February 2014)

Baumüller, J., Esswein, H., Hoffmann, U., Reuter, U., Weidenbacher, S., Nagel, T. and Flassak, T. (2009a). Climate Atlas of a metropolitan region in Germany based on GIS. In: *Proceedings of The 7th International Conference on Urban Climate.* Yokohama, Japan, 29 June–3 July. Available at: http://www.ide.titech.ac.jp/~icuc7/extended_abstracts/pdf/375531-2-090501005214-002.pdf (Accessed 10 February 2014).

Baumüller, J., Hoffmann, U. and Stuckenbrock, U. (2009b). *Urban Framework Plan Hillsides of Stuttgart.* In: *Proceedings of The 7th International Conference on Urban Climate.*Yokohama, Japan, 29 June–3 July. Available at: http://www.ide.titech.ac.jp/~icuc7/extended_abstracts/pdf/375531-1-090501004614-003.pdf (Accessed 10 February 2014).

Beckröge, W. (1988). Climate as a factor of a planning project – demonstrated by the example of Dortmund Bornstrasse. *Energy and Buildings*, 11(1– 3): 129–135.

Beckröge, W., Kiese, O., Otto, W. and Stock, P. (1988). *Klimaanalyse Stadt Recklinghausen.* Essen: Kommunalverband Ruhrgebiet.

Berlin Government (2008). Belüftungsbahnen – Luftaustausch für das Stadtklima. *Landschaftsprogramm einschließlich Artenschutzprogramm, Programmplan Naturhaushalt/Umweltschutz* (Vol. 2004). Berlin, Deutschland.

Bründl, W. (1988). Climate function maps and urban planning. *Energy and Buildings*, 11(1–3): 123–127.

Charalampopoulos, I. and Chronopoulou-Sereli, A. (2005). Mapping the urban green area influence on local climate under windless light wind conditions: The case of western part of Athens, Greece. *Acta Climatologica ET Chorologica*, 38–39: 25–31.

Desplat, J., Salagnac, J-L., Kounkou, R., Lemonsu, A., Colombert, M., Lauffenburger, M. and Masson, V. (2009). EPICEA Project [2008–2010], Multidisciplinary study of the impacts of climate change on the scale of Paris. In: *Proceedings of The 7th International Conference on Urban Climate.* Yokohama, Japan, 29 June–3 July. Available at: http://www.ide.titech.ac.jp/~icuc7/extended_abstracts/pdf/383983-1-090519180457-002.pdf (Accessed 10 February 2014).

Eliasson, I. (2000). The use of climate knowledge in urban planning. *Landscape and Urban Planning*, 48(1–2): 31–44.

ERDF. (2010). *Urban Climatic Map for Arnhem, The Netherlands.* Future Cities – urban networks to face climate change. Arnhem: The Municipality of Arnhem, The Netherlands, The European Regional Development Fund (ERDF), Arnhem, The Netherlands. Available at: http://www.future-cities.eu/uploads/media/report_Urban_Climatic_Map_of_Arnhem_City_02.pdf (Accessed 10 February 2014).

Erell, E., Portnov, B. A. and Etzion, Y. (2003). Mapping the potential for climate-conscious design of buildings. *Building and Environment*, 38(2): 271–281.

Esser, G. (1989). Global land-use changes from 1860 to 1980 and future projections to 2500. *Ecological Modelling*, 44(3–4): 307–316.

Evans, J. M. and de Schiller, S. (1991). Climate and urban planning: The example of the planning code for Vicente Lopez, Buenos Aires. *Energy and Buildings*, 15(1–2): 35–41.

Fehrenbach, U., Scherer, D. and Parlow, E. (2001). Automated classification of planning objectives for the consideration of climate and air quality in urban and regional planning for the example of the region of Basel / Switzerland. *Atmospheric Environment*, 35(32): 5605–5615.

Gal, T. and Unger, J. (2009). Detection of ventilation paths using high-resolution roughness parameter mapping in a large urban area. *Building and Environment*, 44(1): 198–206.

Gao, W. and Ojima, T. (2003). Improving the urban thermal environment of Tokyo through Clusterization. Paper presented at *the 3rd International Symposium on Architectural Interchanges in Asia*. Korea. Available at: http://gao.env.kitakyu-u.ac.jp/japanesesite/publish/Korean20000223/paper.pdf (Accessed July 2006).

Groß, G. (1993). *Numerical Simulation of Canopy Flows*. Berlin: Springer.

He, J. F., Liu, J. Y., Zhuang, D. F., Zhang, W. and Liu, M. L. (2007). Assessing the effect of land use/land cover change on the change of urban heat island intensity. *Theoretical and Applied Climatology*, 90(34): 217–226.

Helbig, A., Baumüller, J. and Kerschgens, M. (1999). *Stadtklima und Luftreinhaltung*. 2nd edition. Berlin: Springer.

Hoffman, U. (1978). City climate of Stuttgart. In Franke, E. (ed.), *City Climate: Data and Aspects for City Planning*. Trans. by Literature Research Company. FBW – A publication of Research, Building and Living, No. 108.

Höppe, P. (1993). Heat balance modelling. *Experimentia*, 49(9): 741–746.

Höppe, P. (1999). The Physiological Equivalent Temperature – a universal index for the biometeorological assessment of the thermal environment. *International Journal of Biometeorology*, 43: 71–75.

Hsie, T. S. (2007). A combined computational method for determining natural ventilation potentials in the planning process. In: Wittkopf, S. K. and Tan, B. K. (eds.), *Proceedings of the 24th International Conference on Passive and Low Energy Architecture (PLEA2007): Sun, Wind and Architecture*. National University of Singapore, Singapore, 22–24 November. Available at: http://www.plea-arch.org/ARCHIVE/2007/html/pdf/DP0214.pdf (Accessed 10 February 2014).

Hsie, T. S. and Ward, I. C. (2006). A GIS-based method for determining natural ventilation potentials and urban morphology. In: *Proceedings of the 23rd Conference on Passive and Low Energy Architecture (PLEA2006)*, Vol.1, 707–712. Geneva, Switzerland, 6–8 September. Available at: http://www.cuepe.ch/html/plea2006/Vol1/PLEA2006_PAPER156.pdf (Accessed 10 February 2014).

IBEC (2006). *CASBEE for Heat Island (CASBEE-HI), Comprehensive Assessment System for Building Environmental Efficiency, Tool 4*. Tokyo: Insitute for Building Environment and Energy Conservation (IBEC). (In Japanese).

Ichinose, T. (2000). Climatic analysis for urban planning, Centre for Global Environmental Research. *NIES News*, 8–9. (In Japanese).

Ichinose, T., Shimodozono, K. and Hanaki, K. (1999). Impact of anthropogenic heat on urban climate in Tokyo. *Atmospheric Environment*, 33(24–25): 3897–3909.

Ichinose, T., Mikami, T., Niitsu, K. and Hirano, Y. (2006). Counteractions for urban heat island in regional autonomies: Activities in Councils of MOE, Japan. In: *Proceedings of the 5th International Conference on Urban Climate*. University of Lodz, Lodz, Poland, 1–5 Septemeber. Available at: http://nargeo.geo.uni.lodz.pl/~icuc5/text/P_5_9.pdf (Accessed 10 February 2014).

Jendritzky, G., Graetz, A., Koppe, C. and Laschewski, G. (2010). How to deal with the urban development – urban climate – human health effect relationship: A contribution to methodology. Paper presented at *The 2010 Urban Heat Island Summit, Clean Air Partnership*. Toronto, 3 May 2010. Available at: http://www.cleanairpartnership.org/pdf/finalpaper_jendritsky.pdf (Accessed 10 February 2014).

Jittawikul, A., Saito, I. and Ishihara, O. (2004). Climatic maps for passive cooling methods utilization in Thailand. *Journal of Asian Architecture and Building Engineering*, 3(1): 109–114.

Katzschner, L. (1988). The urban climate as a parameter for urban development. *Energy and Buildings*, 11(1–3): 137–147.

Katzschner, L. (Cartographer) (1993). *Urban Climatic Analysis Map for Kassel City*.

Katzschner, L. (1998). Designation of urban climate qualities and their implementation in the planning process. In: Maldonado, E. and Yannas, S.: *Environmentally Friendly Cities: Proceedings of PLEA 98, Passive and Low Energy Architecture*. Lisbon, Portugal, June 1998. London: James & James Science Publishers Ltd., 75–78.

Katzschner, L. (2006). Urban climatology and urban planning. Paper presented at *An Expert Forum on UCMap & CFD for Urban Wind Studies in Cities*. Hong Kong Institute of Architects, Hong Kong, 17 October.

Katzschner, L. (2009). Manuel, nicht Kassandra: Frankfurt im Klimawandel. *THEMA DES TAGS*, D2.

Katzschner, L. and Mulder, J. (2008). Regional climatic mapping as a tool for sustainable development. *Journal of Environmental Management*, 87(2): 262–267.

Katzschner, L., Bosch, U. and Röttgen, M. (2003) A methodology for bioclimatic microscale mapping of open spaces. In: *Proceedings of the Fifth International Conference on Urban Climate*. University of Lodz, Lodz, Poland, 1–5 Septemeber. Available at: http://nargeo.geo.uni.lodz.pl/~icuc5/text/P_1_1.pdf (Accessed 10 February 2014).

Kiese, O., Voigt, J., Kelker, J. and Schöpper, H. (1992). Stadtklima Münster. Werkstattberichte zum Umweltschutz. *Umweltamt der Stadt Münster 1/1992*: 247 pages.

Kim, H. O. (2007). *Beitrag sehr hochauflösender Satellitenfernerkundungsdaten zur Aktualisierung der Biotop- und Nutzungstypenkartierung in Stadtgebieten – Dargestellt am Beispiel von Seoul*. PhD thesis. der Technischen Universität Berlin, Berlin, Germany. Available at: http://d-nb.info/985997850/34 (Accessed 10 February 2014).

Klimaatlas (1992). *Nachbarschaftsverband Stuttgart (Stuttgart Regional Federation), Climate study for the area of the Stuttgart Regional Federation and bordering areas of the Stuttgart region*. Stuttgart: Landeschauptstadt Stuttgart, Amt fur Umweltschutz, Abteilung Stadtklimatologie:

Knoch, K. (1951). Uber das Wesen einer Landesklimaaufnahme. *Meteorologische Zeitschrift*, 5: 173.

Knoch, K. (1963). Die Landesklima-aufanhme, Wesen und Methodik. *Ber. Dtsch. Wetterdienst*, No. 85.

The Knowledge for Climate Research Programme (2007). *The Knowledge for Climate Programme*, The VU University, the Royal Dutch Meteorological Institute (KNMI) and the Netherlands Organisation for Applied Scientific Research (TNO).

Kuttler, W. (1997). Climate and air hygiene investigations for urban planning. *Acta Climatologica ET Chorologica*, 31(A): 3–6.

KVR (ed.) (1992). *Synthetische Klimafunktionskarte Ruhrgebiet*. Essen: Kommunalverband Ruhrgebiet, Abt. Öffentlichkeitsarbeit/Wirtschaft.

Lam, C. Y. (2006). On climate changes brought about by urban living. *Hong Kong Meteorological Society Bulletin*, 16(1/2): 15–27.

Lambin, E. F., Baulies, X., Bockstael, N., Fischer, G., Krug, T., Leemans, R., Moran, E. F., Rindfuss, R. R., Sato, Y., Skole, D., Turber, B. L. and Vogel, C. (1999). *IGBP Report No.48 / IHDP Report No. 10: Land-Use and Land-Cover Change – Implementation Strategy*. IGBP Secretariat, The Royal Swedish Academy of Sciences. Available at: http://www.igbp.net/download/18.1b8ae20512db692f2a680006377/1376383119247/report_48-LUCC.pdf (Accessed 10 February 2014).

Lazar, R. and Podesser, A. (1999). An urban climate analysis of Graz and its significance for urban planning in the tributary valleys east of Graz (Austrial). *Atmospheric Environment*, 33(24): 4195–4209.

Lazar, R., Buchroithner, M. F. and Kaufmann, V. (1994). *Stadtklimaanalyse Graz*. Graz: Magistrat Graz, Stadtplanungsamt.

Leung, Y. K., Yip, K. M. and Yeung, K. H. (2008). Relationship between thermal index and mortality in Hong Kong. *Meteorological Application*, 15(3): 399–409.

Lindqvist, S. (1991). *Local Climatological Maps for Planning*. Gothenburg: Department of Physical Geography, University of Gothenburg.

Lindqvist, S. and Mattsson, J. (1989). Topoclimatic maps for different planning levels – some Swedish examples. *Building Research and Practice*, 17(5): 299–304.

Lindqvist, S., Mattsson, J. O. and Holmer, B. (1983). Lokalklimatiska kartor for anvandning i kommunal oversiktlig planering. *Byggforskiningsradet*, 38.

Littlefair, P., Santamouris, M., Alvarez, S., Dupagne, A., Hall, D., Teller, J., Coronel, J.F. and Papanikolaou, N. (2000). *Environmental Site Layout Planning: Solar Access, Microclimate and Passive Cooling in Urban Areas*. UK: Building Research Establishment Press.

Lüttig, G. W. (1972). Naturräumliches Potential I, II und II. In: *Niedersachsen: Industrieland mit Zukunft*. Hannover: Nieders. Min. f. Wirtschaft u. Öffentl. Arbeiten, 9–10.

Lüttig, G. W. (1978a). Geoscientific maps for land-use planning. A certain approach how to communicate by new types of maps. *International Yearbook Cartography*, Vol. 18. Godesberg, Germany: Bonn-Bad, 95–101.

Lüttig, G. W. (1978b). Geoscientific maps of the environment as an essential tool in planning. *Geologie en Mijnbouw*, 57(4): 527–532.

Mattig, U. (1992). Geoscientific maps for land-use planning: A review. *Lecture Notes in Earth Sciences*, 42: 49–81.

Matzarakis, A. (2005). Country Report: Urban climate research in Germany. *IAUC Newsletter*, 11:4–6. Available at: http://www.urbanclimate.net/matzarakis1/papers/UCRE_de_IAUC011.pdf (Accessed 10 February 2014).

Matzarakis, A. and Mayer, H. (1992). Mapping of urban air paths for planning in Munich. *Wiss. Ber. Inst. Meteor. Klimaforsch. Univ. Karlsruhe*, 16: 13–22.

Matzarakis, A. and Mayer, H. (1996). Bioclimate maps of Greece for touristic aspects. In: Hočevar, A., Črepinšek, Z. and Kajfež-Bogataj, L. (eds.), *Proceedings of The 14th International Congress of Biometeorology*, Vol. 3. Ljubijana, Slovenia, 1–8 September. The International Society of Biometeorology, 222–229. Available at: http://www.urbanclimate.net/matzarakis1/papers/icb15_maps.pdf (Accessed 10 February 2014).

Matzarakis, A. and Mayer, H. (2008). Learning from the past: Urban climate studies in Munich. In: Mayer, H and Matzarakis, A. (eds.), *Proceedings of the 5th Japanese-German Meeting on Urban Climatology*. Berichte des Meteorologischen Instituts der Albert-Ludwigs-Universität Freiburg, No. 18. The Albert-Ludwigs-University of Freiburg, Freiburg, Germany, 6–11 October. Freiburg: the Meteorological Institute, Albert-Ludwigs-University of Freiburg, 271–276. Available at: http://www.meteo.uni-freiburg.de/forschung/publikationen/berichte/report18.pdf (Accessed 10 February 2014).

Matzarakis, A., Röckle, R. and Richter, C. J. (2005). Urban climate analysis of Freiburg – An integral assessment approach. Paper presented at *The 4th Japanese-German Meeting on Urban Climatology*. Tsukuba, Japan, 30 November–2 December. Available at: http://www.kenken.go.jp/japanese/information/information/event/jgmuc/report/c3.pdf (Accessed 15 August 2008).

Matzarakis, A., Röckle, R., Richter, C. J., Höfl, H. C., Steinicke, W., Streifeneder, M. and Mayer, H. (2008). Planungsrelevante Bewertung des Stadtklimas – Am Beispiel von Freiburg im Breisgau (Planning oriented assessment of urban climate – the case of Freiburg). *Gefahrstoffe – Reinhaltung der Luft*, 68: 334–340. Available at: http://www.ima-umwelt.de/fileadmin/dokumente/klima_downloads/planungsrelevante_bewertung_stadtklima_freiburg.pdf (Accessed 10 February 2014).

Mayer, H. (1988). Results from the research program 'STADTKLIMA BAYERN' for urban planning. *Energy and Buildings*, 11(1–3): 115–121.

Mills, G. (1997). An urban canopy-layer climate model. *Theoretical and Applied Climatology*, 57(3–4): 229–244.

Mills, G., Cleugh, H., Emmanuel, R., Endlicher, W., Erell, E., McGranahan, G., Ng, E., Nickson, A., Rosenthal, J. and Steemer, K. (2010). Climate Information for Improved Planning and Management of Mega Cities (Needs Perspectives). In: Sivakumar, M. V. K. *et al.* (eds.), *Procedia Environmental Sciences, Vol. 1, Special Issue of World Climate Conference-3*, 228–246. Geneva, Switzerland, 31 August–4 September.

Mochida, A., Sasaki, K., Lun, I. and Oba, H. (2007). Management, control and design of urban climate based on the heat balance analysis of outdoor space. Paper presented at *the ISWE school, Tokyo, Japan.*

MOE (2001). *Annual Technical Report: Investigation on Urban Heat Island Countermeasures.* Tokyo: Urban Heat Island Council, The Ministry of the Environment (MoE) of Japan Government. (In Japanese).

MOE (2002). *Annual Technical Report: Investigation on Urban Heat Island Countermeasures.* Tokyo: Urban Heat Island Council, The Ministry of the Environment (MoE) of Japan Government. (In Japanese).

MOE (2003). *Annual Technical Report: Investigation on Urban Heat Island Countermeasures.* Tokyo: Urban Heat Island Council, The Ministry of the Environment (MoE) of Japan Government. (In Japanese).

MOE (2004). *Annual Technical Report: Investigation on Urban Heat Island Countermeasures.* Tokyo: Urban Heat Island Council, The Ministry of the Environment (MoE) of Japan Government. (In Japanese).

MOE. (2005). *Annual Technical Report: Investigation on Urban Heat Island Countermeasures.* Tokyo: Urban Heat Island Council, The Ministry of the Environment (MoE) of Japan Government. (In Japanese).

MOE (2006). *Annual Technical Report: Investigation on Urban Heat Island Countermeasures.* Tokyo: Urban Heat Island Council, The Ministry of the Environment (MoE) of Japan Government. (In Japanese).

MOE (2007). *Annual Technical Report: Investigation on Urban Heat Island Countermeasures.* Tokyo: Urban Heat Island Council, The Ministry of the Environment (MoE) of Japan Government. (In Japanese).

MOE (2008). *Annual Technical Report: Investigation on Urban Heat Island Countermeasures.* Tokyo: Urban Heat Island Council, The Ministry of the Environment (MoE) of Japan Government. (In Japanese).

Moriyama, M. (2004). *Mitigation and Technique on Urban Heat Island.* Japan: Gakugei Syuppann Sya. (In Japanese).

Moriyama, M. and Takebayashi, H. (1998). Climate analysis for urban planning in Kobe. *Report of Research Center for Urban Safety and Security, Kobe University*, Special Report Vol. 1: 53–62. Available at: http://www.lib.kobe-u.ac.jp/repository/00044717.pdf (Accessed February 2009).

Moriyama, M. and Takebayashi, H. (1999). Making method of 'Klimatope' map based on normalized vegetation index and one-dimensional heat budget model. *Journal of Wind Engineering and Industial Aerodynamices*, 81(1–3): 211–220.

Moriyama, M. and Tanaka, T. (2008). Example of Osaka region: Urban environmental climate maps and plans for the future. Paper presented at *the Workshop on Urban Planning and Climate Change.* Stuttgart, Germany.

Moriyama, M., Takebayashi, H., Shibaike, H. and Tanaka, T. (2005a). Climate analysis for the mitigation of urban heat island in Kyoto city: No.3 urban environmental climate map for the mitigation of urban heat island. Paper presented at *the International Symposium on Sustainable Development of Asia City Environment.* Xian Jiao Tong University, Xian, China, November.

Moriyama, M., Tanaka, T. and Takebayashi, H. (2005b). Urban environmental climate map for neighborhood planning. Paper presented at *The 4th Japanese-German Meeting on Urban Climatology.* Tsukuba, Japan, 30 November–2 December. Available at: http://www.kenken.go.jp/japanese/information/information/event/jgmuc/report/h2.pdf (Accessed February 2009).

Murakami, M. and Sakamoto, K. (2005). Relationship between urban thermal environment and urban form, *Proceedings of The Ninth International Conference Computers in Urban Planning and Urban Management.* University College London, London, U.K., 29 June–1 July.

Narita, K.-i. (2006). Ventilation path and urban climate. *Wind Engineers, JAWE*, 31(2): 109–114.

Nery, J., Freire, T., Andrade, T. and Katzschner, L. (2006). Thermal comfort studies in humid tropical city. In: *Proceedings of The Sixth International Conference on Urban Climate.* Gothenburg, Sweden, 12–16 June. Sweden: University of Gothenburg, 234–237.

Ng, E. (2009a). *Designing High-Density Cities for Social and Environmental Sustainability.* London: Earthscan.

Ng, E. (2009b). Policies and technical guidelines for urban planning of high-density cities – Air ventilation assessment (AVA) of Hong Kong. *Building and Environment*, 44(7): 1478–1488.

Ng, E., Katzschner, L., Wang, U., Ren, C. and Chen, L. (2008a). *Working Paper No. 1A : Draft Urban Climatic Analysis Map – Urban Climatic Map and Standards for Wind Environment – Feasibility Study*, Technical Report for Planning Department HKSAR.

Ng, E., Katzschner, L., Wang, Y., Ren, C. and Chen, L. (2008b). *Working Paper No. 1B: Draft Urban Climatic Analysis Map – Urban Climatic Map and Standards for Wind Environment – Feasibility Study*, Technical Report for Planning Department HKSAR.

Ng, E., Wang, U., Ren, C. and Cheng, V. (2008c). *Technical Input Report: Methodologies and Results of Field Measurement*, Urban Climatic Map and Standards for Wind Environment – Feasibility Study, Planning Department, HKSAR Government, 79 Pages.

Ng, E., Ren, C., Katzschner, L. and Yau, R. (2009). Urban climatic studies for the hot and humid tropical coastal city of Hong Kong. In: *Proceedings of the Seventh International Conference on Urban Climate.* Yokohama, Japan, 29 June–3 July. Available at: http://www.ide.titech.ac.jp/~icuc7/extended_abstracts/pdf/254693-2-090422170338-003.pdf (Accessed 10 February 2014).

Nielinger, J. and Kost, W.J. (2001). *Klimaanalyse der Stadt Sindelfingen, Stadt Sindlfingen: Beluftungsverhaltnisse fur das Stadtgebiet Sindelfingen.* Stuttgart: iMA-Immissionen-Meteorologie-Akustik. Available at: http://www.ima-umwelt.de/fileadmin/dokumente/klima_downloads/belueftungsanalyse_sindelfingen.pdf (Accessed 10 February 2014).

Oke, T. R. (1987). *Boundary Layer Climates.* London: Routledge.

Parlow, E., Scherer, D. and Fehrenbach, U. (2001a). Climatic Analysis Map for Grenchen und Umgebung, *CAMPAS, Klimaanalyse- und Planungshinweiskarten für den Kanton Solothurn.* Basel, Switzerland.

Parlow, E., Scherer, D. and Fehrenbach, U. (2001b). Climatic Analyse Map for Olten and Umgebung, *CAMPAS, Klimaanalyse- und Planungshinweiskarten für den Kanton Solothurn.* Basel, Switzerland.

Parlow, E., Scherer, D. and Fehrenbach, U. (2005). Klimaanalysekarte, *Regionale Klliimaanallyse Südlliicher Oberrheiin (REKLIISO).* Baden-Wuerttemberg, Germany.

Parlow, E., Scherer, D., Fehrenbach, U., Föhner, M. and Beha, H.-D. (1995). *Klimaanalyse der Region Basel (KABA). Analysis of the Regional Climate of Basel/Switzerland.* Available at: http://www.mcr.unibas.ch/Projects/KABA/index.en.htm (Accessed 10 February 2014).

Paszynski, J. (1991). Mapping urban topoclimates. *Energy and Buildings*, 16(3–4): 1059–1062.

Radosz, J. and Kaminski, A. (2003). Topoclimatic mapping on 1:50 000 scale. The map sheet of Bytom. In: *Proceedings of the Fifth International Conference on Urban Climate.* University of Lodz, Lodz, Poland, 1–5 Septemeber. Available at: http://www.geo.uni.lodz.pl/~icuc5/text/P_8_1.pdf (Accessed February 2009)

Ren, C., Ng, E. and Katzschner, L. (2007). An investigation into developing an urban climatic map for high density living—Initial study in Hong Kong. In: Santamouris, M. and Wouters, P. (eds.), *Proceedings of The 2nd PALENC Conference and the 28th AIVC Conference on Building Low Energy Cooling and Advanced Ventilation Technologies in the 21st Century*, Vol. 2. Crete Island, Greece, 27– 29 September. Greece: Heliotopos Conference, 811–817.

Reuter, U. (2008). Urban climate and planning in Stuttgart. Paper presented at *The Workshop on the Application of UCMap in Urban Planning.*

Richards, K. (2002). Topoclimates and topoclimate mapping: What do the scientific abstracts tell us about research perspectives? In: Whigham, P. A. (ed.), *Proceedings of The 14th Annual Colloquium of the Spatial Information Research Centre.* University of Otago, Wellington, New Zealand, 3–5 December. Dunedin: University of Otago, 1–8. Available at: http://www.business.otago.ac.nz/sirc/conferences/2002_SIRC/01_Richards.pdf (Accessed 10 February 2014).

Richter, C. J. and Röckle, R. (2009). *Das numerische Simulationsmodell FITNAH.* Freiburg: iMA Immissionen, Meteorologie Akustik. Available at: http://www.ima-umwelt.de/fileadmin/dokumente/klima_downloads/fitnah_kurzuebersicht.pdf (Accessed 10 February 2014).

Röckle, R. (2008). Urban climate maps and planning. In: *Proceedings of Thermal Comfort in Urban Planning and Architecture under Consideration of Global Climate Change.* University of Kassel, Kassel, Germany, 20–21 February. Kassel: Fachgebiet Umweltmeteorologie, University of Kassel. Available at: https://kobra.bibliothek.uni-kassel.de/bitstream/urn:nbn:de:hebis:34-2008042121208/1/booklet_workshop_kassel_08.pdf (Accessed 10 February 2014).

Röckle, R., Richter, C.-J., Höfl, H.-C., Steinicke, W. and Matzarakis, A. (2003). *Klimaanalyse Stadt Freiburg.* Freiburg: Stadtplanungsamt.

Scherer, D., Fehrenbach, U., Beha, H.-D. and Parlow, E. (1999). Improved concepts and methods in analysis and evaluation of the urban climate for optimizing urban planning process. *Atmospheric Environment*, 33(24–25): 4185–4193.

de Schiller, S. and Evans, J. M. (1991). Bridging the gap between climate and design at the urban and building scale: Research and application. *Energy and Buildings*, 15(1–2): 51–55.

Schirmer, H. (1984). Climate and regional land-use planning. *Energy and Buildings*, 7(1): 35– 53.

SDUDB (2008). *Geoinformation-Berlin Digital Environmental Atlas.* Berlin: Senate Department for Urban Development.

Sera, T. (2006). Japan's policy instruments on urban heat island measures by MLIT. In: *Proceedings of the International Workshop on Countermeasures to Urban Heat Islands.* Tokyo, Japan, 3– 4 August. Available at: http://www.iea.org/Textbase/work/2006/heat/9-d_Sera.pdf (Accessed February 2009).

Shimoda, Y. and Narumi, D. (1998). Climate analysis for urban planning in Osaka. *Report of Research Centre for Urban Safety and Security, Kobe University*, Special Report Vol. 1: 95–99. Available at: http://www.lib.kobe-u.ac.jp/repository/00044721.pdf (Accessed 10 February 2014).

Smith, C. L., Lindley, S. J., Levermore, G. J. and Lee, S. E. (2009). A GIS-based decision support tool for urban climate risk analysis and exploration of adpatation options, with respect to urban thermal environments. In: *Proceedings of The 7th International Conference on Urban Climate.* Yokohama, Japan, 29 June–3 July. Available at: http://www.ide.titech.ac.jp/~icuc7/extended_abstracts/pdf/375805-1-090514233750-003.pdf (Accessed 10 February 2014).

Stanhill, G. and Kalma, J. D. (1995). Solar dimming and urban heating at Hong Kong. *International Journal of Climatology*, 15(8): 933–941.

Steinicke, W. and Streifeneder, M. (2002). *Klimafunktionskarte für das Verbandsgebiet des Nachbarschaftsverbandes Heidelberg-Mannheim*. Mannheim, Germany: Nachbarschaftsverband Heidelberg-Mannheim.

Sterten, A. K. (1982). A thematic mapping system and a description of local climatic conditions developed for urban planning purposes. *Energy and Buildings*, 4(2): 121– 124.

Stock, P. and Beckröge, W. (1985). *Klimaanalyse Stadt Essen*. Essen: Kommunalverband Ruhrgebiet.

Stock, P. and Beckröge, W. (1991). *Klimaanalyse Stadt Bochum*. Essen: Kommunalverband Ruhrgebiet.

Stock, P., Beckröge, W., Kiese, O., Kuttler, W. and Lüftner, H. (1986). *Klimaanalyse Stadt Dortmund*. Planungshefte Ruhrgebiet, PO 18. Essen: Kommunalverband Ruhrgebiet.

Svensson, M. K., Thorsson, S. and Lindqvist, S. (2003). A geographical information system model for creating bioclimatic maps – examples from a high, mid-latitude city. *International Journal of Biometeorology*, 47(2): 102–112.

Swaid, H. (1992). Intelligent Urban Forms (IUF): A new climtate-concerned, urban planning strategy. *Theoretical and Applied Climatology*, 46(2–3): 179–191.

Tablada, A., Troyer, F. D., Blocken, B., Carmeliet, J. and Verschure, H. (2009). On natural ventilation and thermal comfort in compact urban environments – the old Havana case. *Building and Environment*, 44(9): 1943–1958.

Tan, W., Xu, J. and Yue, W. (2005). Analysis of mechanism for formation of urban thermal environment – A case of Shanghai. In: *Proceedings of the International Geoscience and Remote Sensing Symposium*. Seoul, Korea, 25–29 July. IEEE, 1452–1455. Available at: http://ieeexplore.ieee.org/iel5/10226/32596/01525398.pdf (Accessed February 2009).

Tanaka, T. and Morlyama, M. (2004). Application of GIS to make 'Urban Environmental Climate Map' for urban planning. In: *Proceeedings of the Fifth Conference on Urban Environment*. (CD-ROM).Vancouver, BC, Canada, 23–27 August.

Tanaka, T., Yamashita, T., Takebayashi, H. and Morlyama, M. (2005). Urban environment climate map for community planning. In: *Proceedings of The 25th Annual Esri International User Conference*. San Diego, California, 25–29 July. Available at: http://proceedings.esri.com/library/userconf/proc05/papers/pap1156.pdf (Accessed 10 February 2014).

Tanaka, T., Yamazaki, K. and Moriyama, M. (2008). Urban environmental climate map for supporting urban planning-related works in local government: Case study in city of Sakai. In: Mayer, H. and Matzarakis, A. (eds.), *Proceedings of the 5th Japanese-German Meeting on Urban Climatology*. Berichte des Meteorologischen Instituts der Albert-Ludwigs-Universität Freiburg, No. 18. The Albert-Ludwigs-University of Freiburg, Freiburg, Germany, 6–11 October. Freiburg: the Meteorological Institute, Albert-Ludwigs-University of Freiburg, 259–264. Available at: http://www.meteo.uni-freiburg.de/forschung/publikationen/berichte/report18.pdf (Accessed 10 February 2014).

Tanaka, T., Ogasawara, T., Koshi, H., Yoshida, S., Sadohara, S. and Moriyama, M. (2009). Urban environmental climate maps for supporting urban-planning related work of local governments in Japan: Case studies of Yokohama and Sakai. In: *Proceedings of The 7th International Conference on Urban Climate*. Yokohama, Japan, 29 June–3 July. Available at: http://www.ide.titech.ac.jp/~icuc7/extended_abstracts/pdf/376178-1-090520230556-003.pdf (Accessed 10 February 2014).

Taraxacum, e.V. (1999). *klimabewertungskarte Kassel*. Kaofungen.

TMG (2005a). *Guidelines for Heat Island Control Measures [Summary Edition]*. Tokyo: Bureau of the Environment, Tokyo Metropolitan Government (TMG). Available at: http://www.kankyo.metro.tokyo.jp/en/attachement/heat_island.pdf (Accessed 10 February 2014).

TMG (2005b). *The Thermal Environment Map and Areas Designated for the Implementation of Measures against the Heat Island Phenomenon*. Tokyo: Bureau of Environment, Bureau of Urban Development, Tokyo Metropolitan Government (TMG). Available at: http://www.metro.tokyo.jp/ENGLISH/TOPICS/2005/ftf56100.htm (Accessed 10 February 2014).

UN (2008). *State of the World's Cities 2008/2009 – Harmonious Cities United Nations Human Settlements Programme (UN-HABITAT)*. London: Earthscan.

UNFPA (2007). *State of World Population 2007: Unleashing the Potential of Urban Growth*. New York: United Nations Population Fund (UNFPA). Available at: http://www.unfpa.org/swp/2007/presskit/pdf/sowp2007_eng.pdf (Accessed 10 February 2014).

Unger, J. (2004). Intra-urban relationship between surface geometry and urban heat island: Review and new approach. *Climate Research*, 27(3): 253–264.

Ustrnul, Z. and Czekierda, D. (2005). Application of GIS for the development of climatological air temperature maps: An example from Poland. *Meteorological Applications*, 12(1): 43–50.

VDI (1988). *Stadtklima und Luftreinhaltung*. Berlin: Springer-Verlag.

VDI (1997). *VDI-Standard: VDI 3787 Part 1 Environmental Meteorology – Climate and Air Pollution Maps for Cities and Regions*. Berlin: Beuth Verlag.

Vogt, J. (2002a). *Bericht über orientierende Untersuchungen zur lokalklimatischen Funktion der Flächen des Gleisdreieckes in Berlin, Abbildungsteil*, Voruntersuchung im Auftrag der Vivico Management GmbH, unveröffentlicht. Berlin, Germany. (In German).

Vogt, J. (2002b). *Bericht über orientierende Untersuchungen zur lokalklimatischen Funktion der Flächen des Gleisdreieckes in Berlin, Textteil*, Voruntersuchung im Auftrag der Vivico Management GmbH, unveröffentlicht. Berlin, Germany. (In German).

Wang, G. T. (2004). *Urban Climate, Environment and Urban Planning*. Beijing: Beijing Press. (In Chinese).

Ward, I. C. (2003). The usefulness of climatic maps of built-up areas in determining drivers for the energy and environmental efficiency of buildings and external areas. *International Journal of Ventilation*, 2(3): 277–286.

Wirtschaftsministerium Baden-Württemberg (ed.) (1993). *Städtebauliche Klimafibel-Hinweise für die Bauleitplanung*, Vol.2. Stuttgart: Wirtschaftsministerium Baden-Württemberg.

Wong, N. H. and Jusuf, S. K. (2007). GIS-based urban heat island study in university campus. In: Santamouris, M. and Wouters, P. (eds.), *Proceedings of The 2nd PALENC Conference and the 28th AIVC Conference on Building Low Energy Cooling and Advanced Ventilation Technologies in the 21st Century*, Vol. 2. Crete Island, Greece, 27–29 September. Greece: Heliotopos Conference, 1127–1131.

Yamamoto, Y. (2006). Measures to mitigate urban heat islands. *Science and Technology Trends Quarterly Review*, 18(1): 65–83.

Yamamoto, Y. (2007). Measures to mitigate urban heat islands. *Global Change and Sustainable Development*, 1(2): 18–46.

Yoda, H. (2005). Klimaatlas and action program in Fukuoka city. In: *Proceedings of The 4th Japanese-German Meeting on Urban Climatology*. Tsukuba, Japan, 30 November–2 December. Available at: http://www.kenken.go.jp/japanese/information/information/event/jgmuc/report/a6.pdf (Accessed 10 February 2014).

Yoda, H. (2009). Climate atlas in Fukuoka city. In: *Proceedings of The Seventh International Conference on Urban Climate*. Yokohama, Japan, 29 June–3 July. Available at: http://www.ide.titech.ac.jp/~icuc7/extended_abstracts/pdf/384608-1-090514232915-002.pdf (Accessed 10 February 2014).

Yoda, H. and Katayama, T. (1998). Climate analysis for urban planning in Fukuoka. *Report of Research Center for Urban Safety and Security, Kobe University*, Special Report Vol. 1: 63–78. Available at: http://www.lib.kobe-u.ac.jp/repository/00044718.pdf (Accessed February 2009).

Yoshida, A. (1998). Climate analysis for urban planning in Okayama – Field investigation on thermal environments in Okayama. *Report of Research Center for Urban Safety and Security, Kobe University*, Special Report Vol. 1: 100–104. Available at: http://www.lib.kobe-u.ac.jp/repository/00044722.pdf (Accessed 10 February 2014).

Zhou, L., Dickinson, R. E., Tian, Y., Fang, J., Li, Q., Kaufmann, R. K., Tucker, C. J. and Myneni, R. B. (2004). Evidence for a significant urbanization effect on climate in China. *PNAS*, 101: 9540–9544.

Chapter 3

# A summary of key methodologies

*Jürgen Baumüller*

## Introduction

In order to take into account the local climatic situation of a city, it is necessary to take a detailed look at the complex correlation and the effects of the various climatic parameters. The climatic analyses and the recommendations must follow in three steps (see Figure 3.1). The new requirements as a result of climate change also strengthen the need for applied climate information for planning issues.

In the context of the ongoing discussion about new residential and commercial development as well as the urban restructuring of the city, fundamental studies of climate and air are gaining increasing importance for producing qualified land-use planning in densely settled areas. Since planning-related statements refer to specific areas, the use of maps as an informational basis is recommended. Maps (or Urban Climatic Maps) in this context are a very significant tool for the planner, and are also a meaningful method for communicating information with politicians and the interested public. As such, spatially-related cartographic representations are necessary for attaining climatic and air-hygienic goals (VDI, 2008).

The production of climatic maps requires the collection of diverse individual climate parameters. It is possible to get input data to produce spatial climatic maps in different ways: (a) data from

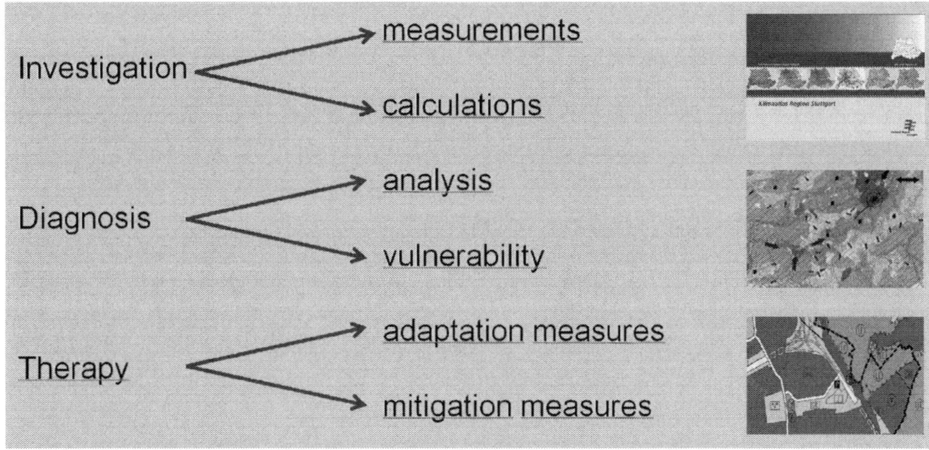


*Figure 3.1* Steps for climate analysis in cities and regions.

Source: Baumüller and Baumüller, 2011

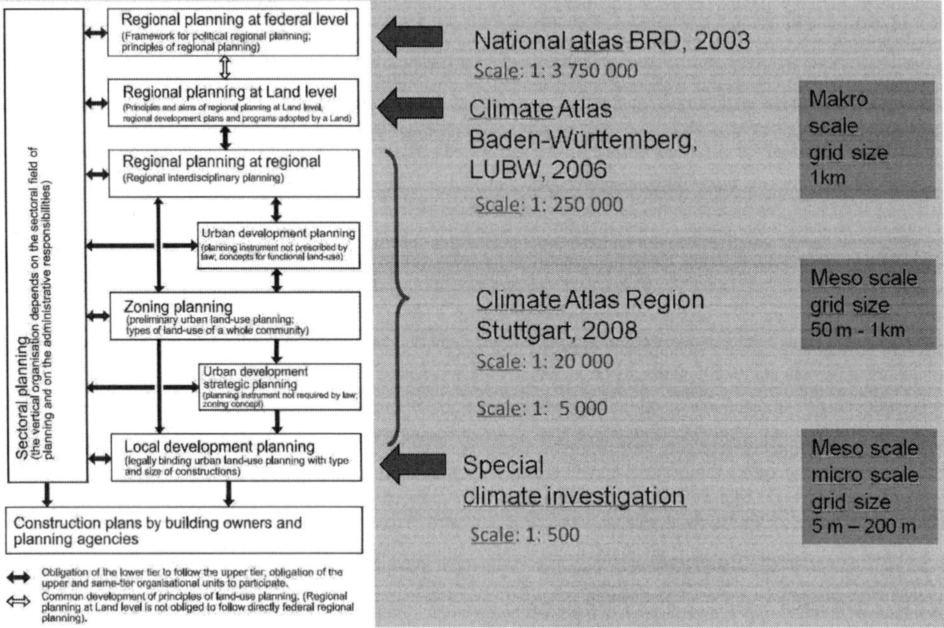


*Figure 3.2* Spatial planning levels, scales and climatic information (example of Germany, VDI-Standard: VDI 3787 Part 9, 2004).

Source: Baumüller and Baumüller, 2011

stationary stations, (b) data from mobile measurements, (c) data from remote sensing (satellite or airplane), and (d) computer simulations.

Data from stationary and mobile measurements are especially useful when interpolated into spatial data. The mathematical and geostatistical tools to do this are available and sometimes integrated in the Geographic Information System (GIS). In principle, we can distinguish 'vector data' or 'grid data' for spatial maps. Grid data is used more for producing climatic maps. The investigations and simulations should be accorded with the different planning levels because of different scales (Lauser, 2007) (see Figure 3.2). The goal of the planning recommendations is first and foremost to motivate the planner towards a stronger consideration of climatic criteria. As such, a planning project should incorporate the standards of the 'Planning Recommendations' map (UC-ReMap).

## Required base maps for climate analysis

Most of the climatic parameters depend on elevation and land use, so for calculations, there is a need to have spatial digital data of this in a good resolution. For air pollution, the car traffic information (number of cars, kind of cars, speed) is necessary because the emission of pollutants is dependant on this.

### *Digital elevation model*

The knowledge of local topography is necessary for many tasks in urban climatology. The use of a 'digital elevation model' (DEM) can be helpful for this, and it is also necessary for many applications in GIS. The DEM contains coordinates for position (mostly Gauss–Krüger system) and elevation (m above sea level), and they are available in a lot of countries and cities. The level of precision amounts to +/−2m in topographically consistent areas. With the help of interpretive programs, contour plans as well as the size and direction of land inclinations or surface curvatures can be derived from this data (Helbig *et al.*, 1999). Especially descriptive are perspective views produced from the data, in which the direction and angle of viewing (i.e. elevation) can be determined at will. Some of these programs (e.g. SURFER) are also available for normal PCs.

### *Digital land use data*

Temperature and wind, and also other environmental parameters, are very strongly affected by the surface character. Land use data is available from satellite data or from local information in the offices of urban planning. Normally, eight land use classes are adequate: (a) industry and commercial use, (b) high building density, (c) low building density, (d) streets, (e) railway areas, (f) open space, (g) forest, and (h) waters.

### *Infrared thermography*

Remote sensing is often used to get information about the radiation surface temperature of cities (see Figure 3.3). The infrared thermography provides indications of variations in temperature structures (e.g. heat islands, cold air collection areas, cold air drainage areas) caused by human settlement in an urban area.

The execution of at least two flyovers (evening and morning) makes possible the generation of information about the cooling behaviour of individual areas. In addition, indications can be

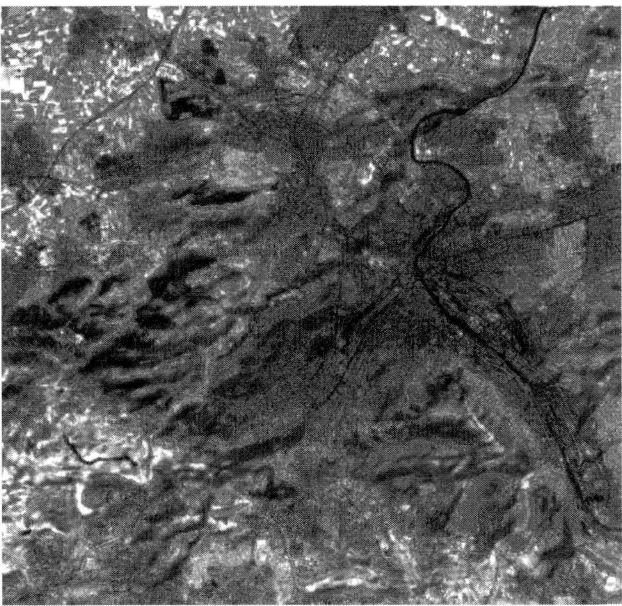

*Figure 3.3* Thermal map of Stuttgart, evening 18 August 1988, combination with DEM.

Source: Author

obtained regarding climatically preferential areas and local climate factors such as local air exchange processes, cold air blockage, and conflicts with existing uses. Strategies can also be developed for more in-depth measurements on the ground. Such conclusions, however, require a realistic conception of the interaction of meteorological parameters in the air layer near the ground, knowledge of the local land conditions, and additional meteorological information.

In a climatic atlas for planning use it is important to give information about the wind field (spatial wind directions) and local wind systems like land–sea breezes or mountain–valley winds. On the other hand, the thermal situation must be taken into account (UHI, heat stress, cold air production areas) as well as the situation of the air pollution in the city.

Based on measurements and calculations, a lot of different climatic and air pollution maps can be produced, as summarised in Table 3.1. In the climate atlas of Stuttgart (Baumüller *et al.*, 1992), the following maps (see Figure 3.4) (e.g.) were worked out: terrain height, land use, thermal maps (evening, morning), total irradiance, mean temperature, mean minimum and maximum temperature, days with heat stress, summer days, hot days, yearly precipitation, cold air drainage flow, thickness of cold drainage flow, areas of cold air, annual wind speed, and air pollution maps.

## Climatic analysis maps or climate function maps

A significant component of a climatic study is the production of climatic analysis maps depicting the local climatic conditions in the region as a cartographic overview (see Plate 3.1). The significant bases for this are the data material described above, topographic maps, city maps, land use plans, aerial photographs and climate maps. The classification of 'climatopes' and coldair collection areas must not be parcel-specific. Tolerances can range up to 50m–100m, since both the contextual definition of borders' relative transient areas and the accuracy of drawings due to the working material used must be taken into account. Technically detailed valuation is necessary for more precise results. The signatures and symbols used in Plate 3.1 correspond largely to VDI 3787, Part 1 (VDI, 1997).

### *Climatopes*

Climatopes describe geographic areas with similar microclimatic characteristics. These are distinguished primarily by the daily thermal variation, the vertical roughness (wind field disruption), the topographical situation or exposure, and above all by the type of material land use. The level of emissions is included as an additional criterion for special climatopes. Since the microclimatic characteristics of built-up areas are determined significantly by the material land use and especially by the type of development, the climatopes are named after the dominant land-use type or building use: Water Climatope, Open Land Climatope, Forest Climatope, Greenbelt Climatope, Garden City Climatope, City Periphery Climatope, City Climatope, Core City Climatope, Commercial Climatope, Industry Climatope, and Railroad Climatope. Detailed descriptions of the climatopes can be found in the VDI-Standard: VDI 3787, Part 1 (VDI, 1997).

Additionally, the following information, sometimes as pictograms, is given in the climatic analysis map (see Plate 3.1): (a) cold air areas and characteristics of the relief structure, (b) pollution from traffic emissions, (c) immissions, (d) pollution pictogram, which emphasises locations with high levels of air pollution in areas at risk of ground inversion effects. These are usually cold air collection areas that cool strongly at night and exhibit high air pollution values because of nearby pollutant emitters: (e) ground/valley fog, (f) elevated inversion, and (g) wind roses that depict the percentage distribution of the average annual frequency of wind direction at a given measurement location.

*Table 3.1* Planning levels and climatic relevant maps.

| | *Wind Situation* | | | | | *Thermal Situation – Bioclimate* | | | | | | *Air Pollution* | | |
|---|---|---|---|---|---|---|---|---|---|---|---|---|---|---|
| *Planning levels* | *Windfield* | *Local Wind* | *Cold airflow* | *Wind comfort* | *Wind Roses* | *Thermal map* | *UHI* | *Irradiance* | *Heat stress* | *Tropical nights* | *Cold air areas* | *$NO_x$* | *$PM_{10}$* | *Climate Change Effects* |
| State Development Plan | ●● | ● | ● | ● | ●● | ● | – | ● | ● | – | – | ● | ● | ● |
| Regional Plan | ●● | ●●● | ●●● | ●● | ●●● | ●● | ●● | ● | ●●● | ●● | ●●● | ●● | ●● | ●● |
| Urban Development Strategy | ●●● | ●●● | ●●● | ●● | ●●● | ●●● | ●●● | ●● | ●●● | ●●● | ●●● | ●●● | ●●● | ●●● |
| Preparatory Land-use Plan | ●●● | ●●● | ●●● | ●●● | ●●● | ●●● | ●●● | ●●● | ●●● | ●●● | ●●● | ●●● | ●●● | ●●● |
| Landscape Plan | ●●● | ●●● | ●●● | ●●● | ●●● | ●●● | ●●● | ●●● | ●●● | ●●● | ●●● | ●●● | ●●● | ●● |
| Urban Framework Plan | ●●● | ●●● | ●●● | ●●● | ●●● | ●●● | ●●● | ●●● | ●●● | ●●● | ●●● | ●●● | ●●● | ●● |
| Local Development Plan | ●●● | ●●● | ●●● | ●●● | ●●● | ●●● | ●●● | ●● | ●●● | ●●● | ●●● | ●●● | ●●● | ● |
| Local Green Structure Plan | ●●● | ●●● | ●●● | ●●● | ●●● | ●●● | ●●● | ●● | ●●● | ●●● | ●●● | ●●● | ●●● | ● |
| Local Design Plan | ● | ●● | ●● | ●● | ● | ●● | ●●● | ● | ●●● | ●●● | ●● | ●●● | ●●● | ● |
| Buildings | ● | ● | ● | ● | – | ● | ●●● | ● | ●●● | ●●● | – | ●●● | ●●● | ●●● |

Note: (very high ●●●; high ●●; middle ●; low ●; no –)

Source: Baumüller, 2011

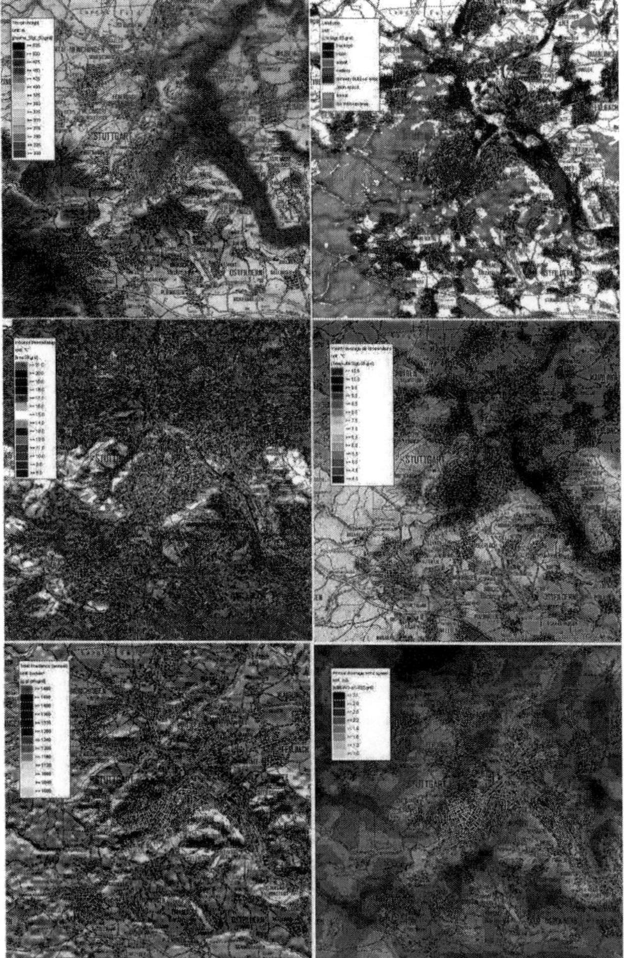

*Figure 3.4* Examples of climatic maps.

Source: Baumüller *et al.*, 1992

## Maps with recommendations for planning

A map with recommendations for planning (see Plate 3.2) contains an integrated assessment of the material represented in the climate analysis map, as it relates to concerns relevant in planning. The symbols give recommendations as to the sensitivity of certain land areas to changes in land use, from which climatically grounded conditions and measures can be derived in the context of planning and zoning.

The recommendations for planning primarily relate to structural changes of land use. For example, a change in the composition of vegetation exerts fewer climatic effects than large-scale soil capping measures and the erection of structures.

The planning recommendations are not specific to the level of individual parcels, and tolerances can range up to 50m–100m. More detailed questions in connection with site plans must be dealt

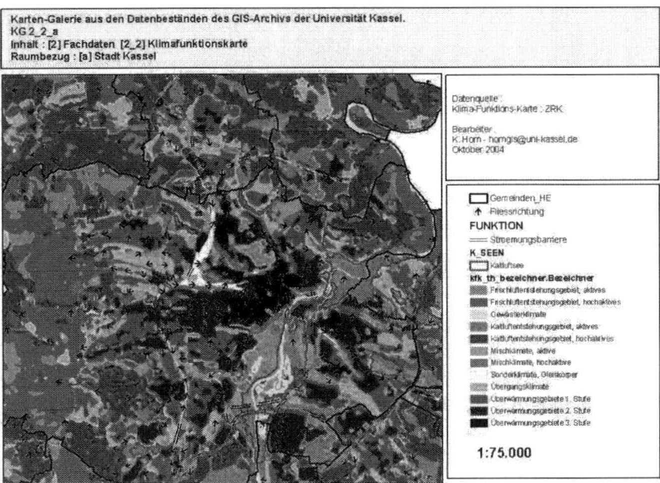


*Figure 3.5* Climate function map of Kassel.

Source: Courtesy of Lutz Katzschner

with through special appraisals when necessary, especially in areas of high climatic and air-hygienic sensitivity.

In addition to local characteristics, the following principles form the basis for the planning recommendations:

(a) Areas of vegetation have an important effect on the local climate, since on the one hand they cause the nightly fresh/cold air production and on the other they exert a balancing thermal effect when they feature a high proportion of trees. Green spaces in the city and nearby areas exert a positive influence on their immediate vicinity in a microclimatic sense; vegetation on the border of developments also contributes to air exchange. Larger, connected green spaces represent the climatic and air-hygienic potential for regeneration. Particularly in the present spatial context of the built-up area, such green spaces are very important for air exchange. As far as possible, therefore, open spaces should not be converted to development from a climatic perspective.

(b) Development in valleys can also be judged as generally negative, since the movement of cold, fresh air takes place in valleys under weak wind conditions, and since valleys serve as air delivery corridors for stronger regional winds.

(c) Hillsides in extended built-up areas should remain undeveloped, especially when development exists in valleys, since intensive cold- and fresh-air transport occurs here (however, development on southern hillsides is desirable from an energy conservation perspective). The same is valid for gullies and ridges along these hillsides.

(d) Saddle-like topographies on the backside of mountains serve as air induction corridors and should not be developed.

(e) The climatic and air-hygienic perspective recommends encircling development with as much green space as possible as well as criss-crossing it with green corridors oriented to topographic features (e.g. ventilation passages; air induction corridors), thus supporting air exchange.

(f) Urban sprawl from numerous developments strewn across the landscape as well as the emergence of disruptive belts of built-up areas, e.g. through the convergence of neighbouring communities, are to be avoided. Urban development must be accompanied by close, large fresh- and cold-air production areas and ventilation corridors.
(g) The development of commercial and industrial enterprises should ensure that the residential areas in the immediate vicinity do not suffer from heightened emissions resulting from the local wind patterns.

More detailed descriptions of the individual symbols on the map 'Recommendations for Planning' are given below.

## Open spaces

*Open spaces with important climatic activity* Direct relation to built-up areas such as green spaces in the city or those that lie upwind from a mountain/valley wind system; undeveloped valleys, ridges, and gaps in terrain; large, connected open spaces near densely settled areas. These open spaces exhibit a high sensitivity to changes in land use; that is, uses involving construction and soil capping lead to precarious impairments of climate. The same is valid for measures that hinder air exchange.

*Open spaces with less important climatic activity* No direct contact with developed areas or only minor cold air production (e.g. rocky or fallow lands); less sensitivity to changes in land use. Large-scale development, as long as it does not substantially obstruct the regional air exchange, is possible.

*Climatically important local characteristics* such as ridges, depressions, brooks, etc. are to be taken into consideration during planning, however. To obtain as small of an impairment on the climate as possible, the preservation of green spaces and corridors, roof and façade greening, the lowest possible building heights, and building orientations open to the wind are recommended.

*Open spaces with minor climatic activity* Lesser influence on developed areas; lying at a distance from development; relatively unimportant for cold- and fresh-air production. Changes in land use are associated with only minor disturbances to climate. This includes, for example, hilltops and large-scale, well-ventilated areas with relatively level topography at a distance from any development.

Development such as skyscrapers or large-scale commercial enterprises is possible in these areas from a climatic perspective. It should be ensured, however, that the ventilation conditions remain unaltered relative to the main wind direction. The existing level of emissions is also to be taken into consideration, so that no sensitive land uses will be planned in the vicinity of enterprises and heavily trafficked thoroughfares.

## Developed areas

*Developed areas with functions of minor climatic relevance* Developed areas without high thermal or air-hygienic burdens that do not significantly impact neighbouring areas of settlement. No noteworthy climatic or air-hygienic sensitivity relative to intensifications of land use or expanded development is assigned to these areas (e.g. developed, well-ventilated hilltops). Care must be taken so that existing ventilation conditions remain intact and that additional emissions do not bring about negative effects on other developed areas. Roof and façade greening and the preservation of green spaces can prevent thermal problems.

*Developed areas with functions of climatic relevance* Thinly developed settlements with green spaces, which cool noticeably during the night and are relatively open to the wind; well-ventilated, dense areas of development (e.g. hilltops). These areas produce neither intensive thermal or air-hygienic problems nor impediments of air exchange, and they generally exhibit low climatic and air-hygienic sensitivity to changes in land use. This includes, for example, infill development and the closure of gaps in buildings, whereby the amount of developed land in the entire area is to remain constant. Planning should attempt to keep soil capping measures in these areas to a minimum. They can be equalised by the creation of green spaces as well as roof and façade greening.

*Developed areas with functions of significant climatic relevance* Loosely developed, strongly greened areas with low building heights on the periphery of communities with nearly undisturbed air exchange; hillsides with development at their feet (although these hillsides also contribute to cold air production); areas with singular freestanding skyscrapers and green spaces; densely developed areas whose climatic and air-hygienic footprint is not exceedingly high. The designated areas exhibit a substantial climatic and air-hygienic sensitivity relative to changes in land use. Further development and soil capping measures lead to negative effects on the climatic situation. Instead, an enlargement of the proportion of green space and the securing or expansion of ventilation spaces is recommended for these areas.

*Developed areas with climatic and air-hygienic disadvantages* Densely developed areas that have strong climatic and air-hygienic problems; including those developed areas whose air exchange is considerably hindered by buildings. These areas require restructuring under urban climatic criteria (increasing the proportion of green space; minimising the amount of soil capping; minimising the level of emissions, especially traffic emissions; creation or expansion of greened ventilation corridors; removal or relocation of disruptive buildings where necessary).

*Roads with high air and noise pollution* Main traffic thoroughfares with a traffic count of more than 15,000 vehicles per day. The resultant high levels of air and noise pollution must be taken into consideration in planning. Sensitive land uses such as residential areas, recreational areas, and agricultural lands should be planned only at sufficient distances from roads or with adequate protection measures. (Important: an emission prognosis is required.)

## References

Baumüller, J. and Baumüller, N. (2011). Urban climate as a factor for climate change adaptation in city planning. Paper presented at *The 11th EMS Annual Meeting*. Berlin, Germany, 12–16 September.

Baumüller, J., Hoffmann, U., Nagel, T. and Reuter, U. (1992). *Klimauntersuchung Nachbarschaftsverband Stuttgart-Klimaatlas*. Stuggart: Nachbarschaftsverband Stuttgart.

Baumüller, J., Reuter, U., Hoffmann, U. and Esswein, H. (2008). *Klimaatlas Region Stuttgart*. Verband Region Stuggart, No. 26. Stuttgart: Verband Region Stuttgart. Available at: http://www.stadtklima-stuttgart.de/index.php?klima_klimaatlas_region (Accessed 16 December 2013).

Helbig, A., Baumüller, J. and Kerschgens, M. J. (eds.) (1999). *Stadtklima und Luftreinhaltung*. Berlin: Springer.

Lauser, K. (2007). *Levels of Spatial Planning*. Capital City Stuttgart: Office of City Planning and Reconstruction.

VDI (1997). *VDI-Standard: VDI 3787 Part 1 Environmental Meteorology – Climate and Air Pollution Maps for Cities and Regions*. Berlin: Beuth Verlag.

VDI (2004). *VDI-Standard: VDI 3787 Part 9 Environmental Meteorology – Provision for Climate and Air Quality in Regional Planning*. Berlin: Beuth Verlag.

VDI (2008). *VDI-Standard: VDI 3785 Part 1 Environmental Meteorology – Methods and Presentation of Investigations Relevant for Planning and Urban Climate*. Berlin: Beuth Verlag.

Chapter 4

# On the issue of scales of urban climatic maps

*Lutz Katzschner*

With respect to urban planning applications, it is important to provide guidelines in order to evaluate urban climate analysis results. When considering climate and air quality within the area of urban planning, it is crucial not only to deal with the presentation of large-scale (global-scale) mean climatic conditions of the earth as a whole, but also to assess differing observations of individual inner city local climates (meso scale and micro scale), including their reciprocal interactions between the environment and the urban built form.

The main urban climate tools are urban climatic maps in different 'scales', which provide relevant information for planning and make qualitative as well as quantitative statements on the thermal and air quality issues of the city. The maps demonstrate the thermal efficiency complex which refers to the effects of the total relevant meteorological aspects of the urban canopy layer (radiant heat, sensible and latent heat, anthropogenic heat, thermal circulation, and wind). From the information taken from the urban climatic maps of the city, it is possible to derive recommendations for design and planning in a particular spatial resolution for decision making. In practice, the maps can be used with reference to the urban development processes in growing or shrinking cities. Recently, there has been a tendency for European cities to make the inner city living more attractive and a preference for a condensed city form over a dispersed one. The aims of different urban planning and planning levels are often combined with climatic evaluation methods in their spatial, temporal and quantitative description and specification.

For plans at the regional level, areas worth protecting for their climatic functions can be noted. Urban development plans and zoning plans, heat load areas, fresh air supply, and ventilation paths can be mapped out and controlled with planning measures. Moving down the scale, the scope of work for the planners also covers the areas of urban planning and architecture, and housing and urban land use planning as well as urban neighbourhood and urban development planning. For the planners, the consideration of climate issues requires detailed knowledge of the reciprocal process between urban factors and the atmosphere.

The results of climatic analyses can be illustrated in urban climatic maps of different spatial resolutions depending on the scale of urban planning and decision making. Specification of research methods and the assessment for the thermal and air quality efficiency complex depend on the level of planning and the available data. The following factors are of interest in urban climatic maps at the larger regional scale (meso-scale):

- regional occurrence and frequency of air masses exchange (ventilation);
- regional seasonal occurrence of thermal and air quality aspects of urban climate (stress areas, insolation rates, shading conditions);

- regional presentation and evaluation of the impact areas and stress areas;
- energy optimisation of a location based on the urban climate analysis with regard to areas with heat load and cold air areas, and building density.

The task of urban climatology relevant to the urban development and building block planning scale (meso-scale to micro-scale) is to improve air quality conditions and thermal conditions. The factors of interest are:

- reducing urban heat islands (heat islands being an indication of thermal comfort/discomfort and open space planning);
- optimising urban ventilation (air exchange, ventilation paths), urban planning and urban development for air quality and thermal comfort;
- preventing stagnating air in stationary temperature inversion conditions, and preventing barriers from obstructing air exchange;
- preserving/promoting fresh air or cold air influx areas to foster air exchange and improve the air quality situation.

The urban climatic map drafting process carries out a comparative evaluation of the city. The results are then put in a classification system based on modelling in the Geographic Information System (GIS), numerical models, or measurements. The classification is evaluated in terms of 'climatopes', which explain thermal and dynamic conditions of urban climate given the land use zoning and activity pattern. For a comparative evaluation of measurement, operation of at least one monitoring station for the recording of climate data over a period of at least one year, if possible, in each representative climatope type is recommended. Alternatively, calculated data can be used if it contains data which is representative for the climatope of the investigated area.

With regard to evaluation, a distinction should be made between evaluating bioclimatic and ambient air quality conditions according to the issue at hand. Both criteria should be extensively investigated for evaluation while the characteristics of all existing types of zoning plan are taken into account. The evaluation of the bioclimatic condition for the categories of thermal stress and cold stress can be carried out according to the four thermal comfort evaluation criteria (air temperature, humidity, mean radiant temperature and wind speed). Meteorological dispersion conditions are differentiated between horizontal and vertical exchange with three evaluation criteria in each case, which can be considered in an assessment. An appropriate choice of criteria and their combinations has to be made for each individual case and matched to each task. Further criteria, which are not listed here for the determination of the categories of thermal stress and cold stress, may also be investigated.

Understanding the concept of scale is therefore very important when drafting an urban climatic map so that the information contained in the map at various scales matches the information needed for the planning process. A sequence of these processes is illustrated in Figure 4.1. With reference to Table 4.1, it can be seen that urban climate analyses require a special resolution depending on the aims of the planning and administration level. They are as follows:

(A) *Urban master plans* characterise areas for city development perspectives. Therefore, climate aspects have to indicate where air paths or the urban heat islands are located. Strategies for the ventilation and mitigation of heat have to be considered holistically and cannot be separated.

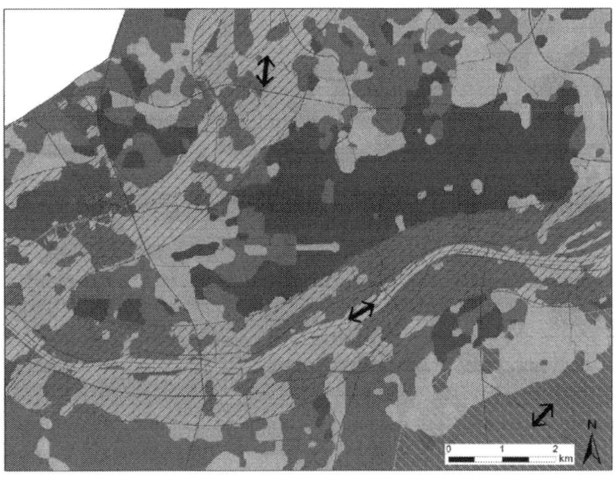


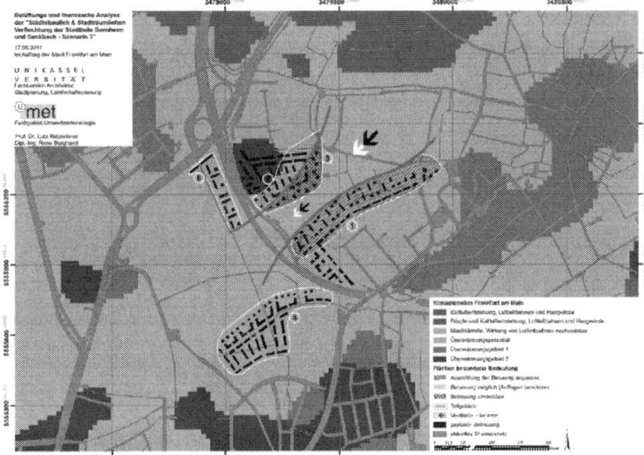

*Figure 4.1* Urban heat load map (top) with air paths, urban design for an air path (middle), and microclimate investigation in a hotspot area (bottom).

Source: Author

*Table 4.1* Planning and urban climate scales.

| *Administration level* | *Planning level* | *Urban climate issue* | *Climatic scale* |
|---|---|---|---|
| Region 1:100,000; city 1:25,000 | Urban development; master plan | Heat island effects; ventilation and air paths | Meso-scale |
| Neighbourhood 1:5,000 | Urban structures | Thermal comfort; air pollution | Meso-scale/micro-scale |
| Streets, block of houses 1:2,000 | Street and open space design | Thermal comfort | Micro-scale |
| Single building site 1:500 | Building design | Radiation and ventilation effects | Micro-scale |

Source: Author

(B) *Zoning plans or neighbourhood plans or blocks (urban structures)* need more detailed specifications. The main planning aspects here are the microclimatic conditions that can be influenced by radiation processes from surfaces and walls combined with ventilation near the ground.

(C) *Building sites (open spaces and buildings)* analyse the building density, street canyons, greenery and open city spaces on a micro-scale level. Many of them can have an isolated impact.

# Part 2

# Large cities

Chapter 5

# Urban climatic map studies in Japan

## Tokyo and Yokohama

*Yasunobu Ashie, Takahiro Tanaka, Satoru Sadohara and Shusuke Inachi*

### The heat island phenomenon in Tokyo

The average global temperature is said to have risen by 0.74°C over the last 100 years. Tokyo, New York, and Paris have undergone relatively large increases in temperature (see Figure 5.1); the average temperature in Tokyo in particular has increased by approximately 3°C in 100 years (Mikami *et al.*, 2003). The rise in temperatures of cities relative to the global average temperature is thought to be due to the effects of urbanisation. Though the rise in temperatures has slowed down in Paris since 1950, Tokyo has shown a consistent temperature rise. The population of Paris has been falling since reaching a peak of approximately 2.9 million in the 1950s, though a slight increase in recent years has brought it up to 2.17 million as of 2007. On the other hand, the population of Tokyo has increased by 8 times in the twentieth century with an era of high economic growth from 1950 to 1970 (1900: 1.5 million; 2000: 12.1 million), making the heat island phenomenon become more marked.

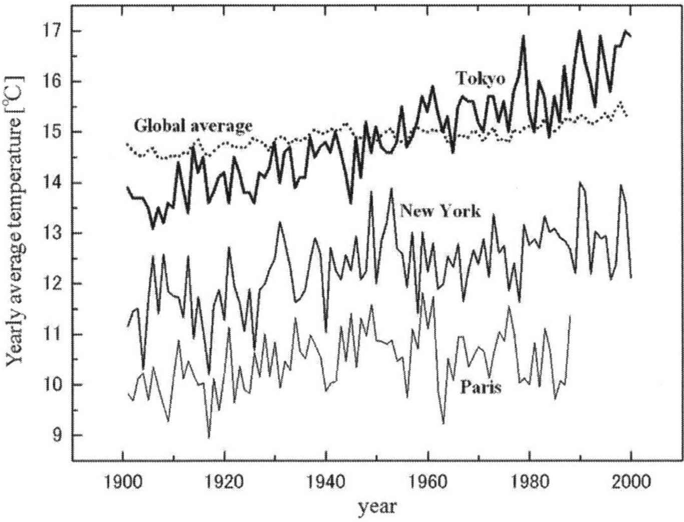


*Figure 5.1* Yearly average temperature for Tokyo and other world cities.

Source: Mikami *et al.*, 2003

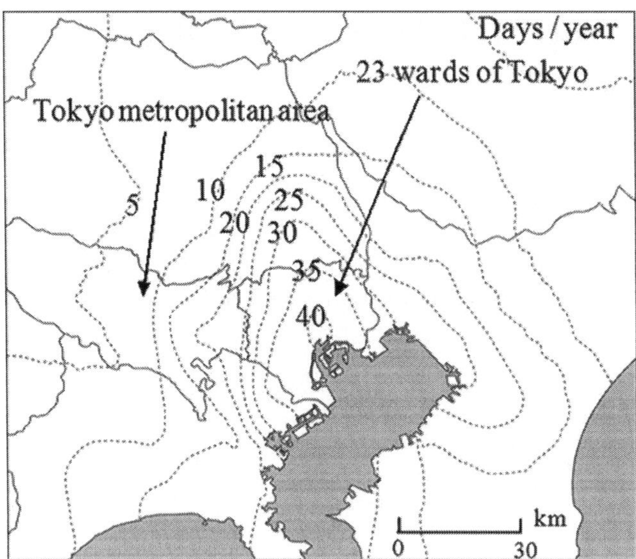


*Figure 5.2* Distribution map of the number of *Nettaiya*.

Source: Ministry of the Environment, Japan

*Nettaiya* (literally 'tropical nights') are nights when the temperature does not fall below 25°C. *Nettaiya* and the heat capacity of buildings combined are known to affect comfortable sleeping times. The number of these nights is used as a benchmark of sleeping difficulties. Figure 5.2 shows the yearly number of *Nettaiya* on contour lines. Though there are 5–20 *Nettaiya* a year in the Tokyo metropolitan area, within the 23 central wards of Tokyo this rises to 30–40 *Nettaiya* a year.

The causes of urban warming are shown in Figure 5.3.The first cause is artificial waste heat. People living in urban areas use vehicles and have air conditioners in buildings, which all require energy. Electricity, gas, petrol, and other forms of energy are gathered from outside the city and consumed, releasing energy loss as exhaust heat into the urban areas and causing the temperature to rise. The amount of artificial waste heat released each summer day in the 23 wards of Tokyo is 2000TJ.

The second cause is the type of land cover. Urban ground surfaces are covered by asphalt and concrete and other construction materials, with few forest or water areas. Buildings and their grounds cover 56 per cent of the land area of the 23 wards, while roads cover 21 per cent, together totalling approximately 80 per cent of the available space. The daytime summer surface heat of asphalt, concrete and other materials reaches 50–60°C, while their heat retaining properties act at nights to prevent temperatures from falling. The third cause has to do with ventilation. Urban areas are filled with innumerable buildings. This causes air to become trapped inside urban areas and fail to disperse upwards, which drives temperatures upwards. In recent years buildings of 200m or higher have been clustered on the Tokyo coastline, a phenomenon known as the 'Tokyo Wall' (see Figure 5.4). The Tokyo Wall, as its name implies, acts as a wall to block breezes blowing off the sea, and is feared to be further worsening the heat island phenomenon.

The heat island phenomenon impacts humans and the environment in a variety of ways. Energy consumption is affected by increases in cooling loads, the number of people affected by heatstroke rises, concentrated heavy downpours of rain occur, and ecological systems are affected. The

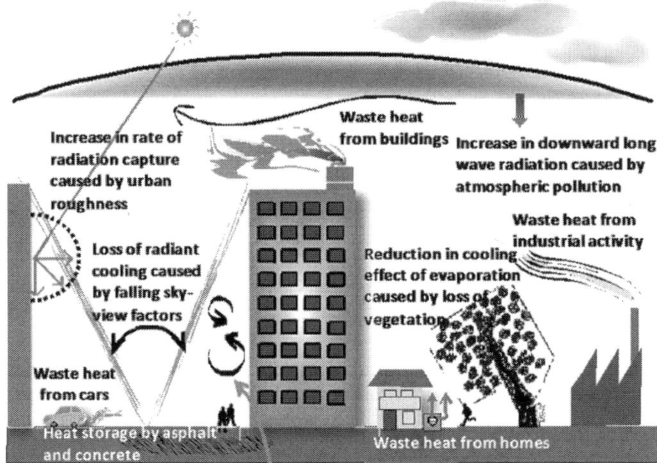


*Figure 5.3* Factors behind rising urban temperatures.

Source: Yasunobu Ashie

*Figure 5.4* Tokyo Wall.

Source: Courtesy of Dr Kagiya, K.

relation between electricity demand and temperatures are shown in Figure 5.5. Electricity demand remains low at 15–20°C, but once temperatures rise above that, electricity demand increases linearly. When summer temperatures in the south of the Kanto region, inclusive of Tokyo, rise by 1°C, electricity demand rises by 1.6–1.7 million kW. This is equivalent to the amount of electricity produced by two medium-sized nuclear reactors.

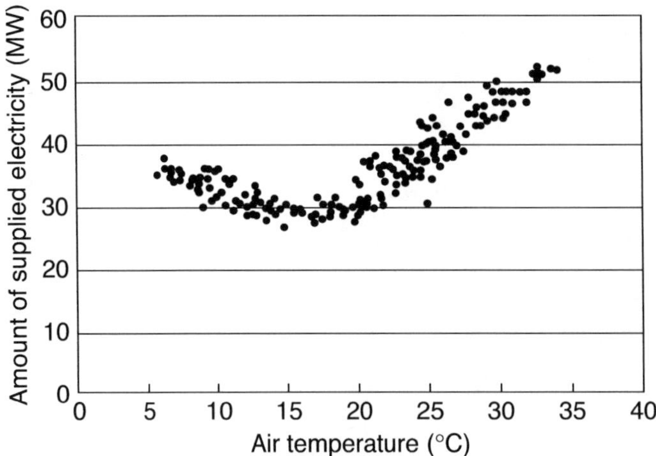


*Figure 5.5* The relationship between electricity demand in office districts and air temperature – using 2003 data (at 5.00 p.m.) from Kansai Electric Power.

Source: Courtesy of Daisuke Narumi

## Countermeasures in Tokyo

Numerous countermeasures against the heat island phenomenon have been undertaken in Tokyo, including the implementation of initiatives focused on public facilities and various systems such as water-retention paving, rooftop greenery, and the grassing over of school grounds. In recent years, water sprinkling activities by non-profit organisations' and citizens' initiatives, e.g. wearing lighter clothes in the summer ('Cool Biz') have been joined by efforts to eliminate the heat island phenomenon (see Figure 5.6). Here we will explain those countermeasures taken in Tokyo against the background of the heat island phenomenon.

Heat island countermeasures imply the involvement of a wide range of entities, and the promotion of countermeasures for private buildings is a key point. The Tokyo Metropolitan Government (TMG) has published the *Guidelines for Heat Island Control Measures* (see Figure 5.7) to involve private sector businesses and citizens in heat island countermeasures in accordance with the local environment when constructing or renovating buildings.

The *Guidelines of Heat Island Control Measures* (TMG, 2005a, 2005b) includes the Heat Environment Map shown in Plate 5.1. The Heat Environment Map analyses the effects of artificial waste heat and land cover of the ground surface on the atmosphere in the 23 wards of Tokyo. Ten types of regions are categorised by the causes of the heat island phenomenon and their distribution is shown from an aerial view at a 500m grid resolution. This map makes explicit the status of various reasons behind the rise in temperatures and it is used as the basis for policies related to heat island countermeasures. The authors of this map formulated the transfer phenomena of the generated heat in urban areas and worked to develop means of estimating temperature figures in urban areas based upon information such as the building land ratio and height of buildings in each city block.

As a result, an urban canopy model has been developed considering urban buildings as multi layered atmospheric structures to handle heat distributions. The name of this tool is the Urban Climate Simulation System (UCSS) (Ashie *et al.*, 1999; Vu Thanh *et al.*, 1999; Hirano and Ashie, 2009). The UCSS is utilised in the Ministry of Land, Infrastructure, Transport

*Figure 5.6* Various activities of heat island countermeasures: (a) sprinking water; (b) Cool Biz; (c) lawn planting in the school ground; (d) water mist spray.

Source: (a) From homepage of Tokyo Metropolitan Government; (b) http://www.frob.co.jp/posterhiroba/poster_h.php?id=1398668364; (c) From homepage of Tokyo Metropolitan Government; (d) Authors

*Figure 5.7* Tokyo Metropolitan Government 'Guideline for Heat Island Control Measures'.

Source: TMG, 2005a

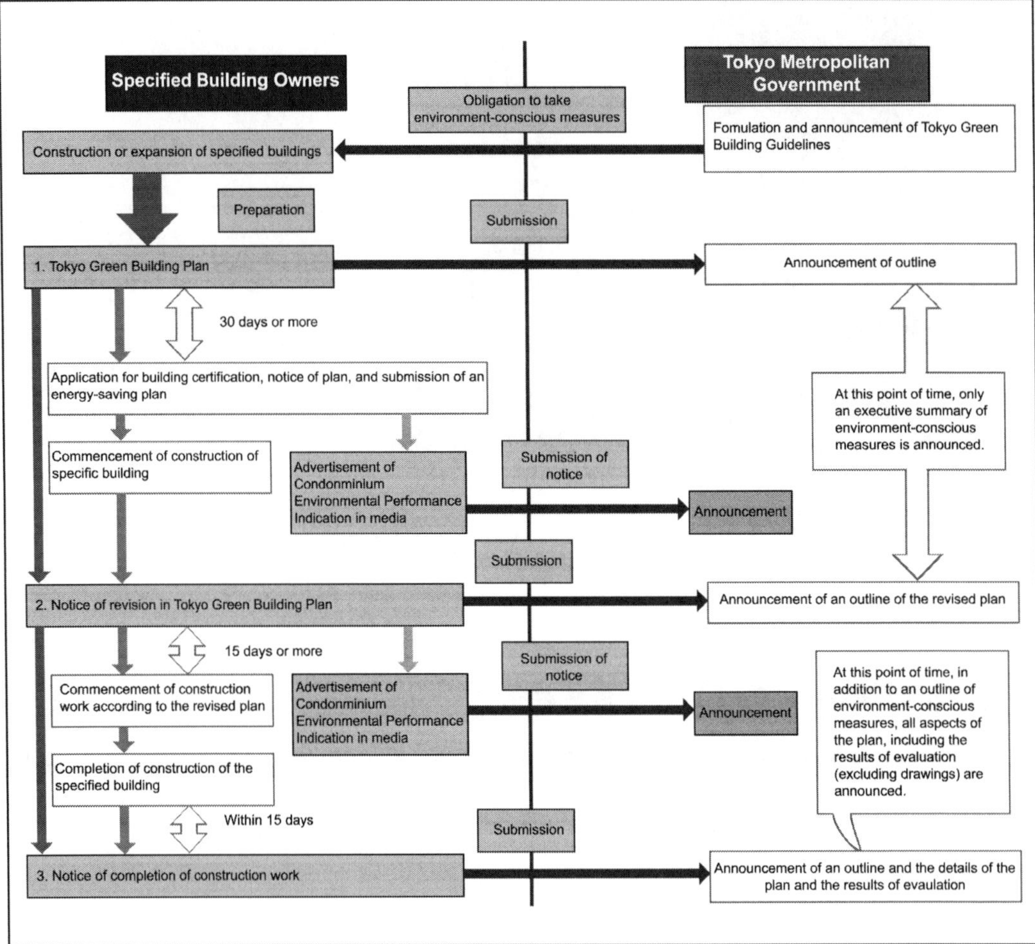


*Figure 5.8* The workflow of the Tokyo green building program.

Source: Tokyo Metropolitan Government

and Tourism's CASBEE-HI (Comprehensive Assessment System for Building Environmental Efficiency for Heat Island Relaxation) system. The Tokyo Metropolitan Government also implemented the Building Environmental Plan System, as shown in Figure 5.8, in 2002 to encourage building owners to take up environmental initiatives voluntarily. The system targets new buildings or extensions of over 10,000m$^2$ (5,000m$^2$ from October 2010), where the submission of a Building Environmental Plan is necessary. Alleviation of the heat island phenomenon is built into reports that consider environmental issues such as the rationalisation of energy usage, the appropriate use of resources, and the protection of the natural environment. These issues have been benchmarked in figures to match the environmental efforts of building owners. In addition, they are posted on the website of the Tokyo Metropolitan Government in the form of a radar chart (see Figure 5.9).

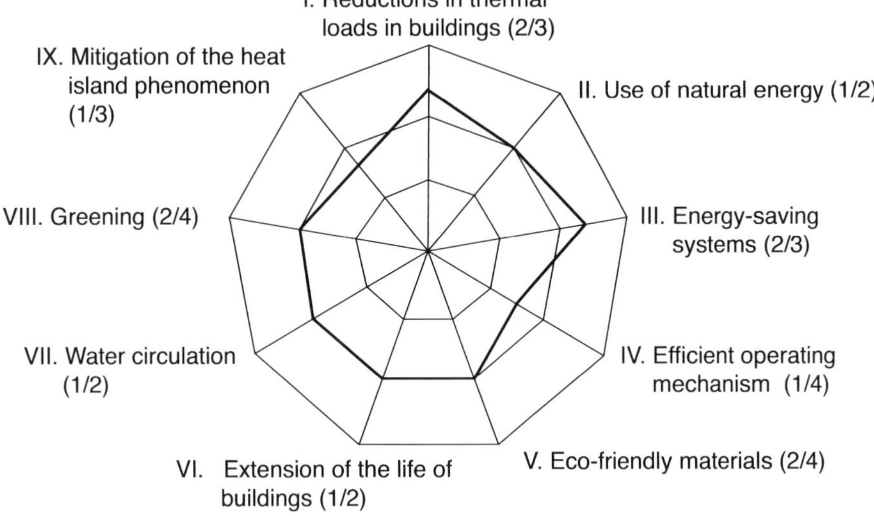


*Figure 5.9* Disclosure to the public.

Source: Tokyo Metropolitan Government

## The Tokyo Station wind passages plan

The centre of Tokyo faces the Tokyo Bay and enjoys cooling breezes from the sea in the summer. Here we will introduce an example of an urban development that brings these cooling sea breezes into the city. Figure 5.10 shows the passage of wind around the Tokyo Station area. A comparison of wind direction and speed at ground level was made using the three methods: on-site observation, wind tunnel experiments, and numerical simulations; and this found a continuous flow of wind through roadways and rivers in every case. Wind blows towards Tokyo Station along Yaesu Road, but the station building (Building A, see Figure 5.12) can be seen to be blocking the path of the wind.

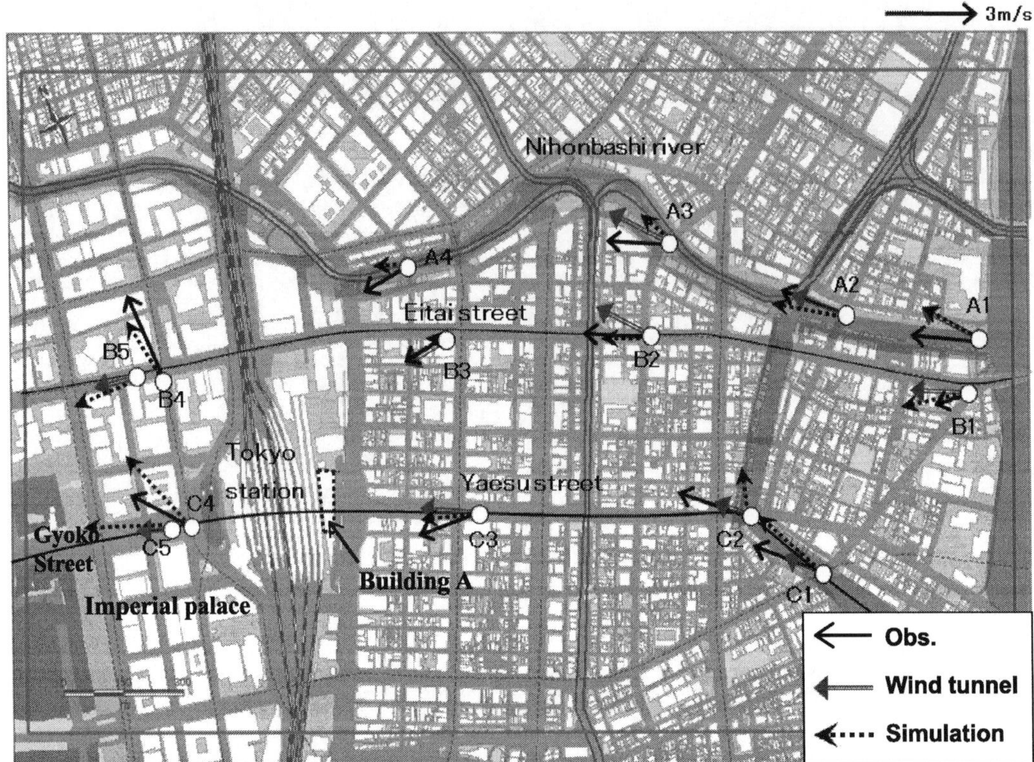


*Figure 5.10* The wind environment around Tokyo Station.

Source: Yasunobu Ashie

The station building is deteriorating with time and needs to be rebuilt or done away with. A plan was thus made to improve the view and secure an open space in front of Tokyo Station from Yaesu Street to the Imperial Palace by removing the station building. The plan was to build new twin towers to expand their floor space. Figure 5.11 shows the site now with the station building (Building A, see Figure 5.12). The offices would be relocated to the twin towers (Buildings B and C, see Figure 5.12). The stores and other tenants of the station building would also be moved to the new twin towers, after which the old station building (Building A) would be demolished.

Figure 5.12 shows a computational fluid dynamics (CFD) study using a supercomputer (the Earth Simulator) in order to compare the flow of wind before and after this redevelopment. (A) Currently, wind flows from Yaesu Street towards Tokyo Station, but the station building (Building A in the Figure) lies in the path of the wind. (B) After the redevelopment, the station building (Building A) is removed, and the twin towers (Buildings B and C) are in place. The calculations show an improvement in the wind flow from Yaesu Street through Tokyo Station and Gyoko Street. Figure 5.13 shows the changes in temperature based on these calculations before and after the redevelopment. Overall, the amount of area with lower temperatures has increased. This is because of enhanced local air exchange efficiency that allows cooler air from above to become admixed through changes to the urban form as a result of the redevelopment.

*Figure 5.11* A view of Tokyo Station.

Source: Yasunobu Ashie

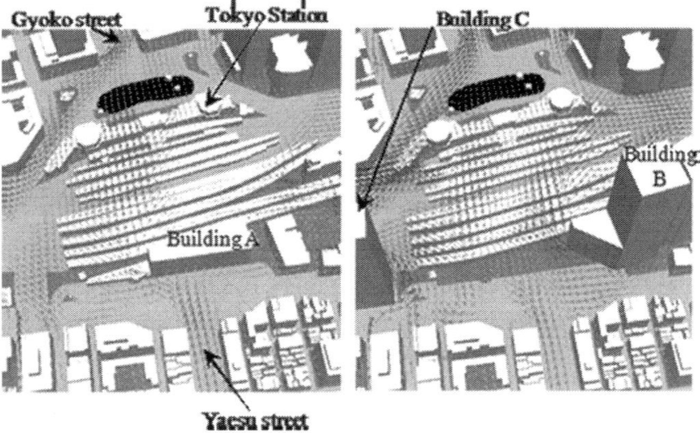


*Figure 5.12* A comparison of wind velocity before (left) and after (right) the redevelopment.

Source: Yasunobu Ashie

However, data remains insufficient due to the analysed results being limited to the summer period alone. A comprehensive analysis of practicable expedients to secure wind passages in urban areas is required, looking at a variety of scenarios by season and time of day through in-depth discussions with urban developers and local bodies.

## The urban climatic map for planning in Yokohama

Like Tokyo, the nearby metro area Yokohama is facing similar kinds of urban climatic issues. Designing and planning it in consideration of urban climate is increasingly important because the urban thermal environment in summer is becoming severe.

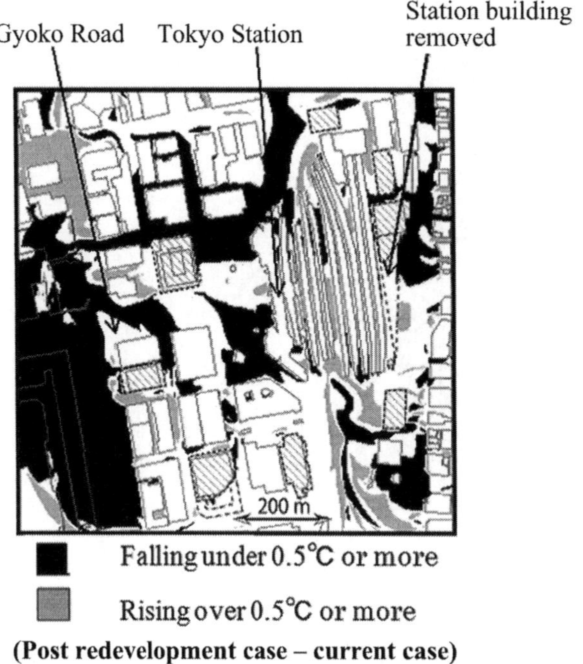


*Figure 5.13* The predicted change in air temperature after the redevelopment (2m above ground). The simulated result clearly shows a fall in air temperature around Tokyo Station.

Source: Yasunobu Ashie

However, stakeholders such as local government officials, planners, and residents cannot consider urban climate in their planning processes because urban climate systems are difficult to understand for non-experts.

To assist planners and local government officials, the urban climatic map (UCMap) for supporting urban planning and design was drafted (Tanaka and Moriyama, 2004). The work makes reference to the method of producing Klimaatlas in Germany (Verband Region Stuttgart, 2008). The UCMap for Yokohama consists of a climate analysis map (UC-AnMap) and a planning recommendations map (UC-ReMap). The latter map was specifically developed to fit into the Japanese planning system.

Drafting the UC-AnMap, the study team analysed the summer urban climatic pattern of Yokohama by using observed climate data such as temperature, wind direction, and wind velocity. A meso-scale numerical study using the Weather Research and Forecasting (WRF) model was conducted (Skamarock *et al.*, 2008). Based on the UC-AnMap and by working with Yokohama's local government officials, urban planners, and designers, the Hint Map was produced. The map contains only the information required by the stakeholders, and leaves out complicated scientific information. During the process of making the planning recommendations map (see Plate 5.2), intense discussions and exchanges were made with the stakeholders. This is vitally important for appropriating scientific knowledge to practical knowledge. The planning recommendations map basically has three pieces of advice. They are:

(1) Guidelines on urban planning and design for using sea breeze effectively: sea breezes are effective in lowering daytime temperatures. Therefore, the authors divided the entire city area into five zones according to wind patterns and showed the guidelines for each zone.
(2) Guidelines on urban planning and design for ventilating effectively: ventilation is effective in lowering daytime temperatures. Therefore, the authors divided the entire city area into two zones according to ventilation conditions.
(3) Guidelines on urban planning and design for greening effectively: greening is effective in lowering night-time temperatures. Therefore, the authors divided the entire city area into four zones according to the necessity of greening and showed the guidelines for each zone.

## References

Ashie, Y., Vu Thanh, C. and Asaeda, T. (1999). Building canopy model for the analysis of urban climate. *Journal of Wind Engineering and Industrial Aerodynamics*, 81(1–3): 237–248.

Hirano, K. and Ashie, Y. (2009). Comprehensive analysis of urban effects on local climate in Tokyo metropolitan region using an urban mesoscale numerical model. In: *Proceedings of The 7th International Conference on Urban Climate*. Yokohama, Japan, 29 June–3 July. Available at: http://www.ide.titech.ac.jp/~icuc7/extended_abstracts/pdf/376129-1-090507141236-004(rev).pdf (Accessed 30 November 2013).

Mikami, T., Ando, H., Morishima, W., Izumi. T., Shioda, T. (2003). A new urban heat island minitering system in Tokyo. In: *Proceedings of the 5th International Conference on Urban Climate*. University of Lodz, Lodz, Poland, 1-5 September. Available at: nargeo.geo.uni.lodz.pl/~icuc5/text/O_3_5.pdf (Accessed 30 November 2013).

Skamarock, W. C., Klemp, J. B., Dudhia, J., Gill, D. O., Barker, D. M., Duda, M. G., Huang, X. Y., Wang, W., Powers., J. G. (2008). *A Description of Advanced Research WRF Version 3, NCAR/TN-475+STR*. Boulder CO: National Center For Atmospheric Research.

Tanaka, T. and Moriyama, M. (2004). Application of GIS to make 'Urban Environmental Climate Map' for urban planning. In: *Proceedings of the Fifth Conference on Urban Environment*. (CD-ROM). Vancouver, BC, Canada, 23–26 August.

TMG (Tokyo Metropolitan Government) (2005a). *Guidelines for Heat Island Control Measures*. Available at: https://www.kankyo.metro.tokyo.jp/en/attachement/heat_island.pdf (Accessed 30 November 2013)

TMG (Tokyo Metropolitan Government) (2005b). *The Thermal Environment Map and Areas Designated for the Implementation of Measures against the Heat Island Phenomenon*. Available at: http://www.metro.tokyo.jp/ENGLISH/TOPICS/2005/ftf56100.htm (Accessed 30 November 2013).

Verband Region Stuttgart (2008). *Klimaatlas Region Stuttgart*. Stuttgart: Verband Region Stuttgart.

Vu-Thanh, C., Asaeda, T. and Ashie, Y. (1999). Development of a numerical model for the evaluation of the urban thermal environment. *Journal of Wind Engineering and Industrial Aerodynamics*, 81(1–3): 181–196.

Chapter 6

# Urban climatic map studies in China

## Beijing

*Xiaoyi Fang, Weimei Jiang and Wenli Guo*

## Introduction

Urban planning guides a city's urban development, construction and management. A scientifically guided urban planning process is key to sustainable urban development; the approach promotes better resource conservation and environmental protection.

Urban planning and urban meteorological understanding should complement each other. Urban planning decisions must be evidence based. The city's development and its human activities invariably change the land uses and surface characteristics that define the local microclimate of the city. If we lack care when developing the city, it will suffer from irreversible consequences. On the other hand, an evidence-based planning approach can help us plan a better city with a good urban atmospheric environment.

In tandem with the urban development process, there is always a need to carry out scientific studies that relate the meteorological environment to the urban morphology (X. Y. Wang *et al.*, 2005a). The studies typically include scientific techniques like map-based calculations, meteorological numerical simulation, and so on. The studies typically aim to establish a causal relationship between urban meteorology and urban planning in an objective and quantitative way. Among other deliverables, the studies allow for the identification of critical areas in the city, and the effects of one's intervention. This kind of map-based study is aligned with the core purpose of urban climatic map (UCMap) studies (Ren *et al.*, 2011).

Our study highlights the work processes and sometimes the dilemmas facing urban planners when they need to consider the urban climatic factors in formulating their balanced planning solutions. This is despite the presence of contradictions that often happen when simultaneously considering many planning-related factors (G. T. Wang *et al.*, 2005a; He *et al.*, 2007). To ease the chore, our study establishes various impact assessment indexes for Beijing's planners based on our multi-scale numerical modelling system that uses Beijing's geographic information as input. Our study concentrates on the urban scale and the urban sub-domain scale (Miao *et al.*, 2006; Jiang *et al.*, 2007). The aim of our study has been to provide a scientific basis for the planner's decision making process (Research Group, 2004; Wang, 2004).

## The concept behind the study

### *Methodology*

Figure 6.1 shows the methodology of our study on Beijing and the impact of urban planning on its meteorological environment. We started with an analysis of the climatic background of the city,

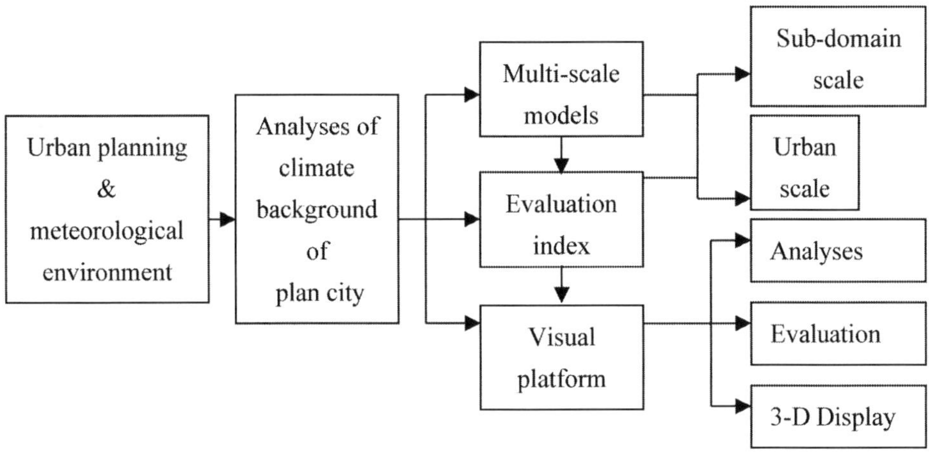


*Figure 6.1* Methodology of the Beijing study.

Source: Xiaoyi Fang, Wenli Guo

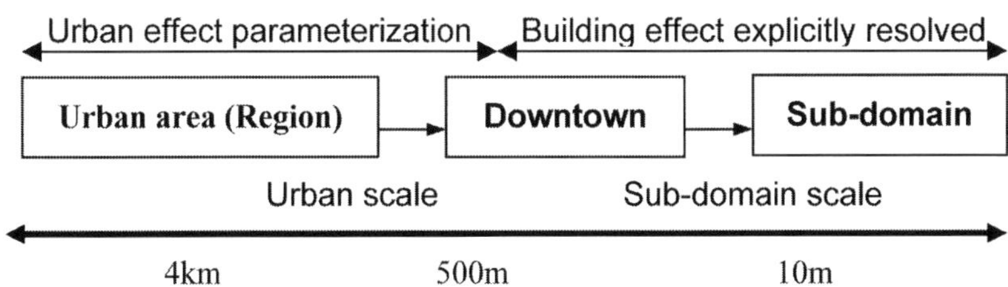


*Figure 6.2* Schema of the multi-scale modelling system.

Source: Xiaoyi Fang, Weimei Jiang

and followed with a number of simulation studies on the planning schemes using our modelling system. We then calculated the results into indexes that enabled us to evaluate their respective performances. Lastly, we represented the results visually for planners. If desired, details of our method can be found in our report (in Chinese) (Research Group, 2004).

### *A multi-scale modelling system for urban planning*

It is important to note that a single-scale study may not be able to address the needs of urban planning. As such, we adopted a multi-scaled modelling approach, as in Figure 6.2. The idea was to nest the different scales of meteorological information one into the next so as to refine the information from a coarser scale to a finer scale (Fang *et al.*, 2004). For the urban-scale modelling, we used the terrain-following coordinates. The model utilises a three-dimensional non-hydrostatic boundary layer model and an atmospheric pollutants transport and dispersion model (Xu *et al.*, 2002; G. T. Wang *et al.*, 2005b; X. Y. Wang *et al.*, 2005b). The urban sub-domain scale numerical model used the Cartesian coordinate system and assumed that the terrain is flat within the district

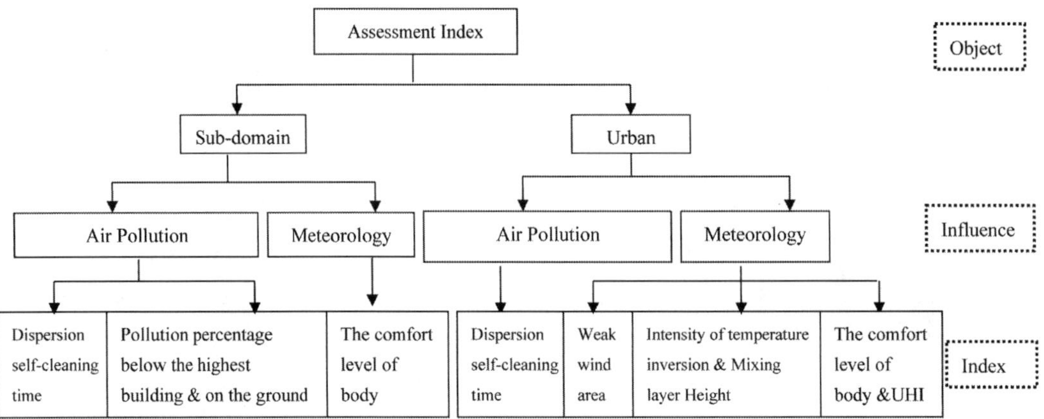


*Figure 6.3* The framework of the assessment indexes.

Source: Xiaoyi Fang, Weimei Jiang, Shiguang Miao, Xiaoyun Wang

and the regional level in the range of the flow field, the temperature distribution and the spread of pollutants (Miao *et al.*, 2002, 2006; Wang *et al.*, 2006). The set-up is suitable for the dispersion and flow field, temperature and pollution distribution fields in the horizontal grid range of 1km to 2km.

### *The assessment index and an understanding of the degree of impact*

The outcome and impact of urban development is often multivalent with multiple targets and hierarchies. Our study therefore adopted a hierarchical process for indicators that correlate the urban development and its resultant urban environment (Jiang, 2004; Xu *et al.*, 2010). The purpose was to find a way to conduct simple and quantifiable calculations that could be easily operated. Figure 6.3 shows our study schema. The assessment indexes were defined in different layers. An expert scoring scheme was applied so that hierarchically the layer indexes could be grouped as they move up the index hierarchy (Miao *et al.*, 2006).

## Case study: Beijing

Some 62 per cent of the city of Beijing is hilly, the rest (38 per cent) is flat. The hills are at the north-east, the north and the west of the city; the city's plains are at the south-east quarters. The city therefore has a topographical aspect towards the sea – the Beijing Bay. Beijing is warm and humid in the summer and cold and dry in the winter. It has high diurnal temperature variation, especially during the spring.

### *An understanding of Beijing's urban climate*

The Beijing urban administration region was simulated using our urban-scale model. The domain of the model is 187.5km × 181.5km. The grid resolution used is 1.5km × 1.5km. Figure 6.4 shows the distribution of the annual average wind speed of the study area. It shows that the plain areas have less wind availability than the surrounding areas (e.g. the south of Shunyi, eastern Chaoyang and Tongzhou areas). Figure 6.5 shows the distribution of the winter wind flow vectors. Flow

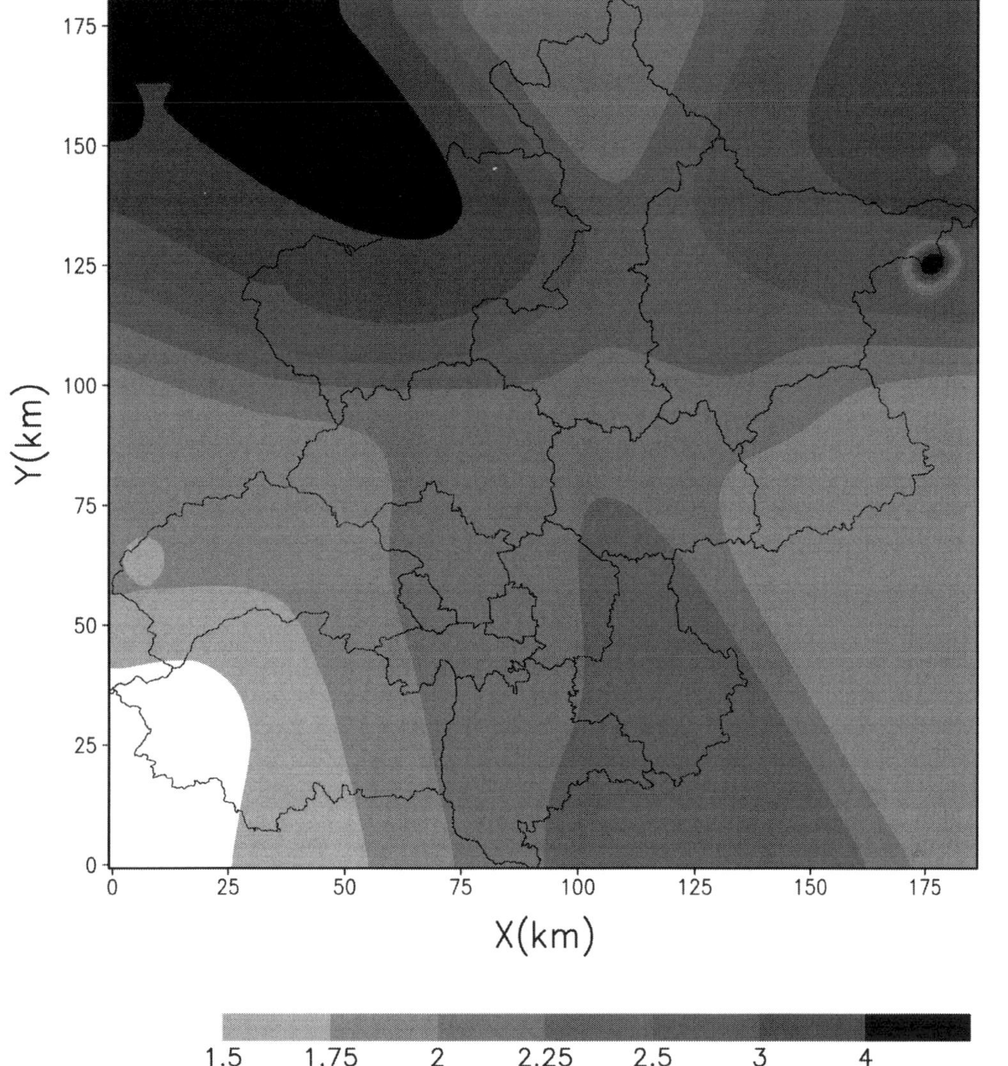


*Figure 6.4* Distribution of the annual average wind speed in Beijing (m/s).

Source: Shiguang Miao, Wenli Guo

convergence can be detected, especially in the Fangshan, Mentougou, Shijingshan areas. Figure 6.6 shows the cleaning hours of pollutants. The hours of higher cleaning of the plain areas can be noted.

## An assessment of Beijing's urban climate

Simulations comparing the planned scenario against the existing conditions have been conducted. Figure 6.7 shows the changes in surface temperature of the planned scenario against the existing condition. Annual average temperature increases of 0.3°C to 0.6°C in the urban areas can be noted.

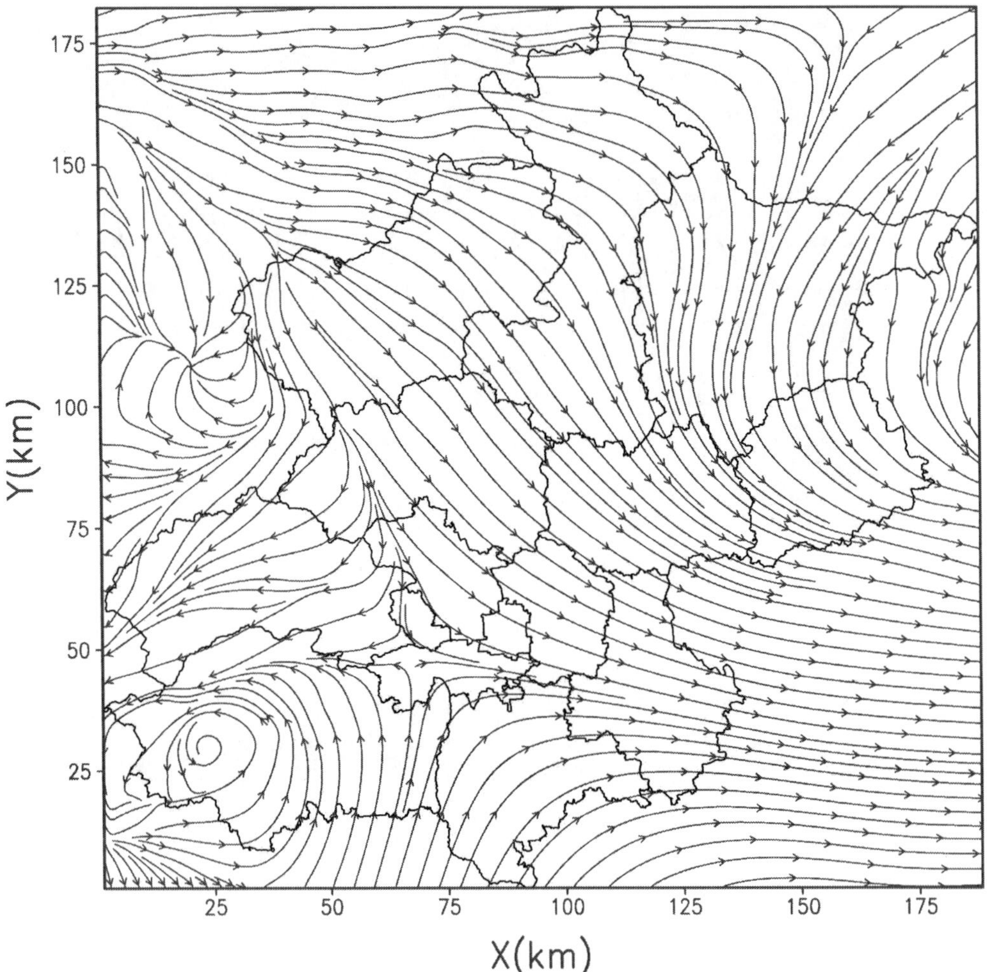


*Figure 6.5* Distribution of wind flow field velocity in Beijing (m/s).

Source: Shiguang Miao, Wenli Guo

## *An assessment of Beijing's master plan*

Based on the numerical studies, the following key observations for planners can be noted:

(1) Urban heat island (UHI) intensity in various urbanised areas in Beijing is severe; the affected areas are expanding and there is a need for mitigation. Greening is recommended.
(2) In areas where intensified greening is planned, air temperature decreases. The available wind is also reduced due to the higher ground roughness caused by the trees. No change in wind speed is detected.
(3) Wind availability in the urbanised metro areas is less than that of the suburban areas, and urban wind availability is decreasing on a year-by-year basis. The suburban areas of Shunyi, Chaoyang, Tongzhou and Daxing have better wind availability; however, in Fangshan and in the metro urban areas, wind is less available.

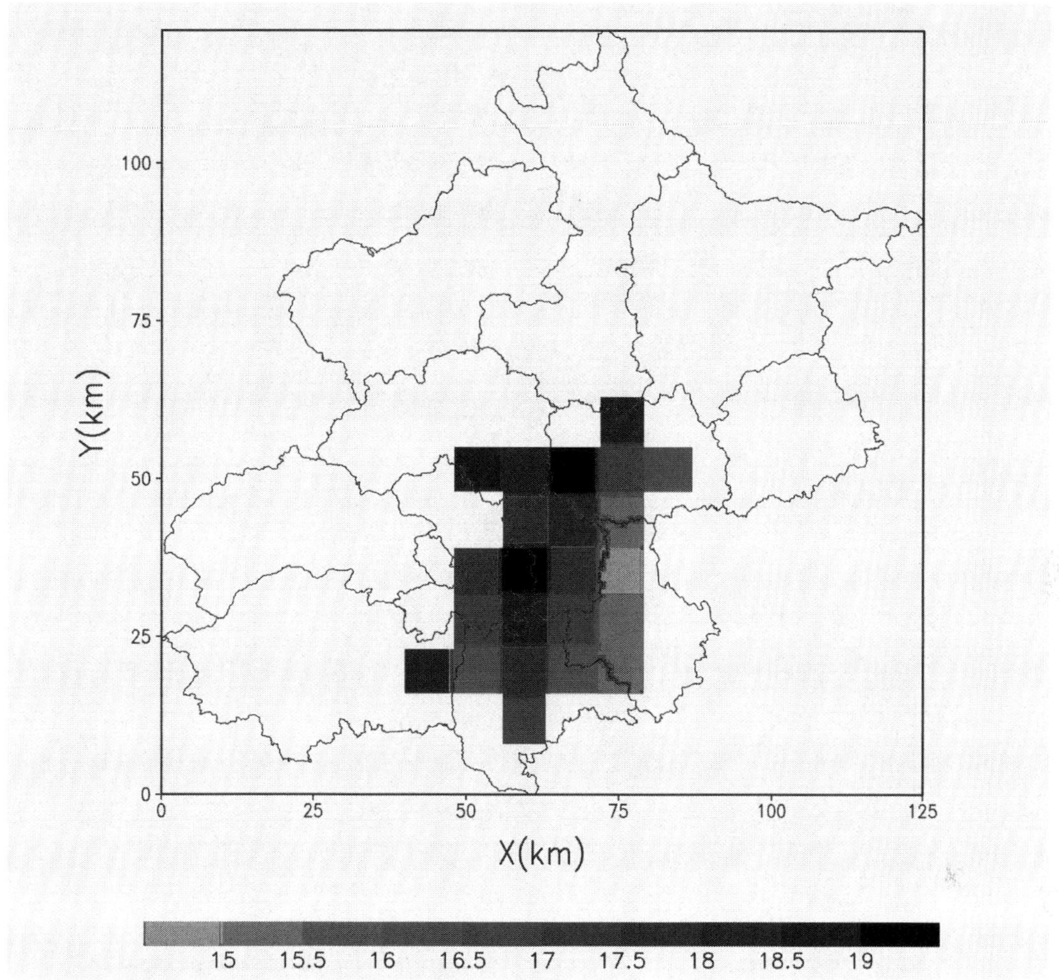


*Figure 6.6* Distribution of the air pollutant dispersion self-cleaning hours (hrs).

Source: Shiguang Miao, Wenli Guo

Based on the study observations, the master plan of 'two axes and smaller multi-centres' was developed. Fangshan, Mentougou, Shijingshan and some other areas were also planned to be used for recreational uses.

## Sub-domain scale studies of Beijing's neighbourhoods – a case study of the Olympic site

Nested within the study of the city as described earlier, we conducted a series of studies that focused on the Beijing Olympic site. The Beijing Wukesong Culture and Sports Centre is located on the intersection of two major roads. The site is flat and mainly surrounded by commercial offices and some residential buildings. Figure 6.8 and Figure 6.9 show two design proposals, Scheme 1 and

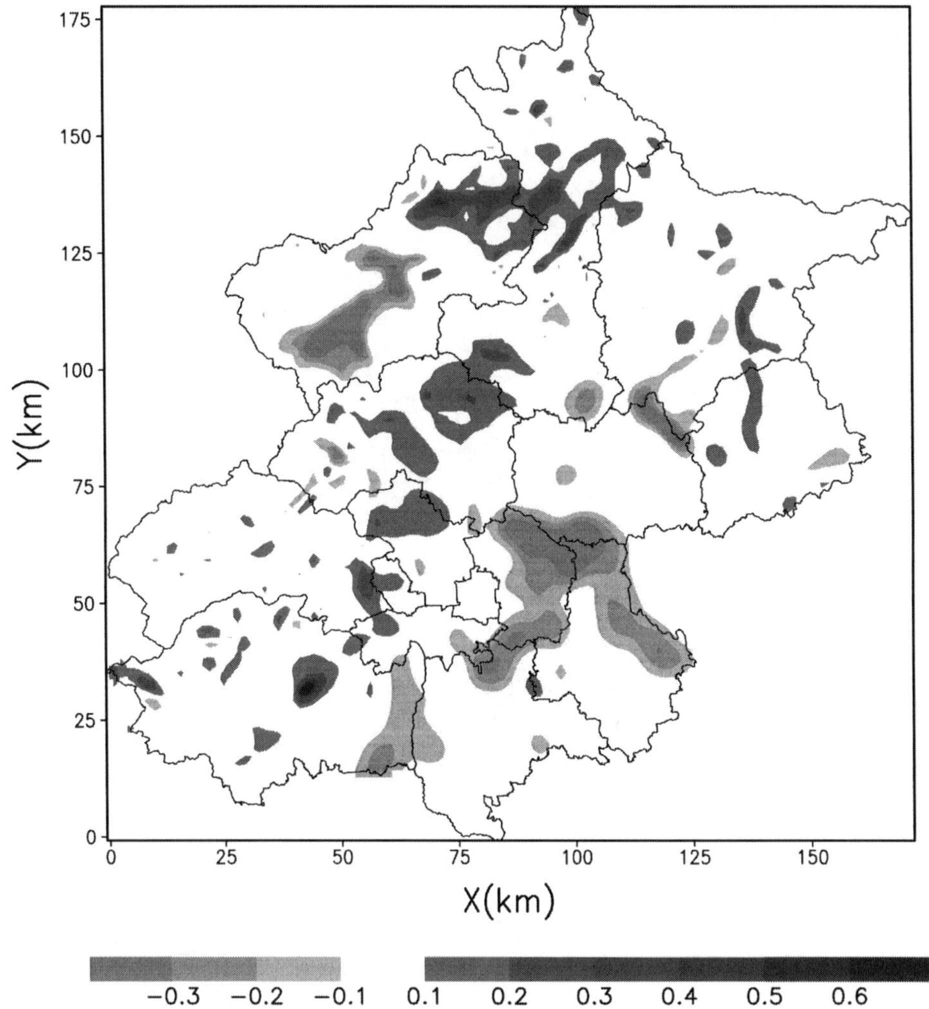


*Figure 6.7* Distribution of the surface temperature changes (planned–existing, unit: °C).
Source: Shiguang Miao, Wenli Guo

Scheme 2 respectively. Scheme 1 has more buildings on-site. There is a large artificial lake in the middle. The greening ratio is 24.06 per cent. Scheme 2 has taller buildings at the north-eastern corner of the project site. The greening ratio is 44.59 per cent.

### *An urban climatic understanding of the two planned scenarios*

Using a sub-domain scale numerical model, a comparative study of the two planned scenarios was conducted. Figure 6.8 shows the prevailing wind flows in the summer months. Scheme 1 has more complicated flow pattern and larger wake areas. The performance is deemed inferior to the flows of Scheme 2. As shown in Figure 6.9 on the wind speed distribution, the large wind wake areas (31.35 per cent of the site) of Scheme 1 that have an average wind speed of equal to or lower

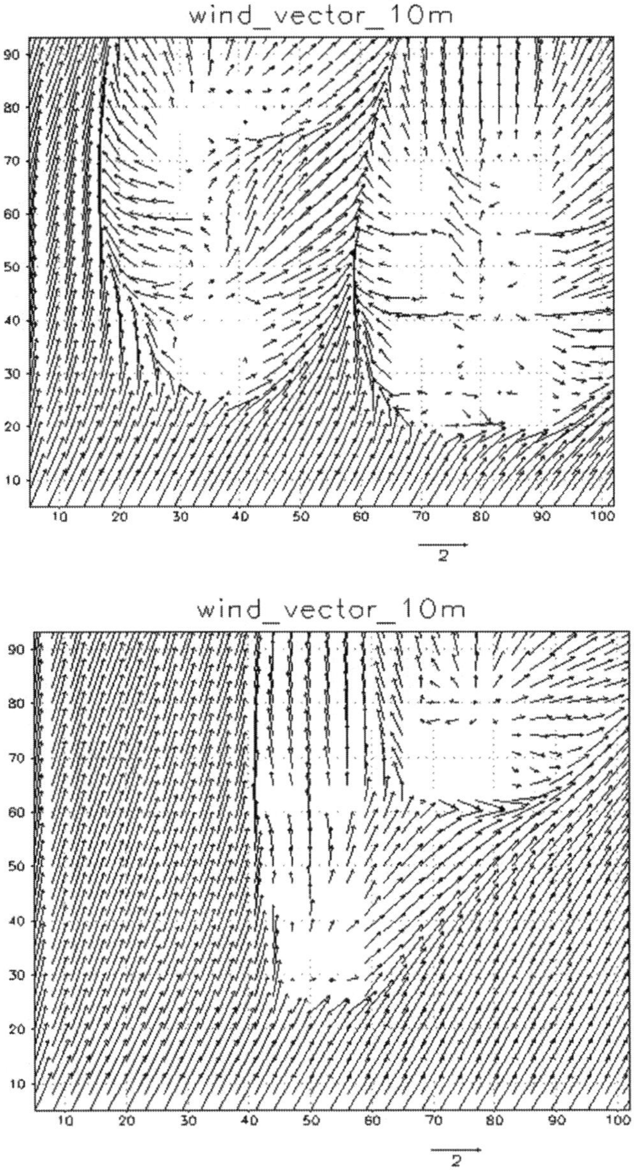


*Figure 6.8* The wind flow vector field in summer: (a) Scheme 1; (b) Scheme 2. (The east-west direction is represented by the X axis, the north-south direction is represented by the Y axis, the grid interval is 10 metre).

Source: Shiguang Miao, Weimei Jiang, Xiaoyun Wang

than 1m/s are apparent. By contrast, only 14 per cent of the site in Scheme 2 has wind wake areas. Beyond wind availability, our study showed that the ground level temperature distribution of Scheme 2 is lower due to its higher greening ratio. Thus, it was concluded that Scheme 2 should be favoured from an urban climatic perspective.

Table 6.1 shows how the two schemes compare based on our assessment schema. Although Scheme 2 does not excel in all aspects, on the whole it still performs better than Scheme 1. Table 6.1 also

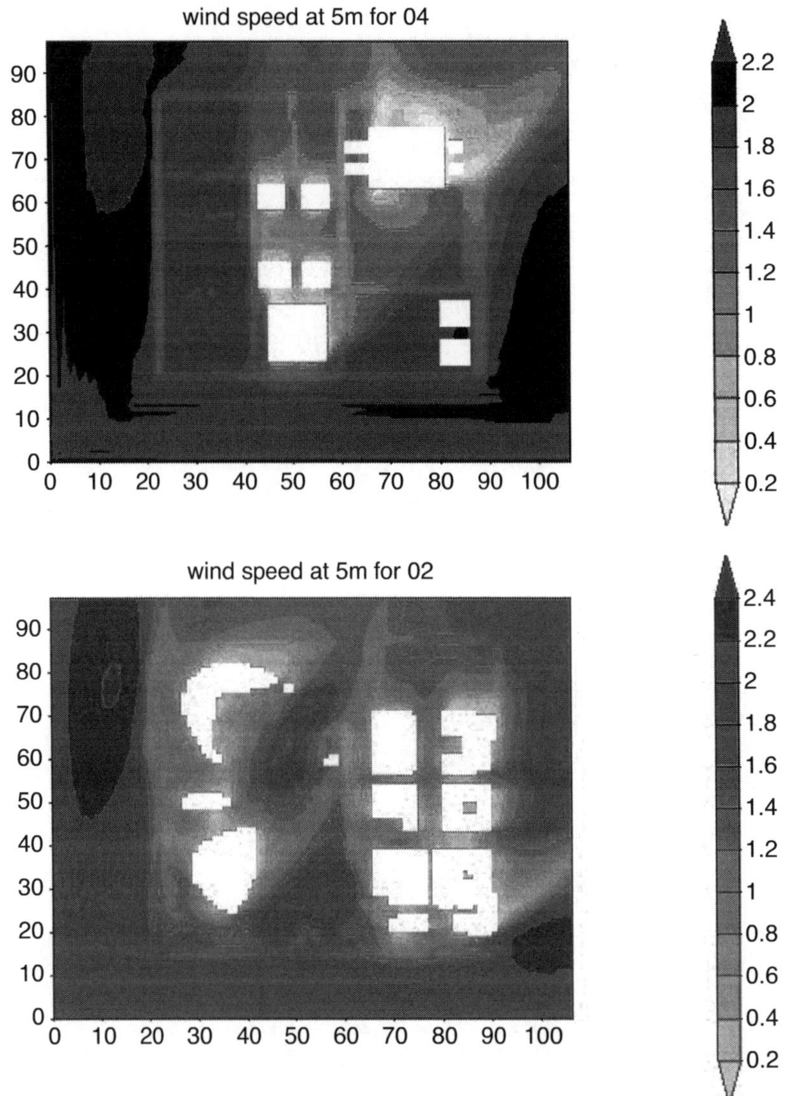


*Figure 6.9* The 5m height wind field (m/s) in summer: (a) Scheme 1; (b) Scheme 2. (The directions of the axis are the same as in Figure 6.8; the white areas in the figures show the buildings).

Source: Shiguang Miao, Weimei Jiang, Xiaoyun Wang

illustrates the importance of considering the priorities and planning values that planners have. No design is perfect, and one needs to judge based on the available information.

## Eco-city, low-carbon city and urban planning

Recently, the issues of eco-city and low-carbon city design have been a topical concern in planners' agendas worldwide. The traditional training of planners has not prepared them for the task, and traditional professional practice has not equipped them with the necessary tools. There is

*Table 6.1* The assessment results of the two schemes.

| *Assessment Index* | *Scheme 1* | | *Scheme 2* | |
|---|---|---|---|---|
| | *Winter* | *Summer* | *Winter* | *Summer* |
| Physiological comfort level | 4.22 | 0.42 | 4.68 | 1.38 |
| Air pollutant concentration on the ground | 3.81 | 4.40 | 4.40 | 3.96 |
| Air pollutant volume around the building | 4.90 | 4.95 | 5.00 | 4.79 |
| Delayed time of air pollutant on building surface | 3.76 | 4.33 | 4.56 | 4.24 |
| Dispersion time | 3.51 | 4.36 | 4.47 | 4.34 |
| Seasonal evaluation index | 3.92 | 3.24 | 4.59 | 3.45 |
| Integrated comprehensive index | 3.58 | | 4.02 | |

Source: Shiguang Miao, Weimei Jiang, Xiaoyun Wang

indeed a dire need for planners to appreciate a performance- and evidence-based way of planning decision-making in our age of climate change and concern about climate.

In the past, the only environmental concern that faced planners was air pollution. This has changed. On 1 January 2009, the Chinese government issued a guideline titled 'Climate Studies and Management Issues'. It demanded a scientific approach to urban climatic concerns. The guidelines require that the urban climate of the city be properly analysed, proper impact assessment studies must be conducted for planning, and climate-related disasters and climate changes must be factored in.

Low-carbon planning is now also an important consideration in China. There are three important planning stages. One must develop policies and technical know-how to guide design. One must conduct a climate and urban climate study for the city for an evidence-based approach. Based on the above context, one must design city-scale strategies for building construction, transportation, greening, energy use, and so on. The variables introduced by a consideration of climate change must be factored in. In short, the process requires a need to combine meteorology and urban planning. A map and spatial-based study are useful tools.

## Conclusions

China has experienced rapid growth in recent years. The high rate of urbanisation is witness to that growth. The process has brought challenges for planners. Couple this with the consideration of climate change and the wish for low-carbon city design, and a deeper climatic and environmental impact assessment is the way forward. It is important to find ways to integrate climate and planning so that better land-use policies and development strategies may be made.

## References

Fang, X. Y., Jiang, W. M. and Miao, S. G. (2004). The multi-scale numerical modelling system for research on the relationship between urban planning and meteorological environment. *Advances in Atmospherica Sciences*, 21(1): 103–112.

He, X. F., Jiang, W. M. and Guo, W. L. (2007). Simulation of local urban planning to the structure of urban boundary layer. *Plateau Meteorology*, 26(2): 363–372. (In Chinese).

Jiang, W. M. (2004). *The Meteorology of Air Pollution*. Nanjing: Nanjing University Press. (In Chinese).

Jiang, W. M., Wang, Y. W. and Liu, G. (2007). Multi-scale urban boundary layer modelling system. *Journal of Nanjing University (Natural Sciences)*, 43(3): 221–237. (In Chinese).

Miao, S. G., Jiang, W. M. and Wang, X. Y. (2002). Numerical simulation of meteorology and pollutant diffusion in urban sub-domain. *Acta Scientiae Circumstantiae*, 22(4): 478–483. (In Chinese).

Miao, S. G., Jiang, W. M., Wang, X. Y. and Guo, W. L. (2006). Impact assessment of urban meteorology and the atmospheric environment using urban sub-domain planning. *Boundary-Layer Meteorology*, 118(1): 133–150.

Ren, C., Ng, E. and Katzschner, L. (2011). Urban climatic map studies: a review. *International Journal of Climatology*, 31(15): 2213–2233.

Research group on the relationship between urban planning and atmospheric environment in Beijing (2004). *Urban Panning and Atmospheric Environment*. Beijing: China Meteorological Press. (In Chinese).

Wang, G. T. (2004). *Meteorological Environment and Urban Planning*. Beijing: Beijing Press.

Wang, G. T., Wang, X. Y. and Miao, S. G. (2005a). The multi-scale evaluated system for the research and application on urban planning and meteorological environment. *Science in China*, Ser. D, 35(supplement I):145–155. (In Chinese).

Wang, G. T., Wang, X. Y. and Miao, S. G. (2005b). A practice on the modern urban planning concept and method: modelling analysis of the atmospheric environment impacts in Foshan town planning. *Urban Planning Forum*, 21(10): 84–87.

Wang, G. T, Wang, X. Y. and Miao, S. G. (2006). The application of numerical simulation of the atmospheric environment in urban sub-domain planning. *Journal of Tsinghua University (Science & Technology)*, 46(9): 1489–1494. (In Chinese).

Wang, X. Y., Wang, G. T. and Fang, X. Y. (2005a). Modern scientific implement of environment conception in urban planning – the atmospheric environmental research of Olympic stadium planning project. *Planners*, 21(10): 84–89. (In Chinese).

Wang, X. Y., Wang, G. T. and Chen, X. Y. (2005b). Research on the response between the urban harmonious developing plan of group of cities and atmospheric environment. *Urban Planning*, 12: 29–32. (In Chinese).

Xu, M., Jiang, W. M. and Ji, C. P. (2002). Numerical modelling and verification of structures of the boundary layer over Beijing area. *Quarterly Journal of Applied Meteorology*, 13 (supplement): 61–68. (In Chinese).

Xu, X. D., Zhou, X. J. and Ding, G. A. (2010). *The Research on Urban Integrated Observations and Atmospheric Environment Dynamics*. Beijing: China Meteorological Press. (In Chinese).

Chapter 7

# Urban climatic map studies in Japan

## Sakai in Osaka

*Takahiro Tanaka and Masakazu Moriyama*

## Introduction

In Japan, large cities have always had a hot and humid climate in summer, but their inhabitants are now exposed to increasingly severe climates caused by urbanisation. Therefore, designing and planning cities in consideration of urban climates is becoming more important because summer urban thermal environments are becoming increasingly severe. Nevertheless, stakeholders (local government officials, planners, residents, and so on) cannot incorporate urban climate information into their design and planning processes because urban climate systems are difficult to understand.

Therefore, the authors have proposed Urban Climatic Maps (UCMaps) for supporting urban design and planning (e.g. Tanaka *et al.*, 2006). Such maps should be made by local governments in the future, and be used for planning-related works in each city. However, UCMaps are rarely made and used by Japanese local governments now, apparently because they do not fit the actual Japanese planning system. For this study, the authors specifically examined applications of UCMaps for urban planning-related works of local government and sought to elucidate how UCMaps should be produced for this purpose. The authors interviewed local government officials (City of Sakai) about UCMap's potential uses and the information that it should provide for them.

## The urban climatic map

We surmised that a UCMap should consist of an Urban Climatic Analysis Map (UC-AnMap) and an Urban Climatic Recommendation Map (UC-ReMap) (see Figure 7.1). The UC-AnMap's role is to represent the actual climate conditions of the target city; the UC-ReMap is intended to represent recommendations for design and planning from the urban climate perspective. Therefore, the UC-ReMap in particular should conform to the actual Japanese planning system.

### *Outline*

For this project, the authors selected Sakai as a study city because it is one of Japan's hottest cities. Furthermore, the local government in this city (City of Sakai) wishes to take some countermeasures against the severe thermal environment in summer. The authors therefore addressed the problem of the mitigation of the summer thermal environment (although the UCMap is also applicable to air pollution reduction) because it is especially necessary in Sakai. In addition, in this project, the authors made urban-scale (1:25,000) UCMaps because their applications in urban planning-related tasks in local government are the target of this study. The authors took three steps: (1) making the UC-AnMap, (2) interviewing local government officials and summarising

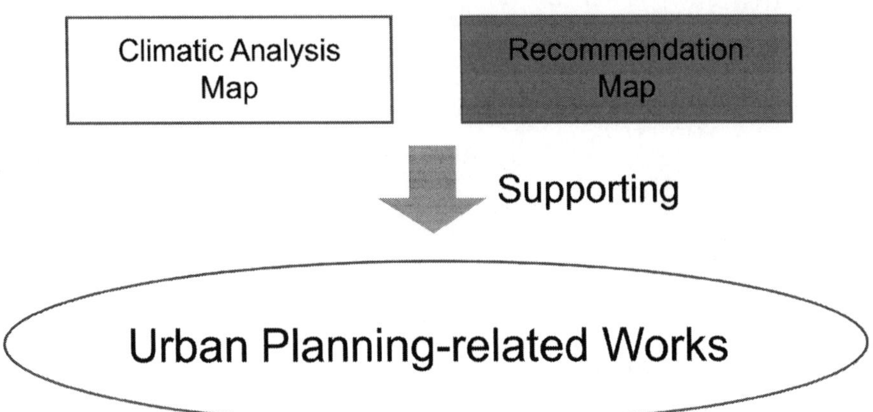


*Figure 7.1* Two component maps included in an urban climatic map (UC-AnMap and UC-ReMap).

Source: Authors

the results, (3) producing an example of a UC-ReMap. From the next section, each result will be described according to these steps.

### *Making the urban climatic analysis map (UC-AnMap)*

For this study, according to previous studies (e.g. Tanaka and Moriyama, 2004), the following four layers are overlaid on the UC-AnMap: (1) Terrain; (2) Wind; (3) Land Use, as categorised by the surface temperature change pattern; and (4) Observed Temperature. Based on this definition, the authors produced a UCMap of Sakai (see Plate 7.1).

### *Hearing from local government officials*

To elucidate the requirements for UCMaps from local government officials in urban planning-related occupations, the authors performed an oral survey of City of Sakai officials. Target departments were the Department of Rivers and Channels, the Department of Green Space, the Department of Urban Planning, and the Department of Environmental Activity. The authors asked the following two questions in addition to others:

(a) What is the urban climate-related work performed in your department?
(b) In what situations will UCMaps be effective? What kinds of information should be represented on the map?

The results were summarised as follows:

**1 Department of Rivers and Channels**

(a) Currently, this department is planning to restore (revitalise) water channels that have disappeared through urbanisation. Furthermore, they expect some additional effects to occur through restoration, such as heat island mitigation and disaster prevention. Consequently, their duties are linked to urban climate indirectly through 'Water'.

(b) It will be effective to represent places where they should restore water channels from the view of urban heat island mitigation on UCMap. Furthermore, it is better to represent areas with a psychological feeling of 'coolness' such as that which water areas provide.

**2 Department of Green Space**

(a) This department performs 'Green' related planning and promotion such as producing a Green Master Plan and promoting the greening of private lands. Consequently, their works are linked to urban climate indirectly through 'Green'.

(b) This department is producing an action plan based on the Green Master Plan. Here, they want to identify places where green space should be conserved. For this purpose, UCMaps are expected to serve as supporting information. In this plan, a 'greening recommendation area' will be defined. This information should also be represented from the viewpoint of urban heat island mitigation on the UCMap.

**3 Department of Urban Planning**

(a) This department is producing an Urban Master Plan as a future vision for the entire city. Furthermore, they promote downtown redevelopment and urban facility arrangement for realising a future vision. Consequently, their works are linked to urban climate indirectly through 'Urban form'.

(b) The UCMap will help to make and remake the Urban Master Plan as part of the support information (they have not considered urban climate yet). A UCMap on a detailed scale (about 1:2,500) will also be effective for producing an urban redevelopment plan (e.g. considering wind patterns created by building site arrangements and green site arrangements).

**4 Department of Environmental Activity**

(a) This department is producing a plan for mitigating urban heat island effects and global warming. Furthermore, they produce energy-saving plans for the entire city. Consequently, to some extent, their duties are linked directly to urban climate.

(b) It is good that the UCMap represents recommendation areas for each countermeasure to urban heat islands (e.g. recommendation areas for use of sea breezes, and recommendation areas for reducing anthropogenic heat release).

Based on the above results, the authors extracted three major requirements for a UCMap as follows:

(A) A UCMap should represent recommended areas for each countermeasure against urban heat island effects, such as 'Recommended areas for restoring water channels', 'Recommended greening areas', 'Recommended areas for using sea breezes', and 'Recommended areas for reducing anthropogenic heat release'.

(B) Another UCMap, with detailed scale (about 1:2,500), will also be needed for urban redevelopment.

(C) A human comfort element also needs to be represented on the UCMap such as the psychological feeling of 'Coolness' that water areas have.

### *Making an urban climatic recommendation map (UC-ReMap)*

To meet Requirement A, the authors attempted to produce an example of a UC-ReMap. Sakai presents clear characteristics of summer wind flow patterns by which sea breezes blow from the west during the day and mountain/land breezes blow from the east in the night-time. Therefore, the authors produced a UC-ReMap that specifically examines 'Wind Use' as one UC-ReMap element (see Figure 7.2). This map was produced based on the results of the meso-scale meteorological model MM5 (Grell *et al.*, 1995). Figure 7.3 depicts an example of the model results.

To meet Requirement B, the authors also attempted to produce an example of a UC-ReMap for neighbourhood design. This neighbourhood includes a small valley. In this area, residential areas will be developed and the summer thermal environment will be severe. Evidently, urban designers

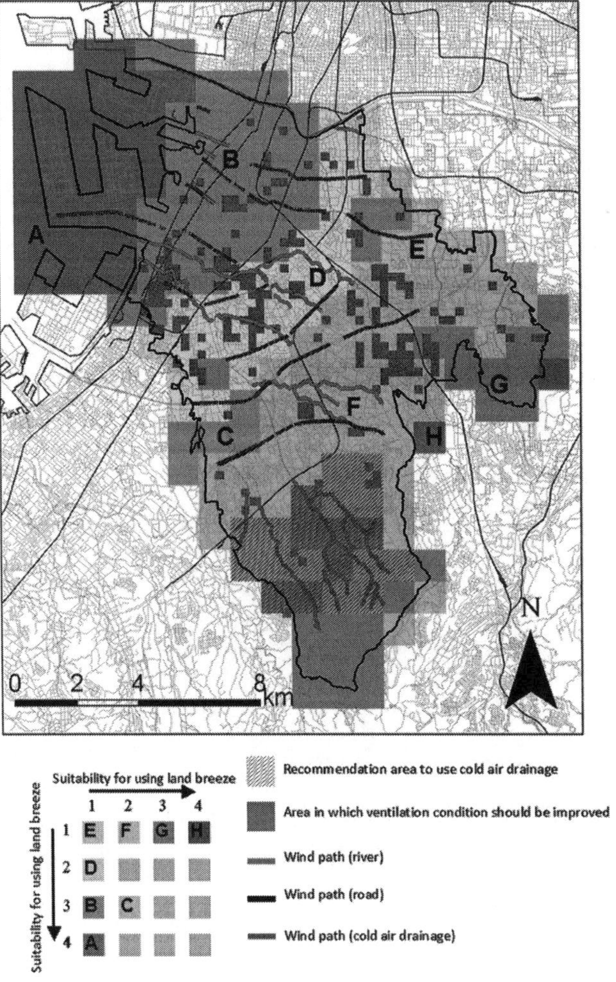


*Figure 7.2* The Urban Climatic Recommendation Map (UC-ReMap) for considering wind use (one UC-ReMap element).

Source: Authors

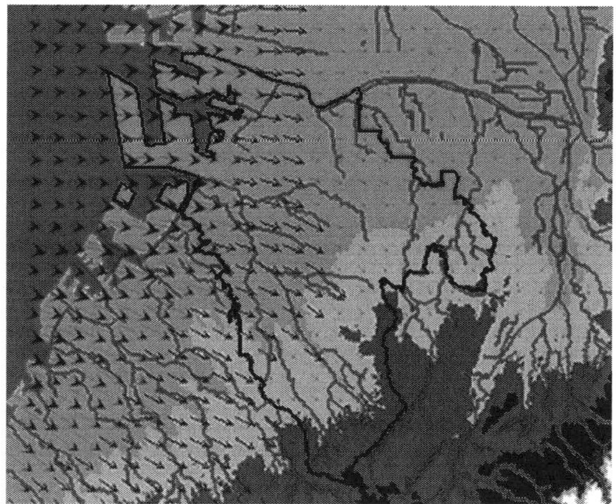

*Figure 7.3* An example of a map produced based on meso-scale meteorological (MM5) model results.

Source: Authors

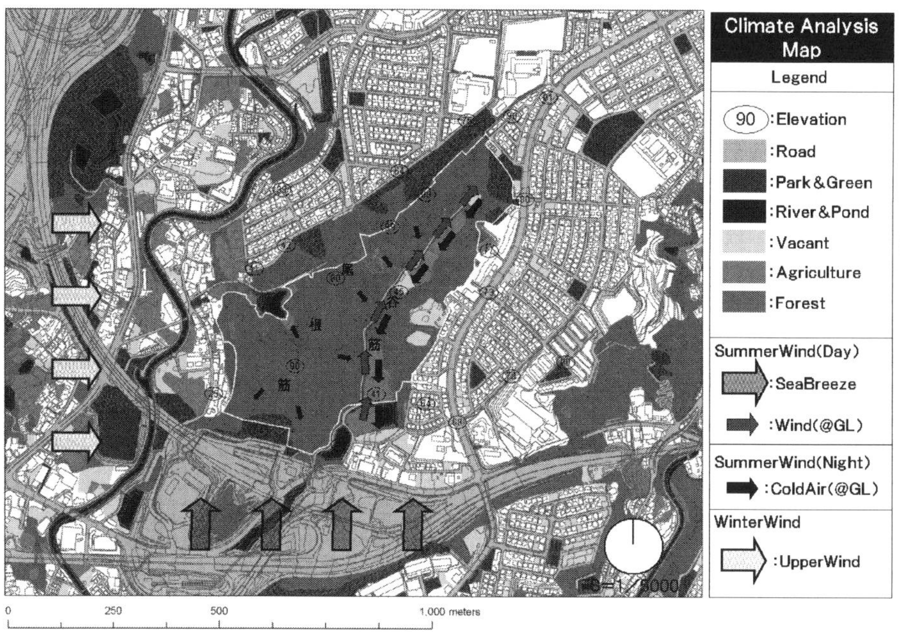


*Figure 7.4* An example of the Urban Climatic Recommendation Map (UC-ReMap) in the neighbourhood scale.

Source: Authors

should design this neighbourhood with local climate. Therefore, the authors produced a UCMap for neighbourhood design (see Figure 7.4). This map describes the wind paths for mitigating severe thermal environments, based on field surveys and computational fluid dynamics (CFD) simulations. Based on this map, a UC-ReMap will be made.

## Summary

In this project, we specifically addressed the application of UCMaps to the urban planning-related duties of a local government. We extracted requirements for the UCMaps based on an oral survey of local government officials. As a next challenge, authors will produce a new UC-ReMap based on that feedback, thereby creating a UCMap that is effective for actual urban planning-related activities.

## References

Grell, G. A., Dudhia, J. and Stauffer, D. R. (1995). *A Description of the Fifth-Generation Penn State/NCAR Mesoscale Model (MM5)*. NCAR (National Center for Atmospheric Research) Technical Note. Available at: http://www.mmm.ucar.edu/mm5/documents/mm5-desc-doc.html (Accessed March 2011).

Tanaka, T. and Moriyama, M. (2004). Application of GIS to make 'Urban Environmental Climate Map' for urban planning. In: *Proceedings of the 5th Conference on Urban Environment*. (CD-ROM). Vancouver, BC, Canada, 23–26 August.

Tanaka, T., Yamashita, T. and Moriyama, M. (2006). Urban Environmental Climate Map for urban design and planning. In: *Proceedings of the 6th International Symposium on Architectural Interchanges in Asia: A+T: Neo-Value in Asian Architecture*, Vol. 1, 688–691. Daegu, Korea, 25–28 October.

Chapter 8

# Urban climatic map studies in Vietnam

## Ho Chi Minh City

*Lutz Katzschner and René Burghardt*

## Introduction

Within the scope of urban planning strategies as well as global climate changes, urban climatic maps are an important tool for master or zoning plans. Moreover, in a changing climate, the analysis is used to mitigate heat stress and heat risk. Aside from analysing thermal comfort conditions, a clean air strategy can also be the result of this analysis. For Ho Chi Minh City, the Urban Climatic Map (UCMap) concept was used as an appropriate tool for presenting climatic phenomena and problems in 2D spatial maps. The UCMap analyses the urban climate of the city and makes recommendations towards the defined *climatopes*. The climatopes represent the heat load situation, which combines the thermal and dynamic effects.

## Urban climatic mapping

The urban climatic mapping method has become widely used for urban planning as it can provide a spatial picture for the planners from the regional scale of 1:100,000 to the urban scale of 1:5,000. By using the Geographic Information System (GIS), a climatic map can be developed together with an analysis on different information layers. Katzschner (2007) carried out a study on thermal comfort in the microclimate, developing a mapping methodology with focus on the spatial analysis of thermal comfort zones. It tried to identify the quality of open urban spaces that contribute to the quality of life within cities. Some methodologies were employed to produce comfort zone maps, such as meteorological field surveys, interviews and urban morphology identification.

The urban climatic map synergistically combines various climatic parameters like wind direction and speed, solar radiation and air temperature with information on city topography, landscape, building bulk, street grids and so on. The UCMap can show how the streets are ventilated, where the more comfortable spots or the most problematic areas are and how the buildings affect the city wind environment (Ng *et al.*, 2007). With information like this, planners and designers can have a better climatic basis for decision making. Apart from physical factors, the development of the UCMap is also based on qualitative and subjective criteria (Scherer *et al.*, 1999).

For the evaluation on Ho Chi Minh City, the urban climatic map was classified into climatopes and parallel recommendations could be derived. These recommendations were achieved in two steps: (A) general climatic-based recommendations and (B) areal recommendations in different climatic zones.

For Ho Chi Minh City, the Urban Climatic Analysis Map (UC-AnMap) and the Urban Climatic Recommendation Map (UC-ReMap) were combined following the latest developments of the 'Klimaplanatlas' of Frankfurt 2009, Kassel 2010 and Berlin 2008 into the UCMap of Ho Chi Minh City.

The analysis explains the above-mentioned phenomena but should be followed by planning recommendations derived from it. The UC-AnMap is a classification system with different *climatopes*, following climatic characteristics of ventilation and urban heat islands. Based on the analysis obtained from the urban climatic analysis, recommendations in the UC-ReMap can be made to show the according planning recommendations together with their rationales. The UCMaps summarise the 'scientific' findings based on the input land and climatic data. The urban climatic recommendation is a comprehension of the UCMaps based on planning comprehension and considerations resulting in a number of guidelines that planners could use as a base for their decisions. In short, planners can simply refer to the analyses in their daily practice. If further details are required, they can always refer to the UCMap together with their urban climatic advisers.

## Methodology

### *Wind*

First, the existing wind characteristic of the city was analysed. For the UCMap, the wind systems of the background wind and the thermally induced winds have to be dealt with separately. Wind roses provide information about the annual wind direction distributions. Combined with low surfaces and the channelling effect, ventilation areas and air paths of the city were derived. Apart from these phenomena, the thermally induced circulations in Ho Chi Minh City were mainly

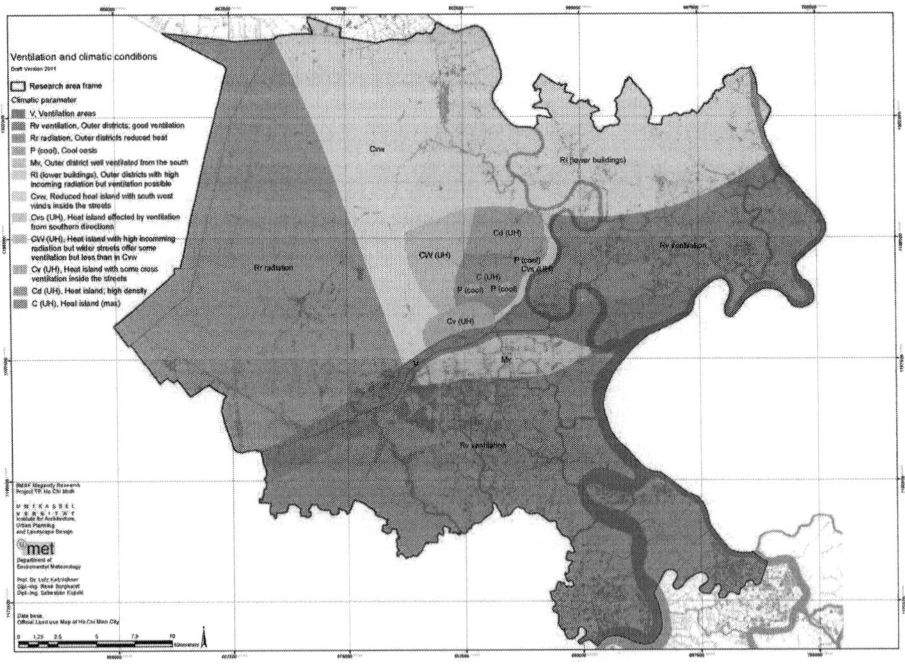


*Figure 8.1* Ventilation Layer Map of Ho Chi Minh City.

Source: Authors

influenced by the oncoming wind into Districts 1 and 3. Both wind systems appear in different dominant or predominant ways (VDI, 1997). For urban ventilation in Ho Chi Minh City, the dominant wind condition directions of 'north-easterly winds' and 'south-westerly winds' depend on the season. Besides, during the afternoon hours, the diurnal wind flow from the Saigon River combines with south-east winds.

For the urban climate analysis this means the following (see Figure 8.1):

### *First case NW*

Wind penetrates the city from the NE using the main streets in Districts 1 and 3 and 5. At the same time, there is a channelling effect which leads to ventilation corridors from Saigon River towards the NW. For the first consideration, the building orientation and streets are important. For the second consideration, the wind entrance of Saigon River into the city should not be blocked. Hence, openness in Districts 1 and 3 should be maintained, and podiums should not be permitted.

### *Second case SW*

The main air path is along the river and the channel system. Orientation, roughness and frontal line against the wind direction have to be observed carefully.

### *Third case SE*

The local and thermally induced afternoon circulations have lower wind speeds and are sensitive to barriers.

## *Climatopes and methodical framework*

Climatic systems describe areas with the same urban climatological characteristics. They are generated and influenced by morphological and city fabric factors. They include thermal load, ventilation and air pollution aspects (VDI, 1997). The climatope information on the territorial level is then used to specify recommendations depending on the existing wind regimes. This can be used to make recommendations for specific planning purposes. The underlying methodology for the map is to combine layers, which are deduced from land use maps or other maps, which are then translated to thermal and dynamic aspects with weighting factors. These weighting factors range from building volume to heat storage, greenery to heat budget, openness to ventilation, roughness to wind speed, and topographical information.

Important intermediate steps are to assess building volume, sealing level and vegetation covering. First, the building volume and the sealing level together with the thermal load potential are used to describe the amount of overheating above the calculated heat capacity. Second, the distribution of green space, which influences the transport routes of air and the cooling capacities, is used to describe the mitigation needed for lowering the calculated heat capacity. The assessment involves climatic functions, its value and the interaction between climatic stress areas and favourable areas. Outdoor areas are examined and evaluated for their potential mitigation impact (air mass transport/air exchange, cold/fresh air production), including their impact on climatic conflict areas. In built-up areas, varying degrees of heat and the issues of air quality and ventilation are important evaluation criteria to describe the preloading on the climatic mitigation impact. The essential applied potential and deficit criteria can be illustrated as follows:

The task of planning-related urban climatology (VDI, 2008) is to improve air quality and thermal conditions:

- reducing urban heat islands (heat islands as an indication of thermal comfort/discomfort), open space planning;
- optimising urban ventilation (air exchange, ventilation lanes), urban planning and urban development for air quality and thermal comfort;
- preventing air stagnation areas (storage areas) and barriers that hinder air exchange;
- preserving/promoting fresh air or cold air influx areas to foster air exchange and to improve the air quality situation.

## Geographical climate data collection and processing

### Relief typing

Elaboration of climatically relevant topographic factors and resultant airflow potential on the basis of the digital elevation model, aerial images and topographic maps as the base material for the thermal and dynamic analysis.

### Structure typing

Elaboration of the use-related roughness, differentiated by climatic relevance (e.g. potential barriers or the channelling of air masses) based on land use data, topographic maps and aerial photographs as important starting products for the dynamic analysis.

### Building volume

Elaboration of the building barrier effect and the reduction of ventilation potential, based on building area and height, and calculation and generalization of volume as a source for dynamic analysis.

### Runoff pathways and flow directions

Elaboration of topographically induced breaks, which can be calculated as a function of building volume and structure typing, and can be used as a supplementary factor for the dynamic analysis.

### Use typing

Elaboration of the thermal importance of different surface uses and summary of microclimate-similar uses (e.g. potential cold air producing areas, potential overheating areas) based on land use data, mapping of buildings and aerial photographs as an important starting material for the thermal analysis.

#### *Building mass*

Elaboration of the building-related thermal stress caused by the heat storage capacity and reflection based on the building mapping derivation of the physical behaviour (both total and urban microclimate).

#### *Sealing level of the surface*

Elaboration of the sealed areas and generalization of certain types of areas based on the real-use mapping, mapping of buildings and land use data (traffic areas) as material for the thermal analysis.

### *High-resolution input layer*

In order to meet the claim of calculating a high-resolution UCMap at the meso-scale, some calculation procedures had to be updated. The calculations for 'Sealing Level', 'Building Volume' and 'Vegetation Covering' were refined.

#### *Sealing level and building volume*

In the last few years computing power has grown very quickly. As such, a new information/resolution level for the used layers of the Ho Chi Minh UCMap could be achieved; the raster size decreased from 100m × 100m in the first draft of the UCMap to the current 25m × 25m in the final version.

#### *Vegetation covering*

The most common way of collecting information on vegetation in a geographic area is by using land use data. The main disadvantage is its low level of detail. Because of that, only large green areas such as parks are ascertainable for the most part. To get a higher level of detail, it is possible to use the 'Normalized Difference Vegetation Index' (NDVI). In this case a 4-band infrared satellite image is used for the collection of vegetation data. For the large research area of Ho Chi Minh City, only normal 3-band 'Red, Green, Blue' (RGB) aerial photographs are available. In order not to lose any important information about vegetation covering, a tool was developed which makes it possible to extract vegetation covering out of normal 3-band aerial views like Google Maps and Bing Maps. The advantage of this tool is the variability of detail level. Depending on research area, computing power and available zooming level in Bing or Google Maps, every resolution size is useable. The use of open source data may be an affordable option.

## Planning zones

The UCMap includes planning orientation as seen in the legend. Based on the analysis obtained from the urban climatic analyses, climatic zones and air paths were developed and recommendations derived (see Plate 8.1). The ventilation aspect is covered by a special ventilation zone V. Here the monsoon wind in the NE and SW directions have to be considered. Since there will be massive future development, the area needs further climatological evaluation for potential building designs. Zone B respects southerly winds (with lower wind velocity) with the recommendation of not permitting the building of barriers. It is recommended to allow for a good permeability as well as to consider the buildings' proper orientation. Zone C is quite open to NE winds and is ventilated well, which is comparable to zone A with the difference being that the main winds come from SW. Zones D to E show the most dense and heat-loaded areas. E is especially influenced by afternoon ventilation.

## References

Katzschner, L. (2007). Klimabewertungskarte als Grundlage für die Regionalplanung Hessen. In: *Geographical Information System*, University Kassel FB6, Vol. 164.

Ng, E., Katzschner, L., Wang, U. and Mulder, J. (2007). *Initial Methodology of Urban Climatic Mapping, Urban Climatic Map and Standards for Wind Environment – Feasibility Study*, Technical Report for Planning Department HKSAR.

Scherer, D., Fehrenbach, U., Beha, H. D. and Parlow, E. (1999). Improved concepts and methods in analysis and evaluation of the urban climate for optimizing urban planning processes. *Atmospheric Environment*, 33(24–25): 4185–4193.

VDI (1997). *VDI-Standard: VDI 3787 Part 1 Environmental Meteorology – Climate and Air Pollution Maps for Cities and Regions*. Berlin: Beuth Verlag.

VDI (2008). *VDI-Standard: VDI 3785 Part 1 Environmental Meteorology – Methods and Presentation of Investigations Relevant for Planning Urban Climate*. Berlin: Beuth Verlag.

Chapter 9

# Urban climatic map studies in China

## Wuhan

*Chao Yuan*

## Introduction

In the last 20 years, major cities in China have undergone rapid urbanisation. Wuhan, with an area of some 8,500km$^2$ and a population of over 10 million, is located inland and west of Shanghai. It is one of the megacities in China and is the country's high-speed rail hub. In the summer months, Wuhan is hot; the average daytime temperature of the city is around 33°C. The city planners of Wuhan have been postulating the idea of urban air paths for a number of years for the making of their master plan. This study to better identify and quantify the wind path idea was commissioned by the City Planning Bureau of the Wuhan City Government in 2012. The study intended to provide an evidence-based basis for Wuhan's planners.

## The study approach

The study of outdoor natural ventilation often requires large-scale aerodynamics modelling. Both physical modelling (wind tunnel) and computational simulation modelling can provide data regarding the airflow within the urban canopy. However, conducting these modelling tests for a particular urban planning exercise is expensive and time-consuming. Modelling results cannot keep up with the quick planning processes; as such, Ng *et al.* (2011) opines that a methodology that uses a rougher understanding of the urban morphological implication to the urban wind environment can be more useful to planners.

With the current high rate of urbanisation, high-density living leads to a more efficient utilisation of land and other resources. However, congested building blocks cause low permeability for airflow in the urban canyon, worsening outdoor urban thermal comfort and air quality, particularly in sub-tropical cites. Given the growing concerns related to the way urban permeability is evaluated and air paths are detected in order to fit the requirements of practical urban planning, this chapter aims to:

- introduce the morphological method to model urban surface roughness and evaluate urban permeability;
- analyse urban permeability to detect potential air paths to improve urban performance in outdoor natural ventilation;
- highlight the implementation of modelling results in urban planning practices and interweave the modelling results into different urban planning stages, such as master and district planning.

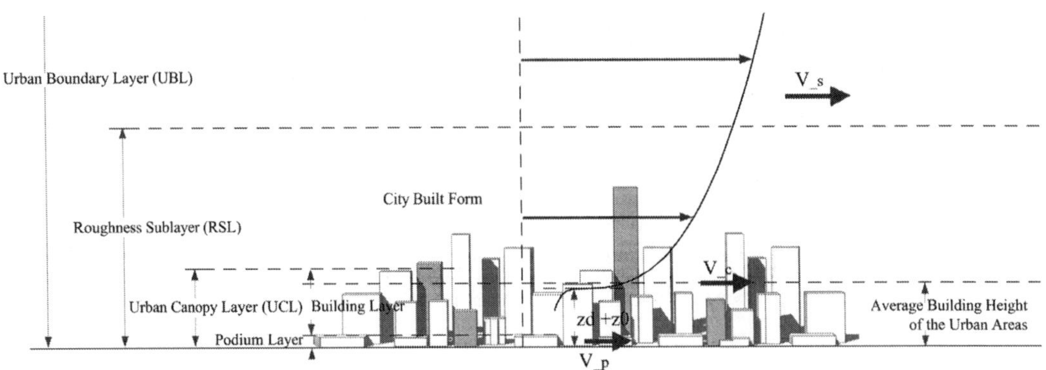


*Figure 9.1* Wind speed profile, podium layer, building layer, urban canopy layer, and roughness sublayer. $V_{\_p}$: pedestrian-level wind speed, $V_{\_s}$: the wind speed at the top of roughness sublayer.

Source: Ng *et al.*, 2011

This case study focuses on Wuhan as an example, a metropolitan city in China famous for its hot and humid summers. By applying the morphological modelling method on Wuhan's local Geographic Information System (GIS) data (3D building database), the planners can easily evaluate the urban permeability to understand the urban ventilation of the city for evidence-based decision making in urban planning.

## *Morphological method*

The morphological method of surface roughness modelling (Lettau, 1969; MacDonald *et al.*, 1998; Grimmond and Oke, 1999) is widely used to estimate the wind profiles in the atmospheric environment, as shown in Figure 9.1. Based on a 3D building database, this modelling method visualizes and maps the spatially averaged site permeability of urban areas to diagnose the urban wind environment (Gál and Unger, 2009).

To make the evaluation of urban permeability more practical for and available to urban planners, this case study uses an urban geometric parameter, the frontal area density ($\lambda_f$), aside from the aerodynamic parameters roughness length $z_0$ and zero-plane displacement height $z_d$.

In particular, the frontal area density ($\lambda_{f(z,\theta)}$) at a height increment of Δz is calculated as (Burian *et al.*, 2002):

$$\lambda_{f(z,\theta)} = \frac{A(\theta)_{proj(\Delta z)}}{A_T} \tag{9.1}$$

where $A(\theta)_{proj(\Delta z)}$ is the frontal area facing the incoming wind direction $\theta$ in the height band Δz and $A_T$ is the site area. In contrast to the frontal area index ($\lambda_{f(\theta)}$), which is an average parameter for the entire urban canyon layer, $\lambda_{f(z,\theta)}$ focuses on the urban morphology at the height band Δz.

To annually evaluate urban permeability, $\lambda_{f(z,\theta)}$ calculated at different prevailing wind directions are averaged, based on the respective annual wind probabilities ($P_{\theta i}$):

$$\lambda_{f(z)} = \sum_1^i \lambda_{f(z,\theta)} \cdot P_{\theta,i} \tag{9.2}$$

where $\lambda_{f(z)}$ is the annually averaged $\lambda_{f(z,\theta)}$, and $P_{\theta,i}$ is the annual wind probability in the $i_{th}$ wind direction $\theta$.

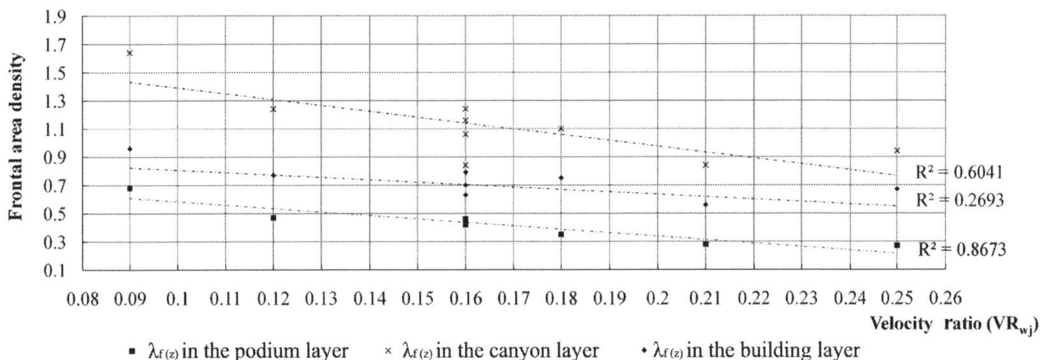


*Figure 9.2* Relationships between $VR_w$ and $\lambda_{f(z)}$ as calculated at the podium, building, and canopy layers.
Source: Ng *et al.*, 2011

### *Validation*

The wind tunnel data from the Hong Kong University of Science and Technology (Hong Kong Planning Department, 2008), i.e. the wind velocity ratio ($VR_w$: the ratio of wind velocity at the pedestrian level to that at the reference height of 500m), is used to test the sensitivities of the site's permeability across the different $\lambda_{f(z)}$ calculated at three height bands $\Delta z$: the podium layer, building layer, and canopy layer (see Figure 9.1).

The cross-comparative results are plotted in Figure 9.2. The $R^2$ values indicate that the pedestrian-level site permeability mostly depends on $\lambda_{f(z)}$ at the podium layer ($R^2 = 0.87$), and is related with $\lambda_{f(z)}$ at the canyon layer ($R^2 = 0.60$). This indicates that the airflow above the urban canyon may not easily enter into deep street gaps because of the high density and tall buildings in metropolitan urban areas, and that the pedestrian-level wind environment mostly depends on the horizontal urban permeability of the podium layer (Ng *et al.*, 2011).

### *Classification*

Based on the linear relationship reported by Ng *et al.* (2011), as shown in Figure 9.3, the values of $\lambda_{f(z)}$ are classified as follows: (1) $\lambda_{f(z)} \leq 0.35$; (2) $0.35 < \lambda_{f(z)} \leq 0.45$; (3) $0.45 < \lambda_{f(z)} \leq 0.6$; and (4) $\lambda_{f(z)} > 0.6$. This classification aims to statistically weigh the effects of different values of $\lambda_{f(z)}$ on the pedestrian-level natural ventilation performance, and to detect the potential air paths (the areas with low surface roughness) in high-density urban areas. For instance, Class 4 ($\lambda_{f(z)} > 0.6$) indicates that the wind velocity ratio ($VR_w$) may be less than 0.1, which implies very poor natural ventilation. In contrast, Class 1 ($\lambda_{f(z)} \leq 0.35$) indicates that $VR_w$ may be larger than 0.2, which implies good natural ventilation (Ng *et al.*, 2011).

### *Modelling settings and results in Wuhan*

To identify the value of $\Delta z$ in Equation 9.1, particularly in the context of Wuhan, this case study calculated the dividing level (27m) of the building height distribution (0m–204m) using the local 3D building database in GIS. The dividing level classifies the height distribution of the city into two classes – an average building height zone of 0m–27m, and a high-rise building height zone of 27m–204m. The urban morphology at the layer ranging from 0m–27m is considered as being

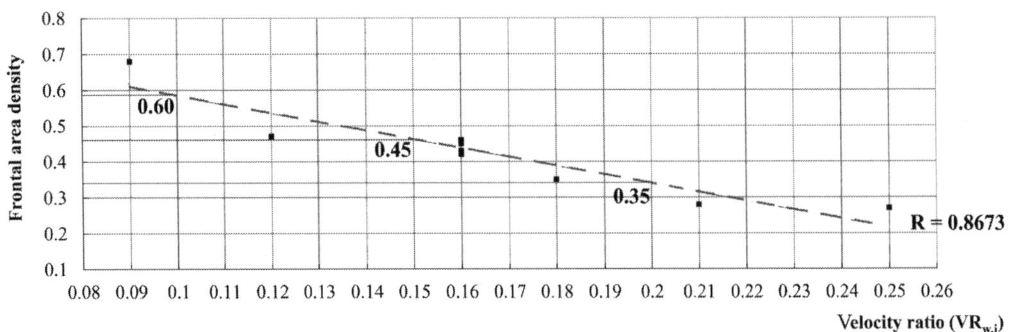


*Figure 9.3* Linear relationship between $\lambda_{f(z)}$ and $VR_w$. The values of $\lambda_{f(z)}$ are classified as: (1) $\lambda_{f(z)} \leq 0.35$; (2) $0.35 < \lambda_{f(z)} \leq 0.45$; (3) $0.45 < \lambda_{f(z)} \leq 0.6$; and (4) $\lambda_{f(z)} > 0.6$.

Source: Ng *et al.*, 2011

much denser than the layer ranging from 27m–204m. The value of $\Delta z$ in this case study is set to 27m.

To identify the local annual prevailing wind probability $P_\theta$ of Wuhan in Equation 9.2, the wind frequency data from Wuhan Observatory was used. The prevailing wind directions were identified as south ($\theta_1 = 90°$), south-east ($\theta_2 = 135°$), and south-west ($\theta_3 = 45°$), and their frequency is generally similar. Therefore, the values of $P_{\theta,i}$ (i = 1,2,3) across the three prevailing wind directions are simplified as 1/3.

After calculating $\lambda_{f(z)}$ at a resolution of 100m × 100m and classifying the results based on Figure 9.3, the urban permeability of the pedestrian-level natural ventilation in Wuhan is mapped as shown in Plate 9.1. Given the uncertainties in the modelling results caused by the linear regression analysis and other assumptions, the modelling results are considered as acceptable for the planning practices in the initial stages of the decision making process.

## Implementation in urban planning

The urban permeability map shown in Plate 9.1 provides urban planners with an intuitive grasp of the natural ventilation of urban areas for the master planning in which the district land use and density are determined. The lower urban permeability areas (Classes 3 and 4) include Hankou, Wuchang, and Hanyang, in the downtown area of Wuhan. It indicates that the airflow in the street canyon is seriously restricted by compact building blocks, and the outdoor natural ventilation may worsen in these areas. By contrast, the surface roughness in the other districts located far from the downtown area is still very low ($\lambda_{f(z)} \leq 0.35$). Compared with these districts in which new development is still acceptable, the urban density at Hankou, Wuchang, and Hanyang should be strictly controlled in the master plan, and particular mitigation strategies in the district planning for these three areas are also necessary.

Based on the above analysis, district-based information is needed, which can be provided by the high-resolution urban permeability map, as shown in Figure 9.4. The areas with low urban permeability occupy most of Hankou. Compared with Hankou, the urban permeability in Hanyang and Wuchang are relatively high. Furthermore, in Hankou, the areas with low urban permeability are wide and close to each other, whereas in Wuchang and Hanyang, they are smaller and more scattered. Correspondingly, different district planning goals and mitigation strategies are suggested in the respective districts:

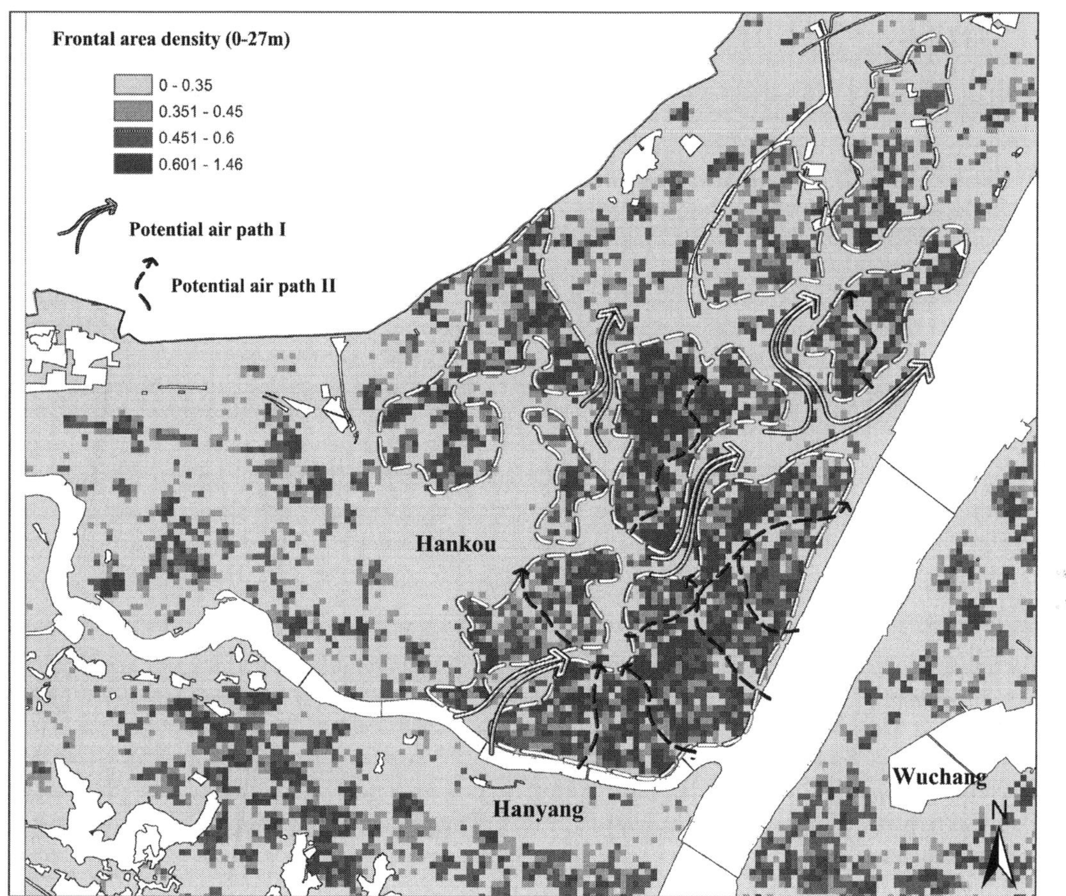


*Figure 9.4* Potential air paths across different scales. The white dashed line marks the boundaries of areas with low urban permeability in Hankou. Potential air path I (urban scale) is represented by the hollow arrows. Potential air path II (neighbourhood scale) is represented by the black dashed line arrows.

Source: Author

1) *Planning goals and mitigation strategies for Hankou*
The planning goal for Hankou district is to identify the key areas to make the potential air paths play a role in encouraging the flow of fresh air into the deeper urban areas of the city. This strategy is more practicable than decreasing the urban density of the whole district because of the presence of wide urban areas with low permeability. According to the planning goal, the corresponding planning strategies are as follows:

- As shown in Figure 9.4, the areas with low permeability are marked by white dashed lines. The gaps between these boundaries, represented by hollow arrows, are characterized by comparatively low surface roughness and are considered as the key areas for the potential air path I. The ground coverage ratio ($\lambda_p$) in these key areas needs to be strictly controlled to make sure air paths are connected to each other – that is, $\lambda_p$ must be less than 30 per cent (Yoshie *et al.*, 2008). The width of air path I ranges from several hundred metres to one kilometre.

The air path II is in the neighbourhood scale, which is detected inside the low permeability areas and is represented by dashed arrows in Figure 9.4. The potential air path II is important in the separation of single and wide low-permeability areas into smaller areas, so that the air can flow into them and thereby mitigate the high intensity of the urban heat island in these areas. The width of the air path II is about 100m. The values of $\lambda_p$ at the air paths need to strictly be kept below 30 per cent (Yoshie *et al.*, 2008).

2) *Planning goals and mitigation strategies for Wuchang and Hanyang*
The low-permeability areas in Wuchang and Hanyang are scattered. As a result, the planning goal for these two districts is to decrease the urban density of the whole district, avoiding the spread of the small and scattered low-permeability areas. No mitigation strategies are viable in creating an air path in these two districts. Based on the above planning goal, the corresponding district planning strategies are as follows:

- The land use density of new development projects needs to be controlled by the ground coverage ratio ($\lambda_p$), which must be less than 50 per cent or, better yet, less than 30 per cent.

## Conclusions

In wind tunnel experiments and computational fluid dynamics simulations, the air in the street canyon is treated as the control volume. By contrast, as a viable alternative, the morphological method is an empirical model based on the relationship between urban morphology parameters and experimental wind data. Because of this characteristic, the complicated calculations associated with fluid mechanics can be avoided during the planning process. Urban planners can easily relate the urban natural ventilation knowledge to the urban planning parameters, by using the local 3D building database.

This case study of Wuhan highlights the practical application of the morphological modelling method, from modelling to the analysis of results to the establishment of planning guidelines for both master and district planning. As our knowledge of roughness parameters improves and as more experimental data becomes available, the morphological modelling method has the potential for broader applications.

## References

Burian, S. J., Velugubantla, S. P. and Brown, M. J. (2002). *Morphological Analyses using 3D Building Databases: Phoenix, Arizona*, LA-UR-02-6726. Los Alamos: Los Alamos National Laboratory.

Gál, T. and Unger, J. (2009). Detection of ventilation paths using high-resolution roughness parameter mapping in a large urban area. *Building and Environment*, 44(1): 198–206.

Grimmond, C. S. B. and Oke, T. R. (1999). Aerodynamic properties of urban areas derived from analysis of surface form. *Journal of Applied Meteorology*, 38(9): 1262–1292.

Hong Kong Planning Department (2008). *Working Paper 2B: Wind Tunnel Benchmarking Studies, Batch 1, Urban Climatic Map and Standards for Wind Environment – Feasibility Study.*

Lettau, H. (1969). Note on aerodynamic roughness-parameter estimation on the basis of roughness-element description. *Journal of Applied Meteorology*, 8(5): 828–832.

MacDonald, R. W., Griffiths, R. F. and Hall, D. J. (1998). An improved method for the estimation of surface roughness of obstacle arrays. *Atmospheric Environment*, 32(11): 1857–1864.

Ng, E., Yuan, C., Chen, L., Ren, C. and Fung, J. C. H. (2011). Improving the wind environment in high-density cities by understanding urban morphology and surface roughness: a study in Hong Kong. *Landscape and Urban Planning*, 101(1): 59–74.

Yoshie, R., Tanaka, H., Shirasawa, T. and Kobayashi, T. (2008). Experimental study on air ventilation in a built-up area with closely-packed high-rise building. *Journal of Environmental Engineering*, 73(627): 661–667. (In Japanese).

Chapter 10

# Urban climatic map studies in China

## Hong Kong

*Edward Ng*

### Introduction

Since 2006, over half of the world's population has lived in cities (UN, 2008). The number of mega- and high-density cities on earth is on the rise. In developing countries, the rate of city growth and urbanisation is increasing. City governments and their planners have the unprecedented task of finding ways to design their cities so that quality living, or merely day-to-day living, can be sustained (Ng, 2009a). Furthermore, given the global needs to reduce energy use in buildings, not only is designing low energy buildings important, creating conducive boundary conditions for the buildings via good city planning is paramount.

2003 is a memorable year for two reasons. The episode of Severe Acute Respiratory Syndrome (SARS) hit Hong Kong and many cities around the world. By the end of the saga, over 900 people unfortunately lost their lives to the disease. In Hong Kong, due to the close proximity of buildings, the spread of the disease via water droplets from one apartment to the next was reckoned to have caused the rapid spread of the germ in the community. SARS was a wake-up call for the people in Hong Kong that the environmental design of cities could have a life and death consequence in our lives. However, while mourning the deaths around us, we seemed to have forgotten a more deadly killer looming around the corner that has silently taken many lives away year after year. That nothing worse than the European heat wave happened in the same year illustrated the deadliness of the silent killer; over 70,000 lives were lost in the few summer months. The vast majority of those who perished during the heat wave lived in cities.

After SARS, the Hong Kong government set up a committee, aptly called Team Clean, to review our urban living situation. Among many agendas on the table, one of was to examine whether Hong Kong had indeed reached the limiting capacity of its high-density built environment. If not, what then would be the carrying capacity? The Planning Department embarked on a number of projects trying to find answers, and more importantly, action plans. The first project was entitled 'Feasibility for Establishment of Air Ventilation Assessment (AVA) System'. It was commissioned in 2003 and completed in 2006. The second project was entitled 'Urban Climatic Map and Standards for Wind Environment – Feasibility Study' and was commissioned in 2006 and completed in 2012. This chapter gives an account of the ten-year journey, scientifically and politically, of the research team who worked on these projects.

The important message of the experience gained was that the aspiration to design better cities could only be realized via the concerted and coordinated efforts of all the stakeholders. It must be a multidisciplinary task. The process can be systematically and logically followed, from science to policy to implementation and to monitoring. But beyond the process itself, the more important factor must be the need for a common community value, the determination to work together as a team, and the courage to step beyond one's own knowledge boundary so as to find a synergy among different disciplines working towards a common goal. Without this, neither scientific know-how, nor any competence in administration, nor any amount of resources invested would be able to yield the desired results. The art of the process must be 'focus' and 'communication' and it must bear 'criticality' and 'prevailing' in mind, and keep everything one utters 'simple' (Ng, 2012).

## *High-density city living in the tropics*

The United Nations (UN) estimates that by 2050, the percentage of urban population will exceed 70 per cent. More and more megacities – cities with over 10 million inhabitants, high-density cities and compact cities are being formed around the world. In 2010, there were over 20 megacities in existence (see Figure 10.1). Some of them, like Mumbai, Tokyo, Seoul, New York City and Mexico City already have more than 20 million inhabitants. It is projected that by 2015, cities like Shanghai, Beijing, Calcutta, Karachi, Jakarta, Lagos and Sao Paulo – many of them located in the tropics and sub-tropics – will be joining them. Apart from these megacities, in 2005, more than 300 cities had inhabitants of over 1 million. This number is increasing rapidly. The UN estimates that by 2025, this number will increase to over 500 cities. China, with its rapid urbanisation process, will have more than 120 cities with over 1 million inhabitants.

Cities with large land mass and higher population have their own urban climate – energy-flux modifications due to land surface changes, ground roughness due to buildings, and anthropogenic heat input due to human activities (Oke, 1988). In 2007, more than 70 cities had a land area exceeding 1,000km$^2$. The city of Tokyo for example has a land mass of 70km by 70km. Furthermore, the number of higher density cities is also increasing. In 2007, eight cities had a density of over 10,000 people per square kilometre, and more than 60 cities had a density of over 1,000 people per square kilometre.

To focus on Hong Kong: it is a city of over seven million living on land of just over one thousand square kilometres. Since over 40 per cent of the territory is hilly and classified as country-park

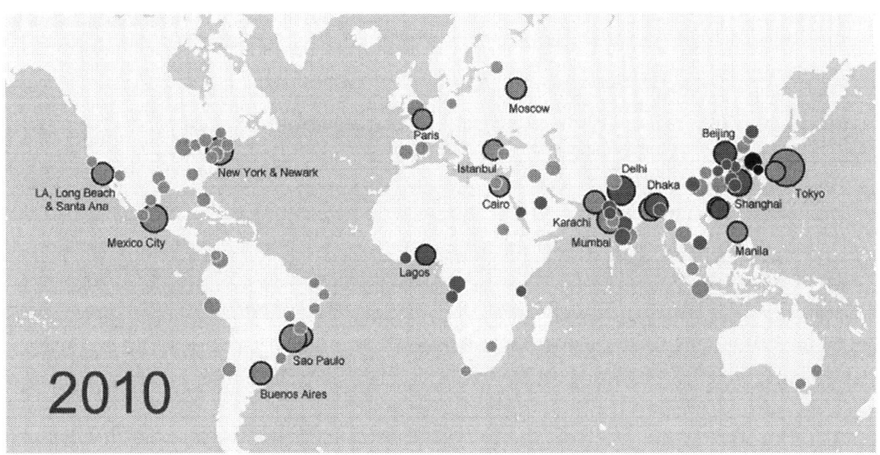


*Figure 10.1* A map of large cities in the world in 2010. The size of the circle represents the city's population size. Circles with a border represent cities with over 10 million inhabitants.

Source: Global development – www.theguardian.com, 2012

*Figure 10.2* A view of Hong Kong's high-density urban living environment.

Source: Photo taken by Cornelius Paas, New Internationalist Magazine, http://newint.org/features/2005/05/01/life/

where no development is allowed by law, only some 25 per cent of the land is urbanised. The urban living density of some metro areas in Hong Kong is 60,000 to 100,000 persons per square kilometre. It is not unusual to find a site level project development with a density of 3,000 persons per hectare or above. Due to its extremely high urban living density, it is common, in the metro areas, to find 50- to 60- storey-high buildings being built very close to each other. This has resulted in, using the local's vernacular, 'wall buildings' blocking the very important sea breezes and urban air movements. The tall buildings have also formed extremely deep street canyons, often as high as a 20:1 height to width (H/W) ratio that traps heat and pollution (see Figure 10.2).

It is not for nothing that the city needs to be critically examined. Using Chinese medicine's terminology, is it possible to apply 'urban acupuncture' strategically to heal our city?

### The Air Ventilation Assessment System

In 2003, the Hong Kong Government Team Clean Committee published its report (Team Clean, 2003: para.20–22). Some of its resolutions were:

> We believe that good urban design can contribute to a healthy lifestyle and environment.
>
> We will introduce measures to apply urban design guidelines to improve the general physical environment, particularly in regards to air circulation.
>
> We are also considering the practicality of introducing an air ventilation assessment for future major planning and development proposals.
>
> We will reduce development intensity where appropriate and feasible.

By the end of 2003, the study 'Feasibility for Establishment of Air Ventilation Assessment (AVA) System' was commissioned to researchers at the Chinese University of Hong Kong (PlanD, 2003). Three years later, in 2006, the Government of Hong Kong adopted the study findings and recommendations, and issued two important policy documents for the construction industry. They are the *Air Ventilation Assessment Technical Circular 01/06* and a new chapter on Air Ventilation Assessment (AVA) in the *Hong Kong Planning Standards and Guidelines* (TC 01/06, 2006; HKPSG, 2011). Basically, unlike guidelines that deal with strong wind issues, AVA is a set of guidelines for weak and stagnant urban wind conditions specifically designed to give information on designs related to the congested urban conditions in Hong Kong (Ng, 2009b).

In a nutshell, the AVA system relies on the Wind Velocity Ratio ($VR_w$) criterion to evaluate how a proposed project affects the urban air ventilation environment of the surroundings. $VR_w$ is a ratio of the wind speed at the top of the urban canopy layer (typically set at 300m to 500m above ground) and the wind speed 2m above ground (refer to Figure 9.1 in Chapter 9). It has three working stages, namely Expert Evaluation, Initial Study and Detail Study. As the project progresses in terms of design, the three stages would be activated progressively. The final Detail Study stage requires the project proponent to subject the design to wind tunnel testing. The results, in terms of $VR_w$, need to be meticulously documented and reported.

In terms of the built morphology, the research team identified four problematic issues, namely the building's site coverage, disposition, height, and permeability (Ng, 2009b). The study recommended nine design strategies and good practice, including: increasing building gaps where needed, reducing buildings' site coverage, orientating buildings to reduce blockage, connecting open spaces around buildings, and so on (HKPSG, 2011).

One example of a major development that had gone through the AVA system was the Government's new headquarters building in Tamar in the Central District. The AVA study necessitated a large hole being carved out of the building so that sea breezes could be channelled inland to the public interchange at the back (see Figure 10.3) (Ng, 2009c). This was the first major building in Hong Kong that designers had to design according to the weak urban air ventilation of the project site.

Since the launch of the AVA system in 2006, the Planning Department of the Hong Kong Government has kept an AVA register on projects that have gone through the test (PlanD, 2013). The list includes major public and private projects.

## The Hong Kong urban climatic map study

Beyond the AVA system, the research team also recommended that one must look beyond the project site boundary and address the urban environment from a city planning perspective. Otherwise, by the time the need for urban air ventilation is demanded in the project, the battle for the project proponent would have been lost. The government took the advice and in 2006 commissioned the same research team to continue. The project was titled 'Urban Climatic Map and Standards for Wind Environment – Feasibility Study'. Instead of looking at the issue from the building and the project site outwards as in the AVA study, the Urban Climatic Map (UCMap) study attempted to examine the issue from the meso-scale downwards. It was hoped that by referring to atmospheric conditions from the start, the nesting down of the planning and design process from the city to the urban area, to the neighbourhood, to the project site, and finally to the building could be more systematically tackled one scale at a time.

*Figure 10.3* Tamar Hong Kong Government Headquarters building. The large hole created is for better urban air ventilation from the seafront to the inland areas behind the building.

Source: Civil Service Bureau, 2011, p.7

### Method and data structure of Hong Kong urban climatic map

The key question to ask at the start was: what would be the deliverables? To whom were the deliverables to be made and for what purpose? From the outset, colleagues of the Planning Department of the Hong Kong Government had made it very clear that it was not going to be another scientific study for data, method or process. The results of the study must be actionable and therefore must have policy implications. Thus, the method to be chosen for the study needed to bear the deliverables in mind (see Figure 10.4).

The second issue was the data structure of the UCMap. The data must be 'useable', not by scientists and researchers, but by planners and policy decision makers. The kind of data, and its appropriate format, giving the kind of information that was needed must therefore be carefully selected and agreed with the planners from the start. Bearing these considerations in mind, and taking into account various recent pieces of research literature on the subject matter, the research team decided to adopt the two important guiding principles of 'criticality' and 'prevailing' when formulating the study methodology. Keeping things simple and not overwhelming became the guiding principles of the data structure (de Schiller and Evans, 1996; Eliasson, 2000; Ng *et al.*, 2010).

#### *Reviews and references*

The scientific understanding of urban climate has been well studied, since the late 1960s, by pioneers such as Chandler, Landsberg, Givoni, Oke, and so on, to name but four (Chandler, 1976; Landsberg, 1981; Givoni, 1988, 1998; Oke, 1988). The International Association of Urban Climate

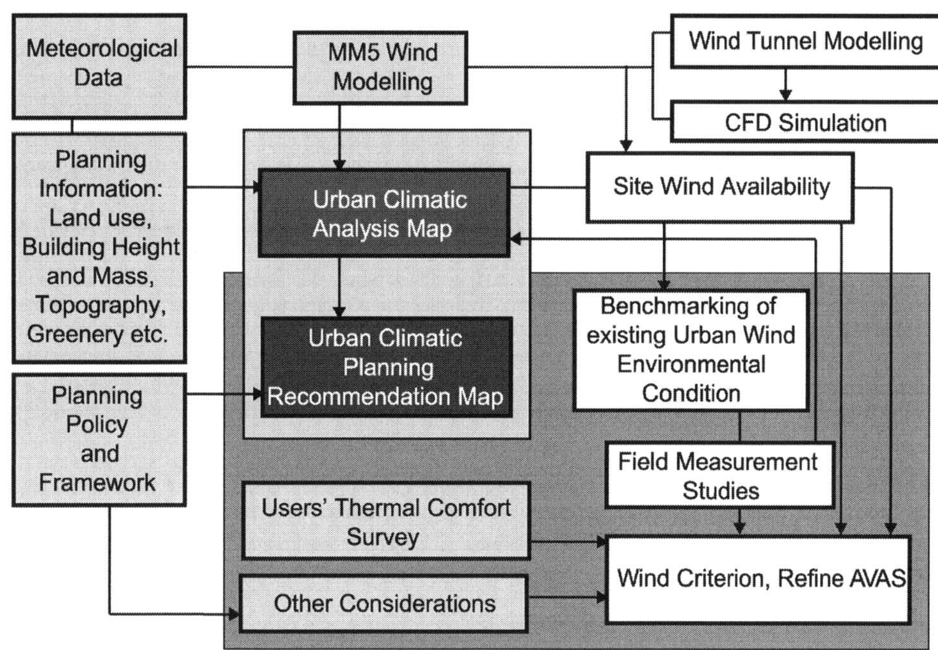


*Figure 10.4* The research framework of the Hong Kong UCMap study.

Source: Author

(IAUC) has, since 2000, organised conferences on the subject and regularly published newsletters and technical texts. From time to time, it also collates urban climate-related resources in the form of bibliographies, thus providing a wealth of study references for students and researchers (IAUC, 2013).

The use of Urban Climatic Maps for guiding city planning is more recent. According to Ren *et al.*'s (2011) excellent review, it seemed to have started in 1978 with Luttig's (1972) suggestion of the use of 'geoscientific maps of the environment' as an essential tool in planning. By 1997, The Association of German Engineers in Germany (Verein Deutscher Ingenieure or VDI) published two important documents on environmental meteorology that also defined the specificities of the making of Klimaatlas (climatic map) (VDI, 1997, 2008).

The VDI guidelines first require an evaluation of the various urban morphological data by classifying them into various data layers of built structure, land use, topography, greenery, roughness, and so on (see Figure 10.5). The positive and negative effects of different layers are then grouped into the consideration of 'Thermal Load' and 'Dynamic Potential' (see Table 10.1) (see VDI, 1997). Basically, Thermal Load considers how a parameter, for example, the built structure or urban greenery, could elevate or lower the urban air temperature. Dynamic Potential considers how a parameter, for example, tall buildings or open spaces, could allow for or diminish the urban wind flow. Apart from the physical and urban morphological data, various meteorological data such as wind speeds and wind directions (Wind Information), air temperature, solar radiation and relative humidity from the last ten years were collected from the Hong Kong Observatory.

The Hong Kong Urban Climatic Map study relied on the aforementioned scientific foundation with two exceptions. First, before the Hong Kong study, no attempt had been made to create a climatic map for a high-density city. More importantly, no attempt had been made to draft a climatic map for city with a highly inhomogeneous city morphology. Second, no climatic map

*Table 10.1* Description of Thermal Load, Dynamic Potential and Wind Information.

| | *Description* |
|---|---|
| Thermal Load | Thermal Load measures the stored or emitted heat intensity of particular localities of urban areas and mainly depends on the building volume (which has an impact on heat storage, blocking the sky view, and slowing the city's cooling at night), the topography, and the availability of green spaces for cooling effect.<br>Thermal Load can be defined as the intra-urban air temperature variations due to the urban forms and surfaces (Evans and de Schiller, 1996). A key problem of urbanisation is the Thermal Load it generates due to buildings and artificial/man-made surfaces. The Thermal Load is considered to be the main reason the intra-urban temperature rises. For Hong Kong's hot and humid sub-tropical climatic conditions, Thermal Load adds to heat stress in the summer months. Inhabitants of the city are less likely to feel comfortable outdoors. In addition, energy consumption within buildings is likely to increase. |
| Dynamic Potential | Dynamic Potential evaluates the ground roughness and therefore the availability of wind and cold air mass exchange of particular localities of urban areas. It mainly depends on the site coverage, availability of natural landscape on slopes, and proximity to openness.<br>Air Ventilation is an effective way to mitigate the adverse effects of Thermal Load as it carries away the excessive heat of the city, replacing it with cooler ambient air (Golany, 1996; Kuttler, 2002; Weber and Kuttler, 2003). Air movement in the hot and humid summer months of Hong Kong could also help reduce heat stress and improve human thermal comfort. |
| Wind Information | Wind Information gives the background wind speed and direction information at the above urban canopy layer (UCL) level, taking into account the surrounding topography. It allows air paths and air mass exchange to be understood. |

Source: Author

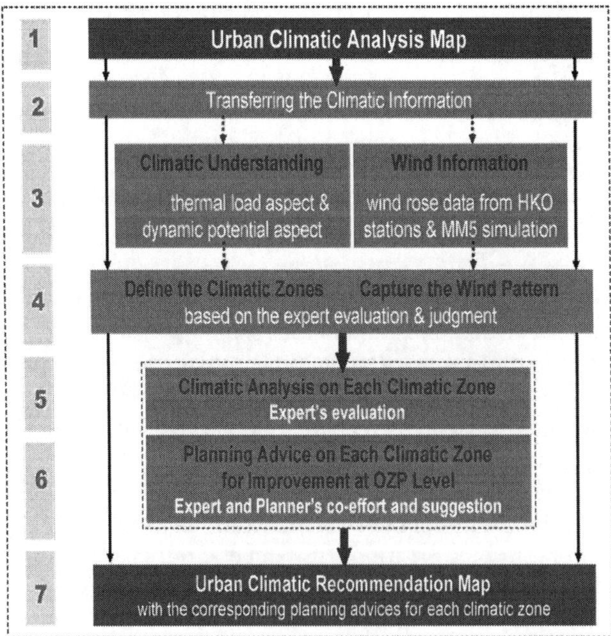


*Figure 10.5* The working process of drafting an urban climatic map.

Source: Author

had been drafted for a city in the tropical regions – the closest was the Environmental Map of the city of Tokyo. As such, the research team needed to approach the study cautiously and sometimes from first principles.

A multidisciplinary research team comprising of more than 20 scientists from over 15 institutions around the world was assembled. The team consisted of experts in building physics, urban climatology, meteorology, human biometeorology, wind engineering, computational fluid dynamics, public health, architecture, and urban and city planning. It was a daunting task at first, requiring the team members to focus, and to speak an 'intelligible language' to the rest of the team members.

### *Focuses and objectives*

The search for a common language boiled down to the focus of 'how a person feels the city' from a bioclimatic point of view. When the word 'feel' was defined, the research team evaluated a number of human body heat exchange thermal models commonly used by researchers. This included the PMV model, the WBGT, the AT model, the SET* model, and the UTCI model. Eventually, the Physical Equivalent Temperature (PET) model was chosen for its wide applicability and ease of use (Höppe, 1999). Eventually, it was more important to calibrate the chosen model to establish the point of criticality than it was to worry too much about the scientific finesse of the model.

A territory-wide user survey was conducted in housing estates, on the roadside and in parks and playgrounds in the summer months of 2006 and 2007. Over 2,700 samples were surveyed. Using micro-meteorological measurement stands, surveyors observed and interviewed the sampled subject in order to establish the relationship between their responses and the immediate climatic variables. The data was then fed into the PET formulation to obtain the subject's range of comfort PET (Ng and An, 2011).

Based on the survey results, the comfort PET of Hong Kong people in the summer months of Hong Kong was found to be PET = 28.1°C. The study results tallied well with other research studies with similar climatic conditions (Cheng *et al.*, 2010; Lin *et al.*, 2013). The study results also correlated well with research studies of public health colleagues in Hong Kong stating that 'An average 1°C increase in daily mean temperature above 28.2°C was associated with an estimated 1.8 per cent increase in mortality', as well as a report by Hong Kong Observatory colleagues (Leung *et al.*, 2008; Chan *et al.*, 2012).

By simplifying the PET formulation for the range of typical summer climatic conditions of Hong Kong, the following formula can be stated:

$$PET = 1.2 \times T_a + 0.52 \times (T_{mrt} - T_a) - 2.2 \times v + c \tag{10.1}$$

$T_a$ being the air temperature in °C, $T_{mrt}$ being the mean radiant temperature in °C, v being the wind speed in m/s, and c being a constant. Shading is assumed and thus the range of $T_{mrt}$ is limited to 2 to 6 degrees above $T_a$ in normal cases. It was immediately obvious that the negative effects of a two degree rise in air temperature could be mitigated with an increase of 1m/s in wind speed. This understanding allowed one to combine the Thermal Load and the Dynamic Potential understandings onto the same map. The Hong Kong UCMap therefore has this bioclimatic basis.

### *The GIS-based layer structure*

Planners use a Geographic Information System (GIS) for their daily work. It is an information platform that they are familiar with. The research team therefore decided to use GIS for assembling the collected data in layers. The next important thing to decide was the grid resolution of the map so that calculations could be operated among the layers. There had been no one correct resolution to use; various resolutions had been tried, for example, the Environmental Map of the city of Tokyo used a 500m × 500m grid. It was deemed sufficient for the highly homogeneous urban structure of the city; this coarser grid was considered sufficient for the planners. However, in Hong Kong, due to the highly inhomogeneous urban structure of the metro areas and the highly complex topography surrounding the city, it was deemed necessary to use a finer grid. Taking into account the results of related research by Nichol and Wong (2008), the need for planning applications and the data sensitivity of the grid size to be used, the research team eventually settled with a 100m × 100m grid. For the Hong Kong UCMap, seven data layers were collated (PlanD, 2012), as in Table 10.2 and Table 10.3.

Each of the seven layers was constructed and classified based on a scientific understanding of how it positively or negatively, in terms of 1 degree in PET, contributes to the Thermal Load and the Dynamic Potential of the urban environment. A detailed account of their working can be found in the *Final Report of the Urban Climatic map and Standards for Wind Environment – Feasibility Study* (PlanD, 2012). As an example, it will suffice here to just illustrate how Layer 1 was put together (see Table 10.4). The result of Layer 1 on GIS is illustrated in Figure 10.6.

## The urban climatic analysis map (UC-AnMap)

Since the data layers were classified based on the parameter's positive and negative effect on PET, collating the Hong Kong UCMap based on the data layers was straightforward (see Figure 10.7 and Plate 10.1, see also Figure 2.5 in Chapter 2).

### Establishing the threshold

Once the UC-AnMap was created, the next questions were 'so what?' and 'what can be done?' This was when the issue of 'criticality' became important (Ng, 2012). Referring to the results of the user survey (neutral PET = 28.1°C) and the average summer month air temperature in Hong Kong of 28.3°C, it was determined that the UC-AnMap classification 3 was to be considered the ambient condition. That is to say, it represented the ambient condition at sea level of Hong Kong if there was no city and everything was natural. Classification 2 and 1 therefore represented potential cooling due to vegetation and elevation. Classification 4 to 8 therefore represented the various degree of urban heat island.

### Calibration and verification

Field measurements in the urban districts of Hong Kong as well as wind tunnel tests were conducted to calibrate the Thermal Load layer of the Hong Kong UCMap. Based on the measurements, the PET under typical summer conditions was calculated and compared to that predicted by the Hong Kong UC-AnMap. The result was reasonable with $R^2 = 0.745$ (Ng *et al.*, 2008a, 2008b; Ren and Ng, 2009; Ng *et al.*, 2010) (see Figure 10.8).

*Table 10.2* The layer structure of the Hong Kong UCMap.

| *Physical Criterion* | *Effect* | *Scientific Basis* | *Input Layers* |
|---|---|---|---|
| **Thermal Load** | Negative | Building bulk | Layer 1<br>Building volume |
| | Positive | Altitude and elevation | Layer 2<br>Topography |
| | Positive | Bioclimatic effect | Layer 3<br>Greenery |
| **Dynamic Potential** | Negative | Urban permeability | Layer 4<br>Ground cover |
| | Positive | Bioclimatic effects – cool air movement | Layer 5<br>Natural landscape |
| | Positive | Air mass change and neighbourhood effects | Layer 6<br>Proximity to openness |
| **Wind Information** | – | MM5 simulation and HKO measured data | Layer 7<br>Prevailing wind directions (summer) |

Source: Author

*Table 10.3* A short description of the data layers of the Hong Kong UCMap.

| *Layer* | *Description* |
|---|---|
| 1 | **Building Volume Map:** Buildings store a significant amount of the solar energy received, which elevates the temperatures (surface and air) of the city, especially at night when it is released back into the sky. A principal cause of high Thermal Load is the blocking of sky view by buildings, which reduces cooling during the night. Buildings built close together block the amount of heat energy that could be released back into the atmosphere. Six classification values are assigned, ranging from Very High heat capacity to No Building. |
| 2 | **Topographical Height Map:** In general, air temperature varies according to altitude, with the higher ground being cooler than the lower ground. Four classification values are assigned, ranging from Low topographical height to Very High topographical height. |
| 3 | **Green Space Map:** Green areas can affect the ground air temperature. Vegetation has a cooling potential to the city and thus mitigates the adverse effects of Thermal Load. Two classification values are assigned: No and Yes. |
| 4 | **Ground Coverage Map:** The amount of land occupied by buildings is known to be directly related to the wind permeability of the location. In general, a neighbourhood with higher ground coverage (by buildings) will have a lower Dynamic Potential. Three classification values are assigned, ranging from High to Low. |
| 5 | **Natural Landscape Map:** Natural vegetation [together with slopes of the hill (Layer 6)] creates cooler air movement. This has a cooling potential to the city. Two classification values are assigned, 'Woodland' and 'Urban area or Grassland'. |
| 6 | **Proximity to Openness Map:** The dynamic movement of air ventilation always mitigates the adverse effects of Thermal Load. There are three sub-layers that are important in this regard.<br>**Layer 6a** Proximity to Waterfront Map: Land and sea breeze is an important consideration for coastal areas. In general, the benefits of sea breeze depend on the location's distance from the sea. Three classification values are assigned.<br>**Layer 6b** Proximity to Open Space Map: Urban open space can benefit its surrounding areas. Two classification values are assigned.<br>**Layer 6c** Slope Map: Cooler air moves downhill and, in general, along the valleys. This cooler air is beneficial. Two classification values are assigned. |
| 7 | **Wind Information Layer Prevailing Wind Directions (Summer):** In addition to the six layers above, Layer 7 is included to give key wind direction and speed information for the prevailing winds of different parts of Hong Kong in the summer. |

Source: Author

*Table 10.4* The working of Layer 1 – Building Volume Map of the Hong Kong UCMap.

| | |
|---|---|
| **Description** | Urban geometry has a complex influence on the microclimate of the urban environment. For example, differences between urban geometry and building density may result in intra-urban air temperature differences (Chandler, 1965; Oke, 1988; Eliasson, 1991). A high building volume not only increases the localised heat capacity (i.e. Thermal Load), but also reduces the sky view factor (SVF) [sky view factor (SVF) is a ratio that ranges from zero to one and represents the proportion of the sky visible from any given locale], which is a major influence in slowing the radiative cooling effect in the city at night. The most important aspect of this effect is that built-up areas predominantly obstruct the open sky and delay the cooling of the surface during clear, calm nights (Oke, 1981). If the building volume density is high, the long-wave radiation could be blocked and the energy would be released back into the sky more slowly. Therefore, the cooling process within the city centre tends to be slower than its surrounding areas leading to relatively higher temperatures. In short, the higher the building volume density, the larger the heat capacity, which in turn, is significant to the increase of Thermal Load. Urban density is also a major factor in determining the urban ventilation conditions and the urban temperature. In general, an urban area having a higher density of buildings would experience a poorer urban ventilation condition and a stronger UHI effect (Givoni, 1998; Hui, 2001). In warm and humid regions such as Hong Kong, these conditions would elevate the level of thermal stress experienced by residents (Leung *et al.*, 2008; Ng, 2009d). To aggravate the problem, the heat produced by air conditioning raises the urban air temperature further still and thus reinforces the Thermal Load. Since wind is one of the major driving forces in mitigating the effect of Thermal Load, the density of building blocks also significantly affects the local micro-wind environment (Niu, 2004). As a result, a high building volume is a major contributor to Thermal Load.<br>For the past three decades, researchers have attempted to analyse the temperature variations particular to urban street canyons caused by the urban geometry, i.e. the height to width ratio (H/W) and SVF. Oke (1981) first developed a scale model to evaluate the role of building geometry on the UHI effect. He showed that the UHI effect is directly related to the SVF, as it controls the rate of the radiative cooling at street level within the city. On the other hand, many studies have demonstrated that the relationship between H/W ratio and SVF can be employed as a measure of urban geometry (Barring and Mattsson *et al.*, 1985; Eliasson, 1991; Goldreich, 1992; Upmanis and Chen, 1999; Svensson, 2004; Unger, 2004; Montaveza, 2008; Unger, 2009). This shows the trends and variations of air temperature in urban and in rural areas. A longitudinal review was given in Unger (2009). Lindberg (2007) has also demonstrated that the areal mean of SVF (r = 100m) is highly correlated to the intra-urban air temperature variations, but is relatively less correlated to the SVF taken from a point source location. The usefulness of areal mean of SVF was further proven by Gal *et al.* (2009). It is important to apply this relationship to urban planning and urban design in order to mitigate the UHI effect.<br>A preliminary investigation of the relationship between SVF and UHI in Hong Kong was given by Chen and Ng (2009, 2010). In this study, the SVF is employed as a means to reflect the building volume information. |
| Input data | From Planning Department, Hong Kong Government:<br>Buildings and Podium .shp data,<br>DEM data (in 1m raster format) and<br>GIS Land Use .shp data. |
| Methodology | This layer is derived from knowledge-based processing. The land use in Hong Kong has been considered in both Layer 1 (Building Volume Map) and Layer 4 (Ground Coverage Map). As discussed, building volume is a major factor in heat capacity and temperature variation in urban areas.<br>Layer 1 contains the building volume information area in a grid size of 100m × 100m resolution and the volume is in cubic meters. However, in the GIS model, the building volume values have to be converted to percentages of the highest volume grid that is found in the region. Six classification values are assigned and ranged from no buildings = 0, |

| | |
|---|---|
| | no building but paved = 1, > 0 and ≤ 4% maximum building volume = 2, > 4% and ≤ 10% = 3, > 10% and ≤ 25% = 4, > 25% = 5.<br>Our parametric model reveals a logarithmic relation between building volume (BV) and SVF, i.e. $SVF = c \times BV^{\alpha}$ (Chen, 2010). This forms the basis for the threshold value of the classification value in Layer 1. SVF is evaluated based on the method proposed by Eliasson and Svensson (2003). The calibration of the SVF is carried out with field measurements and SVF. Hence, the proposed formula for the temperature variation and the SVF is as follows: $\Delta T = 4.18 - 9.09 \times SVF$. Accordingly, the designated threshold values of 4%, 10% and 25% are used. |
| GIS Operation | 1. Derive the correct absolute building height from the value of building top and building base:<br>a. Converting DEM file of topography height to 10m × 10m shapefile (.shp).<br>b. Spatially join the .shp of topography height to building/podium .shp.<br>c. Use the resultant field as a new base and calculate the absolute building height by setting 'height = top − base'.<br>2. Convert the newly joined building and podium .shp to raster file, i.e. raster value = height of 1m x 1m resolution.<br>3. Merge the building and podium raster file by using the 'mosaic' function and select 'maximum' as the option.<br>4. Aggregate the resulting raster file into a 100m x 100m resolution by using the sum option, where the highest value is chosen to be 1,200,000m$^3$ = 100%, being the highest building volume value based on Planning Department 2006 dataset. This is adopted as the basis for the Urban Climatic Analysis Map (UC-AnMap) calibration.<br>5. Divide the raster by the highest value using 'Raster calculation'.<br>6. Classify the result into 5 classes (0%, > 0% and ≤ 4%, > 4% and ≤ 10%, > 10% and ≤ 25%, and > 25%).<br>7. Use the Land Use .shp to select 'no building but concrete areas' and convert to raster of 100m × 100m resolution.<br>8. Use 'mosaic' to add the new raster to the result, choose 'last' option.<br>9. Reclassify and define classification value. |

Source: Author

### *Cross comparative study with UCSS*

Developed by Dr Yasunobu Ashie and his team at the Building Research Institute in Japan, The Urban Climate Simulation System (UCSS) is:

> a numerical model for the simulation of the thermal processes inside the urban canopy layer. The model is coupled with a turbulence closure model for the atmospheric boundary layer with the purpose of analyzing the thermal effects of urban areas. In the model, the buildings and land uses inside each computational grid mesh are averaged by a lumping space-averaging method. Then, a model for the evaluation of momentum loss and heat exchange between the air and the urban canopy is developed. The model accounts for all processes which can generate heat inside the canopy layer such as the heating of wall, roof and the ground surface, the conduction of heat to buildings through windows, wall and roof, and the discharge of artificial heat due to air conditioners. The coupled numerical model was applied for the analysis of heating characteristics of a housing area and an office area and the influence of a housing area on the thermal climate of surrounding vegetative areas.
>
> (Ashie, 2004)

UCSS results were used to cross compare with the Hong Kong UCMap. The correlation was found to be reasonable with $R^2 = 0.67$ (see Figure 10.9). The comparison between the two at the

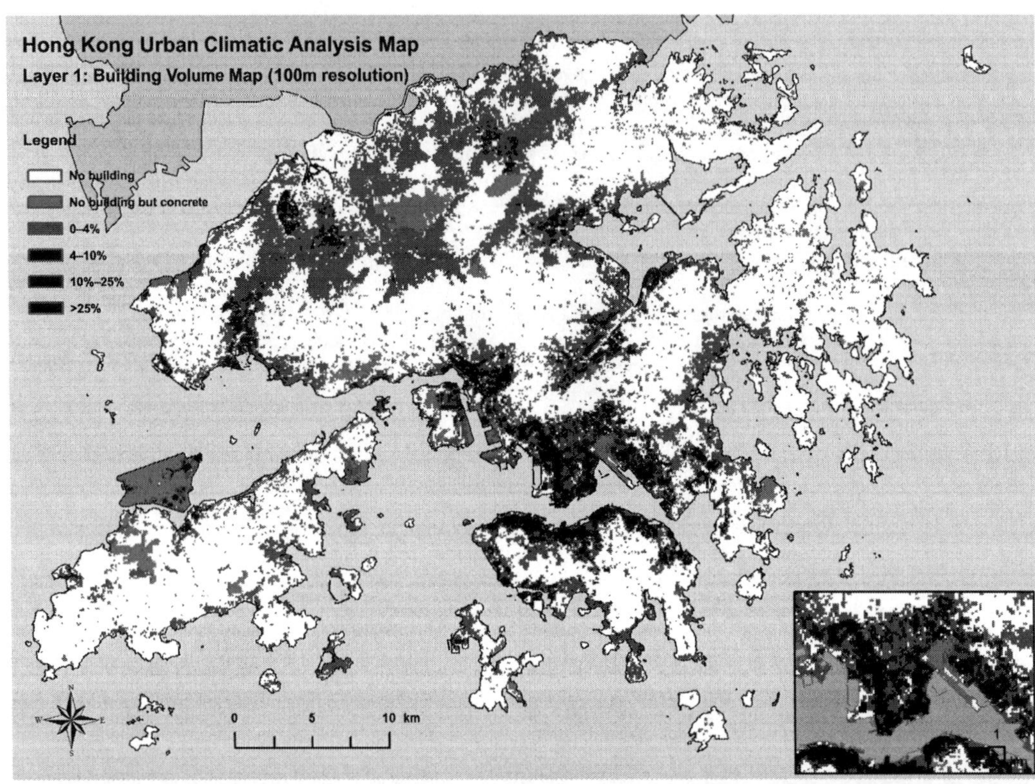


| Thermal Load | Building volume (percentage range) (%) | Tentative Classification Value |
|---|---|---|
| Zero | 0 (no building) | 0 |
| Very low | 0 (paved area only) | 1 |
| Low | >0–4 | 2 |
| Medium | >4–10 | 3 |
| High | >10–25 | 4 |
| Very high | >25 | 5 |

*Figure 10.6* Layer 1 of the Hong Kong UCMap and its six classifications in 100m × 100m rasterised grid.

Source: Author

cooler end of the map (grey and light grey grids) was not as good as that of the hotter end of the map (dark grey and black grids). This was due to the focus of the Hong Kong UCMap, which was to highlight the issues for planning actions. The comparative study further demonstrated the validity of the Hong Kong UCMap.

### *The Wind Information Map*

Once the locations and criticalities of the problems in terms of thermal load and the dynamic potential of the urban characteristics were detected and identified by the Hong Kong UC-AnMap,

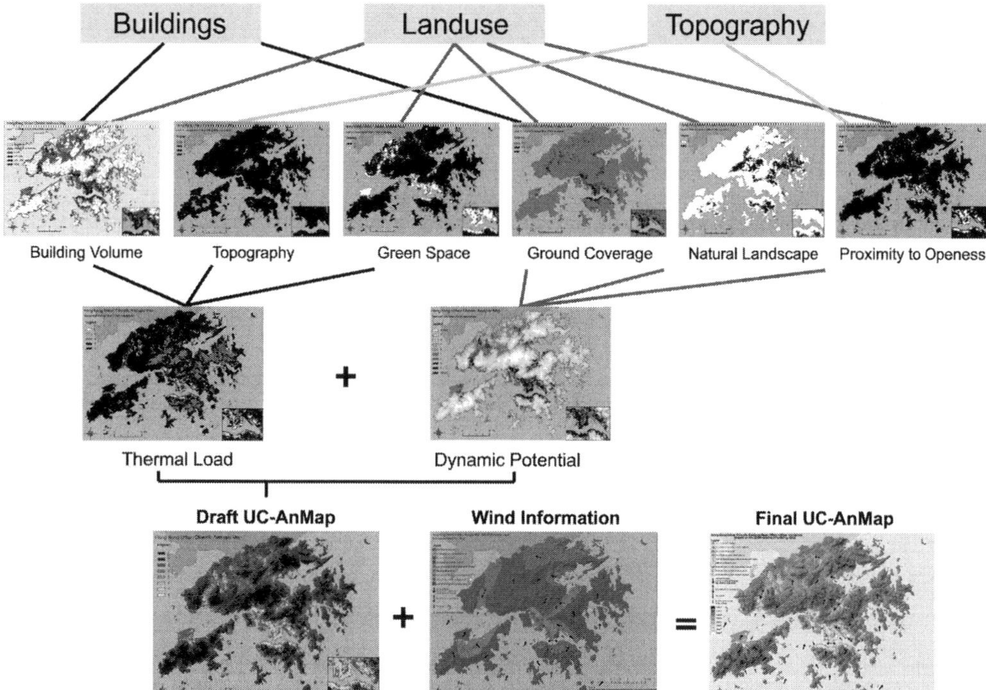


*Figure 10.7* The data layer structure of the Hong Kong UCMap. Results of the data layers were collated into the eight classifications of the Hong Kong UCMap.

Source: Author

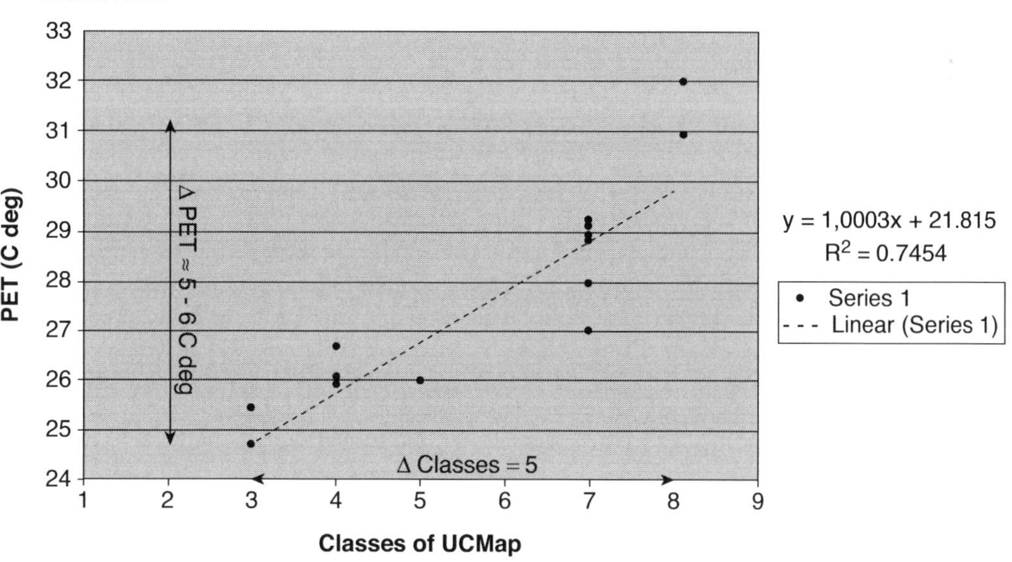


*Figure 10.8* Cross comparative study between results of the field measurements and the Hong Kong UC-AnMap. $R^2$=0.745.

Source: Author

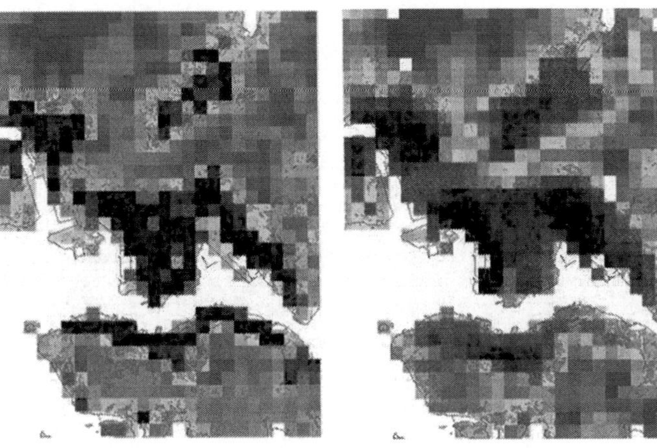

*Figure 10.9* Comparing the results of the UCSS system (right) and the Hong Kong UCMap (left) with $R^2 = 0.67$.

Source: Author

it was deemed necessary for planners to know 'where help is coming from'. For cities in the tropics, providing good urban air ventilation is important.

The research team needed to provide an easy to use Wind Information Map for planners. The key issue was not the technicality of making such a map, but the practical issue of 'information' and 'easy to use'. The first task of the research team was to collate the ten-year measured data from the Hong Kong Observatory and to map the data visually onto the territorial map of Hong Kong (see Plate 10.2). Once the map was made, a number of factors could be discerned: topography, land–sea breezes, and localized katabatic air movements (Ng and Fung, 2008; Ng and An, 2011). First, a number of wind channels were detected. One of them was found to be along the harbour channel between Hong Kong Island and the Kowloon peninsula. Due to the channelling and the shielding effects of the hills, wind was always found to be flowing along the east–west directions. Similarly, at the north-western corner of the territory along the channel between the two parallel hill ranges, wind was found to be always flowing along the north–south directions. Second, by comparing the wind rose of the observatory's reference station (Wanglan Island) on an island at the south-eastern corner of Hong Kong with the stations around Hong Kong, it was obvious that the many south-eastern stations, especially these nearer to the sea front, experienced strong sea breezes from mid-day through to the evening hours. The effect was found to be stronger when the synoptic wind was weak. Third, by examining a few stations nearer to the bottom of the hills, katabatic movements in the evening hours could be detected. All in all, it was decided that the wind regime of the Hong Kong Territory was so complex that the observed data alone might not be able to capture the fine details necessary for planners.

The research team then turned to simulated data. Researchers at the nearby Hong Kong University of Science and Technology have been simulating Hong Kong's wind environment using MM5 coupled with CALMET (Lam *et al.*, 2006; Yim *et al.*, 2007). The data was available at a 100m × 100m grid resolution. The above urban canopy layer wind profiles and wind statistics were available. The terrain followed, 60m above ground prevailing wind directions of the Hong Kong territory were extracted for the summer months from June to Autumn (see Figure 10.10).

Based on the two sets of data, the research team then worked to extract, collate and simplify the data based on the consideration of what planners need for their decision making. The principles of

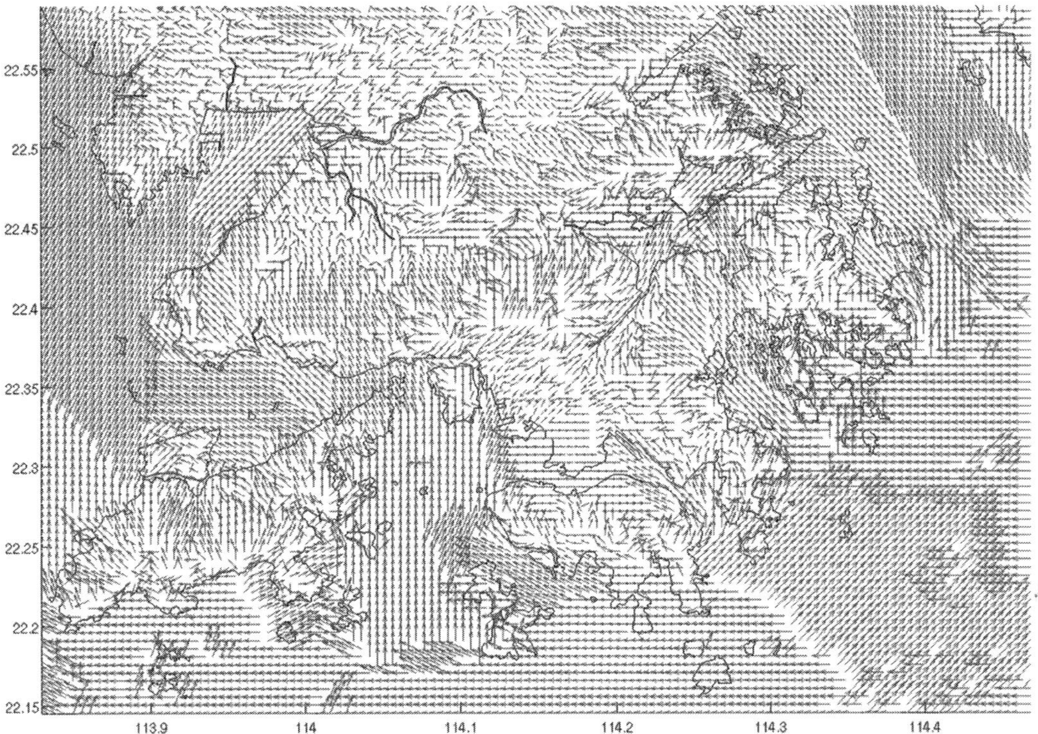


*Figure 10.10* Complex prevailing wind directions of the Hong Kong territory based on MM5/CALMET model simulation.

Source: Courtesy of Professor Jimmy Fung

'criticality' and 'prevailing' were followed in that only the important information and the useful information were shown. The Hong Kong Wind Information Map was created (see Figure 10.11).

The wind regime in different parts of the territory where urban developments were present or were to be planned in the immediate future was zonally demarcated. The prevailing directions in the form of a few simple arrows were marked on each of these zones. A note that accompanied the map to explain the characteristics of the wind regime of the zone was drafted, including, for example, whether typography shielding and channelling wind were dominant, whether sea breezes were present, and whether katabatic wind should be considered. The language used in the notes was planning orientated. When using the map, planners only needed to note the project area in hand and consult the map in terms of the area's prevailing wind characteristics and directions. There would be no need for future information to begin the planning decision making process – the Wind Information Map must not overwhelm, and it must not provide redundant information. However, should the planners need further information, their wind engineers could extract further details like wind statistics, profiles and events from the data embedded in the map's interface.

## *The urban climatic planning recommendation map (UC-ReMap)*

Once the scientific work of the urban climatic analysis map (UC-AnMap) and the wind information map was created, the next task of the research team was to evaluate and translate the

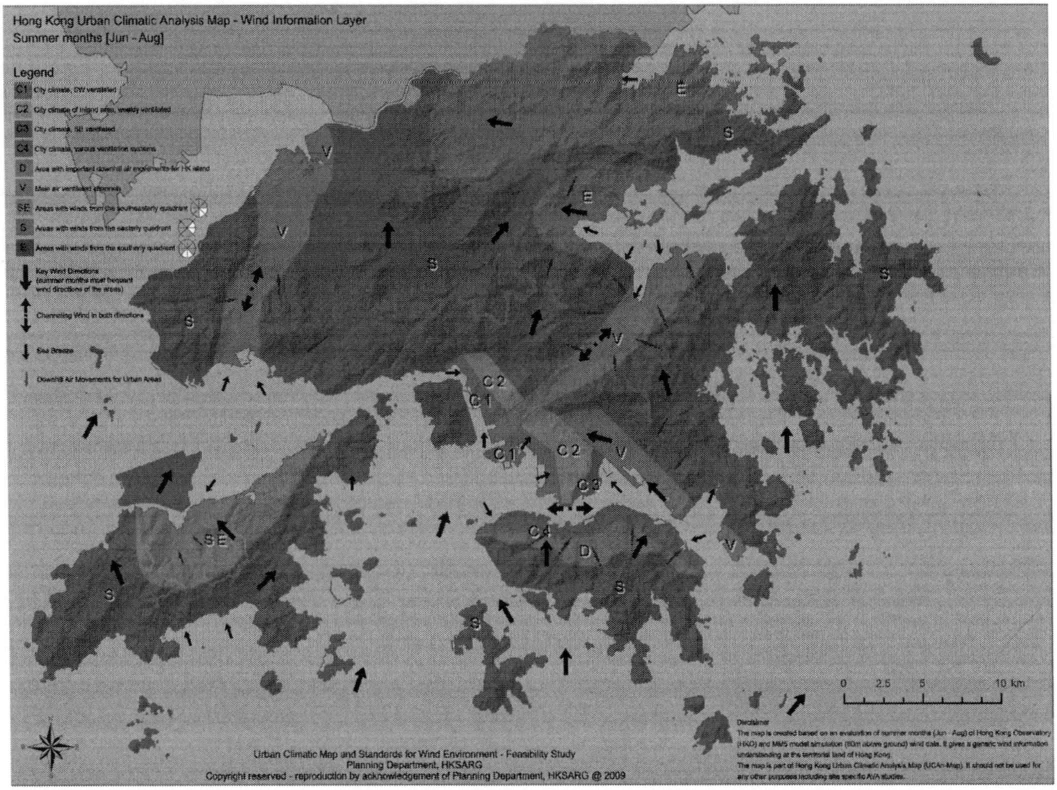

*Figure 10.11* Wind Information Map of the Hong Kong UCMap.

Source: Author

information into a format that would form the working platform of the planners. The process was reflective and interactive. Planning is a multidisciplinary and multivalent process; there is no right or wrong, black or white kind of structure. The 'what needs to be done', 'what can be done', 'when it needs to be done', 'how intensely it should be done' kind of planning decision depends on the ethos, politics and values of the time. The important thing for the Urban Climatic Recommendation Map (UC-ReMap) is to be simple and flexible; it must not be too detailed and too specific too early (see Plate 10.3). However, it must allow for further interrogation should the circumstances warrant the extra effort in cases of important consequences.

### *From science to planning application*

There is no shortage of work on the scientific understanding of urban climate. However, when it comes to practical application, successful results are sparse, if any. Mills *et al.* (2010) highlights the problem in a paper presented at the World Climate Conference 3 in Geneva in 2009. The paper reckons that the context of planning is far richer than that typically appreciated by climatologists. Furthermore, the language of planners is pattern-based and descriptive in nature. Actions need to be impact-evaluated before they can be incorporated. Eliasson (2000) outlines the problem under the issues of 'conceptual', 'knowledge base', 'institutional' and 'technical'. At working level, the issue of the 'knowledge base' is perhaps most fundamental. To achieve this it is necessary to develop good communication, to facilitate which a couple of steps are needed.

First, researchers need to know what planners do and how they do things. It is almost impossible for a specialist like a modeller, a geographer, a meteorologist, and so on to speculate a tool for planning if they themselves have no appreciation or experience of planning; too many tools and methods have been proposed and their usefulness falsely claimed without any example or verification. Ideally, the researcher himself should also be a planner. This way, the knowledge domain crossover can be easier. Second, researchers need to work with planners on an ongoing basis to develop tools and information that is useful at the specific scale and stage of the planning decision making process. Third, overprovision of information should be avoided, and fourth, the impact of an action should always be evaluated and the result presented in planning terms so that the planner may formulate the priority of issues to be considered (Ng *et al.*, 2010).

### *Working with planners and decision makers*

Since the Hong Kong UCMap project was commissioned by the Planning Department of the Hong Kong Government, the research team had access to planners since the early stage of the study. The Planners' hierarchical approach to territorial, district and site planning was understood. The research team then focused the study at the district scale of application – provide information at the Outline Zoning Plan (1:5,000) scale of the planning process whilst also providing information for the boundary condition consideration at the project level of planning operation (see Figure 10.12).

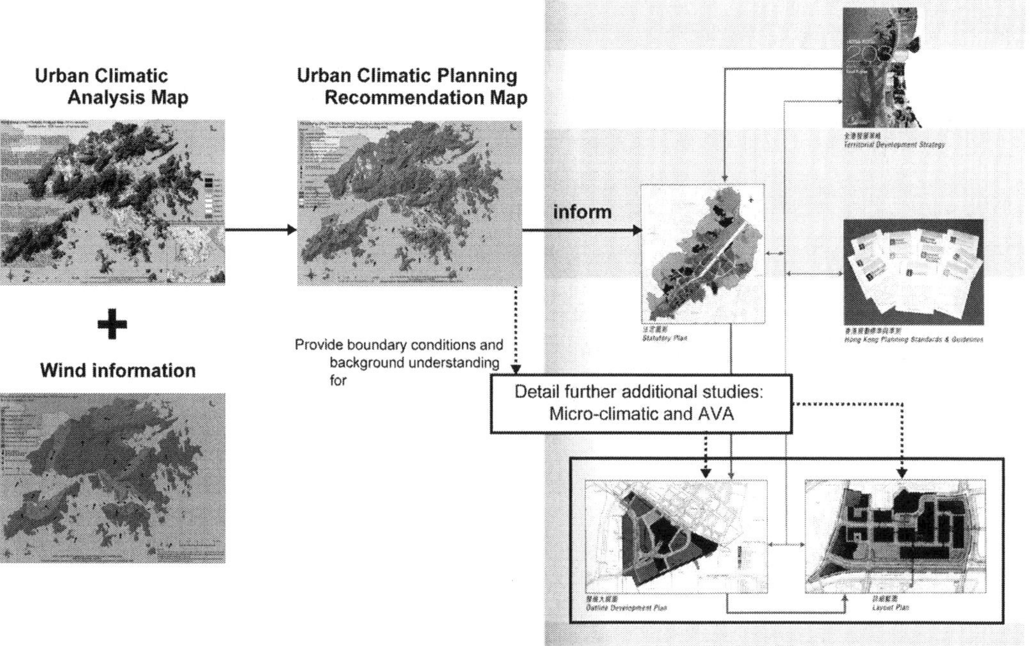


*Figure 10.12* The Hong Kong planning framework and how the Hong Kong UCMap interfaces with it.

Source: Author

### *The five urban climatic planning zones (UCPZs)*

Noting the needs of planners to differentiate actions, the team worked with them to resolve the eight classifications of the UC-AnMap into five Urban Climatic Planning Zones (UCPZs) of the UC-ReMap (see Figure 10.13, see also Figure 2.6 for details).

For UCPZ 1 urban climatically valuable area, the strategic planning action is 'Preservation'. The key planning recommendations are: (A) Preserve the urban climatic conditions. (B) Natural areas at higher altitude and with fewer obstructions to wind act as sources of cool air production and drainage areas, which are beneficial to other areas (e.g. vegetated hill slopes adjacent to urban areas) and should therefore be preserved. Sealing (covering of ground surface) or development should be discouraged. (C) In view of its urban climatic value, there is a general presumption against major development in this zone. (D) Small-scale and essential developments may be allowed in areas other than in natural areas identified in (B) above subject to: (a) careful planning and design of these developments to minimise any disruption to the existing urban climatic characteristics; (b) maximising greenery; and (c) minimising sealing.

For UCPZ 2 urban climatically valuable area, the strategic planning action is 'Maintenance'. The key planning recommendations are: (A) Maintain the urban climatic conditions. (B) These zones are currently urban climatically 'neutral' in terms of urban thermal comfort. They are mostly urban fringe or rural lowland. It is important to maintain their climatic characteristics. (C) General urban climatic characteristics such as lower building volume, open spaces, and greenery should be maintained as far as possible. (D) New low-density individual developments could be allowed subject to: (a) a low building volume and a satisfactory disposition of buildings to align with the prevailing wind directions and preserve existing air paths; (b) a low ground coverage in order not to impede airflow; and (c) maximisation of greenery within development sites. (E) New comprehensive development is possible subject to thorough urban climatic consideration. Prudent planning and building design is necessary to avoid degrading the urban climatic condition. Breezeways and air paths must be carefully designed. Street grids and building disposition must respect prevailing wind directions. High building volume and ground coverage should be discouraged.

For UCPZ 3 urban climatically valuable area, the strategic planning action is 'Mitigation actions are encouraged'. The key planning recommendations are: (A) Some mitigation actions are encouraged where possible. (B) These zones are currently subject to urban climatically 'moderate' impact in terms of thermal comfort. They are mostly in the urban fringe or in less dense development areas. (C) Additional development is permissible subject to: (a) urban climatic evaluation in terms of building volume and green coverage; (b) dispositioning of new buildings in line with the prevailing wind directions, to preserve/enhance existing air paths; (c) reduction of ground coverage in order not to impede air movement; and (d) maximisation of greening, particularly tree planting within development sites and adjoining streets. (D) Greening should be promoted in open areas as far as practicable.

For UCPZ 4 urban climatically valuable area, the strategic planning action is 'Mitigation actions are recommended'. Key planning recommendations are: (A) Mitigation actions are recommended and necessary. (B) These zones are already densely built up. Thermal Load is high and dynamic potential is low. Some strong impact on thermal comfort is expected. (C) Air paths/breezeways, and low-rise, low-density Government, Institution or Community (GIC) sites should be preserved as far as possible. (D) Greenery, particularly tree planting on streets and open areas, should be increased. (E) Additional development should not be allowed unless with appropriate mitigation measures, including: (a) reducing ground coverage to balance against any increase in building volume; (b) respecting existing air paths and introducing new ones if feasible; (c) positioning buildings to align with the prevailing wind directions; and (d) maximising greening within development sites.

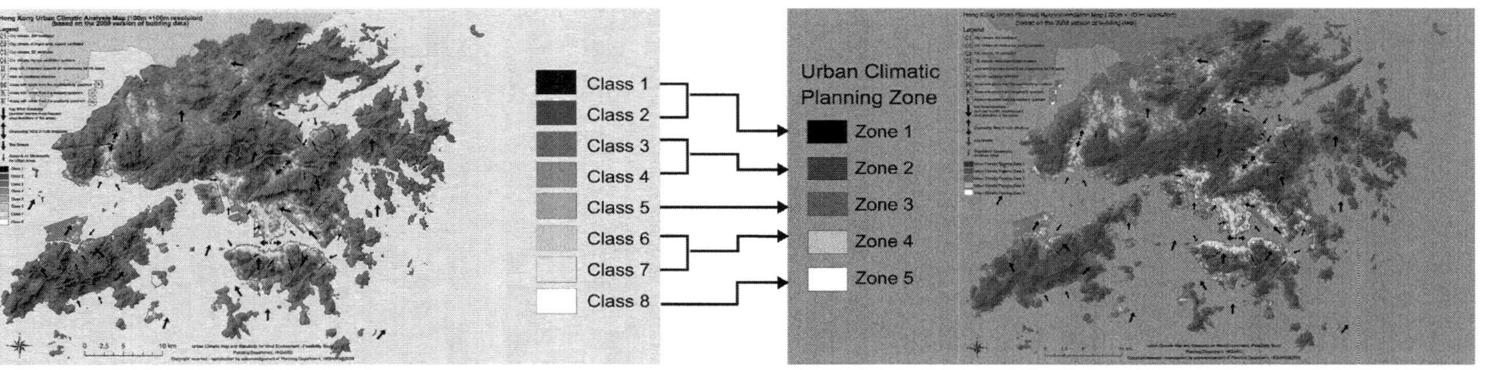


*Figure 10.13* Simplifying the UC-AnMap into the five UCPZs of the UC-ReMap. The strategic planning actions of the five UCPZs are outlined.

Source: Author

For UCPZ 5 urban climatically valuable area, the strategic planning action is 'Mitigation actions are essential'. Key planning recommendations are: (A) Mitigation actions are recommended and essential. (B) These zones are already very densely built up. Thermal Load is very high and dynamic potential is low. Very strong impact on thermal comfort is expected. Frequent occurrence of thermal stress is anticipated. (C) Intensification of GIC sites which serve as a relief to the existing condition should be avoided. Additional and intensified greening within the GIC sites is essential. (D) Additional greenery and tree planting in open areas and streets in this zone is essential and recommended. Intensified greening in 'Open Space' zones is strongly recommended. (E) The existing urban environment should be improved by: (a) identifying, respecting, widening and enhancing existing air paths; (b) creating new air paths; (c) reducing ground coverage, setting back the building line along narrow streets, aligning the long frontage of buildings with prevailing wind directions; and (d) maximising site greening upon development or redevelopment. (F) Intensification of use, adding building volume and/or ground coverage are not recommended unless with strong justifications and appropriate mitigation measures.

### *The 17 urban climate planning districts*

Apart from the UCPZ for the territory in the UC-ReMap as a whole, based on the planner's Outline Zoning Plan (OZP) boundaries (Hong Kong is divided into over a hundred OZPs), 17 district-based UC-ReMaps were drafted, thus providing further information when planners need to work at the district/OZP level. The general descriptions of the five UCPZs were further elaborated contextually. The importance of the localized breezeways and sea breezes zones, the positions of hill valleys, and possible katabatic air mass movements was highlighted on the map, and some of the focus areas were identified (see Figure 10.14).

## Planning design guidelines

Based on the scientific study so far, the research team proceeded to draw up six important planning parameters for planners to formulate action plans. They were: building volume, building permeability, building site coverage, air paths and breezeways, and building heights and greenery. Some quantities were suggested (see Table 10.5).

## The policy implementation process

Once the Hong Kong Urban Climatic Recommendation Map was agreed with the government planners, the process of market transformation was activated. The first step was to consult the industry stakeholders. The purpose was to detect the mechanism that was needed so that the construction industry might buy into the recommendations. It was also designed to educate industry planners and architects in how to alter their working norm for something that might also be important. In addition, it was also structured so that feedback and comments as to how to make the maps more friendly and useable might be obtained. The engagement process took six months; all in all, over 20 workshops and seminars were conducted in 2011 and 2012. Needless to say, at times, the atmosphere of the meeting was a bit tense. There were always some in the construction industry who did not welcome changes. The engagement meetings were recorded and analysed. On the whole, the maps were supported by the community. Surprisingly, feedback from the construction industry was also receptive. To accelerate the market transformation process, the Government of Hong Kong decided to allow a 10 per cent Gross Floor Area (GFA)

*Table 10.5* Quantitative recommendations of the six important planning parameters for better urban climate.

| *Planning parameters* | *Suggestions* |
|---|---|
| Building volume | Site plot ratio of 5 or less. Higher plot area must be mitigated using other planning parameters. |
| Building permeability | 25% to 33% of the project site's frontal elevation. Lower permeability must be mitigated using other planning parameters. |
| Building site coverage | 70% of the site area. Higher site coverage must be mitigated using other planning parameters. |
| Air paths and breezeways | Open spaces must be linked with landscaped pedestrianized streets from one end of the city to the other end in the direction of the prevailing wind. |
| Building heights | Vary building heights so that there is a mixture of building heights in the area with an average aggregated differential difference of 50%. |
| Greenery | 20% to 30% tree planting preferably at grade, or essentially in a position less than 20m from the ground level. Trees with large canopy and a leaf area index of more than 6 are preferred. |

Source: Author

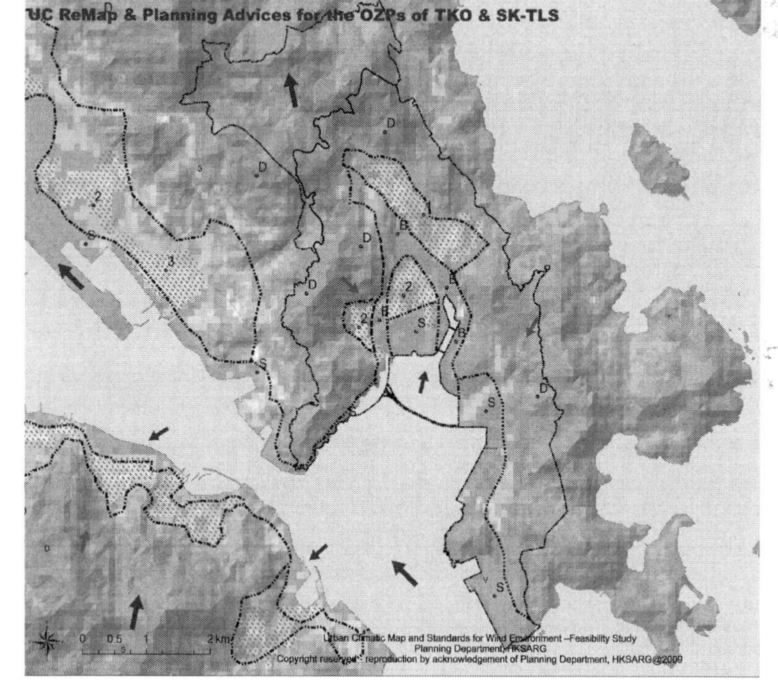


*Figure 10.14* An example of the 17 district-based UC-ReMap.

Source: Author

bonus to project proponents should they choose to follow the planning recommendations as in Table 10.5. Moreover, setting a standard and an example, the Government mandated that all public buildings be required to adhere strictly to the planning recommendations of the Hong Kong UC-ReMap.

*Figure 10.15* The four shortlisted designs of the Central Market as an urban oasis.

Source: Courtesy of Urban Renewal Authority, Hong Kong

Based on the findings of the UCMap project, the Government came to note the problems of some of the more congested metro areas, and started to introduce mitigation measures. One such success story was the Central Market in the busy and congested Central district on the Hong Kong Island, south of Victoria Harbour. The site was originally designated to be sold off for a tall Grade-A office building. However, having consulted the UCMap, the Government decided to conserve the three-storey-high old building and turned it into an urban oasis with intensified greening. A number of designs were shortlisted, the winning design was commissioned (see Figure 10.15).

The Planning Department of Hong Kong adopted the study findings and started to draft a new chapter on urban climate to be incorporated into the *Hong Kong Planning Standards and Guidelines* (HKPSG) (PlanD, 2012). The chapter contains sections on the fundamentals of urban climate and city planning, on the needs for urban climatic considerations and on the impact otherwise; the logic and structure of the UCMap were also explained; the possible action plans, their degree, priority and effectiveness were introduced; the six planning parameters were described; and the implementation process delineated.

## An application

The Planning Department of the Hong Kong Government initiated a comprehensive review process of all of Hong Kong's Outline Zoning Plan (OZP) for the purpose of updating them. Urban

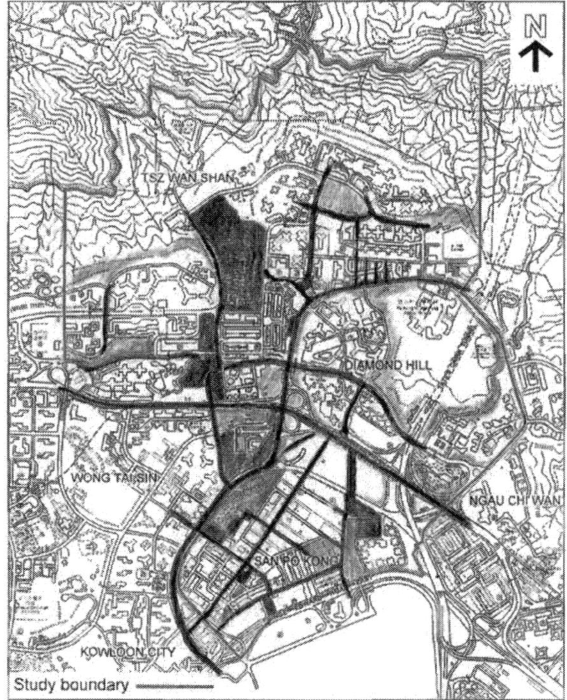


*Figure 10.16* Air path connectivity (black) is integrated into the OZPs open spaces and green areas forming a network of air paths and breezeways.

Source: Author

air ventilation and urban climate have been two important considerations. Detailed studies have been carried out; for example, for one of the OZPs, attempts were made to delineate non-building areas for wind paths, open space connectivity was incorporated, and development heights and densities were controlled (see Figure 10.16).

## Lessons learnt and further development

The key lesson has been that it is always important to maintain communication among all sectors of the map-making team. How to talk to a wind engineer on the one hand and relay his key points to the policymaker has been a challenge. Bearing in mind the wicked problem nature of planning, the process is more of an art form than pure science. All who work on the subject field must be open-minded and be flexible and willing to learn from his teammates.

The drafting of the Hong Kong Urban Climatic Map (UCMap) was completed in 2012. It was recommended to the Planning Department of the Hong Kong Government to continue the effort by establishing an urban climate for planning section within its organization – very much like the practice of the City of Stuttgart. In addition, the research team suggested a minor review by updating the data of the layers once every five years and a major upgrade in terms of science once every ten years.

The UCMap is only a beginning. It was suggested that the Planning Department build on it with additional layers to further understand factors that affect the urban climate of the city. Foremost of all is a set of anthropogenic heat data, another area where the Planning Department may wish to collaborate with the Environmental Protection Department of the Hong Kong Government to incorporate air pollution understanding on a spatial format. In addition, it is reckoned that the urban development of nearby cities would affect Hong Kong. It is useful to expand the Hong Kong UCMap data to include a larger domain.

## Postscript

It has been a while since the research team completed the Hong Kong UCMap project in 2012. As this chapter is written, the Planning Department of the Hong Kong Government is currently putting an Urban Climate chapter into the *Hong Kong Planning Standards and Guidelines* (HKPSG). They are also trying to find ways to draw up practice guidelines on greening and on building disposition (APP-152, 2011). However, progress has been slow. Lately, the political climate of Hong Kong has changed somewhat since the new government took office in 2012. Politicians and government officials now focus only on the immediate need of providing housing units in order to curb the raising prices. It is claimed that there is a mismatch between supply and demand, and therefore the immediate needs must be fulfilled. Gaps in the city and open spaces are rezoned for housing. Higher and higher density developments are planned. Worse still, the many good practice measures of the UCMap project are beginning to be forgotten. Short-termism and quick political return mean that the long-term benefits of creating a sustainable and quality urban living environment has been side lined. The problem is that the current government may, and only may, solve the housing shortage problem now, but it would definitely leave a more difficult to solve problem for our next generations. In a nutshell, there is no sustainable future if its value cannot be embedded in the community and sustained.

I would like to share the following (an extract from the executive summary of the UCMap study) to remind us all:

> It is often said that we do not own the city; we simply borrow it from our children. It is also important to share Sir Winston Churchill's wisdom, which can be paraphrased as: We shape our city and our city will shape us, and our kids.
>
> Cities, ours included, are not made in one day. What we have done in the past had impacted us, and what we are, or are not, going to do will impact our children.
>
> Sustainable development is a matter of balancing environmental, social and economic needs. Urban climate is one of the important considerations in the planning and design process – it must not be neglected.
>
> The Study provides an information platform [on which] informed discussion can be based. In due course, we will shape a future for the next generations. We must believe and value that we all share the same responsibility towards a common future, and we all must do our fair share towards it.

## Acknowledgements

The research team would like to thank colleagues of the Hong Kong Observatory for providing the needed data for the study, as well as critical, insightful and constructive comments throughout the study. Thanks are due to the following team members of the study who endured the long study period (2006–2012) we had with colleagues of the Planning Department, Hong Kong Government.

### Core co-investigators

Ms Betty Ho (PlanArch Consultant Ltd.)
Professor Kenny Kwok (CLP Power Wind/Wave Tunnel Facility, Hong Kong University of Science and Technology)
Professor Lutz Katzschner (Department of Architecture, Urban and Landscape Planning, University of Kassel)
Dr Raymond Yau (Ove Arup & Partners HK Ltd.)
Professor Kam Sing Wong (The Chinese University of Hong Kong)

### Team experts and advisors

Professor Akashi Mochida (Department of Architecture and Building Science, Tohoku University)
Professor Alexis Lau (Institute for the Environment, Hong Kong University of Science and Technology)
Professor Jimmy Fung (Department of Mathematics, Hong Kong University of Science and Technology)
Dr Peter Hitchcock (CLP Power Wind/Wave Tunnel Facility, Hong Kong University of Science and Technology)
Professor Ryuichiro Yoshie (Department of Architecture, Tokyo Polytechnic University)
Dr Nyuk Hien Wong (Department of Building, National University of Singapore)
Professor Baruch Givoni (Department of Architecture, University of California, Los Angeles)
Dr Ing. Bernd Leitl (Meteorological Institute, University of Hamburg)
Dr Marcus O. Letzel (PALM Group, Leibniz University of Hannover)
Professor See Chun Kot (Department of Mechanical Engineering, Hong Kong University of Science and Technology)
Professor Edmund Choi (Department of Building and Construction, The City University of Hong Kong)
Professor Janet Nichol (Department of Land Surveying and Geo-informatics, The Hong Kong Polytechnic University)
Dr Yasunobu Ashie (National Institute for Land and Infrastructure Management, MLITT, Japan)

### Project administration

Professor Chao Ren (School of Architecture, The Chinese University of Hong Kong)
Dr Kevin Lau (School of Architecture, The Chinese University of Hong Kong)

## References

APP-152 (2011). *Buildings Department Practice Note on Sustainable Building Design Guidelines*. http://www.bd.gov.hk/english/documents/pnap/APP/APP152.pdf (Accessed on 27 September 2013).

Ashie, Y. (2004). Developing a three-D urban canopy model by space averaging method, development of the urban climate simulation system for urban and architectural planning part 2. *Journal of Environmental Engineering*, AIJ, 586: 45–51.

Barring, L. and Mattsson, J. O. (1985). Canyon geometry, street temperature and urban heat island in Malmo, Sweden. *Journal of Climatology*, 5(4): 433–444.

Chan, E. Y. Y., Goggins, W., Kim, J. J. and Griffiths, S. M. (2012). A study of intracity variation of temperature-related mortality and socioeconomic status among the Chinese population in Hong Kong. *Journal of Epidemiology & Community Health*, 66(4): 322–327. doi:10.1136/jech.2008.085167.

Chen, L. and Ng, E. (2009). Sky view factor analysis of street canyons and its implication for urban heat island intensity: a GIS-based methodology applied in Hong Kong. In: Demers, C. M. H. and Potvin, A. (eds.), *Proceedings of 26th International Conference on Passive and Low Energy Architecture: Architecture, Energy and the Occupant's Perspective*. Quebec City, Canada, 22–24 June 2009. Quebec: Les Presses de l'Université Laval, 1.2.7.

Chen, L., Ng, E., An, X., Ren, C., Lee, M., Wang, U. and He, Z. (2010). Sky view factor analysis of street canyons and its implications for daytime intra-urban air temperature differentials in high-rise, high-density urban areas of Hong Kong: A GIS-based simulation approach. *International Journal of Climatology*, 32(1): 121–136. doi: 10.1002/joc.2243.

Cheng, V., Ng, E., Chan, C. and Givoni, B. (2010) Outdoor thermal comfort study in sub-tropical climate: a longitudinal study based in Hong Kong. *International Journal of Biometeorology*, 56(1): 43–56. doi.org/10.1007/s00484-010-0396-z.

Chandler, T. J. (1965). *The Climate of London*. London: Hutchinson.

Chandler, T. J. (1976). *Urban Climatology and its Relevance to Urban Design*. Geneva: WMO, no.438.

Civil Service Bureau (2011). *Civil Service Newsletter*, 81. Civil Service Bureau, HKSAR Government. Available at: http://www.csb.gov.hk/hkgcsb/csn/csn81/81e/pdf/csn81.pdf (Accessed 10 February 2014).

Eliasson, I. (1991). Urban geometry, surface temperature and air temperature. *Energy and Buildings*, 15(1–2): 141–145.

Eliasson, I. (2000). The use of climate knowledge in urban planning. *Landscape and Urban Planning*, 48(1–2): 31–44.

Eliasson, I. and Svensson, M. K. (2003). Spatial air temperature variations and urban land use – a statistical approach. *Meteorological Application*, 10(2): 135–149.

Evans, J. M. and de Schiller, S. (1996). Application of microclimate studies in town planning: A new capital city, an existing urban district and urban river front development. *Atmospheric Environment*, 30(3): 361–364.

Gal, T., Lindberg, F. and Unger, J. (2009). Computing continuous sky view factors using 3D urban raster and vector databases: comparison and application to urban climate. *Theoretical and Applied Climatology*, 95(1–2): 111–123.

Givoni, B. (1988). *Guidelines for Urban Design in Different Climates*. Geneva: World Meteorological Organization.

Givoni, B. (1998). *Climate Considerations in Building and Urban Design*. Canada: John Wiley & Sons.

Golany, G. S. (1996). Urban design morphology and thermal performance. *Atmospheric Environment*, 30(3): 455–465.

Goldreich, Y. (1992). Urban climate study in Johannesburg, a sub-tropical city located on a ridge – a review. *Atmospheric Environment, Part B: Urban Atmosphere*, 26(3): 407–420.

HKPSG (2011). *Hong Kong Planning Standards and Guidelines*. Planning Department, HK Government. Available at: http://www.pland.gov.hk/pland_en/tech_doc/hkpsg/full/index.htm (Accessed on 24 September 2013).

Höppe, P. (1999). The physiological equivalent temperature—a universal index for the biometeorological assessment of the thermal environment. *International Journal of Biometeorology*, 43(2): 71–75.

Hui, S. C. M. (2001). Low energy building design in high-density urban cities. *Renewable Energy*, 24(3): 627–640.

IAUC (2013). *International Association for Urban Climate*. Available at: http://www.urban-climate.org/ (Accessed on 24 September 2013).

Kuttler, W. (2002). Local cold air and its significance for the urban climate. Paper presented at *the 4th AMS Symposium on the Urban environment*, 56–57. Norfolk, Virginia, 20–24 May.

Lam, J. S. L., Lau, A. K. H., and Fung, J. C. H. (2006). Application of refined land-use categories for high resolution mesoscale atmospheric modeling. *Boundary-Layer Meteorology*, 119(2): 263–288. doi: 10.1007/s10546-005-9027-3.

Landsberg, H. E. (1981). *The Urban Climate*. New York: Academic Press.

Leung, Y. K., Yip, K. M. and Yeung, K. H. (2008). Relationship between thermal index and mortality in Hong Kong. *Meterological Application*, 15(3): 399–409.

Lin, C. H., Lin, T. P. and Hwang, R. L. (2013). Thermal comfort for urban parks in subtropics: Understanding vsitor's perceptions, behavior and attendance. *Advances in Meteorology*, 2013. doi:10.1155/2013/640473.

Lindberg, F. (2007). Modelling the urban climate using a local governmental geo-database. *Meteorological Application*, 14(3): 263–273.

Lüttig, G. W. (1972). Naturräumliches potential I, II and II. In: *Niedersachsen: Industrieland mit Zukunft. Niedersächs.* Hannover: Minist. Wirtsch, 9–10.

Mills, G., Cleugh, H., Emmanuel, R., Endlicher, W., Erell, E., McGranahan, G., Ng, E., Nickson, A., Rosenthal, J. and Steemer, K. (2010). Climate information for improved planning and management of mega cities (needs perspectives). In: Sivakumar, M. V. K. *et al.* (eds.), *Procedia Environmental Sciences, Vol.1, Special Issue of World Climate Conference-3*, 228–246. Geneva, Switzerland, 31 August–4 September 2009.

Montaveza, J. P., Gonzalez-Rouco, J. F., and Valerob, F. (2008). A simple model for estimating the maximum intensity of nocturnal urban heat island. *International Journal of Climatology*, 28(2): 235–242.

Ng, E. (ed.) (2009a). *Designing High-density Cities for Social and Environmental Sustainability*. London: Earthscan.

Ng, E. (2009b). Policies and technical guidelines for urban planning of high-density cities – Air Ventilation Assessment (AVA) of Hong Kong. *Building and Environment*, 44(7), 1478–1488.

Ng, E. (2009c). Air Ventilation Assessment (AVA) for high-density city – an experience from Hong Kong. In: Demers, C. M. H. and Potvin, A. (eds.), *Proceedings of 26th International Conference on Passive and Low Energy Architecture (PLEA2009): Architecture, Energy and the Occupant's Perspective.* Quebec City, Canada, 22–24 June 2009. Quebec: Les Presses de l'Université Laval, 1.2.8.

Ng, E. (2009d). Wind and heat environment in densely built urban areas in Hong Kong, (invited paper). *Global Environmental Research.* A Special Issue on Wind Disaster Risk and Global Environment Change, 13(2): 169–178.

Ng, E. (2012). Towards a planning and practical understanding for the need of meteorological and climatic information for the design of high-density cities – a case based study of Hong Kong. *International Journal of Climatology*, 32(4): 582–598.

Ng, E. and An, X. P. (2011). City planning with urban wind in complex coastal cities – an experience of Hong Kong. In: Bodart, M. and Evrard, A. (eds.), *Proceedings of 27th International conference on Passive and Low Energy Architecture (PLEA2010).* Louvain-la-Neuve, Belgium, 13–15 July. Presses Universitaires de Louvain, vol. 1, 227–232.

Ng, E. and Fung, J. (2008). Determining site wind availability for Air Ventilation Assessment in Hong Kong's coastal and highly complex topographical conditions, invited paper. In: Choi, C. K. *et al.* (eds.), *Proceedings of 4th International Conference on Advances in Wind & Structures AWAS'08.* Seoul, 29–31 May. (CD-ROM). (http://awas08.kaist.ac.kr).

Ng, E., Kwok, K. and Hitchcock, P.(2008a). *Wind Tunnel Benchmarking Studies – Batch 1, Urban Climatic Map and Standards for Wind Environment – Feasibility Study*, Technical Report for Planning Department HKSAR.

Ng, E., Ren, C., Wang, U. and Katzschner, L. (2008b). *Methodologies and Results of Field Measurement, Urban Climatic Map and Standards for Wind Environment – Feasibility Study*, Technical Report for Planning Department HKSAR, 72 pgs.

Ng, E., Kwok, K. and Hitchcock, P. (2010). *Working Paper 2, Wind Tunnel Benchmarking Studies – Batch 2, Urban Climatic Map and Standards for Wind Environment – Feasibility Study*, Technical Report for Planning Department HKSAR.

Nichol, J. E. and Wong, M. S. (2008). Spatial variability of air temperature and appropriate resolution for satellite-derived air temperature estimation. *International Journal of Remote Sensing*, 29(24): 7213–7223.

Niu, J. L. (2004). Some significant environmental issues in high-rise residential building design in urban areas. *Energy and Buildings*, 36(12): 1259–1263.

Oke, T. R. (1981). Canyon geometry and the nocturnal heat island: Comparison of scale model and field observations. *Internation Journal of Climatology*, 1(3): 237–254.

Oke, T. R. (1988). *Boundary Layer Climates.* 2nd edition. New York: Routledge.

PlanD (2003). *Feasibility Study for Establishment of Air Ventilation Assessment System.* Available at: http://www.pland.gov.hk/pland_en/p_study/comp_s/avas/avas_eng.html (Accessed on 24 September 2013).

PlanD (2012). *Final Report, Urban Climatic map and Standards for Wind Environment – Feasibility Study.* Planning Department, Hong Kong Government. Available at: http://www.pland.gov.hk/pland_en/p_study/prog_s/ucmapweb/ucmap_project/content/reports/final_report.pdf (Accessed on 25 September 2013).

PlanD (2013). *Air Ventilation Assessment Register*. Planning Department, HK Government. Available at: http://www.pland.gov.hk/pland_en/info_serv/ava_register/government.html (Accessed on 24 September 2013).

Ren, C. and Ng, E. (2009). An initial investigation on microclimatic environment in high-density city — spot field measurement study in Hong Kong. In: *Proceedings of 7th International Conference on Urban Climate (ICUC2009)*. Yokohama, Japan. 29 June–3 July. International Association of Urban Climate. (CD-ROM).

Ren, C., Ng, E. and Katzschner, L. (2011). Urban climatic map studies: a review. *International Journal of Climatology*, 31(15): 2213–2233. doi: 10.1002/joc.2237.

de Schiller S. and Evans, J. M. (1996). Training architects and planners to design with urban microclimates. *Atmospheric Environment*, 30(3): 449–454.

Svensson, M. K. (2004). Sky view factor analysis-implications for urban air temperature differences. *Meteorological Application*, 11(3): 201–211.

TC 01/06 (2006). *Technical Circular on Air Ventilation Assessment*. Development Bureau, HK Government. Available at: http://www.devb.gov.hk/filemanager/en/content_679/hplb-etwb-tc-01-06.pdf (Accessed on 24 September 2013).

Team Clean (2003). *Report on Measures to Improve Environmental Hygiene in Hong Kong*. Available at: http://www.legco.gov.hk/yr02-03/english/panels/fseh/papers/fe0815tc_rpt.pdf (Accessed on 24 September 2013).

UN (2008). *United Nations Expert Group Meeting on Population Distribution, Urbanisation, Internal Migration and Development*. New York: Population Division, Department of Economic and Social Affairs, United Nations Secretariat, 21–23 January 2008 [UN/POP/EGM-URB/2008/01]. Available at: http://www.un.org/esa/population/meetings/EGM_PopDist/P01_UNPopDiv.pdf (Accessed on 24 September 2013).

Unger, J. (2004). Intra-urban relationship between surface geometry and urban heat island: Review and new approach, *Climate Research*, 27: 253–264.

Unger, J. (2009). Connection between urban heat island and sky view factor approximated by a software tool on a 3D urban database. *International Journal of Environment and Pollution*, 36(1/2/3): 59–80.

Upmanis, H. and Chen, D. (1999). Influence of geographical factors and meteorological variables on nocturnal urban-park temperature differences – a case study of summer 1995 in Göteborg, Sweden. *Climate Research*, 13(2): 125–139.

VDI (1997). *VDI-Standard: VDI 3787 Part 1 Environmental Meteorology – Climate and Air Pollution Maps for Cities and Regions*. Berlin: Beuth Verlag.

VDI (2008). *VDI-Standard: VDI 3787 Part 2 Environmental Meteorology – Methods for the Human Biometeorological Evaluation of Climate and Air Quality for Urban and Regional Planning at Regional Level, Part I: Climate*. Berlin: Beuth Verlag.

Weber, S. and Kuttler, W. (2003). Analysis of the nocturnal cold air dynamic and quality of a urban ventilation zone (in German). *Gefahrstoffe-Reinhaltung der Luft*, 63(9): 381–386.

Yim, S. H. L., Fung, J. C. H., Lau, A. K. H. and Lot, S. C. (2007). Developing a high-resolution wind map for a complex terrain with a coupled MM5/CALMET system. *Journal of Geophysical Research*, 112(5): D05106. doi:10.1029/2006JD007752.

Chapter 11

# Urban climatic map studies in Germany

## Hesse

*Lutz Katzschner and Sebastian Kupski*

### Introduction

As part of the research project KLIMZUG North Hesse, which deals with the issue of how to adapt to climate change, the Faculty of Environmental Meteorology was commissioned to map the forecast climate changes taking place within the next few decades in the model region of North Hesse in Germany.

One method to make this complex data available and easily accessible for planners and politicians was the use of urban climatic maps (UCMaps) in which the climatic condition of a particular area is analysed and illustrated in terms of average mean temperatures shown in the form of maps. A standard scale for these climate calculations is approximately 1:50,000, which allows greater cities or conurbations to be shown in sufficient detail. The city of Kassel and its surrounding area with approximately 300,000 residents is situated in the area of investigation. UCMaps of this area have constantly been updated since 1990. Sufficient data and expertise make it possible to take the next step and scale up to the entire area of North Hesse. For this purpose, the existing computer model had to be modified, optimising the resolution from 50m to 100m and enlarging the scale to 1:400,000. By technically adapting the computer model, it was possible to analyse the entire area without loss of content and, based on the results of the analysis, to map the impact that climate change has on people.

### Climate analysis by means of urban climatic maps

A UCMap constitutes a climatic assessment that is developed for a certain geographic location. A corresponding data set is a main prerequisite for this complex task. From a climatic point of view, factors such as information on elevation and flowing waters offer clues to illustrate natural conditions. Similarly, anthropogenic factors play a crucial role. Particularly in cities, changes to the ground surface induced by people have the greatest, and in most cases also the most negative, impact. For this reason, data with reference to land use and information on buildings are also required. The more detailed the input data the more precise and detailed will be the analysis.

Next to this geographical information, the knowledge of the parameters relevant to the climate is of equal importance. The ventilation of dense urban areas, in particular, which proves to be highly effective, depends on location with reference to the regional circulation system. However, local as well as regional wind circulations also develop through physical processes and can be calculated as part of an urban climatic map, necessitating, however, a set of measuring data for the calibration of the results. Apart from carrying out continuous and stationary measurements, mobile measurement surveys should be carried out during relevant weather conditions, with a comparatively high spatial resolution. Additional climatic parameters can be derived from the geographic location of the research area.

## Technical implementation of an urban climatic map

When putting together a wide range of technical information, the weighting, or influence, of the individual factor is of great importance. As these factors vary from one location to another for climatic reasons, there is currently no automated system in place for the development of a UCMap (Lohmeyer, 2008). Because of this, only a systematic approach to case studies can be used since the climate classification of each respective generic context has always to be adjusted to suit the particular area.

General climate conditions are very heterogeneous as an outcome of geographical location, the elevation of the research area or continental or maritime influence. Apart from such generic factors, there are a number of small-scale factors. On a smaller scale, various factors, such as inland lakes or valleys, can strongly influence local climate. Therefore, an interim assessment of the climate is crucial while, at the same time, a greater section than that defined by geographical area has to be taken into consideration.

The data material used for the computations contains topographic maps, a digital terrain model (DTM), land-use planning, several aerial pictures and thermal flights, climate studies, as well as continuously collected data from monitoring stations and high-resolution spatial measurement surveys. Several thematic maps are generated from the multitude of input data which are then put together by means of various geo-analytical processes with varying emphases.

After grouping the theme maps into the two climatic components, 'dynamics' and 'thermionics', which both have a distinct impact on different levels of the regional climate, the product will be grouped together by means of appropriate functions and subsequent generalisations in the form of a UCMap. In this example it is shown as a climatope in different colours.

The dynamic component includes the airflow factor and therefore the fresh air and cold air flows which develop, as a physical condition, even without stimulus of the regional flow condition and the main wind direction which, during corresponding weather conditions, determines wind circulation. An additional, relevant theme map of dynamics is the impact of slope lifts. These flows originate from the mountain-valley-wind system which occurs during the day and can gain tremendous strength depending on the prominence of mountain relief (Häckel, 1985). Accordingly, the thematic map has been developed on the basis of the DTM and the flow data. Other criteria, such as roughness measurements of the earth's surface, were also integrated in these computations in order to realistically map the ventilation system and to calibrate the actual degree of impact with the help of the data readings.

The climatic phenomenon, beside the ventilation situation, additionally consists of the thermal property of the earth's surface. Since this component represents the base and has to be universally mapped correspondingly, the current land-use mapping was used as the basis to be able to make a preliminary classification. This detailed input data will then be completed with additional thematic maps whereas the surface sealing grade provides information on the heat storage capacity, as well as open spaces with a low surface roughness which represents areas where cold air is produced. In this context it is the albedo which is a central variable because different reflection and absorption behaviours substantially define the thermal balance of the urban boundary layer (Oke, 2006). In this complex of themes the urban heat island factor is clearly visible because due to the heating of artificial building material, combined with the high heat storage capacity and a slow cooling rate, higher air temperatures are generated in the city than in undeveloped rural areas, especially at night (Baumüller *et al.*, 1993; Hupfer and Kuttler, 1998).

## Urban climatic maps as a resource to illustrate future developments

Aside from mapping current climatic conditions, prognoses of future changes based on these conditions can be modelled. In this way, for instance, climate changes caused by global warming can be outlined. For this purpose, the UCMap with the analysed climatope properties is expanded with prognosticated climate trends of current projections.

The main assumption of future climatic events is the increase of high pressure weather conditions with limited air exchange from which an overall increase of the annual irradiation sum and longer radiation periods will result. In this context, the albedo of the earth's surface becomes more of a concern, and climate change with an increase of heat load is increasing. Starting from this assumption, the climatopes were allocated with specific attributes that allow for a realistic downscaling of regional projections to a user-friendly scale. One clear result is an increase of heat stress in the already disadvantaged areas with a high share of industrial building material, as opposed to unsealed areas with vegetation that are not as affected. A consequence will be an irregular heat load increase in already disadvantaged city districts.

## Urban climatic map for the model region North Hesse

The area comprises the five north Hessian rural districts as well as the city of Kassel. For this area with approximately 6,900km$^2$, a UCMap was developed by means of Geographic Information Systems (GIS) consisting of several theme maps. The main map on which all additional maps are based shows the thermal climatope distribution as well as the climate-relevant system of air channels in the tested area. The bioclimate maps make statements regarding climatic conditions in a human-biometeorological context, i.e. with reference to the impact they have on the human being at present, as well as in 30 years.

With reference to climate functions and the analysed climatope types, there is a statistical refinement (statistic downscaling) of existing regional climate models. This makes it possible to break down the impact of the projected climate change on a regional and user-oriented scale taking into account people's thermal comfort.

The twofold analysis is carried out by subdividing dynamic and thermal aspects (see Figure 11.1). Following this, the reciprocal influence in the sense of an impact study will be examined and correspondingly included:

(A) *Dynamic analysis*

(i) Linking of dynamically relevant (and air-hygiene-relevant) survey levels, and therefore the classification of e.g. the specific activity of cold and fresh air production areas. (ii) Verification through data from meteorological measurements for presenting flow ratios.

(B) *Thermal analysis*

(i) Linking of thermal (and air-hygiene-relevant) characteristics of properties among each other as well as the dynamic impact factors of the relief and the flow structure (evaluation

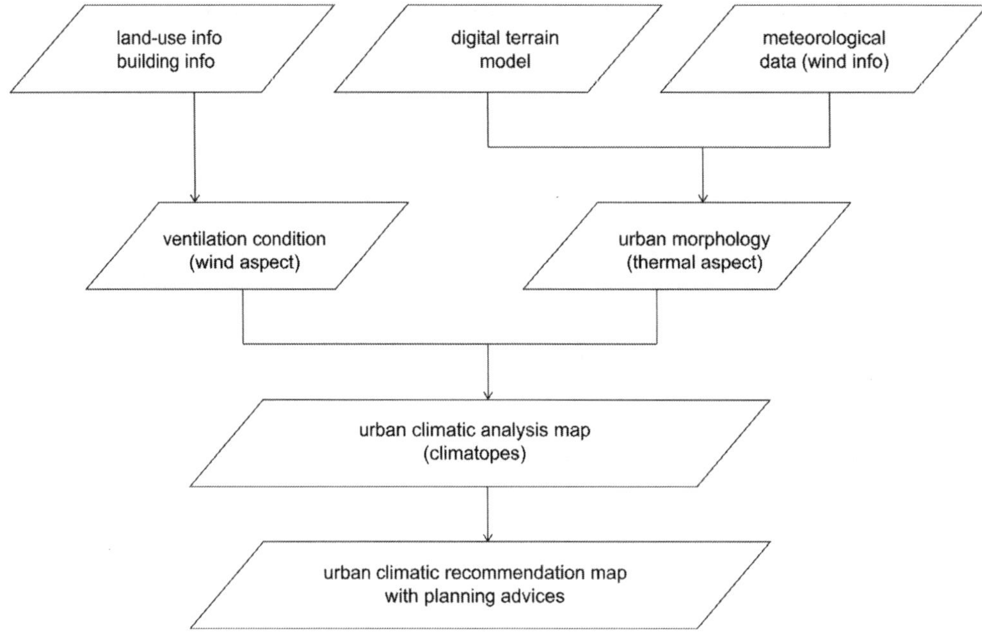


*Figure 11.1* Principle procedure for generating an urban climatic map according to Lohmeyer (2008).

Source: Authors, based on Lohmeyer, 2008

of e.g. the emergence of cold air pockets and the cooling impact on overheated areas). (ii) Verification through data from meteorological measurement for evaluating thermal ratios.

### *Functional synthesis*

A UCMap shows the link between the dynamic and thermal thematic levels with reference to climatic potentials, deficits and functions; it symbolises an ideal rendering of the existing area-related climatic situation as a starting point for the climatic evaluation. Here is where climatopes (areas of similar regional climatic properties) are ultimately generated.

### *Characterization of single aspects and criteria*

Based on the functional analysis and the functional synthesis as well as the assumption of specific questions posed by KLIMZUG North Hesse, an evaluation concerning climate potential areas as well as climate deficit areas is made. For this purpose, there are altogether seven single evaluation criteria listed which are separately looked at and assessed. This serves to be a starting point for a summary of the total evaluation. It furthermore integrates the dynamic component in the form of air channels.

### *Evaluation synthesis and assessment*

With the help of the present map, the areas in North Hesse can be localised and categorised by means of the legend in its climatic complex. Knowledge of the various influences of the complex system allows for technically correct yet user-friendly application of the map during all planning decisions. Thus, a combination of several tools such as guidelines, which are based on the climatope analysis, can easily be implemented.

## Legend

The legend of the UCMap (thermal analysis) is easily decodable due to its clearly identifiable colour scheme and contains not only the designation of the climatopes but also a description of their properties (see Table 11.1). The legend is divided into climatic potential areas and deficits (see Plate 11.1). Furthermore, the level of the air channels is shown as part of the finished product although the climatic impact has already been included in the climatope analysis. This serves to improve orientation and to understand impact correlations.

*Table 11.1* Climatopes and their description of North Hesse's urban climatic map.

| Climatope | Description |
|---|---|
| Natural Climate Altitudes (climate potential area) | • Fresh air and cold air production areas<br>• Altitudes, mountains that are visibly higher than the surrounding investigated area<br>• A reduction of air temperature by adiabatic change due to elevation<br>• Exposed areas for wind and precipitation<br>• Far away from emission sources |
| Natural Climate Forest (climate potential area) | • Mainly fresh air production areas<br>• Commonly high-altitude areas that consist of vegetation and/or slopes and therefore cause a reduced air temperature compared to the regional average<br>• No permanent emission sources |
| Natural Climate Open Land (climate potential area) | • Cold air production areas with direct balancing influence on unfavourable spaces<br>• Natural areas that contain favourable thermal properties, possibly close to populated areas<br>• Low emissions and a high proportion of open areas |
| Mixed and Transitional Climate (climate conflict area) | • Buffer zones between deficit and potential areas<br>• Possibly with built-up areas and other uses, with, however, above-average positive parameters such as slope angle, low surface sealing and/or open spaces nearby |
| Overheating Tendencies (climate deficit area) | • Suburban climate, overheating areas<br>• Characterised by built-up areas with a high proportion of vegetation and/or suitable topographic location<br>• Emissions possibly caused by traffic, industry and household emissions |
| Moderate Overheating (climate deficit area) | • Urban overheated area<br>• Mainly highly dense spaces, causing an unfavourable topographic location in conjunction with unfavourable ventilation conditions<br>• Concentration of air pollutants |
| Strong Overheating (climate deficit area) | • Overheated urban centre<br>• Very high built-up density of a city (Kassel)<br>• High building volume, nearly no vegetation<br>• Greatly reduced ventilation and additionally high emission values |
| Air channels | • Constituent part of the topographically conditioned ventilation and circulation system<br>• Essential factor for bioclimatic conditions and air hygiene |

Source: Authors

### *Bioclimatic analysis*

In order to be able to make statements on climatic conditions that have a direct influence on people, the UCMap was used as output data. Based on that, climate data from measurements and simulations were used to calculate the thermal perception people have at specific locations. By using climate data which can generate data for the future from climate models, it was possible in the next step, beside the existing current one, also to generate a future prognosis for North Hesse.

### *Thermal index as basis for characterization*

To describe the properties and the impact of climatopes of the UCMaps on people and to designate the level of stress, the thermal evaluation index was used as a base of the Physiologically Equivalent Temperature (PET) (Höppe, 1999). The respective categories extend from potential areas (bracing and mild climate), which have a particular positive effect on human well-being, to mixed climatopes and overheating climatopes, that can have a negative effect on people's well-being and health.

PET refers to the subjective perception people have and is allocated in respective categories from cold and cool to hot and very hot. This index contains a complex composition of various climate parameters (air temperature, wind velocity, humidity and mean radiation temperature). By means of comparative measurements, it was possible to calibrate the classification and to transfer it to the entire area of North Hesse. When using measured climate data, the mapping of the bioclimatic situation in reality is possible. In this case, readings provided by Hessisches Landesamt für Umwelt und Geologie (HLUG) [Hessian regional authority for the environment and geology] in conjunction with our own data were applied to illustrate the current bioclimate.

This procedure comprises also the option, beside measured data, to put in modelled weather data from climate models and therefore generate the bioclimate of the future. Consequently, comparing current thermal conditions with those of the future could be possible.

### *Climate regeneration*

For the calculation of the climatic conditions within the climatopes, data from the test runs and future tests of WETTREG 2010, promoted by the global model ECHAM-5, were used for the research area. It is assumed that a change of weather conditions (more frequent occurrences of autochthonous weather conditions) in the area to be researched will cause an increased solar irradiation sum. This will result in a greater significance of albedo which will intensify the already existing urban–rural effect in the future. What is relevant for the people, in this case, is the PET value mentioned in Chapter 10 which refers to a complex formula that due to human-bioclimatic reasons could not be averaged over a period of time. For that reason, the maximum air temperatures, taken from the available data, were measured at a height of 2m over a period of 30 years, and averaged. Mean values of additional parameters were refrained from, and in order to generate the 'climate' based on PET, wind speeds were calculated depending on location, topography, orography, height, slope angle and roughness.

The average radiation temperature was generally calculated for a high pressure weather condition (maximum solar radiation) and placed on 21 June at 1 pm (CET). For the region North Hesse, the global radiation of 790W/m$^2$ is used while the proportion of scattered radiation is approximately 30 per cent.

The impact of humidity or rather vapour pressure in this scale is negligible which means that this value was estimated to be 50 per cent of relative humidity in all climatopes.

For the calculation of the thermal indices, the computer model RayMan version 1.2 was used. Besides the above-mentioned input data, the data for wind velocity was used depending on air channels and height above sea level. In addition, various land uses by means of the albedo value according to T. R. Oke (2006) depending on the climatopes were applied.

For additional calculations a standard person (male; 1.75m tall; 35 years; 75kg) is taken as a base, having a mean energy demand of 80W and a thermal resistance of his clothes of 0.9clo.

## *Applied climate signals*

In order to compare the climatic conditions of the current situation with those of the future prognosis within the respective climatopes, the scheme as in Figure 11.2 was applied.

Starting from an evident urban–rural impact which can arise from a metrological analysis during high pressure weather conditions in the summer in North Hesse, this ratio was transferred to the climatope distribution of the UCMap. Two monitoring stations of the Hessian regional authority for the environment and geology which are situated in the two climatopes most distant from each other were evaluated. The monitoring station, Witzenhausen Wald, according to the climatope distribution, is situated in an area that is categorised as bracing climatope, while the station Kassel Mitte clearly falls in category overheating climatope type 2.

From these comparative and calibrated measurements a temperature, gradient of 5°C was measured during the heat wave in the year 2008. This ratio shows the range of estimated air temperatures for the calculation of the PET. As an average input value an air temperature of 20°C is taken for the 'neutral' climate of mixed and transitional climatope which is enlarged by a spectrum range of −2.5°C to +2.5°C (see Figure 11.2).

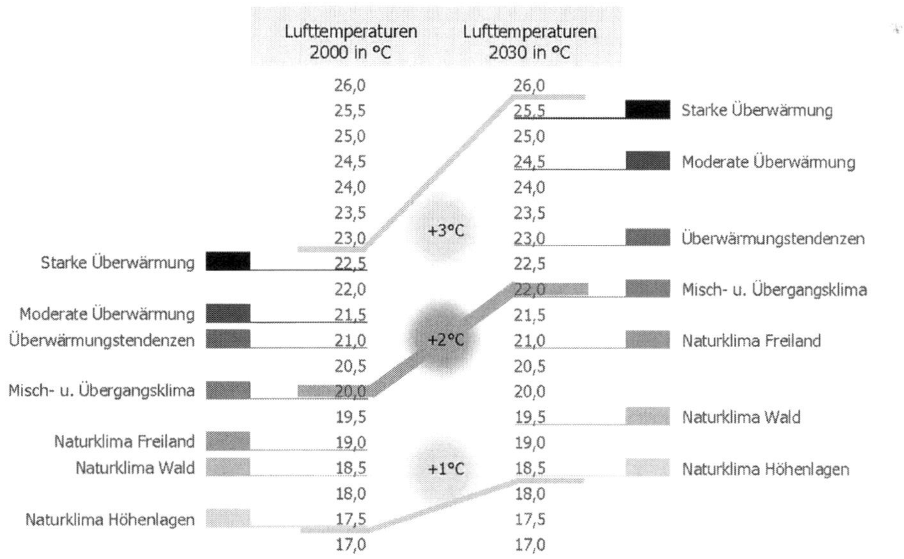


*Figure 11.2* Generation of ambient data, present into the future.

Source: Authors

In order to make an estimate of future change, the mean climate change signal for North Hesse was calculated. Resulting changes in air temperatures are shown in Figure 11.2. Because of the prognosticated rise of air temperature and the solar radiation sum, effecting an increase of the temperature gradient (urban–rural), the values shown are taken as a base for the generation of the data set on the future. It is assumed that there will be a greater span between favourable and unfavourable climates; however, it is expected that the rise in temperatures will not take place in a linear way, which would otherwise result in a uniform rise in air temperature, but rather as a varying temperature rise within the climatopes.

Bracing and mild climatopes will consequently experience a milder increase whereas the overheating climatopes will be characterised by a higher increase than could be expected from the mean climate changing signal.

## References

Baumüller, J., Hoffmann, U. and Reuter, U. (1993). *Städtebauliche Klimafibel – Hinweise für die Bauleitplanung, Folge 2*. Stuttgart: Wirtschaftschaftsministerium Baden-Württemberg.

Häckel, H. (1985). *Meteorologie*. Stuttgart: UTB Ulmer Verlag.

Höppe, P. (1999). The physiological equivalent temperature – a universal index for the biometeorological assessment of the thermal environment. *International Journal of Biometeorology*, 43(2): 71–75.

Hupfer, P. and Kuttler, W. (1998). *Witterung und Klima*. Stuttgart: B. G. Teubner.

Lohmeyer, A. (2008). *Klimafunktions und Klimaplanungskarten*, Lohmeyer Aktuell, 20/2008, Karlsruhe.

Oke, T. R. (2006). *Boundary Layer Climates*. New York: Routledge.

Chapter 12

# Urban climatic map studies in Singapore

*Nyuk-Hien Wong, Steve Kardinal Jusuf, Lutz Katzschner and Edward Ng*

## Singapore urban heat island

Urban heat island (UHI) phenomenon has become a topical concern in many major cities worldwide (Oke and East, 1971; Padmanabhamurty, 1991; Sani 1991; Akbari *et al.*, 1992; Eliasson, 1996; Giridharan *et al.*, 2004) including Singapore (Wong and Chen, 2009). This phenomenon is aggravated due to several factors, such as the loss of greenery area for the purpose of urban development, low wind velocity due high building density, and changes of surface coating materials (Takahashi *et al.*, 2004).

Singapore measures 43km from west to east and 23km from north to south. Singapore's land area has increased by 20 per cent as a result of land reclamation since 1960 (URA, 2008). Singapore is known as a garden city that has no distinct boundary between urban and rural areas. However, most of the built-up areas, such as residential areas, industrial areas and the Central Business District (CBD) area are located in the southern part. Therefore, it is reasonable to categorise the southern part as the 'urban' area, while the northern part is the 'rural' area. In the Singapore UHI study (Wong and Chen, 2009), a thermal satellite image was used to provide a broad and visible surface temperature distribution of the entire Singapore island.

In Figure 12.1, the warm regions, represented in white, are mostly located in the southern part of the island, which has been considered as 'urban' areas. On the other hand, 'rural' areas are relatively cool and they are represented by grey and dark grey colours in the northern part of the island. The image provides evidence that the UHI effect can be observed in Singapore with a clear boundary between 'urban' and 'rural' areas. Based on the island-wide mobile survey, the highest air temperature of 28.4°C was found in the Central Business District (CBD) area, which has less vegetation.

A higher air temperature was also observed in the industrial area. Two different urban morphology characteristics have caused these high temperatures. The first is that the industrial area has a large exposed concrete surface area. The industrial buildings are arranged far apart from one another with no greenery in between. Another characteristic is that the industrial buildings are designed with a combination of metal pitched roofs and flat concrete roofs. Both characteristics contribute to an increase in temperature because of the extensive use of concrete and other heat-absorbing surfaces, by decreasing the surface moisture that is available for the evapotranspiration. Furthermore, more solar radiation is absorbed and re-radiated as heat because dry surfaces have a higher absorptivity.

Meanwhile, the lowest air temperature of 24.0°C was observed in the north-western part of Singapore, where the nature reserve is located. The cooling effect of the nature reserve extends to the nearby built environment; the closer to the reserve, the lower the temperature experienced. Figure 12.2 depicts the UHI profile of Singapore, with the intensity of 4.4K.

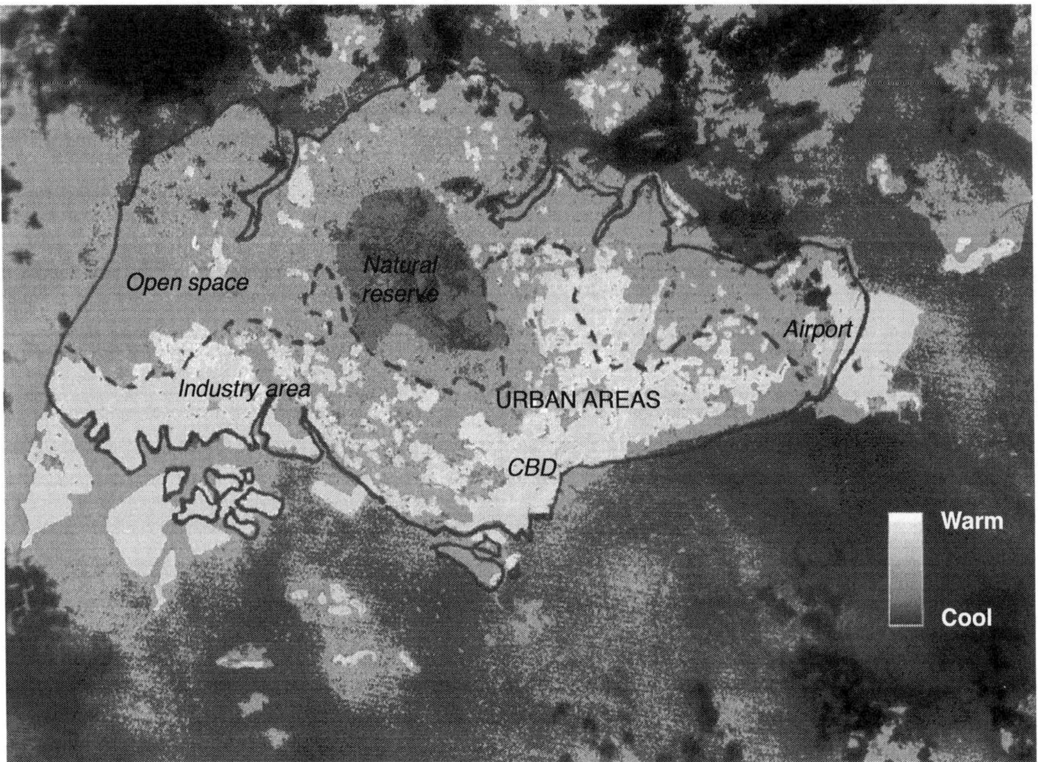


*Figure 12.1* Thermal satellite image coincides with the boundary of 'urban' and 'rural' areas.
Source: Wong and Chen, 2009

A more detailed study, separating the daytime and night-time temperature data (Jusuf *et al.*, 2007), demonstrated the existence of a temperature pattern that is closely related to urban land use. During daytime, the industrial area exhibits a higher temperature than commercial and business areas, and the park area has the lowest temperature. On the contrary, at night, commercial and business areas exhibit a higher temperature than the industrial and airport areas (see Figure 12.3). The industrial areas consist of low buildings, large pavement surfaces, with less vegetation and light roof structures with less shading and extensive use of heat-absorbing building materials. As a result, they have higher temperatures during daytime. On the other hand, they are cool during night-time, since the heat stored during daytime is released to the sky with less obstruction from surrounding buildings. This temperature pattern indicates its relationship with the surrounding distribution of greenery, building and pavement.

## The influence of urban morphology on urban air temperature

At the macro-scale, incident solar radiation controls the climate condition (Kiehl, 1992) and it varies at different latitudes, mainly due to the difference in solar radiation received at the surface. The latitudinal distribution of solar radiation is large at low altitudes and much less near the poles. This latitudinal imbalance of net radiation for the surface-plus-atmosphere system as a whole (positive in lower altitudes and negative in higher altitudes) combined with the effect of the earth's

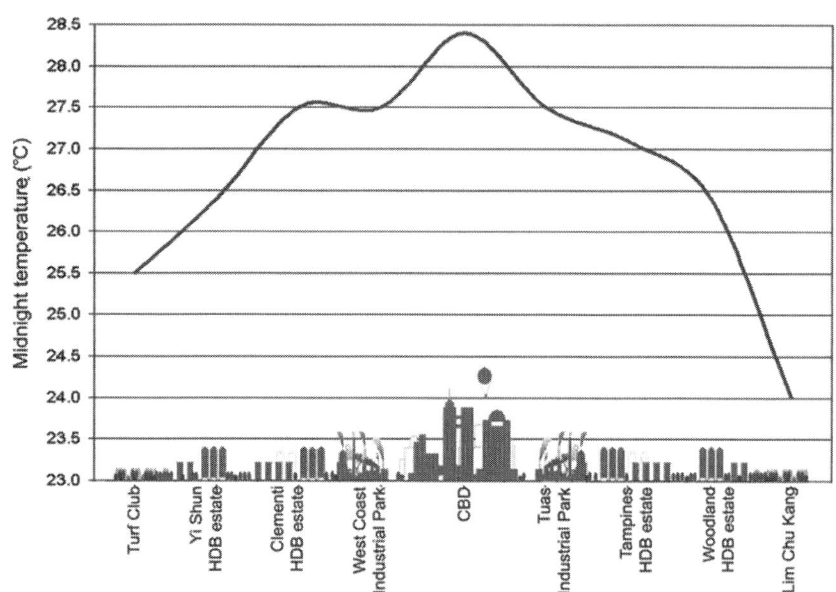


*Figure 12.2* The urban heat island (UHI) profile in Singapore.

Source: Wong and Chen, 2009

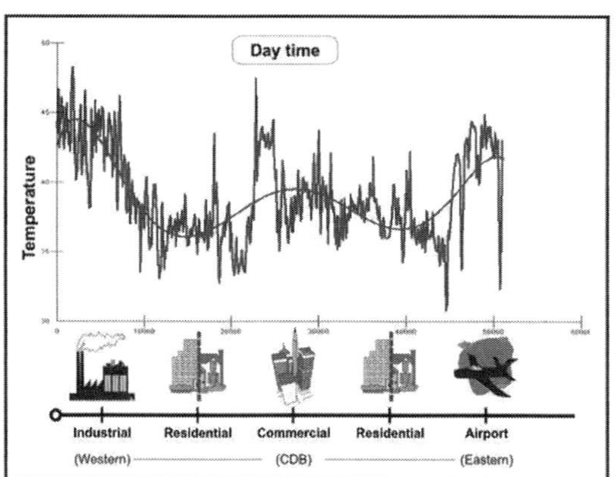


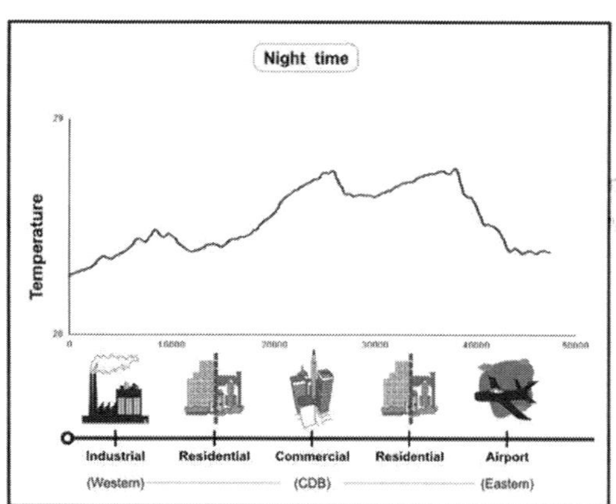


*Figure 12.3* Daytime (left) and night-time (right) temperature profile from west to east of Singapore.

Source: Jusuf *et al.*, 2007

rotation on its axis produces the dynamic circulation system of the atmosphere; see Figure 12.4 (Henderson-Sellers and McGuffie, 1987).

Considering a small island such as Singapore, at the macro-scale, it is logical to assume that Singapore has a uniform temperature above its urban canopy layer. Due to the urban morphologically different urban forms of design and planning, there are temperature differences at different locations in the city, known as '*intra-urban microclimatic air temperature differences*'. The air temperature

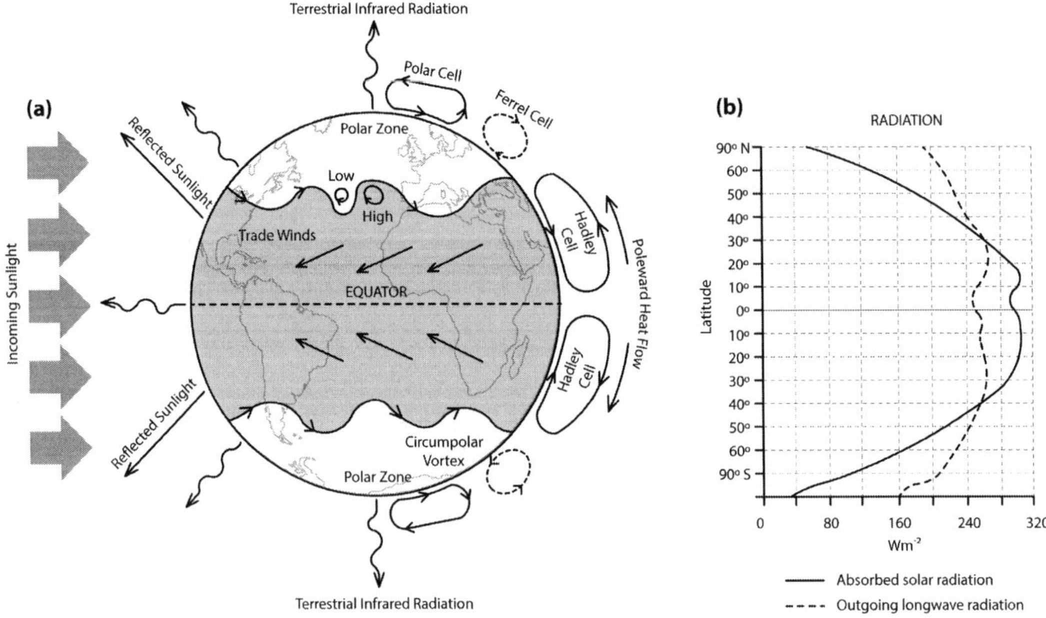


*Figure 12.4* Latitudinal energy balance of the Earth.
Source: Henderson-Sellers and McGuffie, 1987

of a point at a certain height level is a function of the local climate characteristics, which deviates according to the surrounding urban morphology characteristics (building, pavement and greenery) at a '***certain radius***' (see Figure 12.5).

As shown in Figure 12.5, the surrounding habitat, especially building and vegetation, greatly influences the incident solar radiation received by a surface in an urban environment. Building and vegetation determine the 'openness' of a surface, known as the Sky View Factor or SVF (Cleugh, 1995). The SVF is the percentage of a point's field of view that is occupied by the sky as opposed to the buildings, trees or any other object in the landscape. An urban canyon with a large aspect ratio will have a small SVF; flat fields with an unobstructed horizon will have a large SVF.

The correlation between SVF and urban air temperature is complex. Regional factors influence the urban air temperature (Santamouris, 2001). A group of researchers concluded that SVF is one of the UHI problem sources; the lower the SVF, the higher the urban temperature (Oke, 1981; Yamashita *et al.*, 1986; Arnfield, 1990; Chapman *et al.*, 2001). On the other hand, another group of researchers has found a weak correlation between urban air temperature and the SVF, although a good correlation was found between the latter and surface temperature (Barring *et al.*, 1985; Eliasson, 1991, 1996).

Vegetation is another aspect of the urban fabric that reduces the 'openness' to the sky determined by the density of its foliage. Vegetation reduces the radiative heat loss due to the continuous warmth of the buildings and street relative to the trees (Oke, 1989). In Singapore's context, the sky openness of an urban fabric is often as a result of the combination factors of urban geometry and trees, in which the greenery blends between the building arrangements and fills its open spaces.

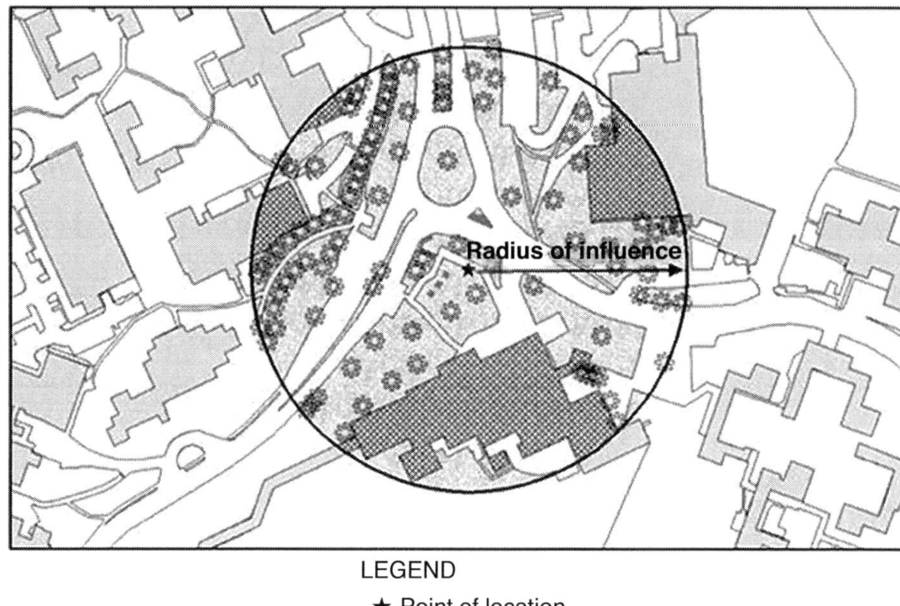


*Figure 12.5* Air temperature of any point is influenced by the surrounding urban morphology condition.

Source: Authors

A comprehensive study in Singapore's green estates concluded that the correlation between SVF and urban air temperature changes according to time (Wong and Jusuf, 2010). During daytime, SVF has a significant and good correlation with air temperature; the higher the SVF, the higher the air temperature. The more open an area is, the more solar radiation is received, which leads to a higher air temperature. Trees reduce the sky openness (i.e. provide shading) and cool the air temperature. At night, the SVF shows a weak correlation with the air temperature. Thus, trees will not reduce the night-time net long-wave loss due to the SVF reduction.

The benefits of greenery on a built environment have been widely investigated (Huang *et al.*, 1987; McPherson *et al.*, 1988; Kawashima, 1991; Akbari *et al.*, 1997; Wong and Chen, 2005). Greenery dissipates incoming solar radiation on the building structures through its effective shading, reduces long-wave radiation exchange between buildings due to the low surface temperatures created by the shading of plants, and reduces the ambient air temperature through evapotranspiration (Wong *et al.*, 2003). Though one tree can already generate the coolness, its impacts are limited only to its surroundings, while clusters of trees and parks are able to extend the cooling effect to the neighbourhood environment (Jaurequi, 1991; Ca *et al.*, 1998; Streiling and Matzarakis, 2003). In Singapore, Chen and Wong (2006) observed that the built environment close to the park has a lower temperature of average 1.3K. Results derived from the TAS simulation showed that every 1K air temperature reduction lowers the cooling energy consumption by 5 per cent. The air temperatures measured inside the parks also have strong relationship with the density of plants, since plants with higher Leaf Area Indexes (LAIs) may cause lower ambient temperatures.

## The methodology behind Singapore's urban climatic map

Similar to other countries' climatic maps, the urban climatic map (UCMap) for Singapore consists of two maps. They are the urban climatic analysis map (UC-AnMap) and the urban climatic recommendation map (UC-ReMap). The UC-AnMap is climate-oriented and presents a classification system of different climatopes, following climatic characteristics of ventilation and urban heat island. It synergistically combines various climatic parameters including the urban morphology parameters described in the previous section as both dynamic potential and thermal load. Later on the climatopes information on the territorial level is used to specify the recommendations in dependence of the existing wind regimes and can also be used for specific planning recommendations. Figure 12.6 shows the principal methodology in deriving UC-AnMaps and UC-ReMaps.

For Singapore's evaluation, the urban climatic map got a classification into climatopes and parallel recommendations could be derived. These recommendations were done in two stages:

- general climatic-based recommendations;
- areal recommendations in different climatic zones.

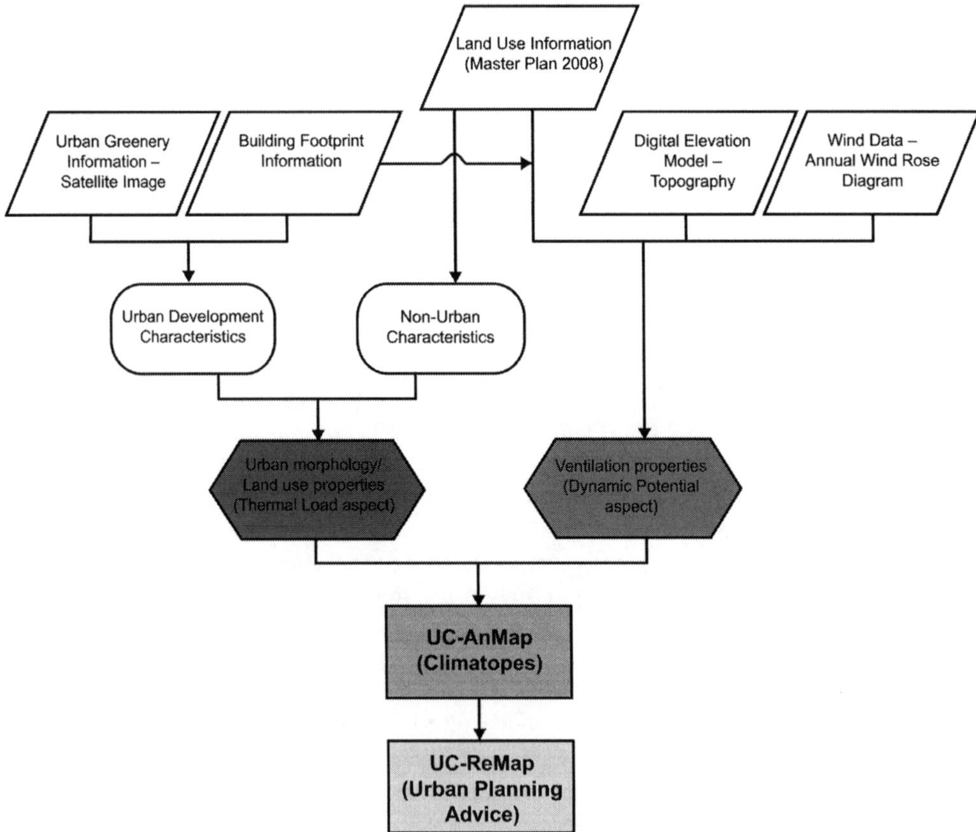


*Figure 12.6* Methodology of a UCMap.

Source: Authors

## Geographical climate data collection and processing

### *Wind information*

Two wind systems of background wind and thermally induced winds were used and analysed separately. Wind roses give information about the annual wind direction distributions. Combined with low surfaces and the channelling effect, ventilation areas and air paths were derived. Besides these phenomena, the thermally induced circulations in Singapore are mainly influenced by the land use differences (sea breeze) and some effects from larger green areas. Both wind systems appear in different dominant or predominant ways (VDI, 1997).

There are two main seasons in Singapore, north-east (NE) monsoon and the south-west (SW) monsoon seasons. The NE monsoon occurs between November and early March with the prevailing wind blowing from the north to north-east. Meanwhile, SW monsoon occurs between June and September with the prevailing wind from the south to south-west. Two short inter-monsoon periods with a duration of two months separate the main seasons.

The wind distribution from three meteorological stations shows that the northerly wind has a slightly higher speed. In the urban climatic analysis, the two dominant wind directions can be dealt with similarly by evaluating the channelling effect. The influence of different weather conditions is marginal. Figure 12.7 shows wind distribution in Singapore.

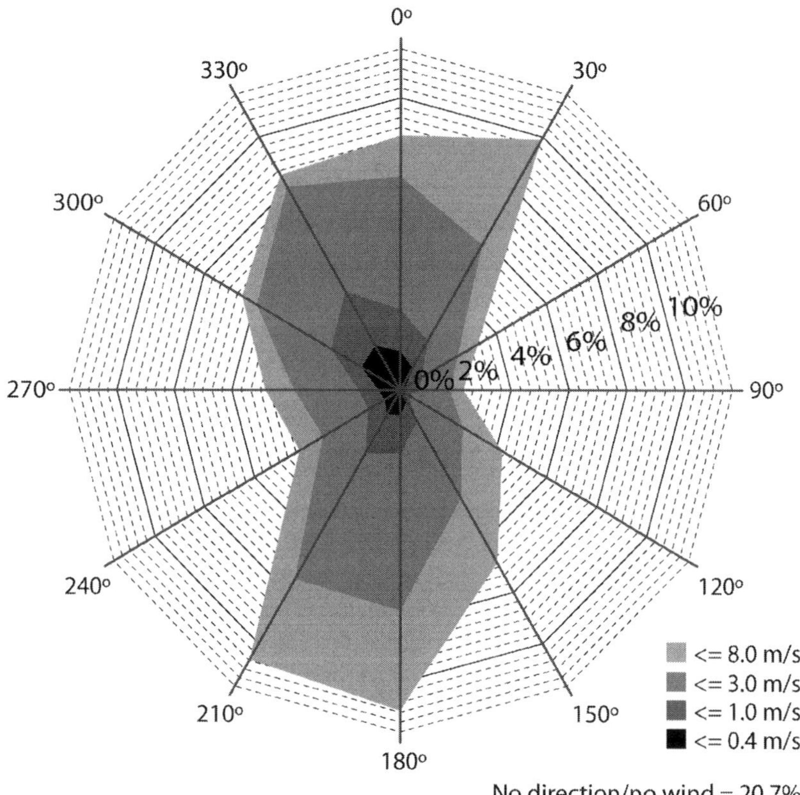


*Figure 12.7* Annual wind distribution of Singapore (Changi airport met. station).

Source: Authors

### Topography

Singapore has a relatively flat terrain, especially in the developed urban areas. The hill is mainly located at the Central Nature Reserve with the highest point at around 160m. This topographical condition makes the temperature differential due to altitude less significant and the downhill convective cooling occurs less intensely. Figure 12.8 shows the topographical condition of Singapore.

### Urban morphology

Understanding its limited land area, the government plans the city as part of the holistic approach of sustainable planning, in which economic sustainability serves as its core and it is supported by other relevant measures of sustainability, including measures such as social, cultural, demographic, educational, political and environmental (Wong and Goldblum, 2008).

Singapore has a rather open urban characteristic in which the greenery blends between the building arrangements and fills its open spaces. It is unique in comparison with typical European cities such as Athens or Rome, which have relatively uniform low-rise buildings with narrow streets, or even with its Asian counterparts such as Hong Kong, which have high-rise high-density urban characteristics (see Figure 12.9).

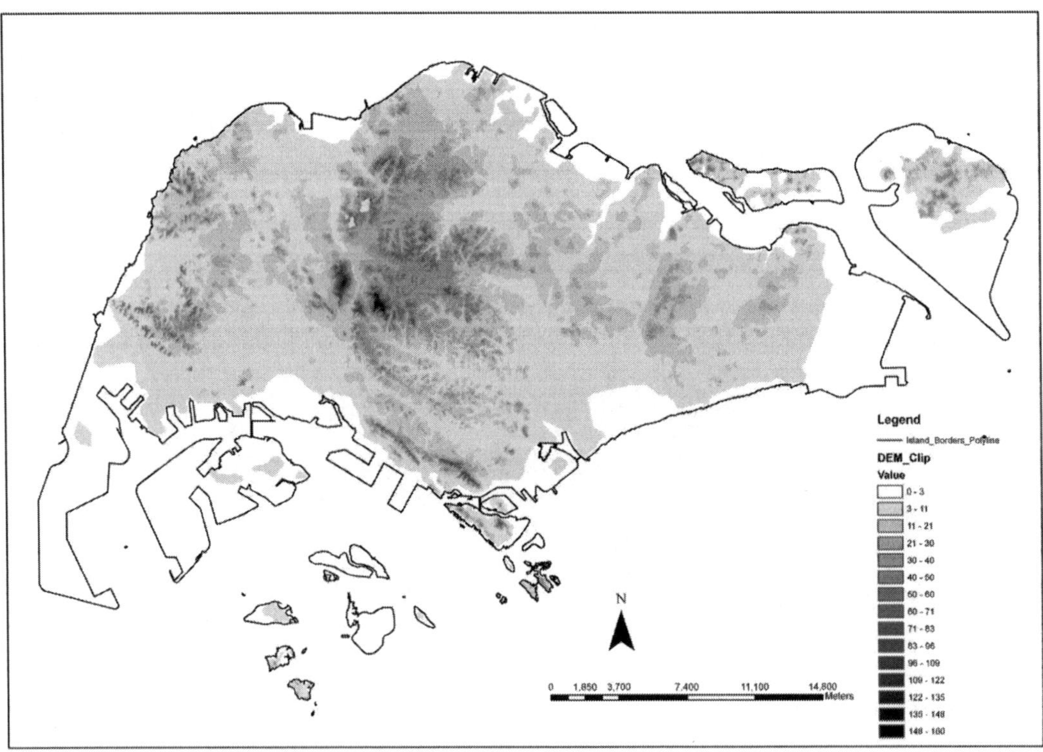


*Figure 12.8* Singapore topography.

Source: Authors

Rome, Italy Athens, Greece Hong Kong, China

*Figure 12.9* Typical urban fabrics in European countries and Hong Kong.
Source: Authors

In examining the urban morphology, several layers are created. They are as follows:

1 Thermal load potential based on land use classifications
2 Potential cold and fresh air areas
3 Sealed areas
4 Building volume.

Figure 12.10 shows that the major developments in Singapore are located at the southern part of the island. The western part of the island is mainly an industrial area. The Jurong island area is characterised by a large exposed concrete surface area. The industrial buildings are arranged far apart from one another with no greenery in between. Another characteristic is industrial buildings, which were designed with the combination of metal pitched roofs and flat concrete roofs. The eastern part of the island is Changi airport with a large paved area, causing a high temperature surface, especially during daytime. However, as compared to the CBD area, it takes less time to release heat, since there are no multiple re-radiations from the surface during night-time (Jusuf *et al.*, 2007). Therefore, due to the different thermal behaviours of different land uses, they are given certain classification values (see Table 12.1). In general, the classification values indicate the thermal load potential of the area; i.e. the higher the value, the higher the thermal load.

Certain land uses have the potential to generate cold and fresh air for the surrounding environment, especially land that is open and planted with vegetation. This includes parks, agricultural land, beach areas and so on (see Figure 12.11). Its potential is determined by the size of the areas; the larger the areas, the higher the cooling potential (see Table 12.2).

The amount of hard surfaces and building bulk determine the heat storage in the city (see Figures 12.12 and 12.13). The cooling process within the city centre is slower than its surrounding areas due to a higher building volume density. The long-wave radiation could be blocked and released slowly. Hence, the trapped radiation within the urban areas has a higher temperature than the surrounding areas at night. The higher building density also reduces the ventilation potential. In short, the higher the building volume density, the larger the heat capacity. Tables 12.3 and 12.4 show the classification values of different amounts of sealed areas and building volume respectively.

## *Vegetation*

The 'Garden City' campaign in Singapore was launched as early as 40 years ago, as part of environmental sustainability measures. Its key focus was to grow a green mantle in the shortest time

*Table 12.1* Classification values of land use layer.

| *Land use description* | *Classification value* |
|---|---|
| Agriculture | 0 |
| Beach Area | 0 |
| Cemetery | 0 |
| Open Space | 0 |
| Reserve Site | 0 |
| Special Use | 0 |
| Waterbody | 0 |
| Airport_Unsealed | 1 |
| Park | 1 |
| Place of Worship | 1 |
| Sports and Recreation | 1 |
| Utility | 2 |
| Educational Institution | 4 |
| Light Rapid Transit | 4 |
| Mass Rapid Transit | 4 |
| Residential | 4 |
| Residential / Institution | 4 |
| Transport Facilities | 4 |
| Airport | 5 |
| Civic and Community Institution | 5 |
| Commercial | 5 |
| Commercial and Residential | 5 |
| Health and Medical Care | 5 |
| Hotel | 5 |
| Residential with Commercial at 1st Storey | 5 |
| White | 5 |
| Business 1 | 6 |
| Business 1 – White | 6 |
| Business 2 | 6 |
| Business 2 – White | 6 |
| Business Park | 6 |
| Business Park – White | 6 |
| Port | 6 |
| Road | 6 |

Source: Authors

possible. The main strategies to achieve this included providing enough space along the road cords for planting trees and shrubs; covering bare concrete structures and bridges with creepers and shrubs; asking developers to plant roadside trees and set aside land for open spaces; and providing parks as city lungs; see Figure 12.14 (URA, 2008).

The importance of the Garden City concept was to soften the harshness of the urban fabric and to create a good image to the investors in the early years (1970s) that Singapore was an efficient place for business. As an example, during the development of Changi International Airport in the mid-1970s, the government instructed planners to complete the expressway (linking Changi at the eastern part of Singapore to the city centre) and its tree planting ahead of the airport completion. Thus, the first visitors in 1981 experienced a beautiful view of mature trees when they travelled from Changi airport to the city centre (Dale, 2008).

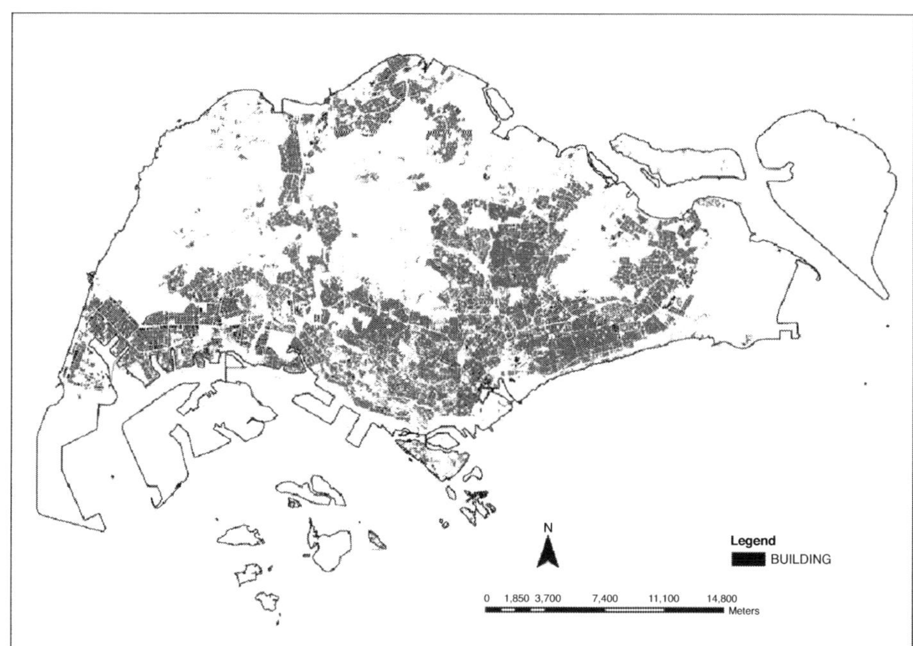


*Figure 12.10* Singapore island, building footprint.

Source: Authors

*Figure 12.11* Potential cold and fresh air production areas.

Source: Authors

*Table 12.2* Classification values of potential cold and fresh air production areas layer.

| *Potential cold and fresh air areas* | *Classification value* |
|---|---|
| ≤ 5km² | −1 |
| 5–10km² | −2 |
| 10–20km² | −3 |
| > 20km² | −4 |

Source: Authors

*Table 12.3* Classification values of sealed area layer.

| *Sealing level in percentage* | *Classification value* |
|---|---|
| 0 | 0 |
| 12.5 | 0.5 |
| 25 | 1 |
| 37.5 | 1.5 |
| 50 | 2 |
| 62.5 | 2.5 |
| 75 | 3 |
| 87.5 | 3.5 |
| 100 | 4 |

Source: Authors

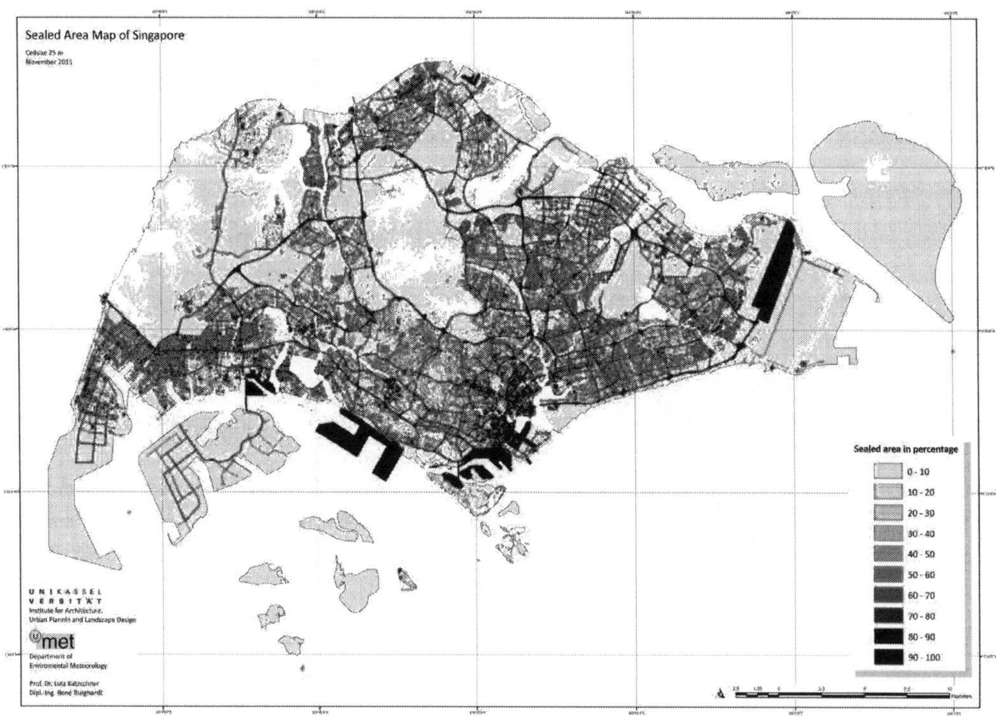


*Figure 12.12* Sealed area map of Singapore.

Source: Authors

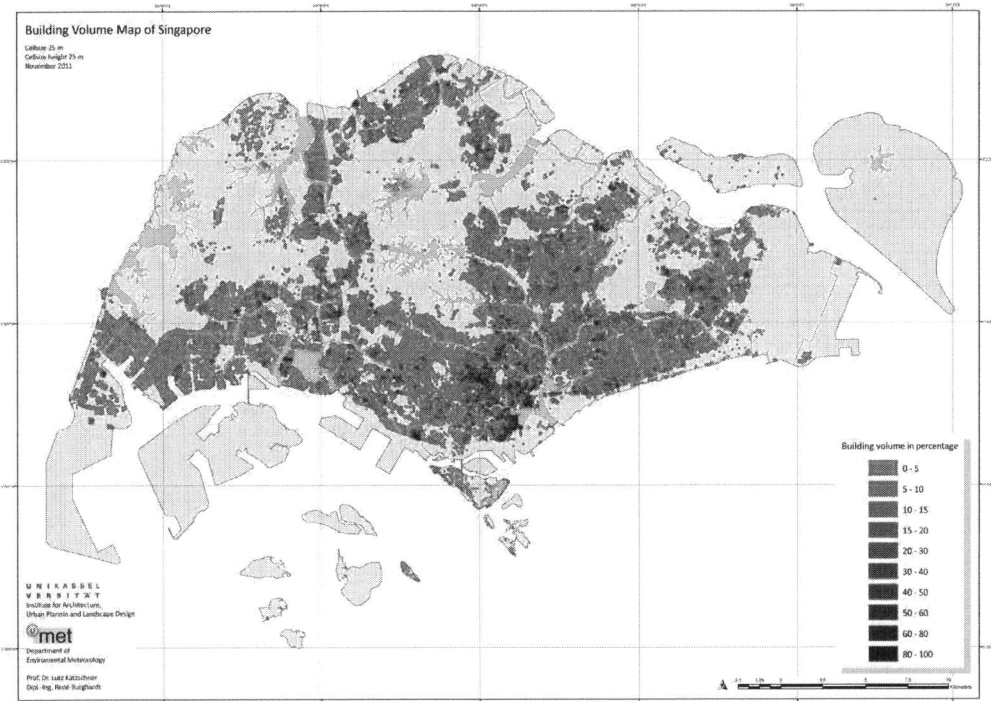


*Figure 12.13* Building volume map of Singapore.

Source: Authors

*Table 12.4* Classification values of building volume layer.

| *Building volume in percentage* | *Classification value* |
|---|---|
| ~16 | 0.8 |
| ~32 | 1.6 |
| ~48 | 2.4 |
| ~64 | 3.2 |
| ~80 | 4.0 |
| ~96–100 | 4.8 |

Source: Authors

The Garden City concept was formalised only in 1992, published as '*The Singapore Green Plan – Towards a Model Green City*'. Later in the revised 2001 Concept Plan, island-wide park connector systems were designed and integrated with leisure (recreational areas for jogging or cycling) and tourism (historical or natural theme parks) (Goldblum, 2008). To date, Singapore has about 300 parks throughout the island and these parks are connected with 70km of park connectors. The government aims to extend the park connectors to 200km by the year 2012 and to over 400km in the long term. Eventually, the whole island will be linked up in a round-island loop. This effort is part of the recent move from the vision of 'Garden City' into 'A City in a Garden' (Cheong, 2008).

*Figure 12.14* Key strategies of the Garden City campaign.
Source: URA, 2008

Figure 12.15 shows the vegetation covers and water bodies across the Singapore Island. Greenery helps to ameliorate the high temperature condition in the city, i.e. reducing the thermal load (Table 12.5).

## The calculations behind Singapore's urban climatic analysis map

Once the layers were prepared, the next step was the calculation with the different weighting and classification values of the individual layer of information. The analysis is performed and compared with the available information based on expert knowledge. From this complex overlay of different kinds of information layers, the climatic features in the urban area were aggregated and processed by calculating the value of each layer and respecting the thermal and dynamic neighbourhoods which influence focal neighbourhood statistics.

The result is the Singapore UC-AnMap 2011 with six different rating categories (potential-, mixing-, stress-climatopes) in equal intervals, see Plate 12.1 and Table 12.6. The displayed map assessed both analysis steps, i.e. the dynamic and the thermal components. The representation of the regional ventilation in the map supports the orientation and can be used to keep in mind the adjustment for new built-up areas.

The six different classifications of a certain climate quality are described in Table 12.6. Air paths, ventilated areas and all these areas without major net loss need to be either protected or improved by means of influencing, long- and short-wave radiation (shadow, albedo) or ventilation by roughness and openness.

*Table 12.5* Classification values of vegetation cover layer.

| *Vegetation cover* | *Classification value* |
|---|---|
| No | 0 |
| Yes | −2 |

Source: Authors

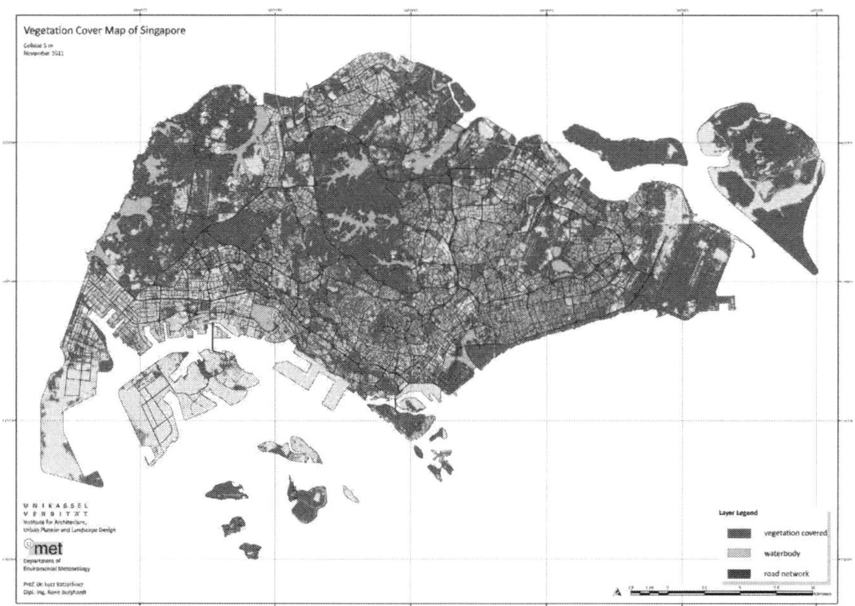


*Figure 12.15* Vegetation cover and water body map.

Source: Authors

The legend (see Table 12.6) is subdivided into multiple columns, so that additional information can be assigned to the climatope classifications. The first and second columns list the respective climatope-categories with their names. These names are generally applied to an understanding of the different climates. Based on the colour of the map, surfaces can be directly assigned to the category. In the third column is placed a short description that characterises the respective category. Based on this classification, the climatological value can be derived. The fourth column of the legend involves the classification and planning information. Planning recommendations were also made here, which thus can be assigned directly to the respective area. Based on results obtained from the urban climatic analysis, climatic zones and air paths can be developed and recommendations derived. Areas showing special characteristics are described (see Table 12.6). Comments range from 'Place which requires an improvement' to 'Place which should be conserved' based on the view of the urban climate. Then, with the aim of mitigating the negative situation and protecting the positive situation, planning advice and guidelines for each zone are offered by both expert and planner.

*Table 12.6* Legend of Singapore UC-AnMap with evaluations and planning recommendations.

| *Category* | *Climatope* | *Description* | *Evaluation/Planning zones* |
|---|---|---|---|
| 1 | Fresh and cool air production zones | Open areas with significant climatic activity, i.e. high potential for air circulation, cool and fresh air production.<br>Climatically active open sites (i.e. high potential area to provide cooling and shading effects) to the housing area.<br>Very high nocturnal cooling. | ***Areas to preserve carefully:***<br>*High sensitivity with respect to intervention which changes in land use. Keep open cold/ fresh air stream by minimizing the existing barrier on air streams. The air movement connections must be fully analysed and understood, including the source of the air stream channels, which may be far away from the area concerned.*<br><br>Very important, preserve and protect.<br>Area [B] has high importance for circulation, green linkages are used; if possible linear greenery should be developed.<br>This category has to be maintained, cool island in area [D] should be maintained. |
| 2 | Cool air production zone | Open areas with less significant climatic activity, i.e. less potential for air circulation.<br>Cool and fresh air with effects to neighbourhoods.<br>Areas with fresh air.<br>High nocturnal heat degradation. | ***Areas to preserve:***<br>*The increasing surface roughness (e.g. further constructions or buildings) should respect slope winds and thermal induced circulation pattern; avoid barriers against main wind directions, Furthermore, redevelopments should be supported by detailed investigation and analysis on climatic function aspect.*<br><br>Important, preserve and protect area [A and B]. This category has to be maintained. |
| 3 | Mixed and transitional climate zone | Strong daily variation through solar radiation, but good cooling effect.<br>Areas with high percentage of vegetation.<br>Low and discontinuous emissions.<br>Buffer zones between different climatopes.<br>Moderate/good nocturnal heat degradation. | ***Areas with possible development:***<br>*These are important linkage areas.*<br>*Future new development should properly consider the orientation and density of new buildings (e.g. new development should be orientated to the prevailing wind, while building density in this zone should not be further increased). Surface roughness should not be increased due to reduction in ventilation, affecting both inside and neighbourhood areas.*<br><br>Take into consideration the circulation direction in building and planning projects.<br>No further increase of heat storage by reducing building mass or using reflective materials. |
| 4 | Heat accumulation potential zone | Some heat storage, but mainly buffered through greeneries and wind.<br>Dominated construction areas with lots of vegetation in the open spaces.<br>Low nocturnal heat degradation. | ***Development allowed:***<br>*No appreciable sensitivity in terms of climate with respect to intensification of use and building agglomeration because increasing building mass will not change the heat load as there is sufficient cooling. Generally redevelopment is possible if they take care about ventilation and if the ratio between built-up area versus green areas is maintained/respected (e.g. by maintaining the existing green* |

| *Category* | *Climatope* | *Description* | *Evaluation/Planning zones* |
|---|---|---|---|
| | | | *area, or if new development that increases the built-up area is required, more greenery must be introduced to maintain the ratio).*<br><br>Thermally vulnerable area (areas at risk of overheating due to high thermal storage), promote porous building design, no increase of areal roughness in area [B]. |
| 5 | Heat accumulation zone | Heat storage significant, but still has some wind effects and cooling potential.<br>Density development with little vegetation in open spaces.<br>Very low nocturnal heat degradation. | ***Areas for improvement and plan actions are necessary:***<br>*Risk of future heat stress with some ventilation. So generally the areas should be maintained or improved, and not worsened. Development should compensate for climate effects, by shadow and surface cooling through evaporation (e.g. greenery).*<br>*The existing air circulation should be analysed before any proposed change so that the urban climate is respected.*<br><br>Promote vegetation, shadow and green facades.<br>For areas [E and F], no barriers against sea breeze. For area [D], radiation aspects (shadow and reflecting materials) should be considered. For area [C], further density has to be buffered by shadow from vegetation. |
| 6 | Overheating zone | Heat storage high.<br>Low cooling potentials and low ventilation.<br>Heavily compressed and sealed inner city areas.<br>No/very low nocturnal heat degradation. | ***Areas for improvement and plan actions are necessary:***<br>*Increase of existing heat stress; due to the accumulated problems on thermal load in the high density built-up area, the climatic condition of this zone should be improved. Development in this zone should ensure enough compensation by surface de-sealing and vegetation shadow. Improving air exchange is one major recommendation together with shadow-providing design. Greenery for façades and surfaces are needed.*<br><br>Thermal high deficits, high heat stress; promote shadowing in the outdoor space (e.g. by planting more trees and using design of building layout; however, in using building layout, be careful of heat trap to prevent UHI) as well as façade- and roof insulation and de-sealing of surfaces (e.g. by planting more surface greenery).<br>Areas [E and F] need gaps towards sea breeze and area [D] needs more shadow. |

Source: Authors

## Conclusions

The origination of the island-wide climatic map of Singapore has taken into account the latest concepts, key methodologies, selected parameters, construction and building procedures, mitigation countermeasures and relevant planning instructions in the field of UCMap studies. The various climatic phenomena, geographic information and planning parameters were discussed and described. It concluded that thermal load through radiation fluxes and air ventilation situations within the urban canopy layer have the most important role in analytical aspects and climatic-environmental evaluation. It also concluded that possible mitigation measures and action plans could be taken by decreasing anthropogenic heat release, improving air ventilation at pedestrian level, providing shading, increasing greenery, creating air paths, and controlling building construction. Future research should be focused on spatial analysis of the bioclimate in urban outdoor areas and climate change impacts and adaptation. It is also important to share lessons learned and experiences with planners and policymakers in the rapidly expanding cities of developing countries and regions.

## Acknowledgement

The research team would like to thank the Ministry of National Development Research Fund Committee for funding and support for this project.

## References

Akbari, H., Davis, S., Dorsano, S., Huang, J. and Winnett, S. (eds.) (1992). *Cooling our Communities – a Guidebook on Tree Planting and Light Coloured Surfacing*. Washington: US Environmental Protection Agency.

Akbari, H., Bretz, S., Kurn, D. M. and Hanford, J. (1997). Peak power and cooling energy savings of shade trees. *Energy and Buildings*, 25(2): 139–148.

Arnfield, A. J. (1990). Street design and urban canyon solar access. *Energy and Buildings*, 14(2): 117–131.

Bärring, I., Mattsson, J. O. and Lindqvist, S. (1985). Canyon geometry, street temperatures and urban heat island in Malmö, Sweden. *International Journal of Climatology*, 5(4): 433–444.

Ca, V. T., Asaeda, T. and Abu, E. M. (1998). Reductions in air conditioning energy caused by a nearby park. *Energy and Buildings*, 29(1): 83–92.

Chapman, L., Thornes, J. E. and Bradley, A. V. (2001). Rapid determination of canyon geometry parameters for use in surface radiation budgets. *Theoretical and Applied Climatology*, 69(1–2): 81–89.

Chen, Y. and Wong, N. H. (2006). Thermal benefits of city parks. *Energy and Buildings*, 38(2): 105–120.

Cheong, K. H. (2008). Strategies for sustainable urban development in Singapore. Speech in Forum on 'Sustainable urbanization in the information age' at the United Nations headquarters, New York, 23 April 2008. Available at: http://www.ura.gov.sg/pr/text/2008/pr08-42.html (Accessed 20 December 2011).

Cleugh, H. (1995). Urban climates. In: Henderson-Sellers, A. (ed.). *Future Climates of the World: A Modelling Perspective*. Amsterdam; New York: Elsevier, 477–516.

Dale, O. J. (2008). Sustainable city centre development: The Singapore city centre in the context of sustainable development. In: Wong, T. C., Belinda, Y. and Goldblum, C. (eds.), *Spatial Planning for a Sustainable Singapore*. London: Springer, 31–57.

Eliasson, I. (1991). Urban geometry, surface temperature and air temperature. *Energy and Buildings*, 15(1–2), 141–145.

Eliasson, I. (1996). Urban nocturnal temperatures, street geometry and land use. *Atmospheric Environment*, 30(3): 379–392.

Giridharan, R., Ganesan, S. and Lau, S. S. Y. (2004). Daytime urban heat island effect in high-rise and high-density residential developments in Hong Kong. *Energy and Buildings*, 36(6): 525–534.

Goldblum, C. (2008). Planning the world metropolis on an island-city scale: Urban innovation as a constraint and tool for global change. In: Wong, T. C., Belinda, Y. and Goldblum, C. (eds.), *Spatial Planning for a Sustainable Singapore*. London: Springer, 17–29.

Henderson-Sellers, A. and McGuffie, K. (1987). *A Climate Model Primer.* New York: Wiley.

Huang, Y. J., Akbari, H., Taha, H. and Rosenfeld, H. (1987). The potential of vegetation in reducing summer cooling loads in residential buildings. *Journal of Climate and Applied Meteorology*, 26(9): 1103–1116.

Jauregui, E. (1991). Influence of a large urban park on temperature and convective precipitation in tropical city. *Energy and Buildings*, 15(3–4): 457–463.

Jusuf, S. K., Wong, N. H., Hagen, E., Anggoro, R. and Yan, H. (2007). The influence of land use on the urban heat island in Singapore. *Habitat International*, 31(2): 232–242.

Kawashima, S. (1991). Effect of vegetation on surface temperature in urban and suburban areas in winter. *Energy and Buildings*, 15(3–4): 465–469.

Kiehl, J. T. (1992). Atmospheric general circulation modeling. In: Trenberth, K. E. (ed.) *Climate System Modelling.* Cambridge: Cambridge University Press, 319–370.

McPherson, E. G., Herrington, L. P. and Heisler, M. (1988). Impacts of vegetation on residential heating and cooling. *Energy and Buildings*, 12(1): 41–51.

Oke, T. R. (1981). Canyon geometry and the nocturnal urban heat island: Comparison of scale model and field observations. *International Journal of Climatology*, 1(3): 237–254.

Oke, T. R. (1989). The micrometeorology of the urban forest. *Philosophical Transactions of the Royal Society of London, Series B, Biological Sciences*, 324(1223): 335–349.

Oke, T. R. and East, C. (1971). The urban boundary layer in Montreal. *Boundary-Layer Meteorology*, 1(4): 411–437.

Padmanabhamurty, B. (1991). Microclimates in tropical urban complexes. *Energy and Buildings*, 15(1–2): 83–92.

Sani, S. (1991). Urban climatology in Malaysia: An overview. *Energy and Buildings*, 15(1–2): 105–117.

Santamouris, M. (2001). The canyon effect. In: Santamouris, M. (ed.). *Energy and Climate in the Urban Built Environment.* London: James & James Science Publishers, 69–96.

Streiling, S. and Matzarakis, A. (2003). Influence of single and small clusters of trees on the bioclimate of a city: A case study. *Journal of Arboriculture*, 29(6): 309–316.

Takahashi, K., Yoshida, H., Tanaka, Y., Aotake, N. and Wang, F. (2004). Measurement of thermal environment in Kyoto city and its prediction by CFD simulation. *Energy and Buildings*, 36(8): 771–779.

URA. (2008). Urban Redevelopment Authority, Singapore Government. Available at: http://www.ura.gov.sg/ (Accessed 8 April 2014).

VDI (1997). *VDI-Standard: VDI 3787 Part 1 Environmental Meteorology – Climate and Air Pollution Maps for Cities and Regions.* Berlin: Beuth Verlag.

Wong, N. H., Chen, Y., Chui, L. O. and Sia, A. (2003). Investigation of thermal benefits of rooftop gardens in the tropical environment. *Building and Environment*, 38(2): 261–270.

Wong, N. H. and Chen, Y. (2005). Study of green areas and urban heat island in a tropical city. *Habitat International*, 29(3): 547–558.

Wong, N. H. and Chen, Y. (2009). *Tropical Urban Heat Islands: Climate, Buildings and Greenery.* London; New York: Taylor & Francis.

Wong, N. H. and Jusuf, S. K. (2010). Air temperature distribution and the influence of sky view factor in a green Singapore estate. *Journal of Urban Planning and Development*, 136(3): 261–272.

Wong, T. and Goldblum, C. (2008). Sustainability planning and its theory and practice: An introduction. In: Wong, T. C., Belinda, Y. and Goldblum, C. (eds.) (2008). *Spatial Planning for a Sustainable Singapore.* London: Springer, 1–13.

Yamashita, S., Sekine, K., Shoda, M., Yamashita, K. and Hara, Y. (1986). On the relationship between heat island and sky view factor in the cities of Tama River Basin, Japan. *Atmospheric Environment*, 20(4): 681–686.

Part 3

# Medium-sized cities

Chapter 13

# Urban climatic map studies in Brazil

## Salvador

*Telma Andrade, Jussana Nery, Tereza Moura and Lutz Katzschner*

### The city of Salvador

Salvador City is located in the north-eastern region of Brazil (see Figure 13.1) at latitude 12° 52′ south and longitude 38° 22′ west on a peninsula that narrows the entrance of the bay – Baía Todos-os-Santos. The city's hilly site, with altitudes varying from sea level to about 100m, is surrounded by the sea on two sides: the Atlantic Ocean on the east coast and the bay on the west. The municipal territory is composed of two geographically distinct spaces – the continent, which comprises about 279km$^2$ and corresponds to approximately 90 per cent of the area, and the bay's islands which together amount to around 30km$^2$ (SEDHAM, 2009).

*Figure 13.1* Salvador City location.

Source: Authors

Salvador was the first city founded in Brazil in 1549, with the purpose of being the capital of the Portuguese colony. It remained as the seat of power until the eighteenth century, which witnessed the beginning of a political and economic decline that produced a long-lasting period of growth stagnation (Andrade and Brandão, 2006). In the second half of the twentieth century, the city resumed its growth path by implementing industrial poles in the metropolitan region, such as Petrobrás (in 1953) and Camaçari Petrochemical Complex (in 1976), attracting migration flows in the process. Salvador expanded inwardly and along the Atlantic coast, generating dense and abrupt occupation of the urban space in a period of three to four decades. The population rose from 656,000 inhabitants in the 1960s to 2.07 million in the 1990s (IBGE, 2010), creating several social and environmental issues as well as spontaneous occupations of municipal land.

Presently, the city has spread out and intensively occupied nearly the entire municipal area at the expense of large areas of vegetation. With a population above 2.7 million inhabitants (IBGE, 2010) and a population density of 87 inhb/ha, the city of Salvador has become one of Brazil's most densely populated cities (SEDHAM, 2009).

Regarding Salvador's total green area, Souza *et al.* (2012) quantified the areas of the polygonal sections as defined by Law No 7.400/2008 of SAVAM[1] (SEDHAM, 2008) and found 100km$^2$ of green areas, which correspond to approximately a third of the city area. The predominantly northern-located green areas were distributed as follows: 47.31 per cent of Environmental Protection Areas; 24.06 per cent of Tree-planted Areas; per cent of Natural Resources Protection Areas; 4.56 per cent of Urban Parks; 0.86 per cent of Urbanised Open Spaces. The values dropped to approximately a third when percentages were calculated in relation to the total area of the city (315km$^2$), revealing the exiguity of these spaces.

## The climate of the city of Salvador

Proximity to the Equator and its peninsular condition lends the city of Salvador a tropical humid climate. Climatologic data from 1961–1990 showed that the average monthly maximum air temperatures were quite homogeneous, reaching the highest value of 30°C in February and March and the lowest of 26°C in July, whereas the minimum was about 24°C in summer and 21°C in winter. Its relative humidity did not vary much annually. Indeed, its average annual range varied from 79 per cent (February) to 83 per cent (May). Typically, the south-easterly Trade Winds characterise the wind pattern of Salvador. The average wind speed does not vary much, from 3.2ms$^{-1}$ in winter to 2.8ms$^{-1}$ in summer. Additionally, June has the lowest insolation with 167 hours and January the highest with 246 hours (Andrade *et al.*, 2004).

Nery *et al.* (1997) stated that the climatic condition of the city promoted positive thermal stress during the whole year, attenuated during the winter months (June, July and August). This condition emphasises the need to provide vegetation shading and to preserve ventilation paths for thermal comfort. Due to its topographic features and patterns of occupation, several microclimate conditions were produced and some might aggravate thermal comfort.

To grasp thermal comfort conditions for the city of Salvador, the researchers applied the Physiological Equivalent Temperature (PET) (°C), proposed by Höppe (1999), for the Test Reference Year (TRY) database obtained from the airport of Salvador meteorological station (Goulart *et al.*, 1998), to calculate the hourly thermal comfort PET index. The results showed that PET values were above 24°C throughout the year from about 10.00 a.m. to 4.00 p.m., reaching peak values of 46°C (Andrade *et al.*, 2004). In summer maximum values of the PET index were around 40°C, reaching 46°C in January. In winter the maximum value was 27°C, with the minimum of 14°C in June at 4.00 a.m. (Nery *et al.*, 2006a).

## Research development on urban climate in the city of Salvador: Meso and topoclimate scales

The urban climate research developed by the authors started by presenting a first approach towards a theoretical climatic zoning of the city. The studies were based on topoclimatic factors from the natural site morphology and its interactions with existing local wind and incoming solar radiation. The research identified three geographic spaces with distinct topoclimatic characteristics, shown in Figure 13.2: Litoral, Inland, and the Bay Seaside (Nery *et al.*, 1997).[2]

The Litoral, characterised by the Atlantic coastal plain, depicted winds originating from an area without roughness, with mild temperatures and high humidity and salinity. Regarding incoming solar radiation, the natural morphology of the Atlantic coast also presented little influence. Hence, taken together these factors tended to produce the following topoclimatic characteristics: higher air speed and humidity, more rainfall and intense solar radiation in comparison with its mesoclimate. The second geographic space, the Bay seaside, located at sea level and facing Todos-os-Santos Bay has a geological fault acting as a barrier to the prevailing winds. Theoretically, these factors implied higher air temperatures, less rainfall, lower wind speed and more radiation in comparison with the mesoclimate. In the Inland, interaction between land reliefs – clover shaped, with solar radiation

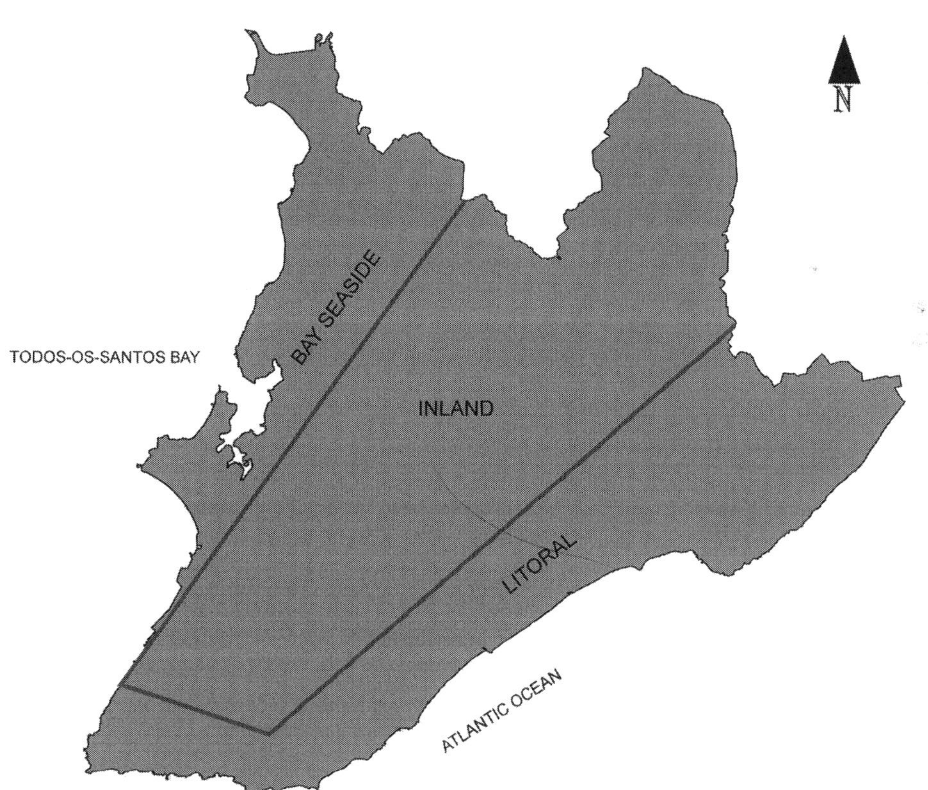


*Figure 13.2* Geographic spaces with distinct topoclimates.

Source: Authors

and winds, forged the appearance of microclimates relative to specific hillside orientations, ridges, grottos and valleys (Nery *et al.*, 1997). The research aimed at achieving a theoretical and comprehensive depiction of conceptual geographic spaces and the implication for the thermal comfort of microclimatic areas.

Ensuing from this, the research focused on mobile measurements which cross-cut Salvador along four transects. From 1998 to 2000, data collection was carried out on two consecutive days: at dawn, early afternoons and early evenings for each season, totalling 116 measurement points and 4,576 measurements, namely: air temperature (°C), relative humidity (%), global radiation ($Wm^{-2}$), speed ($ms^{-1}$) and wind direction (Andrade *et al.*, 2002). The research initially focused on cross-referencing measured climatic variables with observed geomorphologic features of natural and urban structures within a 50m radius of each measurement point, and with the mesoclimatic data from two meteorological stations. This comparative analysis produced a microclimatic classification of the measured points. By aggregating the results, the research constructed new hypotheses regarding urban thermo-hygrometric conditions in Salvador. The study evidenced that homogeneity of thermal conditions across the city, governed by the topoclimate, did not preclude the registry of differences influenced by natural and man-made landscape (mass of vegetation, water bodies, altitude, built density and open areas). It corroborated with the idea that urban design was a potential tool to reduce thermal stress in humid and tropical climates (Freire and Schimmelpfeng, 2001).

A subsequent analysis was made in order to assess thermal comfort based on PET (°C) values for summer and winter seasons using the mobile measured data (Andrade *et al.*, 2002). The results showed that the PET values at dawn and night have a high incidence within the comfort zone – defined by Matzarakis *et al.* (1999) as between 18°C to 23°C, at nearly all measured places, for both seasons. As air temperature and solar radiation increased during the day, comfort conditions tended to deteriorate, especially in summer. The results confirmed that in the summertime, thermal discomfort is sensibly greater than in winter. The PET values found in the city in summer afternoons ranged from 25°C to 43°C, consistently above the comfort zone.

Subsequently, the research centred on the study of land use and occupation patterns in Salvador. Employing urbanistic indices – building heights, setbacks, plot sizes, and widths of streets, the research defined eight occupation patterns, which were mapped and delimited by homogeneous areas obtained from SICAR cartographic and photographic bases,[3] and Salvador's scale model (Prefeitura Municipal da Cidade de Salvador, n.d.).

This phase of the Urban Climate Research correlated land occupation patterns and average local air temperatures from measurements. Results, detailed in the study 'Air Temperature and Occupation Patterns in Salvador' (Nery *et al.*, 2003), underpinned the expected conclusion that the higher the density rate in the occupation patterns, the higher the average air temperatures and vice versa.

Ensuing from this, the research developed an urban climatic map of Salvador, based on principles of urban climatology specifically regarding heat storage and urban ventilation through thematic charts separately developed and later superimposed (Nery *et al.*, 2006b). Because quantitative data of Salvador's urban climate came from (1) two existing meteorological stations – INMET and Airport – both situated on the same topoclimatic spaces of the Litoral, and from (2) the mobile measurements carried out across four transects by our team, the Urban Climatic Map represented a theoretical-qualitative analysis of the potential conditions of the thermal comfort of the city as a whole.

In order to identify the thermal comfort condition over the urban areas, three charts were drawn based on Geographic Information System (GIS) calculations (Katzschner and Horn, 2005), considering different factors for each of them: topographic height, slope, land use and wind potential. For each chart (see Figures 13.3, 13.4 and 13.5) the researchers selected, interpreted and evaluated

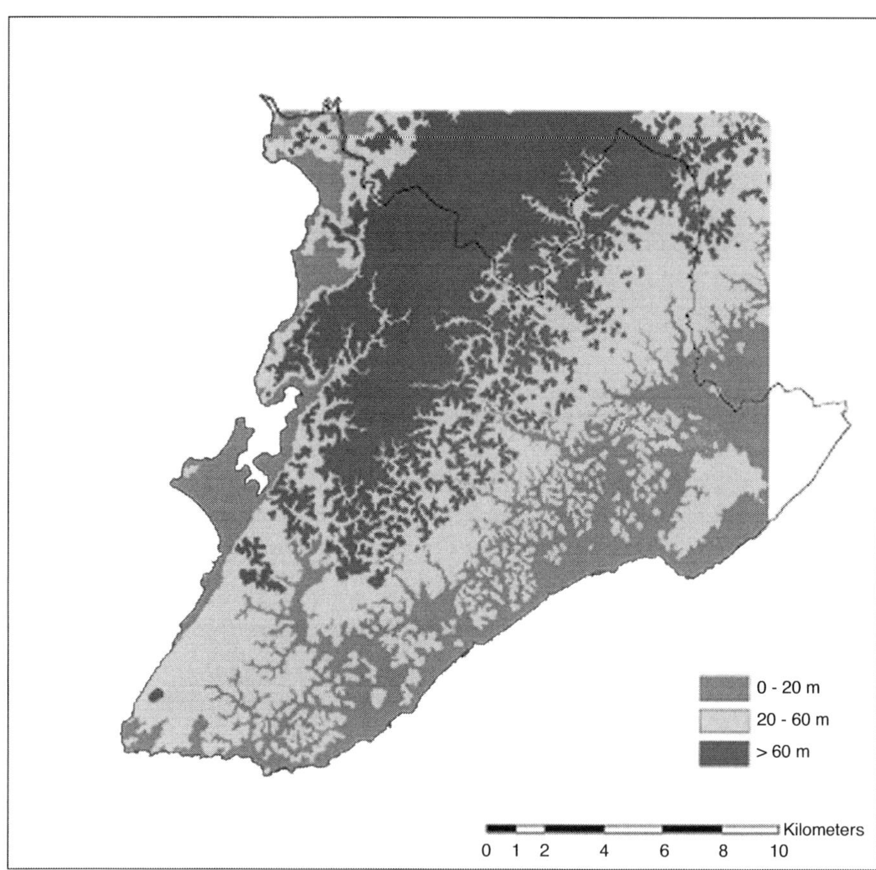


*Figure 13.3* Topographic chart of Salvador.

Source: Authors

*Table 13.1* Topographic height weighting factors.

| *Levels* | *Criteria (height in m)* | *Weighting factors* |
|---|---|---|
| L 1 | h > 60m | −1 |
| L 2 | 20 m < h < 60m | 0 |
| L 3 | h < 20m | −1 |

Source: Authors

three to nine weighting factors according to heat storage levels and ventilation patterns within the urban fabric. The Urban Climatic Map summed up the evaluation of the combined three charts (see Figure 13.6).

The first chart – topographic chart (see Figure 13.3) showed Salvador's topography divided into three different levels: heights over 60m, between 20m and 60m, and below 20m. The criteria to determine the topographic height weighting factors considered that the higher the level, the breezier the area and vice versa, whereas the lower the level, the higher the possibility of shading and the less exposure time to incoming solar radiation (see Table 13.1).

The topographic chart divided the natural morphology into climatic zones accounting for slightly lower temperatures in higher areas as well as for wind exposure, which qualitatively would render areas more thermally comfortable. The chart showed lower areas both on the east (Atlantic Ocean) and west coasts (Baía de Todos-os-Santos seaside), whereas the rest of the municipal area pertained to the middle range height of 20m–60m.

The chart showing land-use classification (see Figure 13.4) drew nine patterns of land occupation (P1 to P9) defined defined in previous research (Nery *et al.*, 2003). Recall that this was determined by actual land use taking building heights, occupation densities, vegetation, and special building areas as criteria for establishing the weighting factors; where the occupation density and height of buildings were higher, the attributed weighting factor was higher (Table 13.2).

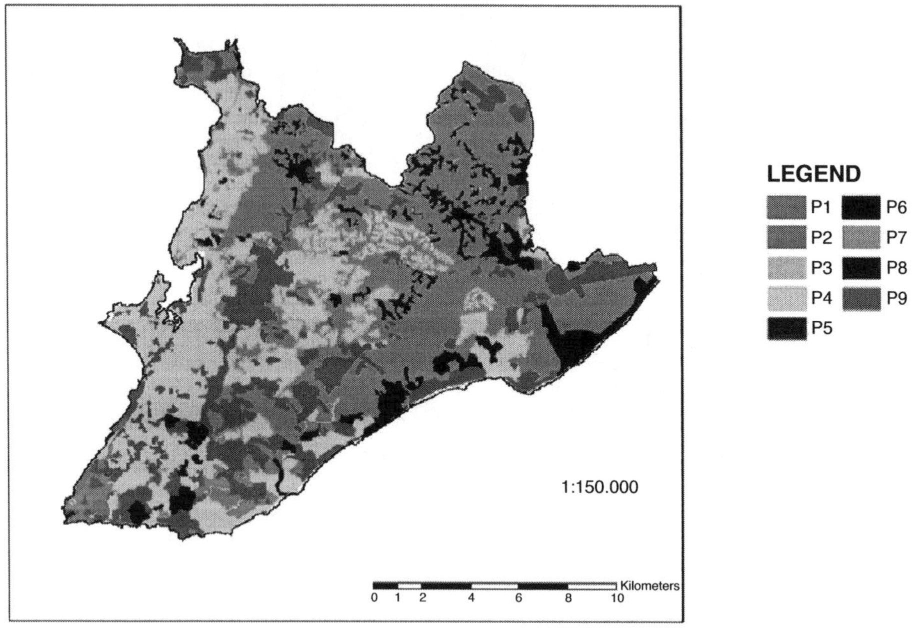


*Figure 13.4* Land use chart of Salvador.

Source: Authors

*Table 13.2* Patterns of occupation and land use weighting factors.

| *Patterns* | *Criteria* | *Weighting factors* |
|---|---|---|
| P 1 | Tall buildings (> 10 storeys) and High density | 8 |
| P 2 | Tall buildings (> 10 storeys) and Medium density | 6 |
| P 3 | Medium-height buildings (1–4 storeys) and Medium density | 4 |
| P 4 | Small buildings (< 4 storeys), Very high density and no vegetation | 7 |
| P 5 | Small buildings (< 4 storeys) and Medium density | 5 |
| P 6 | Small buildings (< 4 storeys), Low density and vegetation | 3 |
| P 7 | Small buildings (< 4 storeys), Low density and no vegetation | 2 |
| P 8 | Specially large structures: industries, shopping centres, hospitals | 1 |
| P 9 | Parks and/or very low density with scattered vegetation | 1 |

Source: Authors

The land-use chart showed that pattern 9 occupied the largest area and included the few existing parks, open areas – with or without ground vegetation or shrubs, and small and scattered houses in between, resulting in very low density.

Although pattern 4 occupied the second largest area, it had the highest density in the whole city. It represented the typical pattern of spontaneous occupation with no open areas or vegetation, small buildings of up to four floors, shared walls on both sides (a type of single-unit attached housing) and narrow access ways (alleyways and lanes), with no possibility of vehicle traffic.

Patterns 5, 6, and 7, each one apart, corresponded to about 9 per cent of the total municipal area. All of them presented low-rise buildings, less than four storeys. Pattern 5 had medium-density occupation, whereas patterns 6 and 7 presented low density, but only the latter had no vegetation despite its low density.

Pattern 8 is a special classification for large buildings such as industries, shopping centres, bus stations and hospitals. Pattern 3 covered about 1 per cent of the city and presented medium-high buildings and medium density. Patterns 1 and 2 corresponded to the high-rise buildings areas of the city, i.e. those with more than ten storeys. The former pattern presented high density and the latter, medium density – their main difference lay on the lateral setbacks between buildings, which were larger in pattern 2. Together they covered about 4 per cent of the total urban area. Even so, their impact should not be underestimated, as they obtained the highest weighting factors. Pattern 4 also received a high weighting factor due to its high-density characteristics.

The chart of wind speed distribution (see Figure 13.5) showed six categories determined by the following set of criteria: distance from the sea, air paths, and roughness. The weighting factors were attributed considering the regional meso-scale wind system. Ventilation for Salvador's mesoclimate functioned as a reduction factor of heat storage since the city's maximum absolute temperature

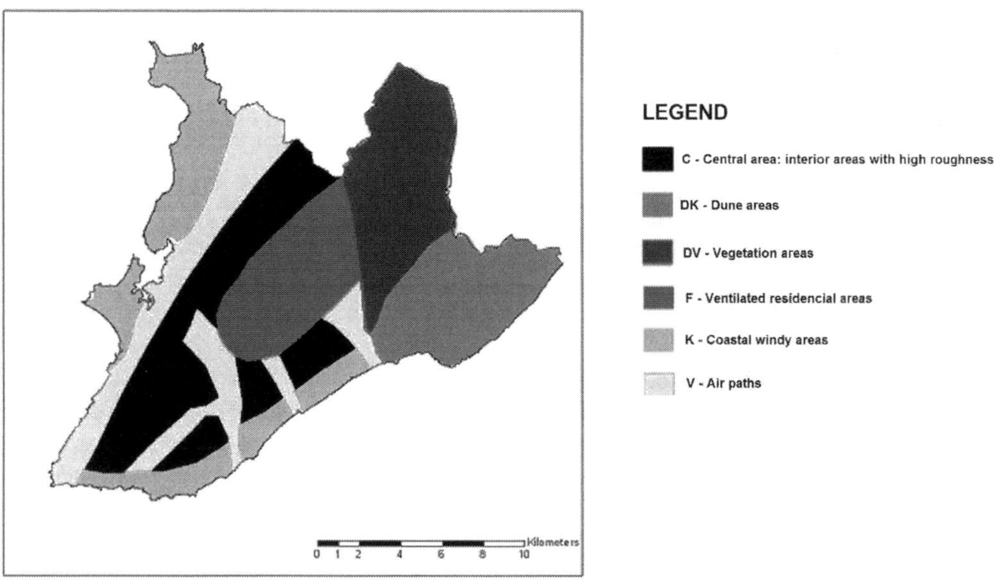


*Figure 13.5* Ventilation chart of Salvador.

Source: Authors

*Table 13.3* Ventilation weighting factors.

| *Patterns* | *Criteria* | *Weighting factors* |
|---|---|---|
| C | Central area: interior areas with high roughness | 0 |
| K | Coastal windy areas | −2 |
| V | Air paths | −3 |
| F | Ventilated residential areas with medium roughness | −1 |
| DV | Vegetation areas with lower roughness under regional wind zone | −1 |
| DK | Dune areas with lower roughness | −2 |

Source: Authors

reached 34.3°C in March 1973 (Brasil, 2009). Furthermore, the closer the area to the ocean and the lower the roughness, the more susceptible the areas become to ventilation. For these areas, the attributed weights were the lowest. Similarly, the same weights were applied to areas within the existing air path corridors (see Table 13.3).

Figure 13.5 presents ventilation areas distributed according to the criteria stated above. It depicts a recommendation map for ventilation derived from the knowledge presented in previous chapters. The air paths highlighted areas that form wind corridors responsible for the refrigeration of central areas of the city – the Inland – and therefore must be kept free of building barriers so that sea breeze and local ventilation can be used for improving thermal comfort.

The largest C area indicated reduced wind speed due to its inner location in relation to the sea coast and urban fabric. The innermost F area also had a reduced regional wind due to its location, but being less dense and having more vegetation, this area was slightly more ventilated than the previous one. The DK and K areas represented the dune wind climate and the coastal ventilation, respectively, both under the influence of the sea breeze. The east coast – the Litoral – was substantially benefited by the intense Southern Trade Winds. These winds penetrated the city fabric through the valleys, leading fresh and humid air into the city, resulting in the wind paths shown in V areas. The DV area had no strong factors influencing the regional wind, no significant urban fabric nor topographic features.

These three charts (see Figures 13.3, 13.4 and 13.5) were superimposed to produce an urban climate evaluation, which was the result of the interaction between all morphological and urban structure data, alongside the ventilation distribution.

The urban climatic map (see Plate 13.1) showed 7 categories, which summarised all studied aspects into different levels of ventilation and heat island, namely: (a) maximum heat island, (b) heat island, (c) reduced ventilation, (d) small heat island, (e) strong ventilation, (f) dune/coast climate, and (g) vegetation climate.

The heat island distribution over the city was quite different from a typical heat island effect for continental cities. As the weighting factors attributed to land use were higher than those to ventilation, inclination and topography, the heat island areas spread all over the built fabric. It occurred even in coastal areas either because of the high densities or wind shadows. The maximum heat island effect took place in older city areas with very high density and reduced wind speed, spreading along the geological fault, followed by the inner areas. Less intense heat islands were scattered in the whole area depending on the integration of the weighting factor of each criteria. The chart shows that strongly ventilated areas occupied a smaller percentage of the total area and were concentrated along the coast and the air path areas.

The urban climatic map shows that greater thermal discomfort was found in the most densely constructed areas, which presented reduced ventilation and no air path benefits, whereas within the same type of city structure, good ventilation provided reasonable thermal comfort. Other central parts of the city with small houses, which in principle would be thermally comfortable, were classified as heat islands due to incoming radiation and less ventilation. The densely constructed areas near the coastal line or those which were within air paths showed reduced heat islands and therefore better thermal conditions. The same held true for high areas above 60m.

The urban climatic map (see Plate 13.1) could be translated into a qualitative thermal classification by applying a thermal comfort scale over the categories of the map above, ranging from +3 to −3, based on Fanger's work (Fanger, 1982). Considering that the thermal comfort condition for humid tropical areas depended on wind effect, 'Strongly ventilated areas' could be taken as a neutral thermal condition (0 value). All of the other categories would represent positive thermal stress, as pointed out by the site measurements and resulting PET indices obtained from previous thermal studies (Nery *et al.*, 2003). 'Dune/coastal climate' and 'Vegetation climate' would be defined as +1, meaning slightly warm as their areas suffered little intervention. 'Small heat island' and 'Reduced ventilation' would be considered +2, meaning warm condition, where low but densely built structures stored heat. 'Heat island' and 'Maximum heat island' could be translated into +3, meaning very warm conditions, as these areas presented the highest heat storage and the minimum ventilation. The different heat island areas identified in the Urban Climatic Map indicated the existence of the severe deterioration of the city's thermal condition, resulting in poor environmental quality.

## Urban climate in micro-scale studies

After developing the Urban Climatic Map, the research focused on studies at the microclimatic scale. It was aimed at finding empirical evidence which supported the theoretical qualitative research developed at the meso and topoclimatic scales. Furthermore, thermal comfort was quantified through the thermal comfort index PET (Höppe, 1999). At this scale, Salvador's inhabitants were investigated regarding the perception of thermal sensation, and the participants' opinions were associated with the environmental variable measurements related to thermal comfort.

Additionally, a simultaneous investigation occurred on two open urban spaces, Cayrú and Piedade Squares (see Figure 13.6), specifically selected for having distinct geomorphologic characteristics (Souza *et al.*, 2011). The former is located in the Lower Town (north-west portion of the city), while the latter is located in the Higher Town (the rest of the city). A geological fault, dividing the city region, defined the two levels. In relation to the Land Use Chart, Cayrú Square was categorised as pattern 1, while Piedade Square was inscribed in the general delimited area of pattern 4. However, because of inhomogeneity, Piedade Square itself differentiated from the surroundings and was closer to pattern 3. In the urban climatic map, both squares lay on a 'Small Heat Island' (see Plate 13.1). Piedade Square, situated in the Inland at approximately 60m was surrounded by medium-sized buildings with some trees, whereas Cayrú Square was situated on the waterfront of the Bay facing west, and next to the hillside generated by the geographic fault (see Figure 13.6).

Comparing the measured data in both squares with data from the INMET Meteorological Station, inserted in pattern 6 (see Figure 13.4) and classified as vegetation climate in the urban climatic map (see Plate 13.1), it could be observed, as expected, that air temperatures reached lower values for the latter pattern.

*Figure 13.6* Photograph of Piedade and Cayrú Squares.

Source: Courtesy of Manu Dias

When compared with each other, Piedade Square presented a tendency to lower air temperatures, however, with lower wind speeds and a lower frequency of winds. In contrast, Cayrú Square presented a tendency to higher air temperatures, higher wind speeds and wind frequency, achieving a higher number of satisfied users. Indeed, 18 per cent of users claimed to be in thermal comfort as opposed to 15 per cent in Piedade Square. For a total of 1,056 interviewed, Piedade Square reached 34 per cent of dissatisfied pedestrians due to heat stress and Cayrú Square, 31 per cent (Souza *et al.*, 2011).

Although Cayrú Square is in a high-density area and shading would be expected, it faces west at sea level, and is more exposed to incoming solar radiation from the west – consequently resulting in higher air temperatures. It was evaluated by pedestrians thermally as more comfortable than Piedade Square, probably due to the higher frequency of ventilation. Importantly, Cayrú Square was not a homogeneous space similar to Piedade Square; rather, it was divided by the Mercado Modelo building, hence creating two distinct microclimates, one facing the Bay on the windward side and the other on the leeward (Souza *et al.*, 2011).

As part of the microclimatic studies, the research targeted two neighbouring, although distinct, areas regarding land occupation patterns: Nordeste de Amaralina and Pituba (Morais *et al.*, 2011)(see Figure 13.7). Nordeste de Amaralina represented a spontaneous occupation, classified in the Land Use Chart as pattern 4, and Pituba, a planned occupation, was classified as pattern 2.

*Figure 13.7* Photograph of neighbourhoods Nordeste de Amaralina and Pituba.

Source: Courtesy of Manu Dias

Nordeste de Amaralina presented greater thermal amplitude, with minimum measured value of 25°C and maximum of 33°C, with 28°C (first quartile) to 30°C (third quartile) as predominant values, and a median of 29°C. At Pituba, air temperatures ranged from 26°C to 29°C, corresponding to the minimum and maximum values respectively, with predominance between 27°C (first quartile) and 28°C (third quartile), and a median of 28°C. There was, therefore, lower data amplitude in air temperature at Pituba. Table 13.4 shows the main descriptive measurements of air temperature regarding both urban spaces.

*Table 13.4* Measurement descriptive of air temperature (°C) in Nordeste de Amaralina and Pituba.

| *Urban space* | *Measurement descriptive of air temperature (°C)* | | | | | | |
|---|---|---|---|---|---|---|---|
| | *Data numbers* | *Media* | *Median* | *Maximum* | *Minimum* | *1° quartile* | *3° quartile* |
| NORDESTE DE AMARALINA | 206 | 29.7 | 29.0 | 33.0 | 25.0 | 28.0 | 30.0 |
| PITUBA | 199 | 28.1 | 28.0 | 29.0 | 26.0 | 27.0 | 28.0 |

Source: Authors

## Conclusions

The drawing of the urban climatic map of Salvador – a tropical city in Brazil – presented the development of ongoing research which has been running for a period of 15 years. Compiling this knowledge revealed the research complexity that sprung from the difficulty of grasping Salvador's urban climate. Composed of differentiated existing microclimates, the urban climate is derived from peculiarities in the city's geography, which had been modified by the land use and occupation patterns compounded since the city's foundation in the early sixteenth century. The dense and abrupt occupation of urban space in a period of three to four decades produced several socio-environmental problems, from the spontaneous land occupation to the decrease of natural vegetation.

The mesoclimate condition of Salvador can be described as having a general tendency towards positive thermal stress during the day all year round, even in wintertime. The different heat island areas identified as the first outcome of the research informed severe deterioration of the city's thermal quality over time, effecting poor environmental quality.

As with the mesoclimatic scale, complexity was also found in the microclimatic studies. However, the latter revealed that better thermal conditions correlated with medium-density land occupation, whereas high-density microclimates, regardless of other characteristics, presented approximately the same thermal environment.

The thermal comfort classification for Salvador inferred from the urban climate situation allowed the identification of areas where potential thermal comfort should be kept at the same level, as well as the critical areas requiring improving. These results may indicate possible actions for urban intervention and, therefore, the feasibility of implementation in an urban master plan.

Urban growth dynamics of cities such as Salvador require urban climate studies to be systematically developed as a continuous process. Similarly, they require validated tools to allow for the evaluation and prediction of the thermal performance of urban structures, which should include the perception of urban dwellers living under differentiated climatic characteristics. Measuring urban climate variables is an important requirement for the identification of the city thermal condition levels of deterioration. This allows for proper public interventions to improve urban climate quality since global climatic changes seem to be inevitable.

Furthermore, the researchers hope that the methodology developed in these studies may encourage and help subsidise future studies on urban climate research aimed at building scenarios considering climate change effects on urban spaces and, hence, establish guidelines to mitigate these effects on the thermal comfort of tropical or otherwise cities around the globe. Indeed, following Monteiro's prophetic words (Mendonça *et al.*, 2003), as a component of the quality of the environment, the treatment of urban climate cannot be rendered meaningless for the modern world.

## References

Andrade, A. and Brandão, P. (2006). *Geografia de Salvador.* Salvador: EDUFBA.

Andrade, T., Nery, J., Moura Freire, T. and Katzschner, L. (2002). Thermal comfort and urban climate of the tropical city of Salvador, Bahia. *TECBAHIA – Revista Baiana de Tecnologia*, 17(3): 34–45.

Andrade, T., Nery, J., Moura Freire, T. Katzschner, L. and Fortuna, D. (2004). Thermal comfort condition for a tropical city, Salvador – Brazil. In: *Proceedings of 21th International Conference on Passive and Low Energy Architecture (PLEA2004).* Eindhoven, Netherlands, 19–21 September. Netherlands: Technische Universität Eindhoven, 19–22.

Brasil (2009). *Normais Climatológicas do Brasil 1961–1990.* Brasília: INMET.

CONDER (Companhia de Desenvolvimento Urbano do Estado da Bahia) (1998). *Sistema Cartográfico da Região Metropolitana de Salvador – SICAR/RMS.* Salvador: CONDER.

Fanger, P. (1982). *Thermal Comfort.* Malabar: R. E. Krieger Pub. Co.

Goulart, S., Lamberts, R. and Firmino, S. (1998). *Dados climáticos para projeto e avaliação energética de edificações para 14 cidades brasileiras.* 2nd edition. Florianópolis, NPC/UFSC.

Höppe, P. (1999). The physiological equivalent temperature – a universal index of the thermal environment. *International Journal of Biometeorology*, 43(2): 71–75.

IBGE (2010). *Sinopse do censo demográfico IBGE 2010*. Available at: http://www.censo2010.ibge.gov.br/sinopse/index.php?dados=68 (Accessed 19 November 2013).

Katzschner, L. and Horn, K. (2005). *Klimabewertungskarte Hessen*. Wiesbanden: Hessisches Minsiterium für Wirtschaft und Landesentwicklung.

Matzarakis, A., Mayer, H. and Iziomon, M. (1999). Applications of a universal thermal index: physiological equivalent temperature. *International Journal of Biometeorology*, 43(2): 76–84.

Mendonça, F. and Monteiro, C. A. F. (org.) (2003). *Clima Urbano*. São Paulo: Contexto.

Morais, J., Andrade, T. and Nery, J. (2011). Caracterização térmica de padrões de ocupação em Salvador - Estudo de caso: Nordeste de Amaralina e Pituba. *XI ENCAC e VIIENLACAC*. Búzios.

Moura Freire, T. and Schimmelpfeng, W. (2001). *Elementos Climáticos e Forma Urbana de Salvador*. Relatório Final do Bolsista. Salvador, UFBA.

Nery, J., Moura Freire, T. Carvalho, L., Freire, M., Andrade, T., Azevedo, H. and Pizzaro, E. (1997). Primeira aproximação para o estudo de clima urbano em Salvador. In: *IV Encontro Nacional de Conforto no Ambiente Construído*. Salvador: FAUFBA/LACAM; ANTAC, 124–128.

Nery, J., Andrade, T. and Lira, I. (2003). Temperatura do ar e padrões de ocupação em Salvador. *ENCAC*.

Nery, J., Andrade, T. and Moura, T. (2006a). Conforto Térmico em Salvador: O índice PET e sua abordagem projetual. *Revista de Urbanismo e Arquitetura (RUA)*, 7(1): 70–77.

Nery, J., Moura Freire, T. Andrade, T. and Katzschner, L. (2006b). Thermal comfort studies in a humid tropical city. *Proceedings of The Sixth International Conference on Urban Climate*, Gothenburg, Sweden, 12–16 June. Sweden: University of Gothenburg, 234–237.

Prefeitura Municipal da Cidade de Salvador (n.d.). *Maquete de Salvador*. Salvador, Bahia, Brazil.

SEDHAM (Prefeitura Municipal de Salvador) (2008). *Plano Diretor de Desenvolvimento Urbano (PDDU)*. Salvador, Brazil.

SEDHAM (Prefeitura Municipal de Salvador) (2009). *Uso e Ocupação do solo, vol.3*. Cadernos da Cidade. Salvador, Bahia, Brazil.

Souza, S., Andrade, T., Pitombo, C., Nery, J., and Freire, M. (2011). Avaliação do desempenho térmico nos microclimas das Preças: Piedade e Visconde Cayrú, Salvador/ BA. *XI ENCAC VII ENLACAC*. Búzios.

Souza, S., Uchôa, P. and Andrade, T. (2012). Avaliação de Conforto Térmico e Cobertura Vegetal na Cidade de Salvador Bahia. *XIV ENTAC – Encontro Nacional de Tecnologia do Ambiente Construído*. Juiz de Fora: UFJF, 3129–3134.

## Notes

1 SAVAM – Sistema de Áreas de Valor Ambiental e Cultural (System of Areas for Environmental and Cultural Value), Salvador City Hall, 2008.

2 Referred to in Nery *et al.* (1997) as BTS – Baía de Todos-os-Santos (Todos-os-Santos Bay).

3 SICAR – Sistema Cartográfico, CONDER – Companhia de Desenvolvimento Urbano do Estado da Bahia, 1998 (Company of Urban Development of the State of Bahia) (CONDER, 1998).

Chapter 14

# Urban climatic map studies in Germany

## Berlin

*Jörn Welsch*

### Introduction

Meteorological-climatological observations started very early in Berlin. They can be dated back to the beginning of the eighteenth century and are among the oldest in the world (Pelz, 2000). The study of urban climate and the application of urban climate knowledge in urban planning were also institutionalised very early in Berlin – at the end of the 1970s in Berlin (West), environmental assessment that integrated urban climate considerations for individual construction projects were already being carried out (Sukopp *et al.*, 1979; Kuttler, 1993). At the start of the 1980s, an active environmental protection policy started in Berlin. A new 'Land Use Plan' and the first 'Landscape Programme' were created. However, during the preparation for the development of the plan, it was apparent that there was a lack of a comprehensive and useable set of spatial information. The administration was largely unprepared for the task at hand. There was environmental data collected in many areas; however, there were no systematically prepared planning documents in existence to assist. This was the context upon which in 1983 the Research Project 'Environmental Atlas Berlin' that was sponsored by the German Environmental Protection Agency started. The coordinators of the project were salaried, and were given official positions. This was, at that time, a far-sighted action. The project was to be pursued with the following two main objectives:

1 to prepare and provide spatial information to be used as a basis for higher-level planning;
2 to give the general public access to information about the state of the environment.

### Initiatives and processes

Much of the data needed was collected from various offices of the Senate Department responsible for urban development and environmental protection. Universities and colleges had also worked from the beginning, developing the Environmental Atlas (EA) and significantly shaping the content of some of the topics. With the data, the Environmental Atlas Working Group assessed and described with accompanying detailed texts that identified the essential environmental problems; they provided information on the origin of the data and the method used for data collection and evaluation; they made the environmental maps and enriched them with graphics, figures and charts that described and interpreted the maps; and they finally provided the readers of the maps with statements and assessments on future developments. As such, the EA started by going far beyond a mere collection of maps; it started to become a key component of environmental reporting for Berlin. An English version of the maps has been provided since the inception. After eight years of research, the task force of the EA was established as a permanent working group in the Senate Department of Urban Development and the Environment (SDUDE, 2013a).

Berlin is the capital of Germany and at the same time one of the three federal city states of Germany; the SDUDE therefore acts like a ministry and is responsible for duties such as: urban planning, regional planning, urban development, housing, transport, construction, recreation, nature conservation, geo-information, forestry, cultural heritage, and environment. Inside these fields of responsibilities, the working group began to fill gaps and systematically build their own databases, since a cross-media description encompassing all aspects of the natural environment was a requirement that had to be met without question. Further milestones of the development were:

1990: Following the reunification of Berlin, the atlas covers the whole city
Since 1995: Implementation of web-technology for publication (parallel to analogue proceedings)
Since 1999: Publication only via internet

Taking into account the principles of sustainability as a concern for the future development of Berlin, the Atlas was recently further developed from a collection of maps into an information system.

This Urban and Environmental Information System (UEIS) enables the preparation, availability, evaluation assessment and graphic presentation of environmental data. The UEIS is composed of several components with various functions. The UEIS enables the application of different methods in synergising geographical and expert data. For example, calculations of pollutant load analyses, effect relationships, conflict descriptions, developments and trends, and presentations of these results in various media with different accents and forms (see Figure 14.1).

## From maps to evaluation and from analogue to internet

The EA of Berlin contains thematic maps for the environmental topics of soil, water, air, biotopes, land use, noise/traffic and climate. In the chapters on land use and traffic it also takes on topics relevant to urban planning, and has meanwhile been extended by a chapter on energy. All data has been

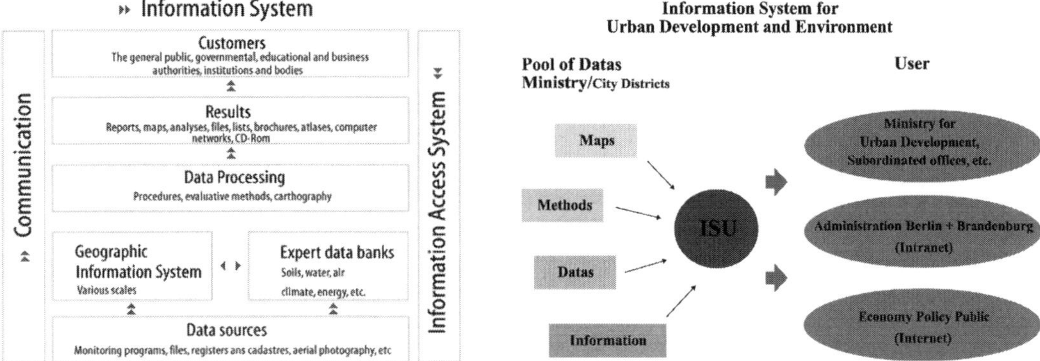


*Figure 14.1* Structure of the Urban and Environmental Information System (UEIS), Senate Department for Urban Development and the Environment, Berlin.

Source: http://www.stadtentwicklung.berlin.de/umwelt/info_system/en/struktur.shtml (Accessed 6 December 2013)

*Table 14.1* Content on the Topic 'Climate' of the Environmental Atlas of Berlin.

| | |
|---|---|
| 04.02 | Long-term Mean Air Temperatures 1961–1990 |
| 04.03 | Near Ground Wind Speeds |
| | 04.03.1 Near Ground Wind Speeds by Day |
| | 04.03.2 Near Ground Wind Speeds at Night |
| 04.04 | Temperature and Moisture Conditions in Medium and Low-exchange Nocturnal Radiation Periods |
| | 04.04.1 Distribution of Air Temperature |
| | 04.04.4 Monitoring Routes and Stations |
| 04.05 | Urban Climate Zones |
| 04.06 | Surface Temperatures Day and Night |
| | 04.06.1 Surface Temperatures in the Evening |
| | 04.06.2 Surface Temperatures in the Morning |
| | 04.06.3 Surface Temperature Differential Evening-Morning |
| 04.07 | Climate Functions |
| 04.08 | Long-term Precipitation Distribution and Runoff Formation |
| | 04.08.1 Winter Half-year 1961–1990 |
| | 04.08.2 Summer Half-year 1961–1990 |
| | 04.08.3 Yearly Precipitation 1961–1990 |
| | 04.08.4 Runoff Quantity (Difference Between Precipitation and Evaporation) |
| 04.09 | Bioclimate – Day and Night |
| | 04.09.1 Bioclimate in the Daytime |
| | 04.09.2 Bioclimate at Night |
| 04.10 | Climate Model Berlin – Analysis Maps |
| | 04.10.01 Air Temperature Entire City 10.00 p.m. |
| | 04.10.02 Air Temperature Entire City 6.00 a.m. |
| | 04.10.03 Near Ground Wind Field and Air Exchange Entire City 10.00 p.m. |
| | 04.10.04 Near Ground Wind Field and Air Exchange Entire City 6.00 a.m. |
| | 04.10.05 Near Ground Wind Field and Air Mass Flow Entire City 10.00 p.m. |
| | 04.10.06 Near Ground Wind Field and Air Mass Flow Entire City 6.00 a.m. |
| | 04.10.07 Air Temperature Detailed Analysis Area 10.00 p.m. |
| | 04.10.08 Air Temperature Detailed Analysis Area 6.00 a.m. |
| | 04.10.09 Near Ground Wind Field and Air Exchange Detailed Analysis Area 10.00 p.m. |
| | 04.10.10 Near Ground Wind Field and Air Exchange Detailed Analysis Area 6.00 a.m. |
| | 04.10.11 Near Ground Wind Field and Air Mass Flow Detailed Analysis Area 10.00 p.m. |
| | 04.10.12 Near Ground Wind Field and Air Mass Flow Detailed Analysis Area 6.00 a.m. |
| 04.11 | Climate Model Berlin – Evaluation Maps |
| | 04.11.1 Climate Functions |
| | 04.11.2 Planning Advices Urban Climate |
| 04.12 | Future Climatic Change and Thermal Load |
| | 04.12.1 Annual Mean Number of Thermal Load Days, 1971–2000 |
| | 04.12.2 Increase in the Number of Thermal Load Days, 2021–2050 |
| | 04.12.3 Increase in the Number of Thermal Load Days, 2071–2100 |
| | 04.12.4 Total of Thermal Load Days, 1971–2000 |
| | 04.12.5 Total of Thermal Load Days, 2021–2050 |
| | 04.12.6 Total of Thermal Load Days, 2071–2100 |

Source: http://www.stadtentwicklung.berlin.de/umwelt/umweltatlas/edinh_04.htm (Assessed 23 February 2015)

available online for several years. Text, graphics and maps are available free of charge. Within the wide spectrum of themes, urban climate has gained more and more relevance in the last few years. Table 14.1 shows the content of the EA; access to different editions of most of the themes is possible.

Urban climatic mapping and all kinds of environmental mapping is strongly influenced by the development of methods and technical requirements. In the last two decades there was an extraordinary change in both concerns. The EA project has always tried to adopt the most up-to-date standards. Thematic challenges that didn't change would remain over the years.

Since the first edition of the EA in 1993 (SDUDE, 1993), the notion of 'Climate Functions' has puzzled planners in Germany: what should be the aims and targets quantitatively? The challenge exists until today that, unlike some environmental topics like air or soil, concrete limits and index values for the appraisal cannot easily be drawn from regulations or guidelines. It was thus necessary to define the particular criteria and goals for the map of climate functions. The guidelines of the German Meteorological Society (DMG, 1989) prescribe a crude framework in that ideally, the city climate should be largely free from pollutants and should offer city dwellers the largest possible diversity of atmospheric conditions without extremes.

Instead of 'climatope', which was the common approach in Germany in the field of urban climatology (Neighbourhood Association Stuttgart [Nachbarschaftsverband], 1992; Local Government Association Ruhrgebiet [KVR], 1992), Berlin decided to go a different way. The initial idea was that the specificity of urban climate is a very complicated effect depending on various parameters, of which the land use characteristics are only one. Therefore, the research group responsible for the Berlin way of evaluating the influence factors decided to go for a more complicated yet appropriate way.

The map 'Climate Function' of edition 1993 (SDUDE, 1993) (see Plate 14.1) pursues an attempt that relies more essentially on the measurements of climate parameters and also further criteria, such as the area, location in the city and/or the surrounding countryside, as well as on a consideration of the mutual interactions among them. Thus the same terrain in the inner city load area would be judged differently than if it were to be situated on the outskirts of town. This is because the factors to which an area is subjected, and/or by which it is influenced, are different from its surroundings. In case of an appraisal based only upon the structure types, the appraisal would be the same in both cases, e.g. type 'villa climate'. Hence the assessment may not be realistic.

The categorised climate functions of the EA should be able to deliver assessment statements of areas which on the one hand have a potential for the relief of other areas, both adjacent to and further away (see Plate 14.1, areas 1a and 1b), and on the other hand add to the other areas' loading (see Plate 14.1, areas 4a and 4b). Between these two extremes, different areas are defined as areas where the climatic conditions are favourable, i.e. no climatic load exists (see Plate 14.1, relieved area 2), and those in which their structures and functions present transitions between Load and Relieved areas (see Plate 14.1, area 3). Apart from the four areas described above, the surroundings and other areas that are assessed to be preferred air exchange areas, i.e. areas that play an important role for the near ground fresh air transport, are also marked. The climatic functions of the areas are always estimated against use intensifications.

The 1993 conceptual ideas making the EA continued into the next edition. The 2001 edition advanced the methodology. Meanwhile, however, by the end of 1997, the new Environmental Meteorology – Climate and Air Pollution Maps for Cities and Regions (VDI, 1997) was published. It recommended the use of 'climatopes', in that homogeneous microclimatic areas are grouped.

The statistical base for integrating the maps of the system was enormous, because the derivation and delimitation of areas according to their climatic function required the collation of different information. Apart from the climate parameters data on use, surface structures as well as surface sealing were evaluated based on the following information:

Annual Mean Air Temperature 1991/92 at 2m Elevation
Near Ground Wind Speeds

Temperature and Moisture Conditions in Medium and Low-exchange Nocturnal Radiation Periods
Urban Climate Zones
Surface Temperatures at Day and Night
Sealing of Soil Surface
Actual Use of Built-up Areas
Inventory of Green and Open Space
Climate-effective Urban Structure Types
Density of Construction
Relief Map of the German Planning Atlases.

Most of the data has already been part of the topics of the EA. Although the data was originally collected in digital format with a universal spatial reference, digital technology was only at an early stage of development back then. Therefore the main procedural steps of the EA were 'handmade' in 1993 and 2001. It was a particularly challenging task and required special skills and expertise, such as

(A) very good knowledge of place in the whole investigation area for analogical conclusions, and
(B) enough time for representative mobile and stationary measurements, in order to bring the mapping of more than 1,200km$^2$ to a successful exclusion.

So, considering the enormous progress in digital methods in the meantime and the application of numerical simulation models, it was obvious that the next steps to improve one's knowledge about the climate system in and around Berlin should use a digital climatic model as a central component of this procedure. The FITNAH-3D procedural package was chosen to be adequate and particularly well capable for this approach of representing the meteorological quanta, which are spatially and temporally very strongly variable, due to the great complexity of the building structure (Groß, 1989, 1993, 2002). This project was carried out in 2003/2004 and updated and improved to a resolution of 50m × 50m in 2008/2009 with the help of the expert team from GEO-NET (http://www.geo-net.de/) and Professor Groß from the Meteorological Institute of the University of Hannover (http://www.muk.uni-hannover.de/206.html?&L=1). Subsequently, all EA data was published on the Internet to give everybody – private or professional – easy and complete access to the data: geo-data as well as the alphanumeric information (factual data) in various databases. This made a spatial search possible via addresses, general maps, city maps, and any so-called spatial units (e.g. toxic-waste sites, neighbourhoods, construction plans), or via coordinates (see Figure 14.2). This climate model approach incorporated the following important advantages:

(A) The comparability of results in the overall area of more than 1,800km$^2$ in Berlin (26.700 GIS units) and the surroundings in the state of Brandenburg was ensured.
(B) In addition to the qualitative statements designed to characterise particular urban climatic phenomena, quantitative statements concerning climate-ecological conditions and exchange processes were also possible.
(C) Climate-ecological compensation and process spaces were localised in the urban area and represented in their spatial dimensions as precisely as possible.
(D) An important aspect of the climate-ecological compensation potential of open areas – the cold air balance – was investigated on a comprehensive city-wide basis for the first time in Berlin. This analytical step in particular represented a necessary addition to the information hitherto available in the EA of Berlin.

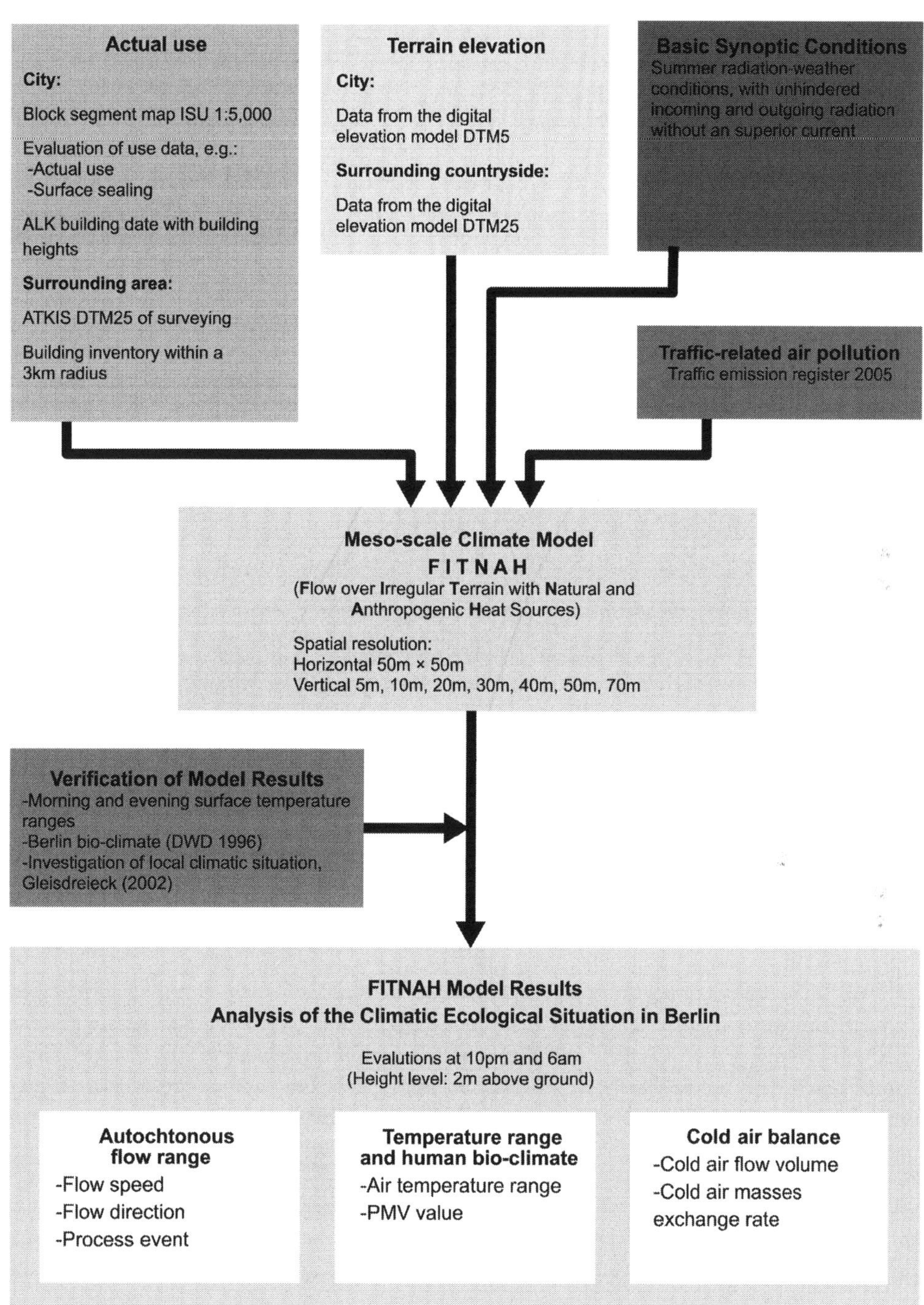


*Figure 14.2* Database and data flow for the application of the climate model FITNAH-3D.

Source: Adapted from www.stadtentwicklung.berlin.de/umwelt/umweltatlas/e_text/eka410.doc (Accessed 23 February 2015)

The results obtained in the context of the application of the climate model FITNAH-3D in the analysis phase led to a comprehensive and actual survey of the climatic situation in the city and the surrounding countryside (SDUDE, 2009a).

The purpose of these maps was to present all important results of the application of the regional model for those users, who are interested not only in the evaluation results but also in the analysis ones. All data should be as transparent as possible, according also to the German Environmental Information Act. In order to achieve comparability with the climate parameters already published in the Digital Environmental Atlas, the distribution of air temperature during two time segments is also presented, although a direct comparison of the map representations based on measurements and analogical conclusions with the results of simulations of model applications requires that the differing frameworks be taken into account (see Figure 14.3). This advice also has to be considered when comparing the results of the both FITNAH-3D model applications of the 2003/2004 edition and the 2009 edition. On the one hand, the scope and level of detail of the input data and, on the other hand, model enhancements may result in differing findings and classifications.

## From urban climate analysis to city planning

The following explanations refer now to phase II of the Climate Model study. The goal of the task is to define spaces of the city according to their different climatic functions, i.e. their effects on other areas, and to evaluate the sensitivity of these functions in relation to the city's structural changes. On this basis, planners may be able to measure results for the preservation and/or improvement of the climatic situation of the city. The actualisation of the level of knowledge on the conditions based on the end of 2005 also permits the comparative consideration of the climatic consequences occurring from structural development since the beginning of the 1990s (see Plate 14.2). Additionally, the sensitivity of these functions regarding structural changes is evaluated in a further step and presented in the form of a digital planning advice map (SDUDE, 2009b) (see Figure 14.4).

The execution into the area-specific, urban-climatic and emission-ecological quality goals debouches in the requirement for recommendations for action (see Figure 14.5). By having a precise attribution of information relevant to planning regarding the importance of climate-ecological process-controlling structural elements, e.g. cold air generating areas, air-stream channels and comfort areas, the planners can act to preserve and protect these areas from negative influences. The planners can also identify the burdened areas with an aeration deficiency and/or polluted air more easily. This methodical procedure provides well-founded conclusions for planners for the scale range from 1:100,000 to 1:20,000. In addition, an outlined evaluation with regard to the impact of planning measures on the level of local development planning can also be made based on the map.

## Technical development to extend the knowledge of Berlin's urban climate at the microclimate scale (2013 onwards)

### *First step: Extraction of building and vegetation height levels*

To further develop the EA, provision has been made for an additional process of upgrading to a model grid size of 10m × 10m to also include the microclimate effects in the evaluation process. Thereby it will be possible to avoid special expert studies at the local level to estimate the current climate situation, as well as to support simulation studies without the need to painstakingly collect the basic data beforehand for every site project.

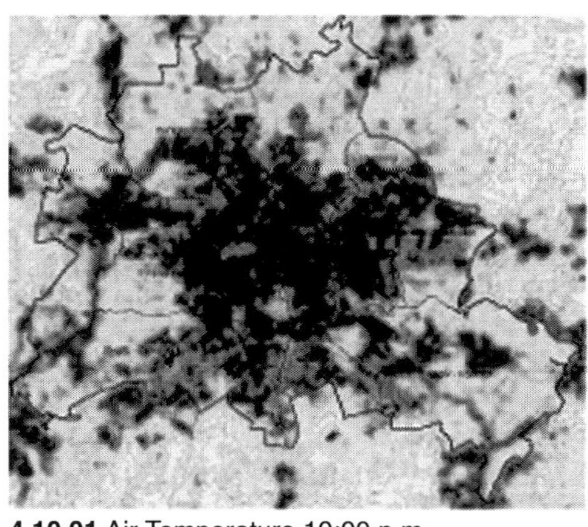

**4.10.01** Air Temperature 10:00 p.m.

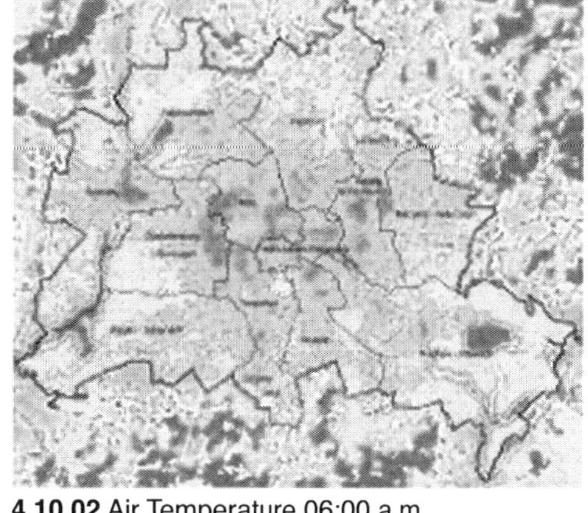

**4.10.02** Air Temperature 06:00 a.m.

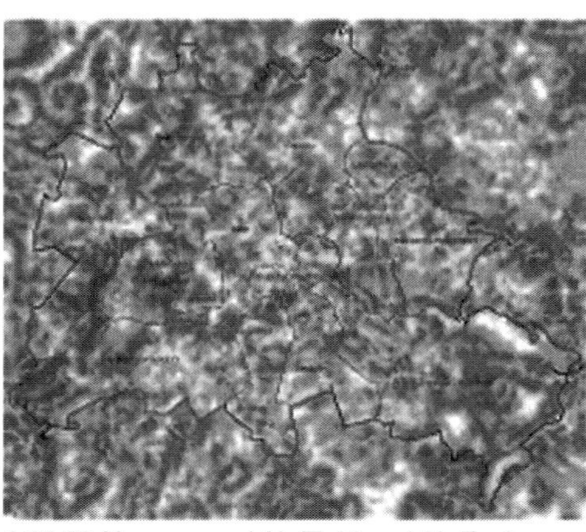

**4.10.03** Near ground Air Field and Air Exchange 10:00 p.m.

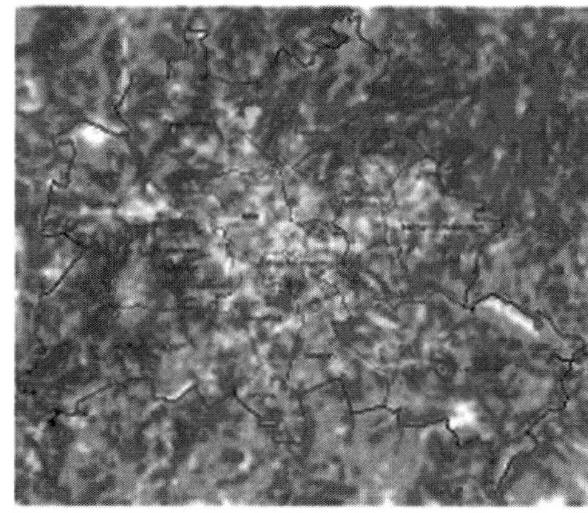

**4.10.04** Near ground Air Field and Air Exchange 06:00 a.m.

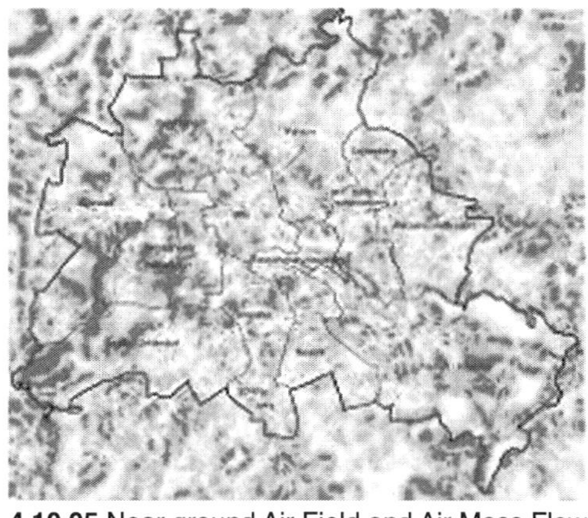

**4.10.05** Near ground Air Field and Air Mass Flow 10:00 p.m.

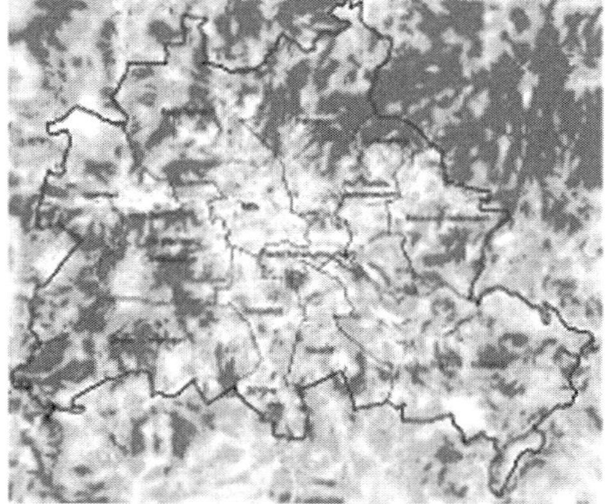

**4.10.06** Near ground Air Field and Air Mass Flow 06:00 a.m.

*Figure 14.3* Topics of the six analysis maps of the Berlin-FITNAH-3D application in 2008/2009.

Source: http://www.stadtentwicklung.berlin.de/umwelt/umweltatlas/eia410.htm (Accessed 23 February 2015)

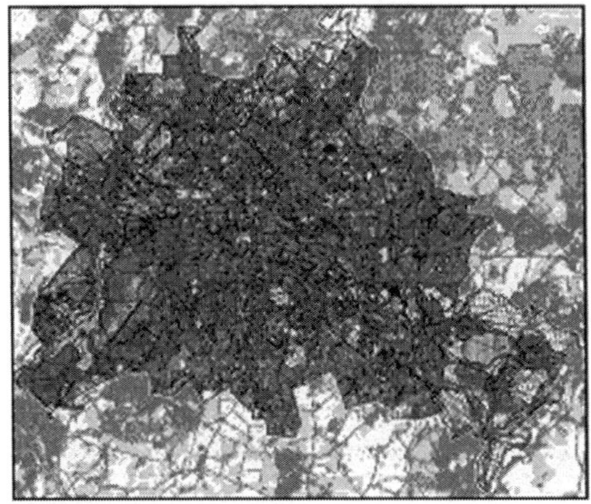


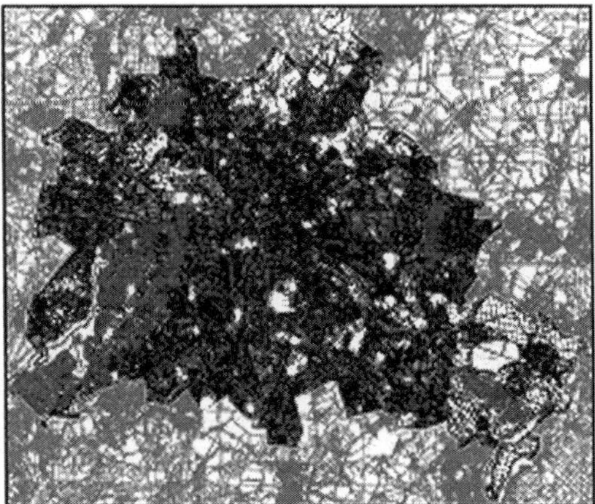


*Figure 14.4* Topics of the evaluation maps of the Berlin-FITNAH-3D application in 2008/2009. (Left): Climate Function Map; (Right): Planning Advice Urban Climatic Map).

Source: http://www.stadtentwicklung.berlin.de/umwelt/umweltatlas/eka411.htm (Accessed 23 February 2015)

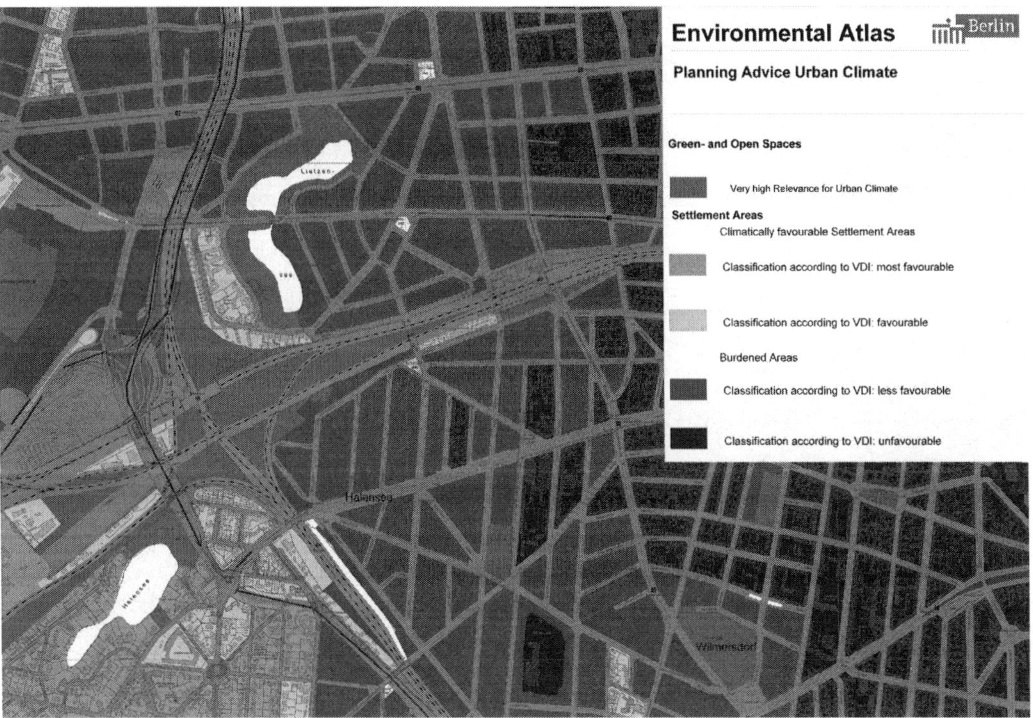


*Figure 14.5* A magnified example of the Planning Advice Urban Climatic Map Berlin 2009.

Source: http://www.stadtentwicklung.berlin.de/umwelt/umweltatlas/eda411_01.htm (Accessed 23 February 2015)

To put this approach into practice, it is necessary to improve our basic model data. Detailed building heights and building volumes, and the different structure and heights of the vegetation in the green public areas and within the building blocks, are needed.

Precise and detailed statements on the height and structure of buildings and vegetation areas can be of great significance for various utilisation purposes. The usefulness of such a database includes its ability to provide information on: (A) the complete mapping of greened roofs; (B) the more precise urban climate modelling; (C) the additional differentiation in the mapping of uses in green areas; and (D) the detailed ascertainment of air and noise pollution in residential areas.

The precision of any modelling depends to a large extent on the quality of the input data. For example, in order to permit a detailed calculation of the course of air channels and ventilation conditions, the aerodynamic surface roughness, including its geometrical dimensions, must be known as precisely as possible. Elevated objects – such as buildings, the entire blocks of buildings, and tall and dense tree structures – constitute barriers, the effect of which may be to block the wind even to the point of complete stagnation. On the other hand, if better planned, they may create a channelling effect that leads to accelerated wind flows.

The main goal of the data collation process is to derive the structure of roofs and roof shapes, as well as the extraction of vegetation height levels for Berlin and the immediate surroundings (DLR, 2013). An additional goal is the preparation of a geo-database with specific object information, and the provision of this data as a basis for further urban analyses. Thus, for the first time, Berlin now has a precise record of the 'vertical extent' of the city (SDUDE, 2013b) (see Plate 14.3).

Especially with regard to vegetation, there is now an information base suitable for many different types of utilisation. For example, it is clear that at least in those parts of the inner city built after 1918, residentially oriented open spaces are of great importance, providing greenery to the city infrastructure (see Figure 14.6).

*Figure 14.6* Classification results in Berlin inner city: (left): Highly impervious inner-city buildings on both sides of '*Friedrichstraße*', and (right): Imperial era block construction with a high share of green space in the area of 'Görlitzer Park' (scale 1:7,500).

Source: http://www.stadtentwicklung.berlin.de/umwelt/umweltatlas/ei610.htm (Accessed 23 February 2015)

### *Second step: Climate model Berlin on the base of high-resolution building and vegetation data*

The project, co-financed by the European Regional Development Fund, started in October 2013 for 1.5 years. The objectives are ambitious:

(A) application of the model with the same grid of 10m × 10m over the entire project area of 1,800km$^2$;
(B) inclusion of single buildings and highly differentiated vegetation structure;
(C) consideration of several initial meteorological situations;
(D) integration and evaluation of health and social criteria with the help of indicators like the sensitivity of social infrastructure or the age distribution of the population;
(E) comprehension of climate change effects to consider future burden and sensitivity; and
(F) development of a concept to integrate changing land use (already at the project level) continuously in the process of monitoring the urban climate.

The first batch of results for this project were due to be available in the middle of 2015.

## Successful application into urban planning for a better future

Continuous and professional urban climatic mapping with comprehensive access to data provides the basis for a successful application of the results into the different planning scales, from the entire city level to the binding land-use plan.

For development planning for Berlin as a whole – urban construction and landscape development – planners will take as much account as possible of the urban climatic requirements for those projects that are connected to the city's function as Germany's capital city, and its need for new housing construction programmes. Special emphasis and priority is now given to development in the existing settlement areas by means of increasing the site density and/or making the best use of land recycling before additional non-built-up areas are used for construction projects (see Figure 14.7).

Nevertheless, conflicts arise, mainly regarding the potential of open spaces that affect climatic conditions. In many areas, open spaces that have a positive influence on the city climate are being used for construction purposes. Examples of this can be seen in the inner-city (*Potsdamer Platz*) and the urban expansion sectors in the North-east (district of *Weißensee*).

However, in every case, the resulting loss in positive climatic potential needs to be balanced out in the obligatory master planning (construction plan). Construction plans are generally binding against everybody. They regularise and determine, for example, the following:

(A) types and dimensions of structural utilisation;
(B) height of structural facilities;
(C) style, positioning and roof orientation;
(D) land areas to be built on/not built on;
(E) size, depth and width of plots of land for buildings;
(F) greening.

The German planning law framework requires that when considering the above during the design and planning process, protection of the environment and nature must be taken into account, e.g. as regulated in the Federal Building Code (BauGB), which states that:

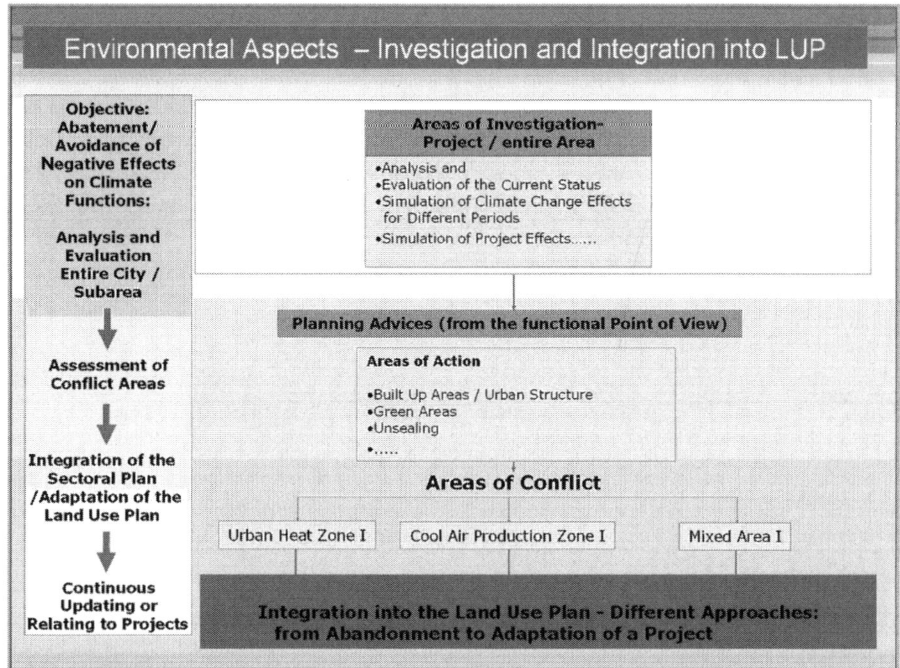


*Figure 14.7* Environmental aspects – investigation and integration into land-use planning.

Source: Author

> the municipal zoning plan and the local construction development plan to contribute to securing an environment consistent with human dignity and to protect and develop the natural basic living conditions, shall also be carried out in such a manner as to meet the responsibility for general climate protection
>
> (Baugesetzbuch, Art.1, Sect. 5, Clause 2)

There are also a number of instruments laid down in various laws. They are integrated into the planning processes and approval procedures. Recently, regulations based on European law have also become applicable (SDUDE, 2006). Therefore, information is needed to produce a workable balance of interests between sustainable resource protection and regional economic development. This balance requires reliable information, available at any time, about the value, the need for protection, the sensitivity, and the load-bearing capacity of smaller, larger, and the entire urban areas. The EA therefore is very useful for the integration of environmental aspects in different planning levels, as below:

***Urban planning level (small and large scale)***

Strategic Environmental Assessment (SEA) for plans and programmes

Environmental Reports for several plans, such as:

- Preparing and binding urban plans
- Land use plan
- Local development plans
- Landscape Programme

***Project level***
Environmental Impact Assessment (EIA)
Impact regulation (nature conservation law)

Thanks to Berlin's comprehensive planning principles, a considerable amount of information and data is already available which does not need to be collected a second time. It is well acknowledged that in all the processes involved during the planning and design stages, recommendations resulting from environmental evaluations can be implemented much better the earlier they are formulated. An exemplary case of this kind of early integration during the planning procedure from the climate point of view can be noted when the development strategy of Tempelhof airport in the centre of Berlin was made. This is discussed in the following section.

## Tempelhofer Freiheit – planning the future in light of climate requirements

### *Historical aspects*

Tempelhof central airport – the 'mother of all airports' (Sir Norman Foster) – ceased operating on 31 October 2008, 85 years after its opening in 1923. After World War II, during the Berlin airlift in 1948/1949, Tempelhof became famous as the main starting and landing point for all airlift operations. During the following decades, Tempelhof remained as one of the two inner-city airports of Berlin (West), but in the course of time Tegel airport in the north of the city adopted the function of Berlin's main airport. After reunification in 1990, Berlin policymakers from the city of Berlin, the state of Brandenburg and the federal Federal Ministry of Transport, Building and Urban Development decided to concentrate all further air traffic at the airport of Berlin–Schönefeld by first closing Berlin–Tempelhof and later on Berlin–Tegel.

The 386-hectare area of the former Tempelhof airport was renamed 'Tempelhofer Freiheit' ('Tempelhof freedom') to illustrate the wide open spaces of more than 2km from north to south (see Figure 14.8). It has been opened as a local recreation area every day since May 2010 without any planning intervention (for spontaneous, unplanned use by so-called pioneers) (see Figure 14.8). For the future, the overall concept of a 'unique urban landscape' is to be developed.

*Figure 14.8* Former Central Airport Berlin-Tempelhof, often called the 'refrigerator' of the city, is situated near the centre of Berlin. After its closure, it has been a very popular local recreation area for the Berliners. Using the always-blowing wind: kite-surfing on the runways of the former Central Airport.

Source: (left) Senate Department for Urban Development and Environment Berlin, photo: Dirk Laubner; (right) Senate Department for Urban Development and Environment Berlin, photo: Margit Schneider

### *Planning processes from the climate point of view*

The future concept and guiding ideas for the 250 hectares green area in Tempelhof have taken into account the local situation of the recreational as well as the environmental requirements. Readers can follow the development of Tempelhofer Freiheit by visiting their website (www.stadtentwicklung.berlin.de/planen/tempelhof).

The design for the Tempelhof park landscape will be implemented in several phases. Step by step, the park will be formed with its wide opening as the theme. In this context the integration of climate aspects into the landscape planning competition is exemplary. The general principle for all steps during the competitions and citizen participations is a transparent and comprehensible procedure. From the beginning, an expert team assisted the planning process with technical contributions and recommendations from the urban climate point of view, e.g. with guidelines for the landscape competition to integrate urban climate requirements into the design process. The technical basics for the climate assessment were delivered from the Berlin urban climatic map and improved with more detailed information at a larger scale. The urban climate recommendations were adapted into the competition brief. In anticipation of the tasks that arrive from the requirements of climate conscious planning, it is an ambitious procedure to harmonise the different competing claims among interest groups. Figure 14.9 illustrates the principal procedure.

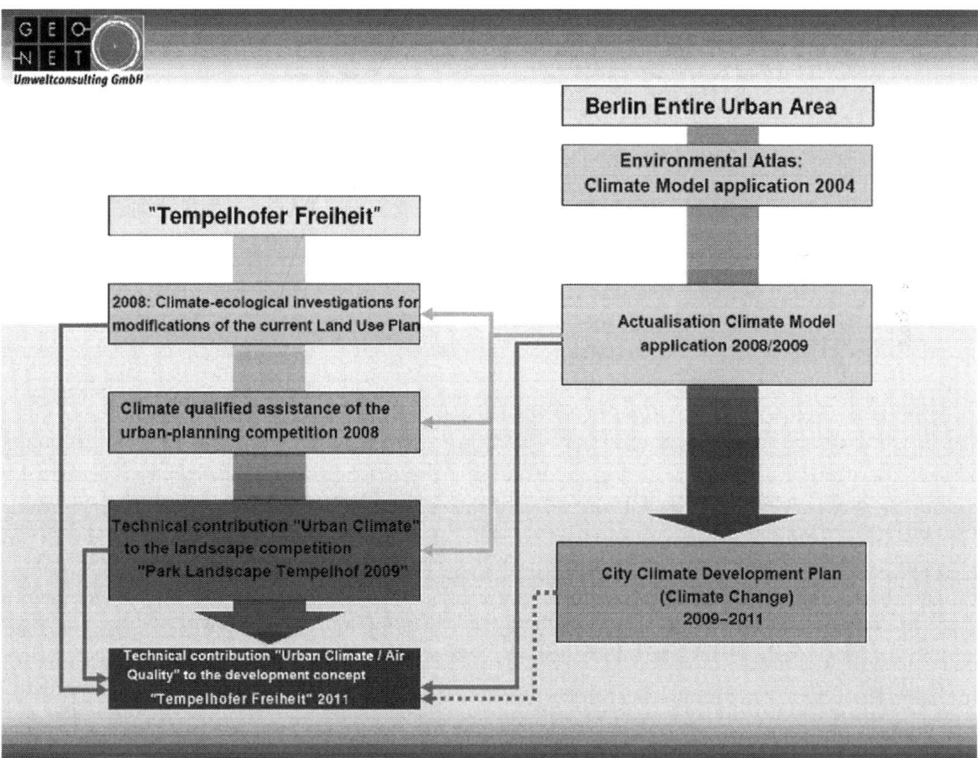


*Figure 14.9* The development concept '*Tempelhofer Freiheit*'/'Tempelhof freedom' for the evaluation of the climate-ecological impacts of the planned land use changes.

Source: Adapted from GEO-NET GmbH, 2012, p.2

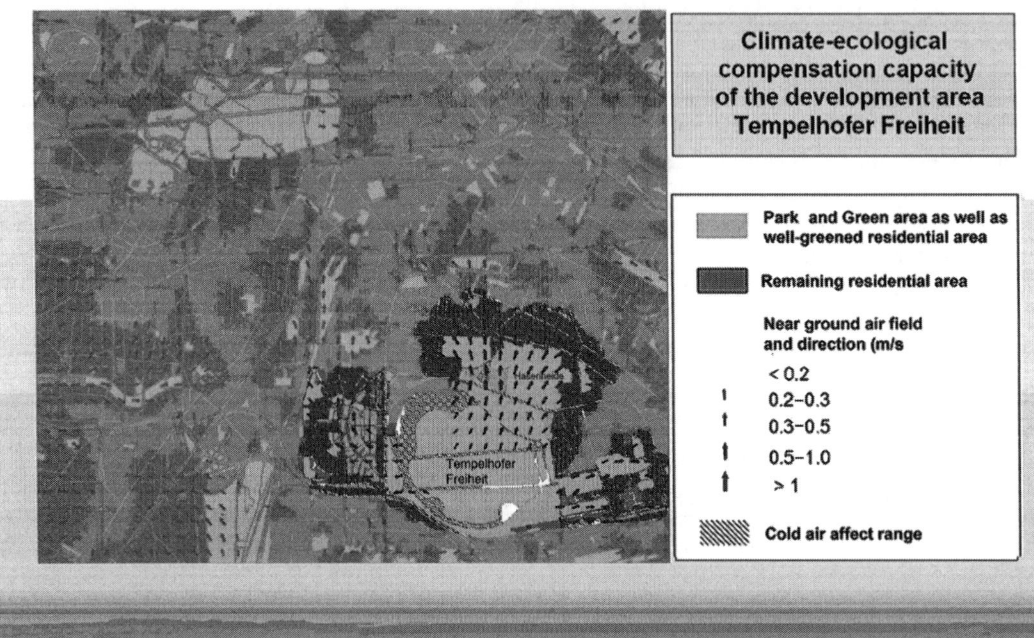


*Figure 14.10* An evaluation of the climate-ecological compensation capacity of the development area of '*Tempelhofer Freiheit*'/'Tempelhof freedom' using the information of the Berlin urban climatic map.

Source: Adapted from GEO-NET GmbH, 2012, p.7

Figure 14.10 illustrates one of the technical steps during the evaluation procedure: the effective range of the cold air-producing areas and flow field near the ground. By better integrating the functionally connected areas, this green area is able to significantly improve a space of about 10.2km$^2$ with a population of about 110,000 inhabitants. This illustrates the importance of 'Tempelhofer Freiheit' as one of the main green and open spaces in Berlin with a positive impact on bioclimatically stressed settled areas in their neighbourhood (see Figure 14.11).

## Climate change, thermal load and adaptation

### *Cooperation agreement with the German weather service (DWD)*

Beyond the scope of 'daily work', the requirements for a regional strategy for climatic prevention and adaptation, resulting from the consequences of worldwide climate change, is an increasingly important task. The presented urban climatic maps for Berlin may also act as an important information basis for this task, because they state the space-relevant status quo demands and recommendations related to the field of urban climate.

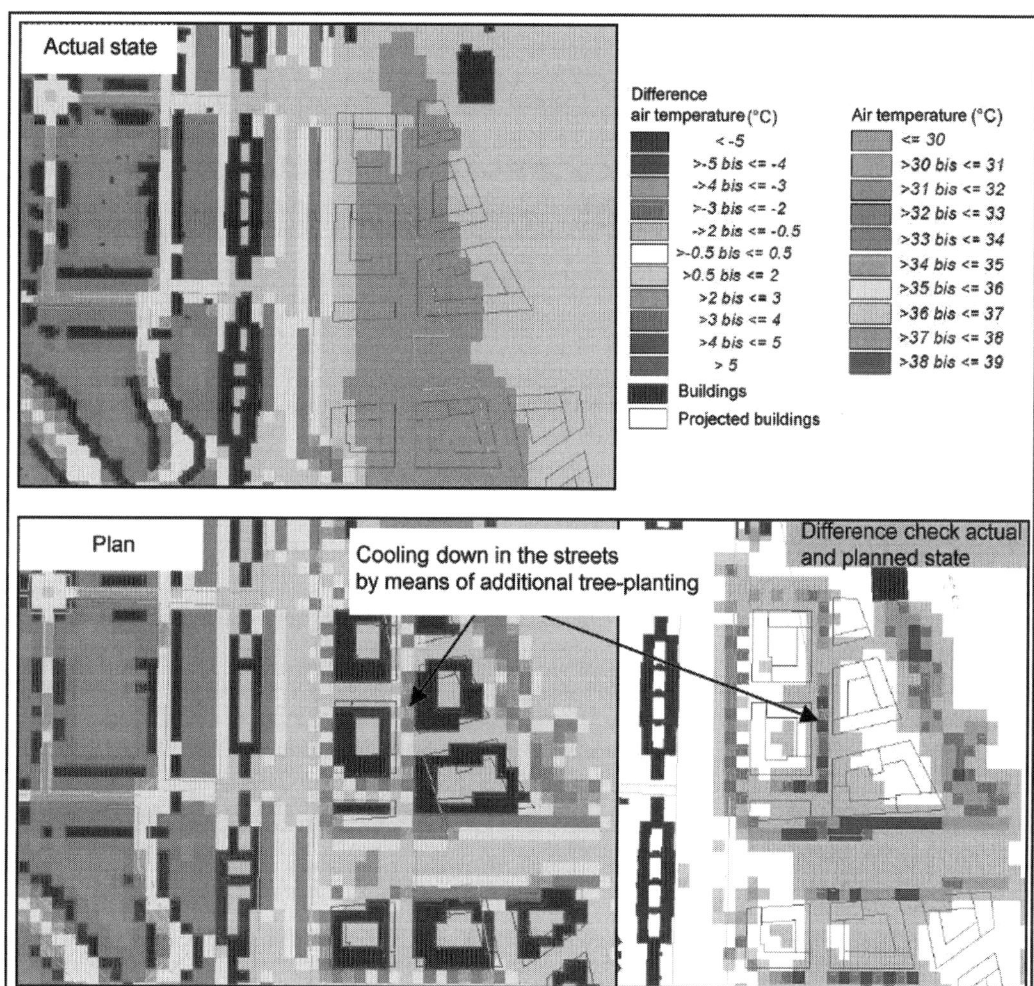


*Figure 14.11* A simulation of the positive climatic influence of greening in the planned streets with additional trees (cooling-down by 4°C–5°C, bottom compared to top).

Source: Adapted from GEO-NET, 2013, p.27

In order to define a necessary framework for the future in a promising way, further activities and processes are needed. This approach requires more than a pure urban climatic map system, and consists of different cross-linked activities which will be intensified in the coming years and can only be mentioned here briefly.

The first action for better assessing the local impact of climate change for Berlin was the cooperation agreement concluded in early 2008 between the Deutscher Wetterdienst (DWD), Climate and Environmental Consultancy Department, and the Berlin State Senate Department for Urban Development, Geo-Information Section, Office of Urban and Environment Information System. The cooperative study was successfully completed at the beginning of 2010. The project report submitted for this purpose has provided essential contributions to the following discussions in this chapter (DWD, 2010). Most of the details concerning the statistical base, the methodology and the results are also online via the EA Berlin (SDUDE, 2010).

The approach of the maps and data presented here address the question as to how thermal conditions might develop in Berlin on the basis of information and model data existing today. This is of special interest because the study may be able to highlight areas of the city that are not yet affected by thermal load but that are likely be subjected to much higher summertime temperatures in coming decades due to climate warming. This applies both to expected absolute temperature peaks and to the duration of heat waves (see Figure 14.12).

As a limitation, one must say that the interpretation of model outputs is subject to the technical limitations imposed by the wide range of possible emission scenarios, the pilot nature of the study and various other factors of influence on the future climate that are impossible to foresee as yet. Nevertheless, the results of this cooperative effort with the DWD provide essential support for the efforts that responsible authorities in the Berlin Senate are making to develop the necessary measures of adjustment to climate impacts already perceived to be inevitable. In addition, they represent an important source of information for the interested public.

### *Urban climate development plan [Stadtentwicklungsplan (StEP) Klima]*

In spite of all efforts to reduce greenhouse gas emissions, temperature and precipitation patterns will change in the future. This will have disastrous effects for the quality of life and health in metropolitan areas. Therefore, one of the greatest challenges for urban policy, even in metropolitan areas, is to question and discuss how to deal with these demands. Berlin, as the most important city and the capital of Germany, has reacted to these challenges amongst others with the urban climate development plan '*Stadtentwicklungsplan (StEP) Klima*'. The framework consists of different fields of activity:

- bioclimate in populated areas;
- green and open spaces;
- water quality and intense rain;
- climate protection.

To identify those areas where the serious consequences of climate change are to be feared, and those green areas with positive climatic impact, much of the aforementioned geo-data from the UEIS formed the basis of this project (SDUDE, 2011a, 2011b):

- maps of the Climate Model Berlin;
- results of the mentioned cooperation with the German Weather Service; and
- additional scenarios for future climate situation on the entire and local city level using the urban structure information from UEIS.

In May 2011, the *Stadtentwicklungsplan (StEP) Klima* was approved by the Berlin city parliament. It has been published via the internet with all the details, maps and figures to inform and consult the citizens. In order to quickly present a high-profile catalogue of pressing and exemplary projects to the public, the *StEP Klima* plan of action has named several projects which combine 'urgency of realisation' with 'potential to serve as models' in order to illustrate the benefits achievable (see Figure 14.13).

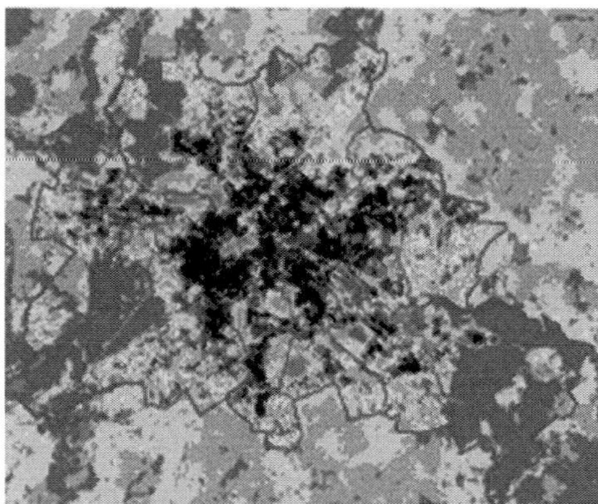

**4.12.1** Annual Mean Number of Thermal Load Days 1971–2000

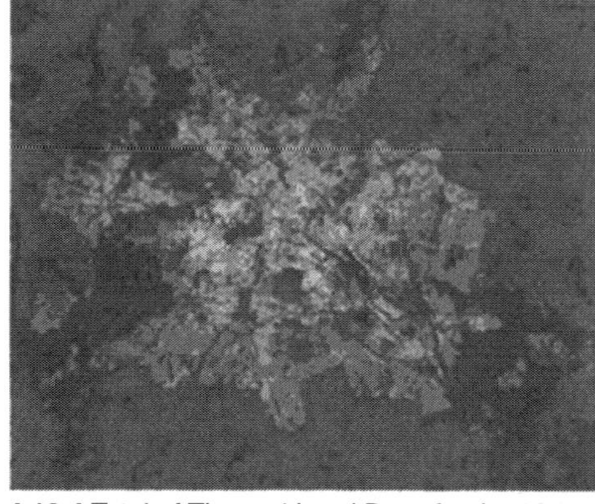

**4.12.4** Total of Thermal Load Days for the 1971–2000 Period

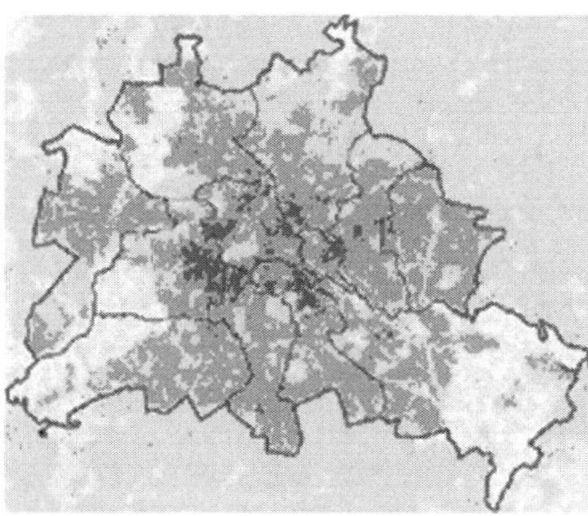

**4.12.2** Increase in the Number of Thermal Load Days 2021–2050

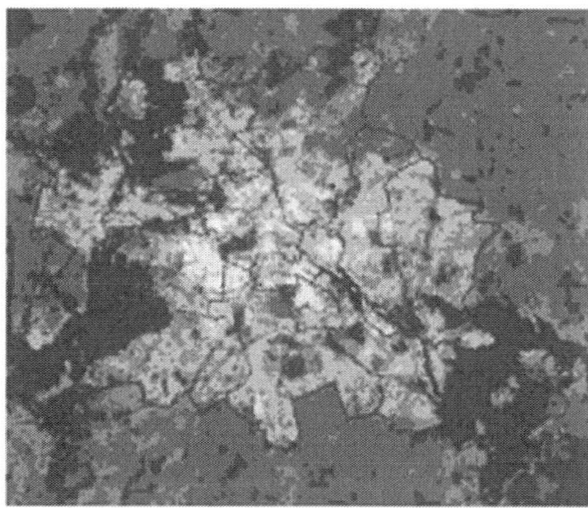

**4.12.5** Total of Thermal Load Days for the 2021–2050 Period

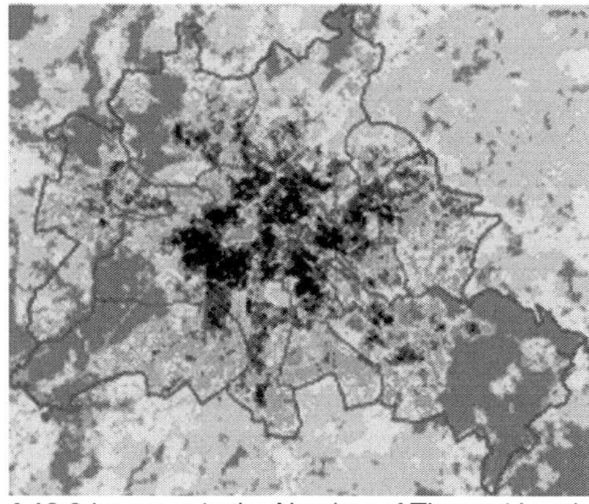

**4.12.3** Increase in the Number of Thermal Load Days 2071–2100

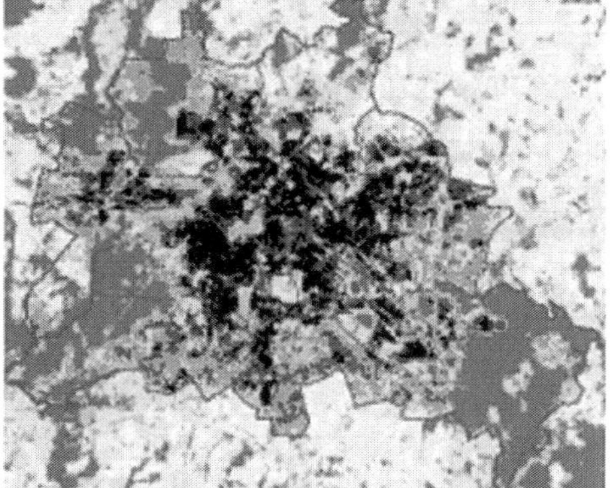

**4.12.6** Total of Thermal Load Days for the 2071–2100 Period

*Figure 14.12* Themes of the six maps of the Environmental Atlas topic 04.12 'Future Climate Change and Thermal Load' in Berlin.

Source: http://www.stadtentwicklung.berlin.de/umwelt/umweltatlas/ei412.htm (Accessed 23 February 2015)

*Figure 14.13* The Urban Climate Development Plan '*Stadtentwicklungsplan* (StEP)' outlines the locations of project areas with urgency of realisation.

Source: http://www.stadtentwicklung.berlin.de/planen/stadtentwicklungsplanung/download/klima/StEP_Klima_Karte_12.pdf (Accessed 23 February 2015)

The *StEP Klima* is not a finished product created once and for all; it stands at the beginning of a process of further planning and discussion. For these coming steps of consolidation and updating, further research and improvement concerning the climate model of Berlin, its details, and its degree of reliance will be necessary. It is a demanding challenge for the future.

## References

Baugesetzbuch (BauGB) (Federal Building Code) amended by the publication of 23 September 2004 (Federal Law Gazette I p. 2414) last amended by the Law of 11 June 2013, Federal Law Gazette I p. 1548.

DLR (2013). *Extraction of Buildings and Vegetation Height Levels for Berlin and the Immediate Surroundings.* Deutsches Zentrum für Luft- und Raumfahrt e.V. Available at: http://www.stadtentwicklung.berlin.de/umwelt/umweltatlas/download/e0610_Edition2013_Documentation_Building_Vegetation_Heights.pdf.

DMG (Deutsche Meteorologische Gesellschaft e.V.) (1989). Fachausschuß BIOMET. In: *Mitteilungen der Deutschen Meteorologischen Gesellschaft*, 3: 51–53.

DWD (Deutscher Wetterdienst) (2010). *Berlin im Klimawandel – Eine Untersuchung zum Bioklima* [Berlin in climate change: an investigation of the bio-climate], final report for the cooperative effort between the Deutscher Wetterdienst and the Senate Department for Urban Development, Section. III, Office of the City and Environment Information System (ISU), Potsdam, Freiburg. Available at: http://www.stadtentwicklung.berlin.de/umwelt/umweltatlas/download/Berlin_Waermebelastung_der_Zukunft_Projektbericht.pdf (Assessed 6 December 2013). (In German).

GEO-NET (2013). *Klimaökologische Untersuchung 'Tempelhofer Freiheit' in Berlin*, final report, expert-study, Tempelhof Projekt GmbH, Berlin, unpublished.

GEO-NET GmbH (2012): *Aspekte zur klimaökologischen Beurteilung der geplanten Nutzungsänderungen durch das Entwicklungskonzept Tempelhofer Freiheit*, interim report, Tempelhof Projekt GmbH, Berlin, not published.

Groß, G. (1989). Numerical simulation of the nocturnal flow systems in the Freiburg area for different topographies. *Beitraege zur Physik der Atmosphaere*, 62: 57–72.

Groß, G. (1993). *Numerical Simulation of Canopy Flows.* Berlin: Springer-Verlag.

Groß, G. (2002). The exploration of boundary layer phenomena using a nonhydrostatic mesoscale model. *Meteorologische Zeitschrift*, 11(4): 295–302.

Kuttler, W. (1993). Planungsorientierte Stadtklimatologie. Aufgaben, Methoden und Fallbeispiele. *Geographische Rundschau*, 45(2): 95–106.

KVR (ed.) (1992). *Synthetische Klimafunktionskarte Ruhrgebiet.* Essen: Kommunalverband Ruhrgebiet, Abt. Öffentlichkeitsarbeit/Wirtschaft.

Nachbarschaftsverband Stuttgart (1992). *Klimaatlas: Klimauntersuchung für den Nachbarschaftsverband Stuttgart und angrenzende Teile der Region Stuttgart.* Stuttgart: Nachbarschaftsverband Stuttgart.

Pelz, J. (2000). Die Wetterbeobachtungsstationen in Berlin und Umgebung. *Beiträge des Institutes für Meteorologie, der Freien Universität Berlin zur Berliner Wetterkarte*, 25/00. Berlin: Verein BERLINER WETTERKARTE e.V.

SDUDE (1993). *Berlin Environmental Atlas, Climate Functions (Edition 1993).* Available at: http://www.stadtentwicklung.berlin.de/umwelt/umweltatlas/ed407_01.htm (Accessed 6 December 2013).

SDUDE (2001). *Berlin Environmental Atlas, Climate Functions (Edition 2001).* Available at: http://www.stadtentwicklung.berlin.de/umwelt/umweltatlas/eia407.htm (Accessed 6 December 2013).

SDUDE (2006). *Environmental Assessment Berlin's Guide for Urban and Landscape Planning.* Berlin: Senate Department of Urban Development and the Environment. Available at: http://www.stadtentwicklung.berlin.de/umwelt/landschaftsplanung/uvp/download/uvp-leit-06_1-koord_en.pdf. (Accessed 6 December 2013).

SDUDE (2009a). *Berlin Environmental Atlas, Climate Model Berlin – Analysis Maps (Edition 2009).* Available at: http://www.stadtentwicklung.berlin.de/umwelt/umweltatlas/eia410.htm (Accessed 6 December 2013).

SDUDE (2009b). *Berlin Environmental Atlas, Climate Model Berlin – Evaluation Maps (Edition 2009).* Available at: http://www.stadtentwicklung.berlin.de/umwelt/umweltatlas/eda411_01.htm (Accessed 6 December 2013).

SDUDE (2010). *Berlin Environmental Atlas, Future Climatic Change and Thermal Load (Edition 2010).* Available at: http://www.stadtentwicklung.berlin.de/umwelt/umweltatlas/ei412.htm (Accessed 6 December 2013).

SDUDE (2011a). *Stadtentwicklungsplan Klima – Urbane Lebensqualität im Klimawandel sichern, Berlin.* Berlin: Senate Department of Urban Development and the Environment. Available at: http://www.stadtentwicklung.berlin.de/planen/stadtentwicklungsplanung/download/klima/step_klima_broschuere.pdf (Accessed 6 December 2013).

SDUDE (2011b). *Untersuchungen zum Klimawandel in Berlin – Dokumentationen der im Rahmen des Stadtentwicklungspklans (StEP) Klima durchgeführten Modellrechnungen.* Available at: http://www.stadtentwicklung.berlin.de/download/StEP_Klima/SenStadt_StEP_Klima_Fachbeitrag_Klimamodellierung.pdf (Accessed 6 December 2013).

SDUDE (2013a). *The Environmental Atlas, Senate Department of Urban Development and the Environment.* Available at: http://www.stadtentwicklung.berlin.de/umwelt/umweltatlas/edua_index.shtml (Accessed 6 December 2013).

SDUDE (2013b). *Berlin Environmental Atlas, Building and Vegetation Heights (2013).* Available at: http://www.stadtentwicklung.berlin.de/umwelt/umweltatlas/ei610.htm (Accessed 6 December 2013).

Sukopp, H. *et al.* (1979). *Ökologisches Gutachten über die Auswirkungen von Bau und Betrieb der BAB Berlin (West) auf den Großen Tiergarten.* Berlin: Senator für Bau- und Wohnungswesen Berlin.

VDI (1997). *VDI-Standard: VDI 3787 Part 1 Environmental Meteorology – Climate and Air Pollution Maps for Cities and Regions.* Berlin: Beuth Verlag.

Chapter 15

# Urban climatic map studies in Taiwan

## Kaohsiung

*Chao Ren*

## Introduction

Currently, cities are becoming increasingly 'high density' or 'mega', as characterised by their compact urban fabric and large urban population (UN, 2002a; Kraas, 2007). This is especially true in developing countries where it has become immensely difficult to achieve sustainable urban development with high-quality living (Ng, 2009). Although scientifically based urban climatic studies have been widely conducted, the application of urban climatic knowledge to urban planning decision making has been, until now, rather limited. One difficulty is the translation between the working languages of scientists and city planners (Bitan, 1984; Oke, 1984; Eliasson, 2000; Mills, 2006; Ng, 2009). From the perspective of planners, the difficulties can include the following reasons:

(A) Planners' lack of a scientific educational background makes it difficult for them to understand the scientific knowledge of climatologists. Planners can have difficulty translating numbers and scientific equations into a meaningful patterns for planning application. It is not easy for them to reconcile the scientific working style of 'precision' and the planning working style of 'balance' (Eliasson, 2000; Ng, 2009; Mills *et al.*, 2010).

(B) Urban climatic information is not normally visualised with spatial information for easy planning application (Bitan, 1988).

(C) Scientific climatic evaluations and knowledge are not normally elaborated in planning language, and effective mitigation measures are not always clear or actionable for planners (Mills *et al.*, 2010).

Finding ways to assemble the immediately necessary information and collating and presenting it in a way that planners find useful is very much required. The use of an urban climatic map offers a possible solution for achieving this goal (Baumüller *et al.*, 2008; Katzschner and Mulder, 2008; Baumüller *et al.*, 2009; Mills *et al.*, 2010).

An urban climatic map (UCMap) is an information and evaluation tool that integrates urban climatic factors and town planning considerations by presenting the urban climatic characteristics on a two-dimensional spatial map in a format that is easily read by city planners (Ren *et al.*, 2011). A UCMap first puts together meteorological, planning, land use, topographical, and vegetation information. Their interrelationships and effects on the urban environment are then analysed and evaluated spatially and quantitatively (VDI, 1997; Scherer *et al.*, 1999; Alcoforado *et al.*, 2009). Based on this information, various spatial 'climatopes' can be defined. A climatope is the basic spatial unit of a UCMap for presenting areas with similar urban climatic conditions and features (Baumüller *et al.*, 1992; VDI, 1997). The spatial distribution of urban climatic characteristics and their significance can be shown easily using climatopes on a UCMap (Scherer *et al.*, 1999; Baumüller *et al.*, 2009a, 2009b). With this understanding, sensitive urban-climatic and environmental problematic areas can be identified so that relevant strategic urban planning recommendations can be made to assist planners in taking appropriate action. The scale of UCMap application normally varies from 1:100,000 to 1:5,000, with urban planning scales ranging from region to city, and down to neighbourhood (Katzschner, 1988; VDI, 1997). For the planning process, UCMaps may assist policymakers and planners to identify suitable locations for new developments. Once the location is defined, the detailed recommendations of the UCMap study may help them to choose the better planning option, and to establish the appropriate land use zones.

The UCMap concept was first developed by German researchers in the 1970s (Matzarakis, 2005). Most German cities have since developed their own UCMaps (Ren *et al.*, 2011). In 1993, to guide the practice of developing UCMaps in Germany, the German National Committee on Applied Urban Climatology published a national guideline: *VDI 3787: Part 1 – Environmental Meteorology Climate and Air Pollution Maps for Cities and Regions* (VDI, 1997). This establishes key methods for drafting UCMaps, defining terms, symbols and representations for UCMaps. It also provides recommendations for applying UCMaps in physical planning. Since the 1980s, UCMap studies have been widely conducted in Europe, Asia, and South America (Scherer *et al.*, 1999; Alcoforado *et al.*, 2009; Baumüller *et al.*, 2009a) (see Figure 2.1). German guidelines have also been referenced by scholars and map makers worldwide (Ren *et al.*, 2011). Currently, most existing studies focus on low-density city planning and design, and UCMap studies for high-density cities are rather rare – the thermal environmental map for Tokyo (TMG, 2005b) and urban climatic map for Hong Kong (Ng *et al.*, 2008, 2009) are two notable exceptions. For the thermal environmental map for Tokyo, it was noted that temperatures in Tokyo had risen by 2°C to 3°C over the past century. In response, the Tokyo metropolitan government (TMG) commissioned the production of the map (see Plate 5.1) in 2000 so as to understand the factors affecting the urban heat island (UHI) intensity of the city. Based on the thermal environment map, the TMG formulated relevant control measures in 2005 that focused on a number of urban design aspects, such as: greening premises, rooftops, and building walls; increasing rooftop reflectance; encouraging water-retentive pavement; and reducing waste heat from buildings (TMG, 2005a, 2005b). In Hong Kong, the urban climatic analysis map (UC-AnMap) (see Plate 10.1) provides urban climatic planning recommendations to city planners based on an evaluation of a number of actionable planning parameters, such as: building density, building volume (floor area ratio), building and site coverage, greenery, open space, air paths and breezeways, and proximity to the waterfront. The urban climatic planning recommendation map (UC-ReMap) of Hong Kong (see Plate 10.3) recommends strategies that focused on the improvement or preservation of existing greenery, creation and protection of ventilation paths, and reduction of thermal load in built-up areas by controlling the urban morphology.

With the above background, the aim of this study is to enhance understanding by developing a map-based planning tool for the high-density city of Kaohsiung. The method of the study mainly follows Part 1 of VDI 3787 of the German guidelines (VDI, 1997), allowing for the quick merging of available climatic data and planning information to generate planning recommendations for planners. The urban climatic environment of Kaohsiung has never been studied systematically at the urban level and applied to the Taiwan Planning System (Tseng, 2007); the study is the first time urban climatic information and knowledge has been applied to the city planning of Kaohsiung.

## Method

The methodology of the Kaohsiung study follows these steps. First, six data layers are input. The urban climatic, environmental and planning parameters, as well as their impact, are then considered in order to evaluate their impact to the thermal load and dynamic potential impact to the city. Second, the prevailing wind data and local land and sea breezes are coded and evaluated as 'wind information', providing an understanding of the wind environment of the city. Third, the synthesised effects of thermal load, dynamic potential and wind information are used to form an understanding of the city's 'climatopes'. Fourth, the analysis eventually leads to the development of a number of planning recommendations.

### *The study area*

Kaohsiung at 23° 30′ N, 120° 27′ E is the second-largest city in Taiwan; it is also the most densely populated city with an average population density of 9,833 persons per square kilometre (KCG, 2003). Located on the south-western coast of the island facing the Taiwan Strait (see Figure 15.1a), the city's downtown areas are centred around the Kaohsiung Harbour, with the island of Chijin on the other side of the harbour acting as a natural breakwater. The Ai River (Love River) flows into the harbour through the old city and downtown areas.

Kaohsiung is located at south of the Tropic of Cancer and its climate is sub-tropical with an average summer month temperature of approximately 29°C, and humidity of approximately 80 per cent (TCWB, 2009). It has 11 administrative districts (see Figure 15.1b). Since 1900, it has experienced three major phrases of urban development (see Figure 15.1c). From 1900 to 1921, Kaohsiung, as a colony of Japan, was constructed as a harbour city, and the main commercial and industrial areas were planned and developed during this period. From 1921 to 1955, the Kaohsiung metropolitan plan was carried out, and more heavy industry was brought to the city. Between 1955 and 1970, the urban area of Kaohsiung sprawled further. From 1970 to 2000, it underwent further redevelopment and urban renewal, especially around its coastal areas with their abandoned factories and industrial areas. Recently, urban climatic adaptation and sustainable development have become two major targets of urban planning in Kaohsiung (KCG, 2009).

Kaohsiung, as an industrial city, has experienced rapid urbanisation in the last few decades, resulting in a wide range of varieties of environmental degradation and a continuous rise in urban temperature due to the UHI (see Figure 15.2) (Huang, 1986; Tseng, 2008; KCG, 2009). Manufacturing and heavy industry have been the major sources of air pollution in the city (Kuo, 1998). High urban density, a result of rapid and extensive urbanisation, is associated with increasing population density. This puts heavy burdens on social amenities and welfare, the natural environment, public health and hygiene. Consequently, the UHI effect has affected the urban areas, causing thermal discomfort and health threats to the general public, especially to the poor and the weak. At the same time, according to meteorological data from the Taiwan Central Weather Bureau, the mean annual air temperature of Kaohsiung has been rising since the 1970s. With this in mind, our study focused on a comprehensive understanding of the current urban climatic and environmental condition of the city by using various urban climatic and planning parameters in order to create a UCMap, and to generate pertinent planning recommendations.

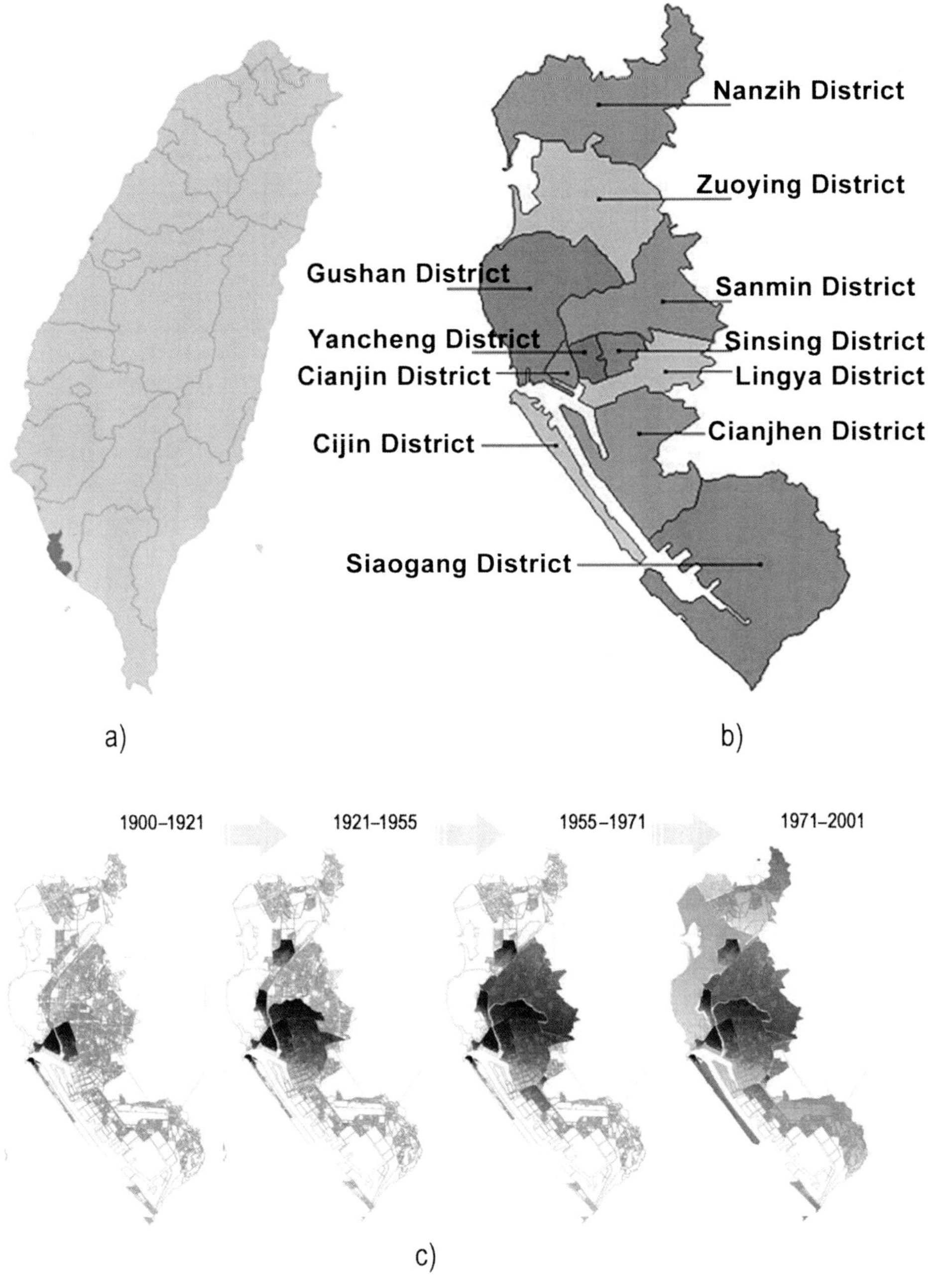


*Figure 15.1* (a) The location of Kaohsiung in Taiwan; (b) the 11 administrative districts; (c) the historical urban development.

Source: KCG, 2009

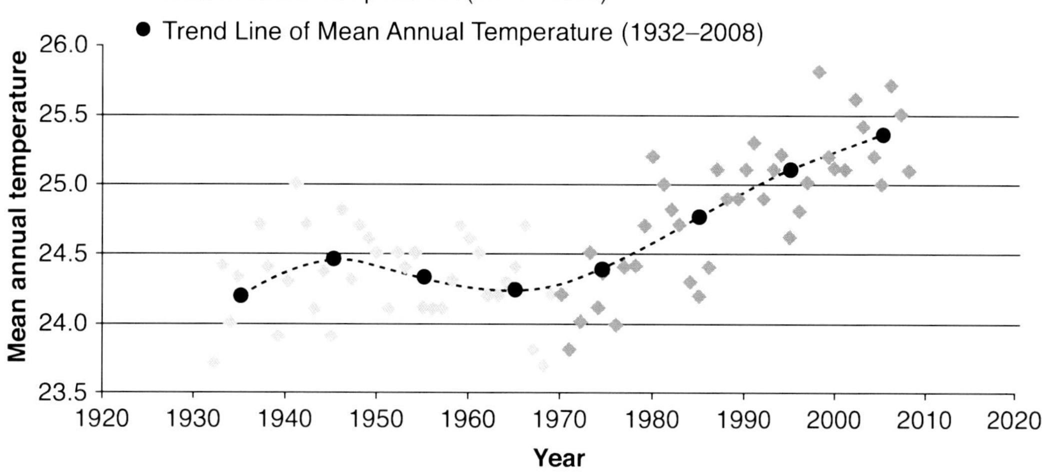


*Figure 15.2* Annual mean temperature from 1932 to 2008.
Source: TCWB, 2009

## *Procedures and data collection*

The study was performed using a Geographic Information System (GIS) as the data platform. The use of the GIS platform ensures that city planners can eventually assess and use the data, as GIS has been a working tool of city planners. The workflow is summarised in Figure 15.3. First, climatic, environmental and planning data and information were collected from the Taiwan Central Weather Bureau, the Urban Development Bureau, and the Department of Budget, Accounting, and Statistics of the Kaohsiung local government. Second, data collation was performed and, based on the data analysis and evaluation, input layers were developed. The selected parameters included population density, land use, UHI intensity, natural landscape, and water bodies. Their impact on the physical urban environment was taken into account when the development of input layers was conducted (see Table 15.1). Third, these input layers were synergised and merged to develop the Urban Climatic Analysis Map (UC-AnMap) for Kaohsiung. The map consists of various climatopes that spatially represent thermal conditions and the wind environment. Based on the urban climatic understanding of the UC-AnMap, problem areas and sensitive areas could be identified. Working with city planners, a number of general urban climatic planning recommendations were summarised into the Urban Climatic Planning Recommendation Map (UC-ReMap).

## *Results*

The UCMap system of Kaohsiung consists of eight layers of input data. It was unified and rasterised into grid cells of 500m × 500m. This provided for a simple area-based spatial understanding to the city planners who would make planning decisions later at the district and neighbourhood levels.

*Table 15.1* Selected parameters and their impacts on the urban environment.

| *Physical urban environment* | *Selected factors for analysis* | *Impact on urban environment* |
|---|---|---|
| Thermal environment | Topography | Negative effect on thermal load |
| | Population density | Positive effect on thermal load |
| | Land use (built-up urban areas) | Positive effect on thermal load |
| | UHI intensity | Positive effect on thermal load |
| | Natural landscape (greenery, open space, forest) | Negative effect on thermal load |
| Wind environment | Water system (sea, river, lake, pond) | Positive effect on dynamic potential |
| | Prevailing wind directions | Wind information |
| | Local wind circulation (land and sea breezes) | Wind information |

Source: Author

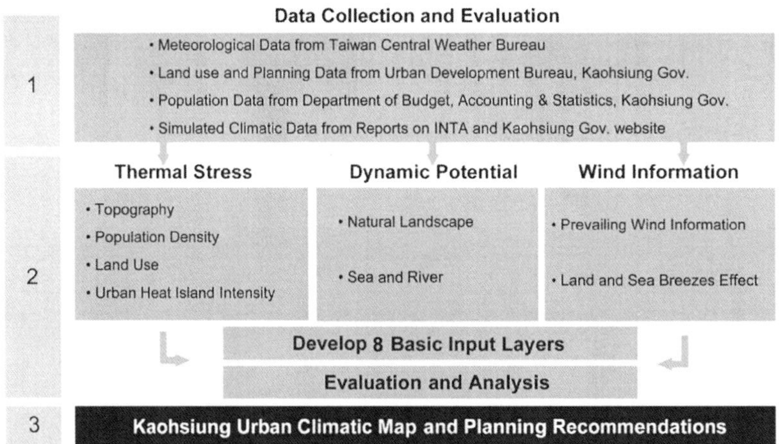


*Figure 15.3* Main procedures of the UCMap study.

Source: Author

### *The thermal load aspect: Layer 1, topography*

Based on the environmental lapse rate, air temperature decreases with height (i.e. adiabatic changes in temperature occur due to changes in the pressure of the gas while not adding or subtracting any heat), and this reduction is approximately 10°C/km for rising air (Golany, 1996). The moist adiabatic lapse rate can be lower at a value of 0.6°C/100m (Aikawa *et al.*, 2006). This layer therefore represented the topographical height in metres according to data obtained from the Urban Development Bureau of the Kaohsiung local government (KCG, 2003; Fung *et al.*, 2009; KCG, 2009). The relatively flat topography of Kaohsiung means that only two small hills needed to be represented. Due to their possible temperature variations and thermal stress contributions, three classes were identified: 0m–150m, 151m–300m, and over 300m (see Figure 15.4).

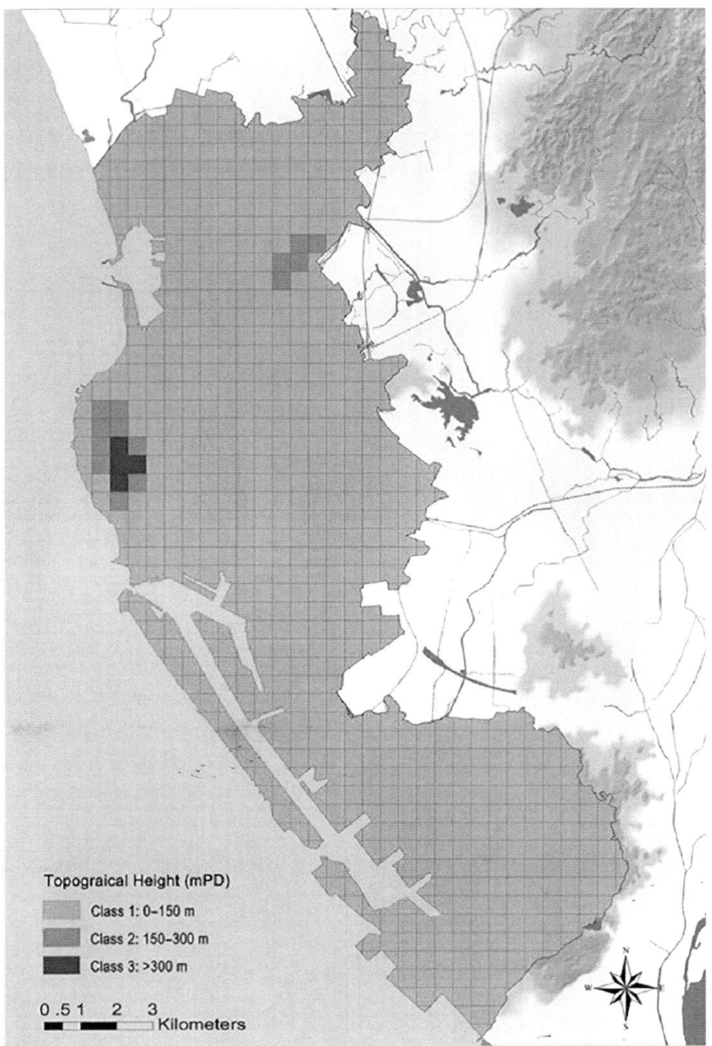


*Figure 15.4* Layer 1: Topographical map of Kaohsiung.
Source: Author

### *The thermal load aspect: Layer 2, population density*

Population density contributes to the intensity of anthropogenic activities and is known to correlate with the urban thermal environment (Oke, 1973, 1987). In addition, building density and volume must increase to accommodate the population. In general, an urban area with a higher density of buildings has poorer urban ventilation conditions and stronger UHI effects (Givoni, 1998; Hui, 2001). Population density contributes to the understanding of thermal loads in a UC-AnMap. This layer (see Figure 15.5) represents the population density in persons per square kilometre. Based on the data obtained from the Department of Budget, Accounting, and Statistics of the Kaohsiung local government (Tseng, 2008), we deduced that the highest population density

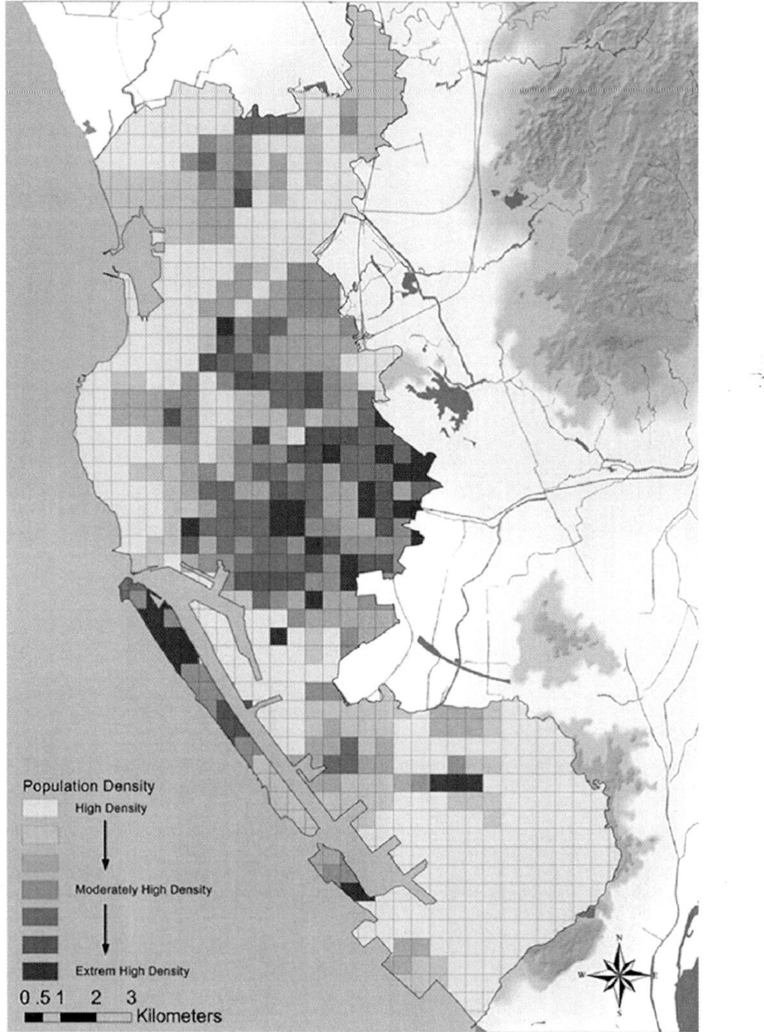


*Figure 15.5* Layer 2: Population density map of Kaohsiung.

Source: Author

in Kaohsiung was over 30,000 persons per square kilometre. Given this high-density scenario (UN, 2002b), the classes of this layer have been defined as high density, moderate high density, or extreme high density (see Figure 15.5).

### *The thermal load aspect: Layer 3, land use*

The urban thermal environment is influenced by land use. Land use determines a wide range of urban parameters, such as building form, urban density, anthropogenic heat release, energy consumption, and transport behaviours. Based on the land use and planning data acquired from the Urban Development Bureau of the Kaohsiung local government and on the Geography Atlas of Kaohsiung (Huang, 2001), the land use layer was rasterized and created (see Figure 15.6). The

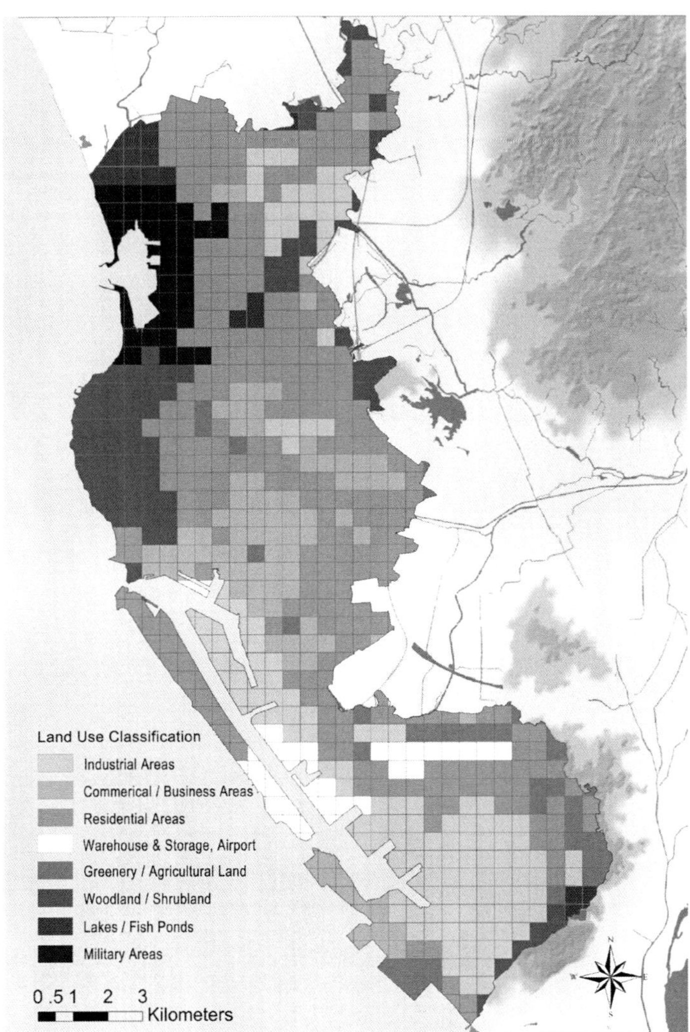


*Figure 15.6* Layer 3: Land use map of Kaohsiung.

Source: Author

grid cells were classified as their respective climatopes. The classification of this layer was based on similarities in urban climatic characteristics for different land uses, such as thermal capacity, surface roughness and anthropogenic heat release (VDI, 1997).

### *The thermal load aspect: Layer 4, urban heat island*

UHI is commonly observed along with the temperature difference between urban and rural areas (Landsberg, 1981). The phenomenon is defined as a metropolitan area having a significantly higher temperature than its surrounding rural areas (Oke, 1973, 1982, 2002), which can be more significant when wind or air ventilation is weak (Oke, 1987). Based on a study by Taiwanese researchers using traverse mobile measurements (Lee, 1999), the UHI intensity in Kaohsiung is approximately

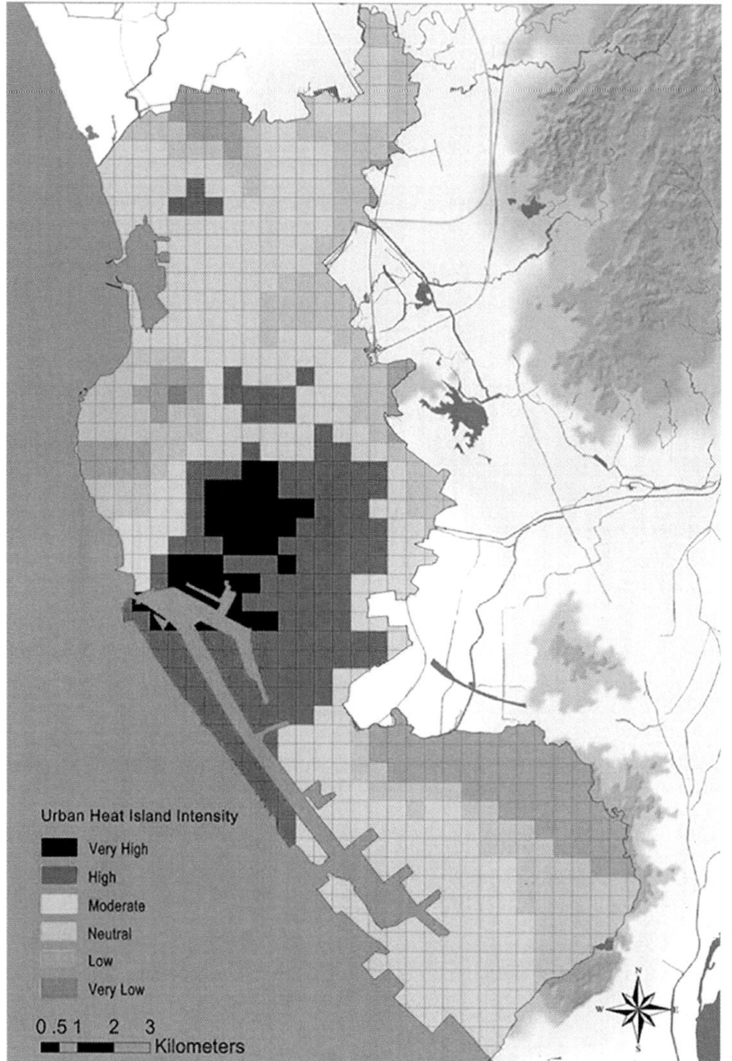


*Figure 15.7* Layer 4: Heat island intensity map of Kaohsiung.

Source: Author

2.5°C–3.0°C. Using a computational fluid dynamics model simulation (Li, 2009; Li *et al.*, 2009), their study results were collated and rasterized, resulting in six classes ranging from very high to very low UHI intensity (see Figure 15.7).

### *The thermal load aspect: Layer 5, natural landscape*

Natural vegetation has cooling effects beneficial to its surrounding areas and can lower thermal load (Bowne and Ball, 1970; Brook, 1972; Landsberg, 1981; Oke, 1987, 1988). The classification of this layer (see Figure 15.8) was based on parks and the types of greenery coverage (KCG, 2003;

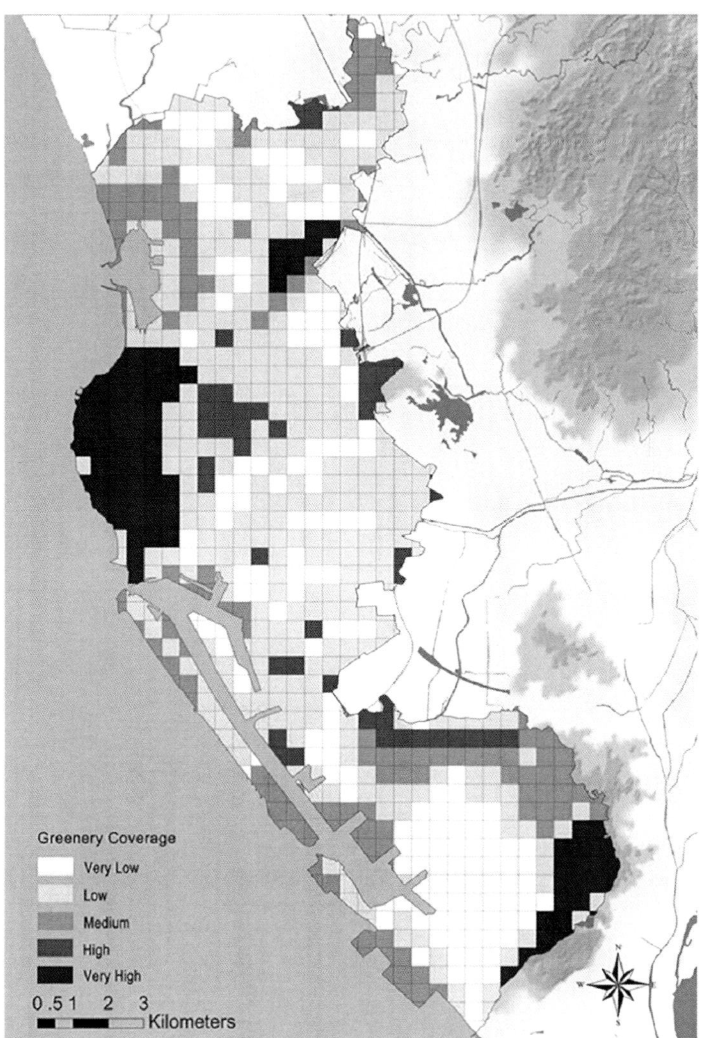


*Figure 15.8* Layer 5: Natural landscape map of Kaohsiung.

Source: Author

Chen, 2006). Areas of no vegetation were classified as very low, while limited coverage is classified as low. Grasslands, agricultural, and military land, which could provide considerable cooling effects to surrounding areas, were classified as medium. Large urban parks, which contribute to the cooling of surrounding urban built-up areas, were classified as high. Forests or large woodlands were classified as very high.

### *The dynamic potential aspect: Layer 6, water system*

In the construction of large-scale climatic maps, the distance to the coastline for sea breezes is included (Svensson *et al.*, 2003). Kaohsiung has a long coastline, with the Love River running

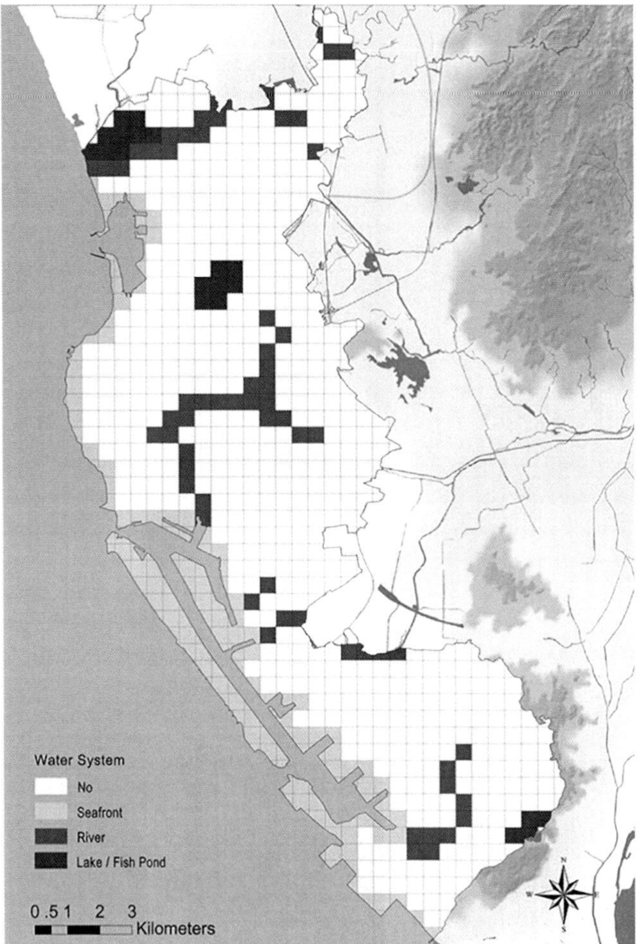


*Figure 15.9* Layer 6: Water body map of Kaohsiung.

Source: Author

through the central urban area and Lianchih Pond in the inland area. Some paddy fields and fishponds are found in the northern part of Kaohsiung. There are two small canals, the Yansheigang Canal and the Cianjhen Canal, within the area. The classification of this layer was based on the potential effects of the different types of water bodies, such as seas, rivers, lakes, and fishponds (see Figure 15.9).

### *The dynamic potential aspect: Layer 7 and 8, prevailing wind, and land and sea breezes*

Most German cities are located inland, therefore for their UCMaps only prevailing wind information is taken into account. However, Kaohsiung is a coastal city that experiences land and sea breezes daily. Thus, in addition to the prevailing wind information, the effects of land and sea

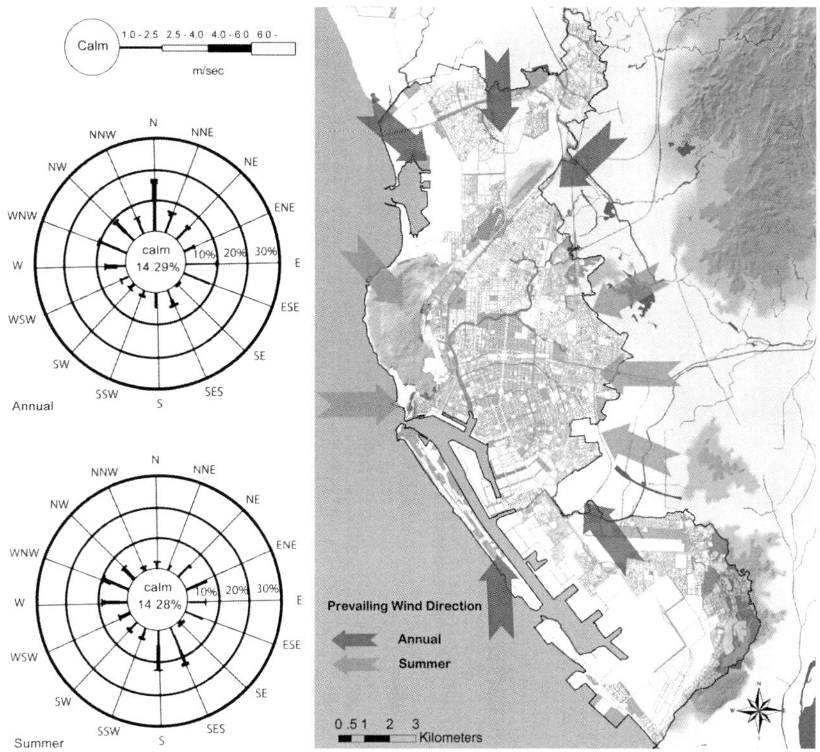


*Figure 15.10* Layer 7: Prevailing wind map of Kaohsiung.

Source: Author

breezes and their respective possible directions were considered and illustrated in the Kaohsiung UCMap.

Prevailing wind information is important in the design of urban settlements. It has great potential in terms of improving the urban thermal environment and in solving problems related to air pollution. Thus, the prevailing summer and annual wind directions were considered in this study. According to the long-term meteorological record, the mean wind speed in Kaohsiung is quite low – approximately 2.7m/s throughout the year (Huang, 1986; Chen, 2006). Annual wind directions are mainly from the N, WNW, NNE, S, and SSE; summer wind directions are mainly from WNW, W, ENE, E, and SSE. In Figure 15.10, the dark grey arrows show the prevailing annual wind direction, while the light grey arrows show the prevailing summer wind direction.

Kaohsiung is a coastal city. Land and sea breezes are prominent (TCWB, 2009). When utilised, they can improve the urban thermal environment. At night, land breezes come from the ENE, N, and SSE directions. Thus, high wind velocity is concentrated in the inland areas, such as the eastern parts of Zuoying District and Cianjhen District. In the daytime, sea breezes come from the WNW, W, and S directions. Thus, high wind velocity is concentrated on the waterfront, such as the outlet of Love River in Cianjin District. In Figures 15.11(a) and 15.11(b), two wind rose diagrams show the land breeze at night-time and the sea breeze during daytime.

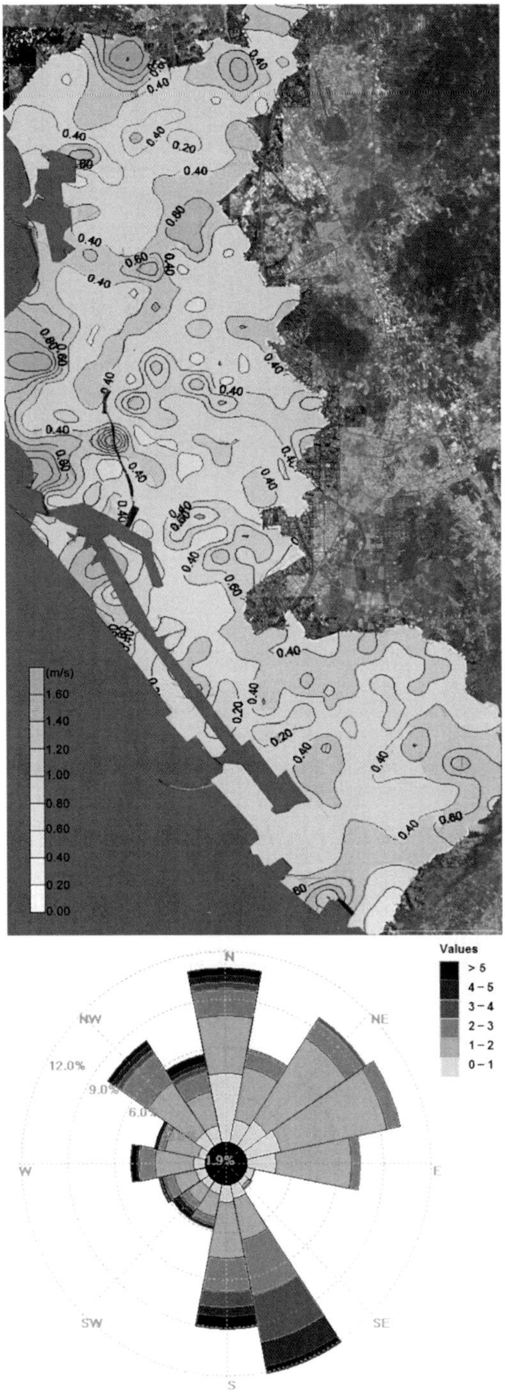

Figure 15.11 (a) Land breezes in Kaohsiung at night-time;

Source: (a) after Li, 2009;

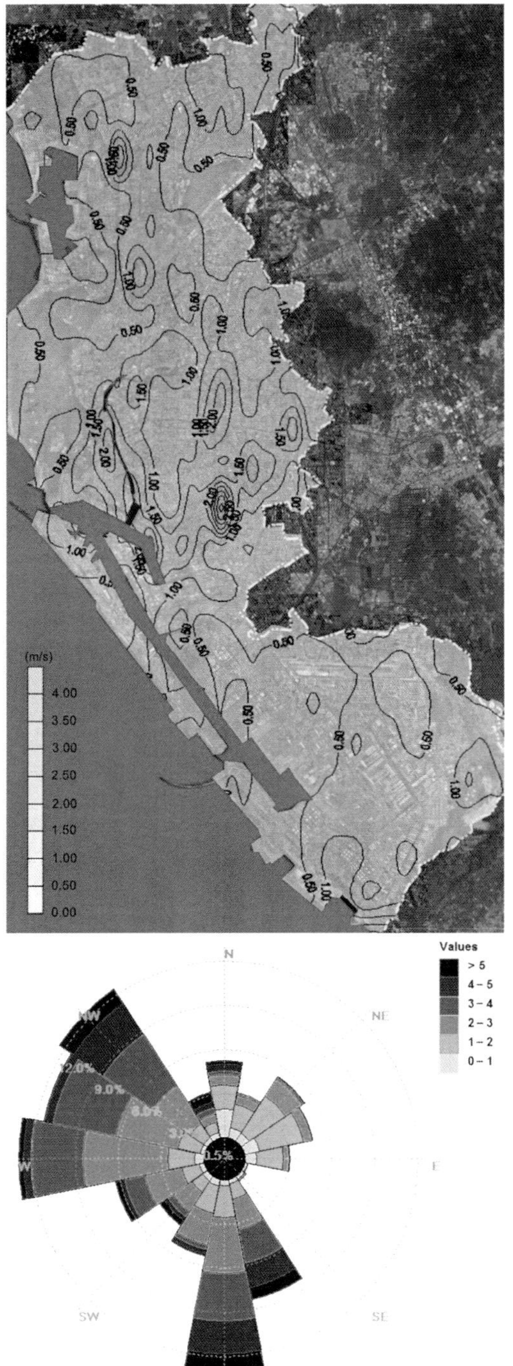


*Figure 15.11* (Continued) (b) sea breezes in Kaohsiung in daytime.

(b) after Li *et al.*, 2009

| Kaohsiung Map | Level of Plan Action | Urban Climatic and Environmental Characteristics | No. | District Name | Menu of Effective Control Measures: Greenery | Shading | Cool Albedo | An-Heat Release | Air Exchange | Air Pollution |
|---|---|---|---|---|---|---|---|---|---|---|
| 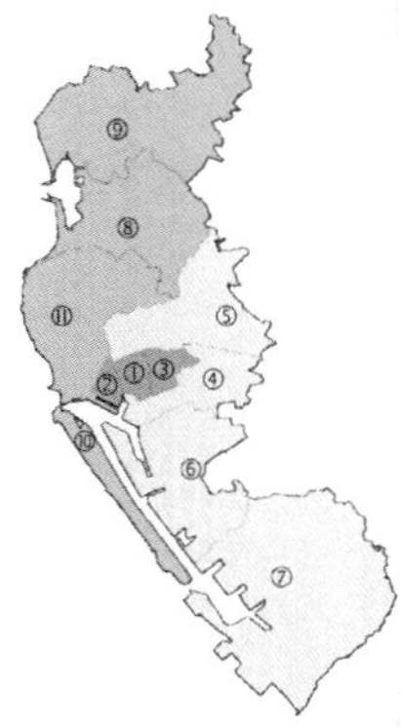 | Mitigation Action Necessary | High to very high thermal stress and low dynamic potential due to high ground coverage, high Anthropogenic Heat (An-Heat) Release, various commercial activities and low greenery coverage | ① | Cianjin | ▲▲ | ▲ | ▲ | ▼▼ | ▲▲ | ▼ |
| | | | ② | Yancheng | ▲▲ | ▲ | ▲ | ▼▼ | ▲▲ | ▼ |
| | | | ③ | Sinsing | ▲▲ | ▲ | ▲ | ▼▼ | ▲ | ▼ |
| | Some Action Required | High to medium thermal stress and low to medium dynamic potential due to low to medium ground coverage, medium An-Heat Release, some commercial activities, lots of industrial activities and low greenery coverage | ④ | Lingya | ▲▲ | ▲▲ | ▲ | ▼▼ | ▲▲ | ▼ |
| | | | ⑤ | Sanmin | ▲▲ | ▲ | ▲ | ▼ | ▲ | ▼▼ |
| | | | ⑥ | Cianjhen | ▲▲ | ▲ | ▲▲ | ▼▼ | ▲ | ▼▼ |
| | | | ⑦ | Siaogang | ▲▲ | ▲ | ▲▲ | ▼▼ | ▲ | ▼▼ |
| | Preserve and Enhance | Medium to low thermal stress and medium to high dynamic potential due to low to medium ground coverage, low An.Heat Release, some commercial and industrial activities and medium to high greenery coverage | ⑧ | Zuoying | ▲ | ▲▲ | ▲ | ▼ | ▲▲ | ▼ |
| | | | ⑨ | Nanzih | ▲ | ▲ | ▲▲ | ▼▼ | ▲ | ▼▼ |
| | | | ⑩ | Cijin | ▲ | ▲ | ▲▲ | ▼ | ▲▲ | ▼ |
| | | | ⑪ | Gushan | — | ▲ | — | — | ▲ | — |

▲: Recommend to improve the existing condition;
▼: Recommend to mitigate the existing condition;
—: Maintain or Protect the existing condition
▲▲: Strongly recommend to improve the existing condition;
▼▼: Strongly recommend to mitigate the existing condition;

*Figure 15.12* Action plan and menu of effective control measures for the 11 districts of Kaohsiung.

Source: Author

### *The urban climatic analysis map (UC-AnMap)*

Based on the eight input layers, the UC-AnMap of Kaohsiung was synthesized based on the urban climatic evaluation of data (see Plate 15.1). The map consists of different climatopes. Different types of land use have been differentiated first for better planning-based understanding: these include areas for commercial/business, residential/education, and industrial, as well as water bodies and greenery. Within such land use types, various areas of similar climatopes are delineated and described. The different climatopes are affected by their constituent parameters of urban morphology, population density, topography, greenery, water bodies, and so on. Their thermal load contributions to the urban environment are likewise differentiated. For example, with regard to commercial/business districts, areas are classified from very high to low thermal load.

## The urban climatic planning recommendation map (UC-ReMap)

Working with planners, three levels of planning action at the city/urban/neighbourhood scales were developed as suggested in Figure 15.12, and the possible effective control measures for each district were elaborated and summarised based on the aspects of greenery, shading, cool albedo and anthropogenic heat release, air exchange and air pollution.

To assist planners and policymakers, urban climatic knowledge must be translated into a planning language that is actionable with regard to policy (Alcoforado, 2006; Alcoforado *et al.*, 2009). Thus, after discussion with local planners concerning the UC-AnMap (see Plate 15.1), a few very high thermal load problem areas and urban climatic sensitive areas in Kaohsiung were identified. They need attention and mitigation measures:

*Level 1*: Central Kaohsiung, including Cianjin, Yancheng, and Sinsing Districts, has very high thermal load and low dynamic potential. This suggests that these areas have intense anthropogenic heat release but limited air ventilation. These areas require specific planning action, such as increasing greenery coverage and reducing anthropogenic heat release.

*Level 2*: Some mitigation planning measures are required in the districts of Lingya, Sanmin, Cianihen, and Siaogang. This is mainly due to their high to medium thermal stress but high dynamic potential. Provision of greenery is encouraged, while anthropogenic heat release must be reduced. In particular, as industrial activities are commonly found here, the problem of air pollution requires specific attention. Industrial restructuring could be considered in these areas.

*Level 3*: For areas with low thermal stress and high dynamic potential, such as Zuoying, Nanzih, Cijin, and Gushan Districts, the current conditions should be preserved and the provision of surfaces of low albedo is encouraged. Because the availability of air ventilation is higher in these areas, air exchange with the surrounding urban areas is encouraged. In particular, possible air pollution problems in Nanzih require specific attention.

The following provides planners with further details of the recommendations.

### Consideration of wind in urban-climatically based planning

Improving urban ventilation in very dense built-up areas in hot humid cities is important, especially in the summer months (Cheng and Ng, 2006; Lin, 2009). Since the surrounding vegetated slopes of the city that can provide fresh cool air to downstream areas can easily be blocked by building development, further consideration and planned action regarding wind environment is recommended for Kaohsiung. Three Focus Areas with better dynamic potential have been identified in the areas surrounding Chanshan, along the riverside or harbour front. In Focus Area 1, the cooling effect from the vegetated hillsides of Chanshan should be carefully considered. In Focus Area 2, the impact of new development on the surrounding vegetated hillsides ought to be minimised. Creating, maintaining, and preserving air paths from the hillside to the downtown areas are recommended. Rivers with low surface roughness can become major breezeways for the city core. In both Focus Areas 2 and 3, buildings found on the riverbanks or the harbour front should be designed appropriately (i.e. with permeability, building gaps, and building height differentials). In so doing, the penetration of urban ventilation can be enhanced. For a coastal city, sea breezes are useful during daytime; thus, sea breeze penetration into the city core should be considered. Buildings forming continuous walls on the harbour front should be avoided. The annual prevailing wind directions are mainly from the N, WNW, NNE, S, and SSE. The N–S-oriented main roads are important major air paths. Buildings should be oriented with respect to the major wind directions and air paths. The prevailing summer wind directions are mainly from the WNW, W, ENE, E, and SSE. The E–W-oriented main roads are important minor air paths. Buildings should be oriented along and set back from the air paths (Li, 2009; Li *et al.*, 2009). The above considerations and specific design strategies are illustrated in Figure 15.13.

### Consideration of water bodies in urban-climatically based planning

Waterfront sites are important areas that allow cool air coming from the water body to penetrate into the city, so further consideration and planned action regarding water bodies is recommended

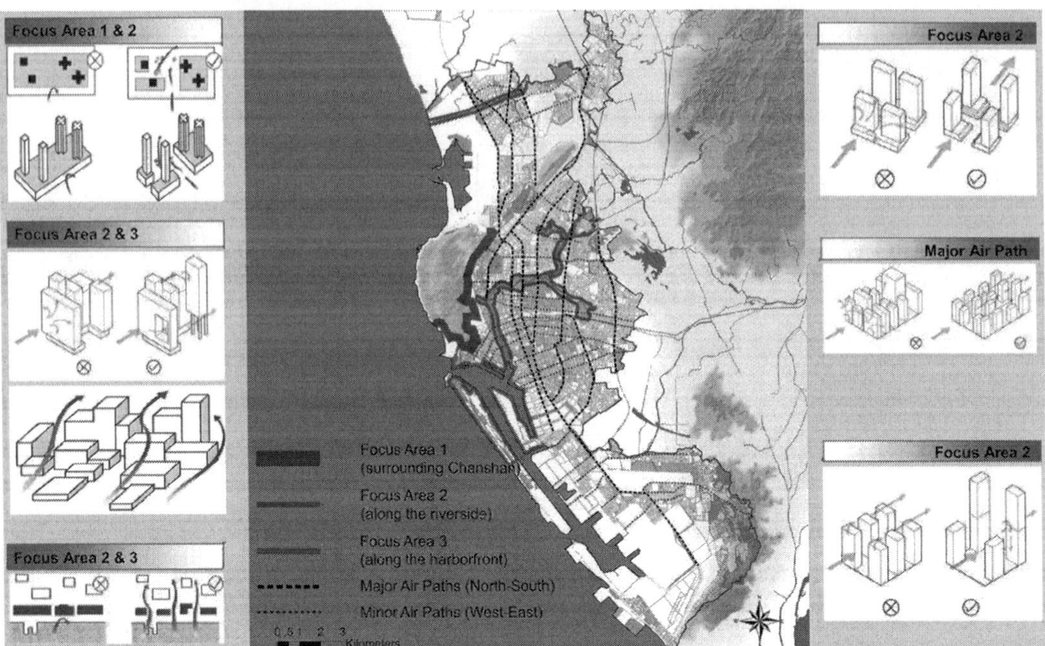


*Figure 15.13* Detailed recommendations on the wind aspect in Kaohsiung.

Source: Author

for Kaohsiung. The cooling effect from water bodies, including rivers, lakes, ponds, and the seafront should be considered and protected, so the impact of development on the waterfront should be minimised. Some cooling branches along major transportation links (highlighted in light grey in the map shown in Figure 15.14) should be formed; placing greenery or designed landscape along these branches is strongly recommended. Lian Chinh Pond, Jinshih Lake, and Chengcing Lake should be linked using vegetation to bring the positive effect of these water bodies to the surrounding areas.

### Consideration of greenery in urban-climatically based planning

As vegetated areas in cities have a positive ecological impact and mitigate UHI effects by acting as oases (Chen and Wong, 2009), further consideration and planned action regarding greenery are recommended for Kaohsiung. Green rail tracks can be adopted to mitigate anthropogenic heat release and air pollution along railways in dense urban areas; green circles should be formed so that the centres of urban areas and 'industrial areas' UHI intensity and anthropogenic heat release can be mitigated, and air pollution can be diluted and constrained; a green link based on the existing greenery system should be created between Chanshan Hill, Lianchih Pond, and Banpinshan to maximise the cooling effect; shade at pedestrian level should be provided to create comfortable walking systems; green fingers should be developed to guide the cooling effect from the Chanshan East hillsides to high-density urban area centres; and greenbelts are needed to bring sea breezes to inner areas and improve air exchange. The above considerations are illustrated in Figure 15.15.

*Figure 15.14* Detailed recommendations on the water aspect in Kaohsiung.

Source: Author

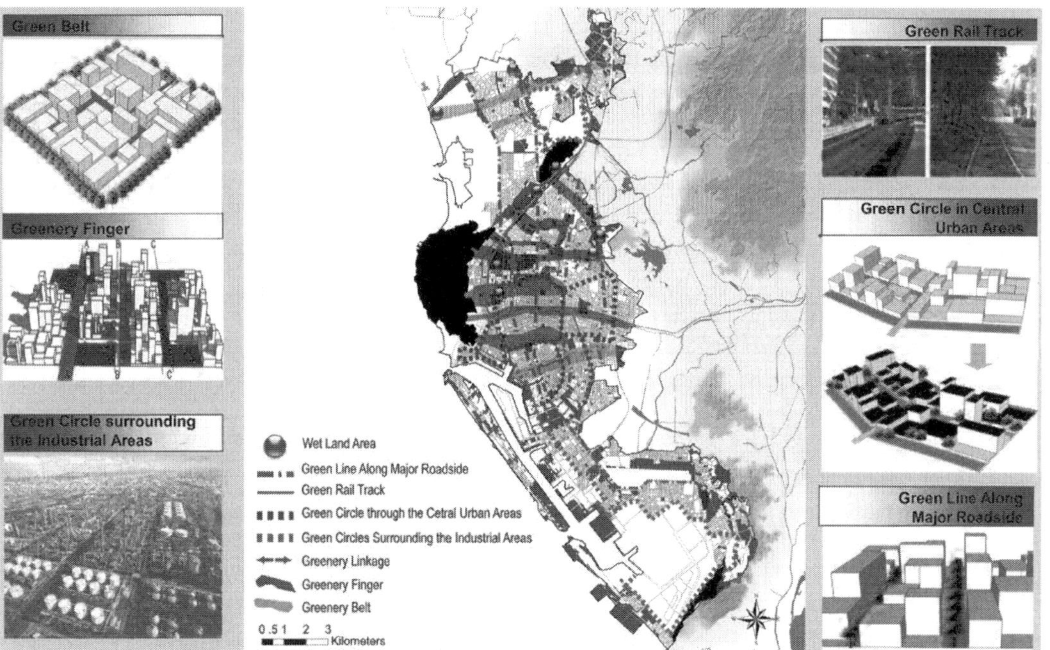


*Figure 15.15* Detailed recommendations on the greenery aspect in Kaohsiung.

Source: Author

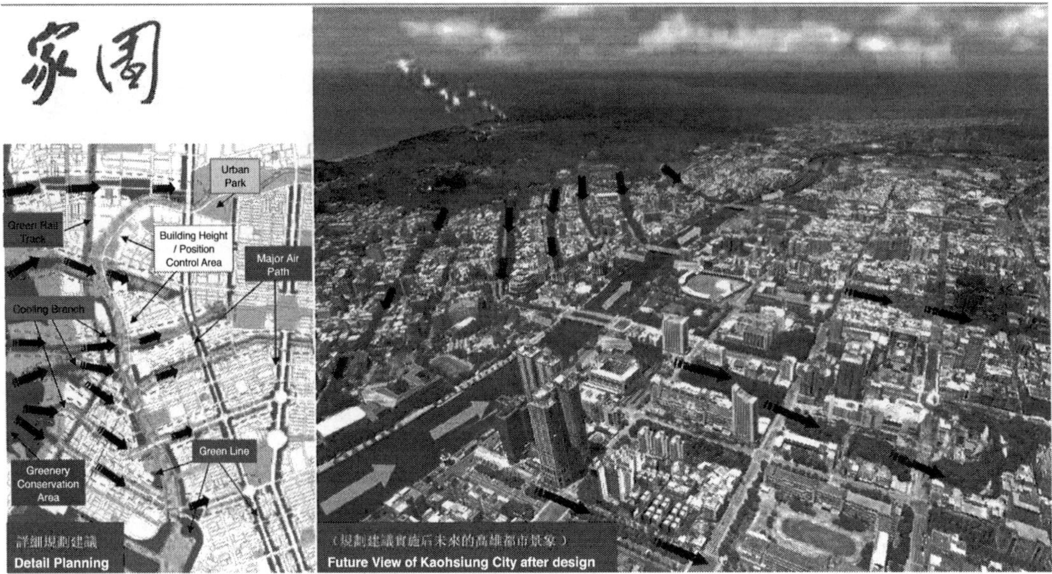


*Figure 15.16* Detailed planning and future view of Kaohsiung centre.

Source: Author

### *Consideration of urban morphology in urban-climatically based planning*

Urban morphology affects urban thermal climate and airflow patterns (Vieira and Vasconcelos, 2004; Matzarakis and Mayer, 2008). Since the urban context of the central areas of Kaohsiung is compact, detailed design and planning recommendations for urban morphology are as follows: building heights and positions should be controlled; bulky buildings and wall-building effects in sensitive areas such as the riverbanks should be avoided; building blocks should be more permeable especially at the pedestrian level; building setbacks on the major E–W roads are recommended to widen air paths for the improvement of urban ventilation; and the greenbelts from the Chanshan East hillsides, parks, and open spaces should be linked together to create a green network. A detailed plan and future view of Kaohsiung is shown in Figure 15.16 as it would be if all these planned actions were to be adopted. If such were to be the case, the study would have achieved its aim of promoting the use of urban climatic knowledge in planning.

## Conclusions

Due to rapid urbanisation in developing countries, high-density or mega-cities will quickly become the norm. Facing climate change and public concern about high-quality urban living, sustainable climatic spatial planning is one of the most important tasks and challenges for planners and policymakers entering an era of mega-urbanisation. However, due to a lack of climatic knowledge and comprehensible climatic-environmental evaluations, the urban climate and environment are easily neglected when planners and policymakers make a new town plan or undertake local construction work. Thus, urban climate science has seldom been applied to urban development in developing countries.

This study provides a social science-based method for developing a UCMap for high-density cities, using Kaohsiung as an example. Eight input layers and a final evaluation UC-AnMap, together with a UC-ReMap, were developed and implemented into a local urban planning system. This method has several advantages: from this interdisciplinary study it can be found that the UCMap may serve as an information platform for planners and policymakers; the structure of the UCMap system is flexible; and all selected climatic data and environmental and planning information is collated and evaluated with the same grid size embedded into GIS. Thus, further urban climatic, environmental and planning information from the UCMap can be updated and managed easily by planners; the current urban climatic condition is also shown visually in map format, so climatic problems and sensitive areas can easily be identified by planners and policymakers; and based on joint efforts from climatologists and planners, the climatic information and evaluation from the UCMap is translated into planning-based language, forming the general effective control measures and planning strategies that can be referred to in the master plan of Kaohsiung.

Regarding the future of the Kaohsiung UCMap, the evaluation of the climatic and environmental conditions still relies on qualitative evaluation. To obtain a specific planning index and urban development intensity of specific areas from an urban climatic point of view, there needs to be further evaluation with empirical study to quantify the UCMap. In addition, the UCMap of Kaohsiung with a 500m resolution was developed for implementation at the city level. Further work at the district and local planning levels are needed.

Climate transcends boundaries, and the need for knowledge sharing and exchange is of paramount importance. The study contributes to the scholarly development of urban climatic mapping for a high-density city based on selected basic climatic data and environmental and planning information with joint efforts from climatologists and planners. In practice, the findings of the UCMap and corresponding climatic planning recommendations concerning wind, greenery, water bodies and urban morphology can provide local planners and governments with a useful reference which could guide them to better climatic spatial planning at the city level.

## Acknowledgements

The author is grateful to Professor Helmut Mayer, Professor Andreas Matzarakis and Professor Tzu-Ping Lin for their valuable suggestions and references. The author would also like to thank the Chinese University of Hong Kong for providing academic assistance for the study.

This chapter was originally published as Ren, C., Lau, K. L., Yiu, K. P. and Ng, E. (2013). The application of urban climatic mapping to the urban planning of high-density cities: The case of Kaohsiung, Taiwan, *Cities*, 31: 1–16. Kind permission has been obtained from Elsevier to reproduce it.

## References

Aikawa, M., Hiraki, T. and Eiho, J. (2006). Vertical atmospheric structure estimated by heat island intensity and temporal variations of methane concentrations in ambient air in an urban area in Japan. *Atmospheric Environment*, 40(23): 4308–4315.

Alcoforado, M. J. (2006). Planning procedures towards high climatic quality cities: Example referring to Lisbon. *Finisterra*, 41(82): 49–64.

Alcoforado, M. J., Andrade, H., Lopes, A. and Vasconcelos, J. (2009). Application of climatic guidelines to urban planning – the example of Lisbon (Portugal). *Landscape and Urban Planning*, 90(1–2): 56–65.

Baumüller, J., Hoffmann, U. and Reuter, U. (1992). *Climate Booklet for Urban Development*. Stuttgart: Ministry of Economy Baden-Wuerttemberg (Wirtschaftsministerium), Environmental Protection Department (Amt fur Umweltschutz).

Baumüller, J., Reuter, U., Hoffmann, U. and Esswein, H. (2008). *Klimaatlas Region Stuttgart*. Stuttgart: Verband Region Stuttgart, Germany. Available at: http://www.stadtklima-stuttgart.de/index.php?klima_klimaatlas_region (Accessed November 2013).

Baumüller, J., Esswein, H., Hoffmann, U., Reuter, U., Weidenbacher, S., Nagel, T. and Flassak, T. (2009a). Climate atlas of a metropolitan region in Germany based on GIS. In: *Proceedings of The 7th International Conference on Urban Climate*. Yokohama, Japan, 29 June–3 July. Available at: http://www.ide.titech.ac.jp/~icuc7/extended_abstracts/pdf/375531-2-090501005214-002.pdf (Accessed 10 February 2014).

Baumüller, J., Hoffmann, U. and Stuckenbrock, U. (2009b). Urban framework plan hillsides of Stuttgart. In: *Proceedings of The 7th International Conference on Urban Climate*. Yokohama, Japan, 29 June–3 July. Available at: http://www.ide.titech.ac.jp/~icuc7/extended_abstracts/pdf/375531-1-090501004614-003.pdf (Accessed 10 February 2014).

Bitan, A. (1984). Climatic data analysis and its use and representation for planners. *Energy and Buildings*, 7(1): 11–22.

Bitan, A. (1988). The methodology of applied climatology in planning and building. *Energy and Buildings*, 11(1–3): 1–10.

Bowne, N. E. and Ball, J. T. (1970). Observational comparison of rural and urban boundary layer turbulence. *Journal of Applied Meteorology*, 9(6): 862–873.

Brook, R. R. (1972). The measurement of turbulence in a city environment. *Journal of Applied Meteorology*, 11(3): 443–450.

Chen, T. W. (2006). *The Study of Relationship between Urban Identity and Landscape Structure on the Natural Environment in Kaohsiung*. Kaohsiung: National University of Kaohsiung. (In Chinese).

Chen, Y. and Wong, N. H. (2009). Thermal impact of strategic landscaping in cities: A review. *Advances in Building Energy Research*, 3(1): 237–260.

Cheng, V. and Ng, E. (2006). Thermal comfort in urban open spaces for Hong Kong. *Architectural Science Review*, 49(3): 236–242.

Eliasson, I. (2000). The use of climate knowledge in urban planning. *Landscape and Urban Planning*, 48(1–2): 31–44.

Fung, W. Y., Lam, K. S., Nichol, E. J. and Wong, M. S. (2009). Derivation of nighttime urban air temperatures using a satellite thermal image. *Journal of Applied Meteorology and Climatology*, 48(4): 863–872.

Givoni, B. (1998). *Climate Considerations in Building and Urban Design*. New York: Van Nostrand Reinhold.

Golany, G. S. (1996). Urban design morphology and thermal performance. *Atmospheric Environment*, 30(3): 455–465.

Huang, H. (ed.) (2001). *Geography Atlas of Kaohsiung*. Kaohsiung: Research, Development and Evaluation Commission of Kaohsiung. (In Chinese).

Huang, S. (1986). *Research Report: New Planning of Aozihdi Urban Downtown Areas*. Taipei: Department of Civil Engineering, National Taiwan University. (In Chinese).

Hui, S. C. M. (2001). Low energy building design in high density urban cities. *Renewable Energy*, 24(3): 627–640.

Katzschner, L. (1988). The urban climate as a parameter for urban development. *Energy and Buildings*, 11(1–3): 137–147.

Katzschner, L. and Mulder, J. (2008). Regional climatic mapping as a tool for sustainable development. *Journal of Environmental Management*, 87(2): 262–267.

KCG (2003). *Guide Book of Kaohsiung Parks and Greenery Areas: Public Works Bureau*. Kaohsiung: Kaohsiung Government (KCG). (In Chinese).

KCG (2009). *Kaohsiung Digital Map and Planning Data*. Kaohsiung: Urban Development Bureau, Kaohsiung Government. Available at: http://urban-web.kcg.gov.tw/airks/web_page/KDA130500.jsp (Accessed November 2013). (In Chinese).

Kraas, F. (2007). Megacities and global change in east, southeast and south Asia. *Asien*, 103(2): 9–22.

Kuo, M. (1998). *The System of Developing Clean Area for Regional Air Quality and Evaluation on its Impact*, (No. NSC87-EPA-P-034-001). Taipei: Environmental Protection Administration Executive Yuan of Taiwan. Available at: http://sta.epa.gov.tw/report/Files/NSC87-EPA-P-034-001.pdf (Accessed November 2013). (In Chinese).

Landsberg, H. E. (1981). *The Urban Climate*. International geophysics series, vol. 28. New York: Academic Press.

Lee, K. P. (1999). *A Study on Urban Heat Island of Four Metropolitan Cities in Taiwan*. Tainan: National Cheng Kung University. (In Chinese).

Li, Y. Y. (2009). The practices and perspectives of Kaohsiung ecocity: Our approaches in Taiwan. Paper presented at the *Twin City Sustainable Development Forum: Hong Kong and Kaohsiung*. The Chinese University of Hong Kong, 21 February 2009.

Li, Y. Y., Lee, T. Y., Chou, P. C. and Yu, C. C. (2009). New paragon of Urban Design: 'Innovation Practice of urban Development toward Environmental Ethics' – The strategic orientation and evaluation of eco-city and green community in Kaohsiung. *Architecture Dialogue*, 126–135.

Lin, T. P. (2009). Thermal perception, adaptation and attendance in a public square in hot and humid regions. *Building and Environment*, 44(10): 2017–2026.

Matzarakis, A. (2005). Country report: Urban climate research in Germany. *IAUC Newsletter*, 11: 4–6. Available at: http://www.urbanclimate.net/matzarakis1/papers/UCRE_de_IAUC011.pdf (Accessed 10 February 2014).

Matzarakis, A. and Mayer, H. (2008). Dependence of the thermal urban climate on morphological variables. In: Mayer, H and Matzarakis, A. (eds.), *Proceedings of the 5th Japanese-German Meeting on Urban Climatology*. Berichte des Meteorologischen Instituts der Albert-Ludwigs-Universität Freiburg, No. 18. The Albert-Ludwigs-University of Freiburg, Freiburg, Germany, 6–8 October. Freiburg: the Meteorological Institute, Albert-Ludwigs-University of Freiburg, 277–282. Available at: http://www.meteo.uni-freiburg.de/forschung/publikationen/berichte/report18.pdf (Accessed 10 February 2014).

Mills, G. (2006). Progress toward sustainable settlements: A role for urban climatology. *Theoretical and Applied Climatology*, 84(1–3): 69–76.

Mills, G., Cleugh, H., Emmanuel, R., Endlicher, W., Erell, E., McGranahan, G., Ng, E., Nickson, A., Rosenthal, J. and Steemer, K. (2010). Climate information for improved planning and management of mega cities (needs perspectives). In: Sivakumar, M. V. K. *et al.* (eds.), *Procedia Environmental Sciences, Vol. 1, Special Issue of World Climate Conference-3*, 228–246. Geneva, Switzerland, 31 August–4 September 2009.

Ng, E. (2009). Policies and technical guidelines for urban planning of high-density cities – Air ventilation assessment (AVA) of Hong Kong. *Building and Environment*, 44(7): 1478–1488.

Ng, E., Katzschner, L., Wang, Y., Ren, C. and Chen, L. (2008). *Working Paper No. 1A: Draft Urban Climatic Analysis Map, Urban Climatic Map and Standards for Wind Environment – Feasibility Study*, November 2008. Technical Report for Planning Department HKSAR.

Ng, E., Ren, C., Katzschner, L. and Yau, R. (2009). Urban climatic studies for hot and humid tropical coastal city of Hong Kong. In: *Proceedings of the Seventh International Conference on Urban Climate*. Yokohama, Japan, 29 June–3 July. Available at: http://www.ide.titech.ac.jp/~icuc7/extended_abstracts/pdf/254693-2-090422170338-003.pdf (Accessed 10 February 2014).

Oke, T. R. (1973). City size and the urban heat island. *Atmospheric Environment*, 7(8): 769–779.

Oke, T. R. (1982). The energetic basis of the urban heat island. *Quarterly Review of the Royal Meteorological Society*, 108(455): 1–24.

Oke, T. R. (1984). Towards a prescription for the greater use of climatic principles in settlement planning. *Energy and Buildings*, 7(1): 1–10.

Oke, T. R. (1987). *Boundary Layer Climates*. London: Routledge.

Oke, T. R. (1988). Street design and urban canopy layer climate. *Energy and Buildings*, 11(1–3): 103–113.

Oke, T. R. (2002). Urban heat islands: an overview of the research and its implications. Paper presented at *North American Urban Heat Island Summit*. Toronto, Canada, 1–4 May. Available at: http://www.cleanairpartnership.org/pdf/uhis_oke.pdf (Accessed 10 February 2014).

Ren, C., Ng, E. and Katzschner, L. (2011). Urban climatic map studies: A review. *International Journal of Climatology*, 31(15): 2213–2233. doi:10.1002/joc.2237.

Scherer, D., Fehrenbach, U., Beha, H. D. and Parlow, E. (1999). Improved concepts and methods in analysis and evaluation of the urban climate for optimizing urban planning process. *Atmospheric Environment*, 33(24–25), 4185–4193.

Svensson, M. K., Thorsson, S. and Lindqvist, S. (2003). A geographical information system model for creating bioclimatic maps – Examples from a high, midlatitude city. *International Journal of Biometeorology*, 47(2): 102–112.

TCWB (2009). *Meteorological Record from Kaohsiung Station (1930-2008)*. Kaohsiung: Taiwan Central Weather Bureau (TCWB). Available at: http://www.cwb.gov.tw/eng/index.htm (Accessed November 2013). (In Chinese).

TMG (2005a). *Guidelines for Heat Island Control Measures [Summary Edition]*. Tokyo: Bureau of the Environment, Tokyo Metropolitan Government (TMG). Available at: https://www.kankyo.metro.tokyo.jp/en/attachement/heat_island.pdf (Accessed November 2013).

TMG (2005b). *The Thermal Environment Map and Areas Designated for the Implementation of Measures Against the Heat Island Phenomenon*. Tokyo: Bureau of the Environment, Tokyo Metropolitan Government (TMG). Available at: http://www.metro.tokyo.jp/ENGLISH/TOPICS/2005/ftf56100.htm (Accessed November 2013).

Tseng, T. F. (2007). *Plan of Changing Urban Space of Kaohsiung*. Kaohsiung: K. C. G. Bureau of Urban Development. (In Chinese).

Tseng, T. F. (2008). A city in transformation – Kaohsiung. Paper presented at *the 2008 International Forum on Community Regeneration, 'Blissful Kaohsiung, Community Regeneration'*. Bureau of Urban Development, Kaohsiung Government, Kaohsiung, Taiwan.

UN (2002a). *World Urbanization Prospects: The 2001 Revision*. United Nations. Available at: http://www.un.org/esa/population/publications/wup2001/wup2001dh.pdf (Accessed November 2013).

UN (2002b). *World Urbanization Prospects: Data Tables and Highlights*. Population Division, Department of Economic and Social Affairs, United Nations Secretariat. Available at: http://www.un.org/esa/population/publications/wup2001/wup2001dh.pdf (Accessed November 2013).

VDI (1997). *VDI-Standard: VDI 3787 Part 1 Environmental Meteorology – Climate and Air Pollution Maps for Cities and Regions*. Berlin: Beuth Verlag.

Vieira, H. and Vasconcelos, J. (2004). *Urban Morphology Characterisation to Include in a GIS for Climatic Purposes in Lisbon: Discussion of Two Different Methods*. Available at: http://www.umbc.edu/cuere/pdf/Vieira_Vasconcelos.pdf (Accessed November 2013).

Chapter 16

# Urban climatic map studies in Portugal

## Lisbon

*Maria João Alcoforado, António Saraiva Lopes and Henrique Andrade*[1]

## Introduction

Urbanised areas have grown significantly throughout Europe. The European Environment Agency reports that between 1950 and 1990 urban area grew between 26 per cent (Sunderland, UK) and 270 per cent (Algarve, Portugal) (Gill *et al.*, 2004). Urbanisation processes strongly impact the environment, mostly in negative ways. Climate is one component of the urban physical environment that may play a role in improving the quality of urban life and the sustainability of cities (Andrade, 2005). However, climate is not often taken into account in urban planning (Oke, 1984; Brazel and Martin, 1997; Eliasson, 2000; Mills, 2006; Oke, 2006) and there is hardly any legislation on climate quality in cities, compared to legislation on air quality and noise.

Climate change is a current and urgent topic as urban areas are particularly vulnerable due to their specific features, such as the urban heat island and the concentration of population, infrastructures and activities. In certain cities, the temperature has already risen to values predicted for the planet's 'global' temperature in 2100 (e.g. Alcoforado and Andrade, 2008, where the relationships between 'global' warming and urban warming are discussed). Furthermore, cities have the potential (in terms of critical mass and technology) to promote innovative solutions that are easily reproducible on a wider scale. So should we not consider cities as privileged places to test different types of adaptive measures to climate change?

As referred by Scherer *et al.* (1999: 4185) 'climate maps presenting features of urban climate relevant for planning are serving as one of the main tools for planners'. Since we agree with this view, the research team Climate Change and Environmental Systems (zephyrus.ulisboa.pt) at the University of Lisbon has endeavoured to acquire data and develop methodologies to model and represent cartographically urban climatic features. This chapter offers a summary. Following the Introduction, the first section starts with an account of how climatic information has been fed into planning, and the second section presents the rationale for these studies. The third section deals with meso-scale climatic maps and the fifth section with maps obtained at the micro-scale. These two sections highlight the documents that support planning. The conclusion includes reference to an information booklet geared to the municipalities.

## Climate information in urban planning

In 1984, Tim Oke wrote that only a small amount of climate knowledge had permeated through to urban planners, due to the 'inherent complexity of the subject, its interdisciplinary nature and lack of meaningful dialogue between planners and the climatological research community' (Oke, 1984: 1). Since then, only a few papers have shown that any steps have been taken towards the introduction of climatological principles in settlement planning. For example, in 1988, Bitan suggested a methodology that would enable planners, as well as architects, to integrate climatic information at all levels of planning, from settlement planning to the design of buildings (Bitan, 1988). The methodology is synthesised in a flowchart divided into five main stages, three of which involve climatological data acquisition and processing (Bitan, 1988: 4).

Also in the same year, i.e. 1988, Zrudlo presented 'A climatic approach to town planning in the Arctic', where a case study was carried out in a wooden house Inuit settlement constructed by the Canadian government near the Hudson Bay. He identified *sun, wind,* and *snow* as the major stress factors in this area. His final plan took into consideration not only individual plans drawn separately for each climate element, but also the conflicts arising from them. He presented a 'synthesized plan which offers maximum solar advantage, wind protection and minimum snow-drifting, contributing [...] to the efficient functioning of the town and to the general well-being, both physically and psychologically, of its inhabitants' (Zrudlo, 1988: 62–63).

Since 1970, Germany has carried out several climatic analyses on urban planning, firstly in the very densely populated *Ruhr* area, then in projects on the urban climate of Bavaria (several cities in southern Germany in the 1980s), followed by many others, including projects Stuttgart 21 (Baumüller, 2005) and BERLIOZ on Berlin (for references and procedure see Matzarakis, 2005). Most of these studies include 'synthetic climate-function maps' and maps containing guidelines for planning. The *Climate Booklet for Urban Development* (Baumüller *et al.*, 2005) provides a very useful tool for planning-related urban climate studies. Within the framework of the KABA Project ('Klima Analyse der Region Basel', Scherer *et al.*, 1999), two types of maps were produced: the climatic analysis maps and climatic recommendation maps for regional and urban planning. The University of Basel work team proposed an automated classification of planning objectives for the consideration of climate and air quality in the Basel region (Fehrenbach *et al.*, 2001: S606). The main objectives were the 'protection of sensitive areas, the improvement of problematic situations, risk assessment and reduction and recommendations for appropriate forms of land use'. This classification has two benefits: it is operator-independent and it can be applied elsewhere.

Meanwhile, other authors have dealt with the potential use of urban climate studies in planning as well as with the difficulties of engaging dialogue among researchers, planners, policymakers and urbanists (Alcoforado, 1999; Eliasson, 2000; Alcoforado, 2006; Mills, 2006; Oke, 2006).

## Background and rationale to our Lisbon Studies

This section deals with a sample of Management Plans (Portuguese Decree-Law 69/90, 2 March), to which information about urban climate and maps might be usefully added. It then moves on to introduce our core applied investigation of urban climatology which was carried out within the Lisbon Master Plan, as detailed below. For climatic phenomena and maps, we follow the scale concepts developed by Oke (2006), who distinguishes three main scales in the analysis of urban space: meso-scale, local scale and micro-scale.

Lisbon is located at 38° 43′ latitude N and lies to the east of the Atlantic seashore (see Figure 16.1), on the bank of the Tagus estuary in a highly differentiated topographic area (see Figure 16.2). Its climate is 'Mediterranean' (Cs in the Köppen classification), that is, the summer corresponds to the dry part of the year. The oldest city districts lie near the river. The highest buildings are concentrated outside of the historical centre (R and Ba in Figure 16.1), on its northern and north-western fringes. There are high-rise buildings near the Lisbon boundaries, but building density is still low in some city districts, for example, near C, PN and M in Figure 16.1.

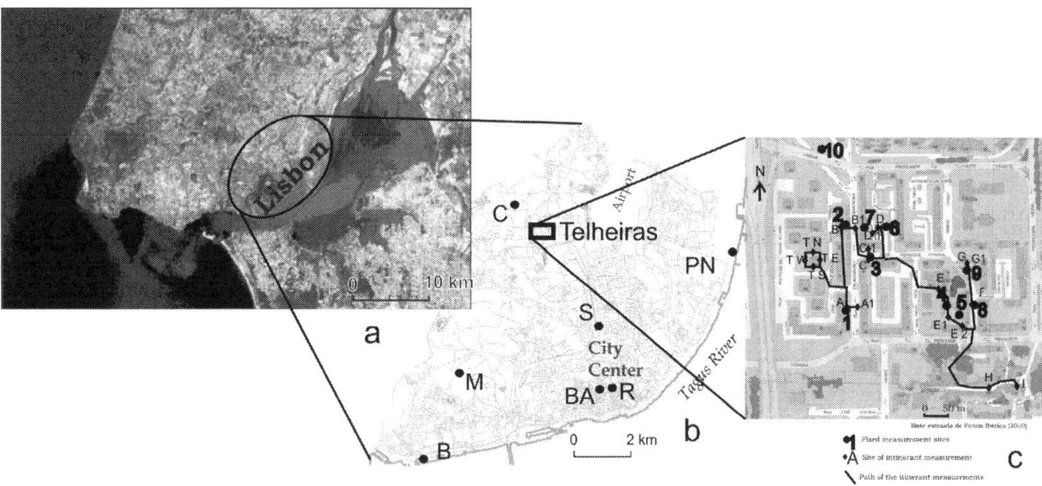


*Figure 16.1* Location maps: (a) Lisbon's region; (b) The city of Lisbon. B = Belém; M = Monsanto; Ba = Bairro Alto; R = Restauradores; S = Saldanha; PN = Parque das Nações (Expo); C = Carnide; (c) Telheiras city district. 1 to 9 = Fixed measurement sites. A, B, etc. = Path of the itinerant measurements.

Source: Authors

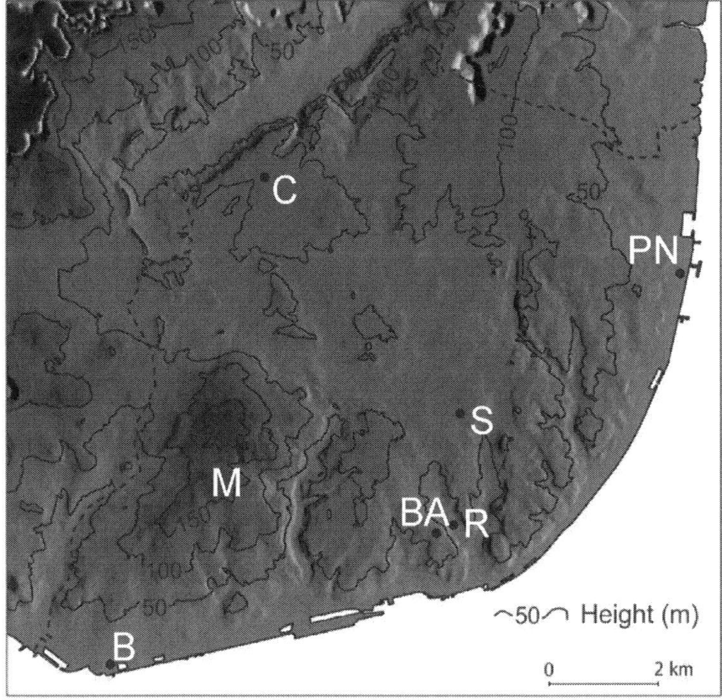


*Figure 16.2* Relief map: The city of Lisbon. B = Belém; M = Monsanto; Ba = Bairro Alto; R = Restauradores; S = Saldanha; PN = Parque das Nações (Expo); C = Carnide.

Source: Authors

The *Municipal Master Plan* (MMP) provides general guidelines for land use, on a municipal scale. Each MMP includes the regulations, the layout master plan map, the constraints map and several other documents, like the biophysical analysis of the area in question (Reis-Machado *et al.*, 1997). The MMP corresponds to the level of 'regional planning' of Bitan (1988) and to the more general aspects of local planning (land use). The MMP concerns a unit of territory administration (municipalities) whose dimension ideally matches the integration of urban climate studies on the mesoclimatic and local scale.

The *Town Master Plans* include the designation of space organisation in the urban environment, the overall layout of urban form and urban parameters, as well as the location of equipment, open-air spaces, road networks and main infrastructure. This type of plan matches the level of *Settlement Planning*; climatic information is predominantly available on a local scale.

The *Allocation Plans* define typologies of occupation of specific municipal areas, land use and general conditions of buildings, the characterisation of façades and the design of open-air areas. These plans match the more detailed aspects of *Settlement Planning,* in that they provide direct constraints to the level of individual building. Here, the more relevant information is clearly on a micro-scale.

In order to analyse how climate information was included in the MMPs, Alcoforado and Vieira (2004) reviewed 18 urban municipalities' MMPs. They concluded that climate is integrated in the biophysical characterisation in 86 per cent of the cases. Several meteorological parameters are included (temperature, precipitation, wind, relative humidity, among others), but only in the form of average values. Data referring to climatic extremes that can be most harmful (heat waves, cold spells, extreme precipitation) are hardly present, as are meteorological stations' metadata; furthermore, data is issued from meteorological stations that, according to the World Meteorological Organisation guidelines, are not (and should not be) representative of urban environments. No information concerning urban climatic characteristics, such as urban heat islands (UHIs), is incorporated, and neither are their possible consequences on the comfort and health of urban dwellers, nor their economic and social effects. Maps are rare and, when available, are prepared at a spatial scale which does not support planning decisions (Alcoforado and Vieira, 2004). The conclusion was that the climatic information supplied by the current MMP is inappropriate for planning purposes.

The main objective of our project was thus to follow Tim Oke's advice (Oke, 1984) to attempt to bridge the gap between scholars and climatic map end-users. The project, titled 'Prescription of Climatic Principles in Urban Planning: Application to Lisbon' (CLIMLIS), was carried out at the Centre for Geographical Studies of the University of Lisbon. After detecting the main climatic problems of Lisbon and predicting the changes that will result from the process of urbanisation, we offered suggestions to reduce the negative climatic local effects of built-up areas and to take advantage of any arising benefits. Drawing on these findings, the municipality of Lisbon (*Câmara Municipal de Lisboa* – CML) financed a second short project that would 'translate' the knowledge we had acquired into simple and spatialised guidelines for urban planning. The main results have been synthesised in a paper (Alcoforado *et al.*, 2009a) and in a report, available at the CML site (Alcoforado *et al.*, 2005), that will be part of the MMP's annexes.

Currently, a new project has been developed in Cascais, a municipality located in the western part of the Lisbon metropolitan area, on the Atlantic ocean. The guidelines for urban planning that we produced were included in the recent revision of the Master Plan and are about to be implemented. A new layer containing the wind power potential for the installation of small wind turbines, which can be used to supply energy for electric vehicles, was added to the urban climatic maps (Lopes and Correia, 2012).

The study at the local scale/micro-scale was also carried out within the CLIMLIS project (in Telheiras city district, see Figure 16.1(b) and (c), but unlike the study integrating the whole urban area, the guidelines for planning at the micro-scale have yet to be presented to planning authorities. They could be of use in town plan master and allocation plans.

## Meso-scale climatic maps

### *Modelling and mapping wind at the meso-scale*

Wind is a weather parameter strongly modified by urban areas. As shown in Figure 16.3, the prevailing winds at Lisbon Airport (located windward of the city, see Figure 16.1b) blow from the N and the NW, particularly during the summer months (Lopes *et al.*, 2011b). Urban roughness decreases air flux and, therefore, the urban logarithmic wind profile is different from that of an open area (Mortensen *et al.*, 1993).

The reduction of wind speed near the ground can be positive in cold climates or cold periods of the year in 'temperate' climates, but it has several disadvantages for the city dweller. First, the removal of air pollutants is less effective in calm weather, and second, in warm periods, particularly during heat waves, the absence of wind aggravates the heat load of the individuals and can lead to discomfort (Givoni, 1998); both situations may cause health problems. In most cities, knowledge of wind systems and patterns is thus important for planners, decisions-makers, and the population (Alcoforado *et al.*, 2009a). Due to great temporal and spatial variability in wind speed and direction, and owing to the complex geometry of urban areas, it is particularly difficult to understand spatial variation of wind patterns in cities. Numerical modelling can be a powerful tool to solve this problem. In order to understand the pattern of summer winds in Lisbon, a simple airflow model was considered appropriate to estimate meso-scale urban boundary layer wind fields: WAsP (Wind

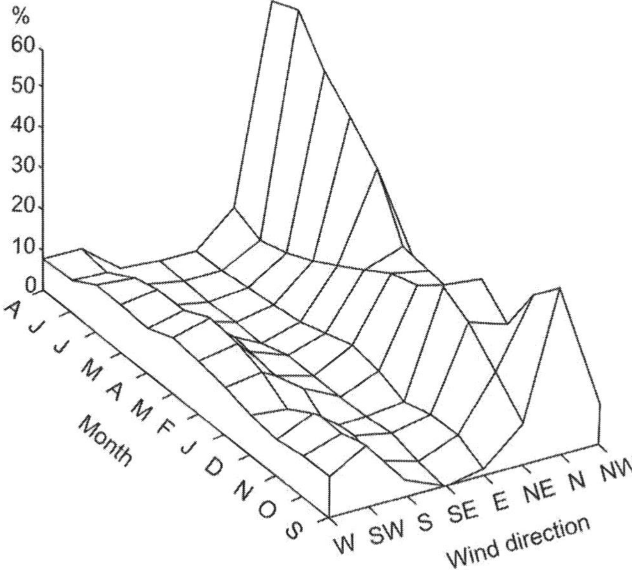


*Figure 16.3* Wind regime in Lisbon.

Source: Alcoforado, 1992

Atlas Analysis and Application Program) is a software developed by Risø National Laboratory in Denmark, which estimates both profiles and spatial data, taking into account the effect of terrain and surface roughness. The model has good agreement with real wind climatology, confirmed by wind tunnel experiments. The methodology and several other experiments are described by Lopes (2002, 2003), Lopes *et al.* (2011b) and Alcoforado (2010).

Lopes spatially represented the average reduction of summer wind speed in the 1980s at several heights above roof level, compared with previous wind situation considering only Lisbon's topography (Lopes, 2003; Lopes *et al.*, 2011b). The objective was to estimate the prevailing moderate and strong north (from 45° to 315°) summer winds' modifications brought about by city growth. Figure 16.4 shows the reduction at 10m high in the 1980s. The greater decrease occurs in the downtown area. The eastern Lisbon districts, which were then less urbanised than nowadays, suffer a smaller decrease. Wind speed is also reduced in the forested Monsanto hill due to its high roughness length ($z_0$ values).[2] If a further reduction of air flux occurs, more frequent calm conditions will be observed and a subsequent impoverishment of air quality, as well as of comfort and health for city dwellers, are to be expected. An update of the map in Figure 16.4 is being carried out in a Masters thesis project at the University of Lisbon. Its author expects not only to obtain a map of current airflow reduction at 10m and 20m high, but also to be able to predict the future situation if the expansion of the city goes on as projected.

Another important feature of the climate in Lisbon is the frequent occurrence of estuary and ocean breezes (30 per cent in summer days), which can provide significant cooling of the riverside

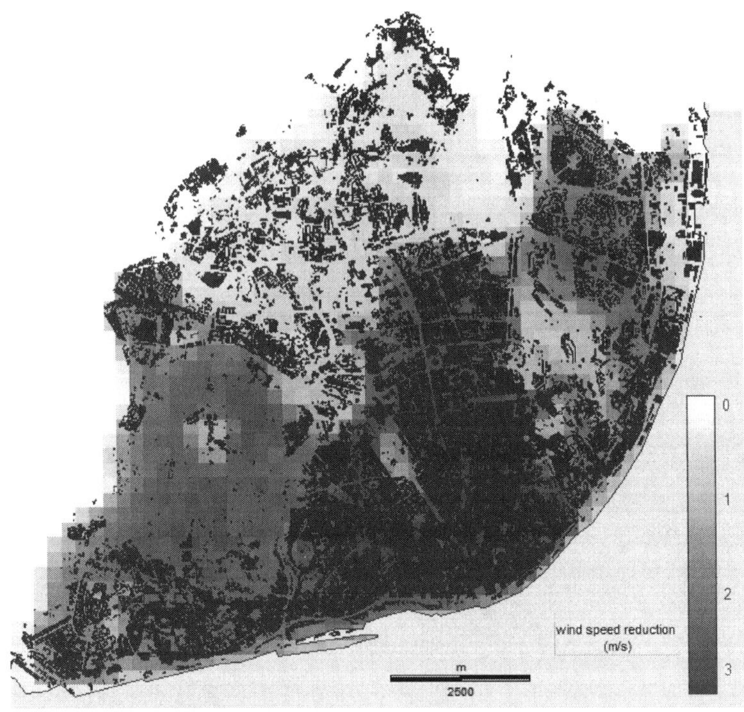


*Figure 16.4* Summer north wind speed reduction: Difference between situation at the end of the 1980s and situation considering only topography (m/s).

Source: Authors

areas. On very hot days, temperature differences of nearly 10°C between these areas and the city centre were measured (Alcoforado, 2006; Alcoforado *et al.*, 2007). Modelling has been devised by Vasconcelos *et al.* (2004). A similar study is being carried out on the city of Funchal (Madeira Island – a travel destination which receives 71 per cent of its tourists from northern European countries, not all of them used to hot environments), where the importance of sea breeze as a cooling factor has been verified (Lopes *et al.*, 2011a). The authors found that the urban structure impoverishes the thermal comfort conditions during heat waves, and that the inner city may be 4°C to 5°C hotter than the coast, where the favourable sea breeze blows frequently on these occasions.

## Measuring, modelling and mapping air temperature at the meso-scale

Knowledge of the urban thermal field is crucial, due to the impact of temperature on urban environmental conditions (Alcoforado *et al.*, 2009a). However, an average situation cannot be assumed; it is necessary to know the frequency of each thermal pattern. Moreover, it is important to understand the consequences of thermal patterns on air quality, human health, thermal comfort and energy consumption.

### Climate data acquisition and statistical procedure

There were several stages in the acquisition of surface and air temperature data for the study of the UHI of Lisbon, with the purpose of solving the insufficient temporal representativeness of the first studies, which were mainly based on itinerant field measurements (Alcoforado, 1986, 1991, 1992, 1994). In these first studies, measuring points were selected along a frequently repeated transverse; at each stop, we carried out measurements with an *Assmann* aspiration psychrometer (see Figure 16.5). Around 60 repetitions of this transverse allowed conclusions about Lisbon's UHI, together with measurements from two thermo-hygrometers (Alcoforado, 1992). As soon as it became financially possible, data loggers were used for data acquisition in a network that included 12 fixed stations equipped with digital thermo-hygrometers (Vieira *et al.*, 2000) in sites with high sky view factors (SVF > 0.65),[3] which were as free as possible from the microclimatic influence of buildings and vegetation (see Figure 16.6b and d; Andrade, 2003). The sensors were first placed in cylindrical shelters, 15cm in diameter and coated in aluminium foil (see Figure 16.5c). These were later replaced by plastic standard multi-plate shelters (see Figure 16.5e; Alcoforado and Andrade, 2006;

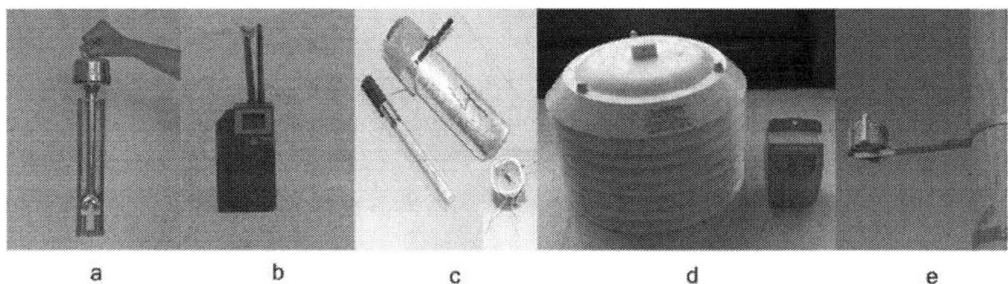


*Figure 16.5* Examples of instruments and shelters: (a) Assmann psychrometer; (b) portable digital thermo-hygrometer; (c) temperature and humidity sensor, Gemini data logger and former shelter; (d) plastic shelter and temperature data logger; (e) plastic shelter located on a lamp.

Source: Authors

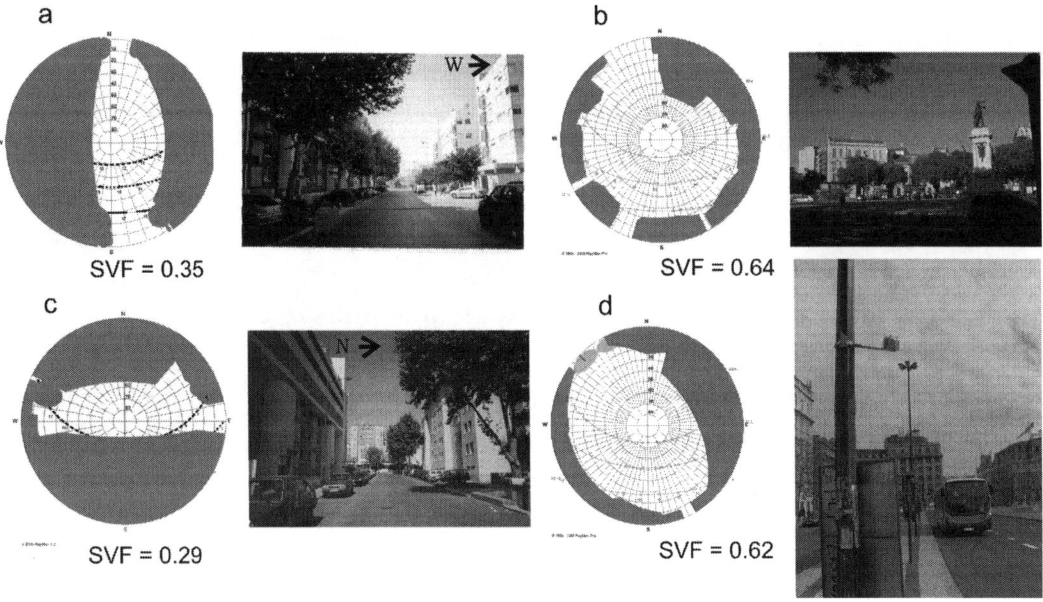


*Figure 16.6* SVFs and solar diagrams with sun paths at the time of the solstices and the equinoxes of four measurement sites in Lisbon:
a and c: two sites of the micro-scale network (low sky view factors)
b (Saldanha) and d (Restauradores): two sites of the meso-scale network (High sky view factors)
See *Figure 16.1* for site location.

Source: Authors

Alcoforado *et al.*, 2007). Part of this meso-scale network has been in place since 2004, supplying data every 15 minutes (for the seven measurement sites, see Figure 16.1b).

A cluster analysis was performed, using the k-means method, with the aim of classifying the spatial thermal patterns at three times of day (Alcoforado and Andrade, 2006). To normalise the values, the difference between each measurement and the average of the temperature at seven sites, available within the city perimeter, was calculated. The spatial generalisation of temperature was obtained through the use of the Geographic Information System (GIS). The statistical models used to estimate the continuous thermal field are described in Alcoforado and Andrade (2006).

### *Thermal patterns*

Two thermal patterns will be described. The first was chosen due to its frequency and the presence of a UHI; the second reflects an interesting situation, showing the influence of the sea breeze.

**Pattern 1** (see Figure 16.7a) is the most frequent (47 per cent) particularly at night (see Figure 16.8), but also on winter days. In these situations, there is a UHI in southern and central Lisbon (due to the urban factors and to topographic shelter from the wind). The cooler areas are the northern ones and the Monsanto Hill (M on Figure 16.1). This pattern is mainly associated with North, North-west and North-east winds.

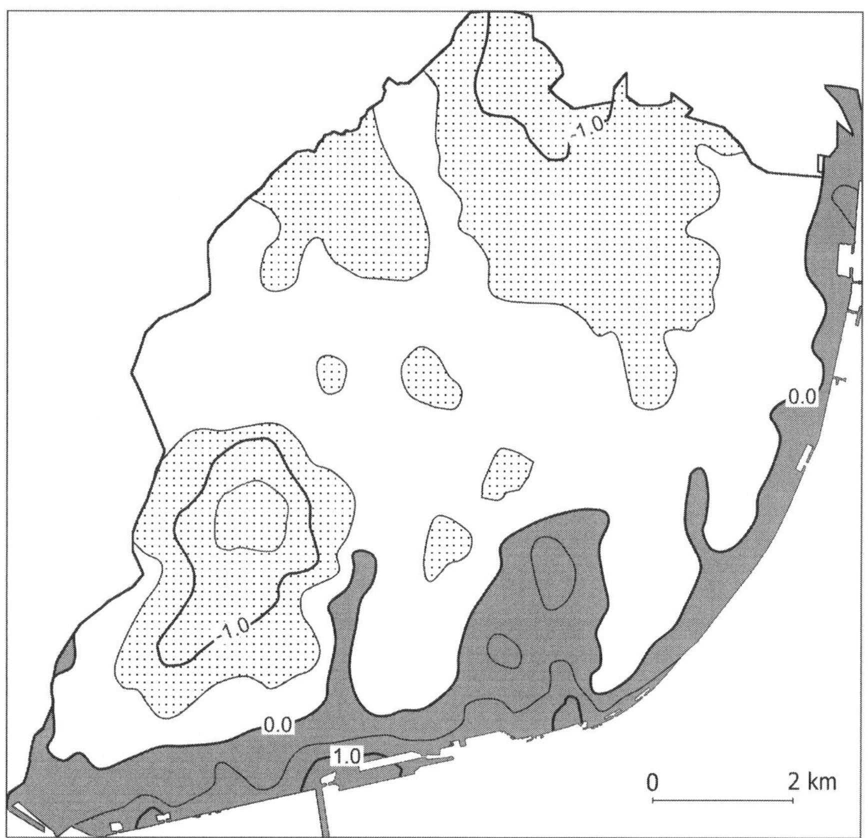


*Figure 16.7* Examples of thermal patterns in Lisbon: Differences between the temperature of each point and spatial temperature average (°C): (a) frequent thermal pattern

Source: Andrade, 2003

**Pattern 2** (see Figure 16.7b) occurs only in 3 per cent of the nights, but it is particularly frequent during summer days (30 per cent at 14h). A synoptic situation with low pressure gradient and mainly Eastern or North-eastern fluxes gives rise to this pattern. It is the one most frequently associated with hot days and also with high $O_3$ and $PM_{10}$ concentrations. Consequently, sea breezes have a strong cooling effect in south-western Lisbon (Alcoforado *et al.*, 2006; Andrade *et al.*, 2011).

## *UHI frequency*

The definition of UHI as the difference between the highest temperature in town and the temperature of the rural area around it (Oke, 1987) may seem quite simple, but the methods to compute UHI have to be adapted to each single city and to the available data. In Lisbon's case, it was calculated through the difference between the highest temperature recorded one of the three measuring points located right at the city centre (S, BA and R on Figure 16.1) and one of the two coolest

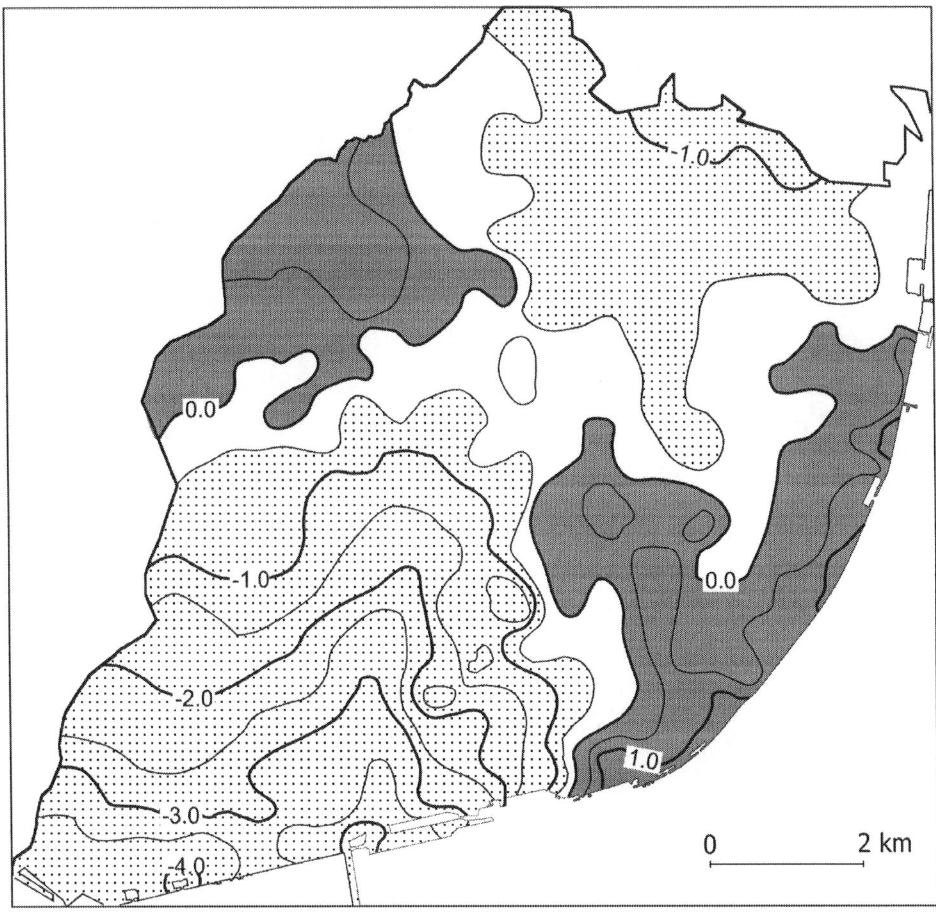


*Figure 16.7* (b) thermal pattern by SW breeze

measuring points outside the urban perimeter (M and C on Figure 16.1). Measuring points Belém and Parque das Nações were not considered, since their riverside position gives them a particular type of climate.

The UHI of the air in the urban canopy layer (below roof level) occurs 95 per cent night-time and 85 per cent daytime. Median intensities range between 1.8°C and 2.1°C (Alcoforado, 1991; Lopes *et al.*, 2013). Lopes *et al.* (2013) recently updated the findings of the initial study with new data (2007–2012) and the sample now (November 2013) encompasses 1,340 days: the average value of UHI intensity was confirmed. The authors also concluded that the strong and very strong UHI values (> 4°C) occurred more often during the summer. The highest frequencies of the UHI occurred with W, NW and N winds, blowing between 2m/s and 6m/s, contrary to the general rule of stronger UHI in windless situations.

To illustrate the daytime situation, the difference from UHI occurrence between 14h and 17h is worth mentioning (see Figure 16.8). During the summer months at 14h, the UHI frequency does not exceed 70 per cent of the cases. This can be explained because Tagus and Ocean breezes blow over the southern city-districts at the same time in about 30 per cent of cases (Alcoforado

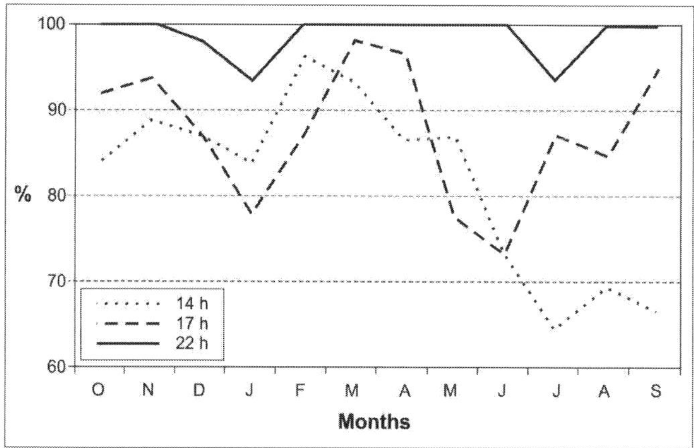


*Figure 16.8* Lisbon Urban Heat Island frequency at 14h, 17h and 22h.
Source: Adapted from Alcoforado *et al.*, 2007

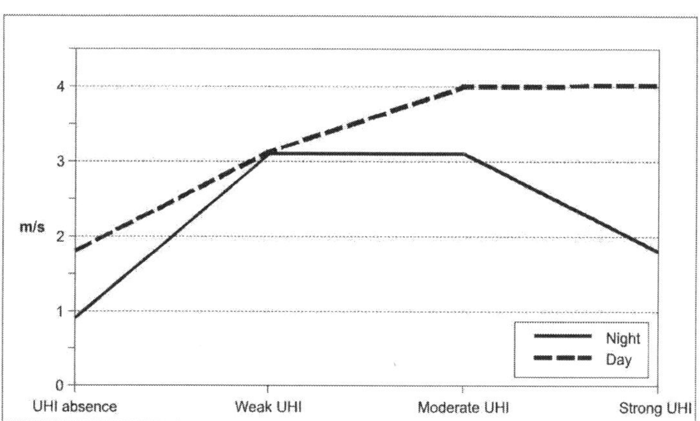


*Figure 16.9* Median wind speed corresponding to several Urban Heat Island intensities.
Source: Adapted from Alcoforado *et al.*, 2007

*et al.*, 2006). At 17h the UHI is more frequent (between 85 and 95 per cent in summer). The explanation lies in the much higher frequency of the north wind during summer late afternoons and evenings, allowing a UHI to form in the southern urban districts.

It is important to notice that Lisbon's UHI is due to both urban and natural factors (wind shelter due to topography). Lisbon's UHI is thus strongly dependent on wind direction and speed, which means that the rules are not always the expected ones, mainly concerning wind speed. The general rule of decreasing UHI with increasing wind speed (Oke, 1987) is not verified in Lisbon, nor in other littoral cities (Carrega, 1998), particularly in what concerns wind speeds < 2m/s measured at the windward side of the city (Lisbon's airport). It is clear from Figure 16.9 that UHI intensity is weak by wind speeds inferior to 2m/s both day and night. This means that when gradient wind is weak, advection from moist and cool air from the estuary and the ocean is made possible and the city centre turns cool; during the day, as wind speed increases up to 4m/s, UHI intensity augments (shelter effect). At night, low wind speeds may also lead to no UHI, as cool air advection may persist during the night in Lisbon.

## *Climatic maps for planning purposes*

These results, together with previous ones, clarified the main features of Lisbon's urban climate (UHI high frequency, wind modifications, the role of breezes, consequences for well-being, etc.) and allowed the subsequent construction of maps that could be of use in planning.

Feedback from city planners and the experience of different authors working on the same topics (quoted above), made it obvious that climatic guidelines can only be of use if they refer to areas whose limits are very precisely drawn on a detailed map. A cartographical representation of Lisbon's physical features had to be carried out, as existing land-use categories were not suitable in that they are mainly based on functional criteria. As a consequence, different types of land use may be included in the same functional class. Different types of residential areas, for example villas and modern apartment towers, will interact with the atmosphere in very different ways, giving rise to dissimilar urban climates. Therefore the cartography considered useful for climatic purposes was based on the parameters that were more important to the urban climate: the topography and the land cover, mainly considering the built density. Our aim was to produce a final map that depicted a set of areas interacting in a homogeneous way with the urban atmosphere. These were named homogeneous climate-response units (HCR Units). This is a concept similar to the 'climatopes', defined by Scherer *et al.* (1999: 4187) as 'areas of characteristic combination of climatic factors and of similar relative significance for their surroundings, operating on a spatial scale of several tenths to hundredths of meters'. The climatic significance of HCR units is potential, in the sense that they are defined and delimited according to *climatic factors* (i.e. features that influence climate, such as topography, urban geometry or land use) and not according to the spatial variation of *climate elements*, such as temperature or humidity. This map was an indispensable tool in defining the limits of the different areas for which climatic guidelines were to be put forth (see Figure 16.14). Figure 16.10 represents the procedure that was followed in pursuing this aim. The built density and the ventilation maps (see Figures 16.11 and 16.12) were produced as an aid to draw the limits of the HCR Units. The methodology to define these units is objective, but there were several final subjective adjustments, such as roughness length ($z_0$) thresholds, altitudinal limit for the low-lying areas, etc. (see below).

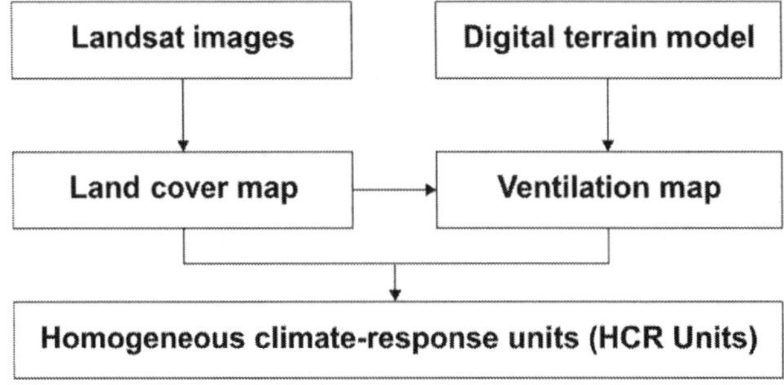


*Figure 16.10* Procedure followed in preparing the Homogeneous Climate-Response Units map.

Source: Alcoforado *et al.*, 2009a

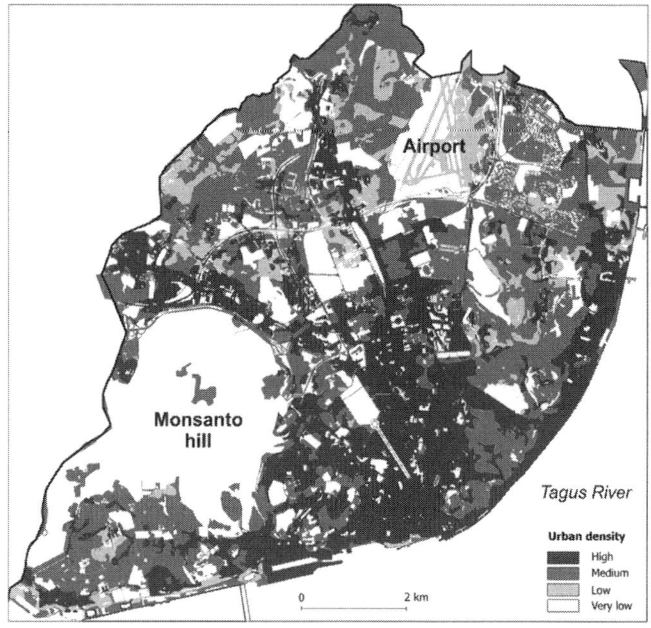


*Figure 16.11* Built density map.

Source: Alcoforado *et al.*, 2009a

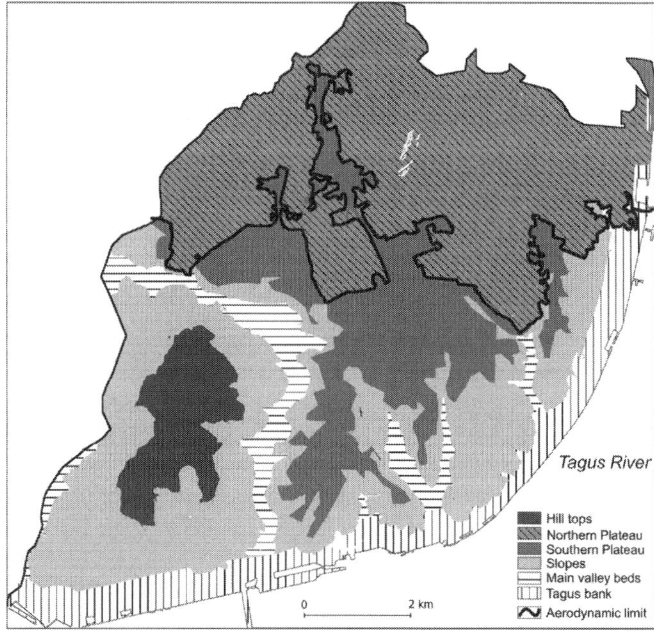


*Figure 16.12* Ventilation map.

Source: Alcoforado *et al.*, 2009a

In the recent project concerning the Cascais municipality, referred to in the third section, the parameters roughness length, urban density, and topographical features (necessary to obtain HCR Units) were automatically computed with a GIS technique. This ongoing work will allow computation of these parameters in any urban area, as long as tri-dimensional information (such as height of the buildings, etc.) exists.

### *Built density map*

The first step involved the classification of land cover, having the urban physical characteristics, particularly built density, as main criteria. The classification algorithm (maximum likelihood) was applied to a February 1992 Landsat image (details in Lopes, 2003 and Alcoforado, 2010). The resulting map was subsequently updated with information provided by the city authorities (mainly referring to green areas) and simplified according to the planners' needs. The following four main groups were obtained (see Figure 16.11): (a) High-density urban areas (where buildings occupy circa 50 per cent of the total ground area). In the central part of the city, between the downtown area (BA and R on Figure 16.1) and the *Avenidas Novas* (northwards from S on Figure 16.1), high-density urban areas prevail and green spaces are conspicuously absent; (b) Medium-density urban areas (where buildings cover between 15 per cent and 30 per cent of the total area); (c) Low-density urban areas (where buildings cover less than 10 per cent of the total area). The northern periphery of the city is characterised by relatively low urban density, particularly around the airport area (see Figure 16.1), where the green spaces essentially consist of grasslands; (d) Very low density urban areas (where green spaces prevail). The largest (mainly forested) green area corresponds to the Monsanto hill (M on Figure 16.1) SW of the city.

### *Ventilation map and the aerodynamic limit*

Wind circulation should not be hampered, in order to improve air quality and to avoid thermal stress. The main factors modifying wind circulation (topography and built density) are synthesised in the ventilation map (see Figure 16.12). Ventilation classes can be defined as areas with 'characteristic combinations of climatic factors controlling local and regional wind fields and vertical air mass exchange processes, resulting in typical and distinctive ventilation conditions' (Scherer *et al.*, 1999: 4189). As the scale of analysis is mesoclimatic, the topography was the main determinant factor in the elaboration of this map (see Figure 16.2). A Digital Terrain Model (DTM) was used, allowing for the identification of the large morphologic units: the valley beds and the tops were limited by subtracting the values of the absolute altitudes from the average values in a particular spatial unit (nine grid cells around the considered location). Slopes with gradients greater than 4° were identified automatically using GIS techniques. The flat areas, in which the slope is lower than 4°, constitute the Plateau. Monsanto is a 200m hill, located to the west of the city's main districts.

The low-lying areas are often sheltered; however, when the frequent north winds are blowing, these areas correspond to paths along which the winds are channelled. The ventilation along the valley beds absolutely must not be hindered, for the sake of air quality and thermal comfort. The low-lying areas near the Tagus, particularly affected by river and ocean breezes, were included in a separate class (Tagus bank), limited by the 20m contour line. This threshold was chosen based on the fact that the estuarine breeze progression to the interior is limited by a topographic 'step' upwards from circa 20m altitude.

As referred to above, it was found that the decrease in wind speed is particularly important in densely built-up southern city districts. The significant differences between built density and building height in northern and southern Lisbon have clear consequences on surface roughness. To quantify this limit, $z_0$ values were assigned to the different city districts, according to the Davenport-Wieringa roughness length classification (Stull, 2000; Lopes, 2003) that was also used for the European Wind Atlas and by the Danish Wind Industry Association. According to this criterion, the city centre and the new centrality area (BA, R, S on Figure 16.1) were assigned a $z_0$ value of 1m, and Monsanto hill (M on Figure 16.1) of 0.7m. In the northern part of the city, open spaces with some houses and green areas were assigned a $z_0$ value of 0.03m, ancient residual farmland and vacant spaces, 0.02m, and the airport runways, 0.01m. In order to include this information, a line representing the aerodynamic limit (see Figures 16.12 and 16.13) has been drawn: it separates the areas where a significant reduction of wind speed occurs, with $z_0$ between 0.7m and 1.0m (mainly in southern Lisbon) from the area with $z_0$ values between 0.01m and 0.05m in northern Lisbon, where wind speed is hardly affected, since the topography is rather flat and the urban density not very high yet. As mentioned earlier, ongoing research deals with a new method to automatically compute these parameters with the GIS.

### *Homogeneous climate-response (HCR) units*

The following step consisted of the creation of a co-occurrence matrix of the land cover/ urban density and ventilation classes (see Figure 16.10 and legend of Figure 16.13). The total number of resulting classes (24) was too high for planning purposes. Moreover, not all of the possible classes actually occurred or, when they occurred, did so with little significant extension. For these reasons, a decision was made to aggregate some of the classes, taking into account the areas for which the guidelines would most likely be similar. Previous knowledge of Lisbon's urban climate showed that this semi-quantitative methodology generated better results than a merely quantitative classification. The classes thus obtained were named homogeneous climate-response units, as referred to above (HCR Units); these are presented in Figure 16.13 and will be briefly described. For the ventilation units (*tops*, *plateau*, and *slopes*), the limits of the HCR units and, consequently, the guidelines for planning were a function of the built density (see Figure 16.13). The other two ventilation units (*Tagus bank* and *Valley beds*) were considered independently of the built density.

HCR Unit 1 refers to areas of very high built density, on hill tops, slopes or the southern plateau.

HCR Unit 2 aggregates areas of medium- and low-built density in southern Lisbon. This aggregation was carried out because on the one hand, the initial six classes from the matrix (see Figure 16.13) were not continuous in space and, on the other hand, the guidelines to be applied were the same.

Delimitation of the green areas (see Figure 16.13, HCR Unit 3) was based solely on their land cover characteristics, i.e. regardless of their topographical position. In the northern plateau the 'green areas' include only arboreal vegetation. Low-lying vegetation was excluded from HCR Unit 3 because it does not hinder wind circulation; it was therefore included in HCR Unit 6.

In the case of the plateau areas to the north of the aerodynamic limit, a decision was made to introduce a further and more detailed subdivision (HCR Units 4 to 6). This decision was based on the fact that the future densification of this area will influence not only the microclimates of the newly created districts, but also the climate of the entire city (for example, if the density of the built-up areas in this part of the city is to increase in such a way that the roughness length increases well beyond its current levels, the prevailing northerly wind would be much less effective in removing pollutants in the southern districts). HCR Units 4 and 5 include high and medium built density areas, while in HCR Unit 6, low built density areas and areas of low-lying vegetation have

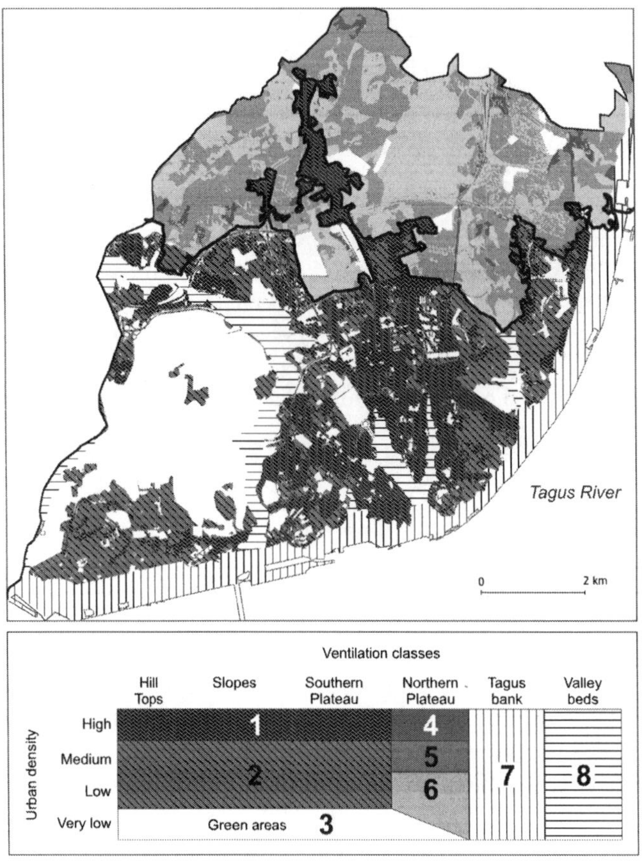


*Figure 16.13* Homogeneous climate-response units (HCR Units).

Source: Alcoforado *et al.*, 2009a

been considered. As stated above, two low-lying areas were delimited without regard for their land cover characteristics. These are the Tagus bank (see Figure 16.13, HCR Unit **7**), an HCR unit that comprises those areas in which the breezes are an important climate resource that must be preserved, and the valley beds (see Figure 16.13, HCR Unit 8), where wind channelling and the cool air drainage are significant factors (most of the valley beds have a North–South orientation, which is also the prevailing wind direction). It was then possible to put forth recommendations of land use transformations aimed at using the delimited areas in more appropriate and efficient ways, or at addressing the problems inherent to their current usage (Scherer *et al.*, 1999).

### *Climatic guidelines for planning*

The aim of our research was to suggest a series of measures aimed at minimising the two sets of climatic problems that were identified: the Urban Heat Island (UHI) (which should be considered as a thermophysiological factor and not simply as a feature of the air temperature field) and poor ventilation. In areas with hot summers, UHI has a very negative effect, increasing the level of discomfort and creating health problems for the city dwellers (Alcoforado and Matzarakis, 2010); furthermore, it raises the level of photochemical pollution and increases energy and water consumption. In global warming scenarios, the UHI will increasingly become a major consideration. In this context, it was decided that the mitigation of the UHI should be a priority. Moreover, new urban developments should not hinder ventilation to an even greater extent. The aim of the suggested guidelines is that they are applicable at city scale and clear enough to be read by non-specialists; therefore, they must be simple and somewhat general in content, with more details supplied at a later date (within the frame of town master plans or allocation plans). As guidelines vary with location within the city, urban density and roughness, as well as with topography, each HCR Unit will be described separately (see Figures 16.13 and 16.14).

**Areas of high urban density in the Southern Plateau (HCR Unit 1)** – They include the old city centre and most of the city that was built before the 1950s. There are hardly any open spaces. The main guidelines are: (i) to avoid increasing built density in valley beds, without a detailed study of the consequences on the ventilation in the valley; (ii) to make sure that the H/W ratio is kept under 1,[4] in those cases where urban development is currently under way; (iii) to maximise the vegetated surfaces, including roof gardens and walls; (iv) when renovating buildings, opt for light colours and materials with low thermal admittance (Doulos *et al.*, 2004).

**Areas of low and medium urban density in the Southern Plateau (HCR Unit 2)** – The main guidelines are: (i) to limit urban developments in valley beds; (ii) to make sure that the H/W ratio is kept under 1; and (iii) to create medium-sized green areas.

**Green areas (HCR Unit 3)** (see also Figures 16.13 and 16.14) – The positive (biophysical, social, cultural, etc.) influence of urban green areas is well known. The diversification of the structure of the inner green areas (ponds, lawns, tall trees, shrubs) would give rise to several types of microclimates, which in turn would favour different types of uses during different times of the year. Besides their influence within the green areas themselves, it is well known that medium- and large-sized parks modify the atmospheric conditions in the surrounding neighbourhoods (Oke, 1989; Eliasson and Upmanis, 2000; Andrade and Vieira, 2007; Oliveira *et al.*, 2011) and filter some of the air pollutants (Kuttler and Strassburger, 1999). Recent studies using mainly modelling techniques have shown that, in some cases, trees do not favour street level air quality (Gromke and Ruth, 2007; Vos *et al.*, 2013). This issue is expressed through the suggestive and grammatically innovative quip, 'To tree or not to tree', from the title of Vos's paper (2013). In their guidelines for planners, Gromke and Ruth (2007: 3302) stress that:

> Tree crowns should not occupy large canyon volumes in order not to suppress the ventilating canyon vortex system and the corner eddies. In particular, sufficient free space between crowns and adjacent walls should be ensured. Otherwise, the air exchange is hindered and the concentration of pollutants rises in the pedestrian level.

Preliminary studies detailing local features (including ventilation conditions and species characteristics) are therefore a must. In most of the cases, it is advisable to (i) preserve the existing green areas and (ii) create new ones wherever there is enough available space. Furthermore, (iii) the new green spaces should have a diversified inner structure and (iv) dense windbreaks should be created windward from leisure areas.

**Areas of low- and medium-urban density in the Northern Plateau (HCR Units 4, 5 and 6)** – The southern limit of this area corresponds to the aerodynamic limit, which means that the gradient wind remains relatively unobstructed by urbanisation. If this situation remains

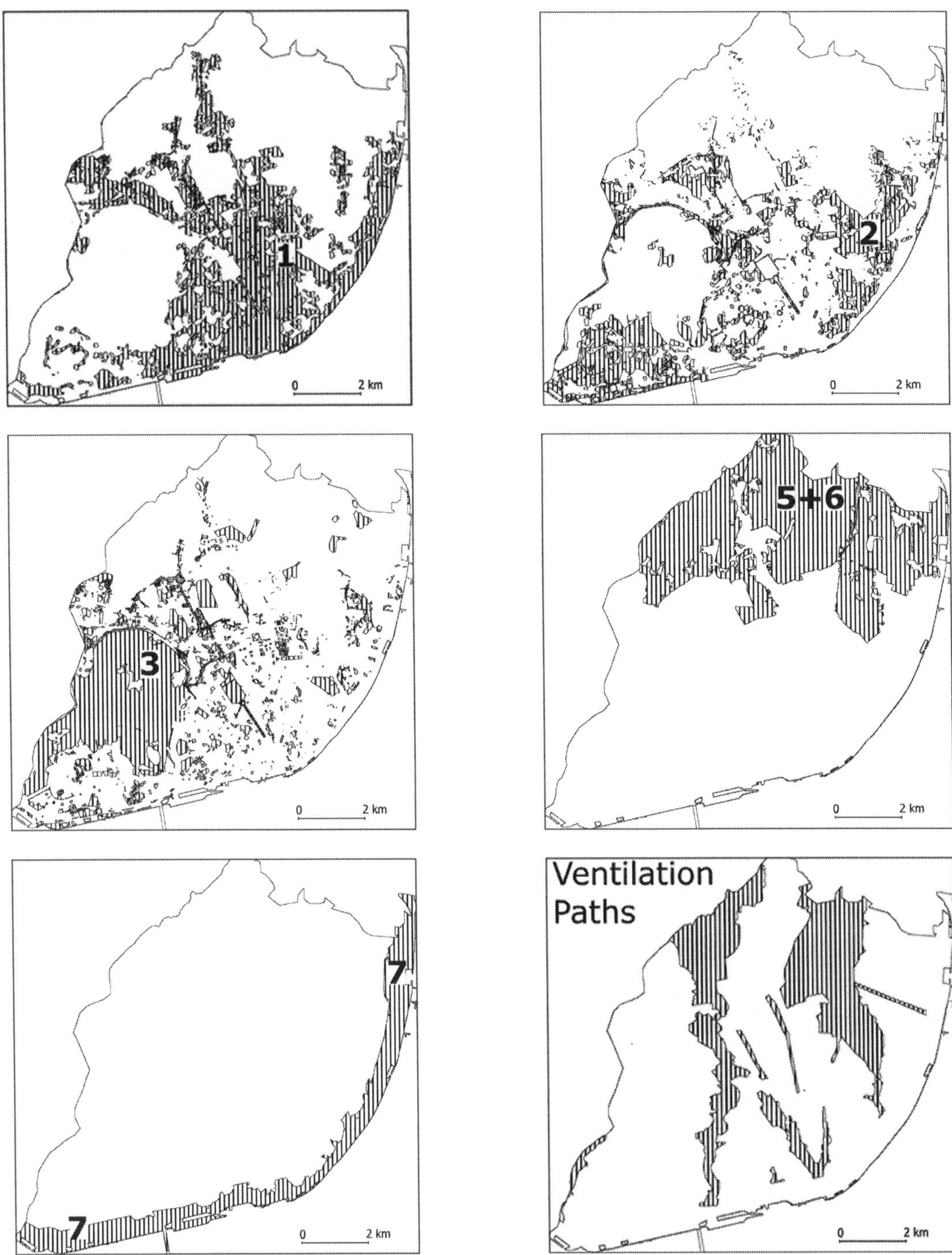


*Figure 16.14* Homogeneous climate-response units for which climatic guidelines were put forth.

Source: Alcoforado *et al.*, 2009a

unchanged, positive consequences are to be expected for the prevention of overheating and of excessively high pollution levels not only for the northern city districts but also for central and southern Lisbon (Burkart *et al.*, 2013). As this is obviously an area subject to great pressure from urbanisation, particularly in its NW sector, the guidelines are the following: (i) to avoid increasing the built density (H/W should be lower than 1); (ii) to promote ventilation paths alongside large freeways or in-between the city districts; and (iii) to create large green areas next to each newly built urbanised neighbourhood quarter. The areas of high density in the northern plateau (HCR Unit 4, see Figure 16.13) are very small and have not been considered at the meso-scale.

**Tagus Bank (HCR Unit 7)** – On the south and south-west Tagus Banks, the built density is already relatively high, although the height of the buildings is, on average, less than 15m. However, new city districts have been created in east Lisbon over the last decade. As urban development proceeds, planners should be aware that buildings whose larger side runs parallel to the river bank prevent the inland penetration of cool air. Thus, the creation of wind corridors with low roughness levels is recommended, in order to allow for the circulation of the estuarine breezes (for example, by keeping $z_0$ under 0.5m, so as to avoid reductions in the wind speed by more than 0.3m/s).

**Ventilation paths** (see Figure 16.14) – Besides the referred HCR Units, it was considered necessary to indicate paths that should be kept free for prevailing wind circulation towards the city core. The ventilation paths were delimited based on a combination of three main factors: topography (in southern Lisbon, it corresponds to the main *valley beds*, HCR unit 8 in Figure 16.13), built density (low-density axes in northern Lisbon, part of HCR Unit 6 in Figure 16.13) and orientation (along a roughly North–South direction). In order to ensure adequate ventilation in these paths, (i) no urban developments (especially tall buildings with an East–West orientation) should be allowed without a detailed study of future consequences on ventilation leeward and (ii) the trees planted along these axes should not form dense windbreaks. Compliance with these guidelines will ensure that good ventilation leads to positive effects in terms of temperature and air quality.

## Local/micro-scale climate maps in a Lisbon city district (Telheiras)

### *Study area*

Microclimatic differentiation is mainly observed in the urban canopy layer (UCL), which shows the direct influence of basic urban features (buildings, streets, trees) at scales of only a few hundred metres. This study was carried out in the city district of Telheiras, in northern Lisbon (see Figure 16.1c). Telheiras is a residential neighbourhood that covers 14 hectares and has a population of 1,800. Altitude varies between 100m and 110m.There is a predominance of apartment buildings that form blocks in lines along the streets; there are also a few villas, buildings used for social facilities and, to the west, a strip of 'tower-like' constructions. The main road axes are oriented either north–south or east–west and vary between 18m and 25m in width. The height of the buildings also varies considerably: the tallest are around 25m. The H/W ratio varies between 0.5 and 1.1. Courtyards are taken up by parking lots, social facilities and small garden areas.

### *Modelling and mapping wind in Telheiras*

A physical model (wind tunnel experiment) and a numerical model (ENVI-met ®) were used to study wind characteristics in the area under scrutiny.

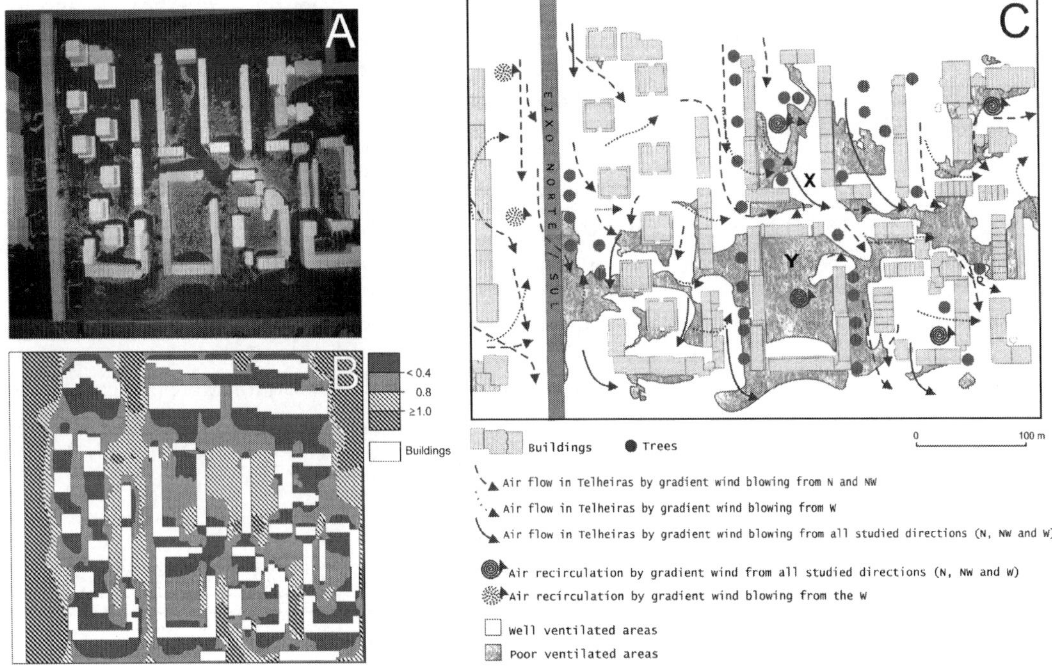


*Figure 16.15* Wind maps in Telheiras (Lisbon): (a) Erosion figures experiment inside a scale model representing Telheiras city-district. The figure refers to the moment when the wind speed had attained 9.3m/s in an undisturbed area on the 'ceiling' of the wind tunnel. (b) North wind in Telheiras as computed by the ENVI-met software (corresponds to wind speed at the airport); (c) Airflow in Telheiras by N, NW and W wind.

Source: (a) Lopes, 2003; (b) Adapted from Andrade, 2003; (c) Adapted from Lopes, 2003.

### *Mapping wind tunnel experiment results (erosion figures and wind profiles)*

Wind measurements inside the scale model were carried out with *Pitot-Prandtl* sensors. Wind profiles showed that if $z_0$ changes from 0.02m to 1.5m in the windward side of Telheiras city district, there would be a severe drop in wind speed: a reduction of 46 per cent near the ground, 30 per cent at 50m high and 10 per cent at 200m (Lopes, 2003).

The erosion figures data obtained by Lopes (2003) also confirm that diverse urban fabrics react differently to wind. Figure 16.15(a) shows an example: a photograph of sand distribution during an experiment by N wind considering a roughness length of 1.5m expectable in the near future, windward of the city district. At the beginning of the experiment (wind speed = 0) sand covered the whole floor of the wind tunnel (not shown). When the photograph was taken, wind speed had increased to 9.3m/s in an undisturbed area on the ceiling of the wind tunnel. When looking at the 'tower-shaped' buildings in the western part of Telheiras, it is clear that ventilation is slightly hindered by this kind of building organisation, and only the southernmost blocks provide some sheltered areas (where the sand has remained on the ground). I- and L-shaped buildings create wind corridors, such as *X* on Figure 16.15, where the N wind is systematically channelled. G-shaped buildings create particularly sheltered areas. Inside the courtyards (such as Y on Figure 16.15c) airflow is trapped and there is no air renewal; there will only be eddies and recirculation of the same air, that may only move local pollutants and particulate matter. As some of these courtyards are used for car parking, one may guess that the air quality inside them will frequently be poor (we have no measurements to prove this as yet). Lopes has conducted numerous other experiments (Lopes, 2003) for the three prevailing wind directions: N, NW and W.

### *Using a numerical model*

A simulation of the average wind speed, by way of the ENVI-met model (Bruse and Fleer, 1998; Bruse, 1999) was also carried out. Simulations were made using the mean wind speed and direction as recorded at the airport, at a height of 10m as the input base. Telheiras was represented on a three-dimensional grid created using the program interface, upon which the buildings and the vegetation were drawn. Each pixel was 5m × 5m. An example for North wind is presented in Figure 16.15(b). Wind speed may decrease to 20 per cent of the wind measured at the airport (mostly southwards of long W–E buildings), although in some N–S streets wind is nearly as strong as at the airport (0.8 to 1; see Figure 16.15b). The urban fabric common to both maps shows shared features, as referred to above. Using two types of models allows validation of results.

### *Synthesis: Airflow in Telheiras*

Figure 16.15(c) synthesises the main airflows in Telheiras and clearly indicates the areas where circulation is disturbed. In most cases, airflow within the city district is similar when gradient wind blows from the N and NW, so the same arrows refer to both gradient wind directions. Western gradient wind originates other flow directions within the city district. It is noticed that the worst ventilated areas (inside G-shaped buildings) correspond to the areas where sand accumulation persisted during the wind tunnel experiments and where eddies as well as (bad quality) air recirculation occurred. The conversion of parking lots into green spaces would certainly improve air quality. The I and L typologies led to wind channelling following the same paths, although parts of the courtyards remain in the 'wind shadow' and generate sheltered areas. In the main W–E street and NW gradient, winds blow from the W, after being channelled between the windward L- and I-shaped buildings. As referred to above, the tower-like buildings allow airflow, although causing deviation as the wind diverges upwind of each tower and converges downwind. The experiments with NW wind have shown that the wind speed will decrease not only due to urban roughness, but also to the fact that the wind forms a 45° angle with the prevailing N–S direction of the buildings. When the wind blows from W the existence of the N–S highway (*Eixo Norte-Sul*), which is higher than the surrounding areas, causes eddies near the slopes of the embankment on which the highway is built. The tower-like buildings hinder wind circulation from W more effectively than from N and NW. The different experiments show clearly that if the city continues to grow windward, the N wind circulation will be progressively hindered inside this city district (and others in similar geographical position), with severe negative impacts on the comfort and health of the inhabitants.

## **Computing and mapping thermal comfort**

Thermal comfort has been estimated by means of the Physiologically Equivalent Temperature (PET) (Höppe, 1999; Matzarakis *et al.*, 1999). This index allows the assessment of the thermo-physiological combined influence of atmospheric parameters which are important for the energy balance of the human being (Matzarakis *et al.*, 1999): air temperature ($T_a$), mean radiant temperature

($T_{mrt}$), vapour pressure (Pa) and wind speed (v). The production of internal heat (80W/m$^2$) and the clothing insulation (0.9clo) were considered constant. For a set of actual atmospheric conditions, PET is equivalent to the air temperature in a room with a standard environment ($T_a = T_{mrt}$; v = 0.1 m/s; Pa = 12hPa) that requires the same thermophysiological response as an actual environment. For example, the combination of $T_a$ = 30°C, $T_{mrt}$ = 45°C, Pa = 22hPa, and v = 2m/s corresponds to a PET value of 34.1°C. This means that the actual thermal environment requires the same thermophysiological response as a standard environment with $T_a$ = 34.1°C, $T_{mrt}$ = 34.1°C, v = 0.1m/s, and Pa = 12hPa. The computation of this index in Telheiras is explained in detail in Andrade and Alcoforado (2008). Data from field measurements in Telheiras, solar radiation data from the airport and modelled data, was used. Spatial interpolation of PET was carried out in the GIS, based on an equation that relates PET to geographical and urban factors. The best predictors for night-time PET were the temperature at the airport, the SVF and the wind speed (Andrade and Alcoforado, 2008).

In simulations with summer weather conditions and wind coming from the north, the level of thermal comfort differed substantially between examples a and b (see Figure 16.16). On a very warm night (see Figure 16.16a), PET exceeded 22°C in places that are more sheltered and are less exposed to the sky. In the streets with a north–south orientation and in the central part of the courtyards, PET values were between 18°C and 19°C and only on their west and north-east peripheries was PET less than 18°C (with a minimum of 17.5°C). Thus, PET values between 18°C and 22°C were predominant and are considered comfortable according to Matzarakis *et al.* (1998). It is worth recalling that PET modelling assumed a level of clothing equivalent to 0.9clo. Under summer conditions, clothing can be considerably reduced: at 20°C, a 0.5clo level of thermal insulation by clothing brings about a decrease in PET of around 3.3°C, which amounts to extending the conditions of light discomfort due to the cool conditions. On nights with characteristics such as these, staying out in the open is clearly an enticing idea, because the sensation of slight thermal discomfort is easily compensated for by small clothing adjustments.

So far, the analysis only concerns outdoor thermal conditions. The assessment of night-time bioclimatic needs must also consider indoor conditions, which are strongly dependent upon heat transfers from the outside (Taesler, 1990–1991). On nights when $T_a$ is close to 20°C, thermal conditions may be comfortable outside, but not indoors. According to Müller-Limmroth (1977, cited in Höppe, 1991), there is significant negative impact upon night-time rest when the $T_a$ is between 18 and 28°C. Höppe (1991) indicates maximum values of 18°C to 21°C for proper night-time rest, but this amplitude varies in function of regional climate, acclimatisation, and cultural factors.

On a night with strong winds from the north (see Figure 16.16b), the thermal conditions were either Cool or Moderately Cool (8°C to 18°C; Matzarakis *et al.*, 1998). In the centre of courtyards, in streets with a north–south orientation and in open areas, PET was lower than 12°C, which requires a considerable increase in the level of thermal insulation of clothing (close to 1.8clo), in order to maintain thermal balance. Obviously, these areas are not suitable for long stays without adequate protection from the wind. When there is such protection, PET increases to values that are just Slightly Cool, which can be compensated for by adjustments in clothing. Simulations for winter are available in Andrade and Alcoforado (2008).

### *Guidelines for planning*

Considering that Lisbon has a climate with thermally contrasted seasons, several guidelines can be suggested to achieve a 'high climatic quality city' (Bitan, 1992) by preventing extreme conditions within city-districts: to favour microclimatic diversity (with several sheltering conditions in relation to the wind, protection/exposure to solar radiation, etc.); to avoid the creation of excessively

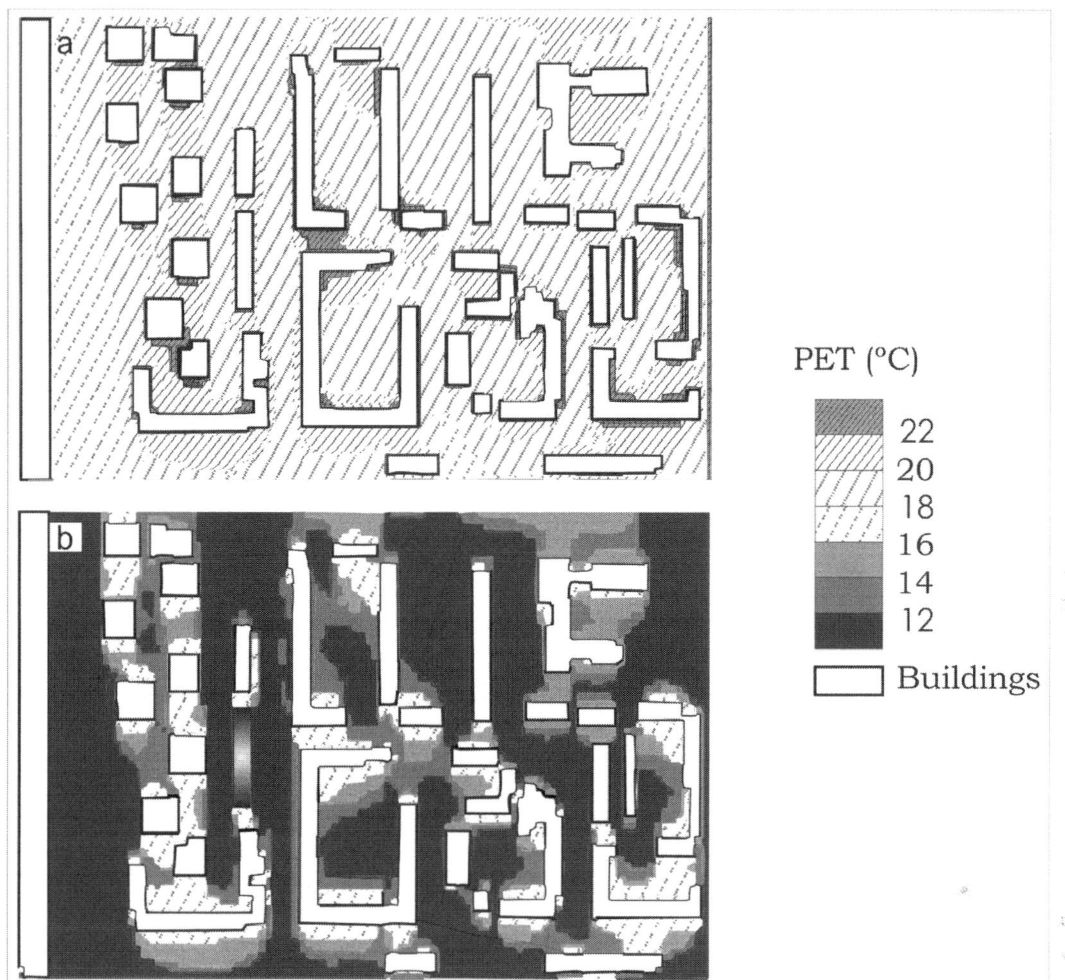


*Figure 16.16* Night-time PET estimates for different dates and times: (a) warm summer night; (b) cool summer night.

Source: Andrade and Alcoforado, 2008

confined spaces; to provide shade in summertime in the passageways and in the areas of permanency outdoors by using deciduous vegetation – the selection of the materials should be carried out according to their albedo, thermal conductivity and heat capacity, and the green area should be maximised, preferably with a diversified internal structure (water plans, grass surfaces, groups of trees with different heights, etc.).

With the purpose of preventing the excessive limitation of the air circulation, it is also suggested to design wide streets, in order to limit the effects of the local acceleration of the wind flux, but to avoid the construction of large roads unevenly located in relation to the surrounding areas, such as in the case of the N–S axis, which can cause undesirable whirlwinds, and to avoid the 'typologies in linear implantation', perpendicular to the direction of the dominant wind and the creation of 'closed typologies' (G type).

On the other hand, it was clear that an increase in roughness due to new constructions windward of the neighbourhood (north and north-west) would limit wind circulation near the surface even further, worsening thermal stress and the concentration of pollutant gases and residues.

## Conclusions

This chapter showed a sample of techniques and methods used in creating urban climatic maps, taking Lisbon (Portugal) as example. The climatic maps support different types of management plan, allowing spatial referencing, on appropriate scales, of climatic problems and potentialities in urban areas. Necessary planning measures are also found in detailed maps, whether to counteract negative elements or to explore climatic resources, thus contributing to enhanced quality of life and assuring sustainability of urban areas.

In addition, government policy for the cities has selected the relationship between climate change and urban development as one of the key issues to be addressed in projects initiated by local authorities and submitted for co-financing. Our studies at both the meso-scale and the micro-scale have been of use in raising awareness of the role of urban planning in responding to urban warming and climate change in cities in Portugal. A booklet on the impacts of climate change in urban areas (Alcoforado *et al.*, 2009b) is one of the actions taken by the Portuguese Directorate General for Spatial Planning and Urban Development (DGOTDU), in collaboration with the University of Lisbon. The DGOTDU is the national authority responsible for the technical implementation of the Policy for the Cities, in order to raise awareness of this issue and stimulate local authorities to carry out projects aimed at enabling urban communities to increase their resilience to climate change. Despite the uncertainties inherent to climate projections for 2100, any mitigation and adaptation measure will largely contribute to ameliorate environmental conditions and is therefore worth implementing. This booklet explains the challenges raised by climate change in Portugal, focusing on urban areas and urban development issues. The content makes use of research by the CliMA group (Centre of Geographical Studies, University of Lisbon), partly referred to in this chapter.

## Acknowledgements

Part of this research was carried out within the scope of two projects, the Urbklim Project (POCI/GEO/61148/2004), financed by FCT and FEDER (Operational Programme for Science and Innovation 2010) and 'Climate Guidelines for Planning in Lisbon', financed by the Municipality of Lisbon. The authors are deeply indebted to Madalena Cruz-Ferreira for her feedback on previous versions of this chapter. Thanks are also due to Rute Vieira for her help with the bibliography and to Joaquim Seixas for redrawing some of the figures.

We would like to dedicate this chapter to the memory of our colleague Henrique Andrade, co-author of this chapter, with whom we worked for two decades, sharing his enthusiasm, his proficiency and his dedication to the study of human bioclimatology and urban climatology and its application to urban planning.

## References

Alcoforado, M. J. (1986). Contribution to the study of Lisbon's heat island: Analysis from an infra-red image. *Freiburger Geographische Hefte*, 26: 165–176.

Alcoforado, M. J. (1991). Influence de l'advection sur les champs thermiques urbains à Lisbonne. *Publications de l'Association Internationale de Climatologie*, 4: 29–35.

Alcoforado, M. J. (1992). *Lisbon's Climate. Contrasts and thermal rhythms*. Memórias, 15, Centro de Estudos Geográficos, Lisbon: 347p. (In Portuguese with abstract in English).

Alcoforado, M. J. (1994). L'extrapolation spatiale des données thermiques en milieu urbain. *Publications de l'Association Internationale de Climatologie*, 6: 493–502.

Alcoforado, M. J. (1999). Aplicação da Climatologia ao Planeamento Urbano. *Alguns apontamentos. Finisterra – Revista Portuguesa de Geografia*, 34(67): 83–94.

Alcoforado, M. J. (2006). Planning procedures towards high climatic quality cities. Example referring to Lisbon. *Finisterra – Revista Portuguesa de Geografia*, 41(82): 49–64.

Alcoforado, M. J. (2010). Assessing and modeling the urban climate in Lisbon. In: Carrega, P. (ed.) *Geographical Information and Climatology*. London: ISTE, and Hoboken: John Wiley & Sons, 125–158.

Alcoforado, M. J. and Andrade, H. (2006). Nocturnal urban heat island in Lisbon (Portugal): Main features and modelling attempts. *Theoretical and Applied Climatology*, 84(1–3): 151–159.

Alcoforado, M. J. and Andrade, H. (2008). Global warming and urban heat island. In: Marzluff, J. M., Shulenberger, E., Endlicher, W., Alberti, M., Bradley, G., Ryan. C., Simon, U. and ZumBrunnen, C. (eds.) *Urban Ecology*, New York: Springer, 249–262.

Alcoforado, M. J. and Matzarakis, A. (2010). Planning with urban climate in different climatic zones. *Geographicalia*, 57: 5–39.

Alcoforado, M. J. and Vieira, H. (2004). Urban climate in Portuguese management plans. *Sociedade e Território*, 37: 101–116. (In Portuguese with abstract in English).

Alcoforado, M. J., Lopes, A., Andrade, H., Vasconcelos, J. and Vieira, R. (2005). *Climatic Principles for Urban Planning*. Geo-Ecologia, 4. Lisboa: Centro de Estudos Geográficos. Available at: http://pdm.cm-lisboa.pt/pdf/RPDMLisboa_avaliacao_climatica.pdf (Accessed March 2010). (In Portuguese with an English summary).

Alcoforado, M. J., Andrade, H., Lopes, A., Vasconcelos, J. and Vieira, R. (2006). Observational studies on summer winds in Lisbon (Portugal) and their influence on daytime regional and urban thermal patterns. *Merhavim*, 6: 90–112.

Alcoforado, M. J., Andrade, H., Lopes, A. and Oliveira, S. (2007). Lisbon's urban heat island. In: Centro de Estudos Geográficos (eds.) *Geophilia*. Lisboa: Centro de Estudos Geográficos, 593–612.

Alcoforado, M. J., Andrade. H., Lopes, A. and Vasconcelos, J. (2009a). Application of climatic guidelines to urban planning. The example of Lisbon (Portugal). *Landscape and Urban Planning*, 90(1–2): 56–65.

Alcoforado, M. J. (coord.), Andrade, H., Oliveira, S., Festas, M. J. and Rosa, F. (2009b). *Alterações climáticas e desenvolvimento urbano*. Série Política de cidades, 4. Lisboa: DGOTDU.

Andrade, H. (2003). *Human Bioclimate and Air Temperature in Lisbon*. PhD Thesis. University of Lisbon. (In Portuguese, with an English summary).

Andrade, H. (2005). O clima urbano – natureza, escalas de análise e aplicabilidade. *Finisterra – Revista Portuguesa de Geografia*, 40(80): 67–91.

Andrade, H. and Alcoforado, M. J. (2008). Microclimatic variation of Thermal comfort in a district of Lisbon (Telheiras) at night. *Theoretical and Applied Climatology*, 92(3–4): 225–237.

Andrade, H. and Vieira, R. (2007). A climatic study of an urban green space: The Gulbenkian Park in Lisbon (Portugal). *Finisterra – Revista Portuguesa de Geografia*, 42(84): 27–46.

Andrade, H., Alcoforado, M. J. and Oliveira, S. (2011). Perception of temperature and wind by users of public outdoor spaces: relationships with weather parameters and personal characteristics. *International Journal of Biometeorology*, 55(5): 665–680. doi: 10.1007/s00484-010-0379-0.

Baumüller, J. (2005). *Stuttgart 21*. Stuttgart: Amt für Umweltschutz. Available at: http://www.stadtklima.de/stuttgart/websk21/Heft13/kap3.HTM (Accessed March 2010)

Baumüller, J., Hoffman, U. and Reuter, U. (2005). *Climate Booklet for Urban Development. References for Zoning and Planning*. Germany: Baden-Württemberg Innenministerium. Available at: http://www.staedtebauliche-klimafibel.de/ (Accessed 23 January 2014).

Bitan, A. (1988). The methodology of applied climatology in planning and building. *Energy and Buildings*, 11(1–3): 1–10.

Bitan, A. (1992). The high climatic quality of the future. *Atmospheric Environment*, 26(3): 313–329.

Brazel, A. and Martin, J. (1997). Town planning, architecture and building. In: Thompson, R. D. and Perry, A. H. (eds.), *Applied Climatology. Principles and Practice*. London: Routledge, 175–186.

Bruse, M. (1999). Modelling and strategies for improved urban climates. In: *Proceedings of The 15th International Congress of Biometeorology & International Conference on Urban Climatology*. Macquarie University, Sydney, Australia, 8–12 November.

Bruse, M. and Fleer, H. (1998). Simulating surface–plant–air interactions inside urban environments with a three dimensional numerical model. *Environmental Modelling & Software*, 13(3–4): 373–384.

Burkart, K., Canário, P., Scherber, K., Breitner, S., Schneider, A., Alcoforado, M. J. and Endlicher, W. (2013). Interactive short-term effects of equivalent temperature and air pollution on human mortality in Berlin and Lisbon. *Environmental Pollution*, 183: 54–63. doi: 10.1016/j.envpol.2013.06.002.

Carrega, P. (1998). Les spécificités de l'îlot de chaleur urbain à Nice. *Nimbus*, 13–14: 33–41.

Doulos, L., Santamouris, M. and Livada, I. (2004). Passive cooling of outdoor urban spaces: The role of materials. *Solar Energy*, 77(2): 231–249.

Eliasson, I. (2000). The use of climate knowledge in urban planning. *Landscape and Urban Planning*, 48 (1–2): 31–44.

Eliasson, I. and Upmanis, H. (2000). Nocturnal airflow from urban parks – Implications for the city ventilation. *Theoretical and Applied Climatology*, 66(1–2): 95–107.

Fehrenbach, U., Scherer, D. and Parlow, E. (2001). Automated classification of planning objectives for the consideration of climate and air quality in urban and regional planning for the example of the region Basel/Switzerland. *Atmospheric Environment*, 35(32): 5605–5615.

Gill, S. (coord.), Pauleit, S., Ennos, R., Lindley, S., Handley, J., Gwilliam, J. and Ueberjahn-Tritta, A. (2004). *Literature Review: Impacts of Climate Change on Urban Environments*. Manchester: University of Manchester. Available at: http://www.sed.manchester.ac.uk/research/cure/downloads/asccue_litreview.pdf (Accessed 23 January 2014).

Givoni, B. (1998). *Climate Considerations in Building and Urban Design*. New York: John Wiley & Sons.

Gromke, C. and Ruck, B. (2007). Influence of trees on the dispersion of pollutants in an urban street canyon – Experimental investigation of the flow and concentration field. *Atmospheric Environment*, 41(16): 3287–3302.

Höppe, P. (1991). Improving indoor thermal comfort by changing outdoor conditions. *Energy and Buildings*, 16(1–2): 743–747.

Höppe, P. (1999). The physiological equivalent temperature – An universal index for the biometeorological assessment of the thermal environment. *International Journal of Biometeorology*, 43(2): 71–75.

Kuttler, W. and Strassburger, A. (1999). Air quality measurements in urban green areas – a case study. *Atmospheric Environment*, 33(24–25): 4101–4108.

Lopes, A. (2002). The influence of the growth of Lisbon on summer wind fields and its environmental implications. In: *Proceedings of The Tyndall/CIB International Conference on Climate Change and the Built Environment*. UMIST, Manchester, 8–9 April 2002.

Lopes, A. (2003). *Urban Climate Changes in Lisbon, as a Consequence of Urban Growth: Wind, Surface Heat Island and Energy Balance*. PhD Dissertation, University of Lisbon. (In Portuguese with English summary).

Lopes, A. and Correia, E. (2012). A proposal to enhance urban climate maps with the assessment of the wind power potential: The case of Cascais Municipality (Portugal). In: Lenka Hájková *et al.* (eds.), *International Scientific Conference: Bioclimate 2012 – Bioclimatology of Ecosystems*. Ústí Nad Labem, 29–31 August. Prague: Czech University of Life Sciences Prague: 68–69.

Lopes, A., Lopes, S., Matzarakis, A. and Alcoforado, M. J. (2011a). Summer sea breeze influence on human comfort during hot periods in Funchal (Madeira Island). *Meteorologische Zeitschrift*, 20(5): 553–564. doi: 10.1127/0941-2948/2011/0248.

Lopes, A., Saraiva, J. and Alcoforado, M. J. (2011b). Urban boundary layer wind speed reduction in summer due to urban growth and environmental consequences in Lisbon. *Environmental Modelling & Software*, 26(2): 241–243.

Lopes, A., Alves, E., Alcoforado, M. J. and Machete, R. (2013). Lisbon Urban Heat Island updated: New highlights about the relationships between thermal patterns and wind regimes. *Advances in Meteorology, Special Issue 'Advances in Urban Biometeorology', Hindawi.* [Online] Available at: http://www.hindawi.com/journals/amet/aip/487695 (Accessed 23 January 2014).

Matzarakis, A. (2005). Country report: Urban climate research in Germany. *IAUC Newsletter*, 11:4–6. Available at: http://www.urbanclimate.net/matzarakis1/papers/UCRE_de_IAUC011.pdf (Accessed 23 January 2014).

Matzarakis, A., Beckröge, W. and Mayer, H. (1998). Future perspectives in applied urban climatology. In: *Proceedings of Second Japanese-German meeting, Report of Research Center for Urban Safety and Security, Kobe University*, Special Report, Vol. 1: 109–122.

Matzarakis, A., Mayer, H. and Iziomom, E. (1999). Applications of a universal thermal index: Physiologically equivalent temperature. *International Journal of Biometeorology*, 43(2): 76–84.

Mills, G. (2006). Progress toward sustainable settlements: A role for urban climatology. *Theoretical and Applied Climatology*, 84(1–3): 69–76.

Mortensen, N., Landberg, L., Troen, I. and Petersen, E. (1993). *Wind Atlas Analysis and Application Program (WAsP)*, Vol. I and II. Roskilde: Risø National Laboratory.

Oke, T. R. (1984). Towards a prescription for the greater use of climatic principles in settlement planning. *Energy and Buildings*, 7(1): 1–10.

Oke, T. R. (1987). *Boundary Layer Climates*. London: Routledge.

Oke, T. R. (1989). The micrometeorology of the urban forest. *Philosophical Translation of Royal Society of London. Series B, Biological Sciences*, 324(1223): 335–349.

Oke, T. R. (2006). Towards better scientific communication in urban climate. *Theoretical and Applied Climatology*, 84(1–3): 179–190.

Oliveira, S., Andrade, H. and Vaz, T. (2011). The cooling effect of green spaces as a contribution to the mitigation of urban heat: A case study in Lisbon. *Building and Environment*, 46(11): 2186–2194.

Reis-Machado, J. *et al.* (1997). Municipal Master Plans for the Lisbon Metropolitan Area (AML). A regional approach. In: Reis-Machado, J. and Ahren, J. (eds.) *Environmental Challenges in an Expanding Urban World and the Role of Emerging Information Technologies Conference*. Lisbon, Portugal. http://www.igeo.pt/servicos/CDI/biblioteca/pdf/AMB_27_33.pdf (Accessed 23 January 2014).

Scherer, D., Fehrenbach, U., Feigenwinter, C., Parlow, E. and Vogt, R. (1999). Improved concepts and methods in analysis and evaluation of the urban climate for optimising urban planning processes. *Atmospheric Environment*, 33(24–25): 4185–4193.

Stull, R. (2000). *Meteorology for Scientists and Engineers*. Pacific Grove: Brooks-Cole.

Taesler, R. (1990–1991). Climate and building energy management. *Energy and Buildings*, 16(1–2): 599–608.

Vasconcelos, J., Lopes, A., Salgado, R. and Neto, J. (2004). Modelling of the estuarine breeze of Lisbon (Portugal): preliminary results. In: García Codron, J. C. *et al.* (eds.), *El Clima entre el Mar y la Montaña.* IV Congreso de la Asociación Española de Climatología. Santander, Spain, 2–5 November. Universidad de Cantabria: 165–169. Available at http://www.aeclim.org/4congr/vasconcelosJ04.pdf (Accessed March 2010).

Vieira, G. T., Mora, C. and Ramos, M. (2000). Registadores automáticos de baixo custo para monitorização de temperaturas do ar, da rocha e do solo. *Finisterra – Revista Portuguesa de Geografia*, 35(69): 139–148.

Vos, P., Maiheu, B., Vankerkom, J. and Janssen, S. (2013). Improving local air quality in cities: To tree or not to tree? *Environmental Pollution*, 183(2013): 113–122.

Zrudlo, L. R. (1988). A climatic approach to town planning in the Arctic. *Energy and Buildings*, 11(1–3): 41–63.

[*Note*: Most of the authors' publications may be downloaded at http://clima.ul.pt or requested to the authors.]

## Notes

1 CliMA-CEG Researcher, deceased 9 January 2013.

2 Roughness length $z_0$ is a measure of the roughness of a surface over which a fluid is flowing/the height above the plane at which the mean wind becomes zero when extrapolating the logarithmic wind-speed profile downwards through the surface layer (AMS glossary/Lopes).

3 The sky view factor (SVF) is 'the ratio of the amount of the sky "seen" from a given point of a surface to that potentially available' (Oke, 1987: 404).
4 The 'Canyon Aspect Ratio' between the height of the buildings (H) and the width of the streets (W) is a parameter used to describe the urban geometry.

Chapter 17

# Urban climatic map studies in Brazil

## Campinas

*Alessandra R. Prata Shimomura, António Saraiva Lopes and Ezequiel Correia*

### Introduction

One of the main components necessary to build urban climatic maps (UCMaps) and to produce climatic guidelines for urban planning is knowledge of the wind regimes of a region. A key issue to assess the urban ventilation is to use at least hourly or sub-hourly wind data and display it in a proper meso-climatic scale of analysis. This can be done by using state of art Computational Fluid Dynamics (CFD) and linearised models. The first category (CFD) has the advantage of accurate wind flows, but needs more computational resources and has a limitation when the integration of all directions is needed. Linear models are better suited to this task because the models are more accessible and real wind data can be used to assess wind speed and directions (Prata, 2005; Prata-Shimomura, 2010; Lopes *et al.*, 2011).

This chapter presents an application where hourly wind data was used along with the WAsP – Wind Atlas Analysis and Application Program – software, the results of which will be included in the analysis of UCMaps in Campinas. The software aids the estimation of profiles in height, and the wind fields on the surface, taking into account the surface roughness, obstacles, and the topography in a mesoclimatic scale. At this time, the characterisation of the roughness length adopted for the analysis which will qualify the areas in the city of Campinas/SP/Brazil will be described, as well as the procedure for developing the maps for use with the software and for the drafting of the homogenous climate-response units (HCR units). Therefore, of the climate variables, the wind will be the main focus of this research, enabling and analysing its behaviour (direction and velocity), taking into account the building characteristics of the city (roughness) and the topography.

At a city scale, the analysis of urban ventilation by macro-zones and the relationships among them are of great importance in suggesting measures and proposing recommendations for the organisation of the areas of the city in macro-zones (see Figure 17.1). The paper we present here is based on the city of Campinas' master plan, as well as on the local management plans (SEPLAMA, 2012).

The need for studies aimed at the application of the knowledge of wind to urban planning is even more important in regions of tropical and hot climates, because air quality and environmental thermal comfort strongly depends on the ventilation patterns. Considering that the quality of urban spaces contributes to the quality of living, the knowledge of the relations between the urban variables and their implications for the users' environmental comfort becomes very important for the analysis of the city. This knowledge provides tools for planning on large-scale projects, enabling a better relationship between people and the urban spaces where they live. The need to apply these studies to urban planning, particularly those aimed at the wind variable for regions in tropical climates, is of great importance to the verification of aspects related to air quality and environmental comfort.

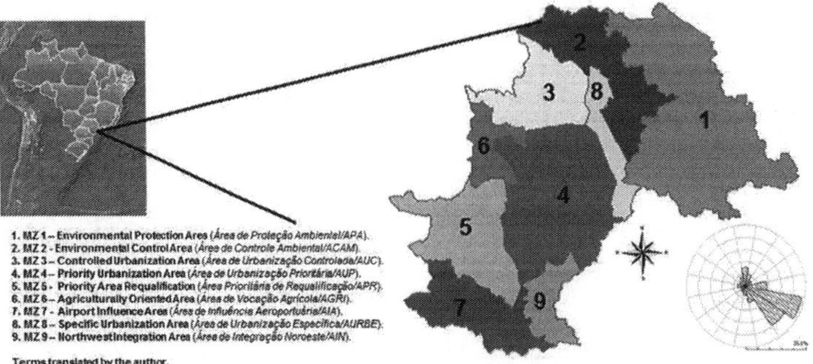


*Figure 17.1* Location of the city of Campinas/São Paulo/Brazil and Macro-zones of the Master Plan.

Source: Authors

The content of this article is an important part of wider research, still being carried out, which will aid in understanding the variables involved in the dynamics of the planning process, with the goal of indicating a methodology for the analysis of the environmental question in cities, where land organisation requires macro-zoned areas. This analysis, on the city-scale, of the use of urban ventilation studies is of great importance to the drafting of recommendations to the planning of the city.

## Study area

The city of Campinas is located on the south-east of the state of São Paulo/Brazil, 100km from its capital (geographical coordinates S 22° 53′ 20″, W 47° 04′ 40″). It occupies a total area of 796.4km$^2$ (urban perimeter 388.9km$^2$, rural perimeter 407.5km$^2$) and its altitude is at about 680m above sea level. Campinas has a tropical altitude climate with hot and humid summers and mild, quasi-dry winters. The prevailing wind direction is from the south-east. The methodology assessment was based on the macro-zoning as proposed by the city's Master Plan (see Figure 17.1).

## Methodology, data and software (WAsP)

The methodology followed work by several researchers (Scherer *et al.*, 1999; Alcoforado *et al.*, 2009; Ng *et al.*, 2009; Ren *et al.*, 2009a, 2009b; Ng, 2012; Ren *et al.*, 2012), which offered guidance in the analysis of questions relating to ventilation in the urban environment and planning process. The use of UCMaps and HCR units as strategies for planning and master planning; the use of the meso-scale models for wind analysis; and the use of Geographic Information System (GIS) were other aids used to combine all the information (see Figure 17.2).

The WAsP software (Mortensen *et al.*, 1993), developed by Denmark's Wind Energy Department – Risø National Laboratory – was used to estimate the height profiles and wind fields, given a roughness and the existing obstacles.

Based on a historical series of wind data (direction and velocity), the WAsP software corrects this data into a new series which describes the wind, generating a wind atlas for the location. Since the software integrates several calculation and extrapolation models, both vertical and horizontal, it can generate wind atlases with measurements taken at 10m.

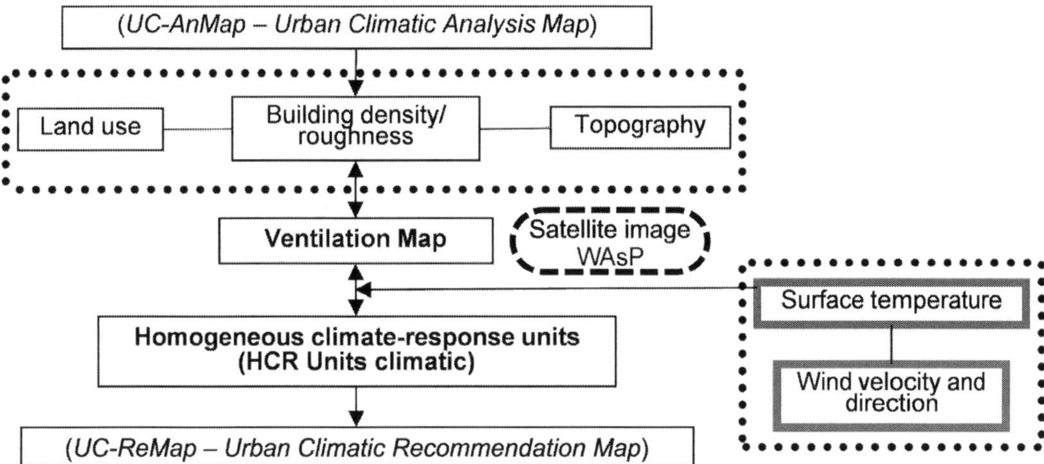


*Figure 17.2* Flowchart methodology.

Source: Authors

The generation of the wind atlas encompasses the acquisition of a wind data series, description of the positioning of the weather station (height of the anemometer), type of roughness of the surface surrounding the weather station, and the roughness of the places for which wind atlases will be generated. For this particular case study in the city of Campinas, data from the Viracopos Airport weather station (hourly wind direction and velocity at 10m height) was used, corresponding to a ten-year period (2000–2010) (see Figure 17.3).

For analysis in the WAsP software, for each macro-zone, topography and roughness maps were generated for the observed urban configuration. The roughness is directly connected to the blockage area put up by the obstacles. For the wind field analysis, WAsP software uses only the parameter $z_0$. The roughness ($z_0$) is described as a length of roughness, defined as the height at which wind velocity is zero. In the present work, the land cover classes used to convert in $z_0$ were derived from Landsat imagery (Landsat 7–21 April 2011) following the research of Alcoforado *et al.* (2009).

There are several references that present typical roughness values: Grimmond and Oke (1999) in urban environment; Davenport-Wieringa (Wieringa, 1996; Wieringa *et al.*, 2001) for areas with construction and green areas; Lettau (1969) presented by Lopes (2003) and Mortensen *et al.* (1993); when there is a need to precisely define the roughness of a certain location, one can use an algorithm or the classification suggested by the European Wind Atlas (Mortensen *et al.*, 1993), adopted by the WAsP software (see Figure 17.4). Table 17.1 presents a description of the macro-zones and their respective classes of roughness, as used in the WAsP simulations, which can aid in future studies.

The nine existing macro-zones were created due to the heterogeneity of the areas of the city of Campinas. Their definition took into consideration physical-territorial, socio-economic, and environmental aspects. For wind analysis in the city of Campinas, the macro-zones' characteristics and roughness values were focused upon Mortensen *et al.* (1993) and Lopes (2003).

Some results from WAsP software are presented in Figure 17.4. In Figure 17.4(a) the simulation was made taking only the topography into account. In Figure 17.4(b), both roughness length and

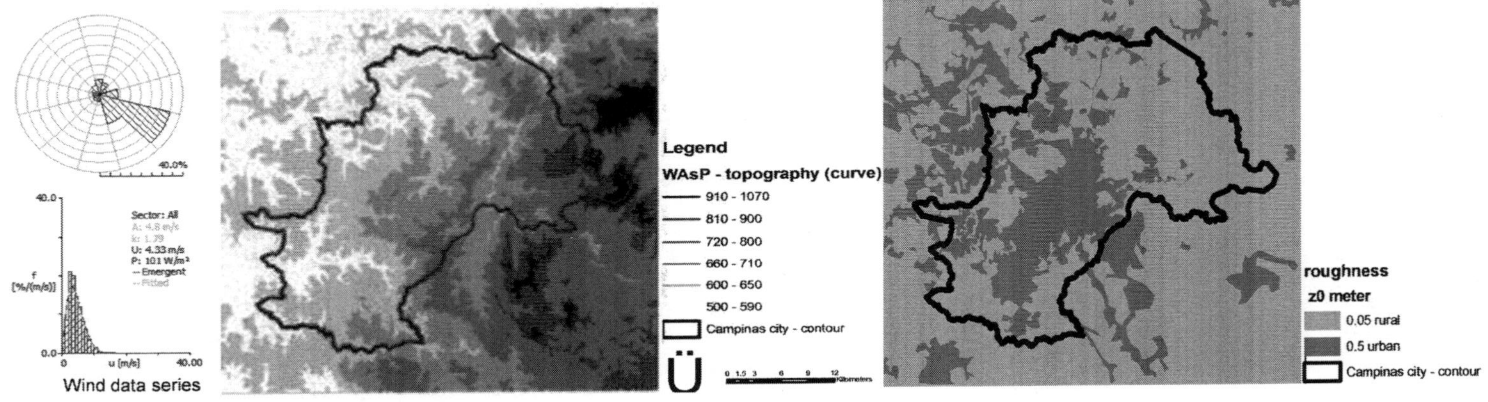


*Figure 17.3* Input data used by the WAsP software (wind data from the Viracopos Airport, 2000–2010, topography and roughness).

Source: Authors

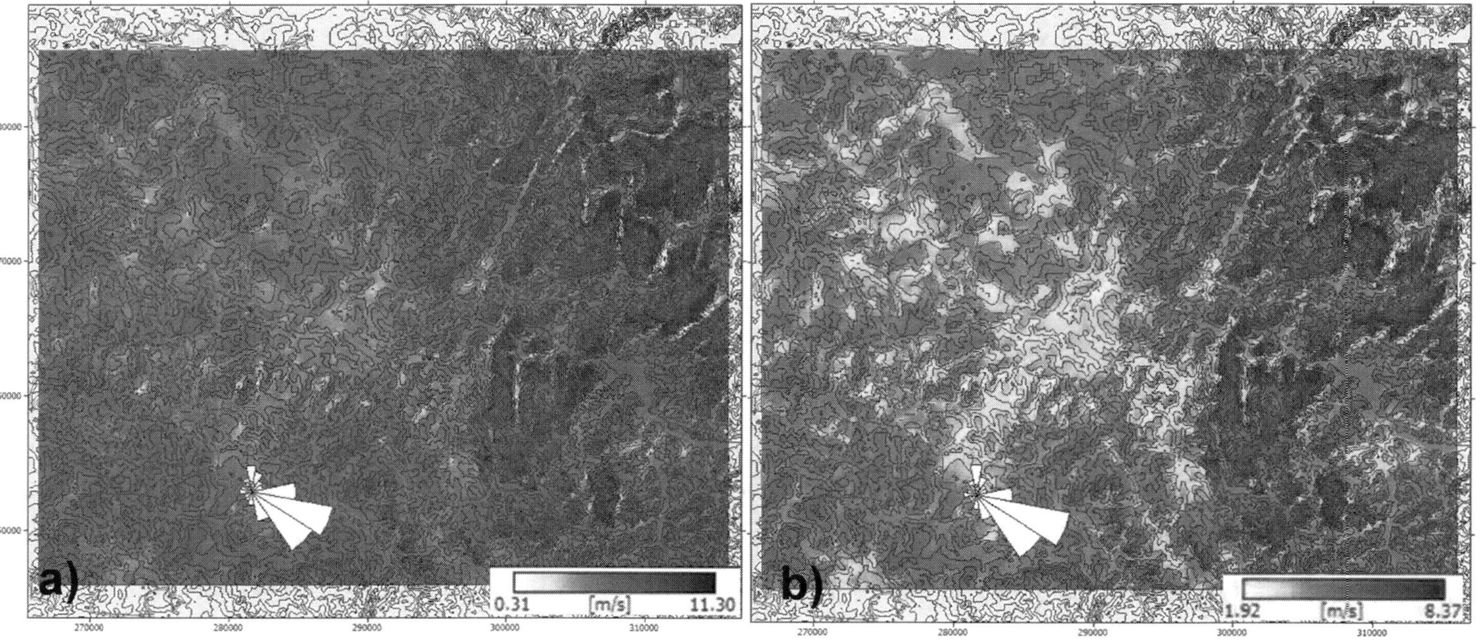


*Figure 17.4* Example of wind output with WAsP software: (a) land with topography but no city roughness; (b) topographical effect and typical roughness lengths of city areas were used ($z_0$ for urban area: 0.50; $z_0$ for rural area: 0.05).

Source: Authors

*Table 17.1* Macro-zones' characteristics and roughness classes

**MZ 1** – **Environmental Protection Area** (*Área de Proteção Ambiental/APA*).
80% of the municipality's rural area, presence of hydric sources, representative vegetal covering, contention of urban expansion, verticalization and densification.
**Green area** – class 2 ($z_0$ 0.05m) and **Urban area** – class 4 ($z_0$ 0.50m) – rural homes and low-density suburban residential areas

**MZ 2 – Environmental Control Area** (*Área de Controle Ambiental/ACAM*).
Rural area, remainders of native vegetation, restrictions to urban expansion for protection of the APA.
**Green area** – class 2 ($z_0$ 0.05m) and **Urban area** – class 4 ($z_0$ 0.30m) – rural homes and low-density suburban residential areas

**MZ 3** – **Controlled Urbanization Area** (*Área de Urbanização Controlada/AUC*).
Urbanization control aimed at guaranteeing functionality conditions for downtown Barão Geraldo, with densities and typologies, avoiding inadequate densification.
**Green area** – class 2 ($z_0$ 0.05m), **Urban area** – class 4 ($z_0$ 0.30m) – rural homes and low-density suburban residential areas and **Verticalized area** – class 4 ($z_0$ 1.00m) – predominantly above 3 floors

**MZ 4** – **Priority Urbanization Area** (*Área de Urbanização Prioritária/AUP*).
Denser area – central area and surrounding neighbourhoods, greater availability of urban infrastructure and services.
**Green area** – class 2 ($z_0$ 0.05m), **Urban area** – class 4 ($z_0$ 0.30m) – rural homes and low-density suburban residential areas, **Urban area** – class 4 ($z_0$ 0.50m) – areas with buildings predominantly up to 3 floors and **Verticalized area** – class 4 ($z_0$ 1.00m) – predominantly buildings above 3 floors

**MZ 5** – **Priority Area Requalification** (*Área Prioritária de Requalificação/APR*).
Environmentally fragile and degraded area, high population density, discontinuous occupation and roadways, natural and man-made barriers.
**Green area** – class 2 ($z_0$ 0.05m) and **Urban area** – class 4 ($z_0$ 0.50m) – areas with buildings predominantly up to 3 floors

**MZ 6** – **Agriculturally Oriented Area** (*Área de Vocação Agrícola/AGRI*).
Predominantly agricultural use – farms, ranches and smaller properties
**Green area** – class 2 ($z_0$ 0.05m) and **Urban area** – class 4 ($z_0$ 0.30m) – rural homes and low-density suburban residential areas

**MZ 7** – **Airport Influence Area** (*Área de Influência Aeroportuária/AIA*).
Viracopos International Airport and its expansion area, surrounding neighbourhoods, part of the productive rural area.
**Green area** – class 2 ($z_0$ 0.05m) and **Urban area** – class 4 ($z_0$ 0.50m) – areas with buildings predominantly up to 3 floors

**MZ 8** – **Specific Urbanization Area** (*Área de Urbanização Específica/AURBE*).
Area surrounded by highways, presence of neighbourhoods and large-size establishments, high-level dwelling communities.
**Green area** – class 2 ($z_0$ 0.05m) and **Urban area** – class 4 ($z_0$ 0.50m) – areas with buildings predominantly up to 3 floors

**MZ 9** – **Northwest Integration Area** (*Área de Integração Noroeste/AIN*).
Conurbated area, low articulation with the remainder of the city due to large non-urbanized areas, area with different urbanization dynamics, resident population concentrated in housing projects
**Green area** – class 2 ($z_0$ 0.05m), **Urban area** – class 4 ($z_0$ 0.50m) – areas with buildings predominantly up to 3 floors and **Verticalized area** – class 4 ($z_0$ 1.00m) – predominantly buildings above 3 floors

Source: Authors

topography were used. Both results are maps at 10m height, with wind direction at 135°. From left to right in Figure 17.4, the wind speed reduction with the growing of the city is shown. The quadrant from 90° to 180° (south-east) shows the predominant direction. Figure 17.4(b) shows that, with the insertion of the roughness data, some areas of the city have higher velocity values due to occupation. In both cases it is clear that low roughness areas in the dominant wind direction quadrant have to be prioritised to aid airflow distribution in the city.

## UCMaps, climatopes and HCR climatic units

The concept of UCMaps started in Germany, in the mid-1970s (Baumüller *et al.*, 1992; Matzarakis, 2005; Katzscher, 2010). At the time there was an intense public clamour, and the political vision, to conduct future planning in a responsible, sensible, and environmentally aware manner. With the intention of guiding the planning decision process, scientists started to focus on research in urban climatology, hatching the proposal for UCMaps (Ng *et al.*, 2009; Ren *et al.*, 2009a, 2009b; Ng, 2012; Ren *et al.*, 2012). Following the introduction of the concept in Germany, it has been widely developed and adopted by other countries in Europe, South America, and Asia after the 1990s.

UCMaps are synthetic tools for the assessment of urban climate factors that should be taken into account in planning processes. It can be said that UCMaps consist, basically, of a series of individual maps (layers), each of which takes into account a specific climate/geography factor which influences the urban climate. The scale of the maps varies in accordance with their scope. For the city, a scale of 1:5,000 can be considered adequate. For a detailed microclimate analysis, on the other hand, scales up to 1:200 can be used. Besides that, both meso- and micro-scales must consider different approaches and methodologies (Alcoforado *et al.*, 2009). UCMaps have two main components (Scherer *et al.*, 1999; VDI, 1997, 2008): the urban climatic analysis map (UC-AnMap) and the urban climate planning recommendation map (UC-ReMap).

With regards to occupation analysis and topography, the 'climatopes' and wind-related variables methodologies will be adopted for the city of Campinas/SP. 'Climatopes' are geographical areas with similar climate characteristics, which can be grouped. These could be daily temperature variation, vertical roughness, vegetation covering, topography, and land use/land cover classes, thus creating HCR units with similar urban-climate characteristics (Alcoforado *et al.*, 2009).

The flowchart in Figure 17.2 shows the steps taken in this study for the drafting of the ventilation map of the HCR units. This process will enable the drafting of the climatic map and recommendations due to natural ventilation in an urban environment for the planning of areas in the city of Campinas/SP/Brazil. The wind data (direction and velocity), along with surface temperature data (obtained by satellite imagery), will aid in future analysis to assess HCR units, on which several recommendations, tailored to the related areas in the macro-zones, will be proposed.

For the creation and handling of the UCMaps, a GIS analysis has been used. The resultant spatial information and computing procedures will permit and facilitate the analysis, management or representation of space and the phenomena taking place therein. With the assistance of GIS, analyses and assessments are carried out for the interrelations between the data and information, as well as their effects under the wind and temperature in the area (Ren *et al.*, 2009a).

Figure 17.5 shows the step-by-step composition of the maps with the HCR units for the analysis of the city. This is done in a GIS environment by superposing topography, roughness and wind maps, generating specific characteristics for each area of the city. This map enables the definition of policies and directives for the occupation of the city, during the design or urban planning processes, aiding the development of master plans.

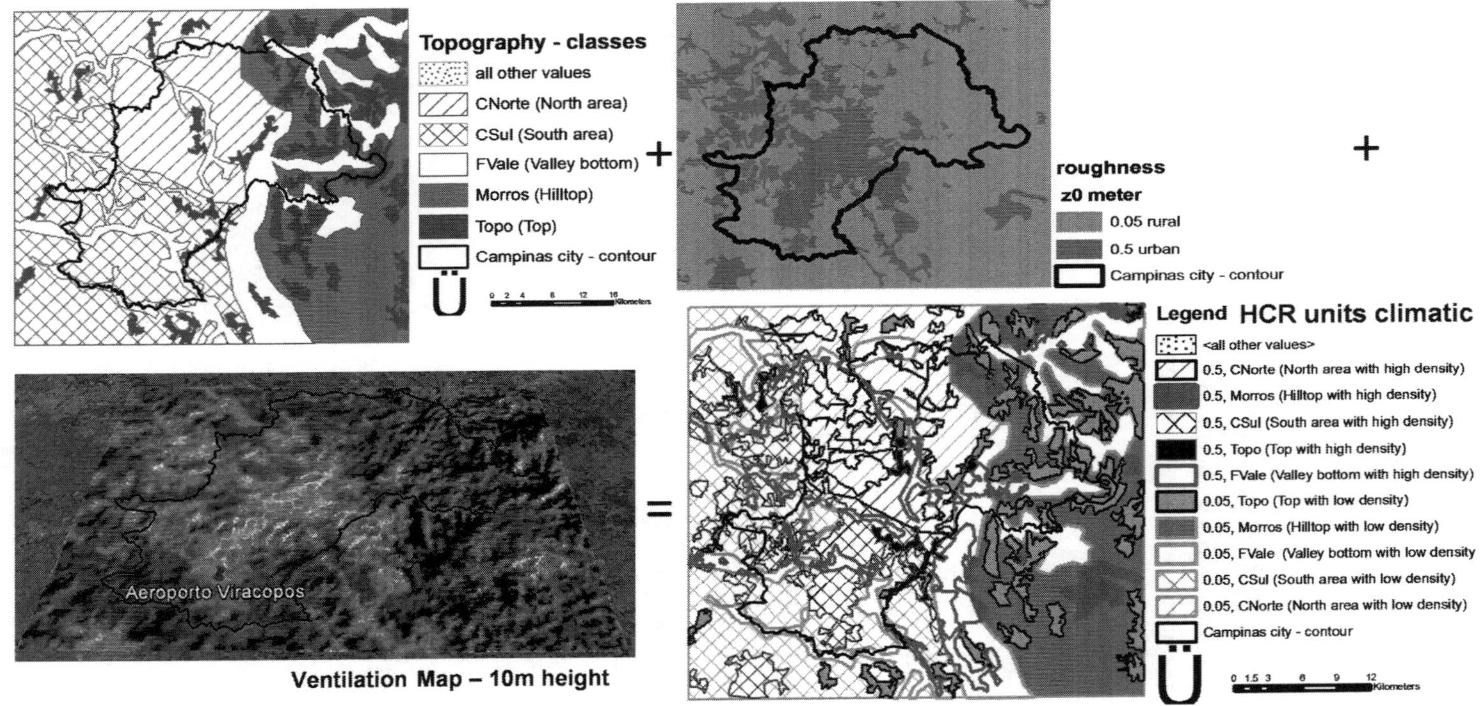


*Figure 17.5* Process for definition of HCR units.

Source: Authors

## Final considerations

The knowledge of the physical characteristics of the land (occupation – especially urban and green areas, and topography – valley bottoms, etc.), along with the expected climate conditions (air temperature, humidity, wind speed and direction, etc.) are of great importance for the correct composition of the homogenous units (HCR or climatopes). Most of the UCMap studies have been conducted in developed countries and cities. There is a necessity to conduct these studies in developing countries and cities, which are undergoing a process of rapid urbanisation and occupation.

The use of the meso-scale model (WAsP) will enable the observation of the influence of urban occupation – as defined in the city's macro-zoning – as well as the effects of the permeability of the urban fabric on the regional wind. With this tool it will be possible to simulate occupation scenarios (different roughnesses) and the analysis of the wind flow in urban environments. Other micro-scale analyses require the use of CFD models which can, through a greater refinement of the urban mesh, represent areas closer to the building/pedestrian scale.

The use of GIS as a tool for the generation of UCMaps brings practicality and a quality, efficient representation. GIS should be more widely used in the area of urban climate research, climate analysis and urban planning, so as to facilitate future studies pertaining to climate and its influences on the development of master plans. Such use permits the assessment of the current conditions of the environment as a whole, which are the measures that need to be taken to improve this situation. Thus, it becomes a very important tool, for it allows the organisation of data and facilitates their visualisation.

Within this study, the decreasing wind speed with urban growth was demonstrated as it is in other areas (Lopes *et al.*, 2011). This information is of great importance in showing the probable impoverishment of the ventilation condition in cities, and should be taken into account in future research.

## Acknowledgements

FAPESP – *Fundação de Amparo à Pesquisa do Estado de São Paulo* for supporting *Auxílio Jovem Pesquisador em Centros Emergentes* – Young Investigators Grants (JP).

## References

Alcoforado, M. J., Andrade, H., Lopes, A. and Vasconcelos, J. (2009). Application of climatic guidelines to urban planning. The example of Lisbon (Portugal). *Landscape and Urban Planning*, 90(1–2): 56–65.

Baumüller, J., Hoffmann, U. and Reuter, U. (1992). *Climate Booklet for Urban Development*. Stuttgart: Ministry of Economy Baden-Wuerttemberg (Wirschaftsministerium). Environmental Protection Department (Amt für Umweitschutz).

Grimmond, C. S. B. and Oke, T. R. (1999). Aerodynamic properties of urban areas derived from analysis of surface form. *Journal of Applied Meteorology*, 38(9): 1262–1292.

Katzschner, L. (2010). Urban climate in dense cities. In: Ng, E. (ed.), *Designing High-Density Cities for Social and Environmental Sustainability*. London: Earthscan: 71–83.

Lettau, H. (1969). Note on aerodynamic roughness-parameter estimation on the basis of roughness-element description. *Journal of Applied Meteorology*, 8(5): 828–832.

Lopes, A. (2003). *Modificações no clima de Lisboa como consequência do crescimento urbano: vento, ilha de calor de superfície e balanço energético*. Tese de Doutoramento em Geografia Física. Universidade de Lisboa.

Lopes, A., Saraiva, J. and Alcoforado, M. J. (2011). Urban boundary layer wind speed reduction in summer due to urban growth and environmental consequences in Lisbon. *Environmental Modelling & Software*, 26(2): 241–243.

Matzarakis, A. (2005). Country report: Urban climate research in Germany. *IAUC Newsletter*, no. 11, 4–6.

Mortensen, N. G., Landerberg, L., Troen, I. and Petersen, E. L. (1993). *Wind Atlas Analysis and Application Program (WAsP), vol 1: Getting Started*. Roskilde: Risø National Laboratory.

Ng, E. (2012). Towards planning and practical understanding of the need for meteorological and climatic information in the design of high-density cities: A case-based study of Hong Kong. *International Journal of Climatology*, 32(4): 582–598.

Ng, E., Ren, C., Katzschner, L. and Yau, R. (2009). Urban climatic studies for hot and humid tropical coastal city of Hong Kong. In: *Proceedings of The 7th International Conference on Urban Climate*. Yokohama, Japan, 29 June–3 July.

Prata, A. R. (2005). *Impacto da altura dos edifícios nas condições de ventilação natural do meio urbano*. Tese (Doutoramento em Arquitetura e Urbanismo, Estruturas Ambientais Urbanas) Faculdade de Arquitetura e Urbanismo. Universidade de São Paulo.

Prata-Shimomura, A. R. (2010). *Relatório de Pós-Doutoramento – Edificação e Desenho Urbano com adensamento e qualidade ambiental: habitação de interesse social na recuperação de áreas urbanas*. Programa MEC/CAPES – PNPD 2009, Processo PNPD no. 02556/09-0, São Paulo.

Ren, C., Ng, E. and Katzschner, L. (2009a). Review of worldwide urban climatic map study for and its application in planning. In: *Proceedings of The 7th International Conference on Urban Climate*. Yokohama, Japan, 29 June–3 July. Available at: http://www.ide.titech.ac.jp/~icuc7/extended_abstracts/pdf/374213-3-090516013120-003.pdf (Accessed 8 February 2014).

Ren, C., Ng, E., Katzschner, L. and Yau, R. (2009b). *Working Paper 1A: Draft Urban Climatic Analysis Map, Urban Climatic Map and Standards for Wind Environment – Feasibility Study*. November, 2009, Planning Department, HKSAR.

Ren, C., Spit, T., Lenzholzer, S., Yim, H. L. S., Heusinkveld, B., van Hove, B., Chen, L., Kupski, S., Burghardt, R. and Katzschener, L. (2012). Urban climate map system for Dutch spatial planning. *International Journal of Applied Earth Observation and Geoinformation*, 18: 207–221.

Scherer, D., Fehrenbach, U., Beha, H.-D. and Parlow, E. (1999). Improved concepts and methods in analysis and evalution of the urban climate for optimizing urban planning processes. *Atmospheric Environment*, 33(24–25): 4185–4193.

SEPLAMA (2012). *Secretaria Municipal de Planejamento, Desenvolvimento Urbano e Meio Ambiente, Campinas – Plano Diretor e Planos Locais de Gestão*. Available at: http://www.campinas.sp.gov.br/governo/seplama/planos-locais-de-gestao (Accessed September 2012)

VDI (1997). *VDI-Standard: VDI 3787 Part 1 Environmental Meteorology – Climate and Air Pollution Maps for Cities and Regions*. Berlin: Beuth Verlag.

VDI (2008). *VDI-Standard: VDI 3787 Part 2 Environmental Meteorology – Methods for the Human Biometeorological Evaluation of Climate and Air Quality for Urban and Regional Planning at Regional Level, Part I: Climate*. Berlin: Beuth Verlag.

Wieringa, J. (1996). Does representative wind information exist? *Journal of Wind Engineering and Industrial Aerodynamics*, 65: 1–12.

Wieringa, J., Davenport, A. G., Grimmond, C. S. B. and Oke, T. R. (2001). New revision of Davenport roughness classification. Paper presented at *3EACWE (3rd European & African Conference on Wind Engineering)*, Eindhoven, Netherlands, 2–6 July.

Chapter 18

# Urban climatic map studies in Germany

## Frankfurt

*Lutz Katzschner and Sabrina Campe*

### Introduction

The investigation carried out by the Faculty of Environmental Meteorology at the University of Kassel on five existing stress areas in the City of Frankfurt am Main during the years 2010/2011 was intended to contribute to the future development of urban space. Microclimatic analyses and corresponding simulations of these areas provide references as to which mitigation measures offer the best solution to reduce heat load and which options for planning arise from the microclimatic condition of the city climate. The City of Frankfurt is characterised by an excessive overheating due to its dense urbanisation and a high degree of sealed surfaces. This cannot entirely be compensated by the functioning wind circulation. The existing wind circulation systems in the Frankfurt area, especially the wind of Wetterau, the air paths along the Nidda and Main rivers, as well as local slope lifts, are of great importance to the thermal and aerial ventilation quality components of the city climate (Magistrat der Stadt Frankfurt am Main, 2009). Due to the issue of global warming, it is assumed that thermal load in the affected areas will continue to rise. The impact of climate change will be more extreme in a densely built-up city than in rural areas (Kuttler, 2009). The number of hot days with peak temperatures higher than 30°C will increase. Local air exchange and the integration of green areas, are, as a result, particularly important since they can improve the city's climatic potential even in areas with insufficient thermal comfort.

### Climate analysis by means of urban climatic maps

The climate classifications (six categories) updated in 2009 for Frankfurt am Main's urban climatic map are oriented towards thermal aspects (thermal index) and the ventilation quality (roughness) of the urban areas, as in Plate 18.1. In built-up areas there are various structural 'environmental factors' depending on their extent which lead to more or less strong overheating tendencies as well as reduced ventilation and a reduction or delay of nocturnal cooling. Such factors include surface sealing, building material, building structure and volumes, or green areas. However, aspects such as topography, location and size of relevant land area and, if applicable, existing compensatory influence of adjacent mitigation sites do play a role. These aspects in combination with emissions, depending on weather conditions and topography, can result in high air pollution which can also have a negative impact on adjacent areas. Barriers caused by building structures affecting flowing air masses are particularly relevant in valleys as air induction corridors can tremendously be affected in their functionality as a consequence (Magistrat der Stadt Frankfurt am Main, 2009).

In order to carry out a microclimate analysis it was essential to know which category the investigated areas were situated in. In this case, they were found primarily in overheating areas of categories 5 and 6 of the urban climatic map. Category 5 describes an overheated area with restricted air exchange. Heat stress days would, in the future, strongly increase in these areas. Category 6 includes overheated areas with highly restricted air exchange. Heat stress days would, in the future, increase tremendously in these areas. For the analysis of affected heat load areas the meso-scale information from the climatic map was applied to each respective location in a downscaling process in order to assess its microclimatic prerequisites. The micro-scale analysis of urban open spaces (public open spaces, streets, green areas, etc.) was carried out in a detailed spatial resolution by means of a numerical simulation. Another basis for the development of evaluation maps with the Physiological Equivalent Temperature (PET), which shows the thermal heat load condition, were interviews and measurements carried out at the same time (Fanger, 1972; Höppe, 1999). The following results should provide information about how planners can integrate climate aspects into their spatial planning and which measures are reasonable.

## Detailed studies of selected urban areas

The selection of the five test areas for the interviews and measurements was based on building density and period so that a range of city structure was available. An example of the study is illustrated in Figure 18.1. The following criteria also played a role: radiation conditions (sky view factor), albedo (solar reflectance) in the city centre area, greening of the area, surfaces (materials), sealing grade and ventilation. For analysing the micro-scale of city spaces, the Faculty of Environmental Meteorology makes use of the program ENVI-met (Bruse and Fleer, 1998). The program generates microclimate maps that comprehensively illustrate a variety of parameters, such as wind speed, mean radiation temperature or thermal indices (e.g. PET). The relevant parameters for the valuation index PET are: air temperature, mean radiation temperature and wind. This biometeorological parameter, taking thermophysiological correlations into account, describes people's thermal comfort (Brandenburg and Matzarakis, 2007) and is therefore a physical parameter for measuring people's general well-being which depends on the thermal complex. The comfort level is around a PET value of 24°C. A balanced sense of well-being predominates if the body absorbs as much heat as it is able to release again.

Urban spaces were evaluated with respect to hot summer days. In this season during daylight hours, the greatest heat stress can be felt by city dwellers in urban open spaces with a greater number of daylight hours than night hours. For the spring and autumn the relevant gradations and distributions on the PET maps of the summer simulations apply, though on a lower level. Due to the different solar radiation angle, the shaded areas are greater so that heat load areas become relatively smaller and the remaining gradations, as a consequence, become proportionately larger. Therefore, spaces which are considered stressed in the summer can be experienced as comfort zones during other seasons. These areas are to be defined by means of graphic presentations of the results.

Based on the PET and wind maps, a specially developed rating scale filtered positive and negative hotspots depending on the area's vegetation and degree of sealing, height and width ratios, orientation of city canyons as well as ventilation grades for each tested area in Frankfurt. According to the simulation results, these hotspots were graded into *very good, good, neutral, bad* and *very bad*.

The basis for the subsequent selection of measurements were the PET values averaged throughout the day (8.00 a.m. to 8.00 p.m. CEST), as illustrated on corresponding maps, as this period is relevant for planning – the length of stay is, after all, not limited to one particular time of the day. Therefore, a compromise had to be found that offered the best solution for any given time of the day during which heat load would affect open spaces. It is, however, impossible to think

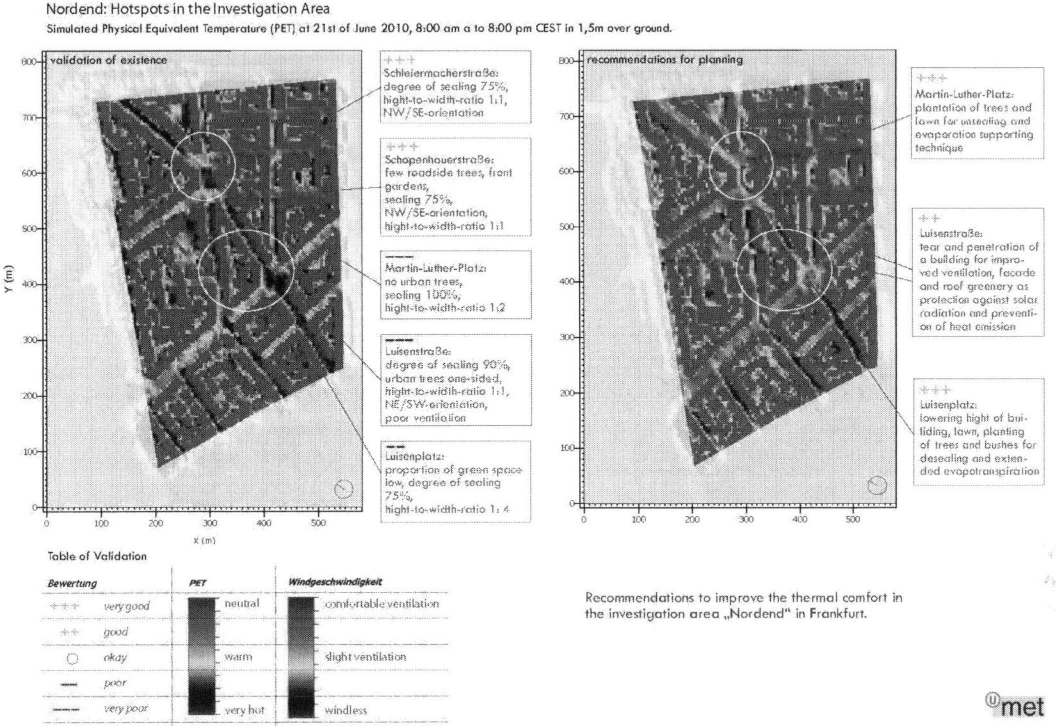


*Figure 18.1* An ENVI-met investigation of an urban area in Frankfurt.

Sources: Authors

that a universal solution can be found for all locations (in street spaces or on city squares). The areas frequented the most by pedestrians should, however, be designed in such a way that make them thermally comfortable. With the help of the evaluation analysis, the potential areas in the respective research area should serve as an example for hotspots with deficits in order to mitigate the impact on stressed areas. By means of reconstructing or changing a plaza or city space, thermal comfort conditions can be improved.

## Planning recommendations

In summary it can be said that, based on this study, a further densification of the inner city of Frankfurt am Main, especially in the overheating areas, is not feasible from an urban climate point of view. However, the city structure should remain compact to maintain suburban cold air influx areas by all means. Effective mitigation measures taken against heat load in condensed urban areas ideally need space, such as the maintenance of ventilation channels and areas for the production of cold air. Suggested measures in the presented project, however, focus on changing existing structures as little as possible, and mitigating the impact on endangered areas with a high heat stress potential as well as using existing potentials as effectively as possible. With that in mind, space-saving measures such as changing façades or roof surfaces and local protection measures against solar radiation were mentioned.

As a principle, the proportion of green space has to be increased in order to make use of water evaporation and to lower surface and air temperatures. It is necessary to plant shading trees to promote evaporation, particularly on the north side of east–west oriented street canyons and open squares. Due to expected and increasingly high summer temperatures and lower precipitation levels, plants tolerant to a dry climate should preferably be planted in the cities (Kuttler, 2011). A most useful remedy to improve the comfort level for city dwellers in urban areas during hot summer periods is to densely line the streets with high deciduous trees as this has proved to give an effective shading of surfaces. Industrial building materials absorb more energy than rural elements. Therefore, the use of plants can mitigate such heating tendencies. The network of green areas plays an important role which, depending on the composition of vegetation, reduces the volume of solar radiation and promotes evaporative cooling. Green spaces provide a varying thermal range, depending on their size (Kuttler, 2010). In a dense city such as Frankfurt am Main, it is crucial to maintain the quality of existing open spaces for all urban residents living at a high level to reduce local heat stress. Most of the green belts in inner cities are, however, too small to provide a quantitatively measurable air circulation to reach adjacent built-up areas. But even small patches of green are essential relatively cool urban outdoor areas for the population to go to during hot summer days as a refuge.

Urban trees not only reduce solar radiation but also slow down wind movements considered as uncomfortable. Coniferous trees provide additional wind protection in winter, which can be of great importance during this season. On the other hand, the wind supply reduces heat load during hot summer periods. Barriers should be removed accordingly in particular areas. In this context it should be taken into account that roadside trees can restrict air exchange, as well as the expansion and the thinning of air pollutants emitted near the ground. Since a majority of trees found in Central European cities are deciduous, the maximum output of these pollutants takes place during the winter months in which the flow obstruction due to treetops is relatively weak. Urban trees also collect dust, especially during the summer (Litschke and Kuttler, 2008; Kuttler, 2010).

Surface materials influence radiation and also the direct heat supply. When choosing façade materials and colours, a selection must be made between the thermal comfort in the building and the thermal comfort outside. The quality of building surfaces and also ground spaces has a great impact on local air temperature quality. The reflection of the sun (albedo) thus plays an important role. The more solar radiation is reflected away from surfaces the less energy from those surfaces is transformed to heat and released into the atmosphere. During the planning it must be considered that highly reflective materials or colours lower the energy need of buildings but may lead to a degeneration of thermal comfort in exterior areas since the albedo is absorbed by pedestrians, and are possibly perceived as uncomfortable. The greening of roofs improves the microclimate of the roof area and protects the building from solar radiation because a major part of the received energy is used to evaporate the stored water. This has, however, only a minor effect on thermal levels close to the ground (Trute, 2011).

The ventilation of the compact urban space has to be improved in several areas. Therefore, according to the data on the urban climatic map, existing air channels must be maintained. This also applies when new buildings go up, and can be achieved by considering storey heights, building orientation and building density. Additional heat factors are to be prevented and measures taken in order to counteract overheating tendencies, such as avoiding further structural densification, building redevelopment, unsealing of surfaces, increased greening and also the installation of artificial shading elements (if trees cannot be planted in certain areas). In any case, it has to be considered that concise local methods cannot automatically be applied to the entire urban space, or possibly to other cities necessitating a classification into the meso-climate. In that case, ventilation, orientation, width and street development as well as surface materials have to be examined to be able to subsequently derive suitable measures.

## References

Brandenburg, C. and Matzarakis, A. (2007). Das thermische Empfinden von Touristen und Einwohnern der Region Neusiedler See. In: Matzarakis, A. and Mayer, H. (eds.), *Proceedings zur 6. Fachtagung BIOMET*. Ber. Meteor. Inst. Univ. Freiburg, 16: 67–72.

Bruse, M. and Fleer, H. (1998). Simulating surface–plant–air interactions inside urban environments with a three dimensional numerical model. *Environmental Modeling and Software*, 13(3–4): 373–384.

Fanger, P. O. (1972). *Thermal Comfort*. New York: McGraw-Hill Companies.

Höppe, P. (1999). The physiological equivalent temperature – a universal index for the biometeorological assessment of the thermal environment. *International Journal of Biometeorology*, 43(2): 71–75.

Kuttler, W. (2009). Zum Klima im urbanen Raum. In: Deutscher Wetterdienst (ed.) (2009). *Klimastatusbericht 2008*, 69–12. Offenbach/M.

Kuttler, W. (2010). Urbanes Klima, Teil 2. Gefahrenstoffe – Reinhaltung der Luft, *Umweltmeteorologie*, 70(9): 378–382.

Kuttler, W. (2011). Klimawandel im urbanen Bereich, Teil 2. Maßnahmen; Climate change in urban areas, Part 2, Measures. *Environmental Sciences Europe (ESEU)*, 23: 21, *Springer open*. Available from: http://www.enveurope.com/content/pdf/2190-4715-23-21.pdf. (Accessed 26 January 2014). doi: 10.1186/2190-4715-23-21.

Litschke, T. and Kuttler, W. (2008). On the reduction of urban particle concentration by vegetation – a review. *Meteorologische Zeitschrift*, 17(3): 229–240. (In German with an English abstract).

Magistrat der Stadt Frankfurt am Main (2009). *Klimaplanatlas Frankfurt am Main, Abschlussbericht*. Kassel: Universität Kassel Fachgebiet Umweltmeteorologie.

Trute, P. (2011). Klimaanpassung – wie viel Klimawandel verträgt Berlin? StEP Klima Berlin als integratives Planungsinstrument. *UVP-report*, 25(2/3): 177–181.

Chapter 19

# Urban climatic map studies in UK

## Birmingham

*Richard Bassett, Xiaoming Cai, John E. Thornes, Richard Rees and Lee Chapman*

### Introduction

Birmingham is a large post-industrial city with a population in excess of one million inhabitants. Due to the nature of the dense, multifaceted buildings contained in the urban sprawl, the city exhibits a strong nocturnal urban heat island (UHI). This effect is strongest several hours after sunset and is related to city size, moisture availability, land use, anthropogenic emissions, building materials and geometry (Oke, 1987). A systematic review of the UHI field can be found in Arnfield (2003) and Stewart (2010).

Early research by Unwin (1980) identified that Birmingham's UHI intensity could be in excess of 5.0°C under anticyclonic conditions. However, a lack of available meteorological sites meant Unwin's (1980) study using a suburban site at Edgbaston (south-west of the city centre) as an urban proxy could potentially underestimate the UHI effect. Johnson (1985) furthered this research by conducting temperature transects across the city, finding an intensity of up to 4.5°C under clear and calm conditions. More recently, surface UHI investigations from Moderate Resolution Imaging Spectroradiometer (MODIS) satellite images by Tomlinson *et al.* (2012) found night-time surface UHI to be typically around 5.0°C, and up to 7.0°C under extremely stable heat wave conditions.

A rise in mean annual air temperature from 9.4°C (1960–1990) to 10.0°C (1991–2007) has indicated that Birmingham is likely to be impacted by the effects of climate change (Kotecha *et al.*, 2008). The 2003 European heat wave was one of the hottest summers on record in Europe; it led to a health crisis in several countries and combined with a drought to create a crop shortfall in Southern Europe. More than 40,000 Europeans died as a result, including 2,091 excess deaths in England and Wales (Johnson *et al.*, 2005) where air temperatures reached 38.5°C. Johnson *et al.* (2005) found the percentage increase in excess mortality of the 2003 heat wave to exceed that found during the 1976 and 1995 heat waves (42 per cent, 16 per cent and 15 per cent respectively). Climate projections show that there could be an average of three heat waves per year during July and two during August by 2080, leading to an increase in mortality, particularly among the elderly and vulnerable. A heat wave experienced in 2020 may lead to 53 per cent more deaths by the 2020s than during the 2003 heat wave (May *et al.*, 2010). However, these projections do not take the complex urban morphology of Birmingham into consideration and unlike any other significant weather event, excess urban heat is rarely treated as an atmospheric hazard.

In 2008 Birmingham City Council (BCC) established the Climate Change Adaptation Partnership to respond to 'National Indicator 188 – adapting to climate change'. The Partnership planned to understand the risks to people and places, both present day and in the future, from the UHI and climate change in Birmingham. However, a lack of previous research meant that only a blanket approach to understanding heat distribution across Birmingham and its impacts on people and places could be used, despite Birmingham being the largest local authority in Europe and the impacts being wide-ranging. In order to understand climate change impacts in Birmingham and the adaptation responses to minimise risks, a new tool was required. As such, BCC led the approach to climate change adaptation by starting the Birmingham Urban Climate Change with Neighbourhood Estimates of Environmental Risk (BUCCANEER) project, a two-year Knowledge Transfer Partnership (KTP) involving BCC, the University of Birmingham and Birmingham Health and Wellbeing Partnership (BHWP). BUCCANEER was to help provide the necessary evidence for Birmingham's 2026 vision – that Birmingham will be the UK's first sustainable global city prepared for climate change impacts.

The BUCCANEER project joined a three-pronged approach at the University of Birmingham whereby the UHI was being researched by satellite (land surface temperatures at 1km resolution), from surface measurements (UHI impact on electricity transformers), and through the modelling presented here. A full description of the approach taken can be found in Tomlinson *et al.* (2013). This chapter puts forward the modelling-based approach used and the application of the results to create the BUCCANEER planning tool.

## Methodology

An applied approach is taken to investigating the UHI in Birmingham. The Joint UK Land Environment Simulator (JULES) model was chosen due to the relative computational efficiency of its urban component when compared to more complex, multilayer models such as Building Effect Parameterization (BEP) (Martilli *et al.*, 2002; JULES, 2012).

JULES is developed from the Met Office Surface Exchange Scheme (MOSES) and has been extensively validated with support from a large user community. Version 2.1.2, used in the project, represents urban areas through a bulk parameterisation and a tiled approach with separate temperature, radiation, and moisture fluxes calculated for each grid cell. This approach modifies parameters to simulate urban areas such as the thermal heat capacity, albedo, and surface roughness. A full model description can be found in Best *et al.* (2011) and Clark *et al.* (2011).

In order to successfully represent the morphology of Birmingham in an urban model, it is vital to correctly determine the land-use input. Models are highly sensitive to changes in land use, and incorrect specifications will lead to inaccurate temperature simulations. Initially, the model was run using Corine Land Cover 2000 data (EEA, 2012). However, simulations indicated that this classification does not demonstrate enough spatial variability within urban areas to correctly reproduce temperatures. JULES calculates a separate surface energy balance per tile for each surface type. To improve model performance, surface types were therefore aggregated from a 37m-resolution satellite-derived urban land-use classification (from the NERC URGENT project; Harrison, lead researcher, 2000), to a 500m resolution. This allowed exact urban and vegetation percentages to be defined for each grid cell; thus no two cells in the simulation were alike. The meteorological input used matches that exchanged by a General Circulation Model if it were coupled. To drive the UHI simulations, JULES was used offline and temperature, radiation, precipitation, pressure, and humidity data were used from a nearby Met Office site at Coleshill (Warwickshire). Meteorological data from a single point was assumed to be constant across the model domain. Variables such as temperature were adjusted to account for topographic changes across the region using environmental lapse rates. Not all variables required to drive JULES were available, so estimations were necessary; for example, incoming long-wave radiation was calculated as a function of the atmosphere using equations from Fassnacht *et al.* (2001). This approach was the best available methodology during the project, but future research will enable improvements.

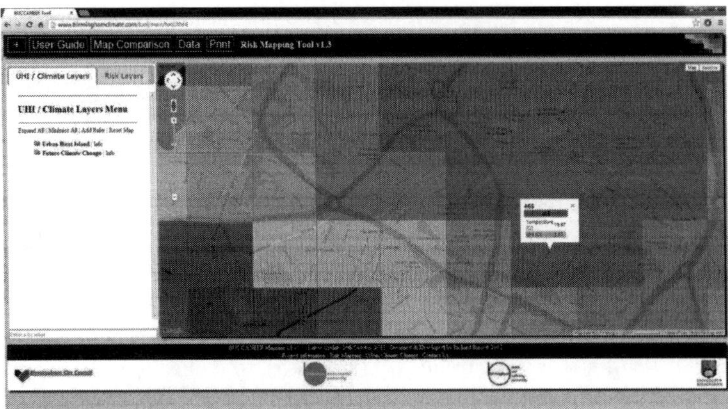

*Figure 19.1* Example of the BUCCANEER tool interface demonstrating how users can extract UHI information.

Source: https://www.birminghamclimate.com

To create the BUCCANEER planning tool model, outputs from JULES along with social and environmental data were imported into the Geographic Information System (GIS). The data was plotted spatially (including geo-referencing) to create the visual and interactive layers. These layers were then converted to a .kmz file format to work with Google Maps Application Programming Interface (API) and stored on a server to allow global access (Google, n.d.). Using Google Maps API, an interactive map was embedded within a website, http://www.birminghamclimate.com (see Figure 19.1). The website which provides the framework for the maps was written using HTML and JavaScript programming and allows the user to control which layer they want to display and provides them with metadata (i.e. data sources). Each layer in the tool is interactive, allowing the user to quickly gather information about their area.

## Results

Model outputs indicate that the UHI in the city centre can exceed 4.0°C under stable conditions. The JULES model was run for a domain covering Birmingham and the West Midlands at a 500m resolution. Averaged over a 12-month simulation (2010), the centre of Birmingham was found to be 0.4°C warmer than surrounding rural areas. Nocturnally, the UHI over this period was 0.9°C. A slight urban cool island was found to develop during the day. The maximum predicted UHI intensity during this simulation was 5.2°C. Two UK Met Office sites were used to evaluate model outputs, Edgbaston (urban proxy) and Winterbourne (suburban). Over the 2010 simulation period, average model outputs accurately predicted the diurnal UHI intensity. A correlation between the observed and predicted values over the 2010 simulation at Edgbaston can be seen in Figure 19.2. Greater variability was found on an hourly basis with a root mean square error (RMSE) of approximately +/− 1.0°C between the observed and predicted temperature values. This was typically found to be an underestimation of the night-time UHI and an overestimation of the daytime cool effect.

Sensitivity tests were conducted on key model parameters such as the heat storage capacity and canopy heights. It should also be noted that when trying to improve the model's performance

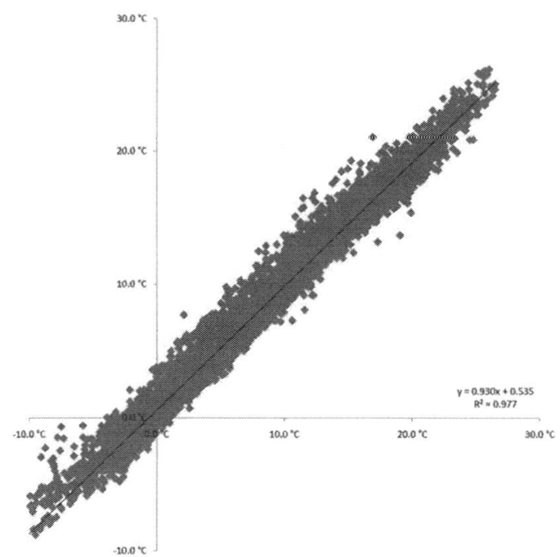


*Figure 19.2* Model validation showing observed versus predicted temperatures using the Met Office site at Edgbaston. For the purposes of this study the site is considered an urban proxy.

Source: BUCCANEER, 2011

through sensitivity tests, trade-offs existed, i.e. improving the model's rural performance may decrease the model's ability to accurately reproduce urban temperatures. Land-use checks using GIS were also made. Exact land-use set-up was found to be critical in delivering good model performance, i.e. the output is only as strong as the input data. Adjustments to the model land use were found to slightly reduce RMSE.

Spatially, the urban core of Birmingham represented the warmest areas, and typical characteristics similar to those described by Oke (1987) were found. For example, a marked temperature gradient, the so-called 'urban temperature cliff', was found when plotting a transect to the city centre. Under a modelled heat wave scenario (July 2006), a temperature gradient in excess of 1°C per kilometre was found. A distribution of the heat across the city with this scenario can be seen in Figure 19.3. The modelled UHI was also found to resemble the satellite-derived surface UHI for Birmingham (Tomlinson *et al.*, 2012) captured by MODIS satellite images. It should be noted that the difference between surface and the near surface temperatures did not allow for direct comparisons.

When considering the sources of uncertainty, the model does perform well. For example, the point locations of the observations may have an entirely different land use to the average land use of the 500m grid cell around it. At this scale, small scale meteorological effects could alter the temperatures enough to explain the slight differences between observed and modelled results. Further to this, limitations in input data driving the model could lead to deviations between observed and predicted values.

## Discussion

The focus of the BUCCANEER, a Knowledge Transfer Partnership between the University of Birmingham and BCC, was the sharing of information to inform policy decisions. It had to be

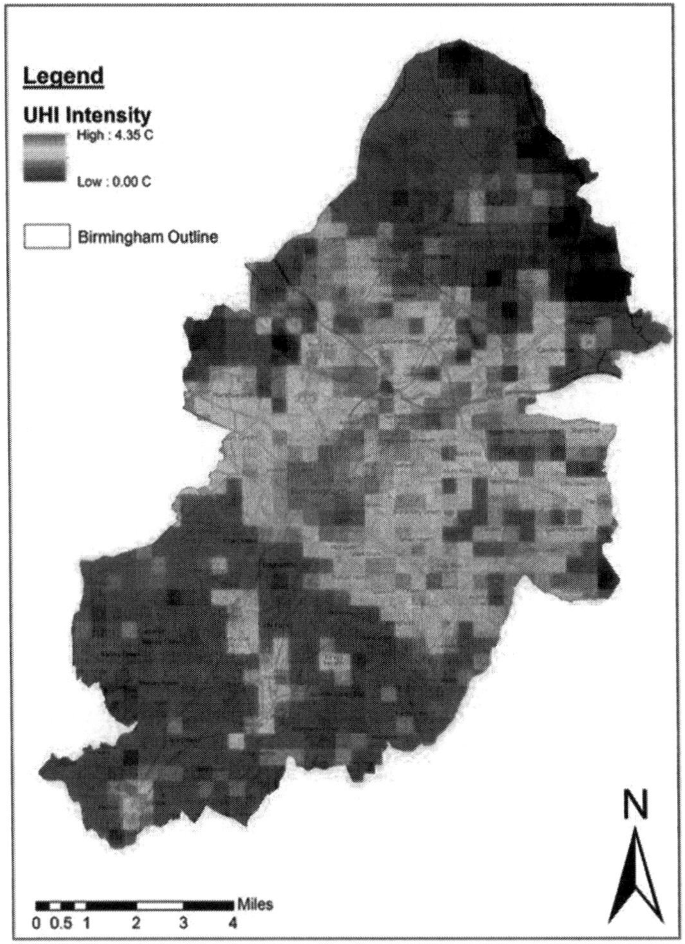


*Figure 19.3* JULES model results showing 1.00 a.m. 18 July 2006 heat wave UHI for Birmingham.

Source: BUCCANEER, 2011

ensured that the science and results were applicable and the research would not remain a technical exercise. To ensure this transition, workshops were hosted for the project to determine requirements and how to convey the findings to a wider audience. To be successful, a tool was required that would combine urban planning and climate change with risk assessment.

The subsequent BUCCANEER planning tool (http://www.birminghamclimate.com; see Figure 19.3) displays visual and interactive layers using Google Maps API embedded within the project website. The tool is available online for anyone to use and will improve risk management, aid strategic decision making, and encourage wider sustainability benefits. The final tool contains mapping on the UHI, infrastructure, health (Birmingham Health and Wellbeing Partnership), air quality, housing, population and life expectancy to help identify vulnerability and risks for people and places. In addition, layers with a combined risk assessment created by Tomlinson *et al.* (2011) were included in the tool; for example, the proportion of people with ill health in high-density housing that will be exposed to excess heat.

The BUCCANEER tool thus provides evidence to support the investment for measures that will help contribute to the sustainability and well-being of the city. It enables BCC to conduct spatial risk assessments. Outlined below are theoretical applications of the tool:

1. **Resource efficiency:** can be achieved through an understanding of where the UHI is most intense to target green infrastructure planning and building-level adaptation to improve thermal insulation that reduces diurnal temperatures. An effective adaptation approach (for example, installing a green roof/wall and trees for shading) will reduce building temperature fluctuations and therefore reduce the demand for energy-intensive temperature controls such as air conditioning or heating. This in turn will reduce the UHI as buildings with effective thermal insulation are not producing excessive heat from cooling the city at night or, indeed, warming it during cold days. Green infrastructure also has wider proven benefits of reducing rain water runoff and water pollution whilst improving air quality, health and biodiversity.
2. **Infrastructure:** Dobney *et al.* (2009), using delay minute costs, estimates the annual average UK rail buckling expenditure during a cool summer to be £3 million. The heat wave summer of 2003 was thought to have costs of up to £12.1 million. However, this extreme may become an average summer by 2050, and in the worst case scenario, an average summer will cost the industry £23 million by 2080 unless adaptation strategies are put in place over the coming years. This is just one example of infrastructure that our cities rely on that will have to face the costs of extreme weather if adaptation planning is not done. The BUCCANEER provides the relevant heat information needed for a wide range of infrastructure organisations to plan for future climates and save money and resources whilst delivering sustainable development. This is demonstrated in Table 19.1 where the user can extract climate and UHI values over their area of interest.
3. **Public health:** Figure 19.4 shows the West Midlands was hardest hit by the effects of heat waves on mortality. The UHI effect can lead to heat stress and exacerbate cardiovascular, cerebrovascular and respiratory diseases which are a major health concern. The estimated increase in overall mortality during heat waves is reported to be between 7.6 per cent and 33.6 per cent with the significant majority of people affected being aged 75 and over (May *et al.*, 2010). By using BUCCANEER, communities in Birmingham that are most likely to need help in adapting to changes in climate can be identified, i.e. areas of dense housing in UHI hotspots. In addition, the practical value of the data in the tool is that it can be used to analyse issues like the spatial pattern of hospital admissions for heat-related illnesses in order to target adaptation.

*Table 19.1* UKCP09 central estimate climate projections (50% probability) added to the UHI values from the 2006 heat wave simulation. This shows the difference in temperatures between assuming the present land use of Birmingham is grassland to what temperatures could be including climate change and the UHI. The model grid cell used was centred over Birmingham New Street Station.

| *Emissions scenario* | *2020* | *2050* | *2080* |
|---|---|---|---|
| Low | 5.6 | 6.4 | 7.0 |
| Medium | 5.5 | 6.7 | 7.9 |
| High | 5.5 | 7.1 | 9.0 |

Source: BUCCANEER, 2011

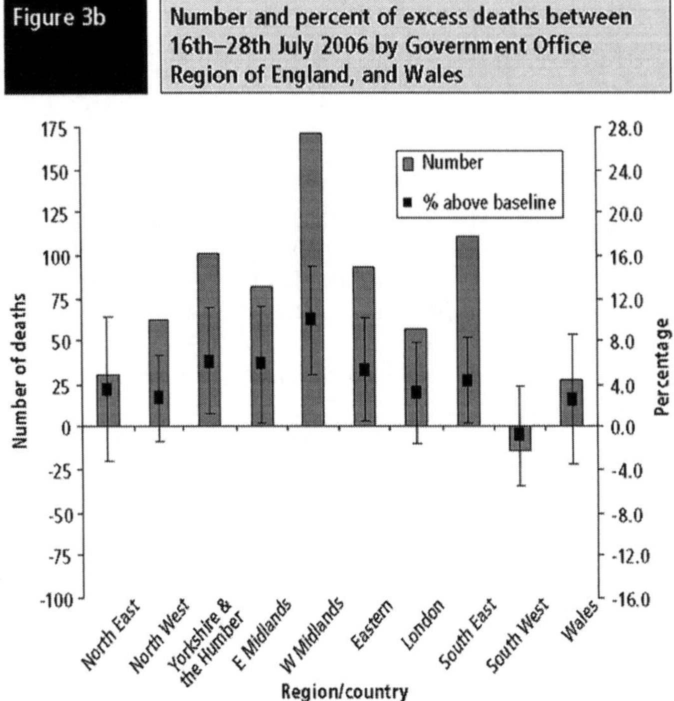


*Figure 19.4* UK regional number and percentage above the baseline excess deaths during a heat wave (18–26 July 2006). The West Midlands, where Birmingham is located, was hardest hit.

Source: ONS, 2006

The tool has been incorporated into Birmingham's planning process with inclusion in the City Council's Emerging Core Strategy and Climate Change Adaptation Action Plan. The Action Plan highlights the risks and vulnerabilities Birmingham faces as a result of climate change, and sets out the core actions that are underway and future actions that need to be developed. BUCCANEER is also being included in the Carbon Roadmap, a strategic plan that is currently being developed to highlight key directions for BCC and its partners to reach an ambitious target of 60 per cent carbon dioxide ($CO_2$) emissions reduction by 2027. The BUCCANEER tool has also been a valuable aid in the redevelopment of Birmingham New Street railway station and for educational purposes in schools.

Despite the appropriateness of the JULES model for assessing the UHI, the model assumes a local equilibrium without considering the wind advection affect, i.e. the predicted air temperature of a cell is unaffected by the land use of neighbouring cells. Recent studies (Bohnenstengel *et al.*, 2011; Heaviside *et al.*, 2014) demonstrate that the UHI pattern can be influenced by wind advection, even at low speeds. To address this, a follow-on project, the BUCCANEER 2, will use the Weather Research and Forecasting Model (WRF) with the BEP urban scheme to further assess heat advection across the city.

The project has also led to exciting new developments such as the creation of a new city centre weather station, sited (unconventionally) in the urban core. Weather data from Birmingham city centre has been previously unattainable due to Met Office stations being located away from any urban influence. Preliminary analysis of the site shows UHI intensities higher than previously observed (Unwin, 1980; Johnson, 1985) or indeed modelled. In addition, an ongoing project, HiTemp (High Density Temperature Measurements in the Urban Environment), is installing over 200 Wi-Fi air temperature sensors across the city (including a fine array in the CBD) alongside 30 fully automatic weather stations. A useful review of meteorological sensors within the urban environment can be found in Muller *et al.* (2013). This will provide real-time UHI monitoring and for the first time allow a meteorological model to be evaluated at a very high spatial resolution in an urban area. This will make Birmingham a leading international urban climate research base and the continued relationship with BCC will help Birmingham achieve its green vision for a sustainable city.

## Conclusions

A successful knowledge transfer partnership has shown that the UHI in Birmingham is a significant phenomenon that can exceed 4.0°C under certain conditions. Model results fit well with observed data and are of a similar magnitude to previous studies in the region. Model simulations were converted for use in a web-based planning tool using GIS and Google Maps API. The product, the BUCCANEER planning tool, is intuitive and interactive, displaying combined UHI and social information. It has been applied within BCC for policy development and has a wider outreach including for infrastructure, health and educational purposes. The project has led to a new generation of urban climate projects that are advancing existing knowledge and transferring this back to the city to ensure a sustainable future.

## References


Arnfield, A. J. (2003). Two decades of urban climate research: A review of turbulence, exchanges of energy and water, and the urban heat island. *International Journal of Climatology*, 23(1): 1–26.

Best, M. J., Pryor, M., Clark, D. B., Rooney, G. G., Essery, R. L. H., Menard, C. B., Edwards, J. M., Hendry, M. A., Porson, A., Gedney, N., Mercado, L. M., Sitch, S., Blyth, E., Boucher, O., Cox, P. M., Grimmond, C. S. B. and Harding, R. J. (2011). The Joint UK Land Environment Simulator (JULES), model description – Part 1: energy and water fluxes. *Geoscientific Model Development*, 4(1): 677–699. doi:10.5194/gmd-4-677-2011.

Bohnenstengel, S. I., Evans, S., Clark, P. A. and Belcher, S. E. (2011). Simulations of the London urban heat island. *Quarterly Journal of the Royal Meteorological Society*, 137(659): 1625–1640.

BUCCANEER (2011). *Birmingham's Urban Climate Change with Neighbourhood Estimates of Environmental Risk*. Available at http://www.birminghamclimate.com/ (Accessed 30 November 2013).

Clark, D. B., Mercado, L. M., Sitch, S., Jones, C. D., Gedney, N., Best, M. J., Pryor, M., Rooney, G. G., Essery, R. L. H., Blyth, E., Boucher, O., Harding, R. J., Huntingford, C. and Cox, P. M. (2011). The Joint UK Land Environment Simulator (JULES), model description – Part 2: carbon fluxes and vegetation dynamics. *Geoscientific Model Development*, 4(3): 701–722. doi:10.5194/gmd-4-701-2011.

Dobney, K., Bajer, C. J., Champan, L. and Quinn, A. D. (2009). The future cost to the United Kingdom's railway network of heat-related delays and buckles caused by the predicted increase in high summer temperatures owing to climate change. *Journal of Rail and Rapid Transit*, 224(1): 25–34.

EEA (2012). *Corine Land Cover 2000*. European Environment Agency (EEA). Available at: http://www.eea.europa.eu/data-and-maps/data/corine-land-cover-2000-clc2000-seamless-vector-database-4 (Accessed 30 November 2013).

Fassnacht, S. R., Snelgrove, K. R. and Soulis, E. D. (2001). Daytime long-wave radiation approximation for physical hydrological modeling of snowmelt: A case study of southwestern Ontario. In: *Proceedings of a symposium held during the 6th Scientific Assembly of the International Association of Hydrological Sciences (IAHS):*

*Soil–Vegetation–Atmosphere Transfer Schemes and Large-Scale Hydrological Models.* Maastricht, The Netherlands, 18–27 July. IAHS Publication, no. 270, 279–286.

Google (n.d.). *Google Maps API.* Available at: https://developers.google.com/maps/ (Accessed 30 November 2013)

Harrison, R., lead researcher (2000). *Natural Environment Research Council, Urban Regeneration and the Environment (NERC URGENT) – Observation, Modelling And Management Of Urban Air Pollution (PUMA COnsortium – PUMACO). NCAS British Atmospheric Data Centre.* Available at: http://badc.nerc.ac.uk/view/badc.nerc.ac.uk__ATOM__dataent_11744364633818458 (Accessed 30 November 2013).

Heaviside, C., Cai, X-M. and Vardoulakis, S. (2014). The effects of horizontal advection on the Urban Heat Island in Birmingham and the West Midlands, UK during a heatwave, Quarterly Journal of the Royal Meteorological Society DOI:10.1002/qj.2452.

Johnson, D. (1985). Urban modification of diurnal temperature cycles in Birmingham, U.K. *International Journal of Climatology*, 5(2): 221–225.

Johnson, H., Kovats, R. S., McGregor, G., Stedman, J., Gibbs, M., Walton, H., Cook, L. and Black, E. (2005). The impact of the 2003 heat wave on mortality and hospital emissions in England. *Health Statistics Quarterly*, 25: 6–11.

JULES (2012). *Joint UK Land Environment Simulator (JULES).* Available at: https://jules.jchmr.org/ (Accessed 30 November 2013).

Kotecha, R., Thornes, J. and Chapman, L. (2008). *Birmingham's Local Climate Impact Profile (LCLIP).* University of Birmingham, Be Birmingham and Birmingham City Council. Available at: http://www.bebirmingham.org.uk/uploads/LCLIP.pdf (Accessed 30 November 2013).

Martilli, A., Clappier, A. and Rotach, M. W. (2002). An urban surface exchange parameterisation for mesoscale models. *Boundary-Layer Meteorology*, 104(2): 261–304.

May, E., Baiardi, L., Kara, E., Raichand, S. and Eshareturi, C. (2010). *Health effects of climate change in the West Midlands: Summary Report.* Defra, HPA, WMPHO, UK Climate Projections, WMCAP and Environment Agency. Available at: http://www.climatesoutheast.org.uk/images/uploads/Health_Effects_of_Climate_Change_in_the_West_Midlands_Summary_Report.pdf (Accessed 30 November 2013).

Muller, C. L., Chapman, L., Grimmond, C. S. B., Young, D. T. and Cai, X-M. (2013). Sensors and the city: A review of urban meteorological networks. *International Journal of Climatology*, 33(7):1585–1600.

Oke, T. R. (1987). *Boundary Layer Climates.* London: Methuen.

ONS (Office for National Statistics) (2006). *Health Statistics Quarterly*, 32. ONS. Available at: http://www.ons.gov.uk/ons/rel/hsq/health-statistics-quarterly/index.html (Accessed 30 November 2013).

Stewart, I. (2010). A systematic review and scientific critique of methodology in modern urban heat island literature. *International Journal of Climatology*, 31(2): 200–217.

Tomlinson, C. J., Chapman, L., Thornes, J. E. and Baker, C. J. (2011). Including the urban heat island in spatial heat health risk assessment strategies: A case study for Birmingham, UK. *International Journal of Health Geographics*, 10:42, *BioMed Central.* Available at: http://www.ij-healthgeographics.com/content/10/1/42. (Assessed 30 November 2013).

Tomlinson, C. J., Chapman, L., Thornes, J. E. and Baker, C. J. (2012). Derivation of Birmingham's summer surface urban heat island from MODIS satellite images. *International Journal of Climatology*, 32(2): 214–224.

Tomlinson, C. J., Priteo-Lopez, T., Bassett, R., Chapman, L., Cai, X-M., Thornes, J. E. and Baker, C. J. (2013). Showcasing urban heat island work in Birmingham – measuring, monitoring, modelling and more. *Weather*, 68(2): 44–49.

UKCP09 (2009). *UK Climate Projections (UKCP09).* Available at: http://ukclimateprojections.defra.gov.uk/ (Accessed 30 November 2013).

Unwin, D. J. (1980). The synoptic climatology of Birmingham's urban heat island, 1965–74. *Weather*, 35(2): 43–50.

Chapter 20

# Urban climatic map studies in UK

## Greater Manchester

*Claire Smith, Gina Cavan and Sarah Lindley*

### Introduction

Manchester City Council is taking a proactive response to the issues of climate change, with respect to both mitigating against further changes to global climate, by reducing greenhouse gas emissions and adapting to unavoidable changes in local climate, to ensure a healthy, safe, and comfortable environment for local inhabitants. In 2009, Manchester's Climate Change Action Plan was endorsed by the Council's Executive Committee and this was subsequently updated in 2013 (Manchester City Council, 2013). An important consideration in relation to the successful delivery of the Plan is the role of planning and sustainable development. This includes themes such as supporting innovative and sustainable planning applications, encouraging climate sensitive-design, managing green infrastructure in response to climate change and setting standards for the quality, accessibility and quantity of open space (Manchester City Council, 2013).

It is also recognised that the impacts of climate are not bounded by administrative borders. With this in mind, a climate strategy for the wider city region of Greater Manchester, which comprises ten local authorities, was developed in 2011 (AGMA, 2011). This builds on the Climate Change Action Plan for Manchester by encouraging a coordinated response to climate change issues across the region through the statutory Combined Authority, which provides an integrated governance structure for the ten authorities. The 2020 vision for Greater Manchester outlined in the strategy incorporates four headline objectives:

1. A rapid transition to a low carbon economy.
2. A reduction in carbon emissions by 48 per cent.
3. Preparation for and active adaptation to a rapidly changing climate.
4. 'Carbon literacy' or in other words '[a]n awareness of the carbon costs and impacts of everyday activities and the ability and motivation to reduce emissions on an individual, community and organisational basis' (Cooler Projects Community Interest Company, 2011) embedded into the culture of organisations, lifestyles and behaviours (AGMA, 2011).

Implicit in the achievement of these objectives, particularly objective 3, is an understanding of how climate events have in the past, and will in the future, impact the city-region, i.e. taking account of both the urban and peri-urban zones associated with the wider conurbation. A knowledge base that includes a spatial assessment of climate risk is a fundamental input to the climate adaptation process, as it can be embedded within strategic planning frameworks. The integration of urban climatic factors with town planning considerations, in the form of an Urban Climatic Map (UCMap), creates a powerful interdisciplinary tool, which can be used to minimise risk and exploit benefits for the local environment and population (Ren *et al.*, 2010).

There are a number of publications concerned with the spatial classification of the urban system (Gill *et al.*, 2008), the climate and air quality conditions within Greater Manchester and/or climate-related risks in the city (e.g. Lindley *et al.*, 2006, 2007; Lawson and Lindley, 2008; Smith *et al.*, 2009; Mölter *et al.*, 2010; Douglas *et al.*, 2010; Kazmierczak and Cavan, 2011; Smith *et al.*, 2011). Despite the existence of some decision-support tools based on project-related outputs (Cavan and Kingston, 2012), there has as yet been no attempt to construct a more comprehensive climatic map of the type discussed by Ren *et al.* (2010). In this chapter we describe the development of a UCMap for Greater Manchester. The outputs from this work provide a valuable additional tool for communicating climate science to the local stakeholder community.

## Study area

Greater Manchester is situated in north-west England (see Figure 20.1). Much of the city region is fairly low-lying (< 100m above sea level) but to the east the altitude reaches 540m above sea level where the region extends into the Pennine hills. The conglomeration of several towns and cities with surrounding areas of designated green belt protecting against urban sprawl has led to the city-region's polycentric urban structure (see Figure 20.2). Almost two-thirds, 62 per cent, of the conurbation is characterised as urban (793km$^2$), just under half of which is residential (29 per cent of the total) (Gill *et al.*, 2008).

With a population of around 2.5 million, Greater Manchester was the third most populous urban area in the UK in 2001 (Pointer, 2005) and has since grown to around 2.7 million according to the 2011 UK Census of Population (Office for National Statistics, 2011). It has a highly variable pattern of social deprivation. Social deprivation is one of the key indicators of social vulnerability (Lindley *et al.*, 2011), and the 2007 English Multiple Deprivation Index ranked Manchester City as the 4th most deprived local authority in England, compared to Stockport Metropolitan Borough Council (MBC) which ranked 161st, and Trafford MBC which ranked 178th, from a total of 354 local authorities (Department for Communities and Local Government, 2007). This, together with other socio-economic and demographic indicators for the city-region, e.g. based on measures of biophysical susceptibility due to age, chronic ill health and/or other dependencies (Department of Health, 2004; Lindley *et al.*, 2006), suggests that there are areas where a significant proportion of the population are potentially vulnerable to the negative aspects of climate change. In 2001, the proportion of people with self-reported limiting long-term illness in Greater Manchester's most socially vulnerable neighbourhood with respect to high temperatures was 30 per cent compared to an English average of 18 per cent (Lindley *et al.*, 2011). There are a range of socio-economic factors which also affect the capacity of the city's population to prepare for, respond to and recover from climate-related events. For example, in 2001 Greater Manchester had a higher proportion (19 per cent) of people living in social housing compared to the national average (17 per cent) (Office for National Statistics, 2001). Those in social or private rented accommodation can be expected to have fewer opportunities to adapt their living environments and therefore experience reduced adaptive capacity relative to homeowners.

Mean annual rainfall at Manchester Airport, in the south of the conurbation (see Figure 20.1), is just over 800mm, with higher amounts falling in autumn and winter. The seasonality in precipitation patterns is accentuated under future climate scenarios, which suggests increasing average winter rainfall amounts in contrast to decreasing summer rainfall (Murphy *et al.*, 2009). The mean daily maximum (minimum) temperature varies from 6.9°C (1.5°C) in January to 20.3°C (12.3°C)

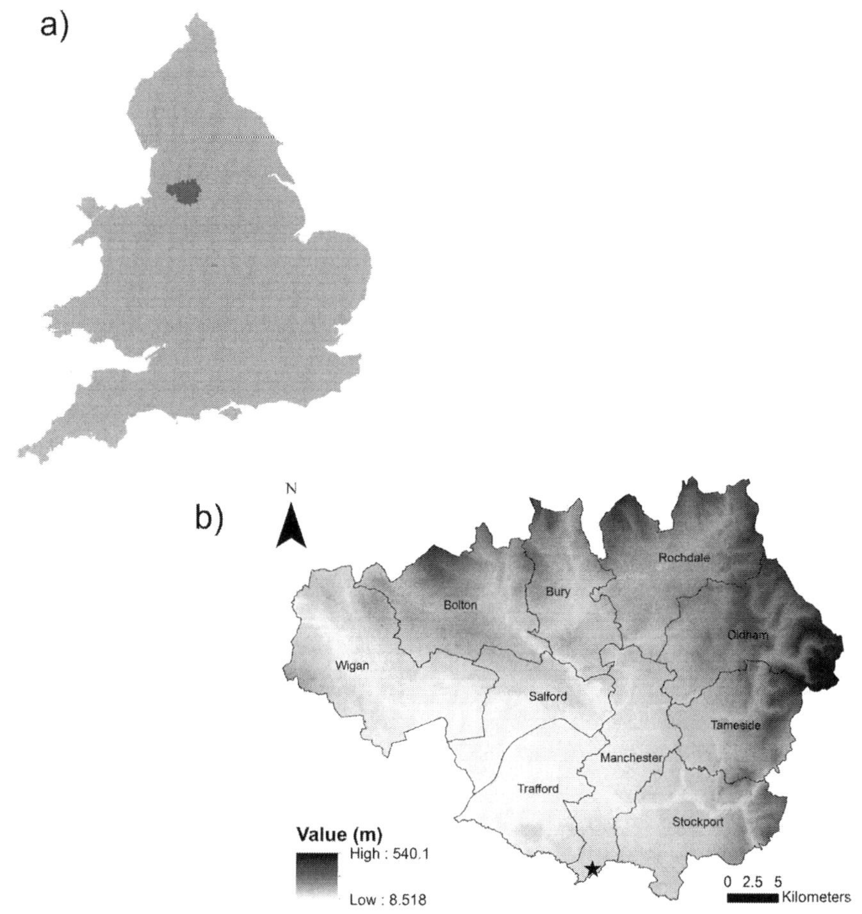


*Figure 20.1* (a) The location of Greater Manchester; (b) digital elevation model of Greater Manchester with the boundaries of the ten administrative authorities. The star in the south of the region indicates the location of Manchester Airport.

Source: Authors. Contains Ordnance Survey data © Crown copyright and database right [2013]

in July. By the 2050s, mean annual daily temperatures across the region are projected to increase by 1.8°C–3.7°C under the high emissions scenario, while maximum summer temperatures could increase by 1.4°C–5.7°C across the region (Cavan, 2011). However, it is the occurrence of weather events that fall at the limits of the statistical distribution for a particular climate variable that often need to be considered when planning for a climate-proof city (Smith and Lawson, 2012). During the 2003 European heat wave, for example, average daily temperatures in Manchester exceeded 20°C in August on eight near-consecutive days (compared to the 1971–2000 daily average of 16.1°C). This resulted in unhealthy living and working spaces (internal temperatures > 30°C) within the urban core and surrounding suburbs (Wright *et al*., 2005). UK urban areas are also recognised as being particularly susceptible to pluvial flooding (Pitt, 2007). The impact of two intense precipitation episodes in the north of the region (in 2004 and in 2006) caused physical damage, with 50 per cent of local residents needing to evacuate homes for up to eight months, and poor health, including liver problems, asthma, stress and depression, for those affected (Douglas

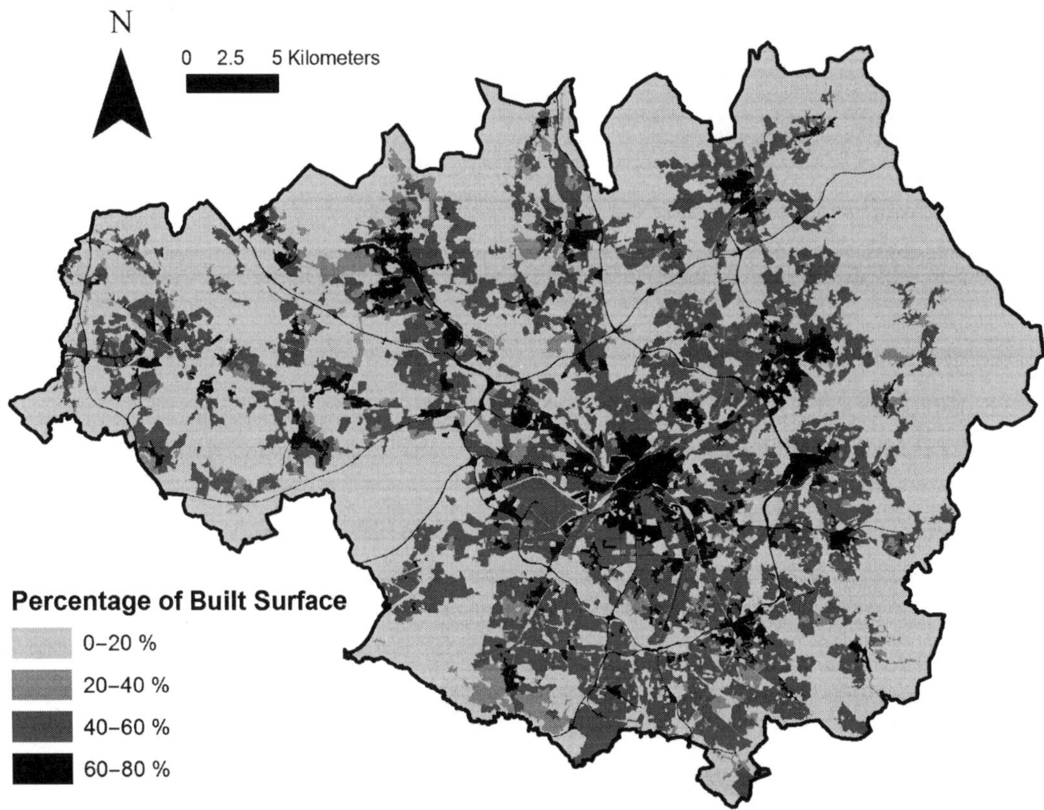


*Figure 20.2* Proportion of built surface cover across Greater Manchester.

Source: After Gill *et al.*, 2008

*et al.*, 2010). Extreme events such as these are likely to increase in frequency and intensity under future climate scenarios for the region (Murphy *et al.*, 2009), indicating that the publication of the Greater Manchester Climate Change Strategy is both timely and pertinent for managing climate-related risks.

Many of the characteristics of Manchester as a city are common to other large European cities. The results presented here are largely specific to the UK in terms of climate and cityscape; however, the methods used are readily applicable to other cities.

## Developing the urban climatic map

In this study the variables temperature and precipitation were considered with the aim of encouraging climate proof planning and adaptive design for heat wave and flooding impacts. A risk-based approach (Lindley *et al.*, 2006) was applied, whereby hazard, exposure and vulnerability components were synthesised within a spatial framework. Two separate risk maps were created for high temperature hazard and flooding hazard, due to the different spatial distributions and indicators of hazard, vulnerability and exposure. Having two risk maps is also helpful to enable spatial planning to develop responses that address different climate impacts. The risk maps are then combined with land use to produce urban climatic recommendation maps (UC-ReMaps), which help to identify priority areas for adaptation. The hazard layers comprise the spatial distribution of the climate variables for the baseline period 1971–2000. These data are produced by the UK Met Office for a 1km × 1km grid (Perry and Hollis, 2005). In particular, summer temperatures (mean, min, max) were used to represent high temperature hazard, and annual average precipitation was used to create the flooding hazard map. The exposure layers combine physical characteristics that influence local exposure to climate impacts and meteorological extremes. For temperature-related exposure these include surface cover (proportion of green/blue and impervious surfaces), building density, building height and anthropogenic heat flux.[1] For exposure to flooding the variables include surface cover, soil type (Gill, 2006) and probabilistic pluvial and fluvial flood risk assessments (Environment Agency, 2006). The exposure variables have been calculated using a 200m × 200m resolution. The vulnerability layers are generated from the results of a socio-spatial vulnerability index which comprises some 80 neighbourhood indicators divided into five dimensions of heat- and flood-related social vulnerability: sensitivity; enhanced exposure, ability to prepare, ability to respond and ability to recover (Lindley *et al.*, 2011).

The data sets and associated summary metadata used to produce the maps are listed in Table 20.1. Datasets were transformed to a normal distribution where applicable, then standardised for consistency. All datasets were then converted to raster grids and reclassified using a 1–10 scoring scale. The 1–10 classification scale used for the climatic mapping provides the user with the relative value of an indicator for a particular location, and allows for inter-comparison between the different variables. The categorisation used here is less prescriptive than existing schemes (e.g. Ren *et al.*, 2010) but is relevant here as climate variables are considered in isolation as well as in combination.

The resolution of the scored datasets was generally consistent with the input data (1km for the climate hazard data; 200m for the exposure data; Lower Super Output Area[2] for the vulnerability data). New data layers were created by averaging the relevant scored datasets for the three independent risk elements: hazard, exposure and vulnerability using an equal weighting scheme (see Figure 20.3). These three layers were combined to produce the overall risk maps (the UC-AnMaps) (Ren *et al.*, 2010) for the two climate risks under consideration (heat waves and flooding) (see Figures 20.4 and 20.5).

Climatic recommendation maps (UC-ReMaps) were then produced by combining the climate analysis with land use data, and overlaying other local planning information, including air quality management zones and major roads (see Figure 20.6 and Plate 20.1). Eight categories are used to define the climate sensitivity and associated adaptation planning guidelines of a particular location, as follows:

- Neutral Areas – Areas where redevelopment is not possible (e.g. transport networks, utilities and infrastructure);
- Climatically Active, Low Risk Areas – Areas of green space which play an important climate regulatory role situated in low risk areas; should have restricted development;
- Climatically Active, High Risk Areas – Areas of green space which play an important climate regulatory role situated in high risk areas; should be protected from development;
- Open, High Risk Area – Areas of unused or previously developed land situated in high risk areas; should have restricted redevelopment to avoid intensification of risk;
- Built-up, High Risk Areas – Urban areas with limited climate regulation situated in high risk areas; should be protected from further development and adaptive interventions should be encouraged;

*Table 20.1* Datasets input to the Greater Manchester urban climatic maps.

| *Data* | *Dataset* | *Source* | *Spatial Resolution* | *Risk Element* |
|---|---|---|---|---|
| Terrain | Digital Terrain Model (Elevation) | NEXTMap | 5m | Display only |
| Planning | Building Heights | LandMap LiDAR data | Individual Building | Exposure* |
| | Built Surface Fraction | Derived from OS MasterMap data | 200m | Exposure |
| | Other Impervious Surface Fraction | Derived from OS MasterMap data | 200m | Exposure |
| | Blue/Green Space Surface Fraction | Derived from OS MasterMap data | 200m | Exposure |
| | Land Use | Urban Morphology Types (Gill *et al.*, 2008) | | UC-ReMap |
| | Air Quality Management Areas | Defra | | UC-ReMap |
| Vulnerability | Socio-spatial heat vulnerability index | Lindley *et al.* (2011) | Lower Super Output Area# | Vulnerability |
| | Socio-spatial flood vulnerability index | Lindley *et al.* (2011) | Lower Super Output Area# | Vulnerability |
| Emissions & air quality | Air pollution emissions: $PM_{10}$ (2009) | NAEI | 1km | Display only |
| | Air pollution emissions: $NO_x$ (2009) | NAEI | 1km | Display only |
| | Background $PM_{10}$ ($\mu gm^{-3}$ gravimetric) (2008) | Defra | 1km | Display only |
| | Background $NO_2$ ($\mu gm^{-3}$) (2008) | Defra | 1km | Display only |
| | Anthropogenic heat emissions ($Wm^{-2}$) | Smith *et al.* (2009) | 200m | Exposure* |
| Climate | Maximum temperature (°C; 1971–2000 average) | UK Met Office | 1km | Hazard* |
| | Minimum temperature (°C; 1971–2000 average) | UK Met Office | 1km | Hazard* |
| | Mean temperature (°C; 1971–2000 average) | UK Met Office | 1km | Hazard* |
| | Annual rainfall (mm; 1971–2000 average) | UK Met Office | 1km | Hazard† |
| | Fluvial flooding (NaFRA0910) | Environment Agency | Urban Morphology Type (Gill *et al.*, 2008) | Exposure† |
| | Pluvial flooding (areas susceptible to surface water flooding) | Environment Agency | Polygons | Exposure† |
| | Runoff | Gill (2006) | Urban Morphology Type (Gill *et al.*, 2008) | Exposure† |

*Note*: *For heat wave risk map only; † For flooding risk map only.
# Lower Super Output Area: Census Units with a mean of 1,500 residents each.

Source: Authors. Contains Ordnance Survey data © Crown copyright and database right (2013).

- Built-up, Very High Risk Areas – Schools and hospitals with limited climate regulation; situated in high risk areas; should be protected from further development and adaptive interventions should be encouraged;
- Built-up, Low Risk Areas – Retail and manufacturing zones with limited climate regulation; situated in low risk areas; should have restricted development;

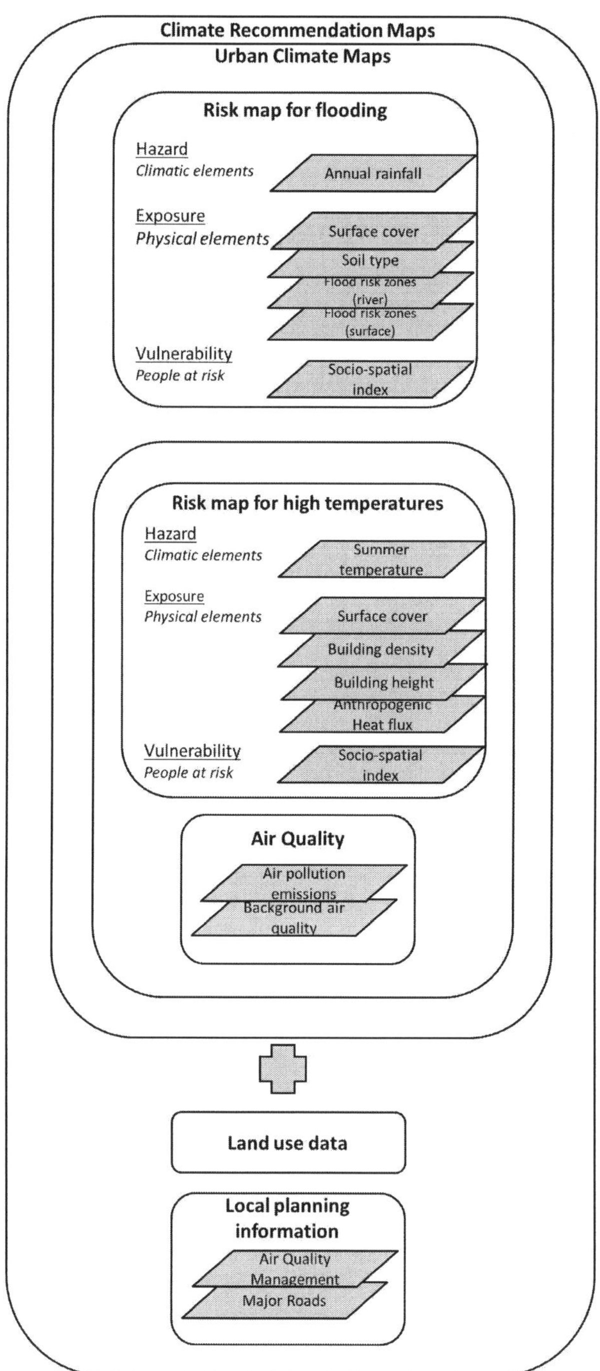


*Figure 20.3* Overview of the datasets and method used to create the risk maps.

Source: Authors

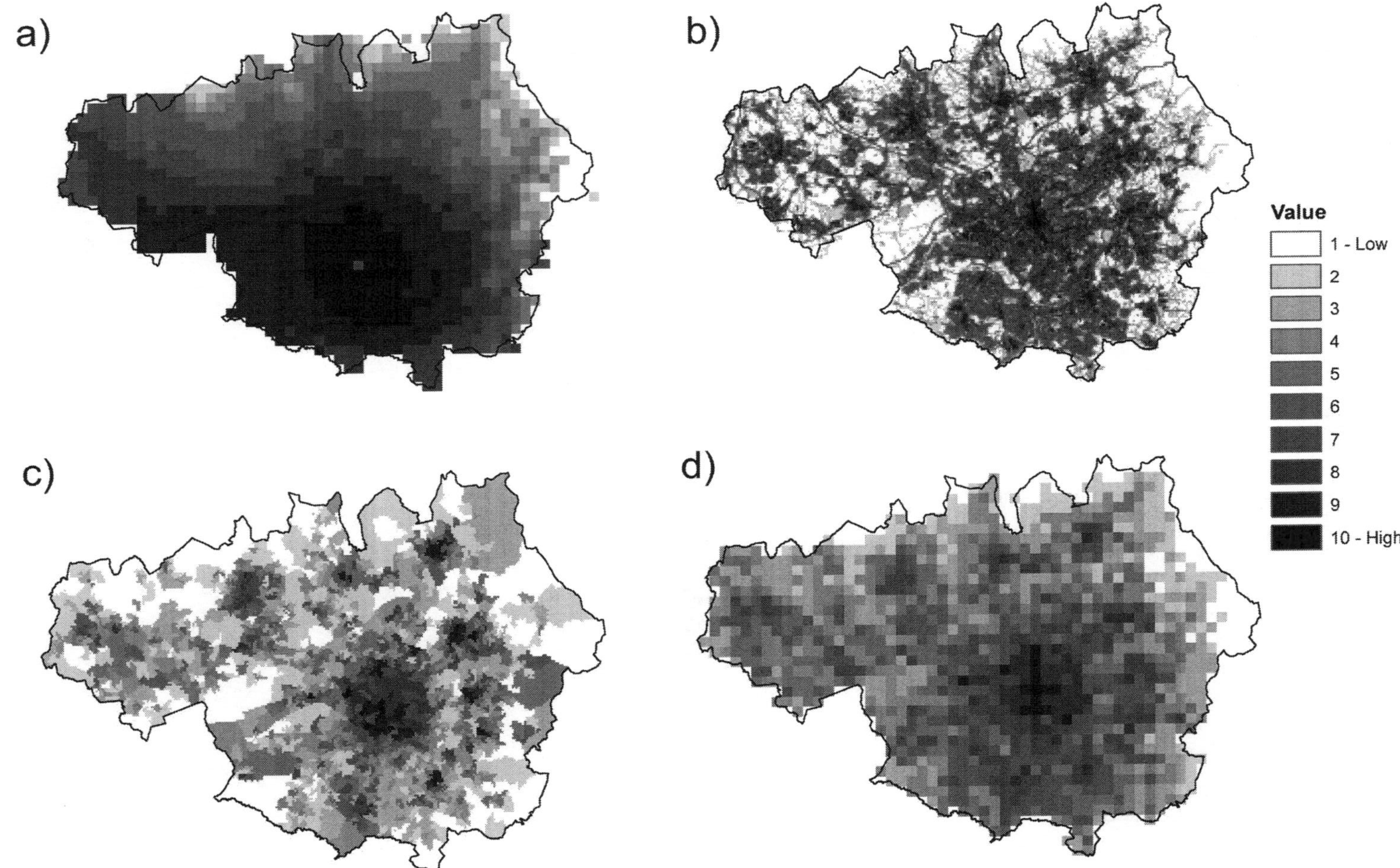


*Figure 20.4* (a) Hazard map; (b) Exposure map; (c) Vulnerability map; (d) Risk map for heat wave events.

Source: Authors. Contains Ordnance Survey data © Crown copyright and database right [2013]

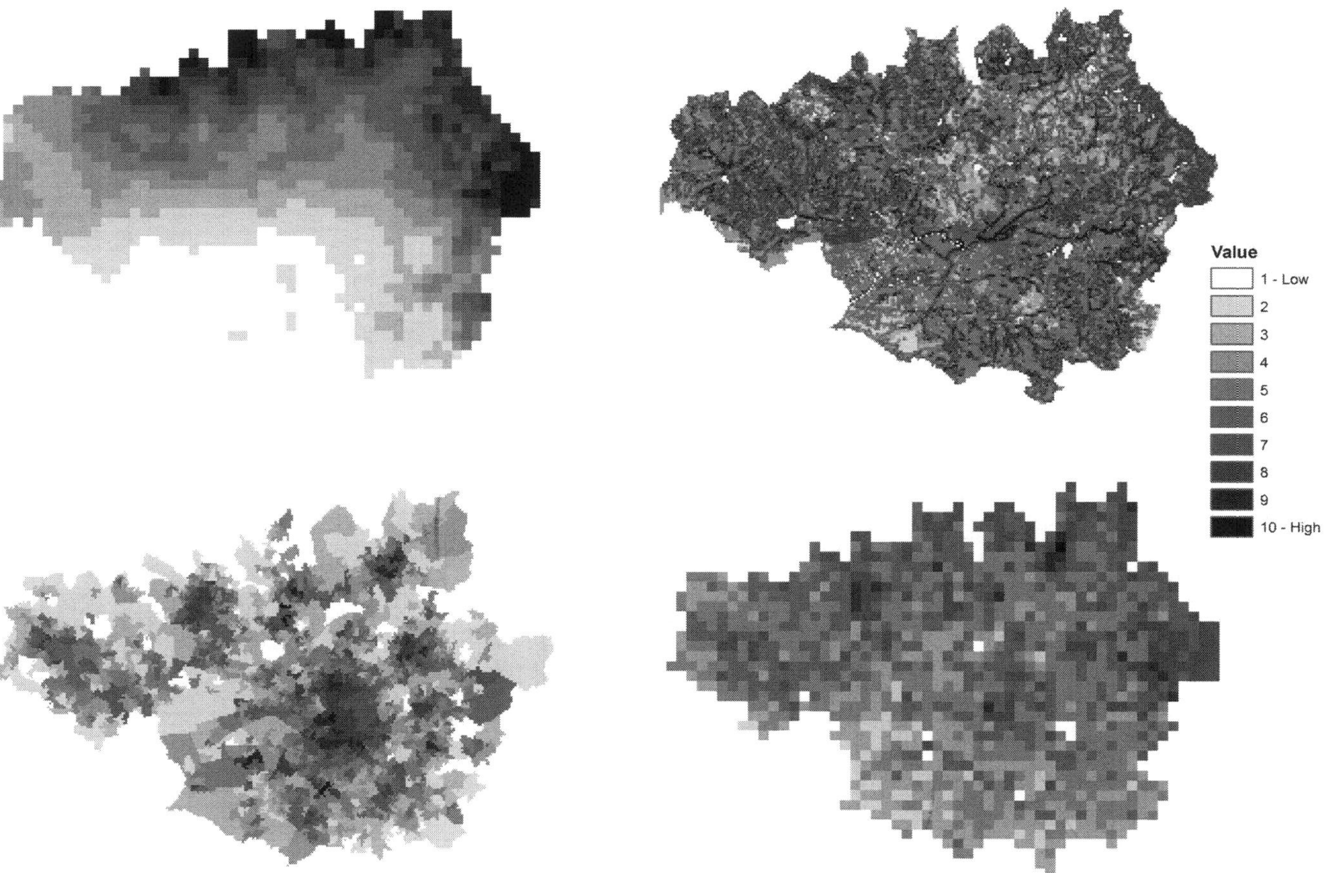


*Figure 20.5* (a) Hazard map; (b) Exposure map; (c) Vulnerability map; (d) Risk map for intense precipitation events.

Source: Authors. Contains Ordnance Survey data © Crown copyright and database right [2013]

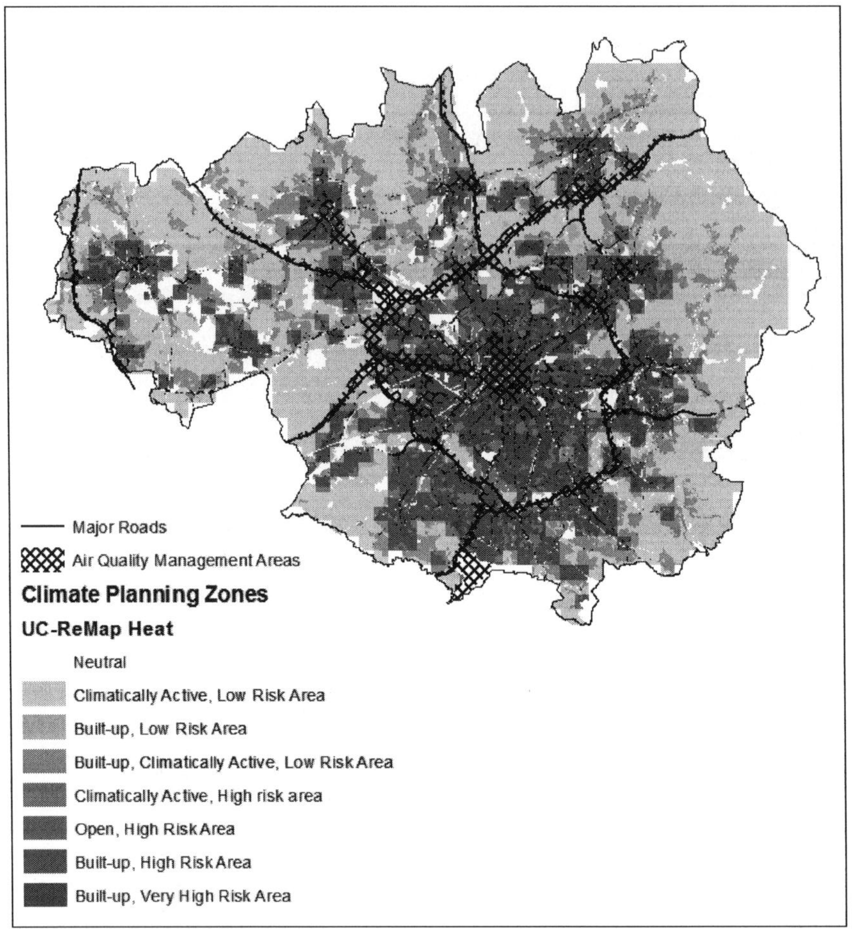


*Figure 20.6* Urban Climatic Recommendation Map (UC-ReMap) for heat wave events shown with air quality management zones and major roads. The colour version of the map is available online: http://www2.le.ac.uk/departments/geography/people/cls53.

Source: Authors

- Built-up, Climatically Active, Low Risk Areas – Schools and residential zones with significant green space, which plays an important climate regulatory role; situated in low risk areas; should have restricted development.

These are based on the current land use (Gill *et al.*, 2008) and the combined climate risk maps. This form of applied climatology acts as an important aid to decision-making, enabling planners to prioritise resources and develop informed and appropriate action plans in relation to climate impacts and extreme weather events (VDI, 1997; Ren *et al.*, 2010).

## Results and discussion

The high temperature risk map (see Figure 20.4d) emphasises the most heavily built-up areas in the conurbation as the locations where there is the greatest chance of seeing high hazard, high exposure and high social vulnerability (see Figure 20.2). Peak values are found in the adjoining centres of Manchester and Salford in the urban core, with elevated risk from high temperatures also seen in the neighbourhoods adjoining the urban core and to a lesser extent in the smaller, surrounding towns. This pattern is also apparent in the exposure and vulnerability layers (see Figures 20.4b and c) and can be attributed to the denser population, increased urbanisation and impervious surface cover, and greater anthropogenic activity found in these areas. The temperature hazard also indicates higher values in the region's urban core (see Figure 20.4a), however, the spatial variation of hazard is primarily a function of elevation (see Figure 20.1). Moreover, these climatologically sensitive zones generally coincide with areas of poor air quality, creating dual pressures which require management through appropriate planning and governance structures.

The risk from flooding associated with heavy rainfall events is spatially disparate. There is less clustering of high values compared to the temperature risk map, and while there are some larger areas of flood risk to the north and east of the region, there are a number of isolated pockets where higher values are evident (see Figure 20.5d). This is due to the differences between the flooding vulnerability and exposure maps, where there is little overlap between high values (see Figure 20.5b and c). Vulnerability to flooding events, as with vulnerability to heat wave events, is elevated in the more urbanised areas. The exposure map, in contrast, is indicative of flood plains and areas of poor drainage, encompassing both pluvial and fluvial events, and therefore includes both developed and undeveloped areas. The precipitation hazard mirrors the temperature hazard, with the highest values coincident with the areas of higher ground to the north and east of the region (see Figure 20.5a).

The final climatic recommendation maps for heat waves and flooding are designed to bridge the gap between urban climatology and urban planning (see Figure 20.6 and Plate 20.1). Areas which are particularly likely to see greater impacts from climate-related events include community services, such as schools and hospitals, where there are vulnerable populations, and built-up areas with limited green space, where the impacts themselves are likely to be exaggerated. These are areas where further development should be discouraged and adaptive interventions should be a priority. There is considerable spread of these areas out from the urban core, highlighting the importance of appropriate management of urban creep, urban infill and the erosion of the conurbation's semi-natural landscapes. The light grey and yellow zones on the maps indicate climatically important areas of green space within these high risk areas. They provide an important role in terms of climate regulation with respect to both flooding and heat wave events. These should be retained, and where possible urban design should encourage the further integration of these valuable features. The areas that are currently identified as 'low risk' ought to be monitored closely in terms of future development to ensure that opportunities are exploited but not at the expense of amplifying climate risks.

## Conclusions

The Greater Manchester UCMap provides an insightful and powerful tool to assist in the interpretation of current climate impacts on the city region. The large amounts of data used to create the UCMap implies that they are a rich and robust source of information, yet the output is presented in a simple, clear and meaningful manner which can be easily interpreted by the end-user. It is the first time that such an extensive database of thematic layers has been synthesised in this way for the region. It demonstrates that each local authority in the conurbation contains some high risk zones in relation to both flooding and high temperatures. The findings underline the need for a multi-layered response which includes directed local activities and a coordinated city-wide response.

Further development of the Greater Manchester UCMap could involve the inclusion of additional climate variables, such as ventilation pathways, which are particularly important in the amelioration of high temperatures. The integration of future scenarios of both climatic conditions and population change would also be valuable, but would introduce an inevitable degree of uncertainty, which would need to be communicated appropriately. It is imperative that climate scientists and planners in the city region continue to work together in order to understand, respond and adapt to the challenges of climate change, allowing for effective management of the conurbation's infrastructure and the creation of a safe, healthy environment for its population.

## References

AGMA (2011). *Transformation, adaptation and competitive advantage. The Greater Manchester Climate Change Strategy 2011–2020.* Manchester: Association of Greater Manchester Authorities (AGMA). Available at: http://www.agma.gov.uk/cms_media/files/gm_climate_change_strategy_final1.pdf (Accessed 23 October 2013).

Cavan, G. (2011). *Climate Change Projections for Greater Manchester. EcoCities Project.* Manchester: University of Manchester. Available at: http://media.adaptingmanchester.co.uk.ccc.cdn.faelix.net/sites/default/files/Climate_change_projections_GM_final.pdf (Accessed 24 October 2013).

Cavan, G. and Kingston, R. (2012). Development of a climate change risk and vulnerability assessment tool. *International Journal of Disaster Resilience in the Built Environment*, 3(3): 253–269.

Cooler Projects Community Interest Company (2011). *A Carbon Literate City – The Manchester Carbon Literacy Project.* Manchester: Cooler Projects Community Interest Company. Available at: http://www.manchester carbonliteracy.com/wp-content/uploads/2012/10/Carbon-Literacy-in-a-single-side.pdf (Accessed 24 October 2013).

Department for Communities and Local Government (2007). Index for Multiple Deprivation for England. Office for National Statistics. Available at http://data.gov.uk/dataset/index_of_multiple_deprivation_imd_2007 (Accessed February 2014).

Department of Health (2004). *Heatwave Plan for England.* Available at: http://webarchive.nationalarchives.gov.uk/+/www.dh.gov.uk/en/Publicationsandstatistics/Publications/PublicationsPolicyAndGuidance/DH_4086874 (Accessed February 2014). Latest version published by Public Health England (2013), available at https://www.gov.uk/government/uploads/system/uploads/attachment_data/file/201039/Heatwave-Main_Plan-2013.pdf (Accessed February 2014).

Douglas, I., Garvin, S., Lawson, N., Richards, J., Tippett, J. and White, I. (2010). Urban pluvial flooding: A qualitative case study of cause, effect and non-structural mitigation. *Journal of Flood Risk Management*, 3(2): 1–14.

Environment Agency (2006). *Understanding Flood Risk: Using Our Flood Map.* Bristol: Environment Agency.

Gill, S. E. (2006). *Climate Change and Urban Greenspace.* Unpublished PhD thesis. School of Environment and Development, University of Manchester.

Gill, S. E., Handley, J. F, Ennos, A. R., Pauleit, S., Theuray, N. and Lindley, S. J. (2008). Characterising the urban environment of UK cities and towns: a template for landscape planning in a changing climate. *Landscape and Urban Planning*, 87(3): 210–222.

Kazmierczak, A. and Cavan, G. (2011). Surface water flooding risk to urban communities: Analysis of vulnerability, hazard and exposure. *Landscape and Urban Planning*, 103(2): 185–197.

Lawson, N. and Lindley, S. (2008) A deeper understanding of climate induced risk to urban infrastructure: Case studies of past events in Greater Manchester. *North West Geography*, 8(1): 4–18. Available at: http://www.mangeogsoc.org.uk/pdfs/lawson_lindley.pdf (Accessed 24 October 2013).

Lindley, S., O'Neill, J., Kandeh, J., Lawson, N., Christian, R. and O'Neill, M. (2011). *Climate Change, Justice and Vulnerability*. York: Joseph Rowntree Foundation. Available at: http://www.jrf.org.uk/sites/files/jrf/climate-change-social-vulnerability-full.pdf (Accessed 24 October 2013).

Lindley, S. J., Handley, J. F., Theuray, N., Peet, E. and McEvoy, D. (2006). Adaptation strategies for climate change in the urban environment: Assessing climate change related risk in UK urban areas. *Journal of Risk Research*, 9(5): 543–568.

Lindley, S. J., Handley, J. F., McEvoy, D., Peet, E. and Theuray, N. (2007). The role of spatial risk assessment in the context of planning for adaptation in UK urban areas. *Built Environment*, 33(1): 46–69.

Manchester City Council (2013). *Manchester – A Certain Future – Updated for 2013*. Manchester: Manchester City Council. Available at: http://www.manchesterclimate.com/sites/default/files/MACF%20Update%202013.pdf (Accessed 24 October 2013).

Mölter, A, Lindley, S., de Vocht, F., Simpson, A., and Agius, R. (2010). Modelling air pollution for epidemiologic research – Part I: A novel approach combining land use regression and air dispersion. *Science of the Total Environment*, 408(23): 5862–5869.

Murphy, J., Sexton, D., Jenkins, G., Boorman, P., Booth, B., Brown, K., Clark, R., Collins, M., Harris, G. and Kendon, L. (2009). *UK Climate Projections Science Report: Climate Change Projections*. Exeter: Met Office Hadley Centre. Available at: http://ukclimateprojections.metoffice.gov.uk/22566 (Accessed 24 October 2013).

Office for National Statistics (2001). *UK Census of Population*. Available at: http://www.ons.gov.uk/ons/guide-method/census/census-2001/index.html (Accessed February 2014).

Office for National Statistics (2011). *UK Census of Population*. Available at: http://www.ons.gov.uk/ons/guide-method/census/2011/uk-census/index.html (Accessed February 2014).

Perry, M. C., and Hollis, D. M. (2005). The development of a new set of long-term average climate averages for the UK. *International Journal of Climatology*, 25(8): 1023–1039.

Pitt, M. (2007). *Pitt Review: Lessons Learned from the 2007 Floods*. London: Cabinet Office.

Pointer, G. (2005). *Focus on People and Migration: The UK's Major Urban Areas*. South Wales: Office for National Statistics. Available at: http://www.ons.gov.uk/ons/rel/fertility-analysis/focus-on-people-and-migration/december-2005/index.html (Accessed 24 October 2013)

Ren, C., Ng, E. and Katzschner, L. (2010). Urban climatic map studies: A review. *International Journal of Climatology*, 31(15): 2213–2233.

Smith, C. L. and Lawson, N. (2012). Identifying extreme event climate thresholds for Greater Manchester, UK: Examining the past to prepare for the future. *Meteorological Applications*, 19(1): 26–35.

Smith, C. L., Lindley, S. J., Levermore, G. J. (2009). Estimating spatial and temporal patterns of urban anthropogenic heat fluxes for UK cities: The case of Manchester. *Theoretical and Applied Climatology*, 98(1–2): 19–35.

Smith C. L., Webb, A., Levermore, G. J., Lindley, S. J. and Beswick, K. (2011). Fine-scale spatial temperature patterns across a UK conurbation. *Climatic Change*, 109(3–4): 269–286.

VDI (1997). *VDI-Standard: VDI 3787 Part 1 Environmental Meteorology – Climate and Air Pollution Maps for Cities and Regions*. Berlin: Beuth Verlag.

Wright, A. J., Young, A. N. and Natarajan, S. (2005). Dwelling temperatures and comfort during the August 2003 heat wave. *Building Services Engineering Research & Technology*, 26(4): 285–300.

## Notes

1 Note that elevation is not included as it has been used to create the climate data sets which form the hazard layers.

2 Census Units with a mean of 1,500 residents each.

Part 4

# Small cities

Chapter 21

# Urban climatic map studies in Japan

## Sendai

*Akashi Mochida and Keisuke Mouri*

### Introduction

Urbanisation is progressing rapidly in many Asian cities. The process of urbanisation has modified the land use from natural environment into built environment. It alters surface heat balance by changing sensible and latent heat fluxes, heat capacity, and surface albedo. It also adds a great quantity of anthropogenic sources of waste heat through air conditioning, cars, and so on. In urbanised cities in Asia such as Hong Kong and Tokyo, enormous numbers of people are exposed to the effects of urban heat islands. The urbanisation process will eventually be exacerbated with the resultant detrimental impacts of climate change. Thus, urban thermal environment is one of the major concerns that have led to much research on this topic (Baumüller and Reuter, 1999; Mayer *et al.*, 1999; Assimakopoulos *et al.*, 2006; Wong, 2006; Ng, 2009). In Japan, the urban heat island effect has caused various problems such as heat stroke, high electric power demand for cooling devices, etc. These problems are not only observed in Tokyo, but are also found in other regional core cities in Japan.

In recent years, various countermeasures for reducing the urban heat island effects, e.g. urban tree planting, high-albedo building surfaces, and the introduction of sea breeze into urban areas have been investigated. The urban climate of each city region is influenced by regional characteristics such as urban scale, geographical features, land use, sea breeze, anthropogenic heat releases, and so on. Thus, the effective countermeasures vary from region to region according to the regional climatic characteristics. In order to make proper choices for appropriate countermeasures, it is necessary to evaluate the factors that significantly influence the urban climate of each region. These countermeasures against heat island effects are generally intended to modify the heat balance mechanism in urban spaces to reduce air temperature. For instance, introducing sea breezes into urban areas can mitigate the incoming heat fluxes advected by wind, and tree planting can reduce the sensible heat flux emitted from the ground surface to the urban space. In order to take full advantage of these countermeasures, a systematic choice of appropriate measures should be made in accordance with the characteristics of the heat balance mechanism in every region of each city.

This chapter describes a map-based method to select appropriate countermeasures for reducing heat island effects based on an evaluation of the heat balance mechanism in each city region, using the data provided by numerical analyses of meso-scale climates (Murakami *et al.*, 2003; Sasaki *et al.*, 2006, 2008). Two examples of the analyses are given here. In the first example, numerical analyses of meso-scale climates in the coastal cities of Tokyo, Sendai, and Haramachi were scrutinised. The heat balance mechanisms of urban spaces were evaluated by using the heat balance model in urban space (Murakami *et al.*, 2003), based on numerical data from the meso-scale climate analyses, in order to clarify the dominant factors that cause urban warming in each city. The second example examined the differences in heat balance mechanisms in various areas inside Sendai city, the core city of the Tohoku district of Japan. The spatial distributions of sensible heat budget inside Sendai city were depicted in the form of a 'heat balance map'. This map indicated the areas where the influence of sea breeze was larger than that of heat generated from urban surfaces and anthropogenic heat release. According to the 'heat balance map', a zoning method that evaluates the ventilation performance of outdoor spaces affected by urban structures was proposed.

## Concept of heat balance model in urban space

The heat balance of a ground surface is described as follows (see Figure 21.1):

$$RS\downarrow - RS\uparrow + RL\downarrow - RL\uparrow \pm H \pm E \pm G = 0 \tag{21.1}$$

where $RS\downarrow$ is the incoming short-wave radiation (solar radiation), $RS\uparrow$ is the reflected short-wave radiation, $RL\downarrow$ is the incoming long-wave radiation, $RL\uparrow$ is the outgoing long-wave radiation, H is sensible heat flux absorbed or transmitted by the ground or the air during a change in temperature, E is latent heat flux released from the ground and G is heat transported by conduction in the ground.

Traditionally, Equation 21.1 has been used to analyse the effects of the changes of land covers on urban climate in many studies. However, Equation 21.1 denotes the one-dimensional (1D) heat balance on the ground surface. The heat balance mechanism of an urban space is a complicated system that involves various entities such as wind advection, turbulent diffusion, anthropogenic heat release, etc. Thus, this traditional approach is obviously not adequate to capture the real situation of the heat balance mechanism in an urban space. Although the effects of land cover on heat transport in a vertical direction can be understood by this traditional 1D method, it is not possible to clarify the heat transport in a horizontal direction due to the advection effects from wind. For this reason, a new method for evaluating the heat balance mechanism in urban space was developed.

Figure 21.2 illustrates the new approach for evaluating the three-dimensional (3D) heat balance mechanism in an urban space (Murakami *et al.*, 2003; Sasaki *et al.*, 2008). The space considered in this study for evaluating the heat balance is a 3D domain (Control Volume, CV). The total heat balance is composed of incoming and outgoing heat fluxes through all the surfaces of the CV by advection and turbulent diffusion; the heat generation is caused by anthropogenic heat release in the CV.

In the following section, numerical analyses of meso-scale climate in three different cities of Japan (i.e. Tokyo, Sendai and Haramachi) are illustrated. The simulations were first carried out for

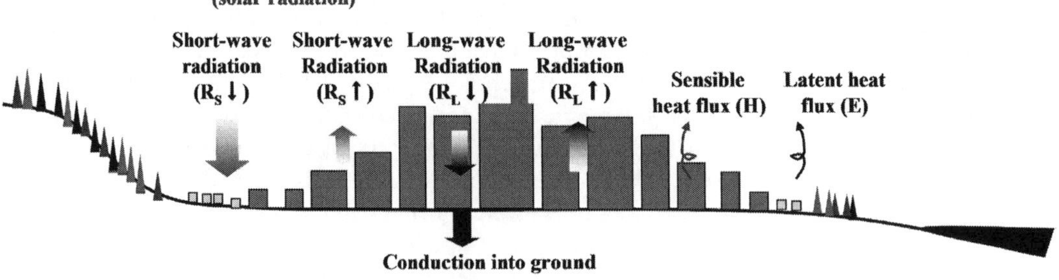


*Figure 21.1* Heat balance on ground surface (1D model).

Source: Authors

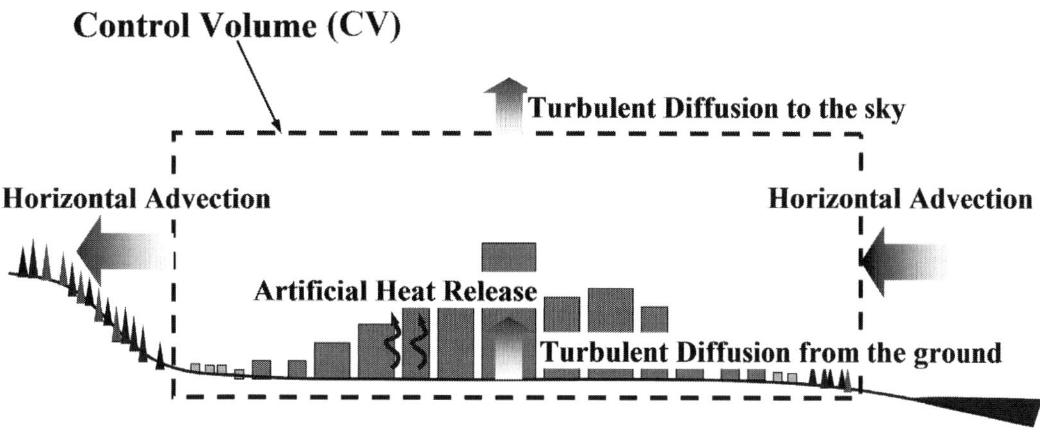


*Figure 21.2* Heat balance in urban spaces (3D model).

Source: Murakami *et al.*, 2003

a typical fine summer day. The climatic mechanism that determines the climatic characteristics of each city was then quantified by applying the aforementioned heat balance model in urban space.

## Comparisons of the heat balance mechanisms between three cities facing the Pacific Ocean

### *Computational domain and grid arrangements*

Numerical analyses of meso-scale climate in Tokyo, Sendai and Haramachi were carried out. Tokyo is the biggest city of Japan. Sendai is a regional core city and Haramachi is a small local city. As indicated in Figure 21.3, all three of these cities face the Pacific Ocean. The populations of the greater Tokyo area, Sendai and Haramachi are about 33 million, 1 million, and 50 thousand, respectively. The grid size and its arrangements for each domain of the three cities are summarised in Tables 21.1 and 21.2. A three-stage nested grid was adopted. Figure 21.4 indicates the domains of Grid 3 and the location of the CV for evaluating the heat balance set in the central part of each city. The Mellor and Yamada 2.5 level turbulence closure model (Yamada and Bunker, 1989) was employed, and all computations presented herein were done by using the function of meso-scale calculation of the Software Platform developed by the present authors (Kondo, 1990; Murakami *et al.*, 2000).

### *Computational conditions*

The simulations started from 6.00 a.m. on 3 August, and a time integration of 42 hours was performed. The initial wind direction and velocity was set from the south at 2m/s at a height of 9.6km from the ground surface in Tokyo. In Sendai and Haramachi, the initial wind direction and velocity were set from the south-east at 4m/s. The initial vertical profile of wind velocity was assumed to obey the similarity theory of Monin–Obukhov, and the details of boundary conditions are given in Mochida *et al.* (1997). The distribution of existing land use was incorporated into the calculation. Here, the ground surface was classified into 12 types of land use, and surface parameters such as albedo, roughness length $z_0$, heat capacity, and moisture availability $\beta$ were set individually

*Table 21.1* Computational domain and grid arrangement (Tokyo).

| | *Computational Domain [x(km) × y(km) × z(km)]* | *Mesh Number* | *Horizontal Node Interval (km)* |
|---|---|---|---|
| Grid 1 | 480 × 400 × 9.6 | 60 × 50 × 49 | 8 |
| Grid 2 | 232 × 200 × 9.6 | 58 × 50 × 49 | 4 |
| Grid 3 – Tokyo | 96 × 96 × 9.6 | 48 × 48 × 49 | 2 |

Source: Authors

*Table 21.2* Computational domains and grid arrangements (Sendai and Haramachi).

| | *Computational Domain [x(km) × y(km) × z(km)]* | *Mesh Number* | *Horizontal Node Interval (km)* |
|---|---|---|---|
| Grid 1 | 400 × 360 × 9.6 | 50 × 45 × 49 | 8 |
| Grid 2 | 120 × 120 × 9.6 | 68 × 60 × 49 | 2 |
| Grid 3 – Sendai | 30 × 30 × 9.6 | 60 × 60 × 49 | 0.5 |
| Grid 3 – Haramachi | 12 × 6 × 9.6 | 24 × 12 × 49 | 0.5 |

Source: Authors

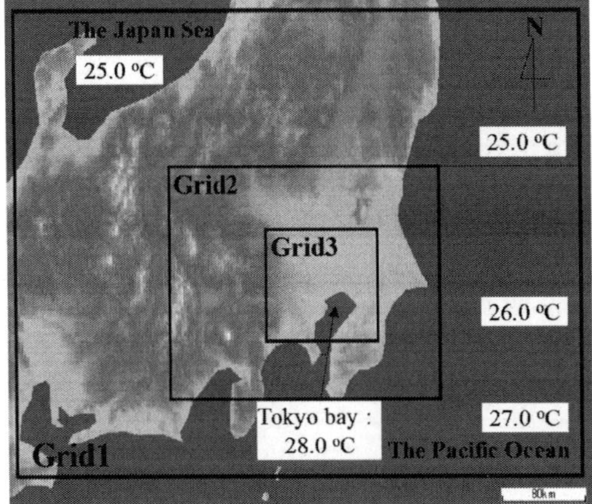


(a)

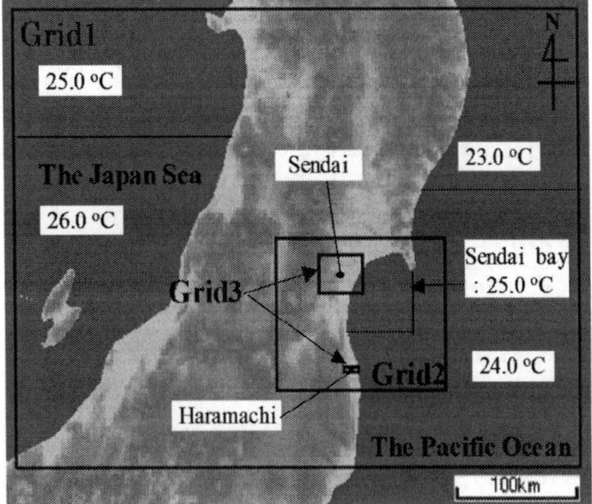


(b)

*Figure 21.3* Domains for one-way three-stage nested grid system: (a) Tokyo; (b) Sendai and Haramachi.

Source: Authors

according to the land-use conditions (see Table 21.3). The situation of land use in Japan is given by utilising the numerical database for land-use compiled by the National Land Agency of Japan (National Land Information Office, 1992).

### Predicted results and comparison with measurement

Figure 21.5 shows the horizontal distributions of wind velocity vectors at a height of 10m at 1.00 p.m. in early August for each city. These figures, Figures 21.5(a) to 21.5(c), are illustrated with the same scale. The sea breeze from the Pacific Ocean is shown in each city at this time.

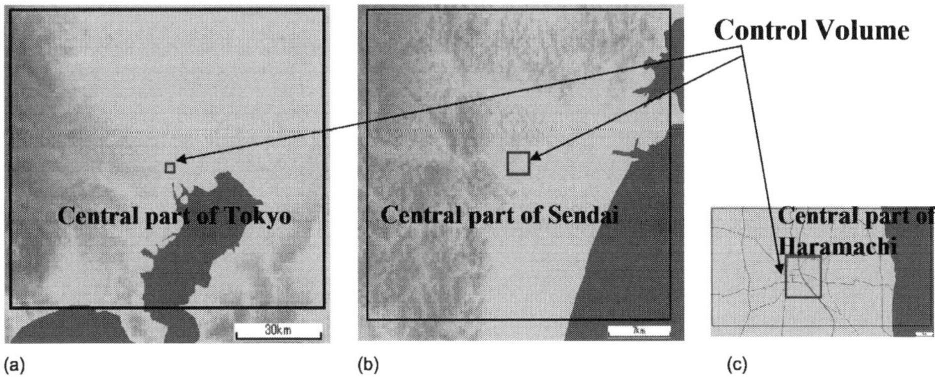


*Figure 21.4* Domain for grid 3 and control volume: (a) Tokyo; (b) Sendai; (c) Haramachi.

Source: Authors

*Table 21.3* Surface parameters.

| | *Albedo (–)* | *Roughness Length $z_0$ (m)* | *Heat Capacity (= × $10^6$) (J/$m^3$K)* | *Moisture Availability β (–)* |
|---|---|---|---|---|
| Rice paddy | 0.20 | 0.050 | 3.0 | 0.5 |
| Farming | 0.10 | 0.010 | 2.0 | 0.3 |
| Orchard 1 | 0.20 | 1.000 | 2.0 | 0.3 |
| Orchard 2 | 0.20 | 0.500 | 2.0 | 0.3 |
| Forest | 0.15 | 2.000 | 2.0 | 0.3 |
| Vacant land | 0.20 | 0.010 | 2.0 | 0.3 |
| Buildings | 0.10 | 1.000 | 2.1 | 0.0 |
| Paved Road | 0.10 | 0.010 | 1.4 | 0.0 |
| Other land | 0.20 | 0.010 | 2.0 | 0.3 |
| River site | 0.03 | 0.001 | 4.2 | 1.0 |
| Coast | 0.30 | 0.005 | 1.3 | 0.6 |
| Ocean | 0.03 | 0.001 | 4.2 | 1.0 |

Source: Authors

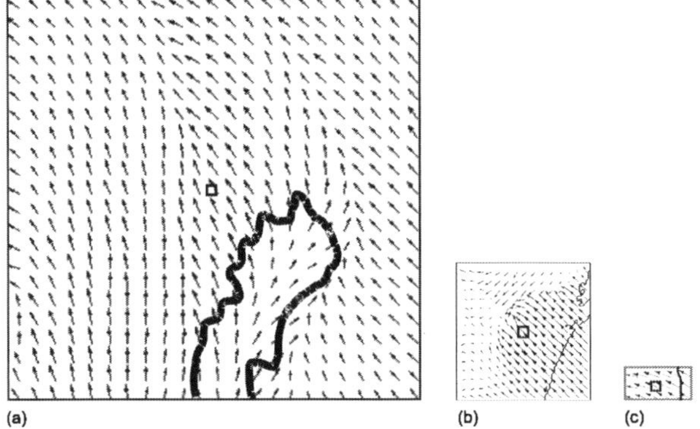


*Figure 21.5* Horizontal distribution of wind velocity vectors (m/s) at 10m height, at 1.00 p.m. on 4 August: (a) Tokyo; (b) Sendai; (c) Haramachi.

Source: Authors

Figure 21.6 shows the horizontal distributions of air temperatures at a height of 10m at 1.00 p.m. in early August for each city. These figures are illustrated with the same scale and temperature range. The air temperature was generally low along the coastal area of each city under the influence of the sea breeze from the Pacific Ocean, while the areas of high temperature were observed in the central parts of all three cities and in the more inland areas. It can be seen that the region of high temperature covers a very wide area in Tokyo in comparison with the other two cities.

Figure 21.7 compares the diurnal variations of air temperature at a height of 10m between the results obtained from numerical analyses and those obtained through measurements (Akasaka *et al.*, 2000).[1] The results of the measurements showed that the peak air temperature occurred at 10.00 a.m. in Haramachi, 12.00 p.m. in Sendai and 2.00 p.m. in Tokyo. This tendency was reproduced well in the results obtained from numerical analyses.

### Comparison of heat balance in urban atmosphere in the central part of three different cities

As shown in Figure 21.7, the tendency of the variations in air temperature was different in the three cities. In order to examine the cause of this deviation, the heat balance mechanisms of urban spaces in these cities were evaluated by using the heat balance model in urban space shown previously (see Figure 21.2). The heat balance in the urban space was evaluated using the numerical results obtained from 0.00 a.m. on 4 August (18 hours after the calculation started) to 0.00 a.m. on 5 August (42 hours after the calculation started). The CV for evaluating the urban heat balance was previously shown in Figure 21.4. The domain of this CV covers an area of 2km × 2km × 80m in $x$-direction (East–West), $y$-direction (North–South), $z$-direction (vertical), respectively.

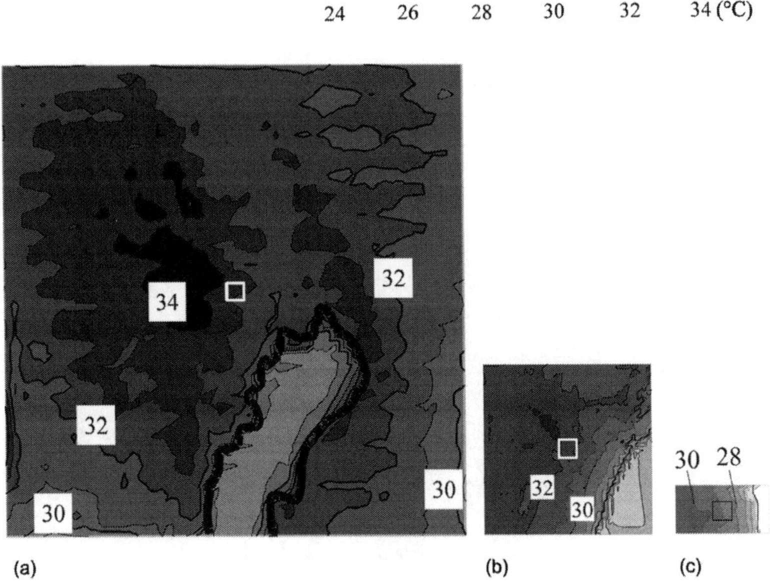


*Figure 21.6* Horizontal distribution of air temperature (°C) at a height of 10m, at 1.00 p.m. on 4 August: (a) Tokyo; (b) Sendai; (c) Haramachi.

Source: Authors

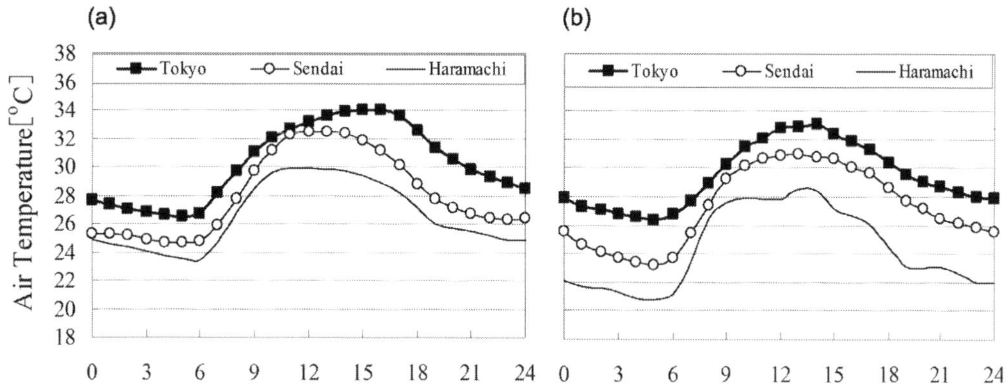


*Figure 21.7* Diurnal variations of air temperature in each city (°C) (comparison of predicted results with measurement): (a) numerical results (in August); (b) measurement (average of typical fine days in July and August).

Source: Akasaka *et al.*, 2000

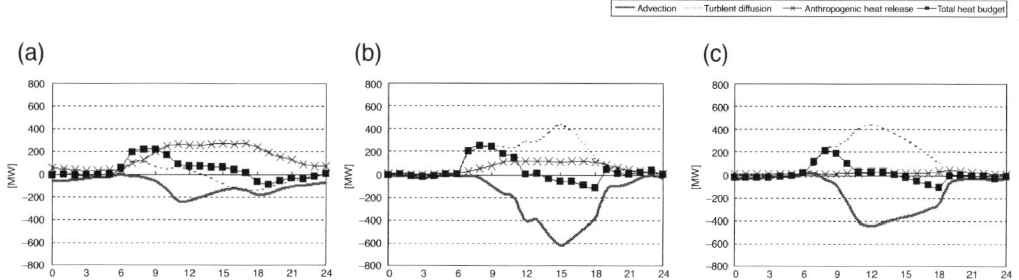


*Figure 21.8* Diurnal variations of sensible heat balance of the control volume by advection, turbulent diffusion, anthropogenic heat release and total heat budget (MW) (+ means incoming heat for control volume): (a) central part of Tokyo; (b) central part of Sendai; (c) central part of Haramachi.

Source: Authors

Figure 21.8 illustrates the diurnal variations of sensible heat balance (incoming fluxes–outgoing fluxes) in the CV by advection, turbulent diffusion and anthropogenic heat release. The total sensible heat budget (advection + turbulent diffusion + anthropogenic heat release, i.e. sum of incoming and outgoing heat fluxes through all surfaces of the CV and heat generation inside the CV) is also shown. Positive and negative signs indicate the heat flow entering and leaving the CV (cf. Figure 21.4). Therefore, the average air temperature over the CV increases when the total heat budget takes the positive value and decreases when the total heat budget is negative.

The negative values of sensible heat balance by advection were found during daytime in all three of the cities, reflecting that the influence of the sea breeze coming from the Pacific Ocean on the air temperature in the central part of each city was significant during this period. On the other hand, the sensible heat balance by turbulent diffusion obtained positive values in all of the cities. These positive values were caused by the incoming heat released from ground and building surfaces. The positive and negative values of the total heat budget indicated that the average air temperature over the CV increased and decreased respectively (see Figure 21.7).

The main factors that greatly governed the increase or decrease in air temperature are shown in Figure 21.8. It is clear from Figure 21.8 that the appropriate countermeasure against heat island effects in the central part of each city is different according to the differences in the regional characteristics of the heat balance mechanisms in these three cities. The effect of sea breeze was found to be more significant in Sendai and Haramachi in comparison to Tokyo. On the other hand, while the effect of sea breeze in Tokyo was also noticeable, the influence of anthropogenic heat release was found to be greater in Tokyo than in Sendai and Haramachi. From these results, effective countermeasures for the central parts of these three cities were selected as follows: (a) in Tokyo, the reduction of anthropogenic heat release is very effective, and the introduction of sea breeze and the modification of land cover are also efficacious; (b) in Sendai, the introduction of sea breeze and the modification of land cover are effective but the reduction of anthropogenic heat cannot mitigate the urban warming significantly; and (c) in Haramachi, the introduction of sea breeze is effective but the modification of land cover, such as tree planting and the impact of the reduction of anthropogenic heat release, is very small.

## Numerical studies on the regional characteristics of heat balance inside Sendai city

In the previous section, it is shown that the heat balance mechanisms in urban spaces are different in the central parts of the three cities, resulting in the different effective countermeasures against the heat island effects. Further studies focused on Sendai city, and this is explained in this section. The main aim of the work is to investigate the regional characteristics of the heat balance of each region inside a city, e.g. city centre, coastal area and inland area, etc., in order to select the most suitable countermeasure for reducing the heat island effects for each region inside a city.

### *Computational domain and grid arrangements*

Numerical analyses of meso-scale climate in and around Sendai city of Japan (see Figure 21.9) were carried out. Computational domain, grid arrangement, and computational conditions are the same as the aforementioned analyses.

### *Comparison of predicted results with measurement*

#### *Diurnal variations of wind velocity and wind direction at the Sendai weather station (Grid 3)*

Figure 21.10 shows the diurnal variations of wind velocity and wind direction at a height of 10m at the Sendai weather station (see Figure 21.9). In this figure, the obtained numerical results are compared with the data measured at the Sendai weather station. Although the wind velocity in this simulation is slightly higher than that of the daytime measurements, the numerical result shows generally good agreement with the measured data for most of the time. Wind direction was well reproduced for a whole day.

#### *Diurnal variations of air temperature at the Sendai weather station (Grid 3)*

Figure 21.11 shows the diurnal variations of air temperature at a height of 10m at the Sendai Weather Station. The predicted results agree fairly well with the measured data. It is seen in the

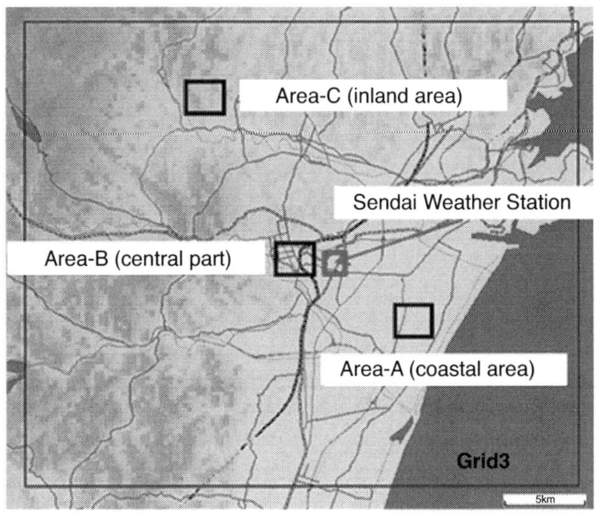


*Figure 21.9* Computational domain: Grid 3 and control volume (Sendai).

Source: Authors



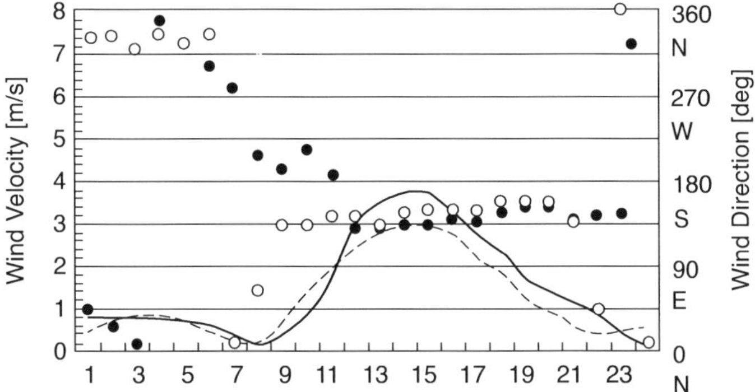


*Figure 21.10* Diurnal variations of wind velocity and wind direction (m/s, deg).

Source: Authors

measurement variation that the increase of air temperature stops at around 11.00 a.m. The sea breeze from the Pacific Ocean reaches the weather station at around this time, and relatively cool air advected by the sea breeze suppresses the temperature increase in this area. This tendency was well reproduced in the numerical result.

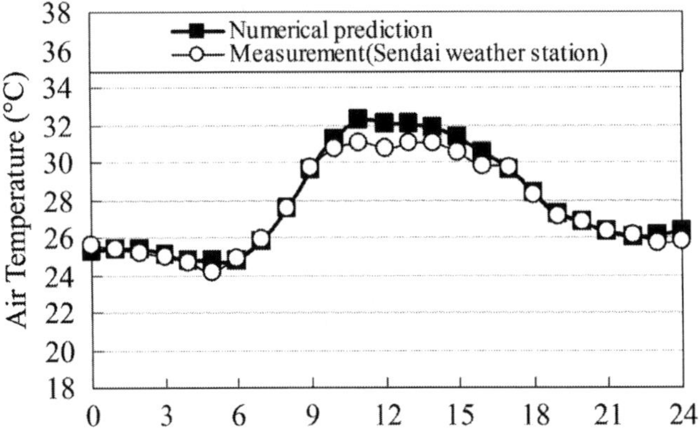


*Figure 21.11* Diurnal variations of air temperature (°C).

Source: Authors

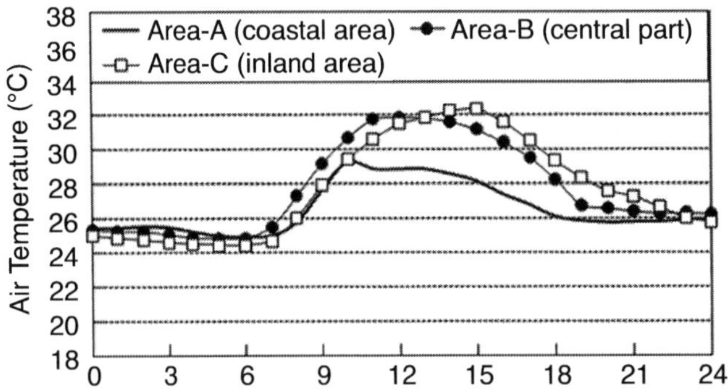


*Figure 21.12* Diurnal variations of air temperature at three areas (Area A, Area B, and Area C, at 10m height).

Source: Authors

### *Diurnal variations of air temperature at three areas inside Sendai city (Grid 3)*

Figure 21.12 compares the predicted diurnal variations of air temperature at three measuring points inside Sendai city (Junimura and Watanabe, 2007). The positions of Area A, Area B, and Area C are around the coast, central part of Sendai, and inland area respectively as indicated in Figure 21.9. The results of the measurements showed that the air temperature at Area A (coastal area) was much lower compared to the other two areas during the daytime due to the influence of the sea breeze from the Pacific Ocean. The highest temperatures were found at 11.00 a.m., 12.00 p.m., and 2.00 p.m. in Area A (coastal area), Area B (central part of Sendai), and Area C (inland area), respectively. This tendency was well reproduced in the numerical analysis results.

### *Comparison of the diurnal variations of heat balance in the urban atmosphere in three areas inside Sendai city*

Hereafter, the total heat balance in a CV within an urban space is discussed (cf. Figure 21.2). As already explained in the section on concept of heat balance model (p. 278), the total heat balance is composed of incoming and outgoing heat fluxes through the surfaces of the CV, as well as heat generation and heat storage in the CV. The 3D heat balance in the urban space was evaluated using the results obtained from 0.00 a.m. on 4 August (18 hours after the calculation started) to 0.00 a.m. on 5 August (42 hours after the calculation started). The CV for evaluating the urban heat balance is shown in Figure 21.9. The domain of each CV covers an urbanised area of 2km × 2km × 80m in *x*-direction (East–West), *y*-direction (North–South), and *z*-direction (vertical), respectively.

Figure 21.13 illustrates the diurnal variations of sensible heat balance (incoming fluxes–outgoing fluxes) in the CV by advection, turbulent diffusion and anthropogenic heat release in three different areas of Sendai. The total sensible heat budget (advection + turbulent diffusion + anthropogenic heat release, i.e. sum of incoming and outgoing heat fluxes through all surfaces of the CV and heat generation inside the CV) is also shown. The positive and negative signs indicate the heat flow entering and leaving the CV, respectively.

The negative values of sensible heat balance by advection were found during the daytime in Area A (coastal area) and Area B (central part of Sendai). These values clearly indicated the significant effect of sea breezes on reducing air temperature. On the other hand, positive values of sensible heat balance by turbulent diffusion were also obtained in Area A (coastal area) and Area B (central part of Sendai). These positive values were caused by the heat released from ground and building surfaces. In Area A (coastal area), the effect of sea breeze (advection) was very large, thus the total heat budget became zero very early in the day. On the other hand, in Area C (inland area), the effect of sea breeze (advection) was very small, hence the total heat budget remained positive until 3.00 p.m. As a result, in Area A (coastal area), the peak air temperature appeared very early in contrast with Area C (inland area) (see Figure 21.12).

In Figure 21.13, the difference in the total heat balance among the three different areas in Sendai is greater than those of the three cities (Tokyo, Sendai and Haramachi) shown in Figure 21.8. Therefore, it is necessary not only to evaluate the regional characteristics of different cities, but also to examine these regional characteristics in various areas inside a city.

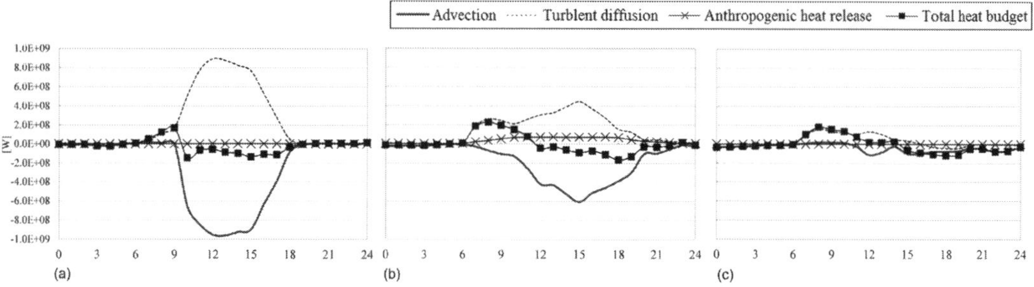


*Figure 21.13* Diurnal variations of sensible heat balance of the control volume by advection, turbulent diffusion, anthropogenic heat release and total heat budget (W) (+ means incoming heat for control volume): (a) coastal area; (b) central part of Sendai; (c) inland area.

Source: Authors

### *Evaluation of the regional characteristic of heat balance in urban space inside Sendai city*

Next, the spatial distribution of sensible heat balance inside Sendai city is discussed. The urban space adjacent to the ground in the domain of Grid 3 (see Figure 21.9) was discretised into 60(x) × 60(y) × 1(z) small domains. The size of each small domain was 0.5km(x) × 0.5km(y) × 80m(z). The heat balances in each small domain were evaluated. Figure 21.14(a) shows the spatial distribution of the total balance of incoming and outgoing sensible heat fluxes through all surfaces of each small domain by advection at 1.00 p.m. The total balance of advective heat transport through each surface of each small domain shows negative values in almost all of the areas. The absolute value in the coastal areas becomes larger compared to that of inland areas, because of the influence of the sea breeze from the Pacific Ocean.

Figure 21.14(b) illustrates the spatial distribution of the total balance of incoming and outgoing sensible heat fluxes through all surfaces of each small domain by turbulent heat transport at 1.00 p.m. In Figure 21.14(b), the total balance of turbulent heat transport shows positive value in almost all the areas. The value becomes large in the coastal area because the outgoing heat fluxes through the top surface of small domains are very small.

Figure 21.14(c) illustrates the distribution of total heat budget in each small domain (advection + turbulent diffusion + anthropogenic heat release, i.e. sum of incoming and outgoing heat fluxes through all surfaces of each small domain and heat generation inside each small domain) at 1.00 p.m. The negative sign in this figure indicates the areas where the outgoing heat flow by advection, mainly due to the effect of sea breeze, is larger than the total incoming heat flow by turbulent diffusion, mainly due to the heat fluxes from the ground surface as well as heat generation by anthropogenic heat release. The temperature in this area is decreased by the effect of sea breezes. Thus, it is expected that the air temperature can be reduced by increasing wind velocity near the ground level with appropriate building arrangements for the wind conditions in this area.

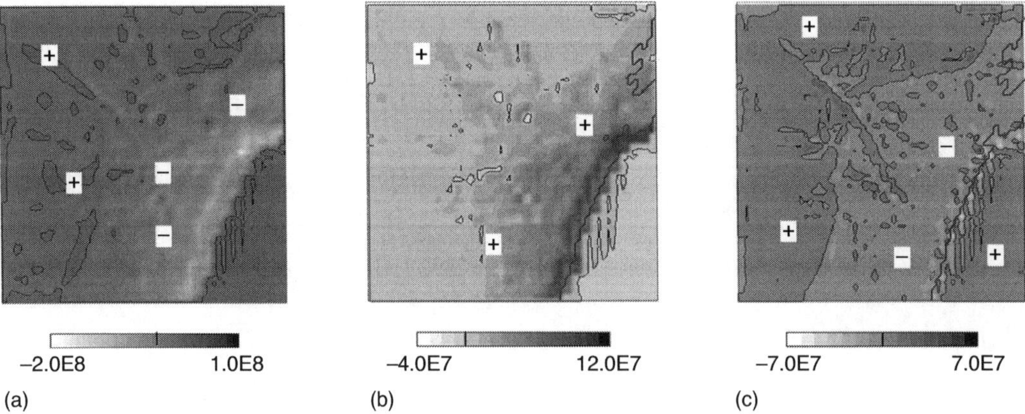


*Figure 21.14* Spatial distribution of sensible heat balance by advection and turbulent diffusion and total sensible heat budget (W) at 1.00 p.m. in early August: (a) total balance of advective heat transport; (b) total balance of turbulent heat transport; (c) total heat budget.

Source: Authors

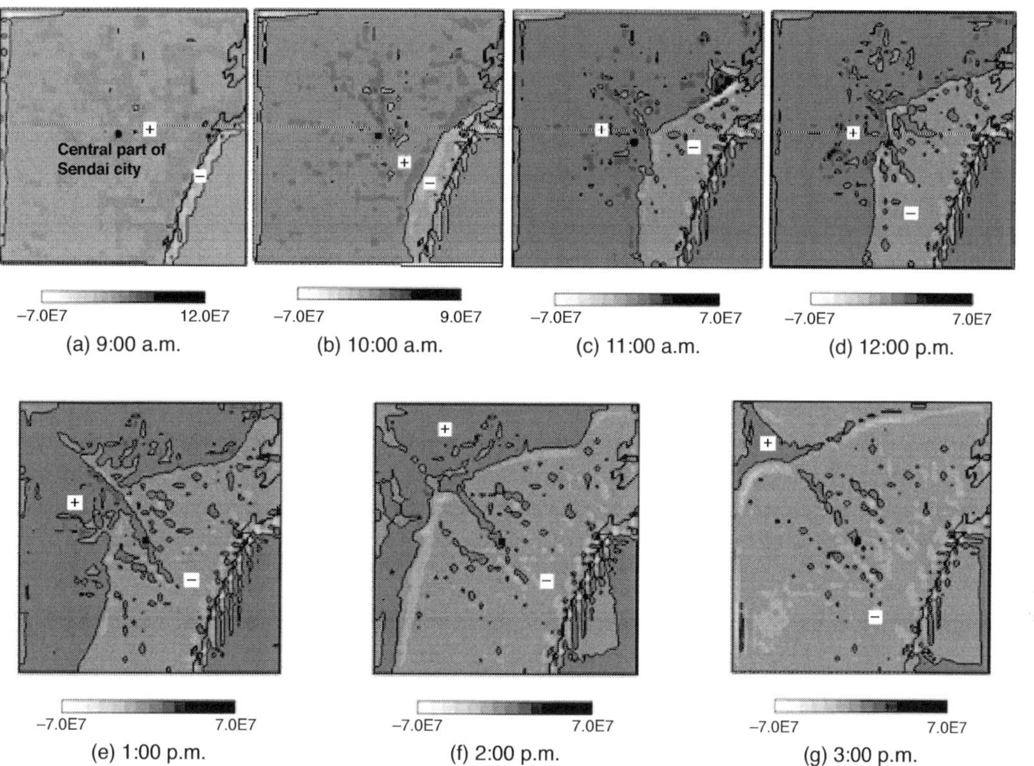


*Figure 21.15* Variations of spatial distributions of total sensible heat budget (W) ('Heat Balance Map', from 9.00 a.m. to 3.00 p.m., in early August).

Source: Authors

The spatial distributions of the total sensible heat budget from 9.00 a.m. to 3.00 p.m. are drawn as a 'Heat Balance Map' and shown in Figure 21.15. At 10.00 a.m., the total heat budget at the coastal area changed from positive to negative due to the effect of sea breeze. Over time, the area where the total sensible heat budget showed negative values extended inland and reached the inland area (Area C) at 3.00 p.m. The period when the sea breeze reduced the air temperature was longer on the coastal side compared to that of the inland area.

## Zone for urban ventilation based on heat balance analysis in urban space

As described in the previous section, the regional characteristics of heat balance inside a city are clearly observed and the heat balance mechanism in each area inside a city is not the same. Hence, the effective countermeasures for reducing air temperature should be selected by examining the differences in the heat balance mechanism in each area. Based on the sensible heat balance map during the day for Sendai city, a new zoning method for the effective use of urban ventilation to mitigate urban warming was proposed.

### *Viewpoints for zoning for urban ventilation*

The effect of urban ventilation was evaluated under the following two viewpoints: (a) Can the natural wind blowing above the urban roughness have the potential to reduce hot air temperature? (b) Is such potential of natural wind blowing above the urban roughness used effectively at pedestrian height within the urban roughness? First, for viewpoint (a), 'the area where the natural wind above the urban roughness has the potential to reduce hot air temperature' was defined. Then, for viewpoint (b), this area was divided into two areas, i.e. 'the area where the natural potential is used effectively' and 'the area where the natural potential is not used effectively'.

### *The area where the natural wind above the urban roughness has the potential to reduce hot air temperature*

According to the sensible heat balance map, the area where the natural wind above the urban roughness has the potential to reduce hot air temperature was defined as the area where the air temperature is decreased by the effect of sea breeze in summer but is not decreased by the effect of seasonal winds in winter.

First, the area where the air temperature is decreased by sea breeze in summer was defined. In this analysis, such an area was regarded as one where the budget of incoming and outgoing sensible heat transported by advection during daytime in summer, which was evaluated from the time-average during 12.00 a.m.–3.00 p.m., is negative and the total sensible heat budget in the daytime in summer is also negative (see Figure 21.16).

Next, in the same way, the area where the air temperature is decreased by seasonal wind in winter was defined. That is, the area was determined as where the budget of incoming and outgoing sensible heat transported by advection in the daytime in winter is negative and the total sensible heat budget during the day in winter is also negative (see Figure 21.17).

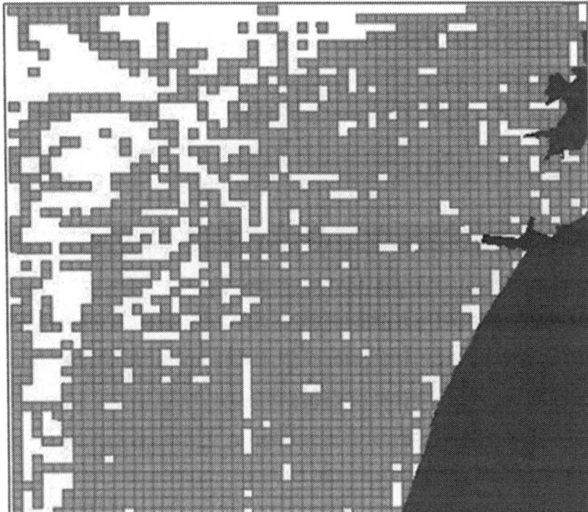

*Figure 21.16* The area where the air temperature is decreased by sea breeze in summer.

Source: Authors

Finally, these two areas were displayed on the same map and the overlapped areas were removed from the areas where the air temperature is decreased by sea breeze in the summer. The remaining areas were defined as 'the areas where the natural wind above the urban roughness has the potential to reduce hot air temperature' (see Figure 21.18).

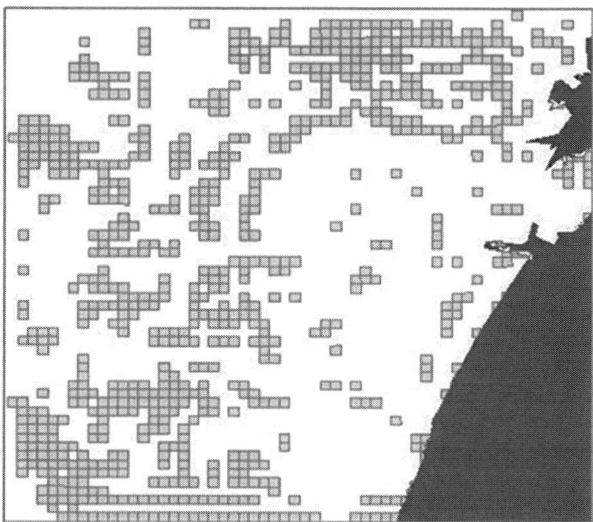

*Figure 21.17* The area where the air temperature is decreased by seasonal wind in winter.

Source: Authors

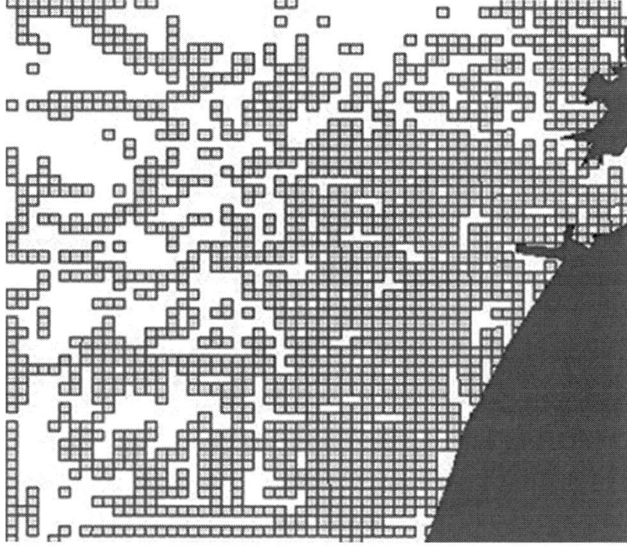

*Figure 21.18* The area where the natural wind above the urban roughness has the potential to reduce hot air temperature.

Source: Authors

### *The area where the potential of natural wind blowing above the urban roughness is used effectively*

As described in the previous section, 'the area where the natural wind above the urban roughness has the potential to reduce hot air temperature' was defined based on the sensible heat budget within the CV at a height of 80m. Next, the area where the potential of natural wind blowing above the urban roughness is effectively utilised to improve the outdoor environment at pedestrian space was defined. Here, the CV was considered to be 3m high and a new zoning method based on the ventilation rate of each CV was proposed. In order to evaluate whether the potential of natural wind that can decrease air temperature is used effectively at pedestrian height of urban space or not, the 'air change rate of urban space' was defined.[2]

Figure 21.19 illustrates the spatial distribution of the air change rate of Sendai urban area by using the method described in Note 2. The air change rate of urban space in the coastal area was large whereas it was small in the central part of Sendai. Figure 21.20 shows 'the area where the natural potential is used effectively' (white coloured grids) and 'the area where the natural potential is not used effectively' (black coloured grids) due to the high densities of buildings.[3] In 'the area where the natural potential is not used effectively', it is expected that the air temperature at pedestrian height within the urban roughness can be reduced by increasing wind velocity near ground level with appropriate building arrangements and configurations to draw the wind blowing above urban roughness into the urban areas.

## Conclusions

In Japan, various countermeasures for reducing urban heat island effects have been proposed and tested in recent years. These countermeasures are intended to modify the heat balance mechanism

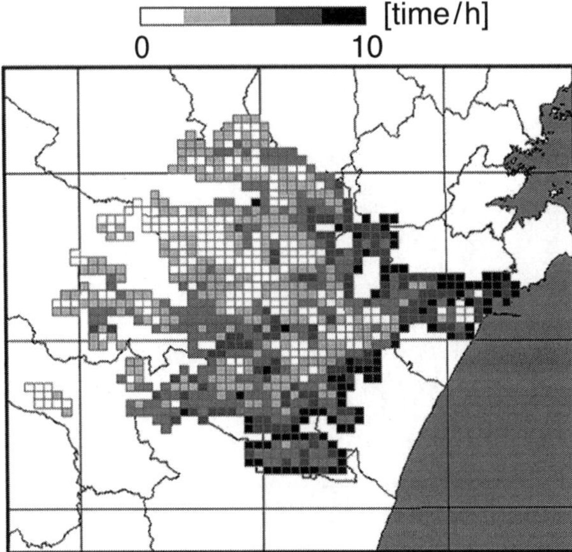


*Figure 21.19* Spatial distribution of air change rate of Sendai urban area.

Source: Authors

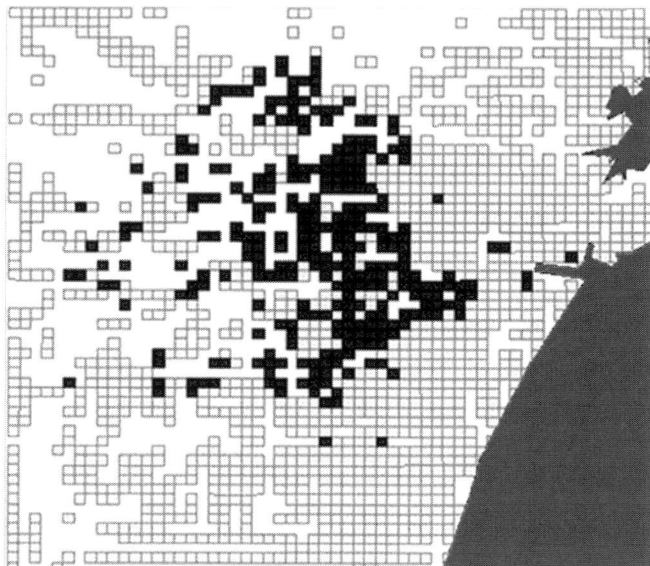

▭ The area where the natural potential is used effectively

■ The area where the natural potential is not used effectively

*Figure 21.20* Zoning map for urban ventilation.

Source: Authors

in urban space so as to reduce the air temperature during the summer. On the other hand, urban climates vary from region to region due to the differences in regional characteristics such as urban scale, geographical features, land use, sea breeze, anthropogenic heat release, etc. Therefore, the selection of the most effective countermeasures for reducing the urban heat island effects in each area should be made according to the regional characteristics. In order to make the proper choice and take full advantage of appropriate countermeasures, it is necessary to evaluate the factors that largely influence the urban climate of each region. It is thus essential not only to evaluate the regional characteristics of different cities, but also to look into the detailed heat balance mechanism inside a city, such as the central part of a city, coastal area, and the inland area.

This chapter has demonstrated a method for selecting appropriate countermeasures against heat island effects, based on an evaluation of the 3D heat balance mechanism in each region, using the data provided by numerical analyses of meso-scale climate. Since most major cities in Japan are located in coastal areas, special attention was paid to the contribution of sea breeze to the heat balance in urban space. The spatial distribution of heat budget inside Sendai was drawn in the form of a 'heat balance map'. Areas where air temperature could be reduced by the introduction of sea breeze were clearly shown on this map. Based on this map, a new zoning method for classifying the areas where the potential of natural wind blowing above the urban roughness is effectively used or not was proposed. Then, the area where the potential of natural wind is not used effectively due to high building densities was defined using the proposed method. In such areas, it is strongly recommended to consider the building arrangement and configuration to enhance urban ventilation through the process of urban planning and building design.

The present situation of the urban heat island effect is mainly as a result of rapid urbanisation. Although it is an unavoidable actuality, there are still options that can be used to ameliorate the impacts. It is hoped that the method illustrated in this chapter can be one of the prescriptions to prevent the city from suffering further elevation of urban air temperature.

## Acknowledgements

Topics shown in this article are the outputs of extended collaborations over the years with Professor S. Murakami (Keio University), Professor R. Ooka (IIS, University of Tokyo), Professor Y. Tominaga (Niigata Institute of Technology), Professor S. Yoshida (Fukui University), Professor H. Yoshino (Tohoku University), Professor H. Watanabe (Tohoku Institute of Technology), Dr K. Sasaki (Shimizu Corporation), Mr T. Yoshida (Tokyo Electric Power Company), and Mr H. Oba (Kajima Construction). The authors are grateful for their valuable contributions.

## References

Akasaka, H. *et al.* (2000). *Expanded AMeDAS Weather DATA*. Tokyo: Architectural Institute of Japan.

Assimakopoulos, V. D., Georgakis, C. and Santamouris, M. (2006). Experimental validation of a computational fluid dynamics code to predict the wind speed in street canyons for passive cooling purposes. *Solar Energy*, 80(4): 423–434.

Baumüller, J. and Reuter, U. (1999). Demands and requirements on a climate atlas for urban planning and design. Paper presented at the *Symposium of Climate Analysis for Urban Planning*. Kobe, Japan.

Junimura, Y. and Watanabe, H. (2007). Actual condition of air temperature distribution in city and influence of wind upon the relationship between green coverage ratio and air temperature in summer season – Analysis based on the results of long-term multi-point measurements for coastal city Sendai in Tohoku region. *Journal of Environmental Engineering (Transactions of AIJ)*, 612: 83–88.

Kondo, H. (1990). A numerical experiment of the 'extended sea breeze' over the Kanto Plain. *Journal of the Meteorological Society of Japan*, 68(4): 419–434.

Kubota, T., Miura, M., Tominaga, Y. and Mochida, A. (2008). Wind tunnel tests on the relationship between building density and pedestrian-level wind velocity: Development of guidelines for realizing acceptable wind environment in residential neighbourhoods. *Building and Environment*, 43(10): 1699–1708.

Mayer, H., Haustein, Ch. and Matzarakis, A. (1999) Urban air pollution caused by motor-traffic. In: *Air Pollution VII*, Advances in Air Pollution 6. Southampton: Wit Press, 251–260. Available at: http://www.urbanclimate.net/matzarakis1/papers/Urban%20air%20pollution%20caused%20by%20motor-traffic.pdf (Accessed 29 January 2014).

Mochida, A., Murakami, S., Ojima, T., Kim, S. J., Ooka, R. and Sugiyama, H. (1997). CFD analysis of mesoscale climate in the Greater Tokyo area. *Journal of Wind Engineering and Industrial Aerodynamics*, 67–68: 459–477.

Murakami, S., Mochida, A., Kim, S., Ooka, R., Yoshida, S., Kondo, H., Genchi, Y. and Shimada, A. (2000). Software platform for the total analysis of wind climate and urban heat island – integration of CWE simulations from human scale to urban scale. In: *Proceedings of The Third International Symposium on Computational Wind Engineering (CWE 2000)*, 23–26. University of Birmingham, 4–7 September.

Murakami, S., Mochida, A., Ooka, R., Yoshida, S., Yoshino, H., Sasaki, K. and Harayama, K. (2003). Evaluation of the impacts of urban tree planting in Tokyo based on urban heat balance model. In: *Preprints of The 11th International Conference on Wind Engineering*. Lubbock, Texas, USA, 2–5 June. Vol. 2, 2641–2648.

National Land Information Office (1992). *National Land Numerical Information*. Japan: Planning and Coordination Bureau, Ministry of Construction Geographical Survey Institute.

Ng, E. (2009). Policies and technical guidelines for urban planning of high-density cities – Air Ventilation Assessment (AVA) of Hong Kong. *Building and Environment*, 44(7): 1478–1488.

Sasaki, K., Mochida, A., Yoshida, T., Watanabe, H. and Yoshino, H. (2006). Comparison of heat balance mechanisms between three cities facing the Pacific Ocean based on numerical analyses of mesoscale climate – Selection of appropriate countermeasures against heat island effects in each city. In: *Preprints of The 6th International Conference on Urban Climate*. Gothenburg, Sweden, 12–16 June. Sweden: Gothenburg University, 342–345.

Available at: http://urban-climate.com/wp3/wp-content/uploads/2011/04/ICUC6_Preprints.pdf (Accessed 29 January 2014).

Sasaki, K., Mochida, A., Yoshino, H., Watanabe, H. and Yoshida, T. (2008). A new method to select appropriate countermeasures against heat-island effects according to the regional characteristics of heat balance mechanism. *Journal of Wind Engineering and Industrial Aerodynamics*, 96(10–11): 1629–1639.

Wong, N. H. (2006). The role of urban greenery in mitigating the urban heat island effect in the tropical climate. *PGBC Symposium 2006 on Urban Climate and Urban Greenery*. Hong Kong Observatory, 2 December. Hong Kong: PGBC, 32–37.

Yamada, T. and Bunker, S. (1989). A numerical model study of nocturnal drainage flows with strong wind and temperature gradients. *Journal of Applied Meteorology*, 28(7): 545–554.

## Notes

1 The measured data was averaged over typical fine days in July and August. The criteria for the selection of a typical fine day are shown as follows. *Tokyo and Sendai*: (a) Extended AMeDAS (Automated Meteorological Data Acquisition System) Weather DATA in July and August in 1994 and 1995 was used. (b) The day when the average wind velocity during the day (6.00 a.m.–6.00 p.m.) blew from South–East directions in the district meteorological observatory in each city was selected, i.e. the day when the sea breeze is observed. (c) The sum of the solar radiation in a whole day of each weather station in Tokyo metropolitan and Miyagi Prefecture was ≥ 20W/m$^2$. Sendai city is the capital of Miyagi Prefecture. *Haramachi*: (a) Daytime weather data observed by field measurements was used. The criteria of selection were the same as those for Tokyo and Sendai, i.e. sea breeze blew on fine day.

2 The air change rate of the CV of 3m was evaluated from the wind velocity at a height of 1.5m within urban roughness. In order to calculate the wind velocity at a height of 1.5m within urban roughness, the following three different wind velocities were considered: (a) $U_{sky}$ (80m): natural wind velocity at a height of 80m blowing above urban roughness obtained from meso-scale simulation; (b) $U_{IN}$ (1.5m): wind velocity at 1.5m height at inflow boundary; (c) $U_{city}$ (1.5m): wind velocity at 1.5m height within the urban roughness. First, by substituting the $U_{sky}$ (80m) value into the log law velocity profile, the $U_{IN}$ (1.5m) value was given. Next, to evaluate $U_{city}$ (1.5m) from $U_{IN}$ (1.5m), the relation between the gross building coverage ratio and the spatially averaged wind velocity ratio within building blocks at pedestrian height proposed by Kubota *et al.* (2008) was applied. The spatially averaged wind velocity ratio [$U_{city}$ (1.5m)/$U_{IN}$ (1.5m)] in each CV was calculated using the Kubota relation. Here, the gross building coverage ratio and the averaged building floor number of each CV were obtained from the Geographic Information System (GIS) data of Sendai. From the $U_{IN}$ (1.5m) value and the spatially averaged wind velocity ratio, $U_{city}$ (1.5m) was estimated. Finally, the air change rate of urban space was evaluated by using $U_{city}$ (1.5m).

3 The former area was tentatively defined as the area where the air change rate of the CV was equal to or larger than the spatial average of the air change rate over all regions shown in Figure 21.19, and the latter area was defined as the remaining area.

Chapter 22

# Urban climatic map studies in Germany

## Stuttgart

*Jürgen Baumüller, Ulrich Reuter*

## PART I: METHODOLOGY

### Introduction and climatic situation

Stuttgart is the capital city of the federal state Baden-Württemberg in the southern part of Germany. With a total population of nearly 600,000, it is the centre of a metropolitan region of about 2.7 million people. The total area covers 207km$^2$ with 50 per cent settlement and 24 per cent forest.

Not without reason, the characteristics of the Stuttgart climate and air hygiene have long been the focus of attention. Indeed the favourable location of Stuttgart, in terms of landscape and climate, masks certain problematic aspects of its urban climate.

Stuttgart's local climate is marked strongly by its site in the wide Neckar basin, shielded by the Black Forest in the West and the Swabian Alb in the South. Further, the city centre lies in a small basin and a valley (see Figure 22.1) with significant influence on all climatic elements like solar radiation, temperature, humidity, precipitation and wind.

Stuttgart's climate is mild with an average annual temperature of about 10°C in the basin of the city and about 8.4°C in the more elevated outskirts. The average wind speed per year is about 1.5m/s in the city centre and about 2.5m/s in the higher regions and is therefore low in general. This low wind condition and the topographical characteristics raise the issue of insufficient natural air ventilation as well as heat island effects, especially in the city centre.

### Development of the city of Stuttgart

Stuttgart's history reveals that its climatic situation has been considered since the seventeenth century. Until 1900, more or less, only the bottom part of the basin was built up. From the nineteenth century, development and construction on the hillsides was restricted by special urban development principles (see Figure 22.2). Development was brought into line with the landscape by limiting the height of the buildings and by defining clearances and construction ban areas. This has allowed for the typical green character of Stuttgart's elevated outskirts until today.

The current land use plan 2010 (FNP, 2010) also contains the goal of preserving the characteristic development of detached houses, which is expressed in the plan as a combination of housing and other green spaces (see Figure 22.3).

The targets of the land use plan 2010 are: compact, urban and green, inner development instead of development in the green open space; integration of urbanism and landscape; and environmentally friendly traffic.

*Figure 22.1* Stuttgart 1698 without hillside development.

Source: City of Stuttgart, 2010

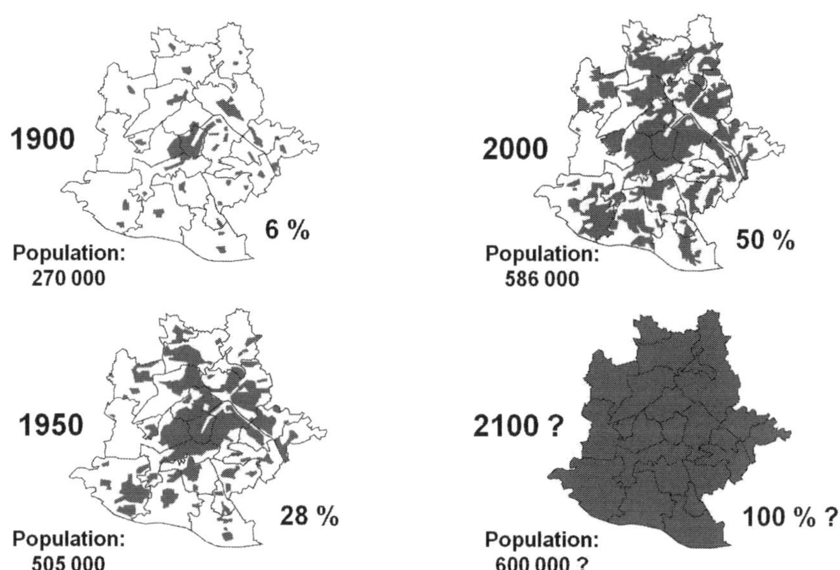


*Figure 22.2* Development of Stuttgart since 1900.

Source: Courtesy of Office of Environmental Protection, City of Stuttgart

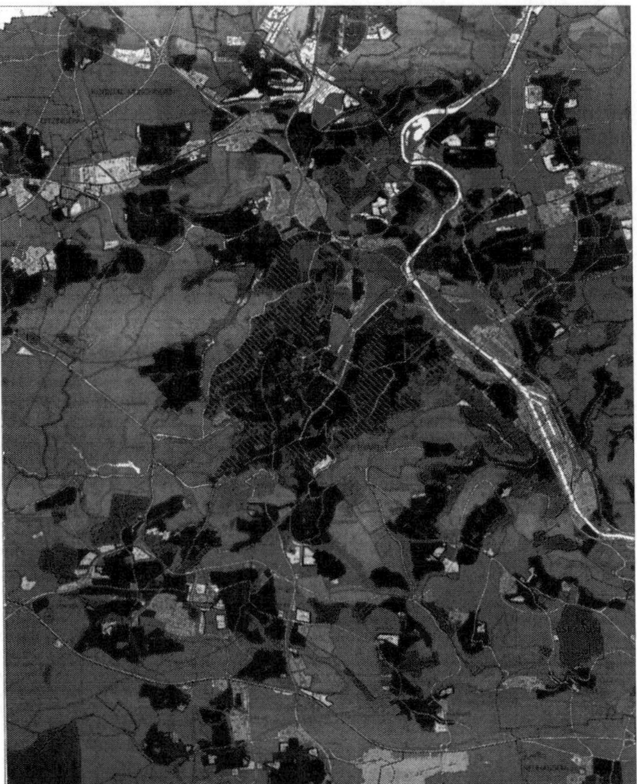

*Figure 22.3* Land Use Plan Stuttgart.
Source: FNP, 2010

## Urban climatology in Stuttgart – historical overview

It was in the year 1938 that the city council decided to employ a meteorologist whose job was to make analyses on the climatic conditions in Stuttgart and to reveal the connection between climate and urban development. Even then, the aspect of climatic hygiene in urban development was recognised as a means of strengthening and preserving the inhabitants' health. The origin of the Department of Urban Climatology dates back to that year (City of Stuttgart, 2010).

To implement climatic aspects in urban planning, it was necessary at first to investigate the local climate and especially the urban climate of Stuttgart. The urban climatologists of Stuttgart already had a lot of data, calculations, and maps of the city (Baumüller, 2006).

The department carried out climate analysis for the territory of the associated municipalities in 1991 and published the results in the climate atlas as a basis of the common land use plan (Klimaatlas, 1992) (see Figure 22.4).

Working methods and results in the context of the drawing up of the climate atlas have influenced the VDI-Standard VDI 3787, Part 1 (VDI, 1997) and allowed the early participation of the Department of Urban Climatology and the consideration of urban climatic interests in all planning stages of the urban development project 'Stuttgart 21' with an underground new main railway station and an inner city development of about 100 hectares.

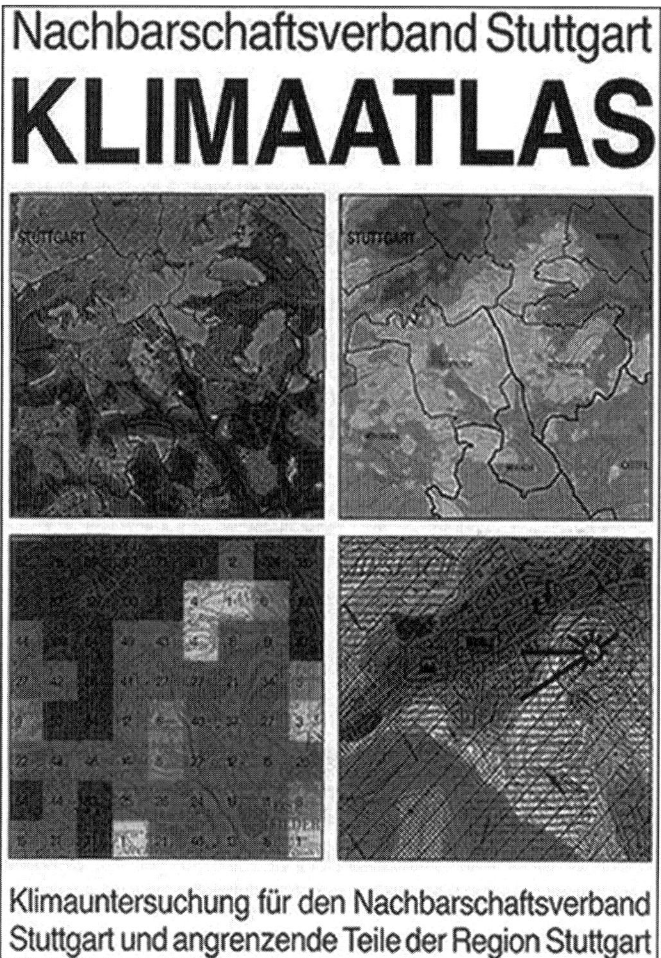


*Figure 22.4* Climate Atlas 1992.

Source: Klimaatlas, 1992

The Ministry of Traffic and Infrastructure of the state of Baden-Württemberg supported by the municipal Department of Environmental Protection financed the publication of the *Climate Booklet for Urban Development – References for Urban Planning* (Ministerium für Verkehr und Infrastruktur Baden-Württemberg, 2012) on the Internet.

## Climate atlas Stuttgart (1992)

In the context of the ongoing discussion about new residential and commercial development, fundamental studies of climate and air were gaining increasing importance for producing qualified land use planning in densely settled areas. Since planning-related statements refer to specific areas, the use of maps as an informational basis is recommended. Maps in this context are a very significant tool for the planner, and are also a meaningful method of communicating information for politicians and the interested public. As such, spatially related cartographic representations are necessary for attaining climatic and air-hygienic goals.

The example of the climate atlas produced by the Planning Association Stuttgart (Klimaatlas, 1992) shows how the concerns of climate and air can be incorporated into cartographic representations for land-use planning.

In the context of the collection of basic data, two infrared aerial images (evening, morning) of the entire study area were taken. Infrared thermography provides one with a picture of the momentary radiation temperature distribution on the earth's surface at high powers of resolution, impossible to obtain with any stationary measurement network. From an airplane, the landscape was scanned line by line with the measuring photometer (with a ground resolution of about 7m by 7m at an altitude of 3,000m).

In addition, for one year the German Weather Service carried out an extensive ground measuring programme (temperature, humidity and wind) and produced cartographic representations of various climatic elements from the collected data. Air-hygienic information was incorporated from the emissions registers, from the data of the immissions registers for the Stuttgart region, and from the air measurement stations of the state measurement network.

The study results are summarised and depicted in the climate atlas with basic maps (1:100,000) and analysis maps of 1:20,000 (which corresponds to that of land-use plans). As an additional step, evaluated maps were produced with climatic and air-hygienic recommendations for planning.

The goal of the planning recommendations is first and foremost to motivate the planner towards a stronger consideration of climatic criteria. As such, a planning project should incorporate the standards of the 'Planning Recommendations' map.

With the assistance of the climatic analysis map and maps with recommendations for planning, the climatologists demand respect for climate-sensitive areas when planning decisions are taken.

### *Climatic analysis maps*

A significant component of the aforementioned study was the production of climate analysis maps depicting the local-climatic conditions in this region as a cartographic overview. The significant bases for this are the data material described above, topographic maps, city maps, land use plans, and aerial photographs.

One of the main features of the maps are 'climatopes'. Climatopes describe geographic areas with similar microclimatic characteristics. These are distinguished primarily by the daily thermal variation, the vertical roughness (wind field disruption), the topographical situation or exposure, and above all by the type of material land use. The level of emissions is included as an additional criterion for special climatopes. Since the microclimatic characteristics of built-up areas are determined significantly by the material land use and especially by the type of development, the climatopes are named after the dominant land-use type or building use.

The classification of climatope and cold air collection areas is not parcel-specific. Tolerances can range up to 100m, since both the contextual definition of borders and relative transient areas, and the accuracy of drawings due to the working material used must be taken into account. Technically detailed appraisals are necessary for more precise results. The signatures and symbols used in the maps correspond largely to the German VDI 3787, Part 1.

The ventilation of built areas with cold airflow has a significant function in Stuttgart, especially during low exchange weather conditions. Areas for cold air production and collection, which provide the nightly fresh-air supply, are therefore characterised distinctively in the climatic map. Also depicted are cold air blockage areas, narrow sections of valleys, winds descending from slopes, mountain and valley winds, and air induction passages for regional winds, along with data for air pollution.

Additionally there is information on the pollution from traffic emissions, on the inversion situation and on the wind distribution.

### *Maps with recommendations for planning*

A map with recommendations for planning contains an integrated assessment of the material represented in the climatic analysis map as it relates to concerns relevant in planning. The symbols give recommendations as to the sensitivity of certain land areas to changes in land use, from which climatically grounded conditions and measures can be derived in the context of planning and zoning. The planning recommendations primarily relate to structural changes in land use. For example, a change in the composition of vegetation exerts fewer climatic effects than large-scale soil capping measures and the erection of structures. Planning recommendations are not specific to the level of individual parcels, and tolerances can range up to 100m. More detailed questions in connection with site plans must be dealt with through special appraisals when necessary, especially in areas of high climatic and air-hygienic sensitivity. In addition to local characteristics, the principles that are given below form the basis for the planning recommendations.

Areas of vegetation have an important effect on the local climate, since on the one hand they cause the nightly fresh/cold air production, and on the other they exert a balancing thermal effect when they feature a high proportion of trees. Green spaces in the city and nearby areas exert a positive influence on their immediate vicinity in a microclimatic sense; vegetation on the border of developments also contributes to air exchange. Larger, connected green spaces represent the climatic and air-hygienic potential for regeneration. Particularly in the present spatial context of the built-up area, such green spaces are very important for air exchange. As far as possible, therefore, open spaces should not be converted to development from a climatic perspective.

Development in valleys can also be judged as negative in general, since the movement of cold, fresh air takes place in valleys under weak wind conditions and since valleys serve as air delivery corridors for stronger regional winds.

Hillsides in extended built-up areas should remain undeveloped, especially when development exists in valleys, since intensive cold- and fresh-air transport occurs here. The same is valid for gullies and ridges along these hillsides.

Saddle-like topographies on the backside of mountains serve as air induction corridors and should not be developed.

The climatic and air-hygienic perspective recommends encircling development with as much green space as possible as well as criss-crossing it with green corridors oriented to topographic features (e.g. ventilation passages; air induction corridors) in order to support air exchange.

Urban sprawl from numerous developments strewn across the landscape as well as the emergence of disruptive belts of built-up areas, e.g. through the convergence of neighbouring communities, are to be avoided. Urban development must be accompanied by close, large, fresh- and cold-air production areas and ventilation corridors.

## Climate information system Stuttgart – interactive module for climate atlas

Climatic studies performed for the project 'Stuttgart 21' and others, as well as the analysis of already existing data like the climate atlas, provided a wealth of information, mainly in digital form. Thus

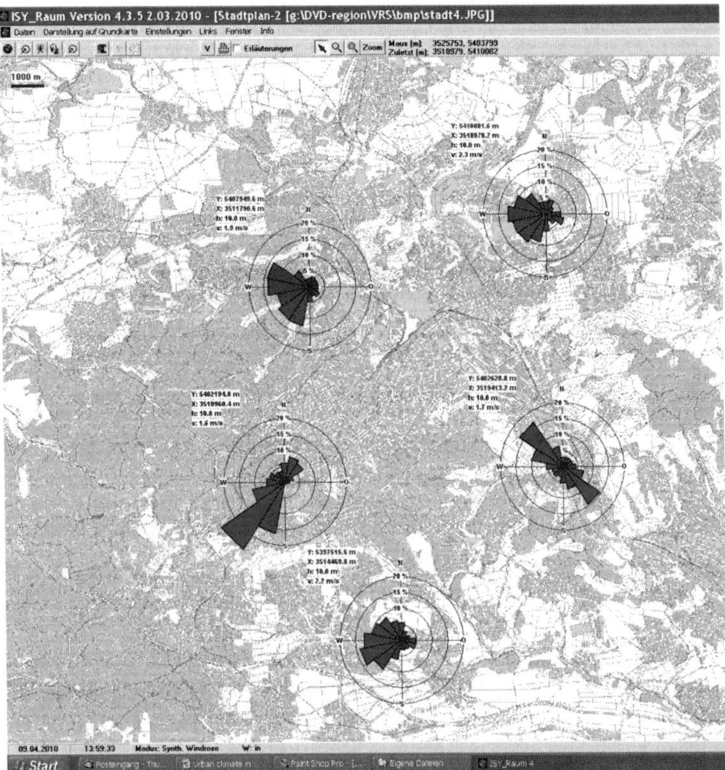


*Figure 22.5* Synthetic wind roses map produced with Urban Climate Information System Stuttgart on DVD.

Source: Urban Climate 21, 2008

it was possible to make the data available to experts as well as to a broader public by means of a special software on DVD-ROM. The new version 5 has been available since September 2008 (Urban Climate 21, 2008). The DVD contains more than 300 areal and line datasets, and a lot of text files, photos, pictures and figures (see Figure 22.5). A lot of maps are now available in the internet (City of Stuttgart, 2014).

## Climate atlas Region of Stuttgart 2008

Sustainable spatial development aims at durably preserving important ecologically protective goods and balancing functions in order to guarantee an environmentally friendly development of housing estates and infrastructure. Large-scale studies on the functions of open space were carried out in the context of the updating of the regional plan in combination with an environmental impact assessment in order to gain essential current information and to account for the planning legislation requirements. The 'Verband Region Stuttgart' (a political organisation for the regional development of Greater Stuttgart) had developed a GIS-based digital information and management system for all relevant protective goods. This data pool is supposed to be made available as a service for towns and municipalities in Greater Stuttgart, e.g. for the purposes of urban land use planning. Data on the protective good climate is one of the main elements of this 'environmental information system'. For this purpose the climate atlas of the Region Stuttgart was worked out by climatologists at the Department of Urban Climatology in the Office of Environmental Protection for the City of Stuttgart.

Climatic balancing functions such as the production of cold air and the transport of cold and fresh air are of great importance for people's health and well-being. This is why the regional plan from 1998 already presented the climatic functions of free spaces, protected as green areas or regional green corridors, on the basis of information and presentations of the landscape structure plan. Data from the climate atlas from 1992 was used for this purpose. This data is only available for parts of the region and it became necessary to update the climate atlas for the Region of Stuttgart on a digital basis.

The necessity for the working up of climatic concerns in the context of the updating of the regional plan is not least the compelling result of the new legal demands of the Strategic Environmental Assessment (SEA). A qualified analysis of the implications of the regional plan for the protection of a good climate was a major requirement for the legal security of the planning.

An important new aspect that adds to the legal requirements concerns global climate change. This can have particularly negative implications for the health of the resident population in the agglomerated areas of the region. Against this background, a forward-looking consideration of climatic balancing functions within spatial planning is of special significance.

The digital climate atlas for the region of Stuttgart from 2008 on the basis of a Geographic Information System (GIS) covers the whole area of the region (3,654km$^2$), for all 176 towns and municipalities. Digitisation allows for further analysis steps thanks to special software, e.g. wind field calculations, cold air drainage as well as the interaction with other relevant environmental data. This is a significant functional improvement compared to the climate atlas from 1992. The climate atlas is published in printed form and as a CD-ROM with a comprehensive set of maps as a PDF file. Texts and maps could be made available as PDF files on the homepage of the Verband Region Stuttgart (http://www.region-stuttgart.org) and the homepage (http://www.stadtklima-stuttgart.de).

In addition to the general accessibility of the information, the data will also be prepared in the context of a GIS-based digital information and management system in order to be available for towns and municipalities in a suitable format for further processing. The basic information within the climate atlas contains a general climatic classification of the region for factors such as wind, solar radiation, temperature and precipitation. Resulting from this, the regional situation of the air and the climatic concerns relevant for the planning are worked up and presented in texts and maps.

### *Thermal maps*

Thermal maps illustrate the results of the measuring flights (infrared thermography), which allow for a snapshot of the temperature distribution on a fine day and for the identification of differences in the temperature structures of a city or a landscape in the context of settlement.

### *Production and drainage of cold air, wind field calculations*

Region-wide calculations of the density and drainage of cold air were carried out on the basis of the digital surface model and land use. Since areas producing cold air and cold air catchment areas during temperature inversion weather conditions bring about fresh air supply during the night, they have a substantial function for the aeration of settlement areas.

The digital climate atlas also provides detailed information on wind conditions. Synthetic wind field calculations allow for an evaluation of local wind conditions in the region. As wind determines the spread of air pollutants, it plays a major role in air hygiene. Knowledge of aeration conditions within settled areas gained from the information about wind and cold air provides an important foundation for assessing spatial planning at both regional and municipal level.

### Climatic analysis maps

Just as within the climate atlas from 1992, climatic analysis maps represent a substantial result of the analysis (see Plate 22.1). The climatic analysis maps, which are now available in digital form for the whole region, show local climatic features as a spatial outline. On the one hand the map gives a differentiated depiction of areas with a particular suitability, such as areas producing cold air, cold air catchment areas or climate-relevant ventilation lanes. These areas are of great significance for the balance of climate and air hygiene. On the other hand the climatic map shows settled areas which are defined as climatopes with certain microclimatic characteristics. They are basically determined by the actual land use and especially by the type of development. Climatic compensation areas and climatopes can be influenced by a change in the land use, especially by sealing and development. This is especially important in the case of planning designations in the spatial and functional context of climatically polluted areas. Climate-relevant open land with a direct connection to polluted settlement areas is highly sensitive to changes of use.

### Maps with recommendations for planning

The climate atlas serves as technical support for the regional plan and land use planning. This is why there are maps for the assessment of aspects relevant for planning, which contain area classifications with different indications for changes of use or the requirements to take particular steps. The indications are summarised in eight categories (see the sub-section 'Maps with recommendations for planning' in 'Climate Atlas Stuttgart (1992), p. 301). They refer to undeveloped free spaces as well as to structurally used areas. The indications refer to the effects of structural uses and changes of use on the climatic situation (see Plate 22.2).

### Prognosis of the implications of climate change

What is studied in more detail apart from the climatic situation are the changes resulting from global climate change on the thermal stress. The climate prognoses by the Intergovernmental Panel on Climate Change (IPCC, 2013) expect a global temperature increase up to 5.4°C in this century. The temperatures in turn have a strong influence on the bioclimate. The term 'bioclimate' is defined as 'the sum of all climatic factors influencing living organisms', in this case especially the influence on human beings. Factors like heat, cold, and air humidity strongly influence people's well-being, working capacity and health. Numerous epidemiological studies prove that the adaptability of sensitive people will be overstrained more quickly in these cases – especially in the case of a predisposition for cardiovascular and respiratory diseases.

For one thing, the climate atlas shows the actual situation of heat stress and cold stress on the basis of long-term measurements. Nowadays an area of about 5 per cent with more than 30 days with heat stress is a result of high perceived temperatures in this region.

Assuming that the number of days with heat stress will double in the case of climate warming, large parts of Greater Stuttgart (57 per cent of the territory) would have to expect more than 30

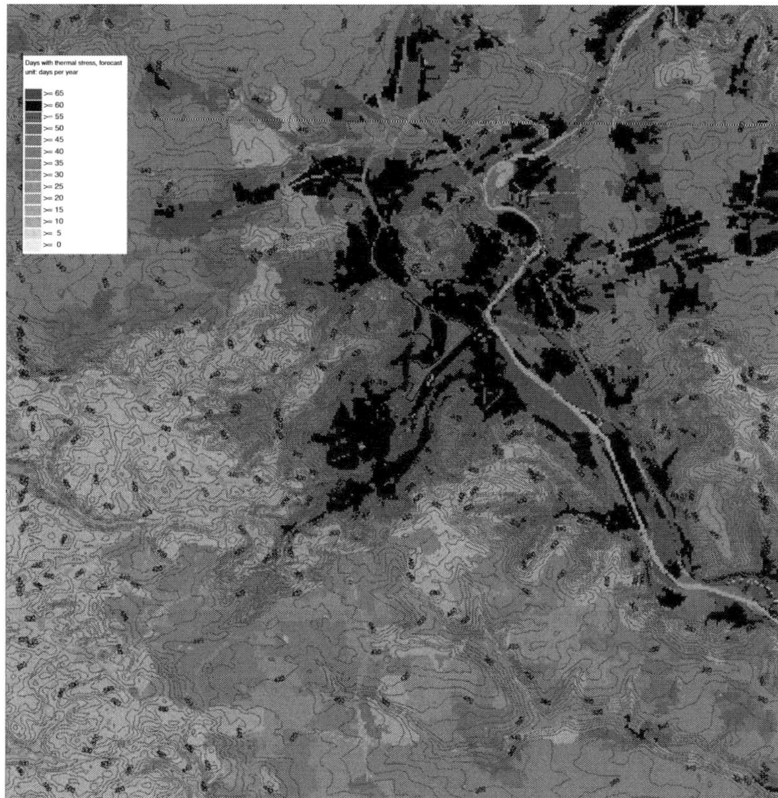


*Figure 22.6* Heat days in the Region Stuttgart 2070–2100.

Source: Verband Region Stuttgart, 2008

days with heat stress and in some parts more than 60 days, i.e. that a significantly higher percentage of people would be exposed to heavy heat pollution in the summer (see Figure 22.6). The prognosis shows that this will be a big challenge for regional planning. What plays a major role in this context are the preservation of climatic compensation areas on which fresh and cold air is produced and sufficient aeration is guaranteed.

## Outlook

The global temperature increase that will also influence the maximum temperatures is a new challenge for the cities because, by reason of the urban heat island effect (UHI), the temperatures in cities are higher than in the surroundings. Further, the vulnerability in cities is high because more and more people are living in cities and in many countries the number of older people is increasing. In Germany about 40 per cent of the people will be over 60 years of age by 2050. For a few years there has been discussion in Germany on urban climate change adaptation strategies (BMU, 2009, 2011). Several cities like Berlin, Hamburg, Stuttgart (Landeshauptstadt Stuttgart, 2013), and others have worked out ideas for climate adaptation. Since levels of vulnerability vary in different regions, particular strategies are necessary.

On 17 December 2008, the Federal Cabinet adopted the German Strategy for Adaptation to Climate Change (BMU, 2009). This created a framework for adapting to climate change impact in Germany. It primarily describes the contribution of the Federation, thus acting as a guide for other actors. The strategy lays the foundation for a medium-term, step-by-step process undertaken in cooperation with the federal states and other civil groups and is aimed at assessing the risks of climate change, identifying the possible need for action, defining appropriate goals and developing and implementing options for adaptation measures. In BMU (2009: 40) it is mentioned, that:

> Spatial, regional and physical development planning represent the start of the risk avoidance chain, since they develop precautionary regional concepts, use planning documents which are legally binding and valid for long periods, and may involve long lead times before the contents of the plans are put into practice. Spatial planning has the important function of reconciling different claims on the same space.
>
> With the existing legal and planning instruments, spatial planning can support both mitigation and adaptation. The fact that natural hazards may occur more frequently can place restrictions on the use of natural resources. At the same time it gives rise to great usage pressure, since adaptation measures frequently require space as well. Spatial planning, by developing models for adaptable and resilient spatial structures, can play a pioneering role in ensuring a robust and flexible response to the impacts of all societal change processes on spatial structure.

In August 2011 the Federal Building Code was amended. Now climate adaptation is a task of equal importance to climate mitigation in all planning processes. Today most of the urban climate atlases show the current climate situation. In the future it will be necessary to also produce prognostic maps for 2050 and 2100. Further maps which show the vulnerability (e.g. heat stress, floods, scarcity of water) are necessary.

## PART II: APPLICATION

### Introduction

Global climate change is upon us. Climate change is a process that is no longer completely stoppable. Extreme weather conditions, such as an increasing incidence of floods, storms, heat waves and droughts, are all clear indicators of climate change and its severe repercussions. Climate change and its impact present us with a dual challenge. The first is climate protection and the associated need to reduce carbon emissions and so minimise climate change. The second is adjustment: in other words, the task of preparing for the effects of inevitable climate change. Equally important is the endeavour to adjust to the inevitable effects of climate change.

One significant way in which to approach the adjustment process is by taking the climate into account in urban planning (City of Stuttgart, 2010). It is evident that the efforts invested over decades by the Section of Urban Climatology of the Office for Environmental Protection in Stuttgart to protect the local climate serve, at the same time, as an effective approach to the process of adjusting to climate change. In Stuttgart, this applies in particular to heat in the city centre. Measures undertaken here include the maintenance and expansion of green spaces such as woodland and parks in the city, safeguarding vital fresh air corridors and air exchange channels, as well as roadside, railway track and roof greening.

The Federal German Building Code (2011), Article 1 provides the main basis for taking climate into account in urban planning. It sets out the objectives and principles of construction management planning, including consideration of environmental concerns, ruling that the natural foundation for human existence, in particular the soil, climate and air, be maintained and safeguarded. This raises 'air and climate' to the status of planning factors.

The statutory category of designations that may justifiably be listed in development plans opens up a range of effective possibilities for the implementation of principles developed from the aspect of urban climatology and of climate protection. The designation of the type and degree of building and land use (Art. 9 para. 1 no. 1) determines, for instance, whether the land is utilised with due consideration to climate protection. Also of significance are the following possible designations admitted by the Code in relation to the creation of green spaces in urban conurbations, providing scope for the planning of green areas and open spaces with due consideration of areas for cold air generation and fresh air corridors:

No.10 spaces to be kept free from built development, with their use;
No.15 public and private green spaces, such as parks, allotment gardens, sports grounds and playgrounds, camping sites and bathing areas, cemeteries;
No.18 (a) agricultural land and
(b) woodland;
No.20 measures for the protection, conservation and development of topsoil, of the natural environment and of the landscape;
No.25 (a) planting of trees, shrubs and greenery of any other kind
(b) obligations relating to planting and to the preservation of trees, shrubs and greenery of any other kind and of water bodies.

## Fresh air corridors

Topographic structures such as stream and meadow valleys provide natural green belts which at the same time represent preferred pathways for ventilation. Keeping these free of encroachment by buildings does not necessitate a great deal of persuasion, given that aspects of landscape and nature conservation also support the urban climatology arguments.

The course is set in favour of retaining undeveloped fresh air corridors within the framework of the Land Use Plan, in which the structures to be developed are already set out in the overriding regional plan by the depicted green belts and green divides.

### *Schelmenäcker district (Stuttgart-Feuerbach)*

In the Schelmenäcker area of Stuttgart Feuerbach, plans were presented for the extension of an existing residential building area near a hillside zone reaching down from the woodland-covered Lemberg Mountain to the centre of the town. The plans envisaged development through the corridor leading up to the hillside. A strip just 7m wide would have remained undeveloped from the hillside zone in the form of roadside greenery.

During the course of the planning deliberations, the urban climatological viewpoint was put forward that the 7m wide planted strip would not be capable of fulfilling any useful urban climatological function in terms of interlocking the natural landscape of the Lemberg range of hills with the densely developed town centre of Feuerbach. It was only by maintaining a green divide of around 100m in width that it would be possible to create the conditions in which the climatic and

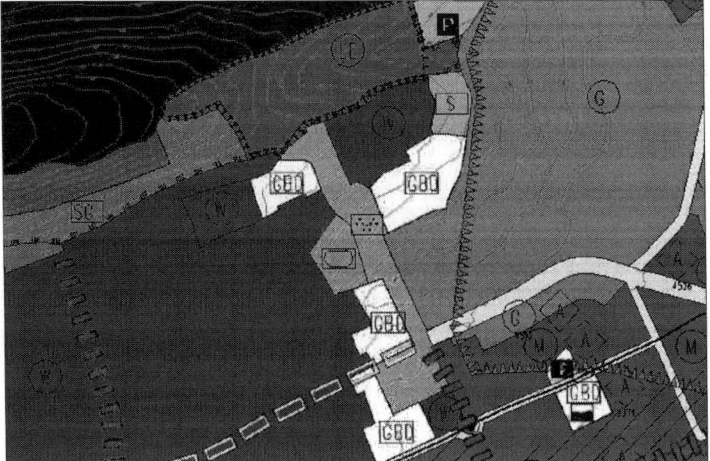

*Figure 22.7* Binding development plan Schelmenäcker with green corridor.
Source: FNP, 2010

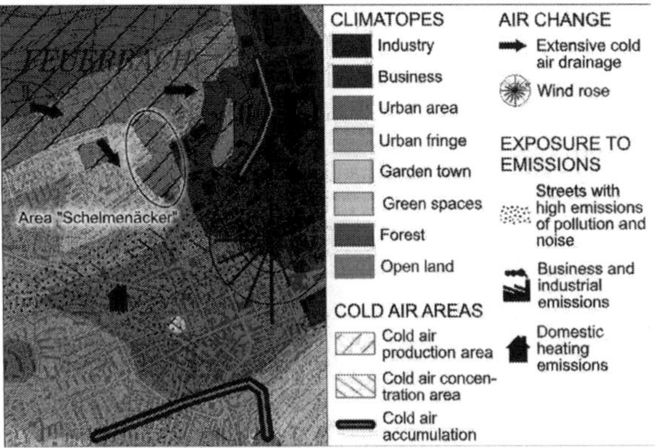


*Figure 22.8* Climatic Analysis map Schelmenäcker district.
Source: Verband Region Stuttgart, 2008

ecological balancing function of the Lemberg area could be able to effectively impact the town close to the ground. Figure 22.7 shows the binding development plan for Schelmenacker with green corridor. Figures 22.8 and 22.9 show the climatic situation and the planning recommendations in the climate atlas for the region of Stuttgart (Verband Region Stuttgart, 2008). Figure 22.10 shows the green corridor.

The urban climatological arguments put forward fell on receptive ears in the urban planning department, and finally resulted in a completely changed development concept. This was then implemented in the form of two separate development islands, each developed outward from their outer boundaries instead of centrally across the hillside zone and separated by a wide green divide.

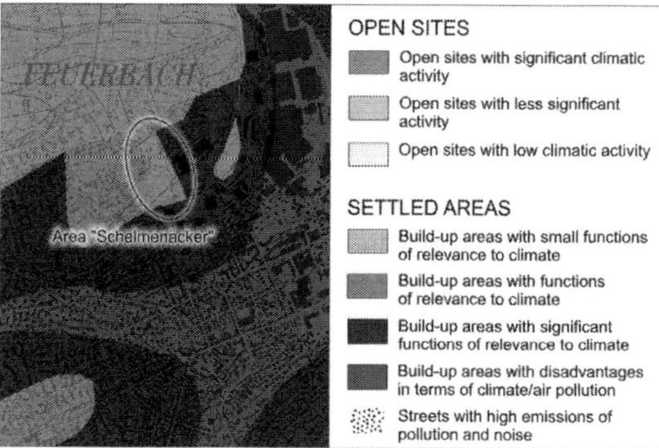


*Figure 22.9* Map with Recommendations for Planning Schelmenäcker district.
Source: Verband Region Stuttgart, 2008

*Figure 22.10* Green corridor Schelmenäcker district.
Source: City of Stuttgart, 2010

The illustrations show the result of the changed land use concept and also the use made of the green space created by the changed plan. This not only upgrades the surrounding residential areas, but also assumes a climatic function which has a positive impact on the town centre.

### *Hillside development plan*

In the form of the hillside development plan (Rahmenplan Halbhöhenlagen) (Landeshauptstadt Stuttgart, 2008), what has been termed a 'different planning model' exists for the districts of Stuttgart's inner city basin formation. Performed prior to the process of urban land use planning, this model has a relevant role to play in urban planning and has helped to ensure the creation and maintenance of green and open spaces in the sensitive system existing in the hillside areas. The climate-active areas of vegetation on the hillsides which are not used for building help support thermally induced air exchange close to the ground, which contributes towards producing

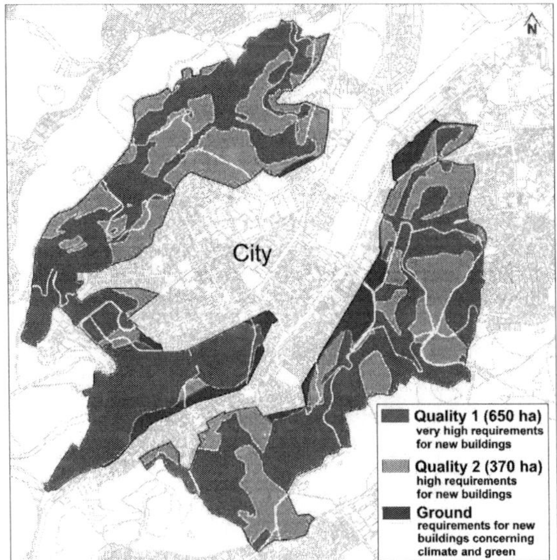


*Figure 22.11* Hillside Development Plan Stuttgart.

Source: Landeshauptstadt Stuttgart, 2008

improved air hygiene conditions in Stuttgart in the form of nightly downslope winds. Both in terms of wind dynamics and also thermally, extended building development in the hillside areas would have a negative impact on the nightly downflow of cold air.

The urban climatological and ecological arguments are summarised in the form of quality areas. These quality areas are assigned to distinctive requirements and measures outlined by the plan (see Figure 22.11).

At the same time, the outline plan takes consideration of the fact that isolated urban climatological assessments of minor individual building projects encounter problems of scale if the changes anticipated as a result of the building project have been described in quantitative terms.

## Urban green

Green belt policy and green space planning are the most promising areas of municipal influence with respect to their impact on urban climatology and climate protection. The provision of green areas and open spaces benefits the urban climate and the appeal of the city in equal measure. Areas of vegetation bind the greenhouse gas carbon dioxide ($CO_2$). Green spaces serve as place-keepers, and in this way eliminate other uses which could negatively impact climate protection due to potential emissions of relevance for the climate. The temperature-sinking significance of areas of vegetation is important.

According to the climate atlas of the region of Stuttgart, the city of Stuttgart is defined as a core city climatope with heat island effect and significant influence on the wind situation; the planning recommendations characterise the areas as built-up areas with disadvantages in terms of climate and air pollution and in need of renewal from the point of view of urban climate.

Besides forests, agriculturally used spaces, and green spaces, the following possibilities for green in the city exist.

### *Greened-over urban railway tracks (grass tracks)*

Stuttgart has plenty of experience in the construction of tram lines with grassed-over tracks (see Figure 22.12). The total rail length of the 'city train' in Stuttgart is about 250km, of which 50km are green rails.

This makes the track construction a comparatively complex process and increases the laying costs for a new track section considerably. In the long term, certain savings may be expected in the process of track maintenance, as the cleaning and exchanging of the rail ballast and tamping are no longer required. Track lawn mowing is still performed manually but is relatively simple; in the future this process is certain to be further rationalised through the use of mechanised alternatives. Also worthy of mention is an experiment carried out by the tram company Stuttgarter Straßenbahnen AG involving the use of turf to retroactively green over existing ballast and sleeper tracks. Should this method prove successful, it would be possible to green over not only new track sections but also suitable stretches of existing stock.

### *Roadside greenery*

There are already around 38,000 trees planted alongside Stuttgart's streets. Almost all traffic islands have already been greened over. By maintaining and expanding this significant existing plant stock, major urban climatological air hygiene objectives and also municipal climate protection targets can be pursued alongside the process of implementing attractive urban planning proposals. The enhanced attraction of these areas for pedestrians and cyclists and also the associated reduction in the traffic speed and volume of private road users where renaturation projects are implemented (reduced lane widths for cars) deserve particular mention.

*Figure 22.12* Green rails in Stuttgart.

Source: City of Stuttgart, 2010

Extensive greening brings about bioclimatic benefits, and avenue-style tree planting not only provides a $CO_2$ reducing effect, which is beneficial as a means of climate protection, but also offers a way of adapting to climate change (providing shade, cooling, and more even moisture balance). Also, importantly, roadside trees with dense foliage help absorb air pollution and filter particulates from the ambient air. The uncapped soil area accommodating the roadside green is able to absorb and store rainwater, helping to relieve the stress on the sewage system which is likely to occur with the expected increasing frequency of heavy rainfall.

### *Roof greening*

Roof greening can also be set out as a legal requirement in the development plan. The benefits of roof greening in terms of the ecology, building structure and architectural/urban planning, have been extensively analysed in the past and have been scientifically proven. To increase green areas in Stuttgart, houses with flat roofs normally have to be built with green roofs. From 1986 to 2010 there was also a municipal grant programme for citizens for roof renewal with roof greening. A new grant programme has started in 2014. This helps alleviate the extreme values of surface temperatures both over different times of day and different seasons. Where planting is present, this brings the annual roof surface temperature fluctuation of around 100°C on ungreened roofs down to only 30°C. The reduced thermal load means lower material wear in the roof construction, which serves to reduce costs.

In summer, a large proportion of the solar energy that radiates from a greened roof is used to evaporate water. This helps to provide protection against summer heat. In winter, the vegetation layer and the roof substrate create an additional component layer to reduce the passage of heat. As a result, roof greening makes a modest contribution towards saving energy used for heating in winter, and for cooling in the summer. This in turn reduces the release of damaging greenhouse gases and helps protect the climate as one of the natural bases for life. Other advantages of green roofs are the retention of rainwater, dust fixation and new living spaces for animals.

In order to maximise on the positive environmental aspects of using solar energy, alongside scope for greening, flat roofs also offer ideal conditions for using solar energy with the installation of a solar thermal or photovoltaic system (see Figure 22.13).

### *Inner development before outer development*

The city of Stuttgart is working towards the sustained development of the city based on the principle of 'inner development before outer development'. In this context it is important to work towards a climate-optimised concentration of urban structures (see Figure 22.14). Although concentration can contribute towards reduced energy consumption and so help to protect the climate, it also serves to intensify the heat island effect and so may be considered counterproductive in terms of adjustment to climate change. In order to counteract the negative effects of concentration, functionally networked free spaces and their careful design are needed, as well as minimal soil capping, the thermal insulation of houses, and also greening and shading effects using deciduous trees.

## Conclusions

Taking urban climatology into account in urban planning has a long tradition in Stuttgart. It is an important topic, which is fixed in the German Federal Building Code. Stuttgart's practices can very well serve as a model for other cities in the world. In facing global climate change, urban

*Figure 22.13* Green roof in Stuttgart.
Source: City of Stuttgart, E. Kohfink

*Figure 22.14* Example of climate-optimised inner development (Area Rossbollengässle in Stuttgart-West).
Source: Unpublished, photo taken by E. Kohfink, City of Stuttgart

climatology is getting more and more important. Urban climatology in urban planning is a very important measure of adaptation to climate change. The city of Stuttgart enforces the efforts on urban climatology. For example in a European project has started on the urban heat island, considering the heat stress with calculations and measurements and with the development of climate adaptation strategies. Future city planning for Stuttgart will instigate a support system for developing the concept of inner instead of outer development. City quarters have to be developed more densely, but with a high quality concerning urban climate.

## References


Baumüller, J. (2006). Implementation of climatic aspects in urban development – the example Stuttgart. In: *Proceedings of PGBC Symposium 2006: Urban Climate + Urban Greenery*. Hong Kong, 2 December. Hong Kong: the Professional Green Building Council.

BMU (2009). *Deutsche Anpassungsstrategie an den Klimawandel (German Strategy for Adaptation to Climate Change)*, adopted by the German federal cabinet on 17 December 2008. Available at: http://www.bmu.de/klimaschutz/downloads/doc/42783.php (Accessed 16 December 2013).

BMU (2011). *'Aktionsplan Anpassung' zur Deutschen Anpassungsstrategie an den Klimawandel*, adopted by the German federal cabinet on 31 August 2011. Available at: http://www.bmu.de/klimaschutz/downloads/doc/47641.php (Accessed 16 December 2013).

City of Stuttgart (2010). *Global Climate Change – Adaptation and Mitigation: The New Challenge Facing Urban Climatology*. Publication series No. 3/2010. Stuttgart: Environmental Protection Office. Available at: http://www.stadtklima-stuttgart.de/index.php?klima_klimawandel_heft-3-2010 (Accessed 16 December 2013).

City of Stuttgart (2014). Urban climate viewer. Available at http://www.stadtklima-stuttgart.de/index.php?climate_urban_climate_viewer.

Federal German Building Code 2012 (Baugesetzbuch, BauGB) (2011). BGBl. I S. 2414 last update: 30.07.2011. Germany: Federal Ministry of Transport, Building and Housing.

FNP (2010). *Flächennutzungsplan 2010*. Stuttgart: Office of Urban Planning and Urban Renewal.

IPCC (2013). *Climate Change 2013: The Physical Science Basis*. Contribution of Working Group I to the Fifth Assessment Report of the Intergovernmental Panel on Climate Change. Cambridge and New York: Cambridge University Press. Available at: http://www.ipcc.ch/report/ar5/wg1/#.UluSMKzokfU (Accessed 16 December 2013).

Klimaatlas (1992). *Nachbarschaftsverband Stuttgart (Stuttgart Regional Federation), Climate Study for the Area of the Stuttgart Regional Federation and Bordering Areas of the Stuttgart Region*. Stuttgart: Landeshauptstadt Stuttgart, Amt fur Umweltschutz, Abteilung Stadtklimatologie.

Landeshauptstadt Stuttgart (2008). *Rahmenplan Halbhöhenlage-(Hillside Development Outline Plan)*. Stuttgart: Office of Urban Planning and Urban Renewal. Available at: http://www.stuttgart.de/img/mdb/publ/15686/29825.pdf (Accessed 16 December 2013).

Landeshauptstadt Stuttgart (2013). *Klimawandel – Anpassungskonzept*. Series of Office of Environmental Protection, 1/2013. Stuttgart: Office of Environmental Protection, Department of Urban Climatology. Available at: http://www.stadtklima-stuttgart.de/stadtklima_filestorage/download/kliks/KLIMAKS-Broschuere-2013.pdf (Accessed 16 December 2013).

Ministerium für Verkehr und Infrastruktur Baden-Württemberg (ed.) (2012). *Climate Booklet for Urban Development – Indications for Urban Land-use Planning*. Stuttgart: Ministerium für Verkehr und Infrastruktur Baden-Württemberg. Available at: http://www.staedtebauliche-klimafibel.de/ (Accessed 16 December 2013).

Urban Climate 21 (2008*). Basic Materials for Urban Climate and for Planning* [DVD-ROM]. Baumüller, J. Available: Office of Environmental Protection, City of Stuttgart.

VDI (1997). *VDI-Standard: VDI 3787 Part 1 Environmental Meteorology – Climate and Air Pollution Maps for Cities and Regions*. Berlin: Beuth Verlag.

Verband Region Stuttgart (ed.) (2008). *Klimaatlas Region Stuttgart*, Verband Region Stuggart, No. 26. Stuttgart: Verband Region Stuttgart. Available at: http://www.stadtklima-stuttgart.de/index.php?klima_klimaatlas_region (Accessed 16 December 2013).

Chapter 23

# Urban climatic map studies in Spain

## Bilbao

*Juan A. Acero and Lutz Katzschner*

### Introduction

Bilbao municipality is part of a big urban area known as Gran Bilbao, which is located in the northern part of the Iberian Peninsula. It is a coastal area beside the Atlantic Ocean and is characterised by complex topography. It includes 22 municipalities in an area of 25km × 10km. The municipality of Bilbao covers the biggest area (10 per cent) of Gran Bilbao.

Bilbao city centre (43° 15′ 42″ N and 2° 55′ 43″ W) is about 17km from the sea. The River Nervión flows through the middle of the urban area that is oriented in a SE–NW direction following two mountain ranges that run parallel to the waterway (see Figure 23.1).

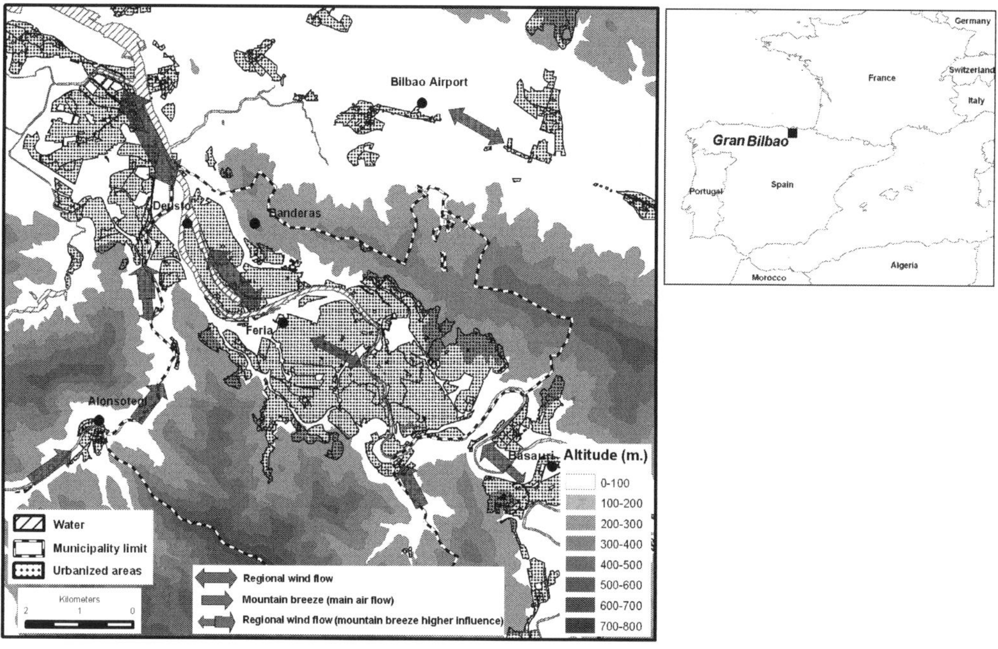


*Figure 23.1* Gran Bilbao's geographical location inside the Iberian Peninsula and representation of predominant wind directions in the surroundings of Bilbao municipality together with the locations of meteorological stations.

Source: Acero *et al.*, 2013a

In recent decades, the urban area has experienced significant change. In the 1970s, heavy industry was the basis of the economy, but nowadays Bilbao has transformed into a city of services; however, the industrial sector is still present in the region. A great amount of effort has gone into regenerating the urban area, improving environmental aspects and changing the land use of the former industrial activities. The municipality of Bilbao reached 351,965 inhabitants in 2011. It can be considered a medium-sized city, quite densely built-up and without many open spaces. Complex topography has always conditioned urban development and most of the population gathers in the lower part of the valley in an area of 16km$^2$ reaching 21,200 persons/km$^2$.

## Background climatic information

In the past, most climatic studies in Gran Bilbao focused on air quality due to the presence of heavily polluting industries (Millan *et al.*, 1984). Sulphur dioxide ($SO_2$) used to be the most problematic atmospheric pollutant several decades ago, causing severe episodes in the late 1960s (Zorraquino, 1971). In December 1977, Gran Bilbao was declared a 'polluted atmosphere zone'. With the implementation of specific actions and efficient policies, air pollution levels improved significantly at the start of the 1990s. However, it was not until the year 2000 that the declaration of 'polluted atmosphere zone' was laid off (Acero *et al.*, 2005).

It is known that complex topography and proximity of the sea are important factors that influence local meteorological conditions in the region (Millan *et al.*, 1984, 1987). Winds at surface levels are usually decoupled from the synoptic situation at higher levels in a way that air masses adapt to the topography (especially under stable atmospheric conditions) following the direction of the valley (Millan *et al.*, 1984; Acero *et al.*, 2007). Bilbao urban area is significantly influenced by sea breeze and cold air drainage winds. Airflow characteristics have significant diurnal and seasonal variations (Acero *et al.*, 2013a) that affect urban heat island (UHI) intensity (see Table 23.1). The cooling potential of sea breezes is responsible for an urban cold island (UCI) after midday that is especially intense during spring and summer when the highest sea breeze intensity occurs (see Figure 23.2). On the contrary, cold air drainage winds are more intense in autumn and enter the urban area especially during the night, causing an important number of surface temperature inversions. These are

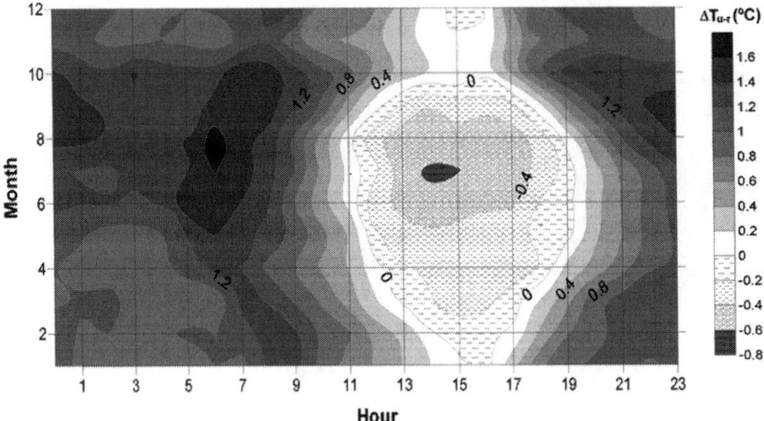


*Figure 23.2* Hourly ΔTu-r along the year between Feria (urban location) and Bilbao Airport (rural location).

Source: Acero *et al.*, 2013a

*Table 23.1* Seasonal and yearly mean ΔTu-r between Feria (urban location) and Bilbao Airport (rural location).

| | *Daily mean ΔTu-r (°C)* |
|---|---|
| Winter | 0.75 (±0.54) |
| Spring | 0.55 (±0.63) |
| Summer | 0.70 (±0.66) |
| Autumn | 0.88 (±0.55) |
| Yearly mean | 0.73 (±0.60) |

Source: Acero *et al.*, 2013a

more frequent in nearby rural valleys than in Bilbao due to UHI effects. During autumn and winter, temperature inversions in Bilbao occur during 30 per cent of the night-time hours while the rural areas reach 60 per cent of occurrence (Acero *et al.*, 2013a). Hourly maximum temperature anomaly (ΔTu-r,max) occurs just after sunrise (see Figure 23.2) and mean UHI intensity is highest in autumn in relation to airflow characteristics during this period of the year (see Table 23.1).

Inside Bilbao municipality, climate variables (e.g. air temperature and wind speed) vary from site to site depending on their location (i.e. exposure to local/regional ventilation systems) and on the characteristics of the urban development. In this context, and considering that municipalities are responsible for their own urban planning, it makes sense to develop a specific urban climatic map (UCMap) for Bilbao. The first UCMap in Bilbao was completed in 2012.

## Method used to develop Bilbao's urban climatic map

The method for Bilbao's UCMap was based on calculations made with different Geographic Information System (GIS) layers, climate measurements and urban climate expert knowledge. The GIS layers included information on the thermal load (i.e. stored heat intensity) and dynamic potential (i.e. air ventilation and exchange capacity) of the urban area. By combining the layers with adequate weighting factors, urban thermal comfort was analysed, and consequently urban planning recommendations were derived. The weighting factors given to each GIS layer were calibrated with specific climate measurements inside the urban area. The results of the GIS calculations showed different climatopes, i.e. areas with relative homogeneous urban climate characteristics that have similar impacts on thermal comfort. These were described in an urban climatic analysis map (UC-AnMap) together with the main airflow characteristics.

Previous to the development of the UC-AnMap, two aspects that condition urban climate were analysed (see Figure 23.3):

- surface thermal load considering land-use characteristics (i.e. type of urban development);
- ventilation properties to account for air exchange capacity and the removal of urban heat.

The required data for the UC-AnMap was:

- general land-use description of the municipality (woodland, farmland, urban, suburban, etc.);
- building characteristics (location, surface covered and height);
- presence of urban vegetation (calculated from satellite images);
- airflow characteristics (regional winds and thermally induced circulation patterns);
- topography (digital elevation model and information on slopes).

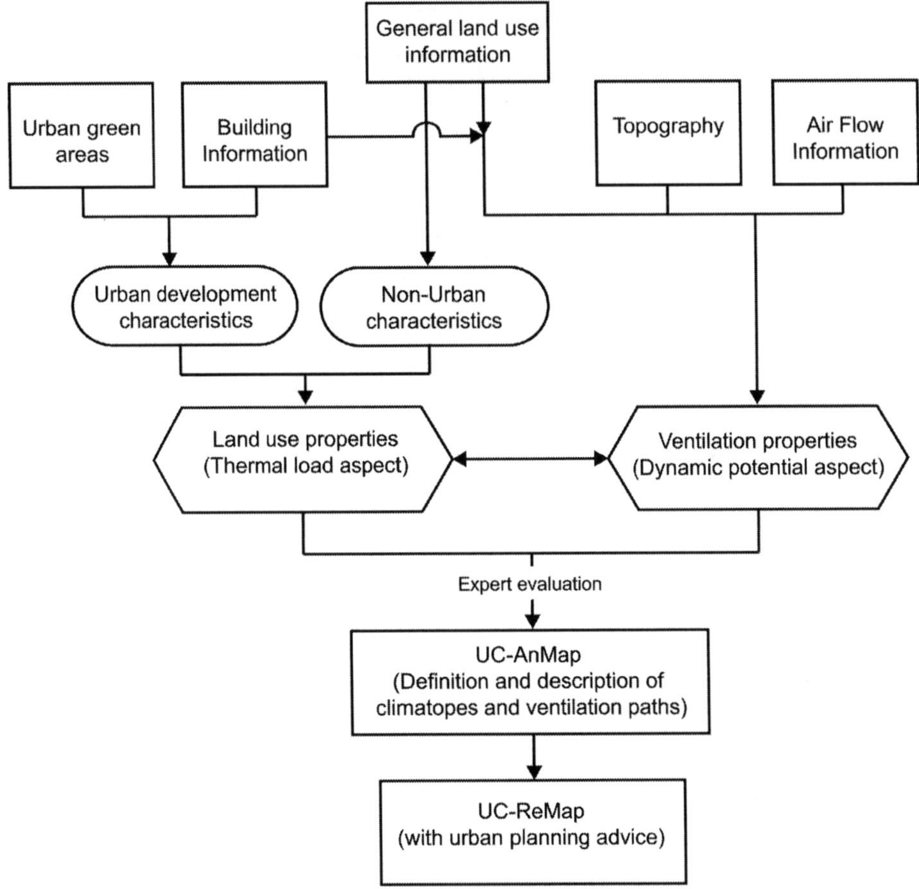


*Figure 23.3* Methodology for Bilbao Urban Climatic Map (UCMap).
Source: Acero *et al.*, 2013b

Finally, thermal load and dynamic potential aspects were integrated in five GIS layers (see Figure 23.4) to derive the Bilbao UC-AnMap with a resolution of 100m. These layers are:

- *Building volume*: affects heat storage capacity due to the trapping of solar radiation and the reduction of sky view factor (SVF) that slows the night-time radiative cooling effect and thus the release of urban heat.
- *Building surface fraction*: describes the effect on heat storage capacity and ventilation due to urban permeability to wind.
- *Green areas*: includes the effect of vegetation on the urban surface energy balance considering that green areas can reduce the air temperature in the surroundings, and thus thermal load.
- *Ventilation paths*: describes the effect on reducing urban heat load by providing cold air to the urban area. These paths are conditioned by the influence of surface roughness and topographical structures in regional winds and thermally induced circulations (e.g. cold air drainage winds).

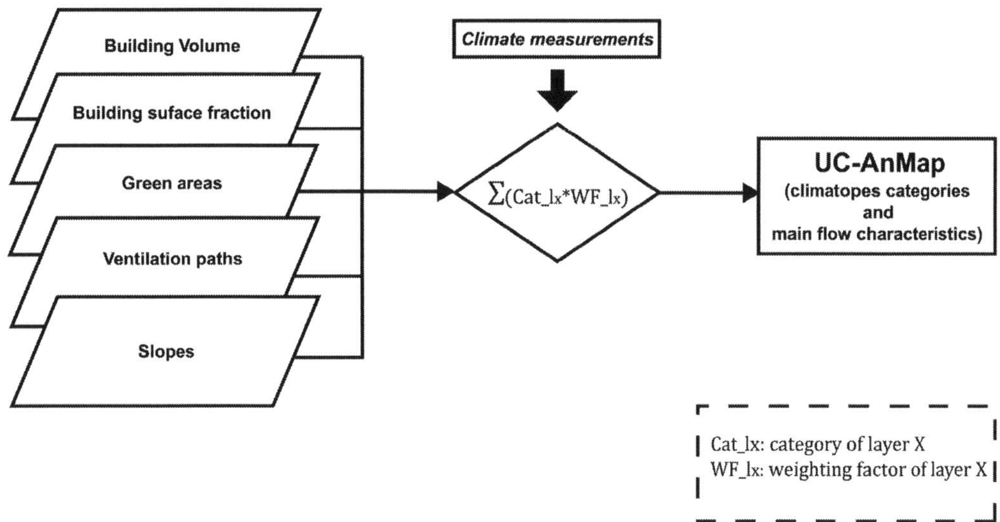


*Figure 23.4* Combination of GIS layers with weighting factors based on measurements.
Source: Acero *et al.*, 2013b

- *Slopes*: includes the effect on ventilation. Especially with regional winds, urban structures at different heights turn out to be more permeable and heat release increases. Also, local thermally induced circulations (i.e. downslope and upslope air movement) can occur inside the urban area.

In addition to the calculations of roughness parameters for the Bilbao urban area (Acero *et al.*, 2013b), urban climate expert knowledge was essential to evaluate regional airflow conditions and define the ventilation properties of the urban area (i.e. ventilation paths). Specific climate measurements inside the urban area turned out to be critical in order to characterise and define climatopes, and finally validate the UC-AnMap (see Figure 23.4). Climate variables was measured during specific time periods and in different areas of the city using stationary and mobile devices. The measuring sites were selected considering: urban development characteristics (i.e. building height, building surface friction, presence of green areas), distance to the bottom of the valley (height/slope), and distance to the non-perturbed sea breeze front in the NW border of the urban area.

The description of the resulting climatopes in Bilbao UC-AnMap was the basis for developing the urban climatic recommendation map (UC-ReMap) that includes specific climate criteria for urban development.

This methodology for the UCMap makes easier to work with different urban planning scenarios.

## Bilbao urban climatic map

Six land-use categories for Bilbao urban area have been defined based on climatic characteristics (i.e. thermal load). Their characteristics and the frequency of occurrence are shown in Table 23.2.

*Table 23.2* Description of urban land-use characteristics for climate purpose in Bilbao.

| | *Building surface fraction (%)* | *Building reference height (m)* | *Presence of vegetation* | *Percentage of occurrence (%)* |
|---|---|---|---|---|
| Open-set high-rise | 10–40 | ≥ 20 | None–Low | 23.8 |
| Open-set mid-rise | 10–40 | 10–20 | None–Low | 25.1 |
| Open-set low-rise | 10–40 | < 10 | Low–Medium | 12.3 |
| Compact mid-rise | ≥ 40 | 20–30 | None | 17.1 |
| Compact low-rise | ≥ 40 | 10–20 | None | 4.8 |
| Extensive low-rise | ≥ 10 | < 10 | None–Low | 12.5 |

Source: Acero *et al.*, 2013b

Considering the topography that surrounds Bilbao and the main airflow characteristics in the area, two types of ventilation paths have been defined in the UCMap:

- ventilation paths that incorporate airflow to the urban area mainly from regional winds channelled along the main valley axis; and
- ventilation paths caused by cold air drainage flow from rural hillsides and other minor valleys.

The combination of the five GIS layers that include information on urban development characteristics (i.e. thermal load) and the ventilation properties (i.e. dynamic potential) of Bilbao result in seven categories of climatopes based on thermal comfort impact: cold air production areas, fresh air production areas, mixed climate, and four areas with different heat levels (from low to high). These are in agreement with climate measurements.

Bilbao UC-AnMap (see Figure 23.5a) includes all the relevant climate phenomena occurring in urban areas and consequently is the basic climate knowledge from which recommendations for urban planning are derived, i.e. the UC-ReMap (see Figure 23.5b). The high dynamic potential of the region is a very important aspect in reducing heat accumulation in Bilbao, and thus conditions significantly pedestrian thermal comfort inside the urban area. The river waterway is a strategic ventilation path that allows cold and fresh air to enter the middle of the city. Similarly, thermal load can also be mitigated by cold air drainage flow provided by topographical features. Both ventilation systems need to be carefully considered during the urban planning process since strategic actions could be taken to extend the cooling effects to wider areas (i.e. low roughness elements, small air corridors, street orientation, and so on.)

The definition of recommendations (see Table 23.3) is focused on relevant aspects of each climatope. These are presented in an easy and clear way for urban planners to understand climate issues. Three urban climate sensitivity zones are defined in Bilbao UC-ReMap: areas to preserve, areas to attend climate, and areas to improve.

Redefinition or actualisation of the recommendations will be necessary to include changes in urban morphology. Thus, before new urban planning starts a revision of the UCMap is mandatory.

Since recommendations in Bilbao UC-ReMap are developed in collaboration between urban climatologists and urban planners, the inclusion of climate aspects during the first stages of urban planning is guaranteed.

Integration of the Bilbao UCMap in the planning process needs to consider that the Urban Plan is conditioned by the Territorial Plan (see Figure 23.6). Despite the fact that most of the specific climate recommendations described in the UCMap should be input during the definition of the Urban Plan managed directly by the municipality, the Territorial Plan for the whole area

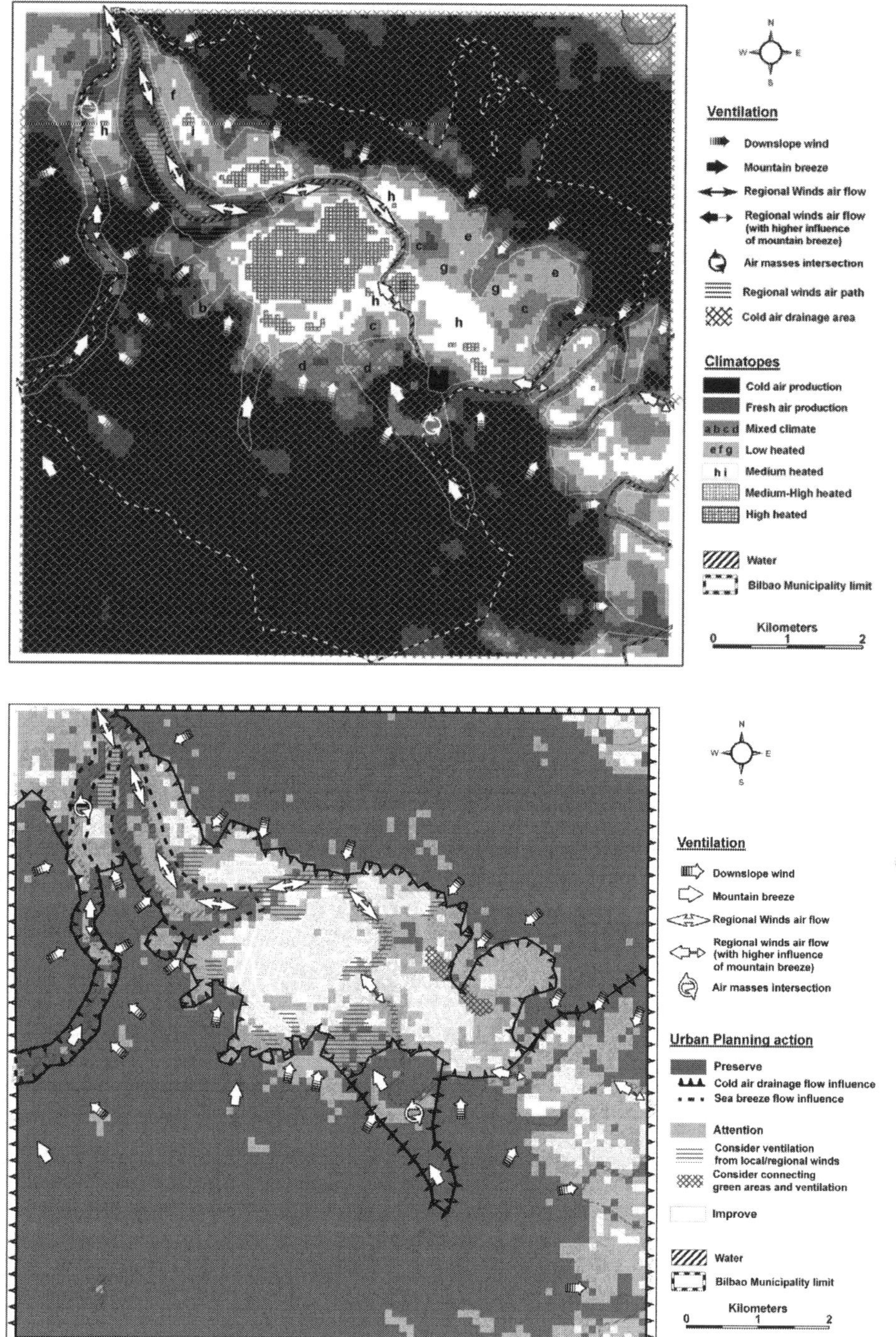


*Figure 23.5* (a) Urban Climatic Analysis Map (UC-AnMap); (b) Recommendation Map (UC-ReMap) of Bilbao city.

Source: Acero *et al.*, 2013b

*Table 23.3* Proposed recommendations in Bilbao UCMap.

| *Climatope* | *Urban Planning Action* | *Planning recommendations* |
|---|---|---|
| 1 Cold air production areas<br><br>2 Fresh air production areas | Preserve | Surface roughness should not increase, so as to allow cold/fresh airflow to enter the urban area. Building volume and ground coverage should be kept low, always trying to increase presence of vegetation.<br>No sealing and conservation of natural characteristics should be mandatory, especially in cold air ventilation paths.<br>Minor development could only be allowed in areas that are not in cold/fresh ventilation paths.<br>Very detailed planning and design is necessary to avoid alteration of climate functions. |
| 3 Mixed climate areas<br><br>4 Low-heated areas | Attention | These areas are quite neutral in terms of urban heat load, so it is important to maintain their climate characteristics.<br>Redevelopment is possible considering that low building volume areas, open spaces and vegetation should be preserved or increased.<br>Ventilation characteristics and air corridors should be analysed. Their preservation in future urban redevelopment is mandatory.<br>Building disposal and orientation should be considered carefully. |
| 5 Medium-heated areas<br><br>6 Medium–High heated areas<br><br>7 High-heated areas | Improve | Impact on urban thermal comfort can be significant.<br>urban heat load should be mitigated.<br>New development should only be allowed if urban cooling effects are included. New scenarios that worsen the existing situation should not be allowed.<br>Increasing vegetation in open spaces and streets is highly recommended. Vegetation planting should be considered carefully so as not to reduce ventilation potential.<br>Air exchange should be a priority; air paths should be analysed in depth before action is taken.<br>Increasing ventilation with open spaces or widening streets is mandatory. Additionally, when redesigning streets, these should be oriented near to the direction of predominant regional airflow. |

Source: Acero *et al.*, 2013b

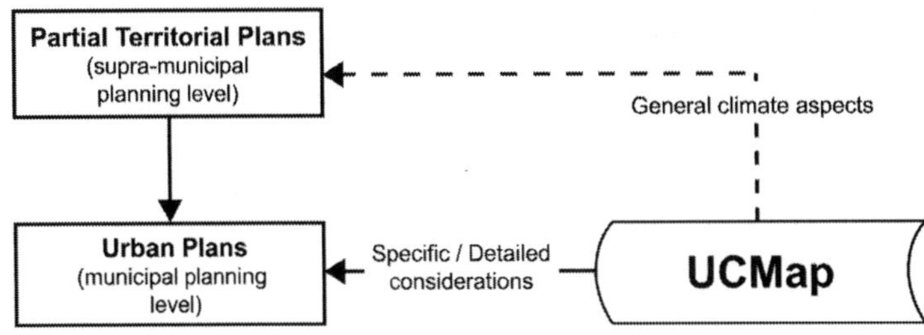


*Figure 23.6* Urban Climatic Map (UCMap) considerations at different planning levels for the case of Bilbao.

Source: Acero *et al.*, 2013b

of Gran Bilbao needs to include certain climatic hints for the planning in other municipalities to avoid climatic inconsistence (e.g. blocking ventilation paths) with the Bilbao UCMap. This fact is important in big urban areas that include different municipalities (e.g. Gran Bilbao).

## References

Acero, J. A., Santa Coloma, O., Albizu, M., Castillo, C. and Barquin, M. (2005). Risk of episodes in the Basque Country. Paper presented at the *5th International Conference on Air Quality*. Valencia, Spain, 29–31 March.

Acero, J. A., Zeberio, U., Azkune, S. and Santa Coloma, O. (2007). Air quality levels in the Basque Country (Spain): Source contribution and meteorology influence. Paper presented at the *6th International Conference on Urban Air Quality*. Nicosia, Cyprus, 27–29 March.

Acero, J. A., Arrizabalaga, J., Kupski, S. and Katzschner, L. (2013a). Urban heat island in a coastal urban area in northern Spain. *Theoretical and Applied Climatology*, 113(1–2): 137–154. doi: 10.1007/s00704-012-0774-z.

Acero, J. A., Arrizabalaga, J., Kupski, S. and Katzschner, L. (2013b). Deriving an Urban Climate Map in coastal areas with complex terrain in the Basque Country (Spain). *Urban Climate*, 4: 35–60. doi: 10.1016/j.uclim.2013.02.002.

Millan, M., Alonso, L., Legarreta, J., Albizu, M., Ureta, I. and Egusquiaguirre, C. (1984). A fumigation episode in an industrialized estuary: Bilbao, November 1981. *Atmospheric Environment*, 18(3): 563–572.

Millan, M., Otamendi, E., Alonso, L, and Ureta, I. (1987). Experimental characterization of atmospheric diffusion in complex terrain with land-sea interactions. *JAPCA*, 37(7): 807–811.

Zorraquino, J. (1971). Datos y comentarios sobre la Contaminación del Aire en Erandio (Bilbao) en 1969. *DYNA*, 1: 19–29.

Chapter 24

# Urban climatic map studies in Sweden

## Gothenburg

*Björn Holmer, Fredrik Lindberg and Sofia Thorsson*

### Introduction

The Urban Climate Group (UCG) in Gothenburg, Sweden, started to develop local climatic maps in the 1970s influenced by the '*Geländeklimatologie*' (landscape climatology) in Central Europe. However, the work was focused more on typical effects under anticyclonic weather conditions (cold air drainage, cold air ponds, urban heat islands, etc.) that were studied during mobile measuring traverses than on the analysis of climate statistics. This choice depended on the low relief of the landscape and the sparse network of meteorological stations and on our own interest in understanding the physical processes. It is well known that the local climate is caused by the synoptic weather situation, but governed by the physical landscape. The beauty of this is that the distribution of local climate effects is repeated each time this weather situation appears and that this distribution can be mapped.

The first attempts to construct local climate maps in Gothenburg were purely scientific, but over time, architects, city planners, and environmental authorities became interested in our work. Some of the maps were initiated by non-university users but in most cases complementary research funding was necessary. The purpose of the local climate maps have been to map, analyse and visualise:

- thermal comfort;
- energy demand for space heating;
- air pollution (these maps will not be discussed here);
- road safety and maintenance (these maps will not be discussed here but see for example Gustavsson and Bogren, 1990; Bogren *et al.*, 1992).

The Swedish climate – especially in the south – has a relatively mild winter climate in relation to its latitude. For example, the average temperature is −1°C in the coldest month in Gothenburg, situated at 58° N on the Swedish west coast. In winter, there are often strong maritime westerly winds but also blocking anticyclonic cells with clear skies and mild wind. Invasions of cold continental air from easterly directions sometimes occur. Summers are not particularly warm with an average air temperature of 17°C in July, but temperatures sometimes exceed 25°C (11 days a year, 1960–1990).

The winter climate has influenced life in Sweden in many ways and has increased the demand for climate information from the society. For example, buildings are designed to reduce the impact of cold and to admit sunshine in winter, giving Swedish cities an open-set, low- to mid-rise city structure. Heat is seldom a problem in Sweden. Nevertheless, during the last decade there has been a growing interest in daytime and summer conditions as a result of changing climate.

An understanding of the concept of scale (space and time) is fundamental to observing and interpreting any aspect of the climate. For detailed planning or to formulate measures to improve the environment, large-scale maps (1:10,000 or larger) have been used. For comprehensive planning maps a lower resolution (1:50,000) is more applied. When working on the development of climatic maps, one soon encounters the problem of 'false accuracy'. For example, if a large-scale map is produced, it is possible to show numerous details and read the location of the information on the map with great accuracy (ten metres or better). However, in reality, it is not possible to delimit local climate effects with such accuracy and resolution. On maps with scales of 1:50,000 or smaller, where the thickness of the lines corresponds to at least 50m, this problem is reduced.

Over the years, methods to obtain climatic maps have varied. The simplest (and earliest) maps were based on map studies only, but soon the need to use measurements to calibrate and evaluate both the intensity and area of the features of the maps was acknowledged. In the early days, measurement trips and mechanical thermo-hygrographs were used, but with the development of small battery-powered loggers it became possible to obtain time series of data at several sites over a surface. The increasing capacity of computers has also provided a useful tool both in data processing and the development of local scale models. Since the 1990s, geographical information technology has been an important tool for analysing and showing spatial climate data (Thornes, 2005).

In the following examples of local climate, maps produced by the UCG in Gothenburg will be presented. The examples are given in time order and thus show the evolution from simple mapping to sophisticated Geographic Information System (GIS) modelling. The examples also show how the intended use of the maps has influenced scale, content and presentation.

## Large-scale maps for future buildings

After the oil/energy crisis of the 1970s, resources were spent on research and on developing projects to reduce the energy consumption for heating houses, especially new buildings. New approaches to building design and construction such as locating the buildings in terrain that takes advantage of the local climate (access to sun, shelter, etc.) and mitigating disadvantages (cold airflows and ponds, wind exposure, etc.) gained increased attention. In a climate study by Holmer and Lindqvist (1980), two areas were compared – a NE–SW valley and a gentle SW oriented slope. The most important local climate effect was presumed to be cold air during anticyclonic nights in the valley area and wind in the slope area. However, the climate statistics showed that south-westerly winds were common and strong and that north-easterly winds were sometimes very cold. Thus wind could also be important in the valley. In this chapter, only the results from the valley area are presented.

The map of the local climate before exploitation is based on walks through the area with a temperature sensor (see Figure 24.1a), the mapping of hoar frost, a few wind measurement sites and the mapping of traces of wind directions during a north-easterly snowfall (see Figure 24.1b). During the anticyclonic evening the whole valley was filled with cold air but there were two depressions that were especially cold. The snow traces showed that there was enough topography in the valley to cause reversals of the local wind.

The local climate map (see Figure 24.2) shows the coldest areas and also a thermal belt along the steep valley slope. The sites that were exposed to wind are also shown. The figure also shows the planned areas with detached houses and how they will be affected by the local climate.

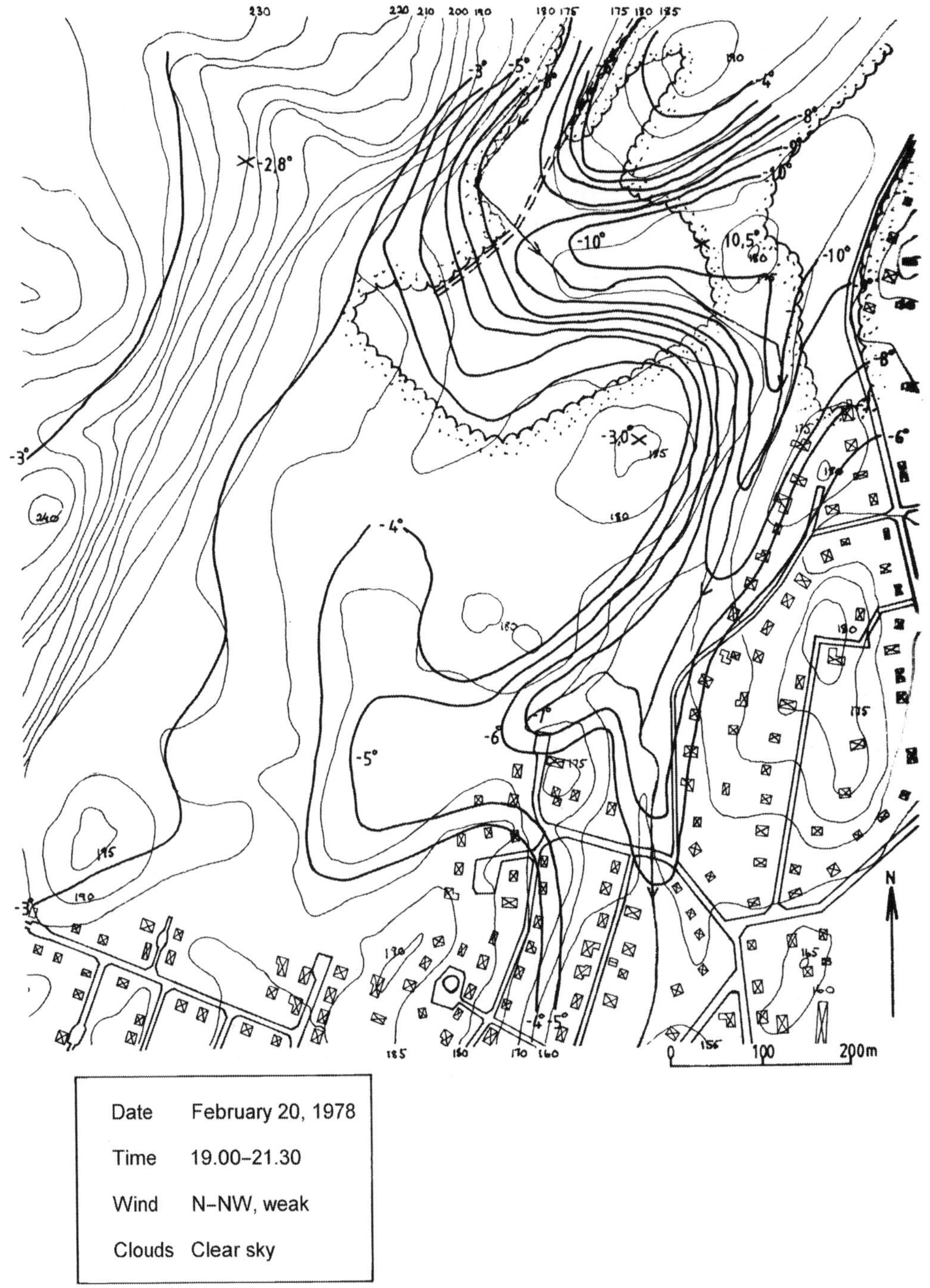


*Figure 24.1* (a) Temperature pattern during an anticyclonic evening;

Source: Holmer and Lindqvist, 1980

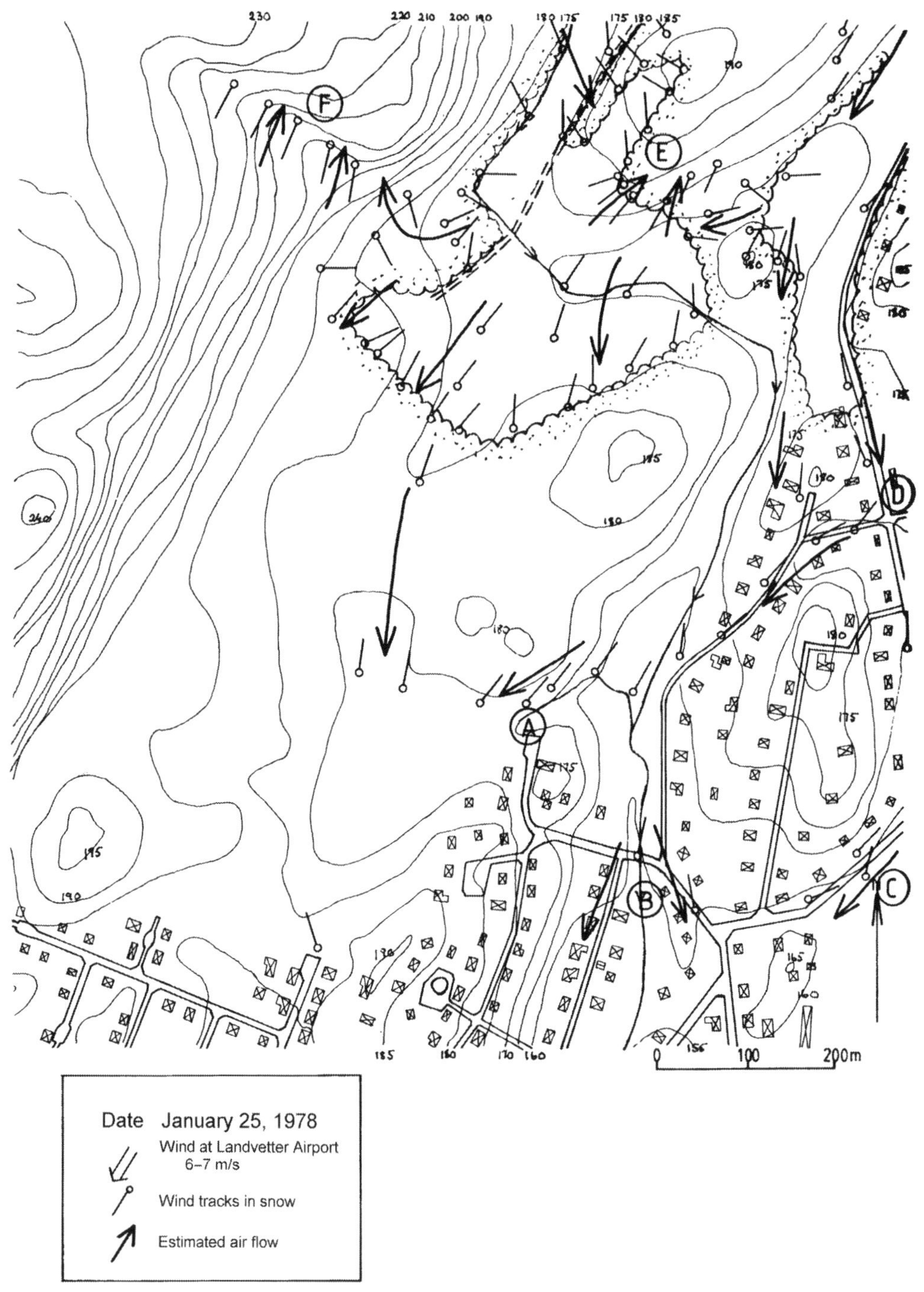


*Figure 24.1* (b) Snow traces showing wind directions during a snowfall from NE.

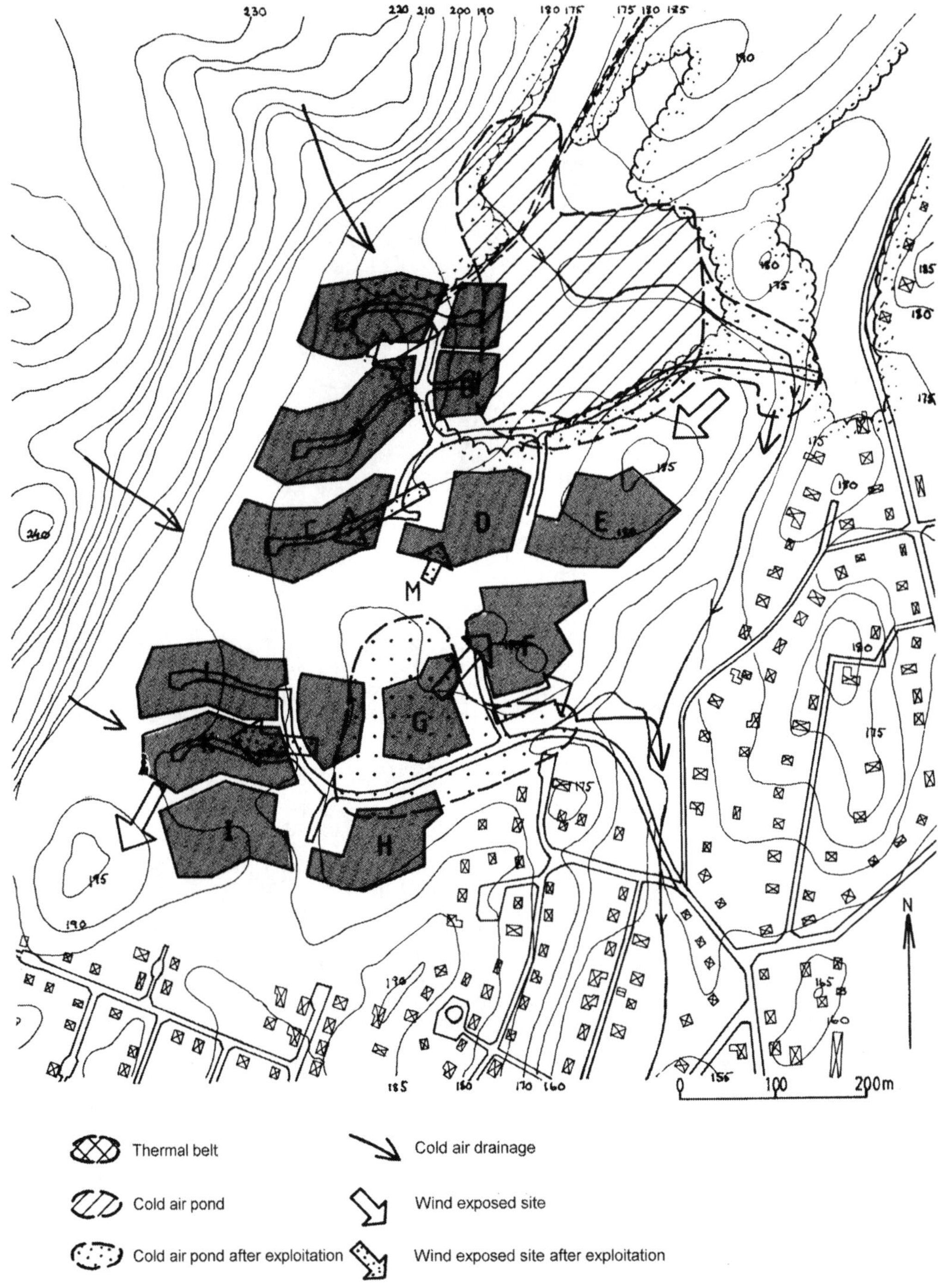


*Figure 24.2* Local climate in the valley and how it will affect the future houses.

Source: Holmer and Lindqvist, 1980

## Small-scale maps for comprehensive planning

In a study by Lindqvist *et al.* (1983), a new method to produce small-scale maps (1:50,000) was established. The method included three different steps. In the first step, areas with special local climate, such as cold air ponds (3 classes), coastal zones with a clear maritime temperature influence (2 classes), cool heights (75–100m a.s.l.), urban heat islands (2 classes), sunny and shady areas, areas with strong winds (2 classes), and areas with mild winds and foggy areas (4 classes) were delimited using topographic maps as shown in Figure 24.3(a). The second step included measurement trips (verification) – most of them focused on temperature but some were concerned with wind direction and speed. In the third and final step, the maps were revised (see Figure 24.3b). The general results showed that trained local climatologists were successful in showing where different local climate effects occur, but it was difficult to assess the magnitude and demarcation of the areas in detail.

## Energy demand for space heating

Increasing energy prices will increase the importance of energy issues in social planning. This includes both existing and planned buildings. With this starting point, a project to estimate the differences in energy consumption for space heating in the municipality of Gothenburg was initiated by Holmer and Linderstad (1985).

The approach is that common meteorological data (temperature and wind) obtained at one site – in this case an airport – could be distributed over an area, depending on the local climates that exist at the same time. First, a map of local climate effects concerning wind speed and temperature was established according to the manual by Lindqvist *et al.* (1983) described above. The next step was to define algorithms to calculate the intensity of the local climate effects that were caused by the present weather (data on wind speed and cloudiness were collected every six hours). This was done in a combination of literature studies and measuring trips. Measurements of wind speed and temperature were taken in a south-west–north-east traverse (perpendicular to the coast line), while temperature was measured in a north–south traverse where the city centre was included. In addition, knowledge and experiences drawn from 15 years of climate measurements in the Gothenburg area were applied. Each local temperature effect, e.g. cold air pond or urban heat island was assigned a maximum value that applied to cloud free skies and no wind. This value was then reduced depending on the observed wind speed, cloudiness and time of the day. Wind speed was assumed to decrease with distance from the coast but was also dependent on wind direction, topography and time of the day. Furthermore, an extra coefficient was applied to account for the increased wind speed on crests. Thus to get the temperature and wind speed at a site, five values are read from the local climate map: (1) topographical temperature effect, (2) the possible effect of urban heat islands, (3) topographical wind effect, (4) wind environment and (5) distance from coast. Temperature and wind speed then determined the ventilation loss of heat and heat flux through the walls and roofs of five types of detached houses and multi-family houses. The heat losses were summed over a period of six years. The most favourable site (the Gothenburg city centre) was used as the basis of the index that was created. Thus all index values for other parts of the Gothenburg municipality will be above 100; thus the index shows how much more energy is needed for heating outside the city centre (see Figure 24.4). The calculations (programmed in BASIC) were carried out in about 60 points in typical areas across the Gothenburg municipality and the resulting index values were also assigned to nearby areas with the same local climate. With the computer technology and power available at that time, one calculation took about six hours. The map shows indices of over 125 along the coast in spite of the positive temperature anomaly

Figure 24.3 Local climate map: (a) based on topographic map only; (b) revised by means of measuring trips;
Source: Lindqvist *et al.*, 1983

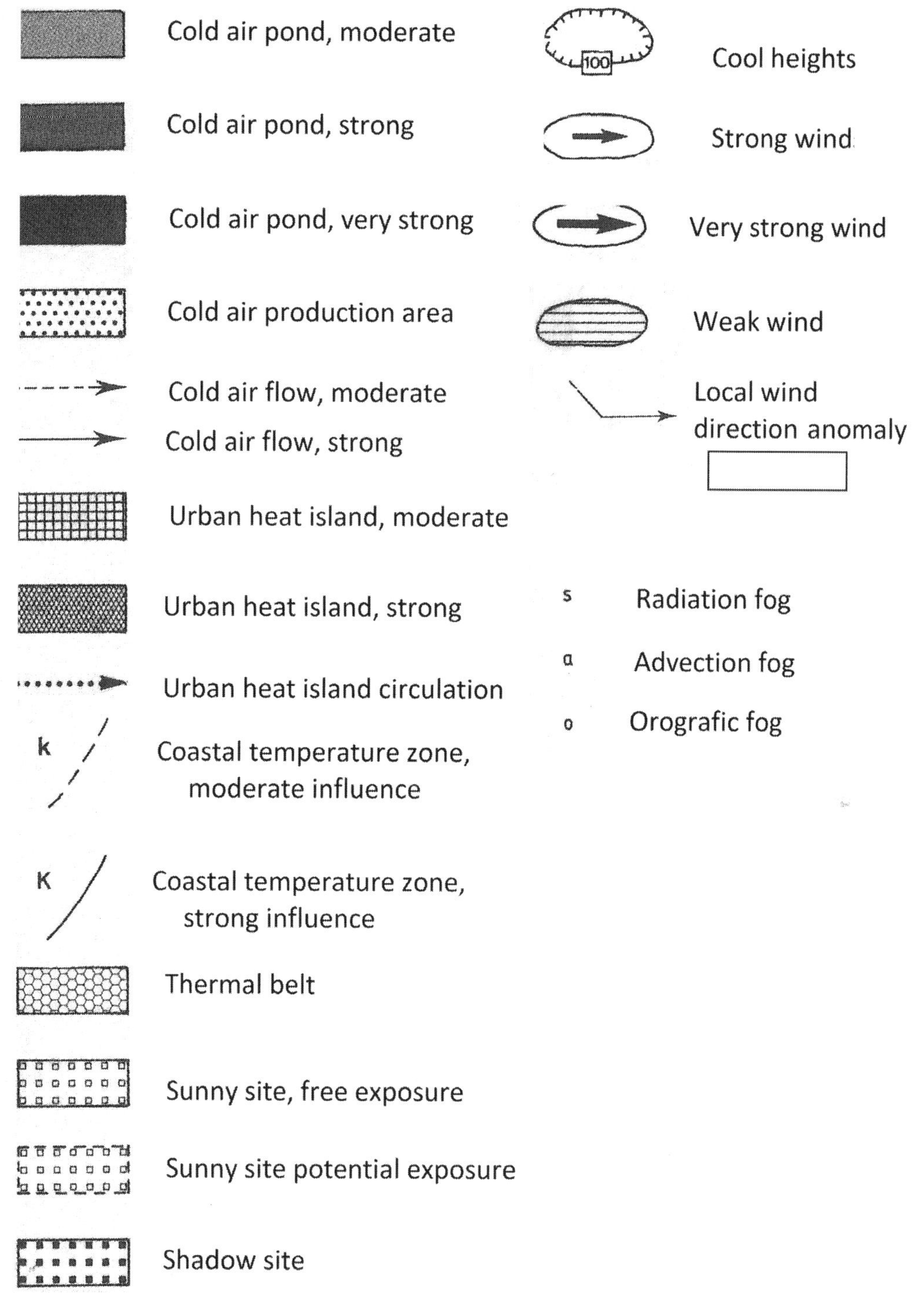


*Figure 24.3* (c) legend.

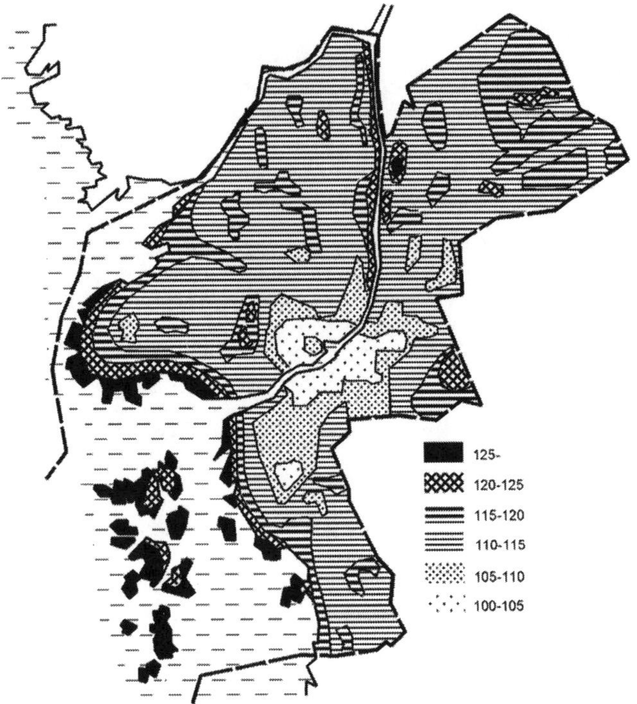


*Figure 24.4* Energy index map over Gothenburg.

Source: Holmer and Linderstad, 1985

brought about by the water. On the other hand, indices of around 115 are found on the mountain plateau in the north-east where the main effect is a drop in temperature due to the height above sea level. The highest index value, 135, was obtained on the wind-exposed edge of the plateau. A closer look at the calculations shows that most of the index variations depend on ventilation loss, where wind speed is most important.

## GIS maps of temperature and wind

In the 1990s it was realised that GIS was an efficient tool for using in preparing, processing and presenting local climate data. Svensson *et al.* (2002) translated the temperature and wind algorithms used to calculate the energy index described above into Matlab algorithms (see Figure 24.5a). These were used as input in a GIS model covering the Gothenburg municipality. The final presentation was performed in IDRISI, which is a raster-based GIS. The resolution is 500m × 500m, a scale that is useful in comprehensive planning.

Figure 24.5(b) shows an evening temperature map simulated for an anticyclonic weather situation in spring. There is a UHI, a mild zone along the coast in the west, a clear cold air pond in the river valley north of the city, smaller cold air ponds scattered over the area and a cool upland area in the northwest. The overall pattern therefore shows what can be expected. However, the simulated temperatures had a rather poor fit ($R^2 = 0.41$) as shown in Figure 24.6. The rather poor fit could, to some extent, be explained by the grid size (500m × 500m), but also to errors in the local climate map.

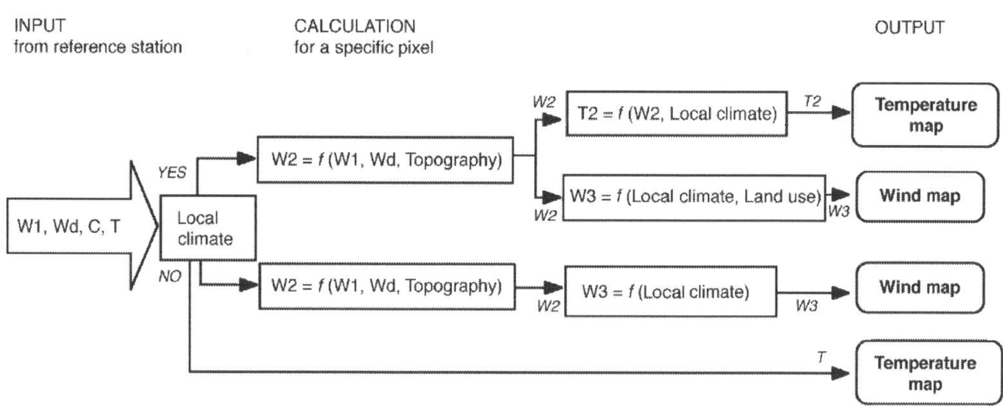


*Figure 24.5* (a) Conceptual framework. Input data to the model are wind velocity (W1), wind direction (Wd), air temperature (T) and cloud amount (C) from the reference station. For every pixel the wind velocity is corrected for topographic features depending on wind direction and used as an input in a regression equation to give temperature. The calculated temperature value depends on the local climate effect of features such as cold airflows and the urban heat island.

Source: Svensson *et al.*, 2002

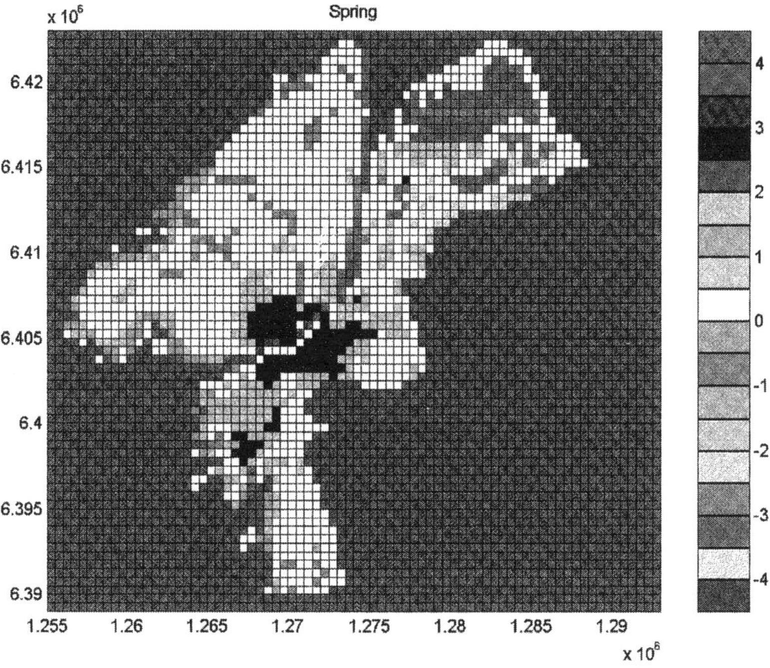


*Figure 24.5* (b) Simulation of the temperature pattern in late March, 3 hours after sunset. Temperatures given are the deviation from the reference station. At the reference station, the wind speed was 1.5m/s and the wind direction 16° N; the temperature was 0.1°C and the cloud amount was 2 octas.

Source: Svensson *et al.*, 2002

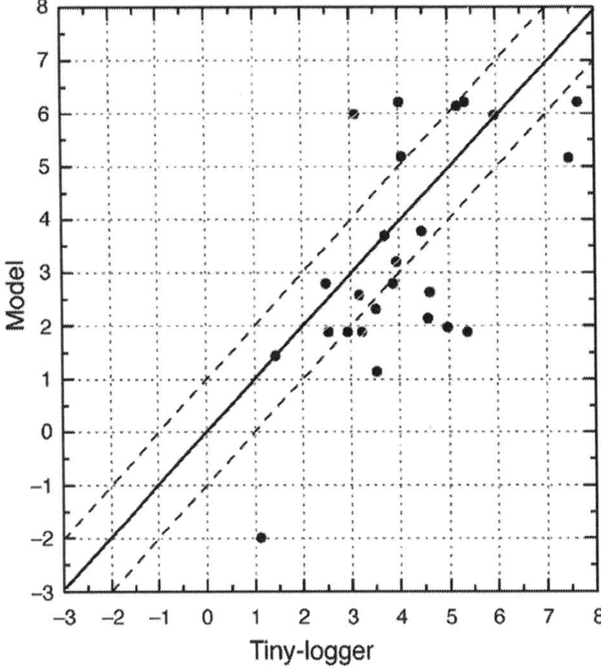


*Figure 24.6* Regression analysis of observed and modelled temperatures.

Source: Svensson *et al.*, 2002

## Bioclimatic maps with GIS

A different approach to simulating temperature differences over the same area as in the study above was used by Svensson *et al.* (2003). In this study, meteorological data (hourly resolution) from 18 temperature stations and 12 wind stations located within the Gothenburg area were linked with information on land cover, altitude and distance to the coast to produce large-scale bioclimatic maps. The method combines an air temperature map (see Figure 24.7a) and a wind map (see Figure 24.7b) using a GIS application in order to create different climate zones for which the thermal component can be calculated.

As shown in Figure 24.7, large spatial variations in air temperature, wind speed and physiological equivalent temperature (PET) exist during calm and clear summer days. Most obvious are the high wind speeds found along the coast, especially at the mouth of the river, but also in the upland areas in the east (see Figure 24.7b). The built-up areas are warmer not only the city centre but in the entire area (see Figure 24.7a). A narrow coastal area is a bit chillier. The resulting PET map (see Figure 24.7c) shows a large influence of both air temperature and wind speed. The influence of temperature is particularly clear in the southern region.

## SOLWEIG – a climate design model

As pointed out by Mayer *et al.* (2008), high spatio-temporal resolution information about human thermal comfort is required for application in city planning. Over the years, several models

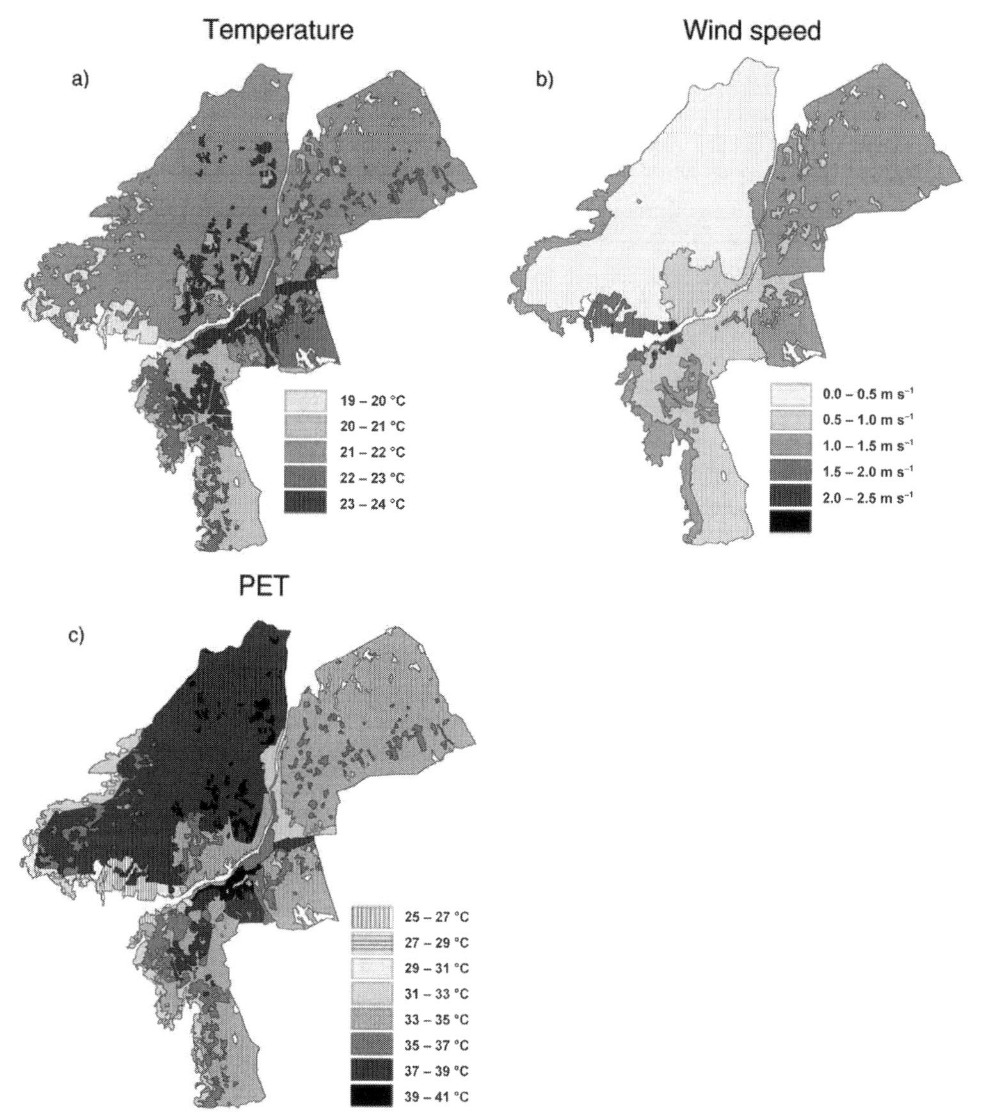


*Figure 24.7* (a) Simulated temperature; (b) simulated wind speed; (c) simulated PET.

Source: Svensson *et al.*, 2003

have been developed to simulate outdoor thermal comfort, such as Rayman (Matzarakis, 2000; Matzarakis *et al.*, 2010), ENVI-met (Bruse, 1999, 2006), TownScope (Teller and Azar, 2001) and SOLWEIG (Lindberg *et al.*, 2008). The SOLWEIG (Solar and Long Wave Environmental and Irradiance Geometry) model developed by UCG is a 2.5-dimensional model in the sense that it applies an urban raster-based Digital Surface Model, DSM (i.e. x and y coordinates with height attributes) consisting of ground and building heights. The model is able to calculate spatial variations of radiant fluxes (upward, downward, northward, southward, eastward and westward) and thus, mean radiant temperature ($T_{mrt}$), which is a central parameter for the evaluation of outdoor thermal comfort in urban areas with a high resolution. The model is based upon the framework of raster analysis of urban form originally presented by Ratti and Richens (1999), where high resolution digital elevation models (DEMs) are used to extract geometrical parameters such as surface shadow patterns and sky view factors (SVF). Commonly available meteorological parameters such as global short-wave radiation, air temperature and relative humidity are used as causal input data for the model (Lindberg *et al.*, 2008). The fact that SOLWEIG is a two-dimensional model makes it suitable for analysing the complex interaction of urban geometry and thermal environment at a neighbourhood or city block scale, or when extended meteorological datasets are used.

If urban green structures are viewed as a climate planning tool they could be used to reduce air temperature through the action of evapotranspiration (latent heat flux), rather than by sensible heat flux; parts of the ground and walls could be shaded, which would result in a reduction of the radiant temperature and would impact wind speed and direction. There are relatively few studies on the influence of vegetation on thermal comfort and the advocacy for its use in urban areas (e.g. Matzarakis *et al.*, 1999; Picot, 2004; Robitu *et al.*, 2006; Ali-Toudert and Mayer, 2007). These studies primarily show that vegetation shadowing can have a large effect in reducing heat stress in urban areas. However, these studies have typically been spatially constrained to one point or a small area such as a square or a street canyon. Developments and a new release (as from version 2) made it possible to take vegetation into account when estimating $T_{mrt}$ within the SOLWEIG model. By using a new type of shadow casting technique, full 3D objects such as trees (consisting of a canopy and trunk zone) can be taken into account (Lindberg and Grimmond, 2011), making it possible to model $T_{mrt}$ on a larger spatial scale including both building structures and vegetation.

Figure 24.8 shows examples of the various input and output data of SOLWEIG. Figure 24.8(a) shows the ground and building DEM which is necessary for the model to work. Figure 24.8(b) shows the vegetation DEM, including trees and bushes. The combination of the two DEMs where all essential 3D objects are present is shown in Figure 24.8(c). Figure 24.8(d) shows simulated spatial distribution of $T_{mrt}$ at 3.00 p.m. on the 23 May 2010 at a square in central Gothenburg using the SOLWEIG.

## Climate change and outdoor thermal comfort

During the 1970s, 1980s and 1990s, most efforts in the production of local climate maps in Gothenburg concerned the adverse effects of low temperatures and high winds, i.e. the cold parts of the year. However, along with a growing interest in the influence of weather for the use of outdoor places, people's place perception and emotions as well as the impact of a warmer climate (trends and heat waves) on outdoor thermal comfort and energy demand for cooling have contributed to the need to emphasise the summer in local climate studies.

In Thorsson *et al.* (2011), augmentation of global/regional climate changes by urban features such as geometry in a compact, mid-rise city structure within the central parts of Gothenburg is explored. The magnitude of spatial and temporal variations of $T_{mrt}$ is quantified using the SOLWEIG model. By using meteorological data from a nearby climate station as well as statistically downscaled data from General Circulation Models, the impact of today's as well as future warmer climates on outdoor thermal comfort in different built structures can be estimated.

Figure 24.9 shows hourly, daytime and yearly average $T_{mrt}$ in central Gothenburg. As shown, large intra-urban differences in $T_{mrt}$ exist within short distances, on hourly, daytime and yearly averages. The spatial variations in $T_{mrt}$ are similar in pattern but smaller in magnitude on daytime and yearly average than on hourly average.

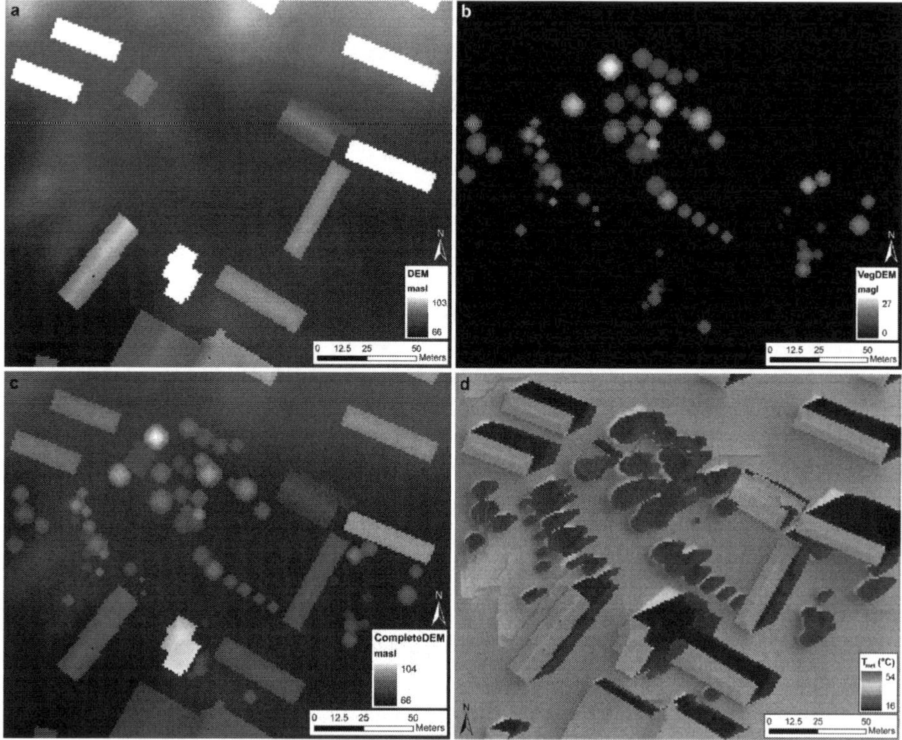


*Figure 24.8* Input and output data of the SOLWEIG model: (a) building and ground DEM; (b) vegetation canopy DEM; (c) complete (building and vegetation) DEM combined; (d) Spatial variations of $T_{mrt}$ (standing man) (°C) covering a square in Gothenburg (Sweden) at 3.00 p.m. on 23 May 2010. The spatial resolution is 1m.

Source: Authors

As shown in Figure 24.9 and Table 24.1, a dense built structure mitigates extreme swings in $T_{mrt}$ and PET, improving outdoor comfort conditions both in summer and in winter. The fact that urban geometry (e.g. street direction, spacing and width, and building height) has a direct impact on $T_{mrt}$ confirms the potential for using geometry to mitigate daytime thermal stress in cities. This is to be compared with air temperature ($T_a$) which is characterised by rather small daytime spatial variations (e.g. Emmanuel and Fernando, 2007; Mayer *et al.*, 2008). Since $T_{mrt}$ is critical to outdoor thermal comfort, mitigation options ought to focus on $T_{mrt}$, rather than $T_a$ alone (Emmanuel and Fernando, 2007).

The number of hours with hot and very hot thermal conditions is expected to triple in Gothenburg by the end of this century according to the ECHAM5-based scenario under the A1B emission scenario (see Table 24.1). This equates to 20–100 hours a year depending on geometry. However, the number of hours with cold and very cold thermal conditions will decrease more, i.e. by 400–450 hours a year. Furthermore, the number of hours with acceptable comfortable conditions (i.e. slight cool, comfortable, slightly warm) will increase by about 200–400 hours a year. This means that, although the problems of excessive temperature will increase in summer, outdoor climate will improve significantly in winter, spring and autumn in a future warmer climate.

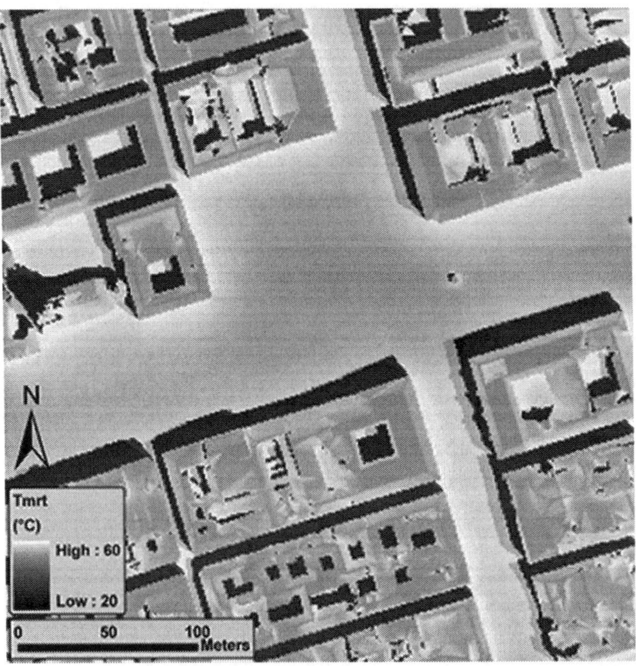


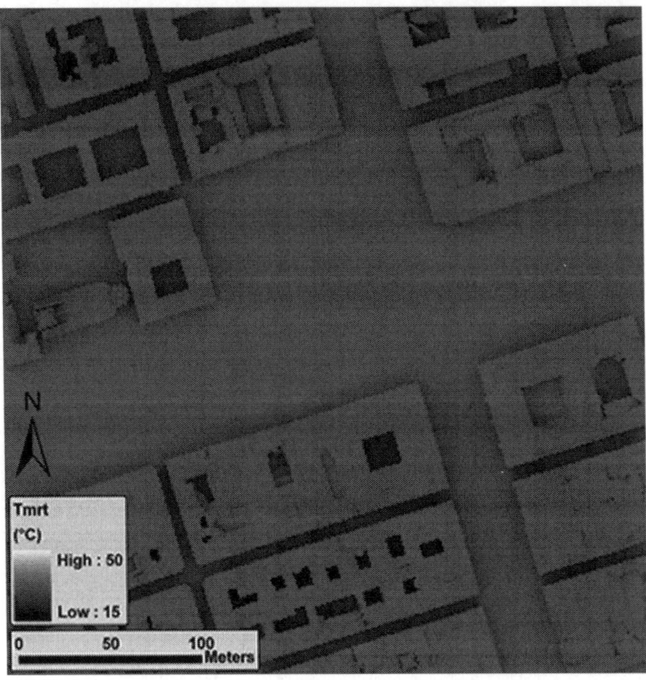


*Figure 24.9* (a) Hourly average (21 June 1977 at 10.00 a.m.; (b) daytime average, i.e. from sunrise to sunset (21 June 1977)

Source: Thorsson *et al.*, 2011

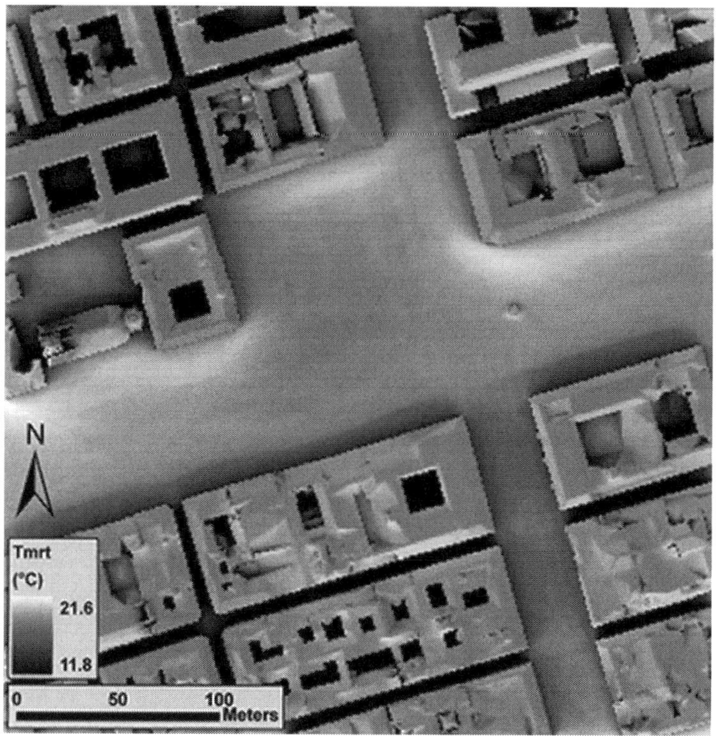


*Figure 24.9* (c) yearly average mean radiant temperature (°C) in central Gothenburg.

*Table 24.1* Average daytime annual numbers of hours with different grades of Physiological Equivalent Temperature (PET); thermal perception according Matzarakis and Mayer (1996) for the period 1980–2000 and change in yearly average number of hours between 1980–2000 and 2080–2100 and the four urban places. The future climate is simulated using statistically downscaled data from ECHAM5/MPI-OM model under the SRES A1B emission scenario.

| *PET (°C)* | *Thermal perception* | *Yearly average number of hours 1980–1999* | | | | *Change in yearly average number of hours (1980–1999 and 2080–2100)* | | | |
|---|---|---|---|---|---|---|---|---|---|
| | | *Place* | | | | *Place* | | | |
| | | *Square* | *N–S canyon* | *E–W canyon* | *Courtyard* | *Square* | *N–S canyon* | *E–W canyon* | *Courtyard* |
| <8 | Cold and very cold | 1941 | 1825 | 1816 | 1785 | −401 | −447 | −448 | −444 |
| 8–13 | Cool | 768 | 887 | 892 | 839 | −59 | −87 | −88 | −75 |
| 13–29 | Acceptable comfortable | 1553 | 1677 | 1707 | 1714 | 192 | 398 | 410 | 348 |
| 29–35 | Warm | 164 | 66 | 51 | 99 | 165 | 105 | 101 | 117 |
| > 35 | Hot and very hot | 50 | 18 | 9 | 37 | 102 | 30 | 24 | 53 |

Source: After Thorsson *et al.*, 2011

## Some concluding remarks

One drawback of the topographical evaluation method is that it depends on the skill of the interpreter. This was informally tested on a course with students who had previously participated in a course in local and micro climatology for a month. One task was to produce a local climate map. It showed that features that are related to temperature were localised at sites that differed little from the supervisor's opinion although the exact borders differed. The correspondence regarding wind was worse.

However, simulation and modelling are not free of subjective elements. There are always several parameters that have to be defined in a program (through the user or predefined by the programmer) that will have considerable influences on the results.

Even for experienced interpreters, it is shown to be difficult to delimit local climate features (see Figure 24.3). Also, the comparison of observed and modelled temperatures in Figure 24.6 sometimes reveals poor agreement. One reason for this is the knowledge of the processes involved. In the case of cold air ponds, the common theory is that they develop as a result of cold airflows along the slopes. However, it is proposed in an increasing number of studies that cooling *in situ* due to wind shelter is the main process (Gustavsson *et al.*, 1998; Whiteman *et al.*, 2004; Vosper and Brown, 2008). This implies that the role of length, steepness, and vegetation on slopes need to be evaluated in a new way and thus both the intensity and areal coverage of cold air ponds must be re-evaluated. The cooling process in urban areas also needs to be considered more (Chow and Roth, 2006; Holmer *et al.*, 2007).

Future research concerning climate mapping within UCG will focus on developing a 2D modelling approach to estimate PET or other thermal indices in the SOLWEIG model. This will require spatial variations of wind speeds to be calculated and the use of a database of parameter values for people related to clothing, age, sex, etc. The major challenge will be to develop a new 2D wind scheme to be incorporated within the model.

Today, most of the work to produce a local climate map is done on a computer and often by some kind of spatial modelling. Grid size, rather than scale, determines the precision of the map. However, there is still a need for measurements both to verify the models used and to form the basis of questions on how to develop the maps.

For many years, climate issues have often had a low impact on the planning process in practice. In the late 1990s, the use of climate knowledge in the urban planning process in three Swedish towns was studied by Eliasson (2000). Planners were interested in climatic aspects. However, the use of climate knowledge had little impact on the planning process. Other constraints were more important, such as economy, predefined projects or architects' vision of design. Some of the identified constraints could be addressed by increasing the awareness of the importance of urban climate among those aside from planners and decision makers; providing good arguments and easy and reliable tools; and improving the communication between researchers, planners and decision makers.

By integrating and implementing climate knowledge at an early stage in the planning process, goal conflicts and synergies between different aspects can be identified and taken into account. This is something that will be done in the new Swedish transdisciplinary project, which aims to adapt cities to climate-induced risks.

Today, it is possible to construct advanced local climate maps. However, even if the software is available free of charge, other resources are necessary (data from climate stations, DEM, altitude data, etc.). This is another purpose for which the local map will be produced. Detailed information is sometimes necessary and thus detailed modelling is suitable, however in other cases (for example in comprehensive planning), approximate delimiting of typical local climate environments is adequate and is therefore a simpler method with which the local climate can be mapped.

## References


Ali-Toudert, F. and Mayer, H. (2007). Effects of asymmetry, galleries, overhanging façades and vegetation on thermal comfort in urban street canyons. *Solar Energy*, 81(6): 742–754.

Bogren, J., Gustavsson, T. and Lindqvist, S. (1992). A description of a local climatological model used to predict temperature variations along stretches of roads. *Meteorological Magazine*, 112: 157–164.

Bruse, M. (1999). *Die Auswirkungen kleinskaliger Umweltgestaltung auf das MikroklimaEntwicklung des prognostischen numerischen Modells ENVI-met zur Simulation der Wind-, Tempertaur-, und Feuchteverteilung in städtischen Strukturen.* PhD Thesis, University Bochum, Germany.

Bruse, M. (2006). *ENVI-met 3 – a three dimensional microclimate model.* Ruhr Universit¨at Bochum, Geographischer Institut, Geomatik. Available at: http://www.envi-met.com (Accessed 5 February 2014).

Chow, W. T. L and Roth, M. (2006). Temporal dynamics of the urban heat island of Singapore. *International Journal of Climatology*, 26(15): 2243–2260.

Eliasson, I. (2000). The use of climate knowledge in urban planning. *Landscape and Urban Planning*, 48(1–2): 31–44.

Emmanuel, R. and Fernando, H. J. S. (2007). Urban heat islands in humid and arid climates: Role of urban form and thermal properties in Colombo, Sri Lanka and Phoenix, USA. *Climate Research*, 34(3): 241–251.

Gustavsson, T. and Bogren, J. (1990). Road slipperiness during warm air advections. *Meteorological Magazine*, 119: 267–270.

Gustavsson, T., Karlsson, M., Bogren, J. and Lindqvist, S. (1998). Development of temperature patterns during clear nights. *Journal of Applied Meteorology*, 37(6): 559–571.

Holmer, B. and Linderstad, H. (1985). Energi-index – lokalklimatets inverkan på energiförbrukningen. *Byggforskningsrådet*, R115: 1985.

Holmer, B. and Lindqvist, S. (1980). Energihushållning i stadsplanen – lokalklimatiska studier. *Byggforskningsrådet*, T6: 1980.

Holmer, B., Thorsson, S. and Eliasson, I. (2007). Cooling rates, sky view factors and the development of intra-urban air temperature differences. *Geografiska Annaler: Series A, Physical Geography*, 89(4): 237–248.

Lindberg, F. and Grimmond, C. S. B. (2011). The influence of vegetation and building morphology on shadow patterns and mean radiant temperatures in urban areas: Model development and evaluation. *Theoretical and Applied Climatology*, 105(3–4): 311–323.

Lindberg, F., Holmer, B. and Thorsson, S. (2008). SOLWEIG 1.0 – Modelling spatial variations of 3D radiant fluxes and mean radiant temperature in complex urban settings. *International Journal of Biometeorology*, 52(7): 697–713.

Lindqvist, S., Mattsson, J. and Holmer, B. (1983). Lokalklimatiska kartor för användning i kommunal översiktlig planering. *Byggforskningsrådet*, R38: 1983.

Matzarakis, A. (2000). Estimation and calculation of the mean radiant temperature within urban structures, *Manual to RayMan*. Freiburg: University of Freiburg, Germany.

Matzarakis, A. and Mayer, H. (1996). Another kind of environmental stress: Thermal stress. *WHO newsletters*, 18: 7–10.

Matzarakis, A., Mayer, H. and Iziomon, M. (1999). Applications of a universal thermal index: physiological equivalent temperature. *International Journal of Biometeorology*, 43(2): 76–84.

Matzarakis, A., Rutz, F. and Mayer, H. (2010). Modelling radiation fluxes in simple and complex environments: basics of the RayMan model. *International Journal of Biometeorology*, 54(2): 131–139.

Mayer, H., Holst, J., Dostal, P., Imbery, F. and Schindler, D. (2008). Human thermal comfort in summer within an urban street canyon in Central Europe. *Meteorologische Zeitschrift*, 17(3): 241–250.

Picot, X. (2004). Thermal comfort in urban spaces: Impact of vegetation growth – Case study: Piazza della Scienza, Milan, Italy. *Energy and Buildings*, 36(4): 329–334.

Ratti, C. F. and Richens, P. (1999). Urban texture analysis with image processing techniques. In: Augenbroe, G. and Eastman, C., (eds.), *Computers in Building: Proceedings of CAAD Futures 99*. Atlanta, GA, USA, 7–8 June. Boston: Kluwer Academic, 49–64.

Robitu, M., Musy, M., Inard, C. and Groleau, D. (2006). Modeling the influence of vegetation and water pond on urban microclimate. *Solar Energy*, 80(4): 435–447.

Svensson, M. K., Eliasson, I. and Holmer, B. (2002). A GIS based empirical model to simulate air temperature variations in the Goteborg urban area during the night. *Climate research*, 22(3): 215–226.

Svensson, M. K., Thorsson, S. and Lindqvist, S. (2003). A geographical information system model for creating bioclimatic maps – examples from a high, mid-latitude city. *International Journal of Biometeorology*, 47(2): 102–112.

Teller, J. and Azar, S. (2001). TOWNSCOPE II – A computer system to support solar access decision-making. *Solar Energy*, 70(3): 187–200.

Thornes, J. (2005). Special issue on the use of GIS in climatology and meteorology. *Meteorological Applications*, 12(1): i–iii.

Thorsson, S., Lindberg, F., Björklund, J., Holmer, B. and Rayner, D. (2011). Potential change in outdoor thermal comfort conditions in Gothenburg, Sweden due to climate change: the influence of urban geometry. *International Journal of Climatology*, 31(2): 324–335.

Vosper, S. B. and Brown, A. R. (2008). Numerical simulations of sheltering in valleys: The formation of nighttime cold-air pools. *Boundary-Layer Meteorology*, 127(3): 429–448.

Whiteman, C. D., Haiden, T., Pospichal, B., Eisenbach, S. and Steinacker, R. (2004). Minimum temperatures, diurnal temperature ranges, and temperature inversions in limestone sinkholes of different sizes and shapes. *Journal of Applied Meteorology*, 43(8): 1224–1236.

Chapter 25

# Urban climatic map studies in Holland

## Arnhem

*Chao Ren, Tejo Spit, Lutz Katzschnerand Anita Kokx*

## PART I: URBAN CLIMATIC MAP AND URBAN PLANNING, THE DUTCH EXPERIENCE

### Introduction

Densely populated cities with compact urban structures can be found all over the world. For the planners and politicians concerned, meeting all the demands and designing a sustainable, healthy, comfortable living environment that its inhabitants can enjoy is no easy job. To achieve success, the planners must include in their processes many factors designed to enhance the development of a safe and comfortable urban area. Climate conditions are a factor worthy of inclusion in these planning processes, particularly with regard to the climate changes to be anticipated. From a scientific perspective, climate conditions must be analysed systematically and introduced strategically into the planning process (Mills *et al.*, 2010). The current global issue of climate change promotes increasing interest between the effects of climate change and spatial planning in terms of adaptation. However, until now, most studies on climate application have been constructed from scientific disciplines such as meteorology, climatology, and physics. None of these studies uses an urban planning perspective. Its absence can be considered an illustration of the huge gap between urban climate research and urban planning (Eliasson, 2000; Mills, 2006). On the one hand, planners, developers and policymakers do not possess enough knowledge of the effects of climate and climate change (Bitan, 1988). Climatic data and scientific research results are not easy for them to understand and integrate into planning processes. On the other hand, climatologists are not familiar with spatial planning procedures and mechanisms, so they cannot provide the appropriate climatic evaluation and information to meet the planners' real needs (Eliasson, 2000). Thus, appropriate assistance is needed on both sides to bridge the gap. In order to enhance the communication between these two worlds, Urban Climatic Maps (UCMaps) may provide an information and evaluation tool that can further the communication between academic climate experts, built-environment professionals, practitioners, and policymakers.

### Review

#### *The concept of the urban climatic map (UCMap)*

The urban climatic map is a climatic information and evaluation tool that helps planners understand climatic-environmental conditions and variations and achieve their aims. The concept of a UCMap is essentially an old one. It was originally generated by German researchers in the 1970s, who named it the 'Synthetic Climate Function Map' (Baumüller *et al.*, 1992). At that time it collated meteorological data, climate information, land-use data, and terrain information, facilitated a comprehensive climate analysis and evaluation, and presented the results in various maps.

This atlas system consists of two major components: the Urban Climatic Analysis Map (UC-AnMap) and the Urban Climatic Recommendation Map (UC-ReMap). The UC-AnMap collates meteorological, planning, land use, topographic and vegetation information; their inter relationships and effects on wind and thermal environment are analysed and evaluated spatially. The scientific understanding of urban heat islands (UHI), urban ventilation, and outdoor human thermal comfort is synergised based on available statistical and interpolation techniques (Matzarakis and Mayer, 2008). The UC-ReMap could be further developed together with strategic urban planning recommendations according to the climatic understanding and evaluation acquired from the UC-AnMap. The UCMap resolves scientific climatic knowledge into guidelines and planning recommendations and could be used to guide planning actions and decision making.

The development of the German UCMap in the 1970s resulted from intense public debate and support, culminating in political willingness to plan for the future with respect to the natural environment in a responsible and sensitive way. According to the German Federal Building Code (BAUGESETZBUCH – BauGB), urban development should be sustainable and beneficial to an environment, fit for people, and protect the natural environment and resources (BauGB, 2004). In line with this ambition, planners, meteorologists, and scientists have worked together to develop UCmaps. Gradually, they succeeded in adding more data into the analysis in order to synergise climatic, topographical, and urban parameters with the objective of providing guidelines for planning processes. Since the 1980s, many European cities in Austria, Sweden, Norway, Switzerland, Hungary, Portugal and so forth have constructed their UCmap studies and similar projects with the same objective. According to the literature review (Ren *et al.*, 2009, 2011), cities in more than 15 countries now have their own UCMaps (refer to Appendix 1). The increasing global concern regarding climate change has generated interest in UCMaps. Countries not only in the western world, (The Netherlands, France, etc.), but also in the developing world (Chile, China, etc.) are starting to develop their own UCMaps or conduct similar research.

Since Germany is a leading country in the field, the metrology of the UCMap used in Europe, Asia, and South America is mostly adapted from the earlier German model and follows the German Guidelines VDI-Standard 3787 Part 1 for drawing up their climate and air pollution maps.

In the original German version, the planning advice could be commissioned by experts and planners aiming not only to improve the urban climate situation (e.g. mitigating urban heat island and improving thermal comfort), but also to decrease air pollution and enhance air quality. It was based on available statistical analysis and interpolation techniques.

## Methodology

The structure of UCMap contains three kinds of maps (see Figure 2.2).

### A basic map

Basic maps present the spatial distribution of climatic parameters and other related parameters such as airflow, air temperature, land use with building and street information, the results of Computer

Fluid Dynamics (CFD) simulations or calculations, anthropogenic heat information, and so on. The map was based on available statistical analysis and interpolation techniques.

### *The urban climatic analysis map (UC-AnMap)*

This 2D map shows the analysis of the climate and an evaluation of the thermal environment and air pollution situation. Urban climatologists, GIS (Geographic Information System) specialists, urban planners and designers met to discuss the presentation of urban climatic analysis and evaluation. For instance, in the partial plan of the UC-AnMap for Stuttgart city (see Figure 2.3). the climatic analysis and evaluation focus on three aspects: climatic variations, wind situation, and air pollution. Different colours were used to present the existing general climatic variations of Stuttgart city, such as the effects of urban greenery, air paths, etc. Arrows demonstrate the wind situation in both daytime and night-time, as well as possible directions, including the downslope wind, mountain breeze, air exchanges, and so on. Other legends, such as a net or dots, show the areas with an air pollution problem.

### *The planning recommendation map (UC-ReMap)*

Zoned homogenous or similar climatic analysis areas from the UC-AnMap are added as basic information to the UC-ReMap, together with advices or measures from the climatic viewpoint that could be conducted in real 3D urban space. The climatic understanding and evaluation gained from the UC-AnMap yield three pillars of recommendation from a climatic perspective for the open space and built-up areas. These are: the wind aspect: its sensitivity to air exchange; the thermal aspect: its density and thermal load; the air pollution aspect: its sensitivity to air pollution.

Thus, in Stuttgart, with the assistance of UCMap, researchers suggest the following goals of climate-sensitive planning:

- Improvement of living conditions relative to climate comfort/bioclimate;
- Improvement of the ventilation of the development;
- Support of fresh-air provision through local wind systems;
- Reduced release of air pollutants and greenhouse gases;
- Proper evaluation of current or expected pollution;
- Proper reaction to pollution situations by adjusting land-use versions.

(Nachbarschaftsverband Stuttgart, 1992; VDI, 1997)

The implementation of Stuttgart's UCMap in spatial planning then concentrates on assisting the preparatory land use plan (in German: 'Flächennutzungsplan' or 'F-Plan' represents the type of land uses arising for the entire municipal territory) from the climatic point of view. The climatic understanding from Stuttgart's UCMap could assist three specific plans: the land-use plan, the green area plan, and the controlling building height plan. It also emphasises the protection and creation of ventilation corridors in urban development.

Apart from Stuttgart's UCMap, considering the spatial plans of Germany, researchers in the Department of Urban Climate of Stuttgart have developed a series of Climate Atlases that contain different climatic information with various scales to help local planners make a better planning decision in their daily practice and to meet their needs from a municipal level to federal level (see Figure 25.1).

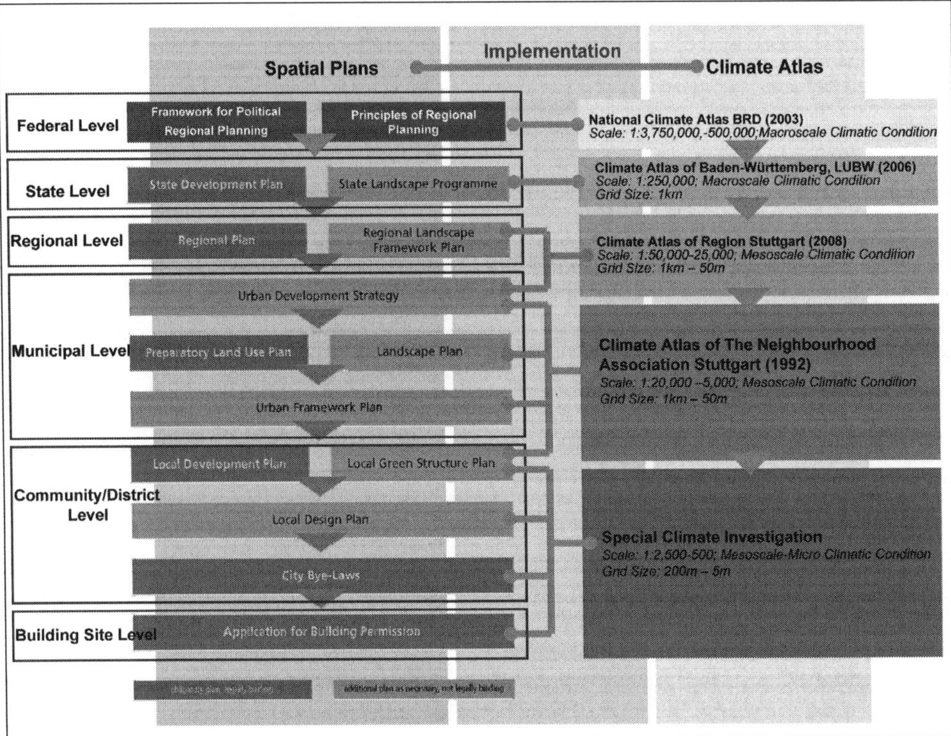


*Figure 25.1* The structure of German Spatial Plans and Climate Atlas.

Source: Baumüller, 2008

## *Development*

Since the 1980s, most German-speaking countries or countries with German as a second language (countries that normally do not speak German), including Switzerland, Austria, Hungary, and Sweden, have initiated UCMap studies. These countries defined their key concerns according to their perceived needs and updated the construction method. In Switzerland, for example, researchers from the University of Basel developed another three kinds of UCMap (Scherer *et al.*, 1999): basic maps of topography [based on digital elevation model (DEM) and digital terrain model (DTM) data], land use information (based on Landsat-TM ERS-1 SAR); and two important maps: a Ventilation Map with different classes and the map of Areal types; a UC-AnMap, named 'The map of climatopes', with planning guidelines. Researchers tried to find an automatic way of defining the climatopes and generating the planning guidelines.

Beyond the European countries, researchers in Asia and South America have also embarked on UCMap studies since the 1990s. Among them, Japan leads the research. In the Japanese method there are three kinds of map: basic data layers; an analysis map of ground covering, air temperature, and wind distribution; and a thermal environmental map. The Japanese paid considerable attention to the scientific analysis and created the thermal balance calculation. For example, in the Tokyo thermal environmental map, three key climatic issues are presented: climatopes, cold airflows in the night-time, and sea breezes (see Figure 25.2).

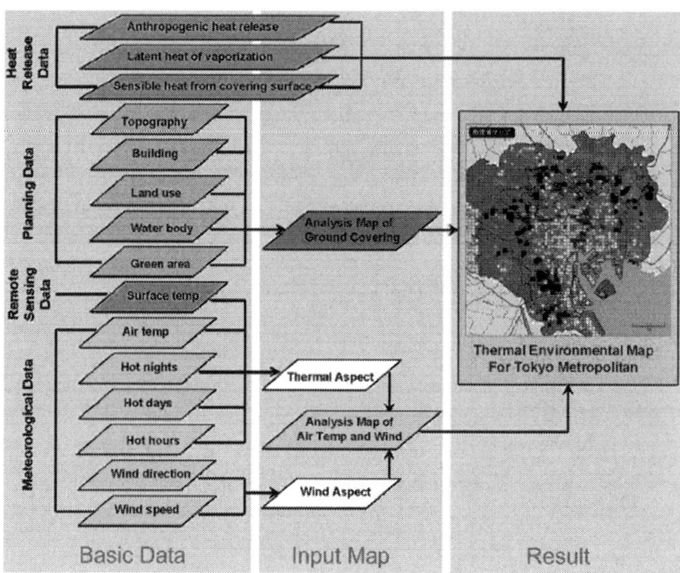


*Figure 25.2* Working flow of creating Tokyo Thermal Environment Map.

Source: after TMG, 2005

Since most Japanese cities experience hot, humid summers, the policy measures in Japan focus on three main aspects for improving the summer condition (TMG, 2005):

(a) Surface covering:
*Increasing greenery*
- Creating a network of urban parks
- Increasing greenery space, in particular, woodland
- Roof and façade greening
- Planting rows of trees along the streets
*Changing building surface covering and street paving*
- Using high-reflection paving for building surfaces
- Using water-permeable street paving

(b) Anthropogenic heat mitigation:
*Improving building performance*
*Controlling the number of automobiles in daytime*

(c) Changing urban morphology and the orientation of streets:
*Urban design and planning considering summer prevailing wind situation*
*Land–sea breeze and valley breeze effect*

Local authorities also created their own countermeasures. For example, according to the thermal environmental map for Tokyo's 23 Wards, the Tokyo Metropolitan Government (TMG) defined four designated areas and formulated corresponding control measures for further development (TMG, 2005). Central Tokyo area, as one of four designated areas, is a business cluster area with both high daytime and night-time temperatures due to the release of large amounts of waste heat from office buildings and the lack of urban air ventilation.

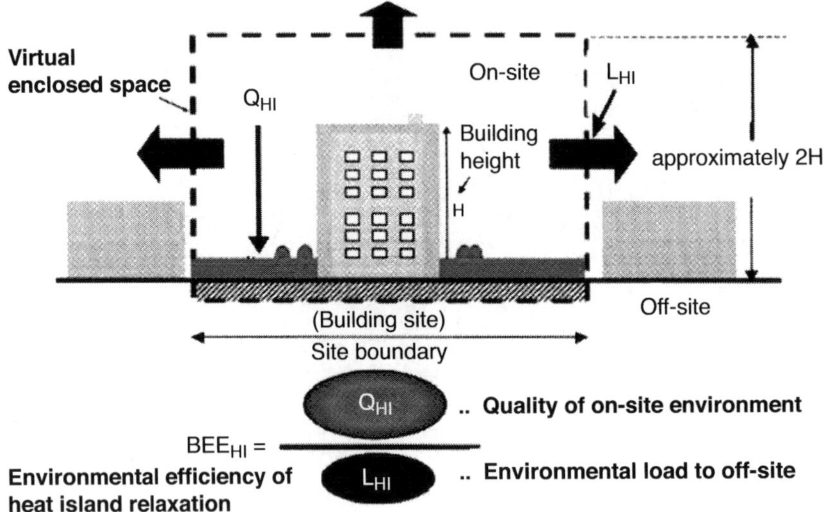


*Figure 25.3* Development of the rating system CASBEE-HI.

Source: IBEC, 2006; Mochida, 2006

Based on the Tokyo Thermal Environmental Map's findings, the Comprehensive Assessment System for Building Environmental Efficiency on Heat Island Relaxation (CASBEE-HI) was developed by the Institute for Building Environment and Energy Conservation (IBEC) in 2005 to guide building design in order to mitigate the UHI effect and evaluate the effects of various countermeasures (see Figure 25.3).

Since people's thermal comfort is greatly influenced by outdoor climatic conditions, they may affect people's use of outdoor urban spaces such as streets, plazas, playgrounds, urban parks, and so on. The issue of outdoor thermal comfort has attracted wide attention in the UCMap research field in recent years. In Sweden, a researcher presented the bioclimatic condition in spatial maps (Svensson, 2002; Svensson *et al.*, 2003). In Hong Kong, local researchers used Physiological Equivalent Temperature (PET), a human thermal index to present the climatic variations of a high-density city based on the analysis of user surveys and field measurements.

Recently, awareness of climate change has increased and the spatial analysis of its impact and consequences for people outdoors has received attention in European countries. For example, French researchers have attempted to incorporate mortality data and spatialise the heat wave impact in Paris (Desplat *et al.*, 2009).

### Climatic implementation in urban planning

Based on the desktop studies of worldwide UCMap studies, it could be summarised that planning action could be carried out from four strategies, albedo, vegetation, shading and ventilation, to improve human thermal comfort and the dynamic potential situation (see Figure 25.4). Their planning timescale ranges from short term to long term and their spatial scales are from urban effect to city effect.

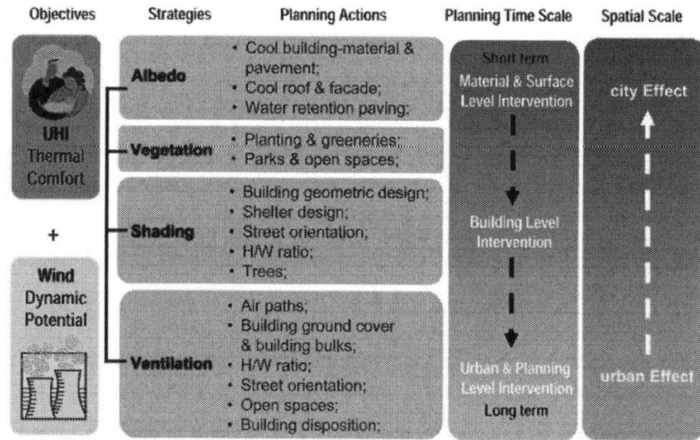


*Figure 25.4* Lessons on strategies and measures for improving urban climate environment.

Source: Ren *et al.*, 2009

## Project set-up and data preprocessing: An example from the municipality of Arnhem, the Netherlands

In order to exemplify the process of making such a UCMap with the most recent example on which the scientific urban climate community worked on, the example of Arnhem is introduced.

### *Study area and background*

The city of Arnhem is situated in the eastern part of the Netherlands (see Figure 25.5a). It is the capital of the province of Gelderland and is situated where the St. Jansbeek River joins the Lower Rhine (Nederrijn) (see Figure 25.5b). The city is full of parks and greenery. Most of the urbanised areas are flat. Only the northern part of city is on hilly terrain, with a top height of 50m to 60m. There are several small valleys in the area.

Arnhem has a mild climate with summer highs of 22°C. Winters range from −0.5°C to 5°C (see Table 25.1). Spring in Arnhem is mildly chilly, ranging from 2°C to 12°C. The weather in autumn ranges from 6°C to 14°C. The annual prevailing wind is from the SW direction and occurs most of the time, but when the wind direction changes to W or E, the wind condition becomes weak. Only the N and NE winds bring chilly climatic conditions.

Researchers from the meteorology and air quality group in Wageningen University (Heusinkveld, 2009) carried out some mobile field measurements in Rotterdam and Arnhem and found that though the air temperature perceived by the human body was 28°C at Zestienhoven (airport), the temperature at the city centre of Rotterdam (in the sun and out of the wind) would feel more than 6°C higher. Similar effects were also measured in Arnhem. In order to understand more about that, ten years (2000–2009) of temperature data at the three stations Rotterdam, Deelen (Chudnovsky *et al.*, 2004) and Volkel (airport) provided by the Royal Netherlands Meteorological Institute were analysed. We used data at Rotterdam to represent the situation of Arnhem because of the lack of data at Arnhem and the similar effect between the two cities found by the Wageningen University and Research Centre (Heusinkveld, 2009). The results showed that the temperature difference from noon to 4.00 p.m. in August can be up to 6.6°C between Rotterdam and the other two stations. It can also be found that around 23 per cent of the time between 7.00 p.m. to 12.00 a.m. in August, the temperature difference between Rotterdam and the other two stations is greater by

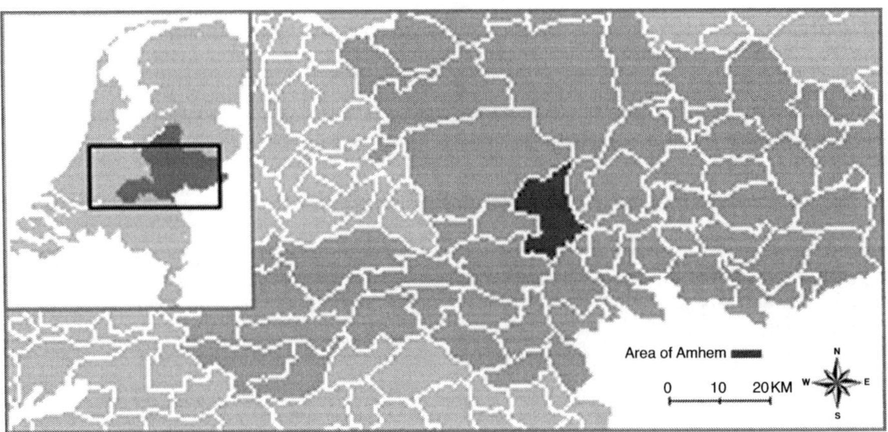


*Figure 25.5* (a) The location of Arnhem.

Source: http://en.wikipedia.org/wiki/File:LocatieArnhem.png

*Figure 25.5* (b) Google ™ map of study area: Arnhem.

Source: Google ™ map

*Table 25.1* Weather data for Arnhem.

| *Weather data for Arnhem, Netherlands* | | | | | | | | | | | | | |
|---|---|---|---|---|---|---|---|---|---|---|---|---|---|
| Month | Jan. | Feb. | Mar. | Apr. | May | Jun. | Jul. | Aug. | Sep. | Oct. | Nov. | Dec. | Year |
| Record high °C | 14.5 | 16.8 | 22.5 | 27.3 | 31.6 | 33.9 | 35.6 | 37.2 | 30.7 | 26.4 | 17.3 | 15.1 | 37.2 |
| Average high °C | 4.6 | 5.6 | 9.2 | 12.8 | 17.7 | 19.9 | 22.1 | 22.3 | 18.5 | 13.8 | 8.5 | 5.7 | 13.4 |
| Average low °C | −0.5 | −0.6 | 1.5 | 3.0 | 7.2 | 9.8 | 11.9 | 11.7 | 9.4 | 6.1 | 2.7 | 0.8 | 5.3 |
| Record low °C | −24.2 | −16.2 | −17.0 | −9.4 | −2.4 | −0.4 | 2.0 | 2.4 | −0.9 | −5.1 | −9.1 | −17.3 | −24.2 |
| Precipitation mm | 83 | 53 | 77 | 50 | 63 | 76 | 72 | 62 | 76 | 76 | 85 | 92 | 865 |

Source: www.knmi.nl

at least 2°C, up to around 7°C. This significant temperature difference should be high enough for the inhabitants in Arnhem to experience heat stress-related issues. Furthermore, the city region of Arnhem–Nijmegen is conducting a new urban development named 'urban planning agreements 2010–2020, which will provide around 26,000 homes in the middle areas between Arnhem and Nijmegen. In order to improve the heat stress situation and create more liveable urban space, the study of the Arnhem UCMap was initiated by the Municipality of Arnhem within the EU-Interreg IVB-project titled 'Future Cities – urban networks to face climate change'. It is a pilot study in the Netherlands and aims to help the Municipality of Arnhem incorporate climate effects in planning processes in a systematic way. Therefore, the implication of this study is to provide climatic reference information for the local planners and policymakers of Arnhem to avoid fuelling the UHI effect and to keep the high quality of city environment for work, living, and recreation.

## Methodology

### Data collection

A cartographical representation of Arnhem's physical features and climatic variations was constructed according to the collected data. In this study, climatically relevant geometrical data (topographical, land use and buildings information) from the Municipality of Arnhem and the Royal Netherlands Meteorological Institute, as well as evaluated data from urban climatologists and wind experts of the consultant team was put into a Geographic Information System (GIS) to become basic input layers and UC-AnMaps.

The collated information is classified and calculated based on the dynamic potential and thermal load contributions to the urban climate. *Thermal load* measures the stored heat load of particular localities of urban areas; thermal load depends mainly on the building volume (which has an impact on heat storage and blocks the sky view, slowing the city's cooling at night), the topography, and availability of green spaces for a cooling effect. *Dynamic potential* evaluates the ground roughness and therefore the potential for air movement for particular localities of the urban areas. Dynamic potential depends mainly on the site coverage, ground roughness, and the proximity to openness. Ground roughness is defined as the intensity of the ground effect influencing the wind speed and turbulence. The rougher the surface, the lower the wind speed and dynamic potential. Thus, the procedure that was followed in developing the UCMap for Arnhem is illustrated in Figure 25.6.

Then, basic input layers including the map of building volume density, a land-use map, and topography were prepared. The urban morphology map and ventilation map were also produced for defining the climatopes and creating the UCAn-Map for Arnhem (see Figure 25.7).

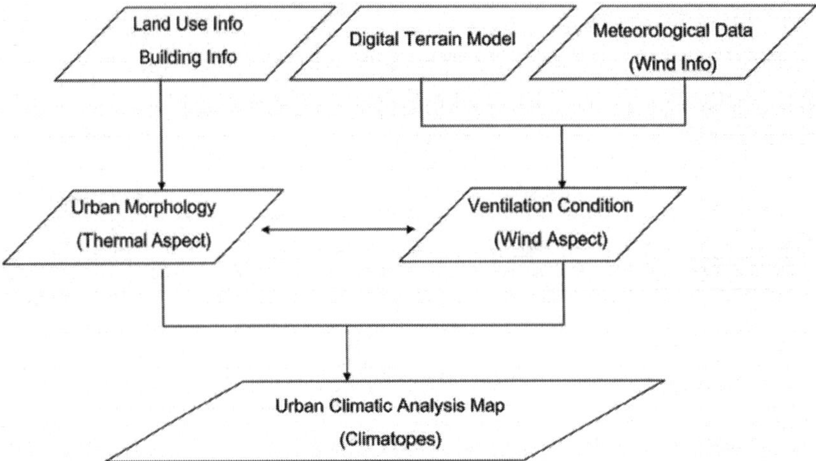


*Figure 25.6* Methodologies of the UCMap for Arnhem.

Source: Authors

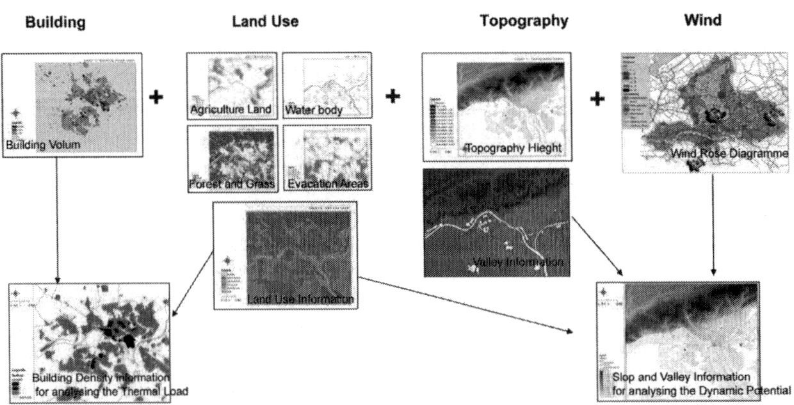


*Figure 25.7* The structure of the UCMap for Arnhem.

*Source: Authors*

### *The urban morphology map of the built-up areas*

Urban geometry has a complex influence on the microclimate of the urban environment. For example, differences between urban geometry and building density may result in intra-urban air temperature differences (Chandler, 1976). High building volume not only increases the localised heat capacity (i.e. thermal load), but also reduces the sky view factor (SVF), which has a major influence in slowing the radiative cooling effect in the city at night and is commonly used as the indicator to quantify the thermal load of built-up areas. The most important aspect of this urban heat island effect is that built-up areas predominantly obstruct the open sky and delay the cooling of the surface during clear, calm nights (Oke, 1981). If the building volume density is high, the long-wave radiation could be blocked, and released slowly. The cooling process within the city centre is slower than its surrounding areas. Hence, the trapped radiation within the urban areas has a higher temperature than the surrounding areas at night. In short, the higher the building volume density, the larger the heat capacity of the built-up areas, and this can contribute to more heat stress.

In this sense, SVF maps for five selected sites with various building densities were generated to provide basic understanding for the classification of building volume and therefore the development of the urban morphology map. A GIS-based software method is used to calculate continuous SVF values of an entire terrain, based on DEM data derived from the geographical building database. The method is introduced in Chen *et al.* (2010) and is proven to give satisfactory result when compared with fish-eye lens photography measurements. The SVF map of five selected areas (see Figure 25.8) provides illustrations of the varieties of thermal load due to building volume differences (see Table 25.2). For understanding the urban morphology of Arnhem, the building volume density and land-use information were synthesised together to develop an urban morphology map of built-up areas with three classifications of density from high (where buildings occupy circa 30 per cent of the total floor area), medium (where buildings cover between 10 per cent and 30 per cent of the total floor area) to low (where building coverage is less than 10 per cent of the total floor area) (see Figure 25.9).

*Figure 25.8* Five selected areas for analysing SVF value.

Source: Courtesy of Liang Chen

*Table 25.2* Area mean value of SVF of five selected areas (size: 1km²).

| No. | *Area 1* | *Area 2* | *Area 3* | *Area 4* | *Area 5* |
|---|---|---|---|---|---|
| **Area Mean Value of SVF** | 0.28 | 0.44 | 0.54 | 0.60 | 0.60 |

* Note: Evaluation range: SVF < 0.3: high thermal load; SVF = [0.3, 0.6]: medium thermal load; SVF > 0.6: low thermal load. The threshold has been examined in Chen *et al.*, 2010.

Source: Authors

*Figure 25.9* Urban Morphology Map of Arnhem.

Source: Authors

### *The ventilation map for Arnhem*

Since the northern part of the city is on hilly terrain with several small valleys, the katabatic winds could be observed, and local variations in topography may greatly affect the wind conditions. This colder air is beneficial. The down-slope winds are only of local significance, especially for the location at the bottom of the slopes (Lazar and Podesser, 1999). Colder air generally moves downhill along the valleys. These winds originate from the production of cold air which is a consequence of the negative balance of radiation. Thus, in the ventilation map for Arnhem, those valleys that can generate the katabatic winds were highlighted by black nets in Figure 25.10 based on the topographic information and evaluation.

Since the St. Jansbeek River joins the Lower Rhine (Nederrijn) in the southern part of Arnhem, the water body areas together with bank and flooding areas were represented by grey dots in Figure 25.10 based on the land use information.

## Results and analysis

### *Defining climatopes*

The climatope is the spatial unit of the UC-AnMap that presents climatic variation (VDI, 1997). A climatope depends mainly on the homogeneous climatic characteristics, surface roughness, and land use. Thus, areal types of Arnhem city were analysed mainly from an area mean value of SVF (see Table 25.2); the roughness length (see Table 25.3), and climatic characteristics were evaluated according to the existing land use information.

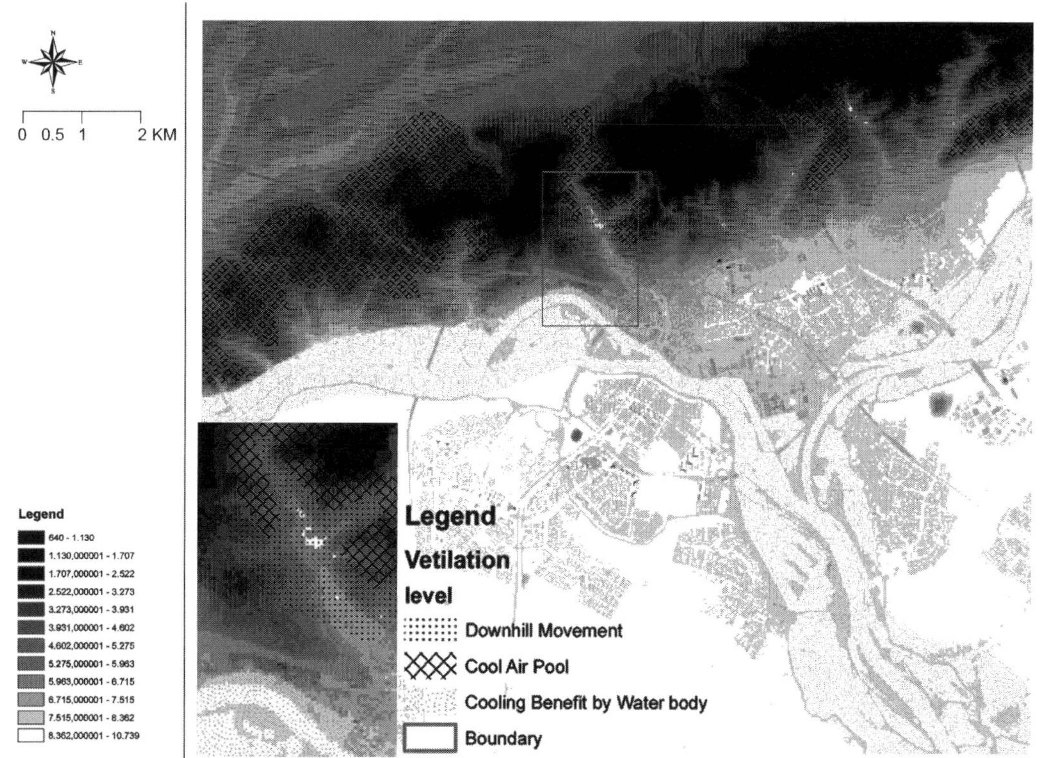


*Figure 25.10* Ventilation Map for Arnhem.

Source: Authors

*Table 25.3* Areal types and evaluation of their climatic characteristics.

| *Areal type* | *Roughness Length* | *Evaluation of Climatic Characteristic* |
|---|---|---|
| **Transportation areas**<br>(railway, road, airport) | 0.03 | Medium thermal stress, high dynamic potential |
| **Built-up areas**<br>(residential, retail and catering, public space, social-cultural facilities, construction site) | > 2.0 | High thermal stress, very low dynamic potential |
| **Semi-built-up areas**<br>(landfill, cemetery, construction site and others) | > 2.0 | High thermal stress, medium dynamic potential |
| **Leisure**<br>(park, sport ground, holiday resort) | 0.03–0.25 | Low thermal stress, high dynamic potential |
| **Agriculture** | 0.10 | Low thermal stress, high dynamic potential |
| **Forest and natural areas** | > 2.0 | Medium thermal stress, high dynamic potential |
| **Water body**<br>Rhine–Meuse River, recreational water areas, flood areas, wet field, water channel | 0.002–0.03 | Low thermal stress, high dynamic potential |

Source: Authors

The determination and classification of climatopes was developed for Arnhem from the land use information and evaluation, based on the urban morphology map (including SVF calculation) and ventilation map. The resulting spatial distribution of areal types and ventilation classes is presented in the urban climatic analysis map in Plate 25.1. It shows the combinations of areal types and ventilation classes in four categories of climatopes. They include the climatopes of built-up areas, greenery areas, water bodies and transport areas. Each climatope range is different according to their climatic characteristics. For example, in the climatope of built-up areas, the dark red represents the downtown area's complex urban morphology, which processes the high thermal load and very low dynamic potential; in the climatope of water bodies, the blue represents the river, which can produce a cooling effect and benefit surrounding areas.

### *Verification of the climatopes of UC-AnMap*

Different climatic factors and planning elements are synergistically taken into consideration to quickly form the Arnhem UCMap. The analysis of various selected factors and information from each basic map of Arnhem UCMap provides an initial understanding of the relationship between the city environment and urban climate of Arnhem and forms the basis of classification of climatopes. This classification is further verified according to the result from the mobile field-measurement study and heat scan study.

Referring to the result of mobile field-measurement study done by the researchers of meteorology and air quality group in Wageningen University (Heusinkveld, 2009) in Figure 25.11(b), it can be found that on a summer day (typical calm winds and clear skies, at 3.00 p.m. on 10 August 2009), the city centre areas of Arnhem (the built-up areas with climatopes of high thermal load to medium thermal load and very low dynamic potential to low dynamic potential) have higher air temperatures than the park areas of Sonsbeek and Zijpendaal (the forest areas with climatopes of low thermal load and low dynamic potential) or the agricultural areas of the southern part of Arnhem (the grassland with climatopes of low thermal load and high dynamic potential). From a heat scan study of Arnhem (see Figure 25.12), it can also be found that in the summertime, the surface temperature of the city centre areas is also higher than the surrounding areas. That means that the classification of the climatopes of the UC-AnMap of Arnhem is in good agreement with the real climate condition on-site.

### *Principles defining the designated areas*

According to the UC-AnMap and the communication with local planners and government, it was possible to point out four designated areas which need to be paid attention to in future development (see Figure 25.11 and Table 25.4). The selection was based on the following:

- the urban climatic analysis map; areas (business cluster areas and high-density residential areas) that have a high thermal load and low dynamic potential on the atmosphere were selected;
- new development or urban renewal where environmentally conscious private-sector development is possible.

In addition, the areas chosen were those where urban development should be systematically directed while preventing future widespread development and incorporating preventative heat island measures and protecting existing climatic resources.

According to the climatic information from the UC-AnMap for Arnhem, the existing problems are pointed out and the effective measures are provided in Table 25.4.

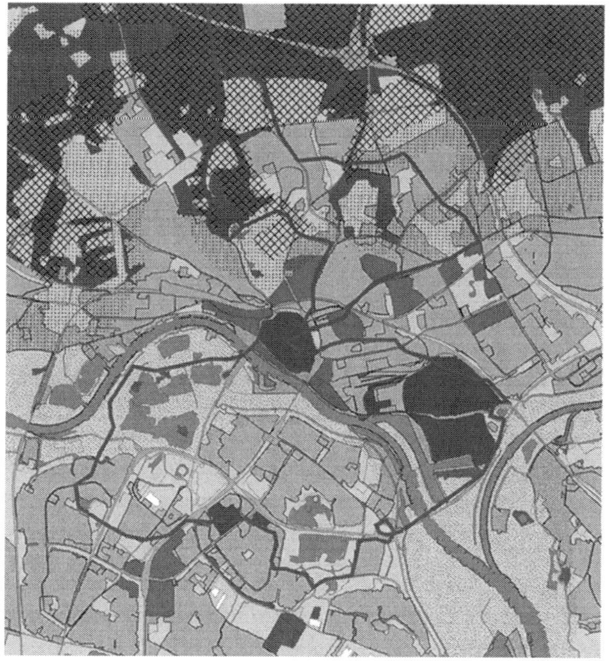

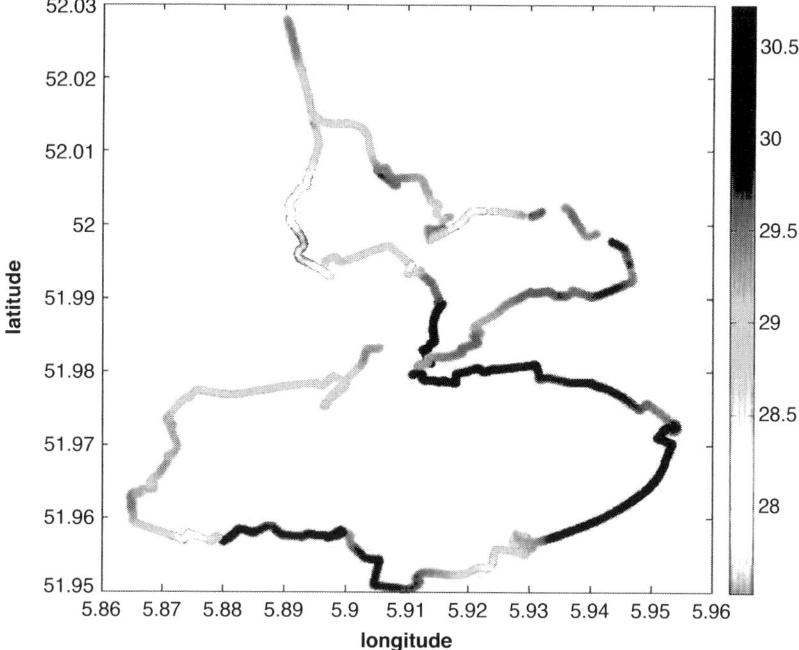


*Figure 25.11* The mobile field-measurement on 10 August 2009: (a) black line shows the measurement route; (b) shows the result of field measurement.

Source: Katzschner, 2010

*Figure 25.12* An image of the surface temperature of Arnhem (heat scan study was carried out at a height of 4 kilometres from an aeroplane, pictures were made by a heat-sensitive camera on a selected summer day in 2009).

Source: Authors

*Table 25.4* Problems in four designated areas and possible effective measures.

| *Designated areas* | *Main climatic condition* | *Areal type* | *Problems and measures* |
|---|---|---|---|
| 1 | Low thermal load and low dynamic potential | Residential areas, forest, park | **The katabatic wind is blocked.**<br>Create air path<br>Create greenery network |
| 2 | High thermal load and very low dynamic potential | Commercial areas, residential areas | **Urban Heat Island is observed.**<br>Create air path for cool breezes to pass through the downtown areas<br>Control the further development |
| 3 | High thermal load and very low dynamic potential | Industrial areas | **Urban Heat Island and air pollution could be observed.**<br>Reduce the anthropogenic heat release |
| 4 | Medium thermal load and low dynamic potential | Residential areas, traffic areas | **Low urban ventilation could be observed.**<br>Create air path<br>Control the further development |

Source: Authors

### *Implementation in the Dutch planning system*

This UCMap of Arnhem could provide an urban climatic information platform at the municipality level of the Dutch planning system (see Figure 25.13). Considering the Dutch planning system (MHSPE, 2000), the recommended measures (see Table 25.4) could be adopted in a structural vision and zoning scheme. This UCMap of Arnhem may also provide boundary conditions and background understanding for detailed additional studies at a microclimatic scale. Thus, the

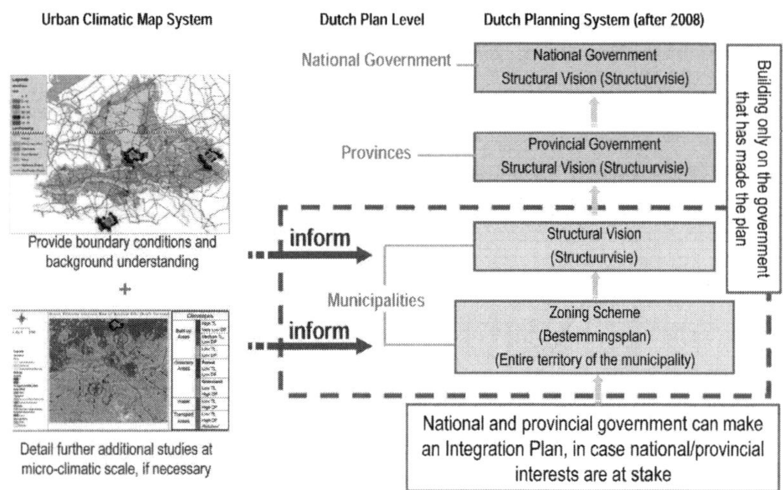


*Figure 25.13* The relationship between the Arnhem UCMap and the Dutch planning system.
Source: Authors

UCMap of Arnhem can assist local planners and policymakers in making better decisions in future development or planning, such as with green master plans, urban renewal plans, future land use plans, new town plans, and so on.

## Discussion on the advantages and limitations of urban climatic maps

The science of the climatic environment is complicated; its application to urban planning is the lively concern of researchers and local governments around the world. To help planners, developers, and policymakers understand urban climatic conditions, we demonstrate how to use limited climatic, environmental, and planning data to quickly construct the basic input layers and the final UCMap and how to formulate the climatic evaluation and recommendation for sustainable planning.

This methodology and construction process has several advantages:

- The method and procedure of constructing a UCMap is easy for non-climatic experts to follow.
- The selected parameters are easy to collect and the study result is useful for planning use.
- The structure of the UCMap system is flexible and easily managed. It consists of basic input layers and a final evaluation map, and all climatic, environmental, and planning information is collated and evaluated in the same grid size embedded within a GIS framework. Thus, further climatic, environmental, and planning information could be updated and managed in the future. UCMaps can be implemented in many cities, even without much existing climate knowledge.
- Various climate data and environmental information is presented spatially and qualitatively according to the UCMap. Planners, built environment experts, developers, and policymakers can gain ready access to knowledge about climatic conditions and their evaluation, and identify

the problem areas and sensitive areas that are in need of strategic attention and improvement from the climatic-environmental point of view.
- The UCMap can also provide a platform for interdisciplinary study; the UCMap visually presents the synthetic evaluation for decision making, construction, and policy actions. Comprehensive climatic understanding at the urban level could be formulated from a UCMap. All climatic knowledge and information is translated into planning-orientated actions and recommendations that could be used in an urban master plan.

However, there are still three main limitations of methodology and implementation:

- The process of climatic evaluation and application in urban planning is mainly on the basis of qualitative and subjective assessment.
- Since the available climatic data and planning information is limited, this result cannot present more details, such as building information and human thermal comfort issues.
- The existing gap between the practical world of spatial planning and the scientific world of climate studies will never be closed. The tool remains just a fragile bridge to cover a huge gap.

At least theoretically, the balance of advantages and disadvantages seem to be in favour of UCMaps. Although there may be many circumstances in which this balance may be judged differently, we expect the tool to be of major assistance in integrating climate knowledge into Dutch urban planning processes.

## Further study

This Arnhem UCMap is an initial, pilot work of urban climatic mapping, which allows local planners and policymakers to get useful information for their daily ongoing works. It attempts to use a quick method to accumulate climatic information and create a platform for planning use. It relies mostly on literature and theoretical understanding that has been well practiced elsewhere. The effort here is to synergise the established understanding for a case at hand and demonstrate how useful guidance can still be made for planners and policymakers. There is a need to further refine and update the Arnhem UCMap when it is needed.

## Conclusions

As can be noted from the empirical studies, the use of UCMaps is growing internationally. It is encouraging that planners are becoming convinced of the importance of the effects of climate change. However, the procedures in urban planning projects are usually long and complicated. A balance has to found in which all the relevant economic and policy conditions and interests are weighted within a strict time schedule. To some extent, the decision-making process is determined by the subject analysis and expert knowledge and experiences, but opportunistic political arguments usually dominate, even when there are direct and huge risks at stake (Flyvbjerg *et al.*, 2003). In those cases, climate information will take last place in the decision-making process in terms of priority as well as in style of communication.

The empirical studies show that the advantages of UCMaps are being recognised, but both climate information and UCMaps still have a long way to go. In order to overcome the implementation problems, the scientific world should endeavour to make its knowledge more accessible.

The practical world of spatial planning must also open up its planning processes to include softer and long-term information in order to cope with the effects of climate change in compact urban areas.

In the Netherlands, people, through the Dutch planning, pursue a quality of life and spatial environment that is sustainable and liveable (van der Valk, 2002). Climatic information is not like other common indicators of the quality of life. It is easily ignored in real planning practice. Based on the learned experience from this pilot study, Arnhem UCMap can be introduced to other similar Dutch municipalities. For example, since the city region of Arnhem–Nijmegen is conducting a new urban development named 'urban planning agreements 2010–2020', which will provide around 26,000 homes in the middle areas between Arnhem and Nijmegen, the next step is to share the learned experience and apply it to the neighbourhood city of Nijmegen. Later on, similar studies will be carried out in all 20 municipalities of this region.

## Acknowledgements

The study was supported by the EU-Interreg IVB-project titled 'Future Cities – urban networks to face climate change' and the Municipality of Arnhem. The authors wish to acknowledge the help from Mr Vincent Kuypers of Wageningen UR Alterra Landscape Centre and Mr Hans van Ammers of the municipality of Arnhem, as well as the researchers of meteorology and air quality group in Wageningen University and the Royal Netherlands Meteorological Institute for providing data needed for the study.

This part of the chapter was originally published as Ren, C., Spit, T., Lenzholzer, S., Yim, H. L. S., Heusinkveld, B., van Hove, B., Chen, L., Kupski, S., Burghardt, R. and Katzschner, L. (2012). Urban Climate Map System for Dutch spatial planning, *International Journal of Applied Earth Observation and Geoinformation*, 18: 207–221. Kind permission has been obtained from Elsevier to reproduce it.

## PART II: TRACING CLIMATE ADAPTATION IN A HARD PLANNING PROCESS, THE DUTCH EXPERIENCE

### Introduction

Throughout the world, cities in delta areas have to deal with the effects of climate change. In the Netherlands, the awareness of this relatively new phenomenon is growing. This can easily be understood when one considers that the Dutch authorities have to deal with rising sea levels as well as rising river discharges. In addition, heavy rainfalls and rising ground water levels are also matters of concern to them. Therefore, water threatens the Dutch cities from multiple sides. Of course, there are also other effects of climate change, such as heavy winds and urban heat islands, but those seem less important within the Dutch context.

The Dutch local government has only recently started to explore the possibilities for coping with the effects of climate change in terms of *adaptation* in urban planning. Adaptation anticipates climate changes that can already be observed, through the use of various physical measures such as adjustments in urban design, temporal water storage, etc. (Kokx, 2012). The impacts of climate change are always locally measured and tackled and therefore have to be tailor-made locally within the institutional arrangements of the local planning system (Blanco *et al.*, 2009). In order to be effective, adaptation should match the institutional arrangements for planning as well as fit into the local planning processes (Kokx, 2012); the latter is part of the local planning process. Also, there is always some sort of cost-benefit balance that has to be taken into account.

### Four challenges

It is important to define what type of challenges the planning system is facing from a climate perspective. Van Buuren *et al.* (2012) defines four challenges: first, the planning system has to deal with the extra uncertainties that come with the issue of climate change. Although we know more and more about the changing climate (see the IPCC reports) and its local effects, there is still much uncertainty about the degree to which it will affect local communities and when and how it will affect them. This uncertainty may result in indecisiveness and hesitation (Giddens, 2009). The second challenge is how to handle the controversial character of climate change in spatial planning. Within local spatial planning processes the issue of climate adaptation has to compete with other interests. As climate adaptation measures mostly require a long-term horizon, it will quickly tend to a so-called weak interest in local decision making processes. The third challenge is its multifaceted character. As climate change can result in dry periods as well as extremely wet periods, the opposite sides of the same coin have to be addressed (see the Australian experiences in 2010). The fourth and last challenge is its complexity. As climate change tends to connect to many other domains and functions, it is not hard to imagine how complex it will be to implement its effects on a local level.

### Towards a successful approach

Together, these four challenges may seem to claim an approach in which flexibility, learning, and experiments are central items in a governance approach (Folke *et al.*, 2005; Huitema *et al.*, 2009). Even flexible coalitions between all kinds of societal actors (Brunner *et al.*, 2005; Pahl-Wostl, 2006), or bottom-up processes of self-organisation aim to increase the resilience of a local community towards climate change. However, adaptation towards climate change through the planning system not only demands flexibility but also robustness (van Buuren *et al.*, 2012). For planning processes, there should always be a balance between the desire to change the built environment and the wish to support legal certainty for those who have possessions in that particular area.

In this part of the chapter we explore the possibilities for integrating the knowledge of climate change into local planning processes in the Netherlands, based on the experiences of some of the larger municipalities in the Netherlands that participate in the research programme Knowledge for Climate: Amsterdam, Rotterdam, The Hague and Arnhem. As the practical experience of this integration is rather young, the analysis remains rather theoretical and explorative. Also, as the debate on this integration is rather fierce, we intend to shed some light on the dilemmas that show up in the debate, as we expect that similar dilemmas will show up all over the world.

## The institutional framework: Integrating adaptation into a functioning planning system

### Urban planning in the Netherlands

From the 1920s onwards in the Netherlands, there has been a growing concern that urban expansion would engulf the whole western part of the Netherlands, forming one huge conurbation (Faludi and van der Valk, 1990). In reality, this was never a serious threat until the 1960s. Then, a major wave of suburbanisation threatened to spread pockets of urban land use across the Green

Heart (Dieleman and Musterd, 1992). From the late sixties onwards, social circumstances began to change. In this period, pressure- and interest groups succeeded more and more in convincing the authorities to focus more attention on predominantly social objectives in urban policy.

The development as described above was mirrored in planning documents from the central government. The *Second Report on Physical Planning in the Netherlands* (Ministry VRO, 1966) included a proposal to divert populations from the crowded western part of the country to the north and south. However, it also took a powerful stand against the suburban sprawl that was developing into a real threat, particularly in the Green Heart (van der Wusten and Faludi, 1992). The proposed alternative was to channel suburbanisation into 'concentrated deconcentration'. More specifically, this meant accommodating new urban growth outside the existing cities in a number of designated overspill centres. Jenks *et al.* (1996) describes this policy as a feasible compromise between concentration and low-density dispersal of urban activities. In Randstad, Holland, it was put into practice in the late 1970s and the early 1980s. Compact urban development has remained the cornerstone of Dutch physical planning ever since. The policy of concentrated deconcentration was successful in the view of Faludi and van der Valk (1990); half a million people moved into the designated growth centres and urban sprawl was stemmed by prohibiting the growth of villages in the Green Heart.

Over the course of the 1980s, the policy of compact urban development changed track. The main cause of the shift was the decline of the old urban cores. Concern about urban decay was first voiced by the cities' administrations. Later the issue was placed on the national political agenda (Ministry VROM, 1983). City officials blamed inner city decline in part on the policy of concentrated deconcentration. Eventually, this policy was abolished. In its place a new concept of compact urban growth was developed and put into practice. Under this new policy the government tried to guide new urban (re)development towards locations within existing cities (towards 'brown' sites) and later on towards new green field sites directly adjacent to the cities of Amsterdam, Rotterdam, The Hague, and Utrecht. Within a ten-year period, a total of some 227,200 dwellings should be built on these sites in relatively compact form. In addition, places of work and service premises will also be built there (Spit and Zoete, 2009).

### Urban planning and climate change

During the process of developing this new course a heated debate on the merits, feasibility, and costs started throughout administrative and policy circles. The arguments used are reminiscent of those brought forward in the international literature on urbanisation processes (see e.g. Richardson and Bae, 2004). The debate showed that the implementation of urban development is no easy task even if there was broad consensus on its merits (Breheney, 1996; Jenks *et al.*, 1996). Within these urbanisation processes the Dutch governance approach already tries to balance too many interests and the introduction of the need to adapt to the effects of climate change further complicates an already very complex decision making process. Based upon the aforementioned challenges it is possible to identify its consequences for the Dutch urban planning processes. In order to deal with the first three challenges, the planning system needs the back up from a legal system that is firmly rooted in broadly accepted values, as well as the flexibility to adjust to local circumstances. This can be considered the backbone of a governance approach needed to adapt to climate change. 'More or less', it guaranties continuity and legal certainty in the otherwise unpredictable processes. It has to guarantee a minimum quality and may certainly not be too detailed. In the latter respect, the Dutch system does not fit this requirement, for the detailed legal system sets limits on the much needed flexibility in urban planning. In trying to address this dilemma some principles may be of help. Van Buuren *et al.* (2012) defined some principles which could be of help in the adaptation process at a local level. We consider that three of them are of utmost importance:

1) the precautionary principle
2) the proportionality principle
3) the cost recovery principle.

Each of these principles play an important role in every decision making process about adaptation towards climate. Ideally these principles should play a more or less equal role in each planning process. In practice, however, it will be more important to prevent an imbalance from occurring between these principles because this will seriously damage public support, and thus frustrate the adaptation process.

The next thing to be handled is the flexibility issue. At this point a new dilemma emerges. With reference to a maximum of protection against the effects of climate change, minimum norms for safety are easily introduced. Generally, it will be expected that the use of norms will raise the general physical quality of the area. However, the use of norms is in contrast with the much-needed flexibility in order to adapt better (in terms of effectiveness and efficiency) to specific local circumstances. Again, some sort of balance needs to be found. Especially in situations of uncertainty and complexity, the need for flexibility in planning rules and planning norms are essential (Bohensky and Lynam, 2005). In order to facilitate this flexibility in the Netherlands, the compensation principle is put into practice more and more. Although the experience with this principle is rather young, the results seem promising, as it enables actors to diverge from planning norms, yet its costs make them cautious.

The fourth challenge deals with complexity. In order to unravel complexity, scientific information might seem to play a role. However, research (Geertman, 2006; Brömmelstroet, 2009) shows that scientific information in general (including GIS tools) is not easily incorporated into planning processes. This applies even more for information about the effects of climate change. Ren *et al.* (2012: 220) concluded from their study on the Dutch city of Arnhem that: 'The existing gap between the practical world of spatial planning and the scientific world of climate studies will never be closed. The tool remains just a fragile bridge to cover a huge gap'.

In order to bridge the gap as described by Ren *et al.* (2012), the earlier identified challenges must be met. In order to do so it is necessary to organise support for the different actors that have a stake in the adaptation process towards climate change. In doing so, a first requisite is the use of a common knowledge base. If there is no agreement between the relevant actors on the basic analysis of the common problems that have to be addressed, there is no chance of a (common) solution. The information from the analysis of UC maps can not only provide this knowledge, but it can also provide it in a common 'language' about the effects of climate change. If the relevant actors agree upon language and analysis, a necessary basis is created for common solutions. The key question that remains is how to organise these solutions.

## Bridging the gap: Towards the conditions for a local adaptation strategy in planning

It is important to realise that a new adaptation strategy has to be integrated in an existing (and functioning) urban planning system. A strategy, firmly supported by a common understanding of the effects of climate change starts with the building of a common ground that can function as a basis for the development of some sort of 'goal entwinement' (see Kokx, 2012). The core characteristic of goal entwinement is the acceptance of differences between actors. This acceptance can not only prevent conflicts of interest, but also provides a basis for a cooperative attitude between actors and the creation of opportunities, e.g. to share costs and resources in the case of an integrated design for area development. In fact, the example illustrates that the introduction of climate-proof elements can provide benefits for public actors as well as private actors as it can easily be attached to day-to-day issues in urban planning such as maintenance issues and replacement investments (see Kokx, 2012).

As the starting position and the role of science become clearer, the next question is: how can public and private actors be mobilised in order to develop such an adaptation strategy? Analytically, some stages can be distinguished in such a strategy. It always starts with a stage in which some kind of *awareness* of the problem has to be created. It is easy to see how the role of information and science fits into this stage which has to end up with some sort of *recognition* of the problem. This recognition, in its turn, has to be translated in the next stage into some sense of *urgency*. Without recognition, the problem will be denied and without some sense of urgency, there is no need for policy actions. In both cases nothing will happen. A common recognition of the problem, in combination with a common sense of urgency are the basic conditions for a joint strategy for the adaptation towards climate change within urban planning processes.

In the third stage a common strategy can be developed in which *priorities* are set, instruments developed and investment schemes agreed upon. This stage can benefit hugely if the strategy is based upon the three principles mentioned above. If the strategy is based upon these principles, it is optimally tailored to the issues, as well as the governance context in which it has been developed.

### *Soft interests in a hard process*

Why is such a careful arrangement for adapting to climate change in urban planning necessary? In order to answer this question, one has to keep in mind that the development of an adaptation strategy will firstly be viewed by the relevant actors as no more than some form of external integrative interest that is eager to penetrate into the urban planning system, as so many sorts of interest do all the time. When it is considered as such, all the usual defence mechanisms will be started up. One may expect that any attempt to start an adaptation strategy will immediately be stamped out as it suffers from a number of characteristics (van Buuren *et al.*, 2012) as a consequence of which it will be interpreted as an extremely weak interest without any economic and/or financial position to back it up. Particularly its long-term character and weak financial position (it will only be considered as an extra cost) are the cause of this relatively weak position of any adaptation strategy in urban planning.

However, if a carefully laid out strategy in stages is accompanied by support from higher tiers of government, this position can change significantly (Driessen and Spit, 2010). As ideological arguments (with a weak economic impact) work better on higher administrative levels of government, it should be possible to arrange support there. As pragmatism rules the lower tiers of government, a lot of support is needed to overcome the existing (and new) barriers to make the adaptation towards climate change in urban planning a success. Although this road may appear a tedious one, it is also an exciting challenge in which practitioners as well as scientists can play an important role.

## Acknowledgement

This research was funded by the Dutch Research Programme 'Knowledge for Climate'.

It is with great respect that we want to dedicate this paper to the memory of Dr Anita Kokx. Her sudden death on 29 December 2012 came as a great shock to us all.

## References


Baumüller, N. (2008). Urban planning in Germany. Paper presented at the *Workshop on 'Climate Change and Urban Planning'*. Office of City Planning and Urban Renewal, City of Stuttgart, Stuttgart, Germany.

Baumüller, J., Hoffmann, U., Nagel, T. and Reuter, U. (1992*). Klimauntersuchung Nachbarschaftsverband Stuttgart-Klimaatlas*. Stuggart: Nachbarschaftsverband Stuttgart.

Bitan, A. (1988). The methodology of applied climatology in planning and building. *Energy and Buildings*, 11(1–3): 1–10.

Blanco, H., Alberti, M., Forsyth, A., Krizek, K., Rodrigues, D., Talen, E. and Ellis, C. (2009). Hot, congested, crowded and diverse: Emerging research agendas in planning. *Progress in Planning*, 71(4): 153–205.

Bohensky, E. and Lynam, T. (2005). Evaluating responses in complex adaptive systems: insights on water management from the Southern African Millennium Ecosystem Assessment. *Ecology and Society*, 10(1): 11.

Brömmelstroet, M. (2009). The relevance of research in planning support systems: A response to Janssen *et al. Environment and Planning B: Planning and Design*, 36(1): 4–7.

Breheny, M. (1996). Centrists, decentrists, and compromisers: Views on the future of urban form. In: Jenks, M., Burton, E and Williams, K. (eds.), *The Compact City, a Sustainable Urban Form?* London: E & FN Spon, 13–35.

Brunner, R., Steelman, T., Coe-Juell, L., Cromley, C., Edwards, C. and Tucker, D. (2005). *Adaptive Governance: Integrating Science, Policy and Decisionmaking*. New York: Columbia University Press.

Chandler, T. J. (1976). *Urban Climate and Its Relevance to Urban Design*. WMO Technical No.149. Geneva: World Meteorological Organization.

Chen, L., Ng, E., An, X., Ren, C., Lee, M., Wang, U. and He, Z. (2010). Sky view factor analysis of street canyons and its implications for daytime intra-urban air temperature differentials in high-rise, high-density urban areas of Hong Kong: A GIS-based simulation approach. *International Journal of Climatology*, 32(1):121–136. doi: 10.1002/joc.2243.

Chudnovsky, A., Dor, E. B. and Saaroni, H. (2004). Diurnal thermal behavior of selected urban objects using remote sensing measurements. *Energy and Buildings*, 36(11): 1063–1074.

Desplat, J., Salagnac, J-L., Kounkou, R., Lemonsu, A., Colombert, M., Lauffenburger, M. and Masson, V. (2009). EPICEA Project [2008–2010], Multidisciplinary study of the impacts of climate change on the scale of Paris, *Proceedings of The 7th International Conference on Urban Climate*. Yokohama, Japan, 29 June–3 July. Available at: http://www.ide.titech.ac.jp/~icuc7/extended_abstracts/pdf/383983-1-090519180457-002.pdf (Accessed 10 February 2014).

Dieleman, F. and Musterd, S. (1992). *The Randstad: A Research and Policy Laboratory*. Dordrecht: Kluwer.

Driessen, P. P. J. and Spit, T. J. M. (2010). De bekostiging van klimaatadaptatie: argumenten voor een legitieme balans van baten en lasten. *Beleid en Maatschappij*, 37(1): 73–84.

Eliasson, I. (2000). The use of climate knowledge in urban planning. *Landscape and Urban Planning*, 48(1–2): 31–44.

Faludi, A. and van der Valk, A. (1990). *De groeikernen als hoekstenen van de nederlandse ruimtelijke planningdoctrine*. Assen: Van Gorcum.

Federal German Building Code (2004). Federal Ministry of Transport, Building and Housing, Germany.

Flyvbjerg, B., Bruzelius, N., and Rothengatter, W. (2003). *Megaprojects and Risk: An Anatomy of Ambition*. Cambridge; New York: Cambridge University Press.

Folke, C. Hahn, T., Olsson, P. and Norberg, J. (2005). Adaptive governance of social-ecological systems. *Annual Review of Environment and Resources*, 30: 441–173.

Geertman, S. (2006). Potentials for Planning Support: A planning conceptual approach. *Environment and Planning B: Planning and Design*, 33(6): 863–881.

Giddens, A. (2009). *The Politics of Climate Change*. Cambridge: Polity Press.

Heusinkveld, B. (2009). Scientists investigate urban climate in Rotterdam and Arnhem. *Newsletter of Wageningen UR*, 27 August 2009. Available at: http://www.wur.nl/uk/newsagenda/archive/news/2009/met090827.htm (Accessed November 2013).

Huitema, D., Mostert, E., Egas, W., Moellenkamp, S., Pahl-Wostl, C. and Yalcin, R. (2009). Adaptive water governance: Assessing the institutional prescriptions of adaptive (co)management from a governance perspective and defining as research agenda. *Ecology and Society*, 14(1): 26.

IBEC (2006). *CASBEE-HI, Comprehensive Assessment System for Building Environmental Efficiency*. Tokyo: Institute for Building Environment and Energy Conservation.

Jenks, M., Burton, E. and Williams, K. (eds.) (1996). *The Compact City, A Sustainble Urban Form?* London: E & FN Spon.

Katzschner, L. (2010). Urban Climate Analysis Map of Arnhem. Paper presented at *the Dutch National Meeting on Urban Heat Island*. Arnhem Municipality Arnhem, Netherlands, 26 May 2010. Available at: http://www.future-cities.eu/uploads/media/katzschner_arnhemII_2010_05_13.pdf (Accessed November 2013).

Kokx, A. (2012). Increasing the adaptive capacity in unembanked neighbourhoods? An exploration into stakeholders' support for adaptive measures in Rotterdam, the Netherlands. Paper presented at the *European Urban Research Association (EURA) Conference in Vienna*, unpubished.

Lazar, R. and Podesser, A. (1999). An urban climate analysis of Graz and its significance for urban planning in the tributary valleys east of Graz (Austria). *Atmospheric Environment*, 33(24–25): 4195–4209.

Matzarakis, A. and Mayer, H. (2008). Learning from the past: Urban climate studies in Munich. In: Mayer, H. and Matzarakis, A. (eds.), *Proceedings of the 5th Japanese-German Meeting on Urban Climatology*. Berichte des Meteorologischen Instituts der Albert-Ludwigs-Universität Freiburg, No. 18. The Albert-Ludwigs-University of Freiburg, Freiburg, Germany, 6–8 October. Freiburg: the Meteorological Institute, Albert-Ludwigs-University of Freiburg, 271–276. Available at: http://www.meteo.uni-freiburg.de/forschung/publikationen/berichte/report18.pdf (Accessed 10 February 2014).

MHSPE. (2000). *Compact Cities and Open Landscapes: Spatial Planning in the Netherlands*. The Hague: Ministry of Housing, Spatial Planning and the Environment (MHSPE).

Mills, G. (2006). Progress toward sustainable settlements: A role for urban climatology. *Theoretical and Applied Climatology*, 84(1–3): 69–76.

Mills, G., Cleugh, H., Emmanuel, R., Endlicher, W., Erell, E., McGranahan, G., Ng, E., Nickson, A., Rosenthal, J. and Steemer, K. (2010). Climate information for improved planning and management of mega cities (needs perspectives). In: Sivakumar, M. V. K. *et al.* (eds.), *Procedia Environmental Sciences, Vol.1, Special Issue of World Climate Conference-3*, 228–246. Geneva, Switzerland, 31 August–4 September.

Ministry VRO (Housing and Physical Planning) (1966). *Second Report on Physical Planning in the Netherlands*. The Hague: Ministry of Housing and Physical Planning.

Ministry VROM (Housing, Physical Planning and the Environment) (1983). *Structuurschets Stedelijke Gebieden*. The Hague: Ministry of Housing, Physical Planning and the Environment.

Mochida, A. (2006). Comprehensive Assessment System for Building Environmental Efficiency on Heat Island Relaxation: CASBEE-HI. In: *Proceedings of the International Workshop on Countermeasures to Urban Heat Islands*. Tokyo, Japan, 3–4 August. Available at: http://www.iea.org/Textbase/work/2006/heat/10-a_Mochida.pdf (Accessed November 2013).

Nachbarschaftsverband Stuttgart (1992). *Klimaatlas: Klimauntersuchung für den Nachbarschaftsverband Stuttgart und angrenzende Teile der Region Stuttgart*. Stuttgart: Nachbarschaftsverband Stuttgart.

Oke, T. R. (1981). Canyon geometry and the nocturnal urban heat island: Comparison of scale model and field observations. *International Journal of Climatology*, 1(3): 237–254.

Pahl-Wostl, C. (2006). Transitions towards adaptive management of water facing climate and global change. *Water Resources Management*, 21(1): 49–62.

Ren, C., Ng, E. and Katzschner, L. (2009). Review of worldwide urban climatic map study for and its application in planning. In: *Proceedings of The 7th International Conference on Urban Climate*. Yokohama, Japan, 29 June–3 July. Available at: http://www.ide.titech.ac.jp/~icuc7/extended_abstracts/pdf/374213-3-090516013120-003.pdf (Accessed 10 February 2014).

Ren, C., Ng, E. and Katzschner, L. (2011). Urban climatic map studies: A review. *International Journal of Climatology*, 31(15): 2213–2233. doi:10.1002/joc.2237.

Ren, C., Spit, T., Lenzholder, S., Yim, H. L. S., Heusinkveld, B., van Hove, B., Chen, L., Kupski, S., Burghard, R. and Katzschner, L. (2012). Urban climate map system for Dutch spatial planning. *International Journal of Applied Earth Observation and Geo-information*, 18: 207–221.

Richardson, H. and Bae, C. (eds.) (2004). *Urban Sprawl in Western Europe and the United States*. Aldershot: Ashgate.

Scherer, D., Fehrenbach, U., Beha, H.-D. and Parlow, E. (1999). Improved concepts and methods in analysis and evaluation of the urban climate for optimizing urban planning process. *Atmospheric Environment,* 33(24–25): 4185–4193.

Spit, T. and Zoete, P. (2009). *Ruimtelijke Ordening in Nederland. Een wetenschappelijke inleiding in het vakgebied.* Den Haag: Sdu Uitgevers. Geheel Herziene Editie (280 pp.).

Svensson, M. K. (2002). *Urban Climate in relation to Land Use, Planning and Comfort.* Gothenburg: University of Gothenburg.

Svensson, M. K., Thorsson, S. and Lindqvist, S. (2003). A geographical information system model for creating bioclimatic maps – examples from a high, mid-latitude city. *International Journal of Biometeorology*, 47(2): 102–112.

TMG (2005). *Guidelines for Heat Island Control Measures [Summary edition].* Tokyo: Bureau of the Environment, Tokyo Metropolitan Government (TMG). Available at: http://www2.kankyo.metro.tokyo.jp/sgw/English/heatislandguideline.pdf (Accessed November 2013). (In Japanese).

van Buuren, A., Driessen, P., Teisman, G., Rietveld, P., van Rijswick, M., Salet, W. and Spit, T. (2012). Spatial planning: Conditions for synchronizing climate adaptation and spatial planning. *Journal of European Environmental Planning and Law.* (forthcoming).

van der Valk, A. (2002). The Dutch planning experience. *Landscape and Urban Planning*, 58(2–4): 201–210.

van der Wusten, H. and Faludi, A. (1992). The Randstad: Playground of Physical Planners. In: Dieleman, F. M. and Musterd, S. (eds.), *The Randstad: A Research and Policy Laboratory*. Dordrecht: Kluwer, 17–38.

VDI (1997). *VDI-Standard: VDI 3787 Part 1 Environmental Meteorology – Climate and Air Pollution Maps for Cities and Regions*. Berlin: Beuth Verlag.

Chapter 26

# Urban climatic map studies in Germany

## Freiburg

*Andreas Matzarakis, Rainer Röckle and Helmut Mayer*

### Introduction

Freiburg belongs to one of the warmest cities in Germany because of its geographical location in the upper Rhine valley (Nübler, 1979; Rudloff, 1993). More than 30 days with heat stress can be detected each year (REKLIP, 1995). During extreme summers like the one in 2003, the number of days with heat stress was much higher. Air pollutants are dominantly produced by car traffic due to the absence of industrial emissions (UMEG, 2003).

Freiburg is located at the foothills or plains of the Black Forest (see Figure 26.1), specifically at the exit of the Dreisam valley. In general, during cloudless and less windy weather conditions, a mountain breeze is formed. During daylight hours, air masses move in the direction of the Black Forest and an air mass exchange is produced. During night-time hours, cold air flows from the valley slopes are formed, and the induced cold airflows to the city of Freiburg from the east, affecting climate conditions there. This local wind system called 'Höllentäler' is very well known and is accompanied with the ventilation of parts of the city of Freiburg (Nübler, 1979; Parlow, 1983; Gross, 1989; Rudloff, 1992, 1993). The cold airflows depend on the synoptic conditions with a diverse intensity and range. In the Dreisam valley the local wind system occurs during 65 per cent of night hours per year (Parlow, 1983).

*Figure 26.1* The investigation area.

Source: Matzarakis *et al.*, 2008

Therefore, Freiburg has a specific role because of its location in the south of Germany and its complex topography. It combines many relevant aspects of climate and the effects of urbanisation and topographical effects, not only due to the Black Forest, but also due to its location in the upper Rhine valley. Nevertheless, since the 1960s, several studies concerning local climates and urban effects in the city have been conducted in the vicinity of Freiburg. In the 1970s, a whole approach was taken for the quantification of the urban climate in Freiburg, and this was the basis for the authorities and decision makers of the city. This was followed by specific urban climate studies and had effects on diverse projects, i.e. new building areas or the modification of sport facilities were only limited in terms of single effects concerning wind conditions. At the start of the twenty-first century, the municipality realised the importance (not only because of climate change issues) of urban climate and demanded a new integral climate analysis for Freiburg (Röckle *et al.*, 2003; Matzarakis *et al.*, 2008; Matzarakis, 2013).

## Method

In order to obtain and quantify the distribution of climatological and air pollution conditions, several approaches based on measurements and modelling have been performed and applied (VDI, 1988; Helbig *et al.*, 1999). Several factors, e.g. air temperature, wind, human-bioclimate, and air pollutants have been aggregated and summarised into maps (Röckle *et al.*, 2003; Matzarakis *et al.*, 2008). Figure 26.2 shows how information and data are interconnected and aggregated into maps.

In detail, the following methods and results have been applied:

- Measurements
  Thermal imaging by airplanes
  Thermal mapping (day and night)
  Screen level measurement campaigns
  Tracer gas experiments
- Modelling
  Cold air drainage flow simulation
  Ventilation analysis
  Analysis of thermal bioclimate
  Analysis of air pollution situation
  Effect analysis
- Maps
  Climate function map
  Planning recommendation map

The aforementioned methods and data were the basis for the development of an integral analysis of the urban climate conditions of Freiburg. The aim of the study was that the produced results were based on the latest scientific methods and findings and are applicable in the urban planning process in Freiburg.

### *Measurements and results*

In this chapter the most relevant information for the production of the final maps are described. First, an inventory of existing data was made and all data was considered for the study. In addition,

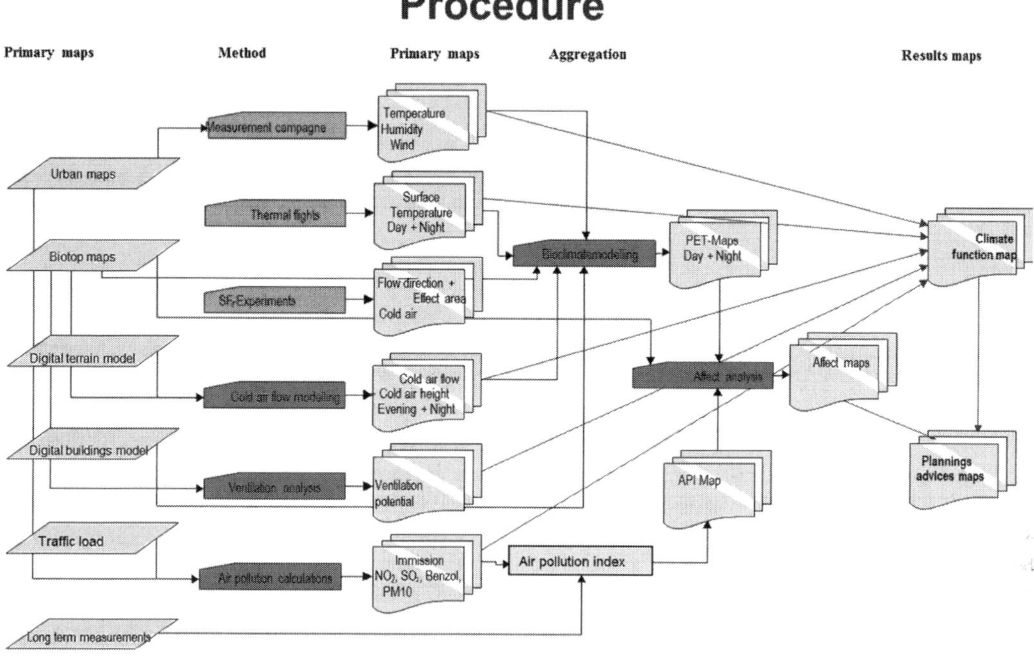


*Figure 26.2* Flowchart of the climate analysis for Freiburg.

Source: Röckle *et al.*, 2003

required data was obtained through measurements and models. This chapter is divided into measured and modelled data.

## *Thermal imaging*

Thermal imaging is a method of acquiring spatial information about the thermal situation of a surface at a very high resolution (usually 3m–5m) (Goßmann, 1987, 1991). Information about cold air drainage flow or air temperature cannot be extracted from these thermal images. In order to detect day and night dynamics, two flights for the period with the highest heating of the surface (8 July 2002, afternoon) and highest surface cooling (9 July 2002, before sunrise) during high pressure weather conditions were carried out. The delivered result is not the surface temperature but the radiation received by the detector of the airplane.

In general, the radiation temperatures are reduced with increasing distance from the city centre due to the lower density of buildings and denser green areas. Inside the less dense building areas, lower temperatures are obtained in areas with a high ratio of green and less pavement. Forests are, during the day, characterised by lower radiation temperatures as shown in the thermal image map (Menz, 1987; Goßmann, 1991). Despite lower radiation temperatures during the night (an average of about 17°C in contrast to the daytime of 26°C), the urbanised areas are significantly warmer than the surrounding areas; the inner city area is significantly dominated by warmer conditions in the nocturnal thermal image. Streets and buildings are heated from the short-wave radiation during the day and release their heat as long-wave radiation to the air during the night. Due to the lower visible horizon (usually expressed by the sky view factor), the cooling in urban canyons is lower compared to the roof level or rural areas. The thermal patterns of the streets are clearly visible on the thermal images. The radiation temperatures of the rural areas are significantly lower than those in urbanised areas and show strong scattering. Forests are of specific matter because they store heat during the day and their cooling strongly depends on their density and location (deciduous/coniferous trees, exposition). At the beginning of the nocturnal cooling period, warm air in the stock area and between the trees limits a more intense cooling (Hildebrandt, 1996).

### *Screen level measurement campaign*

In addition to the thermal images measurements on the 8 and 9 of July 2002, a 24-hour screen level measurement campaign was carried out. Its aim was to record the meteorological variables: wind direction, wind speed, air temperature, and air humidity. These were the basic measurements required in order to have basic variables for estimating the thermal bioclimate of the whole area of Freiburg. The analysis of measured data shows the locations and times at which the highest air temperatures are observed in the investigation area. During times of maximum air temperature e.g. at the main centre of Freiburg, the air temperature is about 2.5°C warmer than in green areas in the west of Freiburg. By contrast, during the times of minimum of air temperature the difference is about 5.5°C, showing that the highest intensity of the urban heat island takes place during the night (Ernst, 1995).

### *Tracer gas experiments*

Using tracer gas (Sulfur hexafluoride, $SF_6$) experiments at six specific locations, the dispersion of gas in the evening and night hours was studied. The dispersion experiments show both the course of the cold air drainage flow and the degree of influence at these specific sites. The results of the tracer gas experiments are in accordance with the cold airflow simulations by modelling.

## **Modelling and results**

### *Cold air drainage flow simulations*

For the cold air drainage flow for the whole area during the nocturnal flow, a numerical simulation model (Hosker, 1984; Röckle, 1992) for a typical weather situation with less wind and radiation was conducted and a 50m spatial resolution was applied. During the night, the area of Freiburg is dominated by a local wind system called 'Höllentäler'. Such an effect is present not only in the eastern parts of Freiburg, which are affected by the Black Forest, but also in the northern parts. The local wind system is evident beyond the small valleys of the Black Forest for some hours after sunset. In early evening hours, the local cold air flows coming from several small- and medium-sized valleys dominate wind flow conditions. They fit the huge east–west flow and are affected strongly by this flow (Gross, 1989; Ernst, 1995).

### *Ventilation analysis*

A ventilation analysis was performed with a numerical wind flow model (Röckle and Richter, 1998). The basis for the analysis was the information on the buildings of the city of Freiburg, allowing for a high spatial resolution of 5m; the 5m resolution was aggregated to 20m for a more appropriate overview. The analysis shows the areas in which the wind fields near the surface are modified the most. The analyses were performed for the main wind directions and allow the detection of ventilation paths, i.e. railway tracks or river areas. The inner part of the city is less ventilated because of the relatively tall and compact buildings. Similar conditions can be also found in other dense areas such as trade districts (Röckle *et al.*, 2003).

### *Analysis of thermal bioclimate*

In applied climatology and biometeorology, thermal comfort is described by using thermal indices, which include the combination of air temperature and/or air humidity or wind speed. Thermal perception and thermal comfort can not only be expressed by air temperature, but also by the influence of radiation conditions (depending on the diurnal and annual variation of solar radiation, shade of buildings and vegetation, infrared radiation of buildings, etc.), wind speed, and also air humidity (VDI, 2008; Matzarakis, 2001). Urban climate is usually characterised by a modified climate and expressed by the urban heat island, which can also be expressed in an urban bioclimate island for humans. This leads to pronounced additional heat stress, which usually occurs during the afternoon hours. In contrast, during the night, the thermal bioclimatic conditions are lower in rural areas due to the course of air temperature and the absence of solar radiation (see Figure 26.3).

Recent methods for the evaluation of thermal bioclimate are well described and applied in several studies (VDI, 2008). For the evaluation of the thermal component of urban climate, this can be also expressed as thermal bioclimate indices, based on the energy exchange of the human body; the Physiologically Equivalent Temperature (PET) is used (Höppe, 1999; Matzarakis *et al.*, 1999, 2007). The calculations are based on different land use information (representing the building mass and other urban characteristics), elevation, measurements from campaigns, and thermal imaging data. A summer day was selected for the construction of maps and the background data used; the PET was calculated for 3.00 p.m. CET by using the radiation and bioclimate model RayMan (Matzarakis *et al.*, 2007, 2010) and is presented in Figure 26.3.

For the entire built-up area, PET values are greater than 33°C, which means that a strong to very strong heat stress occurs at that time in these parts of the city. Heat stress occurs in Freiburg on more than 30 days per year (REKLIP, 1995; Friedrich, 2000), and an increase is expected due to climate change (Matzarakis and Endler, 2010).

The highest PET values are found in locations with increased sealing factors and lower green percentages. The suburban parts of the rural areas are exposed to heat stress, which can be explained by the low buildings that are not able to produce shadows like the taller buildings in the inner parts of the city. In the higher areas of the Black Forest there is no heat stress. During the night-time hours especially at 3.00 a.m. CET, PET values range between 6°C and 11°C, meaning that people are affected by a slight cold stress during that time.

### *Analysis of the air pollution situation*

The air pollution situation in Freiburg, due to the absence of large emission sources, is primarily dominated by car traffic (UMEG, 2000, 2003). Estimations for nitrogen dioxide ($NO_2$), Benzene, and particulate matter ($PM_{10}$) were performed for this source group (UMWELTBUNDESAMT, INFRAS, 1999). For the consideration of the complex topography of the area, five different meteorological dispersion classes were calculated (Richter and Röckle, 1995). The estimated time

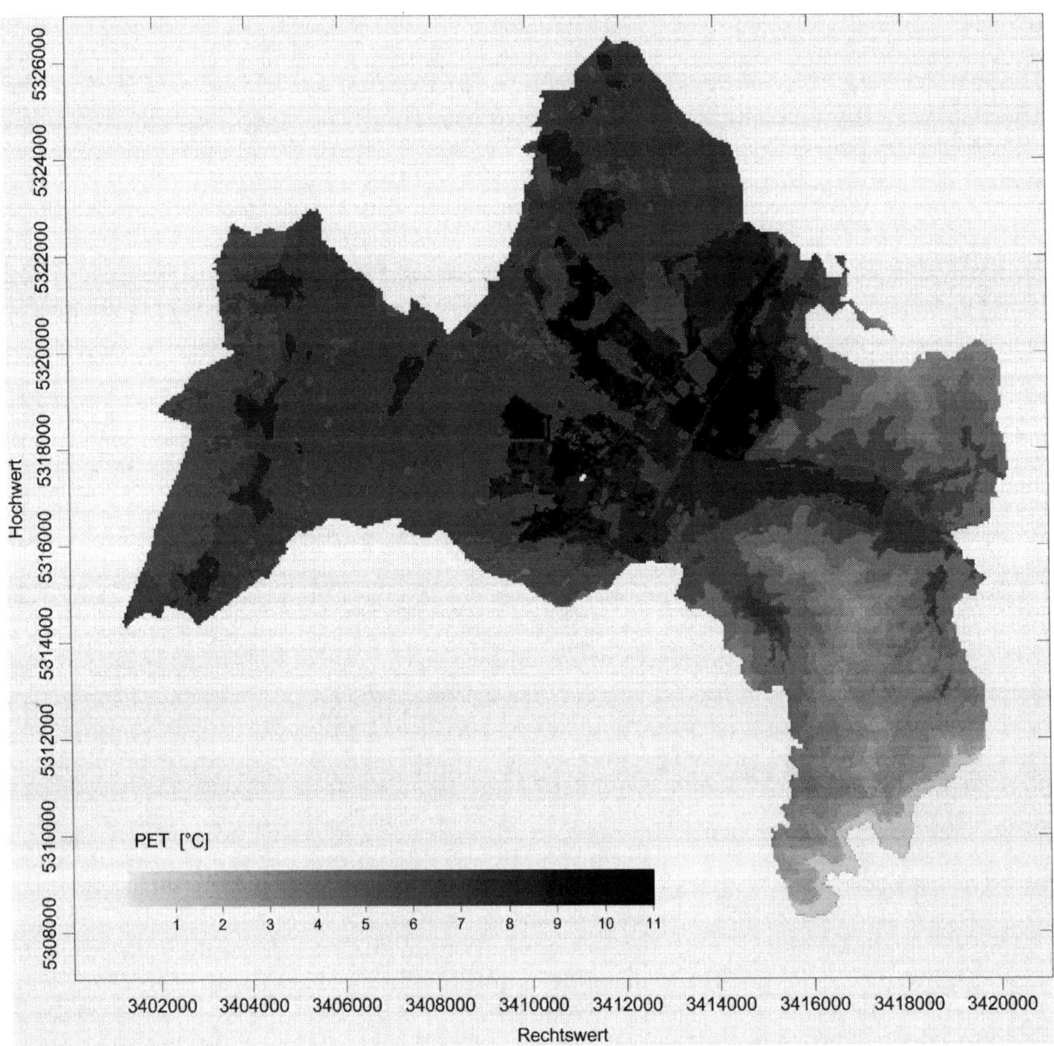


*Figure 26.3* Map of PET.

Source: Authors

horizon was fixed to the year 2005. It is assumed that emissions will be reduced by 2020 because of the specific reductions of air pollutants by cars.

The highest estimated concentrations occur, as expected, along the highway (Autobahn A5), at the crossing points of the highway, and in the portal of the traffic tunnels in the eastern part of Freiburg. The limit values for $NO_2$ can sometimes be exceeded. Based on the estimated values of Benzene, $NO_2$, and $PM_{10}$, an air pollution index for the human-biometeorological quantification was applied (Mayer *et al.*, 2002). Most of the areas of Freiburg are less loaded by air pollutants, apart from the streets and their affected areas. During winter temperature inversions, air pollution is more pronounced, in contrast to the heat stress conditions in summer, as air exchange is limited.

## Results and suggestions for urban planning

### *Effect analysis*

For the assessment of thermal stress or air pollution situation, the intensity as well as the number of people who are affected by these conditions is of importance. For this reason, two maps of effect analysis for day and night were made. During the day, the inner part of the city is characterised by strong heat stress. During the night, the areas in the west of Freiburg with a high density of buildings are related to thermal load. The most urbanised areas are usually found in the 'moderate' and 'strong' class of heat stress during the day and night. The thermal classes 'low' and 'very low' are less frequently found in the urban area. In general, Freiburg shows 'high problem areas', which are a result of thermal stress. Based on that, the importance of green and free areas has to be considered and assessed. In the inner city, most of the areas are characterised by 'high problem areas', especially during the summer. Aside from the daytime situation, the night-time situation is also of importance because of the absence of cooling effects for regeneration from the climatic point of view (cooling of building mass and transportation of polluted air and warm air masses). In this context the ventilation possibilities and especially the cold airflow with less polluted air should not be reduced (Röckle *et al.*, 2003).

### *Urban planning maps*

A climate function map as well as a planning recommendation map was produced based on the information derived above and the knowledge from previous investigations (e.g. Nübler, 1979; Rudloff, 1993; Friedrich, 2000). The spatial dimension of climate information is a possibility for the quantification of the recent and future effects of the structure plan concerning the local climate and air pollution situation in a city.

## Planning-oriented maps

### *Climate function map*

Climate function maps are focused on the spatial and detailed distribution of the present thermal and air pollution conditions (Stock, 1992; Kommunalverb and Ruhrgebiet, 1995). Focus is also placed on the autochthonous weather conditions, i.e. weather situations with high solar radiation and less wind exchange. With the consideration of air paths or ventilation paths based on the long-term wind conditions of the area, a more realistic mean condition approach is reached. Finally, a climate function map is based on a general assessment of several existing climate factors (i.e. slope aspect of topography, land use, etc.), measured climate information (i.e. air temperature, wind, radiation properties of the surfaces, air quality), and results from modelling approaches (ventilation, cold air drainage flow, bioclimate). In the climate function map only atmospheric processes are included, which occur at the screen level considered, so the interactions between different climate relevant areas (climatopes) are not sharply separated (VDI, 1997), i.e. the areas have to be seen as transition areas. In addition, the signatures or legends used have a symbolic character without including exact and quantitative information about, for instance, the range or intensity of flows. The climatopes included in the climate function and planning recommendation maps are based on the *VDI Standard: VDI 3787 Part 1 Environmental Meteorology: Climate and Air Pollution Maps for Cities and Regions* (VDI, 1997).

### *Planning recommendation map*

The aforementioned and explained climatic properties and characteristics are part of the climate function maps. Based on the climate function maps, which are somewhat static, and under the consideration of existing air pollution data (measured and modelled) and the effect analysis maps, a detailed planning *recommendation* map has been constructed (see Plate 26.1). In contrast to the climate function map, where the information is not assessed by specific spaces or areas, information is indicated with a specific value: free spaces based on their climatic/air pollution function and urban structures concerning their sensibility in relation to higher urban density. The urban air paths are separated into polluted and non-polluted quantities (Mayer *et al.*, 1994). Air polluted areas are expressed based on their traffic load. The extracted information is prepared with an emphasis on planning *recommendations* for the level of city planning.

The most relevant and important findings in the planning *recommendation* map are summarised as follows: urban areas are classified into areas of low, medium, and high sensibility in relation to urban development or extension based on the effect value (for the thermal and air pollution situation) and their importance to the surrounding areas. For Freiburg, the free spaces in west to east and north to south directions are conspicuous. Mostly located in the east and south of Freiburg are areas with very high climatic and air quality compensation potential. This means that from those areas, cooler or less polluted air is transported to areas with higher thermal load or higher air pollution. This is an effect of the local wind system formed by the topographical properties of the nearby valley in the Black Forest. This local wind classified as a cool mountain breeze is of importance during specific weather situations and is responsible for the ventilation of the city area, therefore, the source area (forest areas in the south-east and east of Freiburg) of the wind systems is classified as a high priority area. Areas near the river and the small valleys in the eastern and south-eastern part are also classified with the highest climatic priority. Free spaces on the slopes in the south are also of specific climatic relevance, as is the airport area in the north-east and the forest areas in the west of Freiburg. Inner city areas like cemeteries and other green areas have a high climatic potential and are classified by the highest category of positive effects. Free spaces with low and moderate building densities are classified as having improved climatic and air pollution compensation functions. Moderate compensation functions concerning climate have less residential buildings density or moderate trade/industrial areas during weather situations with heat stress. Spaces with no particular cold air production and areas with no residential relation are classified in the category of low climatic air pollution compensation function, but this category does not exist in Freiburg.

Aside from the assessment of free and residential areas, the planning *recommendation* maps also include several elements of the air exchange. The effect of mountain breezes from two different directions during the night and day including the cold air drainage flow of the mountain breeze play an important role in the regional and local significance of the wind conditions in the urban climate conditions of the city of Freiburg. They are an important issue in planning a *recommendation* map and are indicated and quantified by polluted and unpolluted urban air paths. Urban air paths are areas with less roughness, sufficient length and width, and preferably straight courses contributing to the ventilation of urban areas (Mayer *et al.*, 1994). Regional urban air paths are of importance because of the transport of unpolluted air masses from rural environments to city areas. Local urban air paths contribute to the air exchange in urban areas. The efficiency of urban air paths is dependent on the dominant wind direction of a region and/or area.

## Discussion and conclusions

The final aim of assessing areas for future or planned urban development was quantified by an ecological risk analysis. The impact of an area modified by a microclimate is dependent on:

(a) intensity, range, and direction of the effect;
(b) sensitivity and value (significance) of the area in contrast to a specific effect of the modification planned.

For the quantification, the frequency of use by humans (estimated from the land use), the human biometeorological thermal stress (here quantified by PET), and the air pollution situation have been considered. It is a fact that after building up in an area, the physical properties of that area are modified and changed (i.e. heat balance, ventilation, air pollution, and so on). The range of effects on surrounding areas depends on the transport of these properties by synoptic, regional, local wind conditions.

Concerning the human thermal bioclimate, a separation between diurnal and nocturnal conditions has to be performed because of different air exchange conditions during hot days and especially in areas (such as cities) embedded in complex topographies, where local wind systems can be developed. All of the modified conditions have to be estimated based on the microclimatic effects (including bioclimate and air pollution) and the sensitivity of the area of interest. The final climatic consequences for planners can be summarised as follows (Matzarakis *et al.*, 2008):

1. Maintenance of urban climate relevant air paths (for fresh and cold air) transport.
2. Micro-scale climate manipulations to avoid diurnal heating of buildings. Possibilities include planting trees with broad leaves (spending shade), or the surface management of materials with a high reflectance of short-wave radiation (albedo management).

Furthermore, for an improved outdoor quality of life, high climate diversity is an advantage, preferably in short spatial and temporal accessibility. This can be performed by considering effect factors and analysis. It has to be noted that it is less meaningful to analyse and assess separate and single urban structures.

A master analysis with consideration of climatic factors and conditions should be included in any master plan analysis.

The analysis of the specific climate of urban structures and cities should not be an alibi, but the possibility of solid appreciation of values for decision makers should be assessed and known. This is especially valid for cities, which are under expansion pressure and are increasing in the density of their urban structures. The climatic properties of cities are going to be more important not only because of the climate change discussion but also as a factor concerning quality of life. Finally, urban structures and cities in general can use urban climate modifications and manipulations as an opportunity for mitigation and adaptation strategies in the face of climate change (Matzarakis, 2013).

## Acknowledgement

The research work for this chapter is presented on behalf of the City of Freiburg.

## References


Ernst, S. A. (1995). *Tagesperiodische Windsysteme und Belüftungsverhältnisse in Freiburg i. Br. – Planungsrelevante Aspekte eines Bergwindsystems*. Freiburger Geographische Hefte, 49. Freiburg: Institutes für Physische Geographie der Albert-Ludwigs-Universität Freiburg i.Br.

Friedrich, M. (2000). *Die raumzeitliche Differenzierung der thermischen Bedingungen des Menschen im Klima der Stadt*. Dissertation an der Geowissenschaftlichen Fakultät der Albert-Ludwigs-Universität Freiburg i.Br.

Goßmann, H. (1987). Thermalbilder und Oberflächentemperaturen. *Geomethodica*, 12: 117–149.

Goßmann, H. (1991). Infrarot-Thermometrie der Erdoberfläche. *Meteorologische Fortbildung*, 21(1/2): 1–10.

Gross, G. (1989). Numerical simulation of the nocturnal flow systems in the Freiburg areas for different topographies. *Beiträge zur Physik der Atmosphäre*, 62: 57–72.

Helbig, A., Baumüller, J. and Kerschgens, M. J. (1999). *Stadtklima und Luftreinhaltung. 2. vollständig überarbeitete und ergänzte Auflage*. Berlin: Springer-Verlag.

Hildebrandt, G. (1996). *Fernerkundung und Luftbildmessung. für Forstwissenschaft, Vegetationskartierung und Landschaftsökologie*. Heidelberg: Wichmann.

Höppe, P. (1999). The physiological equivalent temperature – a universal index for the biometeorological assessment of the thermal environment. *International Journal of Biometeorology*, 43(2): 71–75.

Hosker, R. P. (1984). Flow and diffusion near obstacles. In: Randerson, D. (ed.), *Atmospheric Science and Power Production*. Oak Ridge, Tenn: Technical Information Center, Office of Scientific and Technical Information, U.S. Department of Energy, 241–326.

Kommunalverband Ruhrgebiet (1995). *Klimaanalyse für die Landeshauptstadt Düsseldorf*. Landeshauptstadt Düsseldorf, Umweltamt.

Matzarakis, A. (2001). *Die thermische Komponente des Stadtklimas*. Berichte des Meteorologischen Institutes, der Universität Freiburg, Nr. 6. Available at: http://www.meteo.uni-freiburg.de/forschung/publikationen/berichte/report6.pdf (Accessed 6 February 2014).

Matzarakis, A. (2013). Stadtklima vor dem Hintergrund des Klimawandels. *Gefahrstoffe – Reinhaltung der Luft*, 73: 115–118.

Matzarakis, A. and Endler, C. (2010). Adaptation of thermal bioclimate under climate change conditions – The example of physiologically equivalent temperature in Freiburg, Germany. *International Journal of Biometeorology*, 54: 479–483.

Matzarakis, A., Mayer, H. and Iziomon, M. (1999). Applications of a universal thermal index: Physiological equivalent temperature. *International Journal of Biometeorology*, 43(2): 76–84.

Matzarakis, A., Rutz, F., and Mayer, H. (2007). Modelling radiation fluxes in simple and complex environments – Application of the RayMan model. *International Journal of Biometeorology*, 51(4): 323–334.

Matzarakis, A., Rutz, F. and Mayer, H. (2010). Modelling radiation fluxes in simple and complex environments – Basics of the RayMan model. *International Journal of Biometeorology*, 54(2): 131–139.

Matzarakis, A., Röckle, R., Richter, C. J., Höfl, H. C., Steinicke, W., Streifeneder, M. and Mayer, H. (2008). Planungsrelevante Bewertung des Stadtklimas – Am Beispiel von Freiburg im Breisgau. *Gefahrstoffe – Reinhaltung der Luft*, 68: 334–340.

Mayer, H., Beckröge, W. and Matzarakis, A. (1994). Bestimmung von stadtklimarelevanten Luftleitbahnen. *UVP-Report 5*, 265–268.

Mayer, H., Kalberlah, F., Ahrens, D. and Reuter, U. (2002). Analyse von Indizes zur Bewertung der Luft. *Gefahrstoffe – Reinhalt. der Luft*, 62: 177–183.

Menz, G. (1987). *Ableitung einer großmaßstäbigen Karte der Wärmebelastung im Raum-Freiburg-Basel mit Hilfe von Satellitendaten*. Freiburg Geographische Hefte, 27. Freiburg: Institutes für Physische Geographie der Albert-Ludwigs-Universität Freiburg i.Br.

Nübler, W. (1979). *Konfiguration und Genese der Wärmeinsel der Stadt Freiburg*. Freiburger Geographische Hefte, 16. Freiburg: Institutes für Physische Geographie der Albert-Ludwigs-Universität Freiburg i.Br.

Parlow, E. (1983). *Geländeklimatologische Untersuchungen im Bereich der Staufener Bucht unter besonderer Berücksichtigung lokaler Ausgleichsströmungen*. Freiburger Geographische Hefte, 20. Freiburg: Institutes für Physische Geographie der Albert-Ludwigs-Universität Freiburg i.Br.

REKLIP (ed.) (1995). *Klimaatlas Oberrhein Mitte-Süd*. Zürich: Vdf Hochschulverlag; Offenbach: IFG; Straßburg: Editions Coprus.

Richter, C. J. and Röckle, R. (1995). Methode zur Ermittlung von Kfz-bedingten Schadstoffkonzentrationen in bebauten Gebieten. *UVP-Report 5*, 233–235.

Röckle, R. (1992). Einsatz mikroskaliger Strömungsmodelle bei Planungsfragen. *Annalen der Meteorologie*, 28: 43–45.

Röckle, R. and Richter, C. J. (1998). Ausbreitung von Geruchsstoffen in Kaltluftabflüssen - Messungen und Modellrechnungen. *VDI-Berichte 1373*, 249–259.

Röckle, R., Richter, C. J., Höfl, H. C., Steinicke, W., Streifeneder, M. and Matzarakis, A. (2003). Klimaanalyse Stadt Freiburg. *Auftraggeber Stadtplanungsamt der Stadt Freiburg*.

Rudloff, H. v. (1992). *Das Freiburger Berg- und Talwindsystem: Eine Bestandsaufnahme*. Freiburg.

Rudloff, H. v. (1993). *Beiträge zum Klima Freiburgs*. Freiburg: Lingg Druck.

Stock, P. (1992). *Synthetische Klimafunktionskarte Ruhrgebiet*. Essen: Kommunalverband Ruhrgebiet, Abt. Offentlichkeitsarbeit/Wirtschaft.

UMEG (2000). *Immissionsuntersuchungen im Raum Freiburg / Emmendingen 1999/2000*. Luftreinhaltung, Bericht Nr. 31-13/2001 im *Auftrag des MINISTERIUM FÜR UMWELT UND VERKEHR*, Baden-Württemberg. Karlsruhe: UMEG Zentrum für Umweltmessungen, Umwelterhebungen und Gerätesicherheit Baden-Württemberg.

UMEG (2003). *Jahresbericht 2002*. Karlsruhe: UMEG Zentrum für Umweltmessungen, Umwelterhebungen und Gerätesicherheit Baden-Württemberg. Available at: http://www.lubw.baden-wuerttemberg.de/servlet/is/14046/ (Accessed 6 February 2014).

UMWELTBUNDESAMT, INFRAS (1999). *Handbuch Emissionsfaktoren des Straßenverkehrs. Version 1.2*. Im Auftrag des Umweltbundesamtes.

VDI (1988). *Stadtklima und Luftreinhaltung*. Berlin: Springer-Verlag.

VDI (1997). *VDI-Standard: VDI 3787 Part 1 Environmental Meteorology – Climate and Air Pollution Maps for Cities and Regions*. Berlin: Beuth Verlag.

VDI (2008). *VDI-Standard: VDI 3787 Part 2 Environmental Meteorology – Methods for the Human Biometeorological Evaluation of Climate and Air Quality for Urban and Regional Planning at Regional Level, Part I: Climate*. Berlin: Beuth Verlag.

Part 5

# Future development

Chapter 27

# Meteorological modelling and its future development for urban climatic map studies

*Steve H. L. Yim*

## Introduction

Meteorological data is an important input for the development of urban climatic analysis maps (UC-AnMaps), which are one of two main components in an urban climatic map (UCMap). Meteorological data, such as air temperature, atmospheric humidity, wind speed and wind direction, describe the local climate environment. There are different means and tools that one could use to obtain meteorological data, such as: ambient measurements of the atmosphere, satellite images, wind tunnels, and numerical models including meteorological models and computational fluid dynamics (CFD). Among these, meteorological models are one of the tools that have been used to provide meteorological data for UCMap studies (Gross, 1993; Ashie *et al.*, 1998; Hirano and Ashie, 2009; Ng *et al.*, 2009; Richter and Röckle, 2009).

Meteorological models solve a set of equations that describe the atmosphere's governing processes. The equations include the momentum equations, the thermodynamic energy equation, the continuity equations for air and total water, and the equation of state. These models typically output three-dimensional atmospheric properties, such as wind velocities, potential temperature, humidity, etc.

There are a number of advantages to using meteorological models for UCMap studies. One advantage is that meteorological models provide a spatial distribution of the required meteorological fields for UCMap development, such as surface wind field. Figure 27.1 depicts an example of simulated surface wind field in Hong Kong (Yim *et al.*, 2007), which was incorporated into the Hong Kong UCMap (Ng *et al.*, 2009). With hourly wind information at each grid cell produced by meteorological models, site wind variations in a study region are better understood using annual wind direction frequency at each grid cell. This spatial and temporal information might not be available from other methods outlined above.

Another advantage is that the land–sea breeze effect can be resolved by meteorological models, providing more representative wind information such as wind direction frequency for UCMap studies. Reproducing the land–sea breeze effect is particularly important for coastal cities. Previous studies have shown land–sea breezes commonly occur at coastal locations (Miller *et al.*, 2003), such as Hong Kong (Ng *et al.*, 2009) and Kaohsiung (Ren *et al.*, 2013). Without taking the land–sea breeze effect into account, estimated wind fields may not be fully representative of the local wind environment in coastal cities. Among the tools for UCMaps, widely used meteorological models such as the PSU/NCAR meso-scale model (MM5) (Dudhia, 1993; Grell *et al.*, 1994) and the Weather Research and Forecasting (WRF) (Skamarock and Klemp, 2008) were demonstrated to be capable of simulating the land–sea breeze effect (Lo *et al.*, 2006; Papanastasiou *et al.*, 2010).

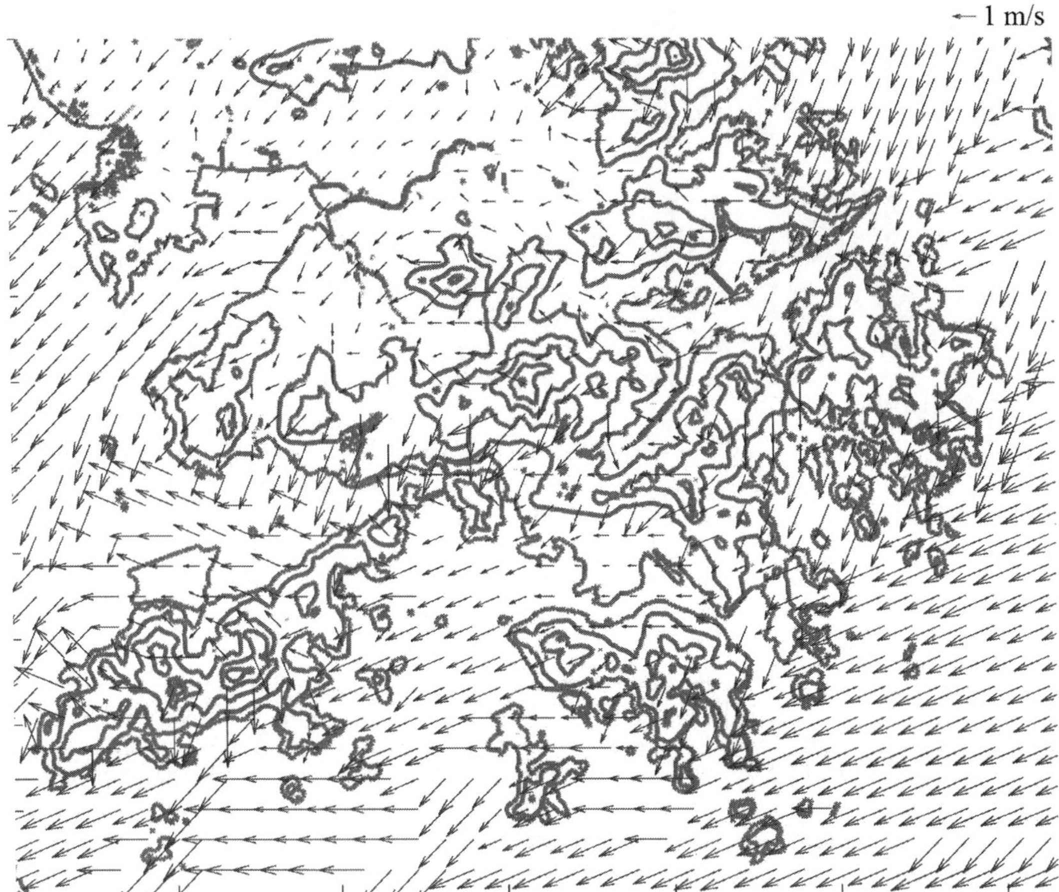


*Figure 27.1* Annual dominant wind (black wind vector) over Hong Kong at 10m above ground in 2004 based on MM5/CALMET simulations. The resolution of the original data is 100m but, to assist visualisation only 1 in every 15 wind vectors is plotted. The isopleths represent terrain height levels of 0m, 100m, 300m, 500m, 700m and 900m.

Source: Yim *et al.*, 2007, 2009

## The application of Weather Research and Forecasting (WRF) in urban climate studies

For urban climate studies a cross-scale atmospheric model is used, capable of simulating meteorological conditions from regional scale (~ 10km) to urban scale (< ~ 1km). WRF, which is the next generation successor to MM5, allows downscaling in order to resolve atmospheric processes at various scales, and is thus widely used in weather and climate studies (Leung and Qian, 2009; Evans and McCabe, 2010; Georgescu *et al.*, 2011; Liang *et al.*, 2012; Li *et al.*, 2013).

In urban climate studies, WRF has been extensively used with a typical spatial resolution of around 1km. For example, Georgescu *et al.* (2011) used WRF to reproduce the diurnal variation of near-surface temperature in summertime in the Phoenix metropolitan area. WRF was configured to downscale the results from 32km to 2km. This study showed that WRF is able to reproduce the monthly diurnal variation in near-surface temperatures, and the WRF results identified two major factors that have an impact on the urban diurnal temperature variations in the study region. Another study, Yang *et al.* (2012), applied WRF coupled with a single-layer urban canopy model (UCM) to simulate the urban climate in Nanjing of eastern China. Three nesting domains were configured with a spatial resolution of 25km, 5km and 1km. Yang *et al.* showed that the model results agreed well with the measurements of surface air temperature, relative humidity, and precipitation frequency and inter-annual variability, even though the precipitation amount was underestimated.

Applications of WRF on urban climatic map meteorological models have also been used in UCMap studies; for example, Ng *et al.* (2009) used a meteorological model to provide the wind information layer for their study. Ng *et al.* developed a UCMap for Hong Kong, in which the wind field layer was provided by a MM5/CALMET model system adopted by Yim *et al.* (2007). The MM5 model was used to simulate the wind conditions in Hong Kong at a spatial resolution of 1.5km. Due to the complex topography of Hong Kong, the MM5 results were then downscaled to 100m using a diagnostic model, CALMET (Douglas and Kessler, 1988), with wind observations obtained from a measurement network operated by the Hong Kong Observatory. The CALMET model uses a two-step approach to calculate wind fields in a study area, taking into account the fine-scale kinematic effects of terrain, slope flows and terrain blocking effects. The model results were compared against the surface and upper air sounding measurements (Yim *et al.*, 2007, 2009), demonstrating that the MM5/CALMET system could reproduce wind field information in Hong Kong. The wind field outputs were thereafter used for the Hong Kong UCMap study (Ng *et al.*, 2009), in which the significant site wind variations in Hong Kong were also identified.

## Future improvement

Even though previous studies in the literature have shown that WRF could provide meteorological fields for UCMap studies, more effort is needed to improve WRF modelling for UCMap developments.

To reproduce representative climate conditions in urban environments, the atmospheric processes at building scale should be explicitly resolved. Due to the limited computational resources in the past, the effects of urban morphology on the atmospheric flow were parameterised in WRF through a bulk urban parameterisation. In this approach, the influences of buildings were taken into account by a group of parameters for all urban areas. Although previous studies in literature showed that WRF could reproduce surface wind speed and temperature that agreed well with measurements, WRF tended to have positive bias in wind speed and negative bias in temperature (Yim and Barrett, 2012), especially in urban areas (Xie *et al.*, 2012). The biases might be partly due to the fact that WRF, with a bulk urban parameterisation, could not resolve the inhomogeneous characteristics of the underlying surface in urban environments. To improve this, current research focuses on coupling WRF with UCMaps (Kusaka *et al.*, 2001; Martilli *et al.*, 2002; Kusaka and Kimura, 2004; Li *et al.*, 2013), or with a CFD model (Tewari *et al.*, 2010; Chen *et al.*, 2011) so as to resolve the atmospheric processes down to the building scale (~ 1m–10m). Literature has shown that WRF coupled with a multilayer UCM or with a CFD model is a promising tool for assessing urbanisation effects (Chen *et al.*, 2004; Holt and Pullen, 2007; Jiang *et al.*, 2008; Lin *et al.*, 2008; Miao and Chen, 2008; Kusaka *et al.*, 2009; Miao *et al.*, 2009a, 2009b; Wang *et al.*, 2009; Tewari *et al.*, 2010). However, this kind of approach is still not practical for the development of UCMaps due to a number of limitations including the expensive computational requirement, the availability of building morphology data, and weather measurements in urban canopies for UCM developments.

A database of building morphology data and weather observations in urban canopies should be developed for the development of UCMaps. To estimate the impacts of building morphology on the atmospheric flow, UCMs require a group of urban canopy parameters such as building height, urban fraction, roof width, road width, etc. These parameters need to be calculated by detailed building morphology data. However, such a data set with a spatial resolution suitable for urban scale studies is not always available. Nowadays, the detailed building morphology data sets are only limited to a few geographical locations. This is one of the current challenges for urban canopy modelling, and thus there is a need to develop these kinds of data sets for UCM simulations. On the other hand, to enhance the capability of UCM, long-term measurements in the urban canopy layer are critical for model validation and verification. However, long-term measurements do not always exist, because the availability of suitable sites for deploying instrumentation in street canyons is limited.

For UCMap studies, WRF modelling should be performed over multiple years. A UCMap requires meteorological data for describing the climate conditions in its studied region. In previous studies, WRF simulations were performed for a maximum of one year, posing a question about the selection of the simulation year. For example, could the meteorology in the simulation year represent the typical climate conditions in the study region? Moreover, a one-year simulation cannot reproduce annual variations in climate conditions, which may be particularly critical in UCMap studies. Now that computational power has become relatively cheaper than it was in the last decade, multi-year WRF simulations have become computationally practical and thus should be performed for UCMap studies.

Apart from multi-year simulations, the influence of climate change should be incorporated into WRF simulations. A UCMap is a tool for planning future city development. Thus, in addition to understanding current climate conditions, future climate should also be taken into account. Previous UCMap studies used historical measurements or simulations. However, these data could not describe the climate in the future. To improve this, one option is to use a general circulation model (GCM) to provide the projected boundary and initial conditions for WRF simulations. This downscaling approach for future projection was widely applied in the literature (Xu and Yang, 2012; Pierce *et al.*, 2013). With this approach, information about future climate conditions can be added into UCMap developments.

## References

Ashie, Y., Kodama, Y., Asaeda, T. and ca, V.T. (1998). Climate analysis for urban planning in Tokyo. *Report of Research Center for Urban Safety and Security Kobe University*, Special Report Vol. 1: 86–94. Available at: http://www.lib.kobe-u.ac.jp/repository/00044720.pdf (Accessed 7 February 2014).

Chen, F., Kusaka, H., Bornstein, R., Ching, J., Grimmond, C. S. B., Grossman-Clarke, S., Loridan, T., Manning, K. W., Martilli, A., Miao, S., Sailor, D., Salamanca, F. P., Taha, H., Tewari, M., Wang, X., Wyszogrodzki, A. A. and Zhang, C. (2011). The integrated WRF/urban modelling system: Development, evaluation, and applications to urban environmental problems. *International Journal of Climatology*, 31(2): 273–288.

Chen, F., Kusaka, H., Tewari, M., Bao, J. W. and Harakuchi, H. (2004). Utilising the coupled WRF/LSM/urban modelling system with detailed urban classification to simulate the urban heat island phenomena over the Greater Houston area. In: *Preprints of Fifth Symposium on the Urban Environment*. Vancouver, BC, Canada, 23–26 August. American Meteorological Society, 9–11. Available at: http://ams.confex.com/ams/pdfpapers/79765.pdf (Accessed 7 February 2014).

Douglas, S. G. and Kessler, R. C. (1988). *User's Guide to the Diagnostic Wind Model (Version 1.0)*. San Rafael: System Application, Inc.

Dudhia, J. (1993). A nonhydrostatic version of the Penn State-NCAR Mesoscale Model: Validation tests and simulation of an Atlantic cyclone and cold front. *Monthly Weather Review*, 121(5): 1493–1513.

Evans, J. P. and McCabe, M. F. (2010). Regional climate simulation over Australia's Murray-Darling basin: A multitemporal assessment. *Journal of Geophysical Research: Atmospheres*, 115: D14114. doi: 10.1029/2010JD013816.

Georgescu, M., Moustaoui, M., Mahalov, A. and Dudhia, J. (2011). An alternative explanation of the semiarid urban area 'oasis effect'. *Journal of Geophysical Research: Atmospheres*, 116: D24113. doi:10.1029/2011JD016720.

Grell, G. A., Dudhia, J. and Stauffer, D. R. (1994). *A Description of the Fifth-Generation Penn State/NCAR Mesoscale Model (MM5)*. NCAR Tech. Note NCAR/TN-398+STR. doi: 10.5065/D60Z716B.

Gross, G. (1993). *Numerical Simulation of Canopy Flows*. Springer Series in Physical Environment, 12. Berlin: Springer-verlag; New York: Springer-verlag.

Hirano, K. and Ashie, Y. (2009). Comprehensive analysis of urban effects on local climate in Tokyo metropolitan region using an urban mesoscale numerical model. In: *Proceedings of The 7th International Conference on Urban Climate*. Yokohama, Japan, 29 June–3 July. Available at: http://www.ide.titech.ac.jp/~icuc7/extended_abstracts/pdf/376129-1-090507141236-004(rev).pdf (Accessed 7 February 2014).

Holt, T. and Pullen, J. (2007). Urban canopy modelling of the New York City metropolitan area: A comparison and validation of single- and multilayer parameterisations. *Monthly Weather Review*, 135(5): 1906–1930.

Jiang, X. Y., Wiedinmyer, C., Chen, F., Yang, Z. L. and Lo, J. C. F. (2008). Predicted impacts of climate and land-use change on surface ozone in the Houston, Texas, area. *Journal of Geophysical Research*, 113: D20312. doi: 10.1029/2008JD009820.

Kusaka, H. and Kimura, F. (2004). Coupling a single-layer urban canopy model with a simple atmospheric model: Impact on urban heat island simulation for an idealised case. *Journal of the Meteorological Society of Japan*, 82(1): 67–80.

Kusaka, H., Kondo, H., Kikegawa, Y. and Kimura, F. (2001). A simple single layer urban canopy model for atmospheric models: Comparison with multi-layer and slab models. *Boundary-Layer Meteorology*, 101(3): 329–358.

Kusaka, H., Chen, F., Tewari, M., Duda, M., Dudhia, J., Miya, Y. and Akimoto, Y. (2009). Performance of the WRF model as a high resolution regional climate model: Model intercomparison study. In: *Proceedings of The 7th International Conference on Urban Climate (ICUC2009)*. Yokohama, Japan, 29 June–3 July. (CD-ROM).

Leung, L. R. and Qian, Y. (2009). Atmospheric rivers induced heavy precipitation and flooding in the western U.S. simulated by the WRF regional climate model. *Geophysical Research Letters*, 36(3): L03820. doi:10.1029/2008GL036445.

Li, X. X., Koh, T. Y., Entekhabi, D., Roth, M., Panda, J. and Norford, L. K. (2013). A multi-resolution ensemble study of a tropical urban environment and its interactions with the background regional atmosphere. *Journal of Geophysical Research: Atmospheres*, 118(17): 9804–9818. doi:10.1002/jgrd.50795.

Liang, X. Z, Xu, M., Yuan, X., Ling, T., Choi, H. I., Zhang, F., Chen, L., Liu, S., Su, S., Qiao, F., He, Y., Wang, J. X. L., Kunkel, K. E., Gao, W., Joseph, E., Morris, V., Yu, T. W., Dudhia, J. and Michalakes, J. (2012). Regional climate – Weather Research and Forecasting Model. *Bulletin of American Meteorological Society*, 93(9): 1363–1387. doi: 10.1175/BAMS-D-11-00180.1.

Lin, C. Y., Chen, F., Huang, J. C., Chen, W. C., Liou, Y. A., Chen, W. N. and Liu, S. C. (2008). Urban Heat Island effect and its impact on boundary layer development and land–sea circulation over northern Taiwan. *Atmospheric Environment*, 42(22): 5635–5649.

Lo, J. C. F., Lau, A. K. H., Fung, J. C. H. and Chen, F. (2006). Investigation of enhanced cross-city transport and trapping of air pollutants by coastal and urban land-sea breeze circulations. *Journal of Geophysical Research: Atmospheres*, 111: D14104. doi:10.1029/2005JD006837.

Martilli, A., Clappier, A. and Rotach, M. W. (2002). An urban surface exchange parameterisation for mesoscale models. *Boundary-Layer Meteorology*, 104(2): 261–304.

Miao, S., Chen, F., LeMone, M. A., Tewari, M., Li, Q. and Wang, Y. (2009a). An observational and modeling study of characteristics of urban heat island and boundary layer structures in Beijing. *Journal of Applied Meteorology and Climatology*, 48(3): 484–501.

Miao, S., Chen, F., Li, Q. and Fan, S. (2009b). Impacts of urbanisation on a summer heavy rainfall in Beijing. In: *Proceedings of The 7th International Conference on Urban Climate (ICUC2009)*. Yokohama, Japan, 29 June–3 July. (CD-ROM).

Miao, S. and Chen, F. (2008). Formation of horizontal convective rolls in urban areas. *Atmospheric Research*, 89(3), 298–304.

Miller, S. T. K., Keim, B. D., Talbot, R. W. and Mao, H. (2003). Sea breeze: Structure, forecasting, and impacts. *Reviews of Geophysics*, 41(3), 1011. doi:10.1029/2003RG000124.

Ng, E., Ren, C., Katzschner, L. and Yau, R. (2009). Urban climatic studies for hot and humid tropical coastal city of Hong Kong. In: *Proceedings of The 7th International Conference on Urban Climate (ICUC2009)*. Yokohama, Japan, 29 June–3 July. (CD-ROM).

Papanastasiou, D. K., Melas, D. and Lissaridis, I. (2010). Study of wind field under sea breeze conditions: An application of WRF model. *Atmospheric Research*, 98(1): 102–117. http://dx.doi.org/10.1016/j.atmosres.2010.06.005.

Pierce, D. W., Das, T., Cayan, D. R., Maurer, E. P., Miller, N. L., Bao, Y., Kanamitsu, M., Yoshimura, K., Snyder, M. A., Sloan, L. C., Franco, G. and Tyree, M. (2013). Probabilistic estimates of future changes in California temperature and precipitation using statistical and dynamical downscaling. *Climate Dynamics*, 40(3–4): 839–856.

Richter, C. J. and Röckle, R. (2009). *Das numerische Simulationsmodell FITNAH*. Freiburg: iMA Immissionen, Meteorologie Akustik. Available at: http://www.ima-umwelt.de/fileadmin/dokumente/klima_downloads/fitnah_kurzuebersicht.pdf (Accessed 7 February 2014).

Ren, C., Lau, K. L., Yiu, K. P. and Ng, E. (2013). The application of urban climatic mapping to the urban planning of high-density cities: The case of Kaohsiung, Taiwan. *Cities*, 31: 1–16. doi: 10.1016/j.cities.2012.12.005.

Skamarock, W. C. and Klemp, J. B. (2008). A time-split nonhydrostatic atmospheric model for weather research and forecasting applications. *Journal of Computational Physics*, 227: 3465–3485.

Tewari, M., Kusaka, H., Chen, F., Coirier, W. J., Kim, S., Wyszogrodzki, A. and Warner, T. T. (2010). Impact of coupling a microscale computational fluid dynamics model with a mesoscale model on urban scale contaminant transport and dispersion. *Atmospheric Research*, 96(4): 656–664.

Xie, B., Fung, J. C. H., Chan, A. and Lau, A. K. H. (2012). Evaluation of nonlocal and local planetary boundary layer schemes in the WRF model. *Journal of Geophysical Research: Atmospheres*, 117: D12103. doi:10.1029/2011JD017080.

Xu, Z. and Yang, Z. L. (2012). An improved dynamical downscaling method with GCM bias corrections and its validation with 30 years of climate simulations. *Journal of Climate*, 25(18): 6271–6286.

Wang, X., Chen, F., Wu, Z., Zhang, M., Tewari, M., Guenther, A. and Wiedinmyer, C. (2009). Impacts of weather conditions modified by urban expansion on surface ozone: Comparison between the Pearl River Delta and Yangtze River Delta regions. *Advances in Atmospheric Sciences*, 26(5): 962–972.

Yang, B., Zhang, Y. and Qian, Y. (2012). Simulation of urban climate with high-resolution WRF model: A case study in Nanjing, China. *Asia-Pacific Journal of Atmospheric Sciences*, 48(3): 227–241.

Yim, S. H. L. and Barrett, S. R. H. (2012). Public health impacts of combustion sources in United Kingdom. *Environmental Science and Technology*, 46(8): 4291–4296.

Yim, S. H. L., Fung, J. C. H., Lau, A. K. H. and Kot, S. C. (2007). Developing a high-resolution wind map for a complex terrain with a coupled MM5/CALMET system. *Journal of Geophysical Research: Atmospheres*, 112: D05106. doi:10.1029/2006JD007752.

Yim, S. H. L., Fung, J. C. H. and Lau, A. K. H. (2009). Mesoscale simulation of year-to-year variation of wind power potential over Southern China. *Energies*, 2(2): 340–361.

Chapter 28

# Future meteorological data and their implications for urban climatic studies

*Kevin Ka-Lun Lau*

## Introduction

Global climate change has received increasing concern in recent decades. According to the Fifth Assessment Report (AR5) of the Intergovernmental Panel on Climate Change (IPCC), global temperature has been increasing since the industrial revolution and will continue to increase in the foreseeable future. Such an increase in temperature results in a wide range of impacts on both the natural and human environment, and can also lead to enormous economic and social costs. In urban environments, the effects of climate change are generally accentuated compared to their rural counterpart since rapid urbanisation involves extensive conversion of vegetated land into concrete surfaces with dense building structures. This results in reduced ventilation, air pollution, and intensive release of anthropogenic heat. The role of urban settlements in the emission of greenhouse gases (GHG) was discussed in the Intergovernmental Panel on Climate Change – *Special Report on Emission Scenarios*. It was also found that land-use patterns and population density in urban areas also significantly affect GHG emissions (Gaffin, 1998; IPCC, 2000).

In response to changing urban climate, more climate-sensitive urban planning and design has a great potential in mitigating the rising air temperature in compacted urban areas (Watkins *et al.*, 2007). However, relevant studies on climate change at an urban scale are generally lacking (Blanco *et al.*, 2009; Hunt and Watkiss, 2011) and there are uncertainties about the assessment of climate change effects (Bentley, 2007; Alcoforado *et al.*, 2009). One of the critical issues is the lack of meteorological data at a fine spatial scale to address the effects of climate change on urban areas and their associated climatic conditions (Wilby, 2008). It leads to insufficient considerations of climate change effects in the urban planning and design framework. The complexities of the built environment of individual districts require extensive data at a fine spatial scale to outline comprehensive strategies in response to climate change (Belcher *et al.*, 2005; Aydin and Çukur, 2012).

The downscaling of future climate change scenarios has become an emerging method for providing data at fine spatial resolutions (Wilby, 2008). One of the widely used approaches is statistical downscaling (SD), which is based on the empirical relationships between large-scale climatic variables from General Circulation Models (GCMs) and local or station scale observations (Wilby *et al.*, 2002; Fowler *et al.*, 2007). The advantages of SD include the low computational cost of generating extensive meteorological data and the incorporation of a large number of climate scenarios for impact assessment studies (Benestad, 2001; Benestad *et al.*, 2008). Since statistical downscaling processes are based on standard and widely accepted statistical procedures, observations can be directly incorporated and other variables that are not available from regional models can be derived (Wilby and Wigley, 1997).

This chapter discusses the potential of using the SD approach in urban climatic mapping and the current practice in Hong Kong. The strengths of various SD techniques in providing future meteorological data at a fine spatial scale are discussed. It concludes with potential applications of statistically downscaled meteorological data in the future development of urban climatic maps (UCMaps) under different climate scenarios.

## The use of statistical downscaling in future climate projection in Hong Kong

The study of climate change effects at an urban scale has been limited in Hong Kong. Previous attempts employed regression-based statistical downscaling to project future maximum, mean and minimum air temperatures, as well as annual rainfall for Hong Kong (Wu *et al.*, 2005; Leung *et al.*, 2007). Ensemble means were employed in order to obtain a comprehensive understanding of the future climate of Hong Kong. Based on the projected data, extreme temperature and precipitation events are calculated, such as very hot days, hot nights, and cold days. Recent advances in climate modelling allow more accurate and reliable climate projection in Hong Kong (Lee *et al.*, 2011a, 2011b).

In general, there were significant trends in temperature extremes in the twentieth century and they are expected to continue into the twenty-first century (Lee *et al.*, 2011a). This results in substantial increases in the number of hot nights and very hot days, while a decrease in the number of cold days is expected (Lee *et al.*, 2011c). However, there are still uncertainties in the model simulations of future climate. One of the uncertainties is the local urbanisation effect, which is not featured in the UCMaps. Lau and Ng (2013) examined the urbanisation effect on local air temperature in various urban and rural areas of Hong Kong. The urbanisation effect was subsequently incorporated into projected air temperature series for urban and rural areas of Hong Kong (Lau, 2013). It was found that future warming in rural areas exceeds that in urban areas, especially during night-time and winter months. Incorporating the urbanisation effect, based on planned and proposed development in different areas, air temperature in rural areas may exceed that of their urban counterparts at the end of the twenty-first century. This implies that more climate-sensitive urban planning and design is required in order to maintain the climatic characteristics of rural areas in future development projects.

The downscaling approach in previous studies was proved to be a successful technique in obtaining future average and extreme climatic conditions. Since subtle changes in average climate conditions and their relative distributions could result in substantial increases in the occurrence of extreme climates (Meehl *et al.*, 2000; Lee *et al.*, 2011a, 2011b), there is an urgent need for adaptation strategies and mitigation measures in response to future climate change. In the context of urban planning and design, SD is able to provide extensive and reliable future climatic data at relatively low computational cost for impact assessments and corresponding sustainable planning and design at an urban scale.

## Statistical downscaling of different meteorological parameters

The primary objective of SD is to obtain future climatic conditions at a fine spatial scale. A wide range of meteorological parameters and their corresponding changes under future climate can be obtained for impact assessments and urban microclimatic studies. The results of studies regarding future changes in urban climate are invaluable for producing relevant UCMaps under different climate scenarios as well as associated impact assessments and the development of adaptation and mitigation strategies. This section introduces the statistical downscaling of various meteorological parameters that are relevant to urban climatic studies, and potential applications of SD are discussed.

## *Air temperature*

As one of the basic meteorological parameters in the assessment of future climate change, a wide range of studies have been conducted for the projection of air temperature under various climate scenarios. Average conditions are important in order to concisely understand the effect of climate change on cities and they are generally used for projecting certain secondary parameters that are a function of future air temperature changes (Belcher *et al.*, 2005). For example, energy consumption due to cooling and heating load can be projected by changes in average air temperature for particular seasons (Mourshed, 2012; Xu *et al.*, 2012). A number of studies have also been conducted to investigate the effect of climate change on air-conditioning energy consumption in Hong Kong (Lam *et al.*, 2010; Wan *et al.*, 2011).

According to the IPCC AR5, it is virtually certain that there will be more hot temperature extremes, and the frequency and duration of heat waves are likely to increase in future. Therefore, the UCMap should be capable of addressing the potential effects of heat waves in the future. Temperature extremes such as maximum and minimum air temperatures can be used to generate different versions of climatic maps in order to feature extreme climatic conditions, particularly in dense urban areas. Ribalaygua *et al.* (2013a, 2013b) adopted a two-step analogue and regression approach to project future maximum and minimum air temperatures in Spain. Extremely hot

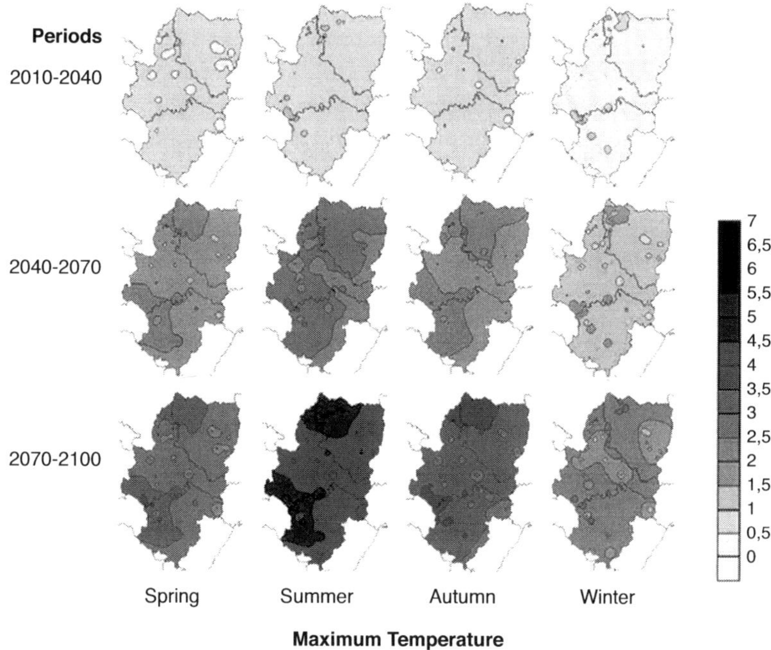


*Figure 28.1* Spatial distribution of maximum temperature increase in Aragón, Spain in the twenty-first century.

Source: Ribalaygua *et al.*, 2013a

days and a certain number of the most similar days are determined in order to select predictors for subsequent downscaling. The spatial distribution of future changes in temperature extremes was determined for different seasons (see Figure 28.1). The downscaled temperature extremes can therefore be applied to examine the changes in local maximum and minimum air temperatures, which are useful for calibrating the UCMap according to future climatic conditions.

### *Wind conditions*

Recent developments in the statistical downscaling of surface wind speed has allowed the study of prevailing wind conditions under future climatic conditions. Various statistical techniques were employed, including neural networks (Sailor *et al.*, 2000), the resampling of probability distribution (Pryor *et al.*, 2005, 2006), transformation of cumulative distribution functions (Michelangeli *et al.*, 2009), and regression-based approaches (Culver and Monahan, 2013). Sailor *et al.* (2000) used neural networks to downscale large-scale predictors to a surface-based variable, i.e. wind speed. Neural network models are particularly suitable for the projection of wind speed since they are able to estimate the non-linear functions that exist in wind-related parameters. They also have a great potential in investigating the variance of average wind speed at the local scale. Despite the difficulties in model interpretation, neural networks are widely used in the statistical downscaling of wind conditions (Bogardi and Matyasovszky, 1996).

Cumulative distribution functions (CDFs) of historical observational data, in general, represent the existing conditions of both local and global wind conditions (Déqué, 2007). The underlying assumption is that the CDFs of large-scale predictors can be translated into CDFs that represent local climatic variables by a transformation function. This is then applied to a future time period so that future wind conditions at the local scale can be determined from GCM outputs. It can be potentially extended to multivariate form, but certain adjustments are required, especially for specific conditions like calm wind (Michelangeli *et al.*, 2009).

Prevailing wind conditions can be used to simulate the wind environment at district level by using numerical modelling methods (Baik *et al.*, 2009). Local wind conditions can be applied to the assessment of wind conditions in individual districts. Such information also contributes to the assessment of wind standards under future climate since the wind environment may be altered due to changes in synoptic wind fields. Potential applications also include pollution transport and dispersion modelling, which affect the quality of the urban living environment.

### *Solar radiation*

Solar radiation plays an important role in outdoor thermal comfort in urban environments. Its effect on thermal comfort is complex due to the interaction of the two components, direct and diffuse radiation, with urban structures. Direct incoming solar radiation has a more prominent effect in open areas and its reflection from building and ground surfaces also leads to thermal discomfort, especially when a person stands close to building walls (Ali-Toudert and Mayer, 2007; Thorsson *et al.*, 2011). Under cloudy situations, diffuse solar radiation increases and affects areas which are shaded under sunny conditions. It implies that global solar radiation should not be considered as the only parameter, and both components have to be addressed in microclimatic analyses within urban environments.

The statistical downscaling of solar radiation has rarely been studied in the past (Dettinger, 2013); previous attempts focused on generating global solar radiation for the assessment of changes in cloud cover (Iizumi *et al.*, 2012; Dettinger, 2013; Rojas *et al.*, 2013). Analogue methods have been widely adopted in weather forecasting and short-term climate prediction. Zorita and von Storch (1999) suggested using analogue methods for downscaling purposes by comparing the large-scale atmospheric circulation to each of the historical observations. The most similar analogues are then used to associate observed local weather to the simulated large-scale conditions. As such, future changes in radiation fluxes can be determined by applying the analogues to the future simulated data series.

## Future development of urban climatic maps in response to climate change

Future climatic conditions obtained by SD can therefore serve as inputs for a wide range of district-level microclimatic analyses which provide site- or district-specific climatic conditions (see Figure 28.2). Such information provides not only an understanding of outdoor thermal comfort under future climate, but also inputs for the calculation of physiological equivalent temperature (PET), which serves as the synergizing indicator in generating the UCMap. As such, the UCMap can be calibrated according to the climatic conditions under different periods and climate scenarios in the future. Scenario-based UCMaps are generated for urban planners and designers to consider the effect of climate change and associated outdoor thermal comfort issues in their practices. It also allows the development of more climate-sensitive urban planning and design with regard to future climate change.

The concept of local climate zones (LCZs) has recently been developed by Stewart and Oke (2012) for the studies of urban heat island phenomenon and urban temperature observations. LCZs are developed according to surface structure and surface cover since they alter the airflow, heat transfer, radiation balance, albedo, moisture, and heating and cooling potential of the ground (Stewart and Oke, 2012; Stewart *et al.*, 2013). It helps to improve the traditional definition of urban–rural difference in terms of climatic conditions according to the surface characteristics of particular localities. Such information contributes to the feature of the urban canopy in numerical

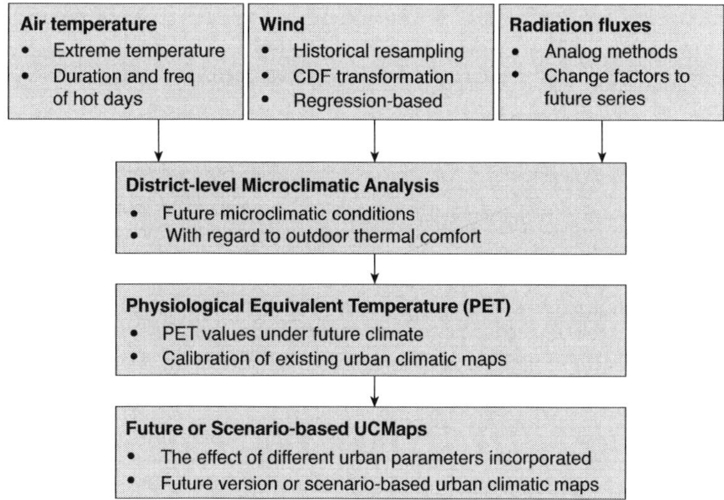


*Figure 28.2* The role of downscaled data and the development of urban climatic maps for future climate.

Source: Author

climate models and weather prediction. Future climate data, together with information provided by LCZs, can therefore be applied to urban-scale climate models in order to generate future climate at the urban scale. Müller *et al.* (2014) performed numerical model simulations for different LCZ classes under four climate scenarios. Adaptation measures were then suggested in terms of modifications to local surface characteristics. It implies that corresponding planning actions are required for different climatic scenarios and it provides the basis for future development of UCMaps in response to climate change.

A recent study conducted by Nichol *et al.* (2013) used satellite images for mapping the spatial variation of the baseline climate in Hong Kong. SD was employed to obtain changes in the future air temperature of a rural station in order to represent the background warming due to climate change. The urbanisation effect, calculated by plot ratio, was then incorporated into projected air temperature so that the spatial variation of future air temperature was obtained. This provides information about the relative changes of air temperature at high spatial resolution over Hong Kong since satellite images are able to provide spatial data at high temporal resolution (e.g. on a daily basis).

Statistically downscaled meteorological data has a great potential in obtaining meteorological conditions under future climate. It facilitates microclimatic studies at district-level and provides essential information for the calibration of existing UCMaps for future climates. In high-density cities like Hong Kong, there is an urgent need for adaptation and mitigation strategies for individual districts due to the complex terrain and surface characteristics. Climate change responses are largely based on more climate-sensitive urban planning and design at territory, district and building levels. Scenario-based UCMaps provide future climatic conditions and the response of urban structures to future climate, and assist with the development of comprehensive adaptation and mitigation strategies at different planning levels.

## References


Alcoforado, M. J., Andrade, H., Lopes, A. and Vasconcelos, J. (2009). Application of climatic guidelines to urban planning: The example of Lisbon (Portugal). *Landscape and Urban Planning*, 90(1–2): 56–65.

Ali-Toudert, F. and Mayer, H. (2007). Thermal comfort in an east–west oriented street canyon in Freiburg (Germany) under hot summer conditions. *Theoretical and Applied Climatology*, 87(1–4): 223–237.

Aydin, M. B. S. and Çukur, D. (2012). Maintaining the carbon-oxygen balance in residential areas: A method proposal for land use planning. *Urban Forestry and Urban Greening*, 11(1): 87–94.

Baik, J. J., Park, S. B. and Kim, J. J. (2009). Urban flow and dispersion simulation using a CFD model coupled to a mesoscale model. *Journal of Applied Meteorology and Climatology*, 48(8): 1667–1681.

Belcher, S. E., Hacker, J. N. and Powell, D. S. (2005). Constructing design weather data for future climates. *Building Services Engineering Research and Technology*, 26(1): 49–61.

Benestad, R. E. (2001). The cause of warming over Norway in the ECHAM4/OPYC3 GHG integration. *International Journal of Climatology*, 21(3): 371–387.

Benestad, R. E., Hanssen-Bauer, I. and Chen, D. (2008). *Empirical-Statistical Downscaling*. Singapore: World Scientific.

Bentley, M. (2007). Healthy cities, local environmental action and climate change. *Health Promotion International*, 22(3): 246–253.

Blanco, H., Alberti, M., Forsyth, A., Krizek, K. J., Rodríguez, D. A., Talen, E. and Ellis, C. (2009). Hot, congested, crowded and diverse: Emerging research agendas in planning. *Progress in Planning*, 71(4): 153–205.

Bogardi, I. and Matyasovszky, I. (1996). Estimating daily wind speed under climate change. *Solar Energy*, 57(3): 239–248.

Culver, A. M. R. and Monahan, A. H. (2013). The statistical predictability of surface winds over western and central Canada. *Journal of Climate*, 26: 8305–8322.

Déqué, M. (2007). Frequency of precipitation and temperature extremes over France in an anthropogenic scenario: Model results and statistical correction according to observed values. *Global and Planetary Change*, 57(1–2): 16–26.

Dettinger, M. D. (2013). Projections and downscaling of 21st century temperatures, precipitation, radiative fluxes and winds for the Southwestern US, with focus on Lake Tahoe. *Climatic Change*, 116(1): 17–33.

Fowler, H. J., Blenkinsop, S. and Tebaldi, C. (2007). Linking climate change modelling to impacts studies: Recent advances in downscaling techniques for hydrological modelling. *International Journal of Climatology*, 27(12): 1547–1578.

Gaffin, S. R. (1998). World population projections for greenhouse gas emissions scenarios. *Mitigation and Adaptation Strategies for Global Change*, 3(2–4): 133–170.

Hunt, A. and Watkiss, P. (2011). Climate change impacts and adaptation in cities: A review of the literature. *Climatic Change*, 104(1): 13–49.

IPCC (2000). *Special Report on Emissions Scenarios – Summary for Policymakers*. Geneva: IPCC. Available at: http://www.ipcc.ch/pdf/special-reports/spm/sres-en.pdf (Accessed 7 February 2014).

Iizumi, T., Nishimori, M., Yokozawa, M., Koteraa, A. and Khang, N. D. (2012). Statistical downscaling with Bayesian inference: Estimating global solar radiation from reanalysis and limited observed data. *International Journal of Climatology*, 32(3): 464–480.

Lam, T. N. T., Wan, K. K. W., Wong, S. L. and Lam, J. C. (2010). Impact of climate change on commercial sector air conditioning energy consumption in subtropical Hong Kong. *Applied Energy*, 87(7): 2321–2327.

Lau, K. L. (2013). *Projecting future air temperature of Hong Kong for the 21st century and its implications on urban planning and design*. PhD thesis, The Chinese University of Hong Kong, Hong Kong.

Lau, K. L. and Ng, E. (2013). An investigation of urbanization effect on urban and rural Hong Kong using a 40-year extended temperature record. *Landscape and Urban Planning*, 114: 42–52.

Lee, T. C., Chan, K. Y. and Ginn, W. L. (2011a). Projection of extreme temperatures in Hong Kong in the 21st century. *Acta Meteorologica Sinica*, 25(1): 1–20.

Lee, T. C., Chan, K. Y., Chan, H. S. and Kok, M. H. (2011b). Projection of extreme rainfall in Hong Kong in the 21st Century. *Acta Meteorologica Sinica*, 25(6): 691–709.

Lee, T. C., Chan, H. S., Ginn, E. W. L. and Wong, M. C. (2011c). Long-term trends in extreme temperatures in Hong Kong and Southern China. *Advances in Atmospheric Sciences*, 28(1): 147–157.

Leung, Y. K., Wu, M. C., Yeung, K. K. and Leung, W. M. (2007). Temperature projections in Hong Kong based on IPCC Fourth Assessment Report. *Hong Kong Meteorological Society Bulletin*, 17: 13–22.

Meehl, G. A., Zwiers, F., Evans, J., Knutson, T., Mearns, L. and Whetton, P. (2000). Trends in extreme weather and climate events: Issues related to modeling extremes in projections of future climate change. *Bulletin of the American Meteorological Society*, 81(3): 427–436.

Michelangeli, P.-A., Vrac, M. and Loukos, H. (2009). Probabilistic downscaling approaches: Application to wind cumulative distribution functions. *Geophysical Research Letters*, 36(11): L11708.

Mourshed, M. (2012). Relationship between annual mean temperature and degree-days. *Energy and Buildings*, 54: 418–425.

Müller, N., Kuttler, W. and Barlag, A. B. (2014). Counteracting urban climate change: adaptation measures and their effect on thermal comfort. *Theoretical and Applied Climatology*, 115(1–2): 243–257.

Nichol, J., To, P. H. and Ng, E. (2013). Temperature projection in a tropical city using remote sensing and dynamic modeling. *Climate Dynamics*, in press. doi: 10.1007/s00382-013-1748-2.

Pryor, S. C., Schoof, J. T. and Barthelmie, R. J. (2005). Empirical downscaling of wind speed probability distributions. *Journal of Geophysical Research: Atmospheres*, 110: D19109. doi: 10.1029/2005JD005899.

Pryor, S. C., Schoof, J. T. and Barthelmie, R. J. (2006). Winds of change? Projections of near-surface winds under climate change scenarios. *Geophysical Research Letters*, 33(11): L11702. doi: 10.1029/2006GL026000.

Ribalaygua, J., Pino, M. R., Pórtoles, J., Roldán, E., Gaitán, E., Chinarro, D. and Torres, L. (2013a). Climate change scenarios for temperature and precipitation in Aragón (Spain). *Science of the Total Environment*, 463–464: 1015–1030.

Ribalaygua, J., Torres, L., Pórtoles, J., Monjo, R., Gaitán, E. and Pino, M. R. (2013b). Description and validation of a two-step analogue/regression downscaling method. *Theoretical and Applied Climatology*, 114(1–2): 253–269.

Rojas, M., Li, L. Z., Kanakidou, M., Hatzianastassiou, N., Seze, G. and Le Treut, H. (2013). Winter weather regimes over the Mediterranean region: Their role for the regional climate and projected changes in the twenty-first century. *Climate Dynamics*, 41(3–4): 551–571.

Sailor, D. J., Hu, T., Li, X. and Rosen, J. N. (2000). A neural network approach to local downscaling of GCM output for assessing wind power implications of climate change. *Renewable Energy*, 19(3): 359–378.

Stewart, I. D. and Oke, T. R. (2012). Local climate zones for urban temperature studies. *Bulletin of the American Meteorological Society*, 93(12): 1879–1900.

Stewart, I. D., Oke, T. R. and Krayenhoff, E. S. (2013). Evaluation of the 'local climate zone' scheme using temperature observations and model simulations. *International Journal of Climatology*, in press. doi: 10.1002/joc.3746.

Thorsson, S., Lindberg, F., Björklund, J., Holmer, B. and Rayner, D. (2011). Potential changes in outdoor thermal comfort conditions in Gothenburg, Sweden due to climate change: The influence of urban geometry. *International Journal of Climatology*, 31(2): 324–335.

Wan, K. K. W., Li, D. H. W., Liu, D. and Lam, J. C. (2011). Future trends of building heating and cooling loads and energy consumption in different climates. *Building and Environment*, 46(1): 223–234.

Watkins, R., Palmer, J. and Kolokotroni, M. (2007). Increased temperature and intensification of the urban heat island: Implications for human comfort and urban design. *Built Environment*, 33(1): 85–96.

Wilby, R. L. (2008). Constructing climate change scenarios of urban heat island intensity and air quality. *Environment and Planning B: Planning and Design*, 35(5): 902–919.

Wilby, R. L. and Wigley, T. M. L. (1997). Downscaling general circulation model output: a review of methods and limitations. *Progress in Physical Geography*, 21(4): 530–548.

Wilby, R. L., Conway, D. and Jones, P. D. (2002). Prospects for downscaling seasonal precipitation variability using conditioned weather generator parameters. *Hydrological Processes*, 16(6): 1215–1234.

Wu, M. C., Leung, Y. K. and Yeung, K. H. (2005). Projected change in Hong Kong's rainfall in the 21st century. *Hong Kong Meteorological Society Bulletin*, 15(1/2): 40–53.

Xu, P., Huang, Y. J., Miller, N., Schlegel, N. and Shen, P. (2012). Impacts of climate change on building heating and cooling energy patterns in California. *Energy*, 44(1): 792–804.

Zorita, E. and von Storch, H. (1999). The analog method – a simple statistical downscaling technique: comparison with more complicated methods. *Journal of Climate*, 12(8): 2474–2489.

Chapter 29

# Local climate zones and urban climatic mapping

*Iain D. Stewart and Timothy R. Oke*

## Introduction

'Local climate zones' (LCZs) are a new development in urban climatology (Stewart and Oke, 2012). They comprise a system of local-scale ($10^2$m to $10^4$m) landscapes that characterise the thermal and morphological conditions of cities, mostly for heat island investigations in the canopy layer, i.e. below the mean height of the roughness elements (e.g. buildings and trees) or below roof level in fully built-up zones. Each of its 17 standard classes exhibits a characteristic surface structure and land cover type (see Table 29.1). LCZs 1 to 10 ('built' types) represent landscapes with roads, buildings, trees, cars, and people; LCZs A to G ('land cover' types) represent landscapes with few paved or no such roads or buildings. 'Built' types broadly correspond with Oke's (2004) 'urban climate zone' (UCZ) scheme, which defines a range of cityscapes by similar criteria to local climate zones. Agreement between the surface property values of the seven UCZ classes and the ten 'built' LCZ classes is therefore good. 'Land cover' classes were developed as an expansion series to the original UCZ system. The 'built' and 'land cover' series together provide a wide range of urban and rural landscapes and local thermal climates.

The thermal climate of each LCZ class is determined by its surface character, which is expressed by urban climatologists as surface *structure* (building and tree height/density), *cover* (permeability), *fabric* (albedo, thermal admittance), and *metabolism* (waste heat from transportation and space heating/cooling) (Oke, 2004). Unique combinations of these properties give each LCZ class a distinctive thermal regime. This is best observed in radiation-type weather that promotes differential heating and cooling of the surface, and in areas where the interference of relief on local climate is relatively minor. Thus we formally define *local climate zones* as 'regions of uniform land cover, surface structure, construction material, and human activity [...] that give a characteristic temperature regime at screen height, and that is most apparent on calm, clear nights and in areas of simple relief' (Stewart and Oke, 2012:1884). The claim that there is correspondence between LCZ/UCZ classes and local thermal climates has independent support from field observations and numerical simulations (e.g. Houet and Pigeon, 2011; Holmer *et al.*, 2013; Muller *et al.*, 2013; Stewart *et al.*, 2014).

The LCZ system is designed to help standardise communication and reporting of site metadata in observational heat island studies. Description and classification of 'urban' and 'rural' field sites in the heat island literature is overly subjective and simplistic (Stewart, 2011), which gives the motivation for a system that facilitates standardised classification of urban and rural sites based on the physical and climatological properties of the local landscape or, more technically, of the thermal source area (or 'footprint') of a screen-level temperature sensor. The LCZ approach is more rigorous than traditional methods of field site classification based on arbitrary, and sometimes erroneous, use of the terms 'urban' and 'rural'. Equally erroneous are surrogates of urban or

*Table 29.1* Select physical properties of the surface for local climate zones.

| *Local Climate Zone (LCZ)* | *Aspect ratio*[a] | *Building surface fraction*[b] | *Impervious surface fraction*[c] | *Height of roughness elements*[d] | *Anthropogenic heat output*[e] |
|---|---|---|---|---|---|
| **BUILT TYPES** | | | | | |
| LCZ 1 *Compact high-rise* | > 2 | 40–60 | 40–60 | > 25 | 50–300 |
| LCZ 2 *Compact midrise* | 0.75–2 | 40–70 | 30–50 | 10–25 | < 75 |
| LCZ 3 *Compact low-rise* | 0.75–1.5 | 40–70 | 20–50 | 3–10 | < 75 |
| LCZ 4 *Open high-rise* | 0.75–1.25 | 20–40 | 30–40 | > 25 | < 50 |
| LCZ 5 *Open mid-rise* | 0.3–0.75 | 20–40 | 30–50 | 10–25 | < 25 |
| LCZ 6 *Open low-rise* | 0.3–0.75 | 20–40 | 20–50 | 3–10 | < 25 |
| LCZ 7 *Lightweight low-rise* | 1–2 | 60–90 | < 20 | 2–4 | < 35 |
| LCZ 8 *Large low-rise* | 0.1–0.3 | 30–50 | 40–50 | 3–10 | < 50 |
| LCZ 9 *Sparsely built* | 0.1–0.25 | 10–20 | < 20 | 3–10 | < 10 |
| LCZ 10 *Heavy industry* | 0.2–0.5 | 20–30 | 20–40 | 5–15 | > 300 |
| **LAND COVER TYPES** | | | | | |
| LCZ A *Dense trees* | > 1 | < 10 | < 10 | 3–30 | 0 |
| LCZ B *Scattered trees* | 0.25–0.75 | < 10 | < 10 | 3–15 | 0 |
| LCZ C *Bush, scrub* | 0.25–1.0 | < 10 | < 10 | < 2 | 0 |
| LCZ D *Low plants* | < 0.1 | < 10 | < 10 | < 1 | 0 |
| LCZ E *Bare rock or paved* | < 0.1 | < 10 | > 90 | < 0.25 | 0 |
| LCZ F *Bare soil or sand* | < 0.1 | < 10 | < 10 | < 0.25 | 0 |
| LCZ G *Water* | < 0.1 | < 10 | < 10 | – | 0 |

[a] Mean height width ratio of street canyons (LCZs 1–7), building spacing (LCZs 8, 9, and 10), and tree spacing (LCZs A–G).
[b] Ratio of building plan area to total plan area (%).
[c] Ratio of impervious plan area (paved, rock) to total plan area (%).
[d] Geometric average of building heights (LCZs 1–10) and tree/plant heights (LCZs A–F) (metres).
[e] Mean annual heat flux density ($W\ m^{-2}$) from fuel combustion and human activity (transportation, space cooling/heating, industrial processing, human metabolism). Varies significantly with latitude, season, and population density.

Source: Stewart and Oke, 2012

*Figure 29.1* Intercity examples of local climate zones (LCZs). Clockwise from top-left: LCZ 1 (*compact high-rise*) in Hong Kong; LCZ 2 (*compact midrise*) in Munich, Germany; LCZ 4 (*open high-rise*) in Jinan, China; LCZ 6 (*open low-rise*) in Seattle, USA.

Source: Photo credit: Stewart, I. D.

rural form, such as land use, population density, and satellite-derived night-light and vegetation (Normalized Difference Vegetation Index, NDVI) indices. LCZs are instead defined by objective criteria (e.g. building height, green cover ratio) that directly influence surface thermal climate and that are easily measured in most cities (see Table 29.1). Their use in heat island studies helps investigators gather and report observations with greater attention to site location, site metadata and data exchange. LCZs might also help substantiate intercity comparisons of heat island observations because they are standardised in name and definition. In future, LCZs can play a key role in developing international guidelines to assess UHI magnitude in the canopy layer. All aspects of the LCZ system, including its historical development, recommended applications, and guidelines for use, are described in Stewart and Oke (2012).

## Climatopes and local climate zones: Mutually beneficial for urban climatic mapping

Here it is important that we introduce a critical distinction between 'climatopes' and 'local climate zones'. The concepts are easily confused because both depict climates at similar spatial scales ($10^2$m to $10^4$m); however, they differ fundamentally in their definition. Climatopes are based on expert knowledge of local topography and climatology in individual cities. Their definition and development criteria are not standardised for all cities, but are specialised to particular settings. The criteria are somewhat selective to each case study, depending crucially on data availability and local knowledge. Consequently, every city exhibits a unique set of climatopes (in name and definition). This means that intercity comparisons and generalisations of climatopes are not straightforward, even though that is not their intended use. LCZs are designed for exactly that purpose. They are based on generalised and simplified knowledge of building form and land cover, and the known influences that these properties exert on surface thermal climate. Their definition and development criteria are consistent across all cities and regions regardless of the purpose or place of an individual study. Unlike climatopes, LCZs are not tailored to the local topography and climatology of one city or study area (e.g. Figure 29.1).

The LCZ classification system offers important metadata – both quantitative and qualitative – to planning and mapping projects that use climatopes and UCMapping techniques. Urban planners and climatologists have suggested that consistent input data are needed to improve the integrity of these projects (e.g. Wilmers, 1991; Scherer *et al.*, 1999). UCMapping follows a layered approach to build its database of spatial information, ultimately to produce analytical and recommendation maps for local planners. These layers ordinarily include air temperature, airflow, land use, land cover, building structure, surface relief, and population density. The layers are quantified and then stacked across local areas to reveal 'climates of special places', or 'climatopes.' Additional information to increase the number of layers in an urban climatic map (UCMap), and to improve consistency in the definition of these layers, is available in the metadata accompanying each LCZ class.

Data that are most valuable to UCMaps can be extracted from the LCZ specification sheets, which contain thermal, radiative, geometric, metabolic, and surface cover properties for all LCZ classes (see Figure 29.2). With these data, planners and climatologists can generate new and well-defined layers to integrate with existing UCMaps. Layers representing city structure and urban heat load are most relevant to LCZs, and are essential to any UCMap. In cities for which surface structure, land cover, and/or anthropogenic heat flux data are unavailable or difficult to acquire, one can instead use the standardised metadata given in the LCZ specification sheets. These data are easily adapted to the local area of a UCMap, and are derived from primary sources, i.e. field measurements in cities. Conventional input for UCMaps, on the other hand, is often based on secondary data for heat islands and city structure, such as population or land use. Thus an advantage of the LCZ system is that not only is it grounded in empirical measurement, but its surface metadata are transferable to any city, and more importantly to cities with limited or restricted access to the resources needed for a climatic mapping study. As such, LCZs facilitate information transfer among UCMap users in different regions, and among urban climate researchers in different disciplines.

A disadvantage of the LCZ system is that they do not account for surface relief, and therefore does not suit climatic mapping studies unless accompanied by additional surface metadata. LCZs account only for land cover, human activity, and height and packing of buildings and trees. This combination gives each class its unique thermal climate. The assumption in this definition is that background relief is relatively simple and consistent among all classes. If this assumption is not met, dynamic effects such as air drainage across LCZ boundaries, or the extra heat loading of slopes with preferential solar exposure, may confound the effects of building form and/or land cover on observed air temperatures. Likewise, if sky conditions are spatially variable, as with cloud streets, standing waves, or moving fronts, the effects of surface form and land cover may again be confounded with those of local weather and sky cover. When used for climatic mapping, LCZs must be integrated with complementary layers for local relief, topography, airflow, and humidity, as is the case for any climatope class. Climatopes are therefore more inclusive of the many surface influences on local climate, and in this way are advantaged over LCZs for climatic mapping.

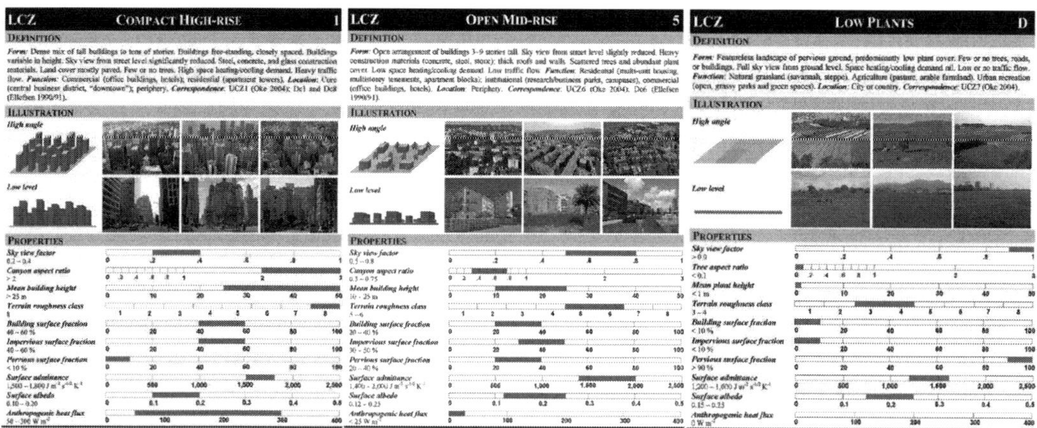


*Figure 29.2* Sample specification sheets for local climate zones. See Stewart and Oke (2012) for full set. ©American Meteorological Society. Used with Permission.

Source: Stewart and Oke, 2012

Arguably, the roles of LCZs and climatopes in UCMapping are mutually beneficial. The former provide a surface classification that is generic and objective, and that introduces standardised information to an otherwise site-specific database. The latter provides a classification that is inclusive yet detailed, and that highlights the pervasive effects of surface relief on local climate. Together, the two classifications can advance scientific and climatological knowledge in UCMaps.

## References

Holmer, B., Thorsson, S. and Linden, J. (2013). Evening evapotranspirative cooling in relation to vegetation and urban geometry in the city of Ouagadougou, Burkina Faso. *International Journal of Climatology*, 33(15): 3089–3105. doi: 10.1002/joc.3561.

Houet, T. and Pigeon, G. (2011). Mapping urban climate zones and quantifying climate behaviors – An application on Toulouse urban area (France). *Environmental Pollution*, 159(8–9): 2180–2192.

Muller, N., Kuttler, W. and Berlag, A. B. (2013). Counteracting urban climate change: adaptation measures and their effect on thermal comfort. *Theoretical and Applied Climatology*, 115(1–2): 243–257. doi: 10.1007/s00704-013-0890-4.

Oke, T. R. (2004). Initial guidance to obtain representative meteorological observations at urban sites. *Instruments and Observing Methods Report No. 81, WMO/TD-No.1250*. Available at: https://www.wmo.int/pages/prog/www/IMOP/publications/IOM-81/IOM-81-UrbanMetObs.pdf (Accessed 6 February 2014).

Scherer, D., Fehrenbach, U., Beha, H. D. and Parlow, E. (1999). Improved concepts and methods in analysis and evaluation of the urban climate for optimizing urban climate processes. *Atmospheric Environment*, 33(24–25): 4185–4193.

Stewart, I. D. (2011). A systematic review and scientific critique of methodology in modern urban heat island literature. *International Journal of Climatology*, 31(2): 200–217.

Stewart, I. D. and Oke, T. R. (2012). Local climate zones for urban temperature studies. *Bulletin of the American Meteorological Society*, 93(12): 1879–1900.

Stewart, I. D., Oke, T. R. and Krayenhoff, E. S. (2014). Evaluation of the 'local climate zone' scheme using temperature observations and model simulations. *International Journal of Climatology*, 34(4): 1062–1080.

Wilmers, F. (1991). Effects of vegetation on urban climate and buildings. *Energy and Buildings*, 15(3–4): 507–514.

Chapter 30

# Future technology developments for urban climatic mapping

*Victor O. K. Li*

## Introduction

The urban environment is greatly influenced by human activities. Some of the influences may be relatively static, such as those due to artificial constructions (the characteristics can now be represented using various kinds of urban climatic maps), while others may be highly dynamic, such as those due to vehicular traffic. Since the urban environment will directly affect the well-being of humans, it is desirable to have high-resolution, near real-time climatic data to guide human living. For example, if we have a real-time climatic map of air pollution in different parts of the city, citizens suffering from respiratory disorders can be alerted to stay away from certain areas.

However, there are many challenges to overcome before we can get accurate, high-resolution, real-time climatic data. Fortunately, with advancements in information technology such as mobile sensor networks, compressive data sensing, and big data stream processing, it is possible to overcome such challenges. In this chapter, we will describe the challenges and explore ways to overcome them. In addition, we will also survey existing research in related areas.

## Challenges of obtaining high-resolution, real-time climatic data

Many cities have monitoring stations providing continuous measurements of major pollutants. However, the number of these stations is usually very small. In Hong Kong, there are fewer than 20 such stations. Since air pollution is highly location-dependent, good coverage of the whole city would require a large number of stations, an economically infeasible solution.

Therefore, the first challenge is obtaining high-resolution data economically. It is also desirable to have near real-time data, requiring the monitoring stations to send data back to the central server frequently. However, with the large number of sensors required to provide high-resolution coverage and the frequent transmissions necessary to have near real-time data, the volume of data being sent to the central server will be tremendous, overwhelming the transmission network.

The second challenge is collecting the data and sending them back to the central server without overwhelming the communication network. Even if we can get the data transmitted to the central server, it may not have the capacity to properly process them so they can be useful to the public.

The third challenge is to develop data processing solutions to process the huge volume of data collected, and to obtain 'value' from them. The fourth challenge is to develop the urban dynamics analysis tool, which is capable of hidden causality detection and prediction once it gets the urban sensing data stream. In addition, the data must be made readily accessible to the public. To summarise, the four technical challenges are:

(1) collecting high-resolution, near real-time data economically.
(2) transmitting the data to the central server efficiently.
(3) processing the huge volume of data collected efficiently.
(4) developing urban dynamics analysis and visualisation tools.

In the next section, we shall explore how we may overcome these challenges.

## Technologies for overcoming the challenges of obtaining high-resolution, real-time climatic data

In this section, we explore ways to overcome each of the four challenges.

### *Mobile sensor networks*

Traditional climatic monitoring stations are bulky and expensive. However, it is now possible to build relatively inexpensive portable sensor units to collect various climatic data. By deploying such portable units on vehicular platforms, it is possible to cover a large area with far fewer units compared to using stationary sensors. Each sensor unit (which may be deployed on buses and taxis, or carried by an individual) is equipped with a location device such as Global Positioning System (GPS), and makes a series of time-stamped and location-stamped measurements as it roams around, thus covering a large region of the city. Due to the city canyon effect, it may be necessary to use hybrid positioning technology with GPS/Wi-Fi in parts of the city with no GPS coverage (Yang *et al.*, 2010).

We have made some preliminary studies on using a public transport system as a platform to monitor air pollution data on Hong Kong Island (Yu, J. J. Q. *et al.*, 2012). In Yu *et al.*'s study, the monitored region was divided into square grids of the same size. We put a sensor on a bus, and the route of the bus was divided into segments according to the boundary of the grids, with each segment's mid-point as the sensing point at which the sensor makes a measurement. The data was transmitted via cellular data service to the data collection centre. Alternatively, the data may be stored and uploaded at the bus terminus.

In our simulation, we selected 91 bus routes from the Citybus transportation system (Citybus Limited and New World First Bus Services Limited, 2011), covering most of the accessible areas on Hong Kong Island. There are 2,277 stations for the 91 bus routes. We divided Hong Kong Island into $16 \times 11 = 176$ 1km $\times$ 1km grids. We say a grid is covered if at least one bus (sensor) passes through that grid in one hour. We have formulated an optimisation problem to select the routes for sensing, finding that with only 14 sensors, we can provide coverage of the whole of Hong Kong Island. If we increase the coverage to a data point every 30 minutes, the number of sensors required becomes 30, a roughly linear increase.

Further increase in spatial and temporal resolutions will require more sensor units, but this preliminary study shows that it is feasible to provide sensing coverage with a relatively small number of mobile sensors. There are locations in the city not covered by bus routes, and units deployed on taxis or carried by an individual may be used to collect data in such areas. Therefore, to overcome the first challenge, mobile sensor networks may be used.

### Compressive sensing

Intuitively, to reduce the volume of data transmitted in the system, we can either reduce the volume of data collected, or reduce the size of the data collected before it is transmitted. By exploiting the correlation of the climatic data, we can reduce the volume of data collected. For example, if we are collecting temperature data, due to the dependence of temperatures in adjacent areas, we do not have to transmit the data at each location. The correlation of data in the time domain means that we can also obtain similar data reduction. In X. Yu *et al.* (2012), data acquisition of urban environment monitoring was described. A cooperative sensing and compression approach was proposed in the vehicular sensor network. The spatial correlation of signals (temperature, humidity, and pollutant concentration) could be utilised for fine-grained signal reconstruction and communication load reduction. In Yu *et al.* (2013), an urban pervasive sensing scheme was proposed, which is capable of acquiring environmental data with good granularity. We also established a spatial-temporal-entangled analysis (STEA) framework to perform efficient analysis of big sensing data and extract clear semantic information. Therefore, compressive sensing techniques may be employed to overcome the second challenge.

### Big data stream processing

To obtain high-resolution, real-time climatic data, we have to generate and process streams of data from many distributed sensors. The volume of data generated will be tremendous. Thus we must solve the big data streaming problem. In Li (2013), we describe a project that aims to develop a complete big data solution for urban dynamic analysis. The basic idea of this solution is presented in Figure 30.1. The sensing network collects and transmits data from the physical world to the cyber world. We propose to deploy vehicular sensor networks to collect the data. Data streams flow into the big data stream processing system, which needs to be scheduled and optimised for both batch processing and stream processing.

Finally, applications are developed to analyse the data. The proposed system consists of three modules: the sensing module, the big data stream processing system module and the urban dynamics analysis module. Figure 30.2 shows details of the three modules. The sensing module is implemented on vehicular sensor networks, collecting data in human dynamics and environment dynamics. Each sensor is equipped with a GPS receiver, and as the sensor roams around the city, a stream of time-stamped, location-aware data is collected. The big data stream processing system constitutes the core of this solution. To overcome the deficiency of Mapreduce, which is a popular big data processing system, but is only efficient in batch processing and not in stream processing, we shall integrate storm-based and Mapreduce-based clusters together, with a control node to decide the suspension and retrieval of computation nodes, based on data stream load prediction and latency feedback. Microsoft's Cloud platform service HDInsight will be suitable for scalable Hadoop cluster deployment. Finally, we develop applications to analyse the data.

### Hidden causality analysis and visualization

In Li (2013), we propose to develop an urban dynamics analysis tool, which is capable of hidden causality detection and prediction once it gets the urban sensing data stream. This tool will output human dynamics and environment dynamics with graphics for visualisation. This visualisation tool will exhibit the city dynamics, especially the human mobility and environment dynamics, to assist the city planners to make strategic decisions.

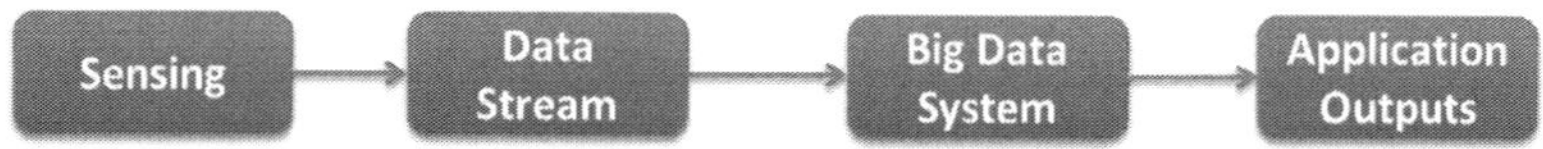


*Figure 30.1* The big data solution framework of urban sensing.
Source: Author

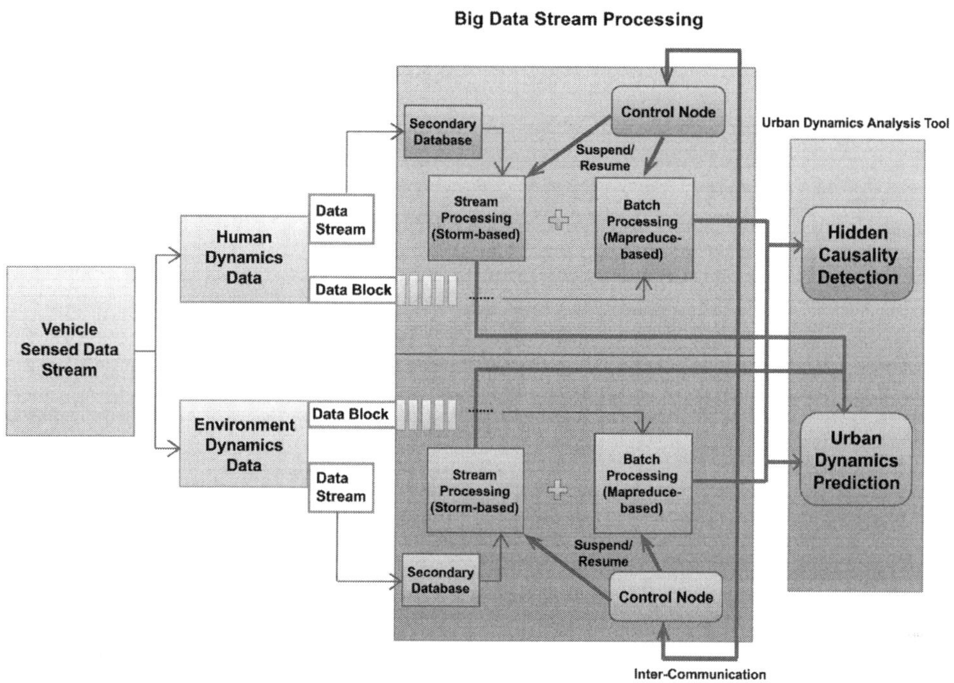


*Figure 30.2* Big data stream processing system for urban dynamics analysis.
Source: Author

## Example studies

The first two technologies described in the last section, namely, mobile sensor network and compressive sensing, are relatively well developed, and there have been a number of studies which utilise these technologies for obtaining real-time, high-resolution climatic data. For example, one such study was performed by the Metropolitan Area Sensing and Operation Network (MASON) project at Tsinghua University. By deploying a sensor platform consisting of a temperature sensor and a GPS receiver on taxis roaming about the city of Beijing, it was possible to obtain a fairly accurate picture of the temperature profile in Beijing (Yu, X. *et al.*, 2012). Since the taxis are constantly moving, resulting in unpredictable network topology, sensor data transmissions are vulnerable to losses, deteriorating data quality. To solve this problem, a cooperative data sampling and compression approach is used. There are similar studies that utilise a mobile sensing network to continuously gather, process, and share location-relevant sensor data (e.g. environment information, road condition, traffic flow) (Hull *et al.*, 2006; Gao *et al.*, 2008; Jung *et al.*, 2008). In addition, smart phones have also received much attention for their potential as mobile sensing platforms (Mohan *et al.*, 2008; Mun *et al.*, 2009; Willett *et al.*, 2010).

## Conclusions

In this chapter, we addressed the problem of how to obtain high-resolution, near real-time climatic data. We have identified four challenges, namely, collecting high-resolution, near real-time data economically; transmitting the data to the central server efficiently; processing the huge volume of data collected efficiently; and developing urban dynamics analysis and visualisation tools. We have also identified technologies to overcome such challenges, and briefly described some existing studies. The idea and methodology here can be deployed in the making of the next generation of 'dynamic' urban climatic maps.

## References

Citybus Limited and New World First Bus Services Limited. (2011). *Route List.* Available at: http://www.nwstbus.com.hk/routes/routesearch.aspx (Accessed 17 November 2013).

Gao, M., Zhang, F. and Tian, J. (2008). Environmental monitoring system with wireless mesh network based on embedded system. In: *Proceedings of 5th IEEE International Symposium on Embedded Computing (SEC).* Beijing, China, 6–8 October, 174–179. doi: 10.1109/SEC.2008.28 (Accessed 17 November 2013).

Hull, B., Bychkovsky, V., Chen, K., Goraczko, M., Miu, A., Shih, E., Zhang, Y., Balakrishnan, H. and Madden, S. (2006). CarTel: A distributed mobile sensor computing system, *Proceedings of the 4th ACM Conference on Embedded Networked Sensor Systems.* Boulder, Colorado, USA, 31 October–3 November. New York: Association for Computing Machinery, 125–138.

Jung, Y. J., Lee, Y. K., Lee, D. G., Ryu, K. H. and Nittel, S. (2008). Air pollution monitoring system based on geosensor network. In: *Proceedings of IEEE International Geoscience and Remote Sensing Symposium.* Boston, Massachusetts, USA, 7–11 July. Vol. 3, 1370–1373. doi:10.1109/IGARSS.2008.4779615 (Accessed 17 November 2013).

Li, V. O. K. (2013). A big data stream processing solution for hidden causality detection of urban dynamics, *Research proposal to Microsoft Research Asia.*

Mohan, P., Padmanabhan, V. and Ramjee, R. (2008). Nericell: Rich monitoring of road and traffic conditions using mobile smartphones. In: *Proceedings of the 6th ACM Conference on Embedded Networked Sensor Systems.* Raleigh, North Carolina, USA, 4–7 November. New York: Association for Computing Machinery, 323–336.

Mun, M., Reddy, S., Shilton, K., Yau, N., Boda, P., Burke, J., Estrin, D., Hansen, M., Howard, E. and West, R. (2009). PEIR, the personal environmental impact report, as a platform for participatory sensing systems research. In: *Proceedings of the 7th Annual International Conference on Mobile Systems, Applications, and Services.* Karaków, Poland, 22–25 June. New York: Association for Computing Machinery, 55–68.

Willett, W., Aoki, P., Kumar, N., Subramanian, S. and Woodruff, A. (2010). Common Sense Community: Scaffolding mobile sensing and analysis for novice users. In: Floréen, P., Krüger, A. and Spasojevic, M. (eds.), *Pervasive Computing: Proceedings of 8th International Conference on Pervasive Computing.* Lecture Notes in Computer Science, Vol. 6030. Helsinki, Finland, 17–20 May. Germany: Springer Berlin Heidelberg, 301–318.

Yang, G., Xu, K. and Li, V. O. K. (2010). Hybrid cargo-level tracking system for logistics. In: *Proceedings of IEEE 71st Vehicular Technology Conference.* Taipei, Taiwan, 16–19 May 2010, 1–5. doi: 10.1109/VETECS.2010.5493655 (Accessed 17 November 2013).

Yu, J. J. Q., Li, V. O. K. and Lam, A. Y. S. (2012). Sensor deployment for air pollution monitoring using public transportation system. In: *Proceedings of IEEE Congress on Evolutionary Computation (CEC).* Brisbane, Australia, 10–15 June, 1–7. doi: 10.1109/CEC.2012.6256495 (Accessed 17 November 2013).

Yu, X., Liu, Y., Zhu, Y., Feng, W., Zhang, L., Rashvand, H. F. and Li, V. O. K. (2012). Efficient sampling and compressive sensing for urban monitoring vehicular sensor networks. *IET Wireless Sensor Systems*, 2(3): 214–221.

Yu, X., Zhang, W., Zhang, L., Li, V. O. K., Yuan, J. and You, I. (2013). Understanding urban dynamics based on pervasive sensing: An experimental study on traffic density and air pollution. *Elsevier Mathematical and Computer Modeling*, 58(5–6): 1328–1339.

Chapter 31

# Future urban climatic map development based on spatiotemporal image fusion for monitoring the seasonal response of urban heat islands to land use/cover

*Juan Wang and Bo Huang*

## Introduction

Rapid urbanisation worldwide has resulted in urban areas covering nearly 0.5 per cent of the earth's total land surface, accommodating approximately half of its population (Ma *et al.*, 1973), which creates a series of urban environmental issues. The most notable one is the urban heat island (UHI) effect, which refers to the temperature over urban areas being higher than that of surrounding rural areas (Oke, 1973). The UHI effect has been attracting much attention because of its impact on air quality, energy use, and comfort in urban areas (Voogt, 2004). Remote sensing (RS) technology has been playing an important role in UCMap and UHI studies because of its spatially continuous, long-term accumulated characteristics (Voogt and Oke, 2003). The surface UHI (SUHI) measured by the land surface temperature (LST) has been extensively reported in previous literatures using RS images (Weng, 2009). It is agreed that SUHI is caused by the replacement of vegetated areas with artificial and impervious surfaces, and the LST over urban surfaces corresponds closely to the land use/cover types in urban areas (Rinner and Hussain, 2011). More accurate assessment SUHI is important for the future development of UC-Maps for planning.

The unique moisture, optical and thermal properties of each land use/cover type in urban areas determines the spatial variation of the LST in urban local environments (Oke, 1982). Exploring the spatial patterns of LST and its relationship with land use/cover types can provide basic information about the generation and development of SUHIs (Ogashawara and Bastos, 2012; Xiong *et al.*, 2012). It has been documented that the optimal spatial resolution for revealing their statistical relationship within the city was around 90m or 120m (Weng *et al.*, 2004; Lu and Weng, 2006). At present, high spatial resolution sensors, such as Landsat Thematic Mapper (TM)/Enhanced TM Plus (ETM+), could provide optimal resolution images for such studies. For example, Xiao *et al.* (2008) investigated the spatial distribution of LST in Beijing and its quantitative relationship with biophysical and demographic parameters using Landsat-5 TM. Xiao *et al.* (2007) examined the impact of impervious surface patterns on LST in Beijing using Landsat TM/ETM+.

These researches often focused on one certain date in the year based on the available images. In reality, the relationship between LST and land use/cover types varies temporally. However, the temporal responses of LST to land use/cover types in urban areas were seldom reported because of the limited available images. Although some satellite sensors, such as Landsat TM/ETM+ can retrieve LST around the optimal spatial resolution (Bechtel *et al.*, 2012), long revisit cycles (approximately 15 days) and frequent cloud contamination have limited their use in monitoring SUHI variations over a period of time. Conversely, Moderate Resolution Imaging Spectroradiometer (MODIS) have high frequency (daily) coverage, but low spatial resolution (ranging from 250m to 1,000m). They would miss the spatial details of urban structures and make it hard to identify the relationship between the LST and land use/cover types in urban environments. The limit facing UC Map makers needs to be addressed.

To improve upon the shortcoming mentioned above, we piloted to explore the seasonal response of LST to land use/cover types using high spatial-temporal resolution NDVI and LST datasets taking the UC Map-making of Beijing city as the study area. The high spatial-temporal resolution NDVI and LST data were first generated using the spatial-temporal image fusion model. Based on the abundant available data support, the seasonal variation of SUHI and the seasonal response of LST to land use/cover types and NDVI are then quantified based on the statistical analysis.

## Method

### Study area

As an international metropolis and the capital of China, Beijing has experienced dramatic urbanisation in recent years and has a distinctive UHI effect (Xiao *et al.*, 2007). Beijing also has four distinct seasons, with a typical sub-humid, temperate, continental, monsoon climate (Wang *et al*, 2007). Influenced by the cold air from western Siberia, winter (December to February) and spring (March to May) in Beijing are cold, windy and dry. Summer (June to August) is relatively hot and humid due to the East Asian monsoon. Autumn (September to November), like spring, sees little rain, but is crisp and short. Almost three-quarters of that total precipitation occurred from June to August (Wang *et al.*, 2007). These climatic attributes make Beijing an ideal setting for exploring the LST's seasonal response to land use/cover types. The study area is the urban area and part of the rural area surrounding the centre of Beijing. Figure 31.1 shows the location of the study area and the land use/cover types.

### Data collection and pre processing

Cloud-free Landsat TM/ETM+ images covering Beijing city (Path/Row: 123/32) were obtained from the United States Geological Survey (USGS) website (http://glovis.usgs.gov/). The time period covers 15 February, 22 May, and 13 October 2002. This L1G-level product has been geographically corrected. Radiation calibration was further accomplished using the parameters given in the metadata. The Fast Line-of-sight Atmospheric Analysis of Spectral Hypercubes (FLAASH) model (Matthew *et al.*, 2000) was applied to the atmospheric correction of bands 1–5, 7.

Two MODIS 1B images (MOD021km) covering the study area on 15 February and 17 August, 2002 were acquired from the National Aeronautics and Space Administration (NASA) (http://ladsweb.nascom.nasa.gov/). They were used to simulate the high spatial resolution Landsat-like NDVI and LST in summer. Geo-correction was implemented using the ground control points (GCPs) in the dataset and the same projected coordinate system with the Landsat TM/ETM+ images (UTM/WGS84, 50N). Radiation calibration was accomplished with the parameters given in the metadata. Because the algorithm used to derive the LST had no requirement on atmospheric correction, no such correction was implemented.

Land use/cover data for the study area in 2000 were obtained from the China National Land Use Database established by the Chinese Academy of Sciences (CAS). The land use data were produced based on Landsat TM/ETM+ images using a two-level hierarchical classification system involving 25 first-level and 6 second-level land use classes (Liu at al., 2005).We considered the

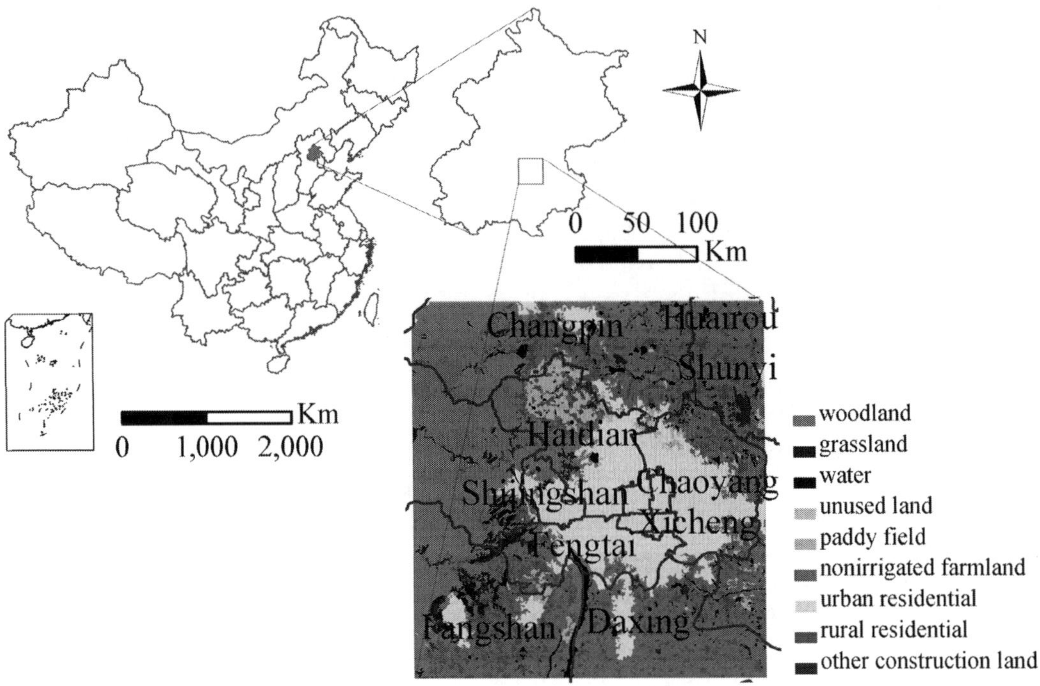


*Figure 31.1* Location of study area.

Source: Authors

dataset to be sufficiently accurate to examine the relationship between the LST and land use/cover types. We obtained nine types of land cover by combining the first-level classifications, as shown in Figure 31.1.

The daily air temperature and relative humidity (RH) in Beijing in 2002 were acquired from the China Meteorological Data Sharing Services System (http://data.cma.gov.cn/). This data was used as the parameters of the algorithm used to retrieve the LST from Landsat TM/ETM+ images.

The details of the datasets used in this paper are listed in Table 31.1. All the image pre-processing, retrieval of LST and NDVI were implemented using the image processing software ENVI/IDL 4.7.

## Methodology

### NDVI calculation

As an indicator of the vegetation density (Purevdorj *et al.*, 1998), NDVI is employed to characterise the land use/cover types and to explore its quantitative relationships with LST. NDVI is calculated as:

$$NDVI = \frac{Nir - Red}{Nir + Red} \quad (31.1)$$

*Table 31.1* Data used in this research.

| *Data* | *Acquired date (Year: 2002)* | *Coverage area* | *Source* |
|---|---|---|---|
| Landsat ETM+ | 15 Feb; 22 May; 13 Oct | Beijing (123/32) | USGS |
| MOD021km | 15 Feb; 17 Aug | Beijing | NASA |
| Land cover | 2002 | Beijing | China National Land Use Database |
| Meteorological data | 15 Feb; 22 May; 17 Aug; 13 Oct | Beijing | China Meteorological Data Sharing Services System |

Source: Authors

Where, Nir and Red refer to the surface reflectance of the near-infrared and red band, respectively. NDVI values range from –1 to 1, with larger positive values signifying vegetated areas and smaller or negative values signifying less or non-vegetated surfaces.

### *LST calculation from TIR*

High spatial resolution LST is derived from Landsat TM/ETM+ images based on the mono-window algorithm (Qin *et al.*, 2001). It has been proven that the mono-window algorithm for deriving LST from Landsat TM/ETM+ images is sufficiently accurate for the urban heat island studies (Liu and Weng, 2009). Moreover, the parameters required by this algorithm can be easily obtained from meteorological stations. Thus, it is widely used in UHI research (Liu and Zhang, 2011). The mono-window algorithm can be summarised using the following equation:

$$LST = \frac{a \times (1 - C - D) + [b \times (1 - C - D) \times T_i - D \times T_a]}{C} \tag{31.2}$$

where $a = -67.355351$; $b = 0.458606$; $T_i$ is the at-sensor brightness temperature (K), which can be derived based on Planck's function; $T_a$ is the effective mean atmospheric temperature; and $C$ and $D$ are determined by emissivity ($\varepsilon_i$) and transmittance ($\tau_i$) on the basis of the following formula:

$$C = \varepsilon_i \times \tau_i;\ D = (1 - \tau_i)[1 + (1 - \varepsilon_i) \times \tau_i] \tag{31.3}$$

Here, emissivity ($\varepsilon_i$) is related to land use/cover and can be estimated via the NDVI according to Zhang *et al.* (2006) and Vandegriend and Owe (1993). Atmospheric transmittance ($\tau_i$) can be determined by the water vapour content ($w_6$), as demonstrated in Qin *et al.* (2001) and Sun *et al.* (2010). The water vapour content ($w_6$, g/cm$^2$) is based on the near-surface air temperature ($T_0$) and RH. Both $T_0$ and RH can be obtained directly from meteorological stations. The mean atmospheric temperature can also be calculated on the basis of the near-surface air temperature ($T_0$) (Qin *et al.*, 2001; Sun *et al.*, 2010).

High temporal resolution LST is derived from MOD021km products based on the split-window algorithm proposed by Mao *et al.* (2005). The basic theory of this algorithm is the same as the mono-window algorithm. The only difference is that there are two thermal bands in MODIS data (band 31, band 32), and thus the combination of the two bands is used to calculate the LST. The split-window algorithm can be written as:

$$LST = \frac{C_{32} \times (B_{31} + D_{31}) - C_{31} \times (B_{32} + D_{32})}{C_{32} \times A_{31} - C_{31} \times A_{32}} \tag{31.4}$$

All of the parameters [i.e. $A_i$, $B_i$, $C_i$, $D_i$, ($i = 31,32$)] are determined by the at-sensor brightness temperature ($T_i$), transmittance ($\tau_i$), and emissivity ($\varepsilon_i$), which can be obtained using the MOD021km data itself. More detail information for this algorithm can be found in Mao *et al.* (2005).

### *Spatial-temporal image fusion model for NDVI simulation*

Spatial-temporal image fusion models are used to generate high spatial-temporal resolution datasets by combining the high spatial resolution images and high temporal resolution images. Because of cloud contamination, there was no available Landsat TM/ETM+ images in summer of 2002. In this research, Landsat-like NDVI in summer was simulated using the most attracted spatial and temporal adaptive reflectance fusion model (STARFM) developed by Gao *et al.* (2006). This model was originally developed to aggregate the surface reflectance from fine- and coarse-resolution homogeneous pixels. It assumes that the high spatial resolution image at date $t_1$ can be simulated by summarising the high spatial resolution image at date $t_0$ and the temporal variation captured by high frequency images between $t_1$ and $t_0$. The influences of the neighbouring pixels can be introduced by a weighting function. In STARFM, the weighting function is dependent on the neighbouring spectral similarity pixels within the searching window size $w$. This model can be expressed using the formula:

$$L(x_{w/2}, y_{w/2}, t_1) = \sum_{i-1}^{w} \sum_{j-1}^{w} w_{ij} \times (M(x_i, y_i, t_0) + L(x_i, y_i, t_1) - M(x_i, y_i, t_0)) \tag{31.5}$$

Where, $w$ is the search window size, ($x_{w/2}$, $y_{w/2}$) is the central pixel of this moving window, and $M$ and $L$ represent the coarse resolution image (MODIS) and fine resolution image (Landsat), respectively.

In this study, the red and near-infrared bands from the post-processed MOD021km and Landsat TM/ETM+ images were used as the inputs of the STARFM, and then the NDVI was computed by the simulated reflectance by the model. Because the STARFM model was originally supposed to simulate Landsat-like surface reflectance, its precision is considered quite promising (Gao *et al.*, 2006). It has also been applied to generate the NDVI in recent research (Liu and Weng, 2012). We suppose it is capable of simulating a high-quality NDVI for the application in this research.

### *Spatial-temporal image fusion model for LST simulation*

The spatial-temporal image fusion model for simulating LST developed by Huang *et al.* (2013) was employed in this research. This model established a new weighting function based on the bilateral filtering to consider all the neighbouring pixels within a certain distance. This feature makes it suitable for characterising the cooling and warming effect of the temperature space (Nichol, 1994; Chen *et al.*, 2012). The improved image fusion model can be expressed as (Huang *et al.*, 2013):

$$T_L(x_i, y_i, t_1) = \frac{\left[\sum_{i-1}^{w} \left(W_{ij} \times \left(T_L(x_i, y_i, t_0) + T_M(x_i, y_i, t_1) - T_M(x_i, y_i, t_0)\right)\right)\right]}{\sum_{i-1}^{w} W_{ij}} \tag{31.6}$$

where, $W_{ij}$ is the new weighting function, which is calculated using a shift-invariant Gaussian filter as the kernel function (Tomasi and Manduchi, 1998). $T_M$ and $T_L$ represent the LST derived from the coarse resolution image (MODIS) and fine resolution image (Landsat), respectively.

*Statistical analysis*

Using the high spatial-temporal resolution datasets, traditional statistical methods and spatial statistical methods were employed to analyse the seasonal variation of SUHI and the seasonal response of LST to land use/cover types and NDVI. The reclassified land use/cover map was firstly overlaid with LST maps to derive the average LST for each land use/cover type in the four seasons. The SUHI intensity (SUHII) was then calculated by the urban averaged LST minus the rural LST. The scatter plot between NDVI and LST were also plotted to explain the response of LST to vegetation cover. The qualitative and quantitative analysis is described as follows.

## Result and discussion

### Seasonal variation of SUHI for UCMap making

Few Landsat images are available in summer because of the cloud contamination caused by the humid and wet summer in Beijing. To investigate the seasonal variation of SUHI, we simulated the LST in the summer of 2002 using the spatial-temporal fusion model (Huang *et al.*, 2013). By combining the MODIS LST on 15 February 2002, 17 August 2002, and Landsat ETM+ LST on 15 February 2002, we simulated the Landsat-like LST on 17 August 2002. The observed and simulated LSTs are presented in Figure 31.2. We can see that the simulated LST on 17 August 2002 has both the detailed information on urban structures captured by Landsat and the temporal dynamics captured by MODIS.

The spatial distribution of LSTs varies greatly in the four seasons (see Figure 31.3). In summer, the LST in the centre of the study area (urban area) is obviously higher than that in the surrounding rural areas, whereas it is quite the opposite in winter. The LST difference between the urban area and rural areas is less in spring and autumn. We also calculated the temperature differences between built-up areas (including urban residential and construction land) and all other land cover types. This average temperature difference between the two categories of land cover was greatest in summer (1.35°C) and had a negative value in winter, indicating an urban cool island. The difference in spring and autumn was relatively small. Although the use of different rural areas influences the value of UHI and its seasonal variation when calculating UHI (Wang *et al.*, 2007), the temperature contrast between the built-up urban area and other raw vegetated areas can reflect the seasonal variation of urban heat island. This study documented that the SUHII in Beijing city has distinguished seasonal variation. The strongest SUHII occurs in summer, which is consistent with previous researches. The other character of SUHI in Beijing city is the urban cool island in winter. The negative heat island effect is also widely recognised by other arid cities (Bounoua *et al.*, 2009; Imhoff *et al.*, 2010). The seasonal dryness in winter in Beijing city may explain the urban cool island. Another possible reason is the low thermal inertia of dry bare soil in rural areas and the high thermal inertia of concrete material used in urban construction.

### Seasonal response of LST to land use/covers

The response of LST to land use/cover types varied in the four seasons (see Table 31.2). In summer, urban residential land has the highest temperature (35.11°C), followed by paddy fields and non-irrigated farmland. Other types of land, such as woodland, grassland, areas of water, and unused land, have relatively low temperatures. In winter, the pattern is the opposite. Urban residential areas have a relatively low temperature (10.69°C), whereas woodland and grassland have a

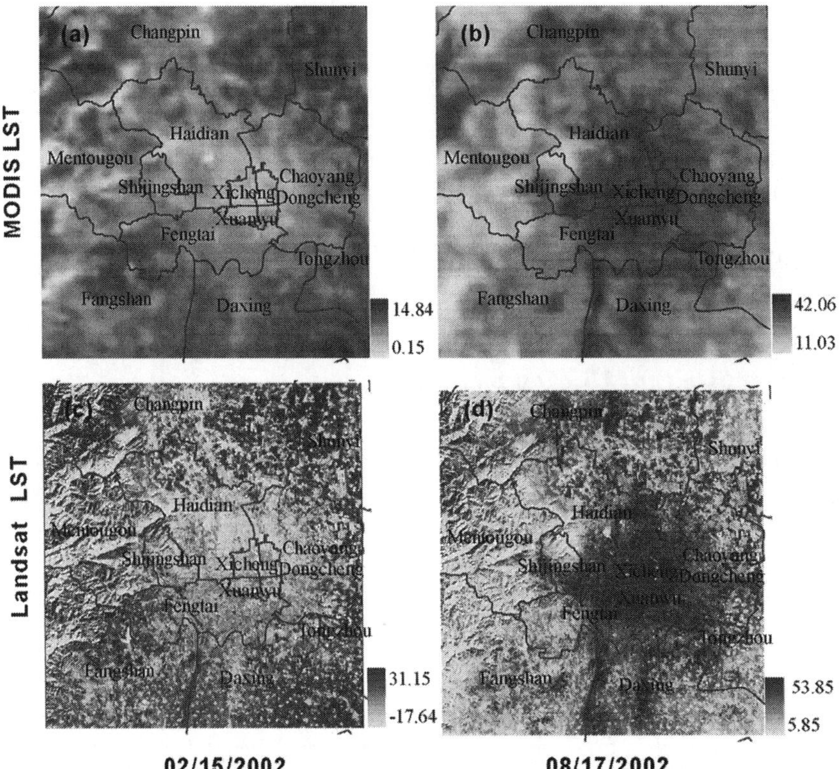


*Figure 31.2* (a) Observed MODIS LST on 15 February 2002; (b) observed MODIS LST on 17 August 2002; (c) observed Landsat ETM+ LST on 15 February 2002; (d) simulated Landsat-like LST on 17 August 2002 (units: °C).

Source: Authors

higher temperature. It is noted that paddy fields and non-irrigated farmland have a relatively high temperature in both summer and winter. In spring and autumn, there is no obvious regular pattern between the LST and land cover. The high standard deviation of LST in 22 May (see Table 31.2) explains the abnormally high value that may be caused by the LST retrieval algorithm.

The temperature vegetation index (TVX) space, which is defined as the scatter plot between the LST and NDVI, is useful for explaining the temporal variation in thermal data and vegetation cover (Amiri *et al.*, 2009). Here, the NDVI on 15 February, 22 May, and 13 October 2002 was computed by the red and NIR bands of the Landsat observations. NDVI on 17 August 2002 was simulated using the STARFM model by combining the red and near-infrared bands of the MODIS observations on 15 February and 17 August and the Landsat observation on 15 February. It can be seen from Figure 31.4 that the spatial pattern of the NDVI is similar in all four seasons; that is, the rural areas have a higher index than the urban areas. This characteristic is most obvious in summer (17 August).

The TVX patterns, in contrast, are quite different in the four seasons (see Figure 31.5). In spring and summer, the LST and NDVI are negatively correlated, whereas in winter they are positively correlated. That is, vegetated areas have a cooler temperature in spring and summer and a higher temperature in winter. In autumn, the relationship between the LST and NDVI is much weaker.

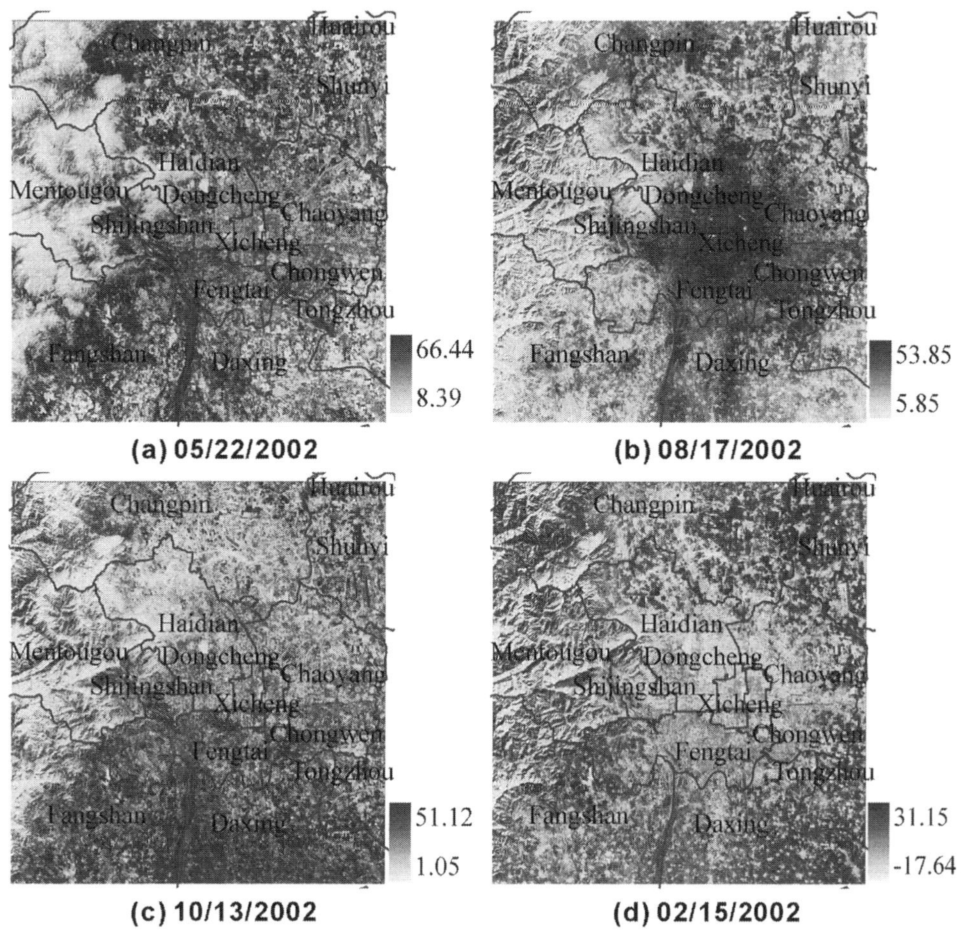


*Figure 31.3* LST spatial patterns in the study area in the four seasons (units: °C).

Source: Authors

The response of LST to NDVI is seasonally varied. According to Imamura-Bornstein (1991), the formation of SUHI is mainly related to the difference of thermal inertia (TI) between adjacent urban and rural surfaces. In the seasonal time cycles, wet rural soils with the highest TI values heat up and cool down most slowly, while the converse is true for dry rural soils with the lowest TI values. Rates for urban concrete and building materials are intermediate. Use of this SUHI formation theory makes it possible to generalise the different contributions of vegetation to SUHI in the four seasons. During the summer, the rural areas covered by dense vegetation have much larger TI than urban areas, which partly accounts for the positive SUHI (Wang *et al.*, 2007). In winter, the positive correlation between LST and NDVI was also found by Sun and Kafatos (2007). Furthermore, soil moisture could also be another important factor related to TI (Peng *et al.*, 2011), although it is not the focus of this paper. Future studies will focus on the most important physical variables, such as soil moisture and evapotranspiration, to study the processes and mechanisms of SUHI and its temporal response to these related variables.

*Table 31.2* Land surface temperature, average value and standard deviation based on cover type (unit: °C).

| | *Average value* | | | | *Standard deviation* | | | |
|---|---|---|---|---|---|---|---|---|
| | *22 May* | *17 Aug* | *13 Oct* | *15 Feb* | *22 May* | *17 Aug* | *13 Oct* | *15 Feb* |
| Woodland | 39.33 | 31.86 | 22.41 | 11.34 | 5.26 | 3.19 | 3.22 | 3.12 |
| Grassland | 44.50 | 32.74 | 25.07 | 12.69 | 4.34 | 2.23 | 2.14 | 2.21 |
| Water | 41.82 | 32.52 | 23.96 | 10.32 | 6.79 | 2.85 | 2.99 | 2.66 |
| Unused land | 43.72 | 30.16 | 23.51 | 10.36 | 2.80 | 2.71 | 1.78 | 1.64 |
| Paddy fields | 44.51 | 34.06 | 23.43 | 12.09 | 5.47 | 1.95 | 2.16 | 1.80 |
| Non-irrigated farmland | 43.40 | 33.73 | 25.45 | 12.67 | 5.05 | 1.96 | 2.48 | 1.68 |
| Urban residential | 44.32 | 35.11 | 24.65 | 10.69 | 2.86 | 1.82 | 1.59 | 1.31 |
| Rural residential | 44.55 | 32.26 | 24.40 | 10.83 | 2.96 | 1.84 | 1.57 | 1.31 |
| Other construction land | 44.36 | 32.55 | 24.64 | 11.15 | 3.26 | 2.07 | 1.79 | 1.61 |

Source: Authors

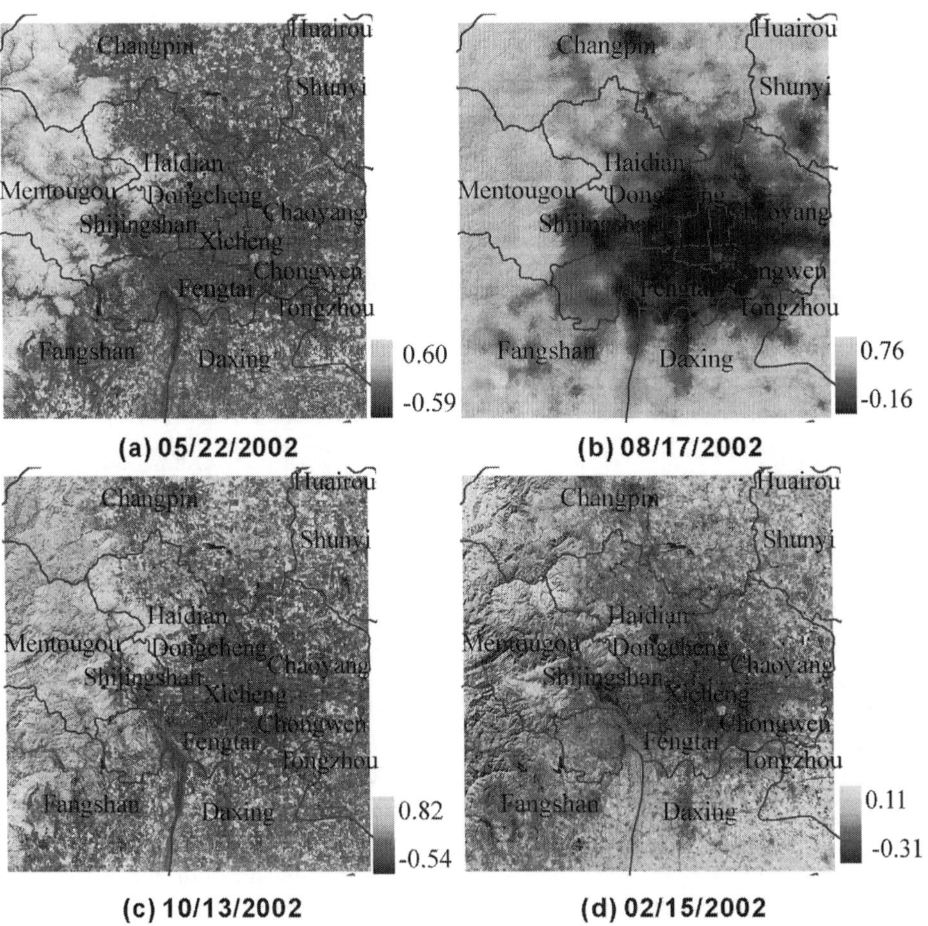


*Figure 31.4* NVDI spatial patterns in the study area in the four seasons.

Source: Authors

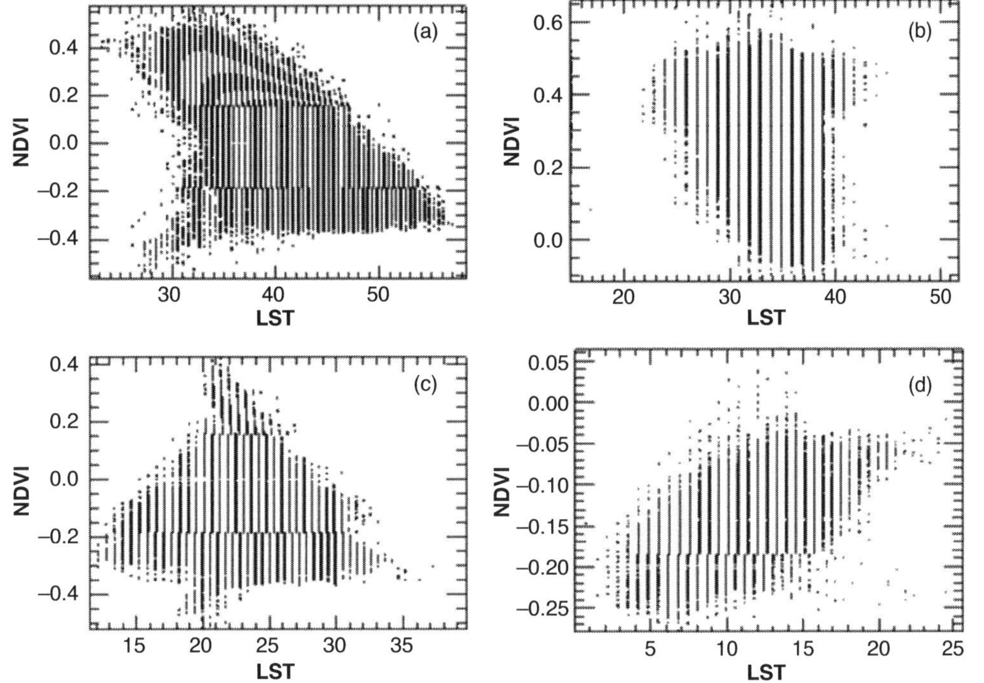


*Figure 31.5* Scatter plots of the LST (X axis, °C) and NDVI (Y axis) in the study area in the four seasons: (a) 22 May 2002; (b) 17 August 2002; (c) 13 October 2002; (d) 15 February 2002.

Source: Authors

## Conclusions

This piloted research presented the seasonal variation of SUHI and its seasonal response to land use/cover types in Beijing based on high spatial-temporal resolution RS datasets. The high spatial-temporal resolution LST and NDVI dataset was first generated using spatial-temporal fusion models. Subsequently, the seasonal variation of SUHI in 2002 in Beijing city and the seasonal responses of LST to land use/cover types and NDVI were analysed using the traditional statistical methods and the TVX space. The seasonal variation of SUHI and the seasonal response of LST to land use/cover in Beijing city were identified.

SUHI in Beijing city has obvious seasonal variation. Summer features an obvious urban heat island, whereas an urban cool island is observed in winter. In spring and autumn, the difference in the LST between the centre of the study area (urban area) and the surroundings (rural areas) is less. The land cover types, particularly vegetation, contribute differently to the spatial pattern of the LST in the four seasons. In summer, urban residential land has the highest temperature, followed by paddy fields and non-irrigated farmland, while the opposite is true in winter. Urban residential land has a relatively low temperature, and woodland and grassland a relatively higher temperature. In spring and autumn, there is no obvious regular pattern between the LST and land cover. Scatter plots between the LST and NDVI also explain the LST's different responses to different types of land cover in different seasons. In spring and summer, the LST and NDVI are negatively correlated and in winter they are positively correlated. This study documented that the correlations between

LST and NDVI depend on the seasons and, thus, the season of the image acquisition should be taken into account when exploring the role of vegetation in UHI studies. This has great value to UCMap making in the future as a more temporal dimension of the city's urban climate could be better evaluated.

As we are pointing to the future, this piloted study has two limitations that should be further advanced. i) The reliability of the results here was largely dependent on the accuracy of the LST data retrieved via thermal infrared remote sensing. Although we adopted the most commonly used mono- and split-window algorithms, their accuracy leaves room for improvement. ii) Considering the available Landsat TM/ETM+ images for evaluating the proposed image fusion model, the study period was limited in the year 2002. The seasonal variation of SUHI and its seasonal response to land use/cover was then analysed. Future researches could focus on the annual variation of SUHI and the urbanisation effect on SUHI in different years by producing high spatial-temporal LST datasets using the proposed model.

## References

Amiri, R., Weng, Q., Alimohammadi, A. and Alavipanah, S. K. (2009). Spatial-temporal dynamics of land surface temperature in relation to fractional vegetation cover and land use/cover in the Tabriz urban area, Iran. *Remote Sensing of Environment*, 113(12): 2606–2617.

Bechtel, B., Zakšek, K. and Hoshyaripour, G. (2012). Downscaling land surface temperature in an urban area: A case study for Hamburg, Germany. *Remote Sensing*, 4(10): 3184–3200.

Bounoua, L., Safia, A., Masek, J., Peters-Lidard, C. and Imhoff, M. L. (2009). Impact of urban growth on surface climate: A case study in Oran, Algeria. *Journal of Applied Meteorology and Climatology*, 48(20): 217–231.

Chen, X., Su, Y., Li, D., Huang, G., Chen, W. and Chen, S. (2012). Study on the cooling effects of urban parks on surrounding environments using Landsat TM data: A case study in Guangzhou, southern China. *International Journal of Remote Sensing*, 33(18): 5889–5914.

Gao, F., Masek, J., Schwaller, M. and Hall, F. (2006). On the blending of the Landsat and MODIS surface reflectance: Predicting daily Landsat surface reflectance. *IEEE Transactions on Geoscience and Remote Sensing*, 44(8): 2207–2218.

Huang, B., Wang, J., Song, H., Fu, D. and Wong, K. (2013). Generating high spatiotemporal resolution land surface temperature for urban heat island monitoring. *IEEE Transactions on Geoscience and Remote Sensing Letters*, 10(5): 1011–1015.

Imamura-Bornstein, I. R. (1991). Observational studies of urban heat island characteristics in different climate zones. PhD Thesis. Institute of Geoscience, University of Tsukuba.

Imhoff, M. L., Zhang, P., Wolfe, R. E. and Bounoua, L. (2010). Remote sensing of the urban heat island effect across biomes in the continental USA. *Remote Sensing of Environment*, 114(3): 504–513.

Liu, H. and Weng, Q. (2009). Scaling effect on the relationship between landscape pattern and land surface temperature: A case study of Indianapolis, United States. *Photogrammetric Engineering and Remote Seminar*, 75(3): 291–304.

Liu, H. and Weng, Q. (2012). Enhancing temporal resolution of satellite imagery for public health studies: A case study of West Nile Virus outbreak in Los Angeles in 2007. *Remote Sensing of Environment*, 117: 57–71.

Liu, L. and Zhang, Y. (2011). Urban heat island analysis using the Landsat TM data and ASTER data: A case study in Hong Kong. *Remote Sensing*, 3(7): 1535–1552.

Liu, J., Liu, M., Tian, H., Zhuang, D., Zhang, Z., Zhang, W., Tang, X. and Deng, X. (2005). Spatial and temporal patterns of China's cropland during 1990–2000: An analysis based on Landsat TM data. *Remote Sensing of Environment*, 98(4): 442–456.

Lu, D. and Weng, Q. (2006). Spectral mixture analysis of ASTER images for examining the relationship between urban thermal features and biophysical descriptors in Indianapolis, Indiana, USA. *Remote Sensing of Environment*, 104(2): 157–167.

Ma, T., Zhou, C., Pei, T., Haynie, S. and Fan, J. (1973). Quantitative estimation of urbanization dynamics using time series of DMSP/OLS nighttime light data: A comparative case study from China's cities. *Remote Sensing Environment*, 124: 99–107.

Mao, K., Qin, Z., Shi, J. and Gong, P. (2005). A practical split-window algorithm for retrieving land-surface temperature from MODIS data. *International Journal of Remote Sensing*, 26(15): 3181–3204.

Matthew, M. W., Adler-Golden, S. M., Berk, A., Richtsmeier, S. C., Levine, R. Y., Bernstein, L. S., Acharya, P. K., Anderson, G. P., Felde, G. W., Hoke, M. P., Ratkowski, A., Burke, H.-H., Kaiser, R. D. and Miller, D. P. (2000). Status of atmospheric correction using a MODTRAN4-based algorithm. *Proceedings of SPIE 4049*, Algorithms for Multispectral, Hyperspectral, and Ultraspectral Imagery VI, 199–207. doi: 10.1117/12.410341.

Nichol, J. E. (1994). A GIS-based approach to microclimate monitoring in Singapore's high-rise housing estates. *Photogrammetric Engineering and Remote Sensing*, 60(10): 1225–1232.

Ogashawara, I. and Bastos, V. (2012). A quantitative approach for analyzing the relationship between urban heat islands and land cover. *Remote Sensing*, 4(11): 3596–3618.

Oke, T. R. (1973). City size and the urban heat island. *Atmospheric Environment*, 7(8): 769–779.

Oke, T. R. (1982). The energetic basis of the urban heat island. *Quarterly Journal of the Royal Meteorological Society*, 108(455): 1–24.

Peng, S., Piao, S., Ciais, P., Friedlingstein, P., Ottle, C., Bréon, F.o.-M., Nan, H., Zhou, L. and Myneni, R. B. (2011). Surface urban heat island across 419 global big cities. *Environmental Science and Technology*, 46(2): 696–703.

Purevdorj, T., Tateishi, R., Ishiyama, T. and Honda, Y. (1998). Relationships between percent vegetation cover and vegetation indices. *International Journal of Remote Sensing*, 19(18): 3519–3535.

Qin, Z., Karnieli, A. and Berliner, P. (2001). A mono-window algorithm for retrieving land surface temperature from Landsat TM data and its application to the Israel-Egypt border region. *International Journal of Remote Sensing*, 22(18): 3719–3746.

Rinner, C. and Hussain, M. (2011). Toronto's urban heat island—exploring the relationship between land use and surface temperature. *Remote Sensing*, 3(6): 1251–1265.

Sun, D. L. and Kafatos, M. (2007). Note on the NDVI-LST relationship and the use of temperature-related drought indices over North America. *Geophysical Research Letter*, 34(24): L24406.

Sun, Q. Q., Tan, J. J. and Xu, Y. H. (2010). An ERDAS image processing method for retrieving LST and describing urban heat evolution: A case study in the Pearl River Delta region in South China. *Environmental Earth Sciences*, 59(5): 1047–1055.

Tomasi, C. and Manduchi, R. (1998). Bilateral filtering for gray and color images. In: *Proceedings of Sixth International Conference on Computer Vision*. Bombay, India, 4–7 January. IEEE Computer Society, 839–846.

Vandegriend, A. A. and Owe, M. (1993). On the relationship between thermal emissivity and the normalized difference vegetation index for natural surfaces. *International Journal of Remote Sensing*, 14(6): 1119–1131.

Voogt, J. A. (2004). Urban heat islands: Hotter cities. Available at: http://www.actionbioscience.org/environment/voogt.html (Accessed 7 April 2014).

Voogt, J. A. and Oke, T. R. (2003). Thermal remote sensing of urban climates. *Remote Sensing of Environment*, 86: 370–384.

Wang, K., Wang, J., Wang, P., Sparrow, M., Yang, J. and Chen, H. (2007). Influences of urbanization on surface characteristics as derived from the Moderate-Resolution Imaging Spectroradiometer: A case study for the Beijing metropolitan area. *Journal of Geophysical Research: Atmospheres*, 112: D22S06. doi: 10.1029/2006JD007997.

Weng, Q. H. (2009). Thermal infrared remote sensing for urban climate and environmental studies: Methods, applications, and trends. *ISPRS Journal of Photogrammetry and Remote Sensing*, 64(4): 335–344.

Weng, Q. H., Lu, D. S. and Schubring, J. (2004). Estimation of land surface temperature-vegetation abundance relationship for urban heat island studies. *Remote Sensing of Environment*, 89(4): 467–483.

Xiao, R. B., Ouyang, Z. Y., Zheng, H., Li, W. F., Schienke, E. W. and Wang, X. K. (2007). Spatial pattern of impervious surfaces and their impacts on land surface temperature in Beijing, China. *Journal of Environmental Science*, 19(2): 250–256.

Xiao, R. B., Weng, Q. H., Ouyang, Z. Y., Li, W. F., Schienke, E. W. and Zhang, Z. M. (2008). Land surface temperature variation and major factors in Beijing, China. *Photogrammetric Engingeering and Remote Sensing*, 74(4): 451–461.

Xiong, Y., Huang, S., Chen, F., Ye, H., Wang, C. and Zhu, C. (2012). The impacts of rapid urbanization on the thermal environment: A remote sensing study of Guangzhou, South China. *Remote Sensing*, 4(7): 2033–2056.

Zhang, J., Wang, Y. and Li, Y. (2006). A C++ program for retrieving land surface temperature from the data of Landsat TM/ETM+ band6. *Computers and Geosciences*, 32(10): 1796–1805.

Chapter 32

# Urban large-eddy simulation (LES)

## Advanced computational fluid dynamics for urban climatic maps

*Marcus Oliver Letzel*

## Introduction

This chapter aims to give a brief look beyond the current state-of-the-art micro-scale urban flow and dispersion models used in the making of urban climatic maps (UCMaps) today. It introduces the innovative atmospheric turbulence modelling technique 'Large-Eddy Simulation' (LES) as an advanced component in the making of UCMaps. The chapter will deal with the following questions:

- What is urban LES and how can it aid UCMap makers in the process of UCMap making today and in the future?
- Which UCMap improvements are possible and which UCMap questions can be answered that today's state-of-the-art models cannot answer?
- Why is urban LES not used routinely in UCMap making?
- How can urban LES be incorporated into the portfolio of models for UCMap making?

The chapter begins with a brief comparison of LES with other turbulence modelling approaches in computational fluid dynamics (CFD) and gives some examples. It concludes with 'homework' suggestions for UCMap makers, UCMap developers and LES model developers.

## Classification of turbulence modelling approaches in microscale urban computational fluid dynamics (CFD)

LES is one of the three main turbulence modelling approaches in CFD. LES is an intermediate compromise in terms of *quality* and *cost* between the two other main approaches, on the one hand the purely academic Direct Numerical Simulation (DNS), and on the other hand the industry-standard conventional turbulence modelling based on solving the Reynolds-averaged Navier-Stokes (RANS) equations.

Details on the theory and classification of turbulence modelling, as discussed for example in the textbooks by Pope (2000) and Ferziger and Perić (2002), are beyond the scope of this text. Here, it shall suffice to state that DNS goes all the way down to the millimetre scale to explicitly resolve even the finest scales of turbulence. For the simulation of full size, fully turbulent urban CFD problems DNS will remain out of reach for the computational capabilities in the foreseeable future (Voller and Porté-Agel, 2002). On the contrary, in RANS models turbulence on all scales is filtered out and needs to be parameterized, which limits the accuracy and universal applicability of RANS models and leads to known deficiencies in building wakes (Rodi *et al.*, 1997; Mochida und Lun, 2008) and urban weak wind regions (Yoshie *et al.*, 2007).

LES, conceptually in between the two former, only applies a low-pass filter, so it explicitly simulates large, energy-containing eddies (hence its name), while parameterizing small-scale turbulence (Sagaut, 2006). In a nutshell, LES is a good compromise in terms of *quality* and *cost* between DNS and RANS and can overcome the RANS problems mentioned above. In recent years the advance in computational resources has made the application of LES for practical urban CFD applications affordable (Tamura, 2008).

### Comparison between LES and RANS

The nature of LES explicitly resolving all relevant scales of turbulent motion means that LES is capable of capturing the inherent unsteadiness of turbulent flow and dispersion in the urban canopy. Consider, for example, a tall urban building: many readers will have experienced times and/or locations of unpredictable gustiness at pedestrian level especially near its corners, likely due to vortex shedding. LES resolves this unsteadiness, which RANS is unable to do.

To avoid a common misunderstanding, it should be pointed out that RANS models can be used to simulate transient flow phenomena, sometimes referred to as URANS (unsteady RANS). However, URANS results merely reflect variations in the forcing of the flow (e.g. the diurnal variation of the boundary conditions), but not the inherent unsteadiness of turbulent flow and dispersion in the urban canopy.

This has two main consequences. First, and most obviously, one can directly compute higher-order statistics from the fluctuating LES time series, such as wind gusts and peak concentrations, but cannot do so from RANS. Second, possibly less obviously, but relevant to UCMap makers, this also affects the quality of *time-mean* flow and dispersion results, particularly in the near-field of bluff bodies – this is what the urban canopy layer is all about, especially in high-density megacities (Ng, 2010). The latter difference between urban LES and RANS has been confirmed by several comparative studies since the 1990s and attributed by some to the inability of (U)RANS to capture the inherent urban flow unsteadiness (see Rodi *et al.* 1997; Xie and Castro, 2006; Gousseau *et al.*, 2011; Salim *et al.*, 2011; Tominaga and Stathopolous, 2011; Yoshie *et al.*, 2011; Tominaga and Stathopolous, 2012; Tominaga *et al.*, 2013).

The improvements of LES over RANS come at increased computational cost, which calls for the use of supercomputers and hence the use of parallel programming, which in turn increases the complexity of LES code development. Quality and quantity demands on initial and boundary conditions increase.

In the light of the advantages of urban LES over RANS, how can it aid UCMap makers in the process of UCMap making today and in the future?

According to Reuter and Kapp (2012), micro-scale urban CFD (RANS) models are particularly used for small-scale urban planning questions, for example near buildings or in case of high building density. In this area of application urban LES outperforms RANS according to turbulence theory as well as the aforementioned comparative studies. UCMap makers can expect more accurately predicted pedestrian-level ventilation or pollutant dispersion from urban LES, especially in high-density megacities. Moreover, urban LES allows UCMap makers to incorporate more sophisticated parameters in the map-making process, for example wind gustiness and pollutant peak concentrations.

Despite these promising advantages, however, there is a reason why urban LES is not used routinely in UCMap making so far. In the field of urban CFD modelling, as of today, it is probably fair to describe the status of LES modelling as a cutting edge, state-of-the-art approach in atmospheric *science*, but not yet established as a routine tool in environmental *consulting*. The historical, technical, computational and economic reasons responsible for the current status are discussed in depth by Hertwig (2013). The scientific and technological development of RANS started much earlier than that of LES. From rather early on, RANS has attracted interest from the engineering community. Several model validation and best practice guidelines for urban RANS modelling have been compiled (VDI, 2005; Franke *et al.*, 2007; Tominaga *et al.*; 2008). Urban RANS is now an established standard CFD tool. Meanwhile, due to its higher computational demand and due to lacking computational resources at the time, LES was more confined to science. Urban LES did not attract the same level of interest in validation as RANS.

In recent years, technological advances in the development of LES and computational resources have demonstrated the potential for practical urban LES applications (see e.g. recent reviews by Blocken *et al.*, 2011; Sabatino *et al.*; 2013; Tominaga and Stathopolous, 2013). Meanwhile, there are quite a number of LES validation studies specific to practical urban LES applications (Patnaik *et al.*, 2007a, 2007b; Harms *et al.*, 2011; Nozu and Tamura, 2012; Gousseau *et al.*, 2013; Tominaga *et al.*, 2013; Leitl *et al.*, 2014). A comprehensive account on the validation of atmospheric LES is given by Hertwig (2013). Urban LES validation is part of the scope of the current COST (European Cooperation in Science and Technology) action ES1006 (Evaluation, improvement and guidance for the use of local-scale emergency prediction and response tools for airborne hazards in built environments). A comparison and harmonization of these validation attempts aiming at the compilation of best practice guidelines specifically for practical LES applications such as urban LES is suggested for future work.

In the absence of best practice guidelines about when/how to apply urban LES for UCMap making, the question from the UCMap maker's point of view is where to commission urban LES. At present, it is suggested this decision is based on expert advice.

## Case study of Tsim Sha Tsui, Kowloon, Hong Kong

As an example of urban LES for UCMap making, consider the case study of Letzel *et al.* (2012) for Tsim Sha Tsui, Kowloon, downtown Hong Kong, using the LES model PALM (Raasch and Schröter, 2001; Letzel *et al.*, 2008, 2012). PALM (Parallelized Large-Eddy Simulation Model) is a parallelized LES model suitable for urban applications. It has been validated for urban flow/flow around solid obstacles (Letzel *et al.*, 2008; Kanda *et al.*, 2013). PALM has been applied to real urban morphologies of European and Asian type (Letzel *et al.*, 2008; Tack *et al.*, 2012, Kanda *et al.*, 2013; Park *et al.*, 2013), also with respect to urban planning (Esau, 2012; Letzel *et al.*, 2012).

Figure 32.1 shows the horizontal distribution of the pedestrian-level ventilation $VR_w$ in the assessment area of Tsim Sha Tsui for East wind approach flow calculated by PALM. The wind velocity $VR_w$ serves as a simple indicator of ventilation, defined as the ratio of mean wind speed at pedestrian level, 2m above ground, and the velocity at the top of the model domain, well above the roof tops. For computational details of the simulation refer to Letzel *et al.* (2012). One can see from Figure 32.1 that sites fronting the waterfront, open spaces and streets aligned in parallel with the incoming wind enjoy a high $VR_w$, whereas deep in the urban canopy, especially streets perpendicular to the incoming flow experience very low ventilation levels. Based on a zonal comparison with wind tunnel reference data for the same assessment area, Letzel *et al.* (2012) demonstrated that both LES and the wind tunnel capture all relevant differences in pedestrian-level ventilation $VR_w$ between different urban morphologies. The authors also highlighted the ambivalence of two isolated tall buildings: they locally enhance $VR_w$ but reduce wind availability up to three building heights downstream. Letzel and Gaus (2008) produced a corresponding animation illustrating the turbulent nature of urban flow in Tsim Sha Tsui and the strong vertical dispersion induced by one of the isolated tall buildings.

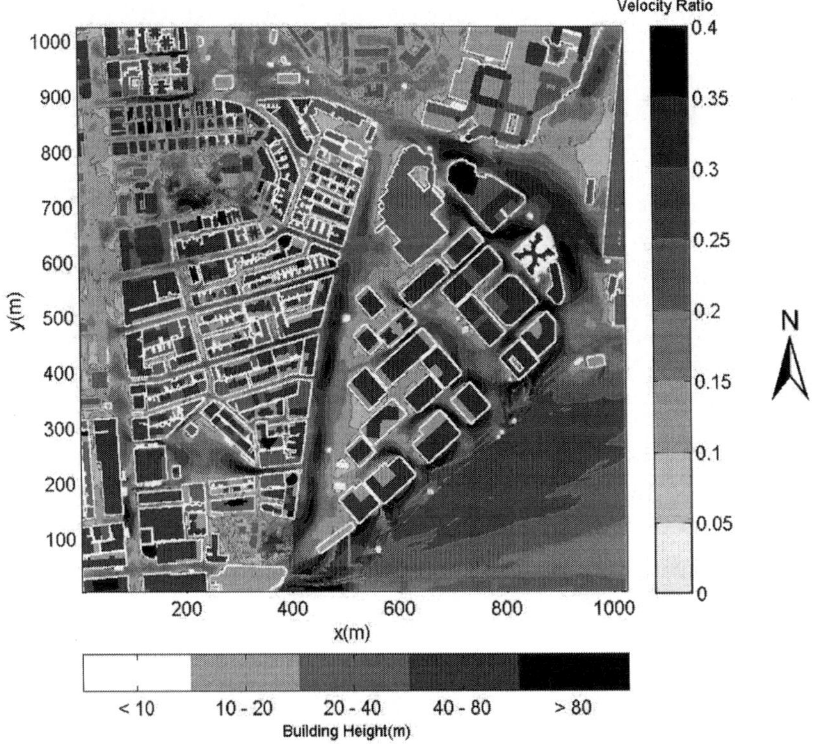


*Figure 32.1* Pedestrian-level ventilation in Tsim Sha Tsui under East wind approach flow obtained from the LES model PALM.

Source: Letzel *et al.*, 2012. Permission by Schweizerbart Science Publishers (www.schweizerbart.de).

Other urban LES studies with realistic urban geometry of ~ 1km scale or larger have been reported; e.g. by Patnaik *et al.* (2007a, 2007b), Xie and Castro (2009), Liu *et al.* (2011), Kanda *et al.* (2013), Onodera *et al.* (2013), Park *et al.* (2013) and Leitl *et al.* (2014).

## Present tasks and future vision

This chapter has shown that the development of urban LES for UCMap making is not complete and thus suggests tasks for the different players involved.

Public authorities or UCMap makers should consider urban LES if the building density at their UCMap site is high or if UCMap input data such as ventilation or dispersion data within the near-field of buildings is of interest. Whenever possible, experimental data should be collected alongside the LES study for sake of comparison.

UCMap developers and urban LES modellers would ideally work together to establish criteria

- to quantify the superiority of LES over RANS and its relevance for the purpose of UCMap making, and
- to decide when the benefit is worth the extra cost of urban LES.

It is worth jointly evaluating the importance of *thermal effects* (stratification, solar radiation, artificial heat release) and other *physical* or *chemical processes* for UCMap making on parameters such as ventilation, dispersion, and gustiness. So far, urban LES studies on thermal effects have focussed on idealized urban morphologies (Yoshie *et al.*, 2011; Park *et al.*, 2012; Cai, 2012; Xie *et al.*, 2013).

Valuable lessons can be learned from the RANS modellers' experience concerning the importance of model validation as well as best practice guidelines (e.g. Yoshie *et al.*, 2007; Eichhorn and Kniffka, 2010; Hertwig *et al.*, 2012; Grawe *et al.*, 2013; Tominaga *et al.*, 2013; Rakai and Franke, 2014). Using LES-specific concepts, urban LES should follow the RANS example.

Looking beyond, there are at least two fields that might be worth keeping an eye on.

Models allow scenarios for *pro-active urban planning*. This is not confined to testing different building or neighbourhood plans under the current climate. According to Mills *et al.* (2010) *future climate projections* should be considered in urban planning (cf. Früh *et al.*, 2011). For urban LES, this approach may require nudging or nesting in larger-scale models (see recent attempts by Schlünzen *et al.*, 2011; Xie, 2011; Neggers *et al.*, 2012; Wyszogrodzki *et al.*, 2012; Michioka *et al.*, 2013).

Innovative developments may be expected from the supercomputing centres. For example, Kieferle and Wössner (2001) demonstrated that early stages of the urban planning process may benefit from 'interactive' urban RANS. Ashie and Kono (2011) performed a 40km scale urban RANS of the entire Tokyo region on the Earth Simulator supercomputer at 5m resolution, while Onodera *et al.* (2013), using graphics accelerators on the Tsubame 2.0 supercomputer, performed a 10km scale urban LES of Tokyo.

## Acknowledgements

The author wishes to thank several of the authors cited below for fruitful discussions on this review. Financial support of the case study by the Chinese University of Hong Kong Social Science Panel Direct Grant, by the German Research Foundation (DFG) under grant RA 617/15-1/2 and by the German National Academic Exchange Service (DAAD) is gratefully acknowledged. Figure 32.1 has been reproduced from Letzel *et al.* (2012) with kind permission from the publisher (www.schweizerbart.de).

## References

Ashie, Y. and Kono, T. (2011). Urban-scale CFD analysis in support of a climate-sensitive design for the Tokyo Bay area. *International Journal of Climatology*, 31(2): 174–188.

Blocken, B., Stathopoulos, T., Carmeliet, J. and Hensen, J. L. M. (2011). Application of computational fluid dynamics in building performance simulation for the outdoor environment: An overview. *Journal of Building Performance Simulation*, 4(2): 157–184.

Cai, X.-M. (2012). Effects of wall heating on flow characteristics in a street canyon. *Boundary-Layer Meteorology*, 142(3): 443–467.

Eichhorn, J. and Kniffka, A. (2010). The numerical flow model MISKAM: State of development and evaluation of the basic version. *Meteorologische Zeitschrift*, 19(1): 81–90.

Esau, I. (2012). A health damage pattern due to street-level pollution in the Central Paris Area estimated with a turbulence-resolving model. In: Rassia, S. T. and Pardalos, P. M. (eds.), *Sustainable Environmental Design in Architecture*, London: Springer, 307–324. doi: 10.1007/978-1-4419-0745-5_18.

Ferziger, J. H. and Perić, M. (2002). *Computational Methods for Fluid Dynamics*. 3rd edition. Berlin: Springer.

Franke, J., Hellsten, A., Schlünzen, H. and Carissimo, B. (2007). Best practice guideline for the CFD simulation of flows in the urban environment, *COST Action 732*. Germany: University of Hamburg. Available at: http://

www.mi.uni-hamburg.de/fileadmin/files/forschung/techmet/cost/cost_732/pdf/BestPractiseGuideline_1-5-2007-www.pdf (Accessed 22 March 2014).

Früh, B., Becker, P., Deutschländer, T., Hessel, J.-D., Kossmann, M., Mieskes, I., Namyslo, J., Roos, M., Sievers, U., Steigerwald, T., Turau, H. and Wienert, U. (2011). Estimation of climate-change impacts on the urban heat load using an urban climate model and regional climate projections. *Journal of Applied Meteorology & Climatology*, 50(1): 167–184.

Gousseau, P., Blocken, B., Stathopoulos, T. and van Heijst, G. J. F. (2011). CFD simulation of near-field pollutant dispersion on a high-resolution grid: A case study by LES and RANS for a building group in downtown Montreal. *Atmospheric Environment*, 45(2): 428–438.

Gousseau, P., Blocken, B. and van Heijst, G. (2013). Quality assessment of Large-Eddy Simulation of wind flow around a high-rise building: Validation and solution verification. *Computers & Fluids*, 79: 120–133.

Grawe, D., Schlünzen, K. H. and Pascheke, F. (2013). Comparison of results of an obstacle resolving microscale model with wind tunnel data, *Atmospheric Environment*, 79: 495–509.

Harms, F., Leitl, B., Schatzmann, M. and Patnaik, G. (2011). Validating LES-based flow and dispersion models, *Journal of Wind Engineering and Industrial Aerodynamics*, 99(4): 289–295.

Hertwig, D. (2013). *On aspects of Large-Eddy Simulation validation for near-surface atmospheric flows*. PhD thesis. University of Hamburg. Available at: http://nbn-resolving.de/urn:nbn:de:gbv:18-62898 (Accessed 22 March 2014).

Hertwig, D., Efthimiou, G. C., Bartzis, J. G. and Leitl, B. (2012). CFD-RANS model validation of turbulent flow in a semi-idealized urban canopy. *Journal of Wind Engineering and Industrial Aerodynamics*, 111: 61–72.

Kanda, M., Inagaki, A., Miyamoto, T., Gryschka, M. and Raasch, S. (2013). A new aerodynamic parametrization for real urban surfaces. *Boundary-Layer Meteorology*, 148(2): 357–377.

Kieferle, J. and Wössner, U. (2001). Showing the invisible – seven rules for a new approach of using immersive virtual reality in architecture. In: *Proceedings of 19th eCAADe: Architectural Information Management*. Helsinki, Finland, 29–31 August. Helsinki: Helsinki University of Technology (HUT), 376–381.

Leitl, B., Hertwig, D., Harms, F., Schatzmann, M., Patnaik, G., Boris, J., Obenschain, K., Fischer, S. and Rechenbach, P. (2014). Large eddy simulation of accidental releases. In: Talamelli, A. *et al.* (eds.), *Progress in Turbulence V: Proceedings of the iTi Conference in Turbulence 2012*, Springer Proceedings in Physics, 149. Switzerland: Springer International Publishing, 133–147. doi: 10.1007/978-3-319-01860-7_22.

Letzel, M. O. and Gaus, G. (2008). Turbulent flow in a densely built-up area in Kowloon, downtown Hong Kong. *Dynamic Visualization in Science*, 13118. Available at: http://palm.muk.uni-hannover.de/wiki/gallery/movies/city#dyvis_13118 (Accessed 22 March 2014).

Letzel, M. O., Krane, M. and Raasch, S. (2008). High resolution urban large-eddy simulation studies from street canyon to neighbourhood scale. *Atmospheric Environment*, 42(38): 8770–8784.

Letzel, M. O., Helmke, C., Ng, E., An, X., Lai, A. and Raasch, S. (2012). LES case study on pedestrian level ventilation in two neighbourhoods in Hong Kong, *Meteorologische Zeitschrift*, 21(6), 575–589. doi: 10.1127/0941-2948/2012/0356.

Liu, Y., Cui, G., Wang, Z. and Zhang, Z. (2011). Large eddy simulation of wind field and pollutant dispersion in downtown Macao. *Atmospheric Environment*, 45(17): 2849–2859.

Michioka, T., Sato, A. and Sada, K. (2013). Large-eddy simulation coupled to mesoscale meteorological model for gas dispersion in an urban district. *Atmospheric Environment*, 75: 153–162.

Mills, G., Cleugh, H., Emmanuel, R., Endlicher, W., Erell, E., McGranahan, G., Ng, E., Nickson, A., Rosenthal, J. and Steemer, K. (2010). Climate information for improved planning and management of mega cities (needs perspectives). In: Sivakumar, M. V. K. *et al.* (eds.), *Procedia Environmental Sciences, Vol. 1, Special Issue of World Climate Conference-3*, 228–246. Geneva, Switzerland, 31 August–4 September 2009.

Mochida, A. and Lun, I. Y. F. (2008). Prediction of wind environment and thermal comfort at pedestrian level in urban area. *Journal of Wind Engineering and Industrial Aerodynamics*, 96(10–11): 1498–1527.

Neggers, R. A. J., Siebesma, A. P. and Heus, T. (2012). Continuous single-column model evaluation at a permanent meteorological supersite. *Bulletin of the American Meteorological Society*, 93(9): 1389–1400.

Ng, E. (ed.) (2010). *Designing High-Density Cities For Social and Environmental Sustainability*. London: Earthscan.

Nozu, T. and Tamura, T. (2012). LES of turbulent wind and gas dispersion in a city. *Journal of Wind Engineering and Industrial Aerodynamics*, 104–106: 492–499.

Onodera, N., Aoki, T., Shimokawabe, T. and Kobayashi, H. (2013). Large-scale LES wind simulation using Lattice Boltzmann Method for a 10km x 10km area in Metropolitan Tokyo. *Tsubame ESJ*, 9: 2–8. Available at: http://www.gsic.titech.ac.jp/en/TSUBAME_ESJ. (Accessed 22 March 2014).

Park, S.-B., Baik, J.-J., Raasch, S. and Letzel, M. O. (2012). A large-eddy simulation study of thermal effects on turbulent flow and dispersion in and above a street canyon. *Journal of Applied Meteorology & Climatology*, 51(5): 829–841.

Park, S.-B., Baik, J.-J. and Han, B.-S. (2013). Large-eddy simulation of turbulent flow in a densely built-up urban area. *Environmental Fluid Mechanics*, 1–16. doi: 10.1007/s10652-013-9306-3

Patnaik, G., Boris, J. P., Young, T. R. and Grinstein, F. F. (2007a). Large scale urban contaminant transport simulations with MILES. *Journal of Fluids Engineering – transactions of the ASME*, 129(12): 1524–1532.

Patnaik, G., Grinstein, F. F., Boris, J. P., Young, T. R. and Parmhed, O. (2007b). Large-scale urban simulations. In: Grinstein, F. F., Margolin, L. G., Rider, W. J. (eds.), *Implicit Large Eddy Simulation*. Cambridge; New York: Cambridge University Press, 502–530. doi: 10.1017/CBO9780511618604.019.

Pope, S. B. (2000). *Turbulent Flows*. Cambridge: Cambridge University Press.

Raasch, S. and Schröter, M. (2001). PALM – A large-eddy simulation model performing on massively parallel computers. *Meteorologische Zeitschrift*. 10(5): 363–372. doi: 10.1127/0941-2948/2001/0010-0363.

Rakai, A. and Franke, J. (2014). Validation of two RANS solvers with flow data of the flat roof Michelstadt case, *Urban Climate*, 10(4): 758-768. doi. 10.1016/j.uclim.2013.11.003.

Reuter, U. and Kapp, R. (2012). *Climate Booklet for Urban Development – Indications for Urban Land-use Planning*. Stuttgart: Ministerium für Verkehr und Infrastruktur Baden-Württemberg. Available at: http://www.staedtebauliche-klimafibel.de/?lng=ENG (Accessed 22 March 2014).

Rodi, W., Ferziger, J. H., Breuer, M. and Pourquié, M. (1997). Status of large eddy simulation: Results of a workshop. *Journal of Fluids Engineering*, 119: 248–262.

Sabatino, S. D., Buccolieri, R. and Salizzoni, P. (2013). Recent advancements in numerical modelling of flow and dispersion in urban areas: A short review. *International Journal of Environment and Pollution*, 52(3–4): 172–191.

Sagaut, P. (2006), *Large Eddy Simulation for Incompressible Flows*. Berlin; Heidelberg; New York: Springer.

Salim, S. M., Buccolieri, R., Chan, A. and Di Sabatino, S. (2011). Numerical simulation of atmospheric pollutant dispersion in an urban street canyon: Comparison between RANS and LES, *Journal of Wind Engineering and Industrial Aerodynamics*, 99(2–3): 103–113.

Schlünzen, K. H., Grawe, D., Bohnenstengel, S. I., Schlüter, I. and Koppmann, R. (2011). Joint modelling of obstacle induced and mesoscale changes – Current limits and challenges. *Journal of Wind Engineering and Industrial Aerodynamics*, 99(4): 217–225.

Tack, A., Koskinen, J., Hellsten, A., Sievinen, P., Esau, I., Praks, J., Kukkonen, J. and Hallikainen, M. (2012). Morphological database of Paris for atmospheric modeling purposes, *IEEE Journal of Selected Topics in Applied Earth Observation and Remote Sensing*, 5(6): 1803–1810.

Tamura, T. (2008). Towards practical use of LES in wind engineering. *Journal of Wind Engineering and Industrial. Aerodynamics*, 96(10–11): 1451–1471.

Tominaga, Y. and Stathopoulos, T. (2011). CFD modeling of pollution dispersion in a street canyon: Comparison between LES and RANS. *Journal of Wind Engineering and Industrial Aerodynamics*, 99(4): 340–348.

Tominaga, Y. and Stathopoulos, T. (2012). CFD modeling of pollution dispersion in building array: Evaluation of turbulent scalar flux modeling in RANS model using LES results. *Journal of Wind Engineering and Industrial Aerodynamics*, 104–106: 484–491.

Tominaga, Y. and Stathopoulos, T. (2013). CFD simulation of near-field pollutant dispersion in the urban environment: A review of current modeling techniques. *Atmospheric Environment*, 79: 716–730.

Tominaga, Y., Mochida, A., Yoshie, R., Kataoka, H., Nozu, T., Yoshikawa, M. and Shirasawa, T. (2008). AIJ Guidelines for practical applications of CFD to pedestrian wind environment around buildings. *Journal of Wind Engineering and Industrial Aerodynamics*, 96(10–11): 1749–1761.

Tominaga, Y., Iizuka, S., Imano, M., Kataoka, H., Mochida, A., Nozu, T., Ono, Y., Shirasawa, T., Tsuchiya, N. and Yoshie, R. (2013). Cross comparisons of CFD results of wind and dispersion fields for MUST experiment: Evaluation exercises by AIJ. *Journal of Asian Architecture and Building Engineering*, 12(1): 117–124. doi: 10.3130/jaabe.12.117.

VDI (2005). VDI-Standard 3783 Part 9 Environmental Meteorology – Prognostic Microscale Wind Field Models – Evaluation for Flow Around Buildings and Obstacles. Berlin: Beuth Verlag.

Voller, V. and Porté-Agel, F. (2002). Moore's law and numerical modeling. *Journal of Computational Physics*, 179(2): 698–703.

Wyszogrodzki, A. A., Miao, S. and Chen, F. (2012). Evaluation of the coupling between mesoscale-WRF and LES-EULAG models for simulating fine-scale urban dispersion. *Atmospheric Research*, 118: 324–345.

Xie, Z.-T. (2011). Modelling street-scale flow and dispersion in realistic winds – towards coupling with mesoscale meteorological models. *Boundary-Layer Meteorology*, 141(1): 53–75.

Xie, Z. and Castro, I. P. (2006). LES and RANS for turbulent flow over arrays of wall-mounted obstacles. *Flow Turbulence Combust*, 76(3): 291–312.

Xie, Z.-T. and Castro, I. P. (2009). Large-eddy simulation for flow and dispersion in urban streets. *Atmospheric Environment*, 43(13): 2174–2185.

Xie, Z.-T., Hayden, P. and Wood, C. R. (2013). Large-eddy simulation of approaching-flow stratification on dispersion over arrays of buildings. *Atmospheric Environment*, 71: 64–74.

Yoshie, R., Mochida, A., Tominaga, Y., Kataoka, H., Harimoto, K., Nozu, T. and Shirasawa, T. (2007). Cooperative project for CFD prediction of pedestrian wind environment in the Architectural Institute of Japan. *Journal of Wind Engineering and Industrial Aerodynamics*, 95(9–11): 1551–1578.

Yoshie, R., Jiang, G., Shirasawa, T. and Chung, J. (2011). CFD simulations of gas dispersion around high-rise building in non-isothermal boundary layer. *Journal of Wind Engineering and Industrial Aerodynamics*, 99(4): 279–288.

Chapter 33

# Issues of application – from urban climatic map to urban planning

*Edward Ng*

## Toward mega, compact, and habitable cities

Since 2006, more than half of the world's population has lived in cities (UNFPA, 2009). The number of cities and megacities is on the rise; the urban population, especially in Asia, is on the rise as well. There are now more than 20 megacities (i.e. cities with populations of more than 10 million) on earth, and more cities are being added to the list. In addition, more than 400 cities now have populations in excess of 1 million. The conversion rate of agricultural land and rural areas into concrete-paved and tarmac-sealed land, especially in rapidly developing regions such as China, is increasing (Seto and Fragkias, 2005). The United Nations estimated that the urban population in less developed countries would rise from 0.5 to 3 billion by 2030. Urbanisation and higher density-living is now an irreversible trend of human urban development (UNFPA, 2009).

There are commercial and political reasons for high-density living in mega and compact cities (Walker, 2003). Higher-density and more compact city designs conserve valuable land resources, reduce transport distance (and consequently the energy needed), and make public transport more viable (Smith, 1984; Betanzo, 2007). Advocates argue that high-density cities are more economically efficient. There are, of course, downsides and concerns (Phoon, 1975), such as the stress of crowed living and 'high density, low diversity' (Freedman, 1975; Travers, 1977). Doubtless, concerns are mostly based on past unhappy episodes of squatters, high-rise council flats, and slums. Nonetheless, the need for appropriate designs for high-density cities is clear. Designs that take urban climate into consideration are a puzzling agenda for planners and urban climatologists.

Mega and high-density compact cities suffer from large conglomerates of urban land mass with high thermal capacity and urban heat island (UHI) intensity (Oke, 1973). In addition, they have higher ground roughness and poorer urban ventilation (Landsberg, 1981; Oke, 1987). High anthropogenic heat and pollution emissions are also problems under weak synoptic wind conditions (Taha, 1997; Hamilton *et al.*, 2009; Narumi *et al.*, 2009). High-density compact cities, by their own urban morphological nature, have tall and bulky buildings, which lead to high frontal area density, high building height to street width ratio, restricted sky view factors, and low solar access (Yamashita *et al.*, 1986). They are also lacking in open and green spaces (Jim, 2004).

Urban landscape creates an urban climate that affects human comfort and environmental health (Tzoulas *et al.*, 2007; Poggio and Vrščaj, 2009). Generally, the use of climatic knowledge in land use and urban planning is lacking (Oke, 1984; Pressman, 1996). Planners and policymakers either do not pay sufficient attention to this increasingly important issue, or cannot fully engage the missing link. Understanding this lack of integration between urban climatic and urban planning

*Table 33.1* Some examples of mega and compact cities in tropical and sub-tropical South-East Asia, and their key urban and climatic characteristics.

| *City* | *Context* | *Population (millions)* | *Urban area (KM²)* | *Mean summer air temperature (°C) and RH (%)* | *Max. UHI* | |
|---|---|---|---|---|---|---|
| Manila, Philippines | c | 20 | 1425 | 28 / 90% | 3 | Tiangco *et al.* (2008) |
| Mumbai, India | c | 21 | 777 | 30 / 85% | / | |
| Guangzhou, China | I | 12 | 2590 | 29 / 83% | 6 | Jiang *et al.* (2007) |
| Jakarta, Indonesia | c | 24 | 2720 | 27 / 92% | / | |
| Taipei, Taiwan | I, v, h | 7 | 440 | 28 / 91% | 6 | Lin *et al.* (2008) |
| Singapore | c | 4.5 | 479 | 27 / 79% | 7 | Chow and Roth (2006) |
| Hong Kong | c, h | 7 | 272 | 28 / 80% | 8 | Nichol (2009) |
| Kuala Lumpur, Malaysia | I, h | 6 | 2137 | 27 / /95% | 8 | Mohammed (2004) |
| Bangkok, Thailand | I | 9 | 1502 | 29 / 91% | 3.5 | Boonjawat *et al.* (2000) and Elsayed (2006) |
| Dhaka, Bangladesh | I | 10 | 344 | 29 / 79% | / | |
| Key for context | c | Coastal | I | Inland | | |
| | v | Basin | h | Hilly | | |

Source: Author

knowledge is important, especially for planners of mega, high-density, and compact cities (de Schiller and Evans, 1996; Evans and de Schiller, 1996; Scherer *et al.*, 1999; Eliasson, 2000).

Many mega, high-density, and compact cities are located in the tropical and subtropical South East Asia, which have hot and humid climatic conditions (see Table 33.1) (Roth, 2007). Many of these cities are on the coastline. Past ill planning in Hong Kong has resulted in tall buildings that limit incoming sea breeze to inland areas (Ng *et al.*, 2009). For cities next to hills, vegetation is not protected, resulting in lesser katabatic wind and air mass exchange benefits. Cities situated in the basin suffer from low wind penetration and higher air pollution, especially when important air paths through the city are blocked (Mayer, 1999).

In mega, high-density, and compact cities located in the tropical and subtropical region of south-east Asia, heat stress-related mortality and morbidity is on the rise (Yan, 1997, 2000; Yip *et al.*, 2006; Leung *et al.*, 2008). This has raised the alarm for local politicians and city planners. Given the inevitable event of global warming and extreme weather, the health implications of increasing urban heat stress in cities are of topical concern (McGeehin and Mirabelli, 2001; Kovats and Jendritzky, 2006). Heat waves are becoming more frequent, longer in duration, and higher in intensity. One study in Hong Kong has indicated that the occurrence of 'heat spells' – defined as six continuous very hot days (Tmax over 33°C), counting from the first day of the occurrence – can increase from 11 times to 97 times under a UHI of 3°C in the daytime. The increase of very hot nights (Tmin over 28°C) from 10 times to 127 times has also been reported under the same UHI conditions. In a nutshell, with 3°C of UHI, inhabitants of the city would live almost every day and night under high thermal heat stress during the summer (Ng, 2009). Apart from the impact on health, higher urban temperature also means higher energy consumption for air conditioning (Fung *et al.*, 2006), thereby increasing energy use and carbon dioxide ($CO_2$) emission.

Noting the inevitable implications of urban climatic issues on health and comfort, the green and sustainable movement for city planning has gathered momentum in recent years. Since 2002, the Cabinet in Tokyo has had a general task force comprising the ministries concerned to address such issues. In 2005, the Hong Kong government established the first sustainable development strategy for Hong Kong; in 2006, it launched feasibility studies for the establishment of an air ventilation assessment system. Since 2004, the Singaporean government has been finding ways to understand these problems and has attempted to address them by commissioning various studies. Since 2009, the city government of Taipei has begun to pay attention to these same problems. At least for some quickly urbanising areas, political will is present; only the methods remain a concern for the planners and politicians.

## The missing link

Very few planners are familiar with the work of Luke Howard (1772–1864). However, planners would most likely know Sir Ebenezer Howard (1850–1928) and the details of his contribution to garden city and modern urban and land-use planning (probably in terms of good urban climatic sense cloaked in planning language). Sir Ebenezer's three-magnet-diagram mentions 'foul' and 'pure' air, 'murky sky', 'bright homes and gardens', and 'no smoke' (Howard, E., 1902). Sir Ebenezer knew and probably had read what Luke Howard discovered and published in his book, *The Climate of London,* in 1818 (Howard, L., 2009). Luke Howard vividly wrote his observations of the sky and air of the city of London. He describes the situation as 'this volcano of a thousand months would, in winter be scarcely habitable.' Apart from Luke Howard's understanding of the sky and air of the city of London, he has also been attributed as one of the first, if not the first, to have noted that urban temperature is higher than rural temperature (Howard, L., 1833). This is now known as the heat island intensity (UHI). In hindsight, the garden city movement of Sir Ebenezer is perhaps the best solution to the problem that planners face today.

Landsberg, in the preface of his book, *The Urban Climate,* wishes that the text 'will not only be useful for boundary layer meteorologists, but also for city planners and developers [...]' (Landsberg, 1981). Unfortunately, 30 years on, the number of planners and developers who are familiar with even the title of the book, let alone the content of urban climate knowledge essential to planning-related decision making, remains small. Eliasson observes that, although planners may claim an interest in urban climate, the use of climate knowledge in their work is unsystematic and has a low impact on the planning process (Eliasson, 2000). She attempts to outline the missing link based on five explanatory variables: conceptual- and knowledge-based, technical, policy, organisation, and the market. The onerous task, she reckons, is for urban climatologists to provide suitable methods and tools for the planners, and not, as typically argued, for planners to learn from urban climatologists. Echoing Eliasson in the 2009 World Climate Conference 3, Grimmond and Mills have presented two papers that gather the views of over 20 international co-authors (Grimmond *et al.*, 2010; Mills *et al.*, 2010). The authors argue that there is a 'technical' need for information, especially for fast-growing cities and megacities in the tropics and sub-tropics. There are also 'communication' needs for programmes and dialogues. More importantly, Mills calls for an integrated hierarchical model that can address planning needs at various planning scales. This is an important acknowledgement by urban climatologists that planning is a hierarchical process that sequentially deals with issues based on an important working parameter called 'scale'. This demands from urban climatologists an appreciation of the kind of urban climatic information that must be tailored for various scales of planning. Hence, avoiding information overload is crucial as it has the inevitable side effect of causing planners to believe, as Eliasson observes in her study, that they are not well-equipped (Eliasson, 2000).

## Discerning the missing link with reflective practice

To further understand the missing link, an investigation protocol commonly known in the design field as 'reflective practice' is used. The concept was introduced by Donald Schön (Schön, 1983,

1985), and is based on an older conceptual protocol known as the Meditations of Marcus Aurelius (Mac Suibhne, 2009). A planner himself, he understands the thinking process of professionals, especially under new and uncharted circumstances. He realises that professionals seldom follow technical rationality as the grounds of professional knowledge. Bryant *et al.* (1997) appropriately sums up the crisis Schön identifies: technical-rationality is a positivist epistemology of practice. It is 'the dominant paradigm which has failed to resolve the dilemma of rigor versus relevance confronting professionals.' Schön notes that design professionals work by referring to a repertoire of metaphors and images that allow for different ways of framing a situation. The repertoire of known metaphors and images provides what Schön sees as the 'stable state', which practitioners seldom cross. Unless new information can be framed within the repertoire, the information is more likely to be overlooked (Schön, 1973). The beginning paragraphs of the section on 'the missing link' in this chapter about the two Howards illustrate this mismatch.

Reflective practice means that one studies one's own working process critically to understand what can be improved. The process is associated with learning from experience and is an important strategy for lifelong learning. There are typically three phases of reflective practice: 'reflection for action', 'reflection in action', and 'reflection on action' (McAlpine and Weston, 2000). 'Reflection in action' is likely the more suitable protocol used as the disserting tool in this study. Since 2003, the author of this study has worked 'reflectively' with city planners of the Planning Department of the Hong Kong Government on a number of projects. They range from district-level land-use planning to new town planning to urban-level and site-level planning where the urban climatic issue is regarded as a concern by top government officials and politicians. The working process has allowed for observations that may shed light on the so-called missing link.

## From meteorological observations to urban planning

The starting point of all urban climatic understanding of urban planning typically begins with meteorological information from local observatories. Meteorological observations (e.g. air temperature, rainfall, wind speed, and relative humidity) are routinely collected by meteorological services at stations around the world at quarter-hourly or shorter intervals (WMO, 2003) to monitor weather conditions in both synoptic and local scales. Data from weather stations with long periods of observation provide climatic information for a specific area, and are essential for planners and architects to understand its 'prevailing' and 'critical' climate conditions. Moreover, meteorological data depicting ambient climate conditions are often used in downscaling studies as well as spatial evaluation of data related to detailed urban planning, building design, and environmental impact assessments.

When assessing climatic information, the keywords for planners are 'prevailing' and 'critical'; these translate into 'how often' and 'how important' respectively. The 'how often' aspect of information is normally well presented in tables and diagrams; unfortunately, the 'how important' aspect of the information is typically missing. Rather than knowing the average air temperature in the month of July, understanding the human-biometeorological implications is more important to planners. Hence, overlaying basic climatic information with human-biometeorological information (see Figure 33.1) is far more useful (Cheng and Ng, 2006). The consequences of urban climatic conditions that fall outside the human-biometeorological threshold should also ideally be stated and explained to planners when climate information is presented (Li and Chan, 2000; Yan, 2000; Yip *et al.*, 2007; Chau *et al.*, 2009). Most importantly, to avoid information overload, information should be presented in a simple and sequential manner to fit the hierarchical process of planning and land-use decision making.

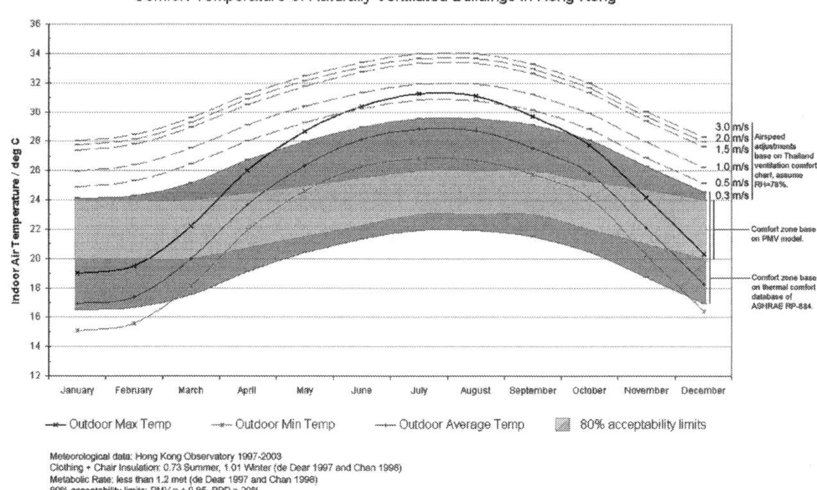


*Figure 33.1* The monthly minimum, average and maximum air temperatures are graphed. It is then overlaid with the human-biometeorological comfort zones of the locals after taking into account human acclimatization. The importance of wind for the summer months of June to August is highlighted. The important message to the planners is that urban wind must be optimized.

Source: Cheng and Ng, 2006

For air temperature, the monthly air temperature from the Hong Kong Observatory coupled with the human-biometeorological threshold of local inhabitants taken from user survey data reveal that in the months of May and September, daytime maximum air temperature can be a problem (see Figure 33.1). Planners have learned that 'critically', every 1°C beyond the threshold can mean an increase of four times the incidence of heat stress-related mortality (Leung *et al.*, 2008). Designing the city to limit daytime maximum heat island to within 2°C, while simultaneously maximising urban wind to the order of one metre per second is crucial. By themselves, these simple objectives allow planners and politicians to realise the goal. This is the situational metaphor, as identified earlier (under the subheading of 'The missing link'), which design professionals need. In this case, criticality of the images includes heat related mortality issues. Furthermore, planners in Hong Kong should also focus on 'prevailing' issues in terms of timing (i.e. in the months of June to August). During the working process with planners, climatic terms, such as air temperature, wind speed, and so on, have little meaning in terms of planners' mental metaphors and images. These have to be constantly brought back to concerns of criticality that have social and economic implications, otherwise, little of the meteorological data would make sense to planners, let alone to politicians who often direct what planners should or should not do.

## The planning process

During the observation period of working with planners, the need for planners and architects to understand how climate information can be usefully incorporated into decision making is realised (Chandler, 1976; de Schiller and Evans, 1996). Climatologists, in turn, need to appreciate planners' and architects' work in design. For planners, a plan is a systematic arrangement, configuration or

*Table 33.2* Rittel and Webber's ten characteristics of 'wicked' problems of planning.

1. There is no definitive formulation of a wicked problem.
2. Wicked problems have no stopping rule.
3. Solutions to wicked problems are not true or false, but better or worse.
4. There is no immediate and no ultimate test of a solution to a wicked problem.
5. Every solution to a wicked problem is a 'one-shot operation'; because there is no opportunity to learn by trial and error, every attempt counts significantly.
6. Wicked problems do not have an enumerable (or an exhaustively describable) set of potential solutions, nor is there a well-described set of permissible operations that may be incorporated into the plan.
7. Every wicked problem is essentially unique.
8. Every wicked problem can be considered to be a symptom of another problem.
9. The existence of a discrepancy representing a wicked problem can be explained in numerous ways. The choice of explanation determines the nature of the problem's resolution.
10. The planner has no right to be wrong (planners are liable for the consequences of the actions they generate).

And

1. The solution depends on how the problem is framed and vice-versa (i.e. the problem definition depends on the solution).
2. Stakeholders have radically different world views and different frames for understanding the problem.
3. The constraints that the problem is subject to and the resources needed to solve it change over time.
4. The problem is never solved definitively.

Source: Ritchey, 2007

outline of elements (such as buildings and their related functions) or important parts (land-use zones like roads and open spaces) for the accomplishment of an objective. Professionals dealing with the built environment need to bridge a very large spatial and time-scale difference of understanding (Oke, 2006). In addition, multiple and sometimes contrasting data has to be reconciled. Most of the time, a compromise, and not an optimised result, emerges. Indeed, planning is a political process that needs to balance the interests of different stakeholders and factors. Most of the time, there is a need to strike a reasonable solution, rather than an accurate or precise one. Scientists commonly find this unscientific manipulation and balancing act by planners difficult to appreciate. Borrowing from Schön's theory of reflective practice, a big difference is observed in the repertoire of known metaphors and images of framing a situation between a design professional dealing with complicated 'wicked' problems (see Table 33.2) (Rittel and Webber, 1973) and an urban climatologist wishing for precision and definitive solutions.

Examining the planning process further reveals three process scales in Hong Kong (Cullingworth and Nadin, 2006) and, commonly, in other places in the world: regional, district, and master layouts. The decisions and climatic information required are different at each of the three stages.

## Regional planning

Typically, regional planning in the form of territorial or country plans involves a spatial scale of tens or hundreds of kilometres or larger, with decision time-scale implications of 10 to 30 years and a map scale in the order of 1:20,000 or larger. In the past, planners planned the future of an area mostly by addressing socio-economic needs. They made decisions in terms of land use, development density, transportation, resources, and energy flows; all of which take into account characteristics of the region and the infrastructural constraints. The political aspirations and values of citizens allowed prioritisation of various factors to be considered; these affected the outcome of planning. For example, town planners commonly proposed a plan in the year 2000 for 2030 with a subtext of 'towards a city of 10 million', 'a better connected social network', or 'sustainable eco-city'. In the past, 'climate information' was rarely considered seriously when planning at this strategic level. A number of reasons underlined this lack of consideration. First, climate was considered a 'constant' entity. The advent of the issue of climate change (IPCC, 2007) and a better understanding of UHI (Mills, 2005) and other urban climatic issues are slowly changing the perception or repertoire of known metaphors and images of framing a situation. Furthermore, the political quest for sustainability and energy efficiency has somehow required planners to find ways to address issues and explain plans accordingly to the public. There is a need to appreciate the changing climatic boundary conditions of planned areas. Second, climate was not perceived as an important issue because there were more pressing socio-economic needs and wishes. Public perception is slowly being altered due to an increased awareness of environmental concerns (Evans and de Schiller, 1996).

In Hong Kong, government planners have developed the 2030 strategic plan (see Figure 33.2), and sustainability and city design have been mentioned in the working process. The planning keywords are 'infrastructure capacities' in terms of the environment, 'quality living space' in terms of urban spaces and environment, 'air quality' in terms of emission and dispersion, and 'waste management and energy consumption' in terms of resources management. Regardless of the parametric concerns of planning, in spatial design (i.e. laying down the morphology of the future city on paper), the need to spatially appreciate concerns is ever-present; issues of 'prevailing' and 'criticality' are already assumed. How should urban climate at this scale be presented spatially, with both notions incorporated?

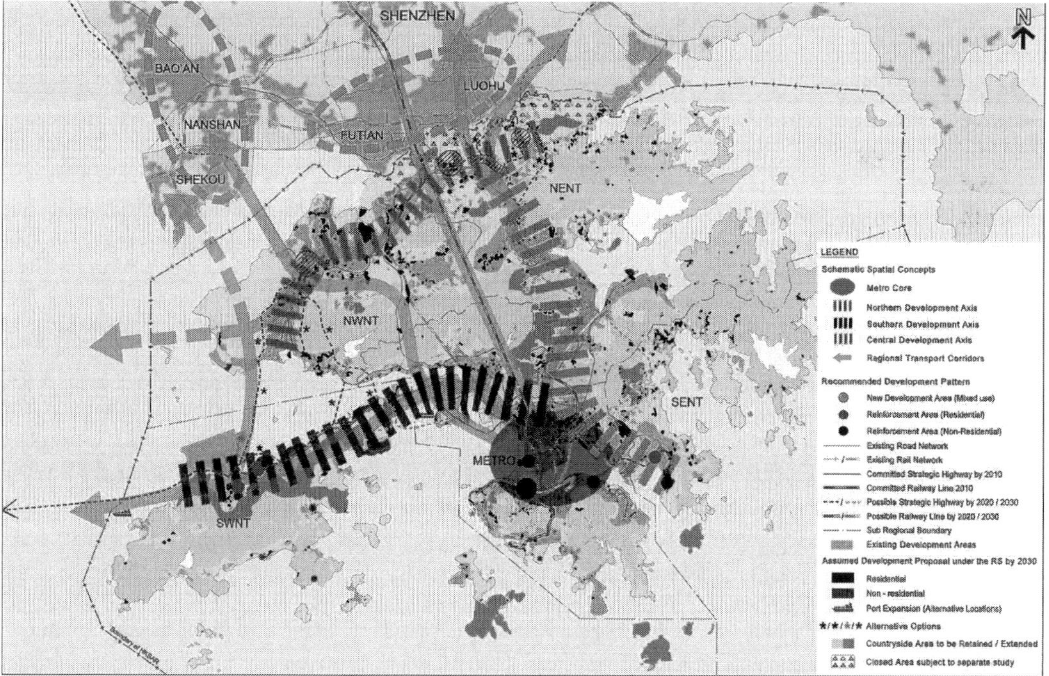


*Figure 33.2* The recommended development plan under Hong Kong 2030 Planning Vision and Strategy.

Source: HKGSAR, 2007b

Climatic maps (klimaaltas) are powerful and, more importantly for planners, more easily understood visual tools. The method originated in Germany (Mayer, 1988; VDI, 1997; Scherer *et al.*, 1999), and is now popular in other places in the world (Alcoforado, 2006). Earlier climatic maps were hand-drawn; however, lately, the use of Geographic Information System (GIS) has become common. The climatic map synthesises various kinds of climatic, topographic, and urban morphological information into synergetic understanding (see Figure 33.2). Human-biometeorology, urban noise, and air pollution interpretations based on these maps can be formulated. When necessary, mitigation measures can be detected and planned at the regional spatial scale. The making of a climatic map relies on a careful collection and collation of available meteorological data from the National Meteorological and Hydrological Service (NMHS). Long-term air temperature, precipitation, wind, cloud, and solar radiation data are input into the map and evaluated. The Berlin digital environmental atlas contains 11 layers of information on climate ranging from 'long-term mean air temperature' to 'bioclimate day and night'. The Hong Kong urban climatic map has nine layers of information on climate and planning ranging from wind formation to building volume and building ground coverage (Ng *et al.*, 2009).

In making the urban climatic map, supplementing observed meteorological data with simulation and experimental data (Schirmer, 1984) is necessary. Meso-scale models (e.g. MM5) have been used. Some simulations involve a nesting strategy to bring the resolution down to a few hundred metres and, parametrically, at the urban canopy level. Use of the prognostic model FITNAH for the Berlin atlas; the Urban Canopy Simulation System (UCSS) for the Tokyo Environmental Map; and the MM5/CALMET model for Hong Kong (refer to Figure 10.12 in Chapter 10) are examples. The crucial step is to simplify results of the model simulation for planning. In Hong Kong, rather than presenting complicated wind rose and frequency information of wind availability, only the prevailing wind direction in the summer months is extracted. This represents the critical condition for planning to try to make a reasonable decision.

In some cases, tracer gas experiments, wind tunnel tests, and mobile traverse air temperature measurements are conducted in monitoring stations in the city, mostly in the form of short-term case-based studies. Currently, due to the sparse data density of weather observing networks (mostly not within the city) and the expense of conducting field case studies, the case-based data could at best be described as 'snapshots', and may not be entirely robust both for its representativeness and for post-design evaluation purposes. For planners, without long-term site-specific meteorological records, snapshots in critical conditions are still the 'no better alternative' solution. Again, the information is useful for making 'reasonable' planning decisions.

At this scale of climatic understanding, planners need to first discern 'the general patterns', such as the generic climatic zones, the regional wind directions, the locations of the breezeway, and the major air mass exchange routes. Second comes the 'important issues' of the climate of the city. These typically do not need to be too exact or detailed. This is very important to appreciate because urban climatologists or scientists have a tendency to provide too much complicated information, which could overload the planners too early in the process. As explained, providing 12 monthly wind-rose values may be scientifically accurate; however, the planners need only to have the prevailing wind flow of an area at critical times for their work. Based on the results of model simulation and with reference to the observatory data in Hong Kong, planners and urban climatologists sat down and made a simple interpretation of the wind dynamics of the city and produced the wind information map of Hong Kong (see Figure 10.10). This map is an evaluated simplification of the observed and modelled simulated data into a generalised understanding for planning.

For planners, the 'criticality' of climatic information is important. Rather than simply showing the variations of daily/monthly air temperature in tables and graphs, planners need to see the relevance of data if the 'how important' aspect of the data is represented. Researchers in Japan (Masumoto, 2009) have calibrated air temperature data into hot days and nights. As such, planners have a clearer map-based spatial picture of the consequences of air temperature data and are in a better position to act when there is a need to address the issue from a political and planning point of view. In Hong Kong, the urban climatic analysis map classifies territories into eight classes using the human-biometeorological assessment index and the physiologically equivalent temperature (PET), developed by Mayer and Höppe (1987). The urban climatic map takes into account information on building volume, topography and greening as the bases of the thermal load evaluation. The map also takes into account building ground coverage, ground roughness, and proximity to open space as the bases on which to evaluate the dynamic potential of the urban area in a 100m × 100m grid. Calibrations are conducted using field measurements and wind tunnel studies (Cheng *et al.*, 2008; Ng *et al.*, 2009; Ren and Ng, 2009; Chen *et al.*, 2010). The eight classes are elaborated with explanations of their likely thermal and dynamic effects and planning actions needed (see Figure 33.3). This spatially based urban climatic information is very useful to planners as it can be directly overlaid to strategic plans.

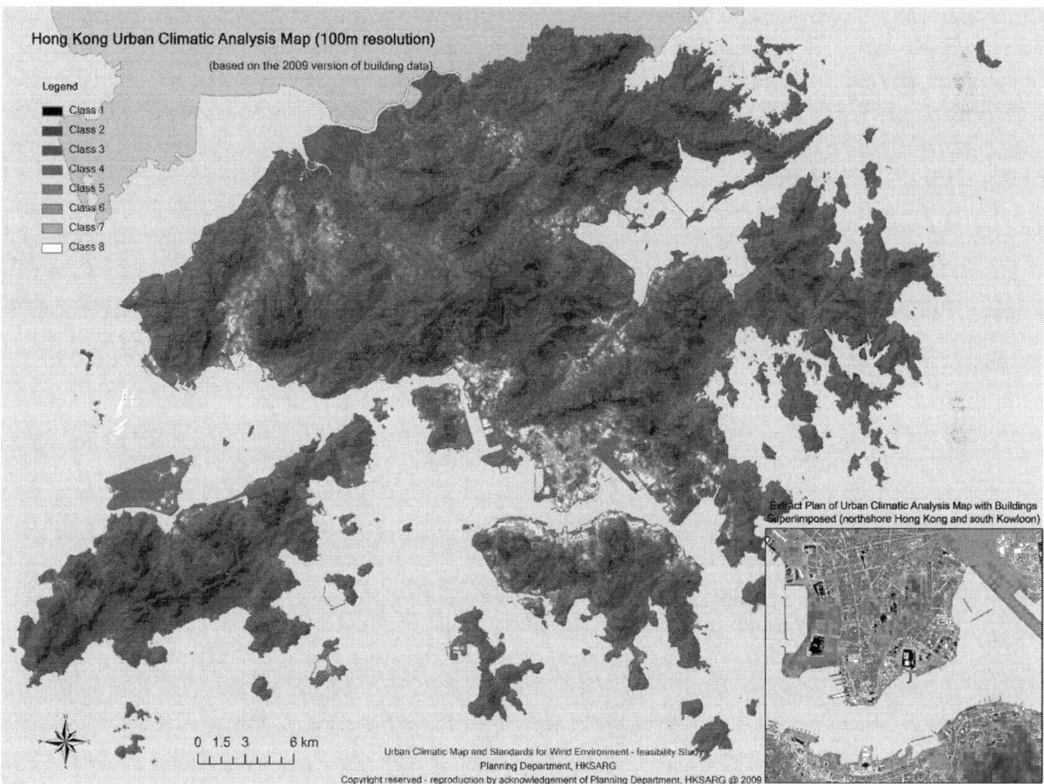


*Figure 33.3* The Urban Climatic Analysis Map of Hong Kong. The classes denote the predicted Physiological Equivalent Temperature (PET) differentials under typical summer daytime conditions. The map allows the planners an overview of the regional human-biometeorological characteristics of the territory. Detail investigations (inserted diagram at the lower right) can be identified for their next stage of planning works.

Source: Author

Furthermore, consequential 'urban parametric variations' (i.e. what one should do and how much one needs to respond) of climate information, even broadly speaking, are necessary. Knowing the density of buildings, even roughly, is important (Stone and Rodgers, 2001); percentages of ground coverage and greenery may be balanced to achieve a desirable result given a certain understanding of intra-city air temperature variations. For the subtropical summers of Hong Kong, to thermally mitigate the negative effects of high-density and bulky buildings in the city, 20 to 30 per cent greenery is deemed to be reasonable, desirable, and practical (Wong, 2009; Wang and Ng, 2010). This information translating urban climatic understanding into a planning actionable understanding, rough as it may be, is more useful to architects, planners, regulators, and policymakers.

## District planning

Once regional (territorial) planning has been strategically developed, planners in Hong Kong and typically in other places need to zoom into district level. The scale of operation is typically at a map scale of 1:5,000 to 1:10,000 and at the spatial scale of a few or tens of kilometres. In Hong Kong, this is the planning scale of the statutory Outline Zoning Plan (OZP). The plan is statutory and is the daily working plan of planners. OZPs show the proposed land uses and major road systems. Areas covered by such plans are zoned for such uses as residential, commercial, industrial, open space, government, and comprehensive development areas. Attached to each OZP is a set of notes setting out the uses that are always permitted; otherwise, permission must be sought with the Town Planning Board. The explanatory statement reflects the planning intentions and objectives of the various land-use zones.

At this scale, the city structure, land-use parcels, development density, building heights, and non-building areas, as well as infrastructural routes of transportation, can all be defined and mapped. A parametric understanding of the urban morphological characteristics is possible at this scale. Ground roughness length ($z_0$), ground sealing percentage, tree area ratio, settlement extent and density, and anthropogenic input can all be estimated and planned. Coupled with this is a fundamental understanding of the climate of the locality and climatically conducive local natural settings, such as the surrounding mountains and the sea. In addition, the urban climatic characteristics of the district can be computed. Sophisticated computational fluid dynamics (CFD) techniques are available and, due to the recent increase of computational power, feasible. The input boundary conditions are normally based on the results of meso-scale modelling. Alternatively, they can be based on representative typical conditions likely to be of critical interest. A canopy closure model, or a simpler k-ε type model can be nested to provide more detailed urban, or even street-scale, information (Oguro *et al.*, 2008); sub-grid scale urban elements can also be factored in (Green, 1992; Hiraoka, 1993; Kikuchi *et al.*, 2007; Mochida *et al.*, 2008a, 2008b). Guidelines for properly carrying out CFD are now available (Franke *et al.*, 2004; Tominaga *et al.*, 2008). Apart from CFD, the use of wind tunnels has commonly been employed to investigate urban ventilation and pollution dispersion, as well as air temperature fields of the urban environment (Kubota *et al.*, 2008).

None of what has been explained would be of interest to planners. For planners, two levels of urban climatic information are typically needed. First is the 'descriptive' information of how a city behaves, preferably at a city scale and presented as a map (see Figure 33.4). This gives planners a holistic appreciation of the urban climatic characteristics of the area. A very large-scale CFD (wind and thermal) study of Tokyo has recently been simulated within a five metre grid (Ichinose *et al.*, 2003; Ashie *et al.*, 2005). With this district scale information, strategic decisions of urban planning as to what needs to be done and where attention is needed can be elaborated; action plans can be formulated by the policymakers. In Japan, a *kaze no michi* (wind path) study has recently been

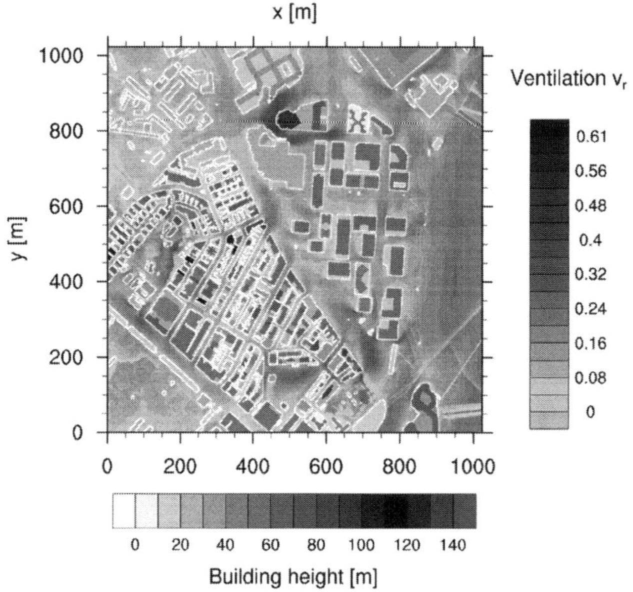


*Figure 33.4* A district-based Large Eddy Simulation study of an urban area in Hong Kong. The district scale wind velocity ratios (the ratio of measured pedestrian level mean wind speed to the reference mean wind speed at a height of 400m above sea level) have been presented. At this scale, for example, the important wind paths can be identified.

Source: Weinreis *et al.*, 2008

conducted as a basis to revitalise an area near Tokyo Station (AIJ, 2008). In Hong Kong, based on the urban climatic map, a district of 300 hectares of urban area (roughly the scale of one OZP in Hong Kong) has been wind tunnel- and CFD-studied to establish wind and urban ventilation characteristics. Based on this information, street grids in newly planned areas can be better laid out (see Figures 33.5 and 33.6).

Second, for planners, the 'predictive' and 'parametric' understanding of 'if this, then that' kind of causal relationship between a planning parameter and its consequent urban climatic and human-biometeorological performance is what is important (Katzschner, 1998). Planners have in their scope the ability to alter only a few urban morphological parameters (e.g. land use and their arrangements, building density, design heights and dispositions, open spaces and greeneries, roads, and infrastructure). Urban climatologists and planners must work together to parametrically understand how to balance such parameters. In Hong Kong, tests have been conducted on how building ground cover, building density, and building heights with regard to urban climate can be parametrically understood for planners (Ng *et al.*, 2003; Ng, 2007, 2008; Yoshie *et al.*, 2008). Based on this understanding, the optimal building site coverage, an important planning parameter, can be decided.

For planners, in addition to detailed modelling and experimental or simulation studies, ensuring layman-level qualitative information of 'dos and don'ts' is important because planners have to find ways to explain a decision in jargon-free language to the general public and policymakers. Planning-related urban climatic guidelines are useful. In the city of Stuttgart, an urban climatic booklet has been published (Stuttgart, 2008). In Hong Kong, a set of urban climatic references has

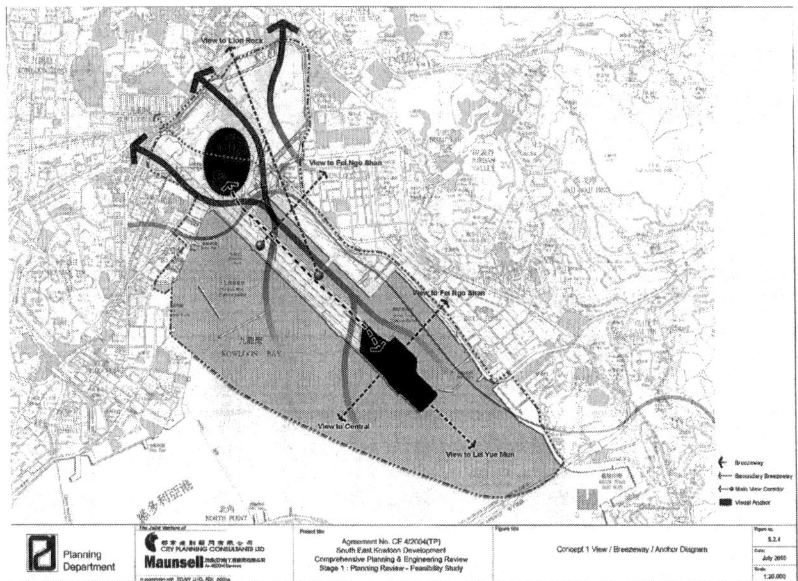


*Figure 33.5* The replanning of the old airport site relies on urban climatic information input. The breezeway directions proposed to the city planners based on CFD model simulation results.

Source: HKGSAR, 2007a

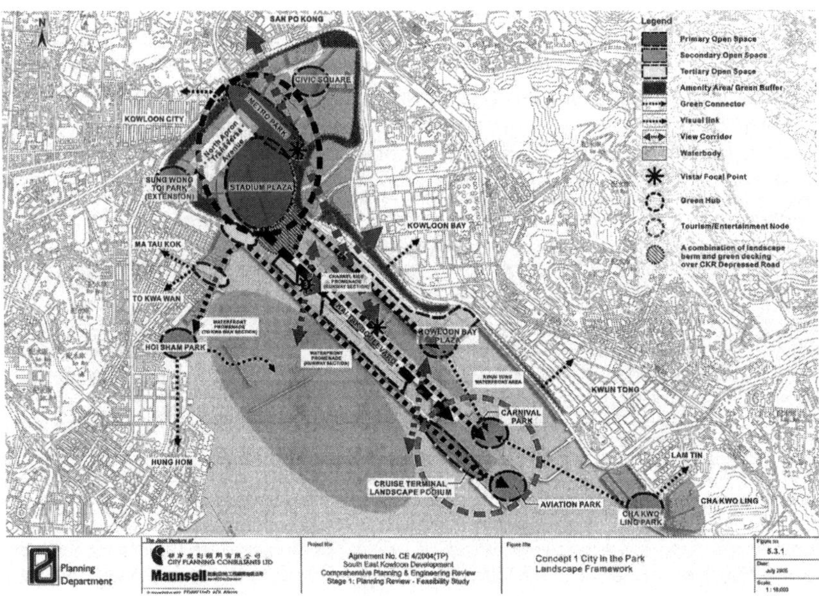


*Figure 33.6* The replanning of the old airport site relies on urban climatic information input. The green open spaces and their connectivity is a planning interpretation of the urban climatic needs.

Source: HKGSAR, 2007a

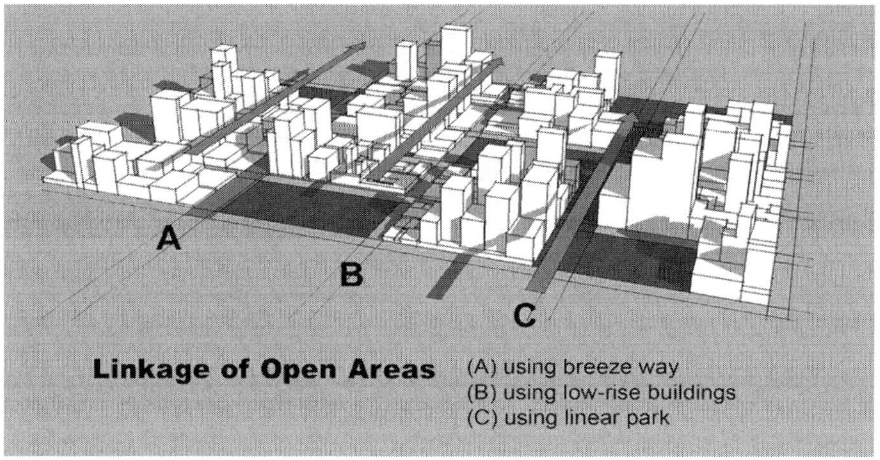


*Figure 33.7* A planning recommendation in *Hong Kong Planning Standards and Guidelines* to note the planners the possible design alternatives establishing and maintaining air paths in the city.

Source: HKPSG, 2008

been incorporated into the government of Hong Kong's planning standards and guidelines (HKPSG, 2008). Although they are mostly rule-of-thumb qualitative recommendations, they have proved to be of extreme value to councillors and lay board members when applying urban climate knowledge to planning and urban design decision-making. For planners, councillors, and lay board members, a diagram is better than numbers, figures or equations (see Figure 33.7).

In many cities, 'metro areas' are developed from 'existing' districts that require renewal and intervention. The planning process is slightly different because intervening within an existing urban area is politically difficult and expensive. The cores of most mega and compact cities belong to this planning scope. Areas designed in the past were based on very different urban conditions from today. Many of the streets were not designed for cars (Abdul-Wahab and Al-Arairni, 2004); the living pattern and demography have changed; economics and citizen aspiration have risen; and most of the land has been built up. Urban renewal plans have been necessary. How the urban climatic conditions can be improved to provide a quality living environment while respecting its current pattern remains a concern.

For planners, there is a need to understand the 'needs', 'wishes', and 'perceived rights' of existing stakeholders as to what quality environmental living is about, and how much effort/compromise they consider worthwhile. User survey and resident focus group discussions are needed. There is also a need to obtain comprehensive 'as is' urban climatic information of streets, spaces, and buildings to evaluate merits and deficiencies of the existing urban fabric. With this information, informed discussions with the stakeholders can be logically conducted. Again, there is a need for layman-oriented urban climate information.

Understanding of an existing district can be achieved with field measurements. Measurement programmes such as these are expensive to mount. A recent study in Tokyo included mounting 190 weather observation points in an area of approximately ten square kilometres (AIJ, 2008). Case study information may be useful for providing a sense of what is going on; for example, studies on urban air temperature, pedestrian-level air ventilation, micro-climatic, and intra-urban variations have been done in many cities that can provide planners with general references (Lazar and Podesser, 1999; Erell and Williamson, 2007; Ren and Ng, 2007; Wong *et al.*, 2007). The more important concern is not data per se, but how data can be visually understood. In Hong Kong, urban ventilation and intra-urban air temperature field study results have been collated to become the physiological equivalent temperature (PET) map, with associated planning recommendations (see Figure 33.8). Again, information is best graphically represented. Figure 33.8 shows the new town area of Tuen Mun in the western part of Hong Kong, which has six hundred thousand inhabitants living on a land area of approximately 10 square kilometres. The PET-devised district-level planning recommendation map has defined five urban climatic planning zones (UCPZs). For example, UCPZ 5 contains the following guidelines.

Very highly urban climatically sensitive area:

1 Mitigation actions are recommended and are considered essential.
2 These zones are very densely built. Thermal load is very high and dynamic potential is low. Very strong impact on thermal comfort is expected. A high frequency of thermal stress is anticipated.
3 Further adding of building volume and/or ground coverage is not encouraged and, if absolutely essential, should be carefully considered. Mitigation measures to 'improve' the existing conditions should be considered.
4 Existing air paths must be identified, respected, enhanced and widened. New air paths may need to be created. The prevailing wind directions and air mass movement must be considered when buildings are redeveloped and repositioned 'to improve' the existing situation. Strategic mitigation measures (air paths, open spaces, urban greenery, street widening, building setbacks, and so on) must be considered 'to improve' the existing situation.
5 A strategy to utilise all government, institution or community (GIC) sites to relieve the existing condition is recommended. No additional tall structure is encouraged on all these GIC sites. Intensive greening is recommended.
6 Additional greenery and tree planting on streets in these zones is essential and is recommended. Intensive greening in 'open space' zones is strongly recommended.

Apart from the UCPZs, various district-based zonal understanding is also incorporated. For example, B on the map is the 'breezeway zone' and has the following planning recommendations:

1 Sea breezes from the waterfront are beneficial to Tuen Mun East and Tuen Mun South areas and must be respected.
2 Open spaces on the waterfront allow sea breezes to penetrate further inland. They must be retained with increased green coverage.
3 Developments near to and along the waterfront must be very carefully designed for urban air ventilation. In particular, developments along the waterfront must not form a continuous barrier to sea breezes. Buildings must be arranged and positioned so that sufficient gaps between building blocks are left for air ventilation and urban permeability. Ideally, building heights should be restricted so that only lower buildings immediately fronting the shoreline are allowed, enabling sea breezes to penetrate further inland. Site coverage of buildings on the waterfront should be reduced to allow larger air spaces at the pedestrian level for better air ventilation. Reduced podia, non-building zones within private development sites connecting with air paths, and setbacks along site boundaries are examples of useful design features.
4 Streets perpendicular to the waterfront leading into the urban areas, including Lung Mun Road, Wu King Road, Hoi Wong Road, Tuen Mun Heung Sze Hui Road, and So Kwun Wat Road, are important air paths. They must be maintained and, if possible, widened and landscaped.

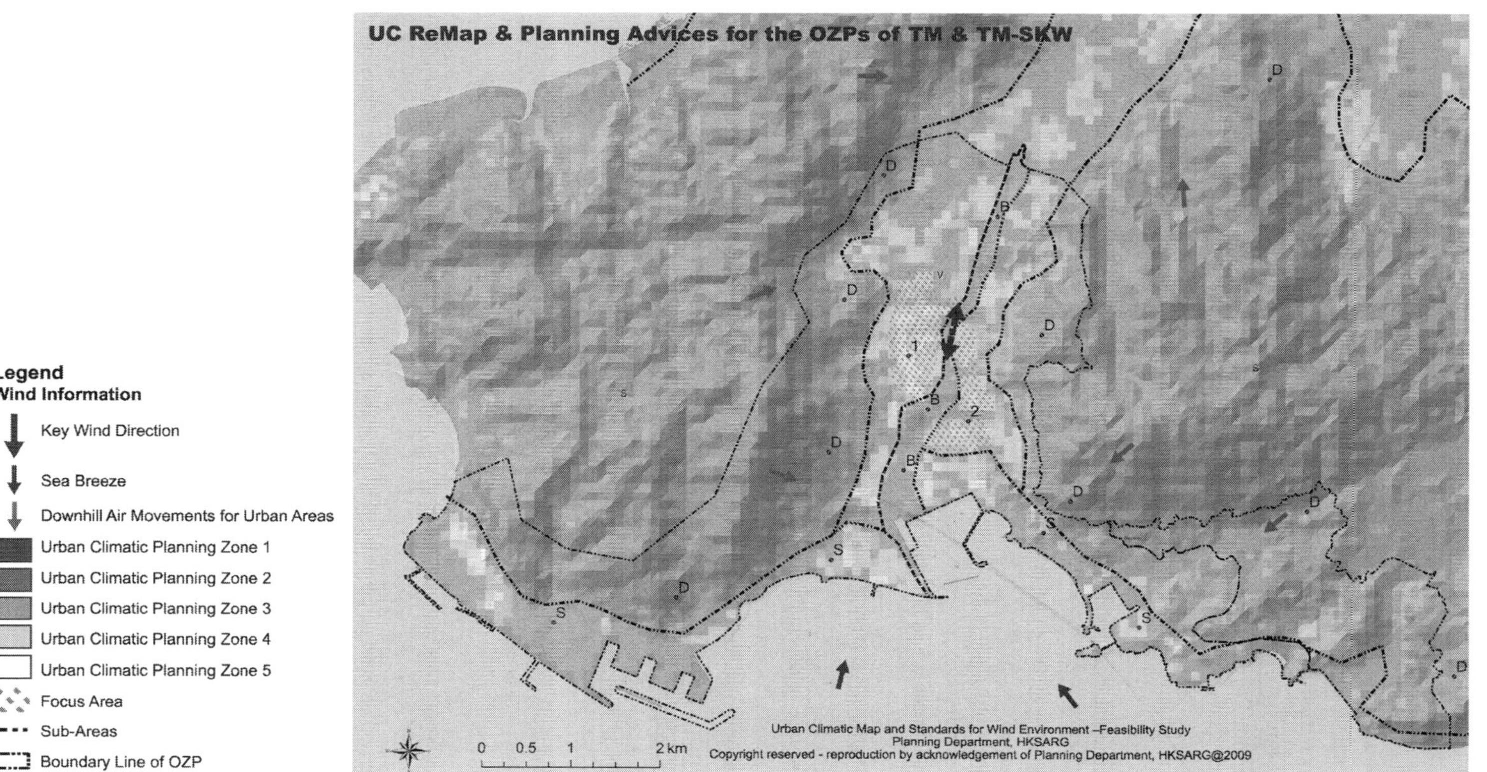


*Figure 33.8* A district-level planning recommendation map. Various urban climatic planning zones (based on PET understanding) have been identified spatially. A zonal understanding of urban climatic factors has also been spatially presented (B = breezeway, S = see breeze areas, D = downhill air mass exchange areas, 1 and 2 = focused areas).

Source: Author

5 In addition, due to the cooler sea breezes, shaded and landscaped walkways along the waterfront are thermally neutral for human comfort in the summer months of Hong Kong. They are good design features of good resting and amenity spaces for the enjoyment of the city inhabitants. These provisions are recommended.

For planners, before and after urban climatic scenarios of an intervention are valuable. As such, there may be a need, before redevelopment is scheduled, to obtain data of the existing condition. The rather limited planning interventions permissible within the existing urban fabric should be considered, and any field measurements should be framed accordingly. There is little need for a full-scale scientific-oriented research. In Tokyo, there is a recommendation for large urban redevelopment to monitor on-site wind, air temperature, and relative humidity information at the pedestrian level for a year before and after building construction.

## Master layout planning building design

Further down the scale is the master layout planning at the neighbourhood and building spatial scale of half a kilometre or less with a map scale of approximately 1:500–1:2,000. This is typically referred to by urban climatologists as the urban canopy layer scale at the micro-level (Oke, 2006). Many scholars have provided good understanding and design procedures (Page, 1976; Givoni, 1998; Szokolay, 2004; Emmanuel, 2005; Kwok and Grondzik, 2007). Observed climate data at this layout scale of planning and design normally does not exist and one needs to rely on model simulations or experimental studies. The boundary conditions can be extrapolated from nearby meteorological data.

At the layout and building scale, for planners and architects, knowing the consequences of failure or non-action, or more positively, the advantages and 'value-added-ness' of a decision is necessary. Cost-performance studies are most useful. A priority list of actions can thus be stated. The economic and socio-economic benefits need to be stated as well. Urban climate information should be resolved and related to human comfort, health, human acceptance, and work productivity understanding.

In the past, the use of micro-urban and building-level simulation for environmental study was possible but uncommon (Augenbroe, 1992; Wong *et al.*, 2000). This is slowly changing, especially in view of the need for building environmental assessments, such as Leadership in Energy and Environmental Design (LEED), in many project requirements. The site aspect portion of the assessment system typically requires an understanding of project impact to the surroundings. In Hong Kong, the BEAM+ system gives credits for projects that demonstrate good 'neighbourhood-ness' by conducting air ventilation assessment studies (Ng, 2009). Currently, the need to address the notion of 'Zero Carbon' development also requires designers to refer to climatic information as the basis for calculations.

At this scale, consideration of alternative design schemes and detailed design mitigation measures (see Figure 33.9) is more crucial. Figure 33.9 shows the existing condition versus the proposed design of the project site (two blocks of land in the centre of the figure) in terms of ground level urban ventilation. Given the high-density high-rise nature of the urban area, the CFD study demonstrates that the reduction of ground coverage of the proposed design allows for better urban ventilation. This is due to the fact that the proposed design has more air volume at ground level and better connected air paths through the site.

The typical meteorological year (TMY) of a locality is commonly used by building service engineers as input to building performance simulations. This provides a 'static' and 'typical' baseline

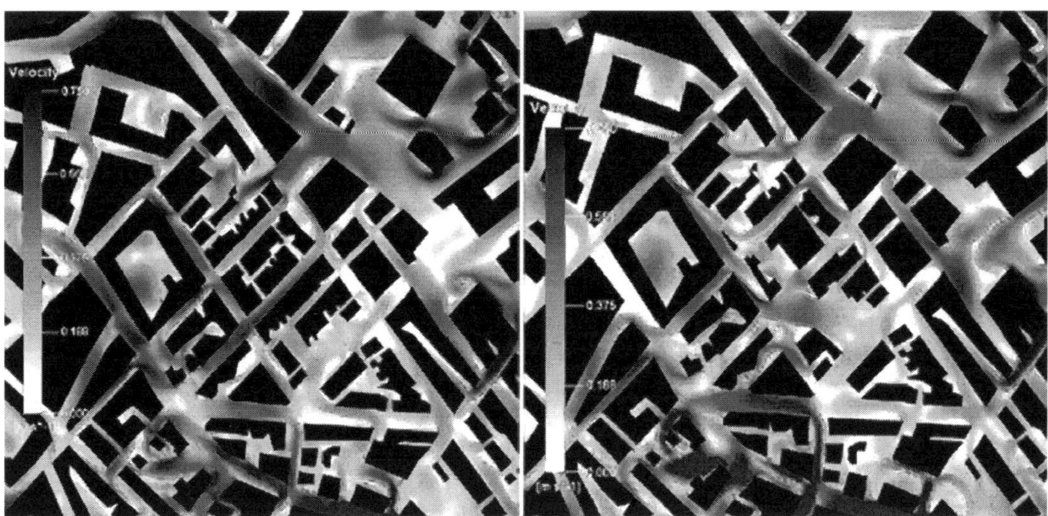

*Figure 33.9* Two CFD model simulation studies of a dense and compact urban condition in Hong Kong. Showing the existing condition (left) and the proposed design (right), planners can evaluate the implication of a design.

Source: Graphics courtesy of Arup and Partners HK Ltd

upon which designs could be studied. However, the dynamic and site-specific quality of the urban climate is not normally factored. For a closed-box, steady-state, air-conditioned artificial indoor environment, this may be fine; however, for designs that aim to use passive and natural means to create a more varied and diversified living environment both spatially and temporally, a static view of site-level urban climate is hardly satisfactory. Currently, planners and designers are often assisted by building services and mechanical engineers. For the engineers to move outside the building envelope, input from urban climatologists may be needed. A dynamic study based on real-time or synthesised typical meteorological data on an hourly time step is needed to demonstrate, at the least, the percentage of time that the system may not work as designed. Given the ease and power of today's computers, this goal is practical and feasible.

## Looking forward – cities of the future

For urban climatologists aiming to assist planners, the topical issue of a healthy, sustainable eco-city needs further thought. As part of the World Health Organization (WHO) Healthy Cities project, a guide to reorienting urban planning towards Local Agenda 21 entitled 'Towards a New Planning Process' has been published by the WHO Regional Office for Europe (WMO, 1999). Apart from the more conventional text on social and economic trends, an urban environment towards health for all has been emphasised. The need for human-biometeorological design is now an important agenda for planners, not just for now, but also for the future, taking into account various changes, including climate change (Loveland and Brown, 1989; Smith, 2005; Isaac and van Vuuren, 2009).

At the regional and district scale of planning, the term 'eco-city' has increasingly been coined in many new town developments, especially in China and in south-east Asia. One of the recent higher-profile offerings is the Dongtan eco-city project in China jointly promoted by the UK and the Chinese governments (Wood, 2007). Climatic information has been factored for the design of buildings, open spaces, and the possibility of renewable energy production. Based on the study, the potentials for zero- or low-energy neighbourhoods and architecture have been proposed. Another example is the Masdar eco-city in Abu Dhabi where wind information has been used to establish renewable energy potential, making planning scale and density of development possible (Foster and Partners, 2010; Masdar, 2010).

At the layout and building design scale of planning is the advent of intelligent building information management systems and clever electronics, means that allow the building to find a way to actively engage changing weather on an hourly or instantaneous manner (Elmualim, 2009). A smart system may adjust windows and ventilation systems to cope with a possible change of weather in a few hours' time, taking into account thermal lag and activity changes in the building (Lo *et al.*, 2007). Estimating daylight availability and solar irradiation based on weather forecasts, the intelligent system can work out its light switching pattern, and cooling load needs also becomes possible (Ng *et al.*, 2007). The next step is for NMHS to provide a quality forecast of weather parameters in a predefined format for the system to self-calibrate and to work out a pattern. The possibility of adapting such innovations in the refurbishment of a large share of existing building stock is similarly imminent for an overall improvement of the city.

Most importantly, there is a real need to plan a city to cope with climate change (LCCP, 2002; IPCC, 2007). In Germany, the KLIMES project aims to 'develop a set of guidelines and test its implementation in planning concepts with respect to the goal to achieve an improved climate protection of human beings under changing climate conditions and extreme weather events' (Mayer *et al.*, 2008). Climate adaptation strategies need to be established at the city planning level (ASCCUE, 2006; London, 2007). Based on various global and regional climatic modelling, prediction, and scenarios, the future change in climatic parameters can be estimated and various likely-to-be-encountered critical issues are identified. More research and interdisciplinary collaboration are required to investigate and ascertain the implications of climate change on urban planning (Burton, 1997; Adger *et al.*, 2003).

## Conclusions

Based on a reflective in-action working process with planners and upon appreciating the wicked problem-solving nature of their work, the needs of and the missing link between urban climate and city planning have been elaborated. Information requirements and data characteristics for planners have been explained. Some examples have been illustrated.

Urban climatic patterns at the regional planning scale in prevailing and critical conditions need to be understood by planners. Overall criticality needs to be stated so that planners can find ways to prioritise issues. Parametric understanding linking urban climate and urban morphology needs to be established. The urban climatic description of the urban fabric needs to be understood at the district scale of planning. Information in map form is encouraged. Qualitative guidelines assisting planners to explain urban climatic matters to councillors and board members can be very useful. At the layout and building design scale, building services engineers must be assisted by urban climatologists to establish a more dynamic understanding of issues beyond the traditional closed-box approach. The advent of rapid urbanisation in the age of climate change further endows urban climatologists with the burden of developing appropriate and easily understandable urban climate knowledge for planners. Resolving something complicated into something that is simple is the only way forward. Instead of the need for precision and accuracy, planners need to make balanced and therefore reasonable decisions. Simplicity is required from urban climatologists.

In her study, Eliasson notes the need for urban climatologists to provide planners with good arguments; this has been supported. The issue then is what defines a good argument. This paper presents the words 'prevailing' and 'criticality' as the foundations for such an argument. The term 'prevailing' gives laymen a sense of the frequency of occurrence and how often they may be affected, whereas the word 'criticality' gives a sense of how important the issue is and what the implications could be.

For the issue of communication, this paper presents the view that keeping information simple and graphical is the key. An arrow on a map, albeit rough and imprecise, can be better for planners at the early district levels of the planning process. The advent of public awareness of issues related to climate change allows urban climatologists a platform to engage the public, stakeholders, and the government. This study aims to make a small contribution.

Planners and architects need to be trained more thoroughly in sustainability and environmental design (de Schiller and Evans, 1996). The Royal Institute of British Architects has mandated that all architectural students be conversant in sustainability upon graduation. The task is for urban climatologists to engage this enthusiasm by providing course materials and easily understandable concepts and data to facilitate learning. The key message to urban climatologists is to keep reports graphical and simple, and to simply state what is prevailing and critical.

## Acknowledgement

This chapter was originally published as Ng, E. (2012). Towards a planning and practical understanding for the need of meteorological and climatic information for the design of high-density cities – a case-based study of Hong Kong, *International Journal of Climatology*, 32(4): 582–598. Kind permission has been obtained from John Wiley and Sons to reproduce it.

## References

Abdul-Wahab, S. A. and Al-Arairni, A. (2004). Environmental considerations in urban planning. *International Journal of Environmental Studies*, 61(5): 527–537.

Adger, W. N., Huq, S., Brown, K., Conway, D. and Hulme, M. (2003). Adaptation to climate change in the developing world. *Progress in Development Studies*, 3(3): 179–195.

AIJ (2008). *Newsletter on Urban Heat Island and Countermeasures. Vol. 4, August 2008.* Japan: Architecture Institute of Japan.

Alcoforado, M. J. (2006). Planning procedures towards high climatic quality cities. Example referring to Lisbon. *Finisterra: Revista Portuguesa de Geografia*, 41(82): 49–64.

ASCCUE (2006). Available at: http://www.k4cc.org/bkcc/asccue (Accessed 8 October 2010).

Ashie, Y., Tokairin, T., Kono, T. and Takahashi, K. (2005). *Wind Condition of 10km Square Area in Tokyo.* Japan: Building Research Institute.

Augenbroe, G. (1992). Integrated building performance evaluation in the early design stages. *Building and Environment*, 27(2): 149–161.

Betanzo, M. (2007). Pros and cons of high density urban environments. *Build*, April/May: 39–40.

Boonjawat, J., Niitsu, K. and Kudo, S. (2000). Urban heat island: thermal pollution and climate change in Bangkok. *Journal of Health Science*, 9(1): 49–55.

Bryant, I., Johnston, R. and Usher R. (1997). *Adult Education and the Postmodern Challenge.* London: Routledge.

Burton, I. (1997). Vulnerability and adaptive response in the context of climate and climate change. *Climatic Change*, 36(1–2): 185–196.

Chandler, T. J. (1976). Urban climate and urban planning. In: *Urban Climate and Its Relevance to Urban Design*. Geneva: World Meteorological Organization, chapter 3.

Chau, P., Chan, K. and Woo, J. (2009). Hot weather warning might help to reduce elderly mortality in Hong Kong. *International Journal of Biometeorology*, 53(5): 461–468.

Chen, L., Ng, E., An, X., Ren, C., Lee, M., Wang, U. and He, Z. (2010). Sky view factor analysis of street canyons and its implications for daytime intra-urban air temperature differentials in high-rise, high-density urban areas of Hong Kong: A GIS-based simulation approach. *International Journal of Climatology*, 32(1): 121–136. doi: 10.1002/joc.2243.

Cheng, V. and Ng, E. (2006). Thermal comfort in urban open spaces for Hong Kong. *Architectural Science Review*, 49(3): 236–242.

Cheng, V., Ng, E., Chan, C. and Givoni, B. (2008). An experiment of urban human thermal comfort in hot and humid sub-tropical city of Hong Kong under high density urban morphological conditions. In: Mayer, H. and Matzarakis, A. (eds.), *Proceedings of the 5th Japanese-German Meeting on Urban Climatology*. Berichte des Meteorologischen Instituts der Albert-Ludwigs-Universität Freiburg, No. 18. The Albert-Ludwigs-University of Freiburg, Freiburg, Germany, 6–11 October. Freiburg: the Meteorological Institute, Albert-Ludwigs-University of Freiburg, 179–184. Available at: http://www.meteo.uni-freiburg.de/forschung/publikationen/berichte/report18.pdf (Accessed 10 February 2014).

Chow, W. T. L. and Roth, M. (2006). Temporal dynamics of the urban heat island of Singapore. *International Journal of Climatology*, 26(15): 2243–2260.

Cullingworth, B. and Nadin, V. (2006). *Town and Country Planning in the UK*. 14th edition. London: Routledge.

de Schiller, S. and Evans, J. M. (1996). Training architects and planners to design with urban microclimates. *Atmospheric Environment*, 30(3): 449–454.

Eliasson, I. (2000). The use of climate knowledge in urban planning. *Landscape and Urban Planning*, 48(1–2): 31–44.

Elmualim, A. (2009). Integrated building management systems for sustainable technologies: Design aspiration and operational shortcoming. In: Howlett, R. J., Jain, L. C. and Lee, S. H. (eds.), *Sustainability in Energy and Buildings: Proceedings of the International Conference in Sustainability in Energy and Buildings (SEB' 09)*. Springer Berlin Heidelberg, 275–280.

Elsayed, I. S. M. (2006). *The Effects of Urbanization of the Intensity of the Urban Heat Island: A Case Study on the City of Kuala Lumpur*. PhD thesis. International Islamic University Malaysia.

Emmanuel, M. R. (2005). *An Urban Approach to Climate-Sensitive Design: Strategies for the Tropics*. London and New York: Spon Press, Taylor & Francis Group.

Erell, E. and Williamson, T. J. (2007). Intra-urban differences in canopy layer air temperature at a mid-latitude city. *International Journal of Climatology*, 27(9): 1243–1255.

Evans, J. M. and de Schiller, S. (1996). Application of microclimate studies in town planning: A new capital city, an existing urban district and urban river front development. *Atmospheric Environment*, 30(3): 361–364.

Foster and Partners (2010). Projects / Masdar Development. Available at: http://www.fosterandpartners.com/Projects/1515/Default.aspx (Accessed 8 October 2010).

Franke, J., Hirsch, C., Jensen, A. G., Krus, H. W., Schatzmann, M., Westbury, P. S., Miles, S. D., Wisse, J. A. and Wright, N. G. (2004). Recommendations on the use of CFD in wind engineering. In: *Proceedings of the International Conference on Urban Wind Engineering and Building Aerodynamics (COST ACTION C14)*. Sint-Genesius-Rode, Belgium, 5–7 May.

Freedman, J. L. (1975). *Crowding and Behavior: The Psychology of High-Density Living*. New York: Viking Press.

Fung, W. Y., Lam, K. S., Hung, W. T., Pang, S. W. and Lee, Y. L. (2006). Impact of urban temperature on energy consumption of Hong Kong. *Energy*, 31(14): 2623–2637.

Givoni, B. (1998). *Climate Considerations in Building and Urban Design*. Canada: John Wiley & Sons, Inc.

Green, S. R. (1992). Modelling turbulent air flow in a stand of widely-spaced trees. *The PHOENICS, Journal of Computational Fluid Dynamics and Its Applications*, 5(3): 294–312.

Grimmond, C. S. B., Roth, M., Oke, A., Best, M., Betts, R., Carmichael, G., Cleugh, H., Dabberdt, W., Emmanuel, R., Freitas, E., Fortuniak, K., Hanna, S., Klein, P., Kalkstein, L. S., Liu, C. H., Nickson, A., Pearlmutter, D., Sailor, D. and Voogt, J. (2010). Climate and more sustainable cities: Climate information for improved planning and management of cities (producers/capabilities perspective). In: Sivakumar, M. V. K. *et al.* (eds.), *Procedia Environmental Sciences, Vol. 1, Special Issue of World Climate Conference-3*, 247–274. Geneva, Switzerland, 31 August–4 September 2009.

Hamilton, I. G., Davies, M., Steadman, P., Stone, A., Ridley, I. and Evans, S. (2009). The significance of the anthropogenic heat emissions of London's buildings: A comparison against captured shortwave solar radiation. *Building and Environment*, 44(4): 807–817.

Hiraoka, H. (1993). Modelling of turbulent flows within plant/urban canopies. *Journal of Wind Engineering and Industrial Aerodynamics*, 46–47: 173–182.

HKGSAR (2007a). *Kai Tak Planning Review*. Hong Kong Government Development Bureau and Planning Department. Available at: http://www.pland.gov.hk/pland_en/p_study/prog_s/sek_09/website_chib5_eng/english/index.html (Accessed 7 March 2010).

HKGSAR (2007b). *Hong Kong 2030 Planning Vision and strategy*. Hong Kong Government Development Bureau and Planning Department. Available at: http://www.pland.gov.hk/pland_en/p_study/comp_s/hk2030/eng/home (Accessed 7 March 2010).

HKPSG (2008). *Hong Kong Planning Standards and Guidelines (HKPSG)*. Planning Department, HK Governement. Available at: http://www.pland.gov.hk/pland_en/tech_doc/hkpsg/ (Accessed 10 February 2014).

Howard, E. (1902). *To-morrow: A Peaceful Path to Real Reform, 1898. Republished as Garden Cities of Tomorrow*. London: Swann Sonnenschein.

Howard, L. (1833). *The Climate of London Deduced from Meteorological Observations*. 3rd edition. London: Harvey & Darton.

Howard, L. (2009). *The Climate of London*. London: General Books LLC.

Ichinose, T., Ashie, Y., Hisano, Y. and Kono, T. (2003). The high resolution numerical model of heat island phenomena. *CGER's Supercomputer Activity Report*, 12: 115–121.

IPCC (2007). *IPCC Forth Assessment Report: Climate Change 2007*. Available at: http://www.ipcc.ch/ipccreports/assessments-reports.htm (Accessed 8 October 2010.)

Isaac, M. and van Vuuren, D. P. (2009). Modeling global residential sector energy demand for heating and air conditioning in the context of climate change. *Energy Policy*, 37(2): 507–521.

Jiang, X. D., Xia, B. C, Guo, L. and Li, N. (2007). Characteristics of multi-scale temporal-spatial distribution of urban heat island in Guangzhou. *Ying Yong Sheng Tai Xue Bao = The Journal of Applied Ecology*, 18(1): 133–139. (In Chinese).

Jim, C. Y. (2004). Green-space preservation and allocation for sustainable greening of compact cities. *Cities*, 21(4): 311–320.

Katzschner, L. (1998). Designation of urban climate qualities and their implementation in the planning process. In: Maldonado, E. and Yannas, S.: *Environmentally Friendly Cities: Proceedings of PLEA 98, Passive and Low Energy Architecture*. Lisbon, Portugal, June 1998. London: James & James Science Publishers Ltd., 75–78.

Kikuchi, A., Hataya, N., Mochida, A., Yoshino, H., Tabata, Y., Watanabe, H. and Jyunimura, Y. (2007). Field study of the influence of roadside trees and moving automobiles on turbulent diffusion of air pollutants and thermal environment in urban street canyons. In: *Proceedings of the 6th International Conference on Indoor Air Quality, Ventilation & Energy Conservation in Buildings*, 137–144. Sendai, Japan, 28–31 October.

Kovats, R. S. and Jendritzky, G. (2006). *Heat Waves and Human Health*. Published on behalf of the World Health Organization Regional Office for Europe. Springer: Heidelberg, Germany.

Kubota, T., Miura, M., Tominaga, Y. and Mochida, A. (2008). Wind tunnel tests on the relationship between building density and pedestrian-level wind velocity: Development of guidelines for realizing acceptable wind environment in residential neighborhoods. *Building and Environment*, 43(10): 1699–1708.

Kwok, A. G. and Grondzik, W. T. (2007). *The Green Studio Handbook: Environmental Strategies for Schematic Design*. London: Elsevier Inc.

Landsberg, H. E. (1981). *The Urban Climate*. New York: Academic Press.

Lazar, R. and Podesser A. (1999). An urban climate analysis of Graz and its significance for urban planning in the tributary valleys east of Graz (Austria). *Atmospheric Environment*, 33(24): 4195–4209.

Leung, Y. K., Yip, K. M. and Yeung, K. H. (2008). Relationship between thermal index and mortality in Hong Kong. *Meteorological Applications*, 15(3): 399–409.

Li, P. W. and Chan, S. T. (2000). Application of a weather stress index for alerting the public to stressful weather in Hong Kong. *Meteorological Applications*, 7(4): 369–375.

Lin, C. Y., Chen, F., Huang, J. C., Chen, W. C., Liou, Y. A., Chen, W. N. and Liu, S. C. (2008). Urban heat island effect and its impact on boundary layer development and land–sea circulation over northern Taiwan. *Atmospheric Environment*, 42(22): 5635–5649.

Lo, S. C., Ma, H. W and Chao, C. W. (2007). Identifying priorities of carbon dioxide reduction policy for buildings using life-cycle approach. In: *Proceedings of 3rd International Conference on Life Cycle management (LCM 2007)*. University of Zurich at Irchel, Zurich, 27–29 August. Available at: http://www.lcm2007.ethz.ch/paper/449.pdf (Accessed 10 February 2014).

LCCP (2002). *London Warming – The Impacts of Climate Change on London*. London: London Climate Change Partnership (LCCP). Available at: http://climatelondon.org.uk/publications/londons-warming/ (Accessed 8 October 2010).

London (2007). *"Rising to the Challenge – The City of London Corporation's Climate Adaptation Strategy."* City of London Corporation.

Loveland, J. E. and Brown, G. Z. (1989). *Impacts of Climate Change on the Energy Performance of Buildings in the United States*. Office of Technology Assessment, United States Congress, Center for Housing Innovation, University of Oregon. Available at: http://hdl.handle.net/1794/10747 (Accessed 10 February 2014).

Mac Suibhne, S. (2009). Wrestle to be the man philosophy wished to make you: Marcus Aurelius, reflective practitioner. *Reflective Practice*, 10(4): 429–436.

Masdar (2010). Masdar City. Available at: http://www.masdarcity.ae/en/ (Accessed 8 October 2010).

Masumoto, K. (2009). Urban heat island in Osaka city – distribution of 'Nettaiya' and 'Moushobi' degree hours and characteristics of air temperature. In: Mayer, H. and Matzarakis, A. (eds.), *Proceedings of the 5th Japanese-German Meeting on Urban Climatology*. Berichte des Meteorologischen Instituts der Albert-Ludwigs-Universität Freiburg, No. 18. The Albert-Ludwigs-University of Freiburg, Freiburg, Germany, 6–11 October. Freiburg: the Meteorological Institute, Albert-Ludwigs-University of Freiburg, 15–20. Available at: http://www.meteo.uni-freiburg.de/forschung/publikationen/berichte/report18.pdf (Accessed 10 February 2014).

Mayer, H. (1988). Results from the research program 'stadtklima bayern' for urban planning. *Energy and Buildings*, 11(1–3): 115–121.

Mayer, H. (1999). Air pollution in cities. *Atmospheric Environment*, 33(24): 4029–4037.

Mayer, H. and Höppe, P. (1987). Thermal comfort of man in different urban environments. *Theoretical and Applied Climatology*, 38(1): 43–49.

Mayer, H., Holst, J., Dostal, P., Imbery, F. and Schindler, D. (2008). Human thermal comfort in summer within an urban street canyon in Central Europe. *Meteorologische Zeitschrift*, 17(3): 241–250.

McAlpine, L. and Weston, C. (2000). Reflection: Issues related to improving professors' teaching and students' learning. *Instructional Science*, 28(5): 363–385.

McGeehin, M. A. and Mirabelli, M. (2001). The potential impacts of climate variability and change on temperature-related morbidity and mortality in the United States. *Environmental Health Perspectives*, 109(Suppl 2): 185–189.

Mills, G. (2005). *Urban Form, Function and Climate*. U.S.: Environmental Protection Agency. Available at http://www.epa.gov/hiri/resources/pdf/GMills4.pdf (Accessed: 8 October 2010).

Mills, G., Cleugh, H., Emmanuel, R., Endlicher, W., Erell, E., McGranahan, G., Ng, E., Nickson, A., Rosenthal, J. and Steemer, K. (2010). Climate information for improved planning and management of mega cities (needs perspectives). In: Sivakumar, M. V. K. *et al.* (eds.), *Procedia Environmental Sciences, Vol. 1, Special Issue of World Climate Conference-3*, 228–246. Geneva, Switzerland, 31 August–4 September 2009.

Mochida, A., Hagishima, A., Tanimoto, J., Maruyama, T., Kikuchi, A., Tabata, Y. and Kikuchi, Y. (2008a). CFD Prediction of flow around car-shaped molds using vehicle canopy model. In: Mayer, H. and Matzarakis, A. (eds.), *Proceedings of the 5th Japanese-German Meeting on Urban Climatology*. Berichte des Meteorologischen Instituts der Albert-Ludwigs-Universität Freiburg, No. 18. The Albert-Ludwigs-University of Freiburg, Freiburg, Germany, 6–11 October. Freiburg: the Meteorological Institute, Albert-Ludwigs-University of Freiburg, 131–138. Available at: http://www.meteo.uni-freiburg.de/forschung/publikationen/berichte/report18.pdf (Accessed 10 February 2014).

Mochida, A., Tabata, Y., Iwata, T. and Yoshino, H. (2008b). Examining tree canopy models for CFD prediction of wind environment at pedestrian level. *Journal of Wind Engineering and Industrial Aerodynamics*, 96(10–11): 1667–1677.

Mohammed, S. Z. (2004). *The Influence of Urban Heat Towards Pedestrian Comfort and the Potential use of Plants and Water as Heat ameliorator in Kuala Lumpur City Centre Area.* MSc Thesis. Universiti Putra Malaysia.

Narumi, D., Kondo, A. and Shimoda, Y. (2009). Effects of anthropogenic heat release upon the urban climate in a Japanese megacity. *Environmental Research*, 109(4): 421–431.

Ng, E. (2007). An investigation into parameters affecting an optimum ventilation design of high density cities. In: Santamouris, M. and Wouters, P. (eds.), *Proceedings of The 2nd PALENC Conference and the 28th AIVC Conference on Building Low Energy Cooling and Advanced Ventilation Technologies in the 21st Century*, Vol. 2. Crete Island, Greece, 27–29 September. Greece: Heliotopos Conference, 697–701.

Ng, E. (2008). An investigation into parameters affecting an optimum ventilation design of high density cities. *The International Journal of Ventilation*, 6(4): 349–357.

Ng, E. (2009). Policies and technical guidelines for urban planning of high-density cities – Air Ventilation Assessment (AVA) of Hong Kong. *Building and Environment*, 44(7): 1478–1488.

Ng, E., Chan, T. Y., Leung, R. and Pang, P. (2003). A daylight design and regulatory method for high density cities using computational lighting simulations. In: Chiu, M. L. *et al.* (eds.), *Digital Design: Research and Practice: Proceedings of the 10th International Conference on Computer Aided Architectural Design Futures*. Boston: Kluwer Academic Publishers.

Ng, E., Gadi, A., Wong, F., Mu, J. and Lee, M. (2007). Predicting daylight availability based on forecast of a weather observatory. *Lighting Research and Technology*, 39(1): 69–80.

Ng, E., Ren, C., Katzschner, L. and Yau, R. (2009). Urban climatic studies for hot and humid tropical coastal city of Hong Kong. In: *Proceedings of the 7th International Conference on Urban Climate (ICUC2009)*, Yokohama, Japan, 29 June–3 July. Available at: http://www.ide.titech.ac.jp/~icuc7/extended_abstracts/pdf/254693-2-090422170338-003.pdf (Accessed 10 February 2014).

Nichol, J. (2009). An emissivity modulation method for spatial enhancement of thermal satellite images in urban heat island analysis. *Photogrammetric Engineering & Remote Sensing*, 75(5): 547–556.

Oguro, M., Morikawa, Y., Murakami, S., Matsunawa, K., Mochida, A. and Hayashi, H. (2008). Development of a wind environment database in Tokyo for a comprehensive assessment system for heat island relaxation measures. *Journal of Wind Engineering and Industrial Aerodynamics*, 96(10–11): 1591–1602.

Oke, T. R. (1973). City size and the urban heat island. *Atmospheric Environment*, 7(8): 769–779.

Oke, T. R. (1984). Towards a prescription for the greater use of climatic principles in settlement planning. *Energy and Buildings*, 7(1): 1–10.

Oke, T. R. (1987). *Boundary Layer Climates*. 2nd edition. London: Methuen & Co.

Oke, T. R. (2006). Towards better scientific communication in urban climate. *Theoretical and Applied Climatology*, 84(1–3): 179–190.

Page, J. K. (1976). *Application of Building Climatology to the Problems of Housing and Building for Human Settlements*. Technical Note No. 150, WMO-No. 441. World Meteorological Organization.

Phoon, W. O. (1975). The medical aspect of high-rise and high-density living. *The Nursing Journal of Singapore*, 15(2): 69–75.

Poggio, L. and Vrščaj, B. (2009). A GIS-based human health risk assessment for urban green space planning - an example from Grugliasco (Italy). *Science of The Total Environment*, 407(23): 5961–5970.

Pressman, N. E. P. (1996). Sustainable winter cities: Future directions for planning, policy and design. *Atmospheric Environment*, 30(3): 521–529.

Ren, C. and Ng, E. (2007). An investigation of ventilation at ground level in high density cities – an Initial study in Hong Kong. In: Wittkopf, S. K. and Tan, B. K. (eds.), *Proceedings of the 24th International Conference on Passive and Low Energy Architecture (PLEA2007): Sun, Wind and Architecture*. National University of Singapore, Singapore, 22–24 November. Available at: http://www.plea-arch.org/ARCHIVE/2007/html/pdf/P0189.pdf (Accessed 10 February 2014)

Ren, C. and Ng, E. (2009). An initial investigation on microclimatic environment in high density city – spot field measurement study in Hong Kong. In: *Proceedings of the 7th International Conference on Urban Climate*

*(ICUC2009)*. Yokohama, Japan, 29 June–3 July. Available at: http://www.ide.titech.ac.jp/~icuc7/extended_abstracts/pdf/374213-2-081130213537-002.pdf (Accessed 10 February 2014).

Ritchey, T. (2007). *Wicked Problems: Structuring Social Messes with Morphological Analysis*. Swedish Morphological Society. Available at: http://www.swemorph.com/pdf/wp.pdf (Accessed 7 March 2010).

Rittel, H. and Webber, M. (1973). Dilemmas in a general theory of planning. *Policy Sciences*, 4(2): 155–169.

Roth, M. (2007). Review of urban climate research in (sub)tropical regions. *International Journal of Climatology*, 27(14): 1859–1873.

Scherer, D., Fehrenbach, U., Beha, H. D. and Parlow, E. (1999). Improved concepts and methods in analysis and evaluation of the urban climate for optimizing urban planning processes. *Atmospheric Environment*, 33(24–25): 4185–4193.

Schirmer, H. (1984). Climate and regional land-use planning. *Energy and Buildings*, 7(1): 35–53.

Schön, D. A. (1973). *Beyond the Stable State: Public and Private Learning in a Changing Society*. Harmondsworth: Penguin.

Schön, D. A. (1983). *The Reflective Practitioner: How Professionals Think in Action*. London: Temple Smith.

Schön, D. A. (1985). *The Design Studio: An Exploration of its Traditions and Potentials*. London: RIBA Publications for RIBA Building Industry Trust.

Seto, K. C. and Fragkias, M. (2005). Quantifying spatiotemporal patterns of urban land-use change in four cities of China with time series landscape metrics. *Landscape Ecology*, 20(7): 871–888.

Smith, P. F. (2005). *Architecture in a Climate of Change: A Guide to Sustainable Design*. Oxford: Architectural Press.

Smith, W. S. (1984). Mass transport for high-rise high-density living. *Journal of Transportation Engineering*, 110(6): 521–535.

Stone, B. and Rodgers, M. O. (2001). Urban form and thermal efficiency: How the design of cities influences the urban heat island effect. *Journal of American Planning Association*, 67(2): 186–198.

Stuttgart (2008). *Climate Booklet for Urban Development*. Available at: http://www.staedtebauliche-klimafibel.de/ (Accessed 8 October 2010).

Szokolay, S. V. (2004). *Introduction to Architectural Science: The Basis of Sustainable Design*. Oxford: Architectural Press.

Taha, H. (1997). Urban climates and heat islands: Albedo, evapotranspiration, and anthropogenic heat. *Energy and Buildings*, 25(2): 99–103.

Tiangco, M., Lagmay, A. M. F. and Argete, J. (2008). ASTER-based study of the night-time urban heat island effect in Metro Manila. *International Journal of Remote Sensing*, 29(10): 2799–2818.

Tominaga, Y., Mochida, A., Yoshie, R., Kataoka, H., Nozu, T., Yoshikawa, M. and Shirasawa, T. (2008). AIJ guidelines for practical applications of CFD to pedestrian wind environment around buildings. *Journal of Wind Engineering and Industrial Aerodynamics*, 96(10–11): 1749–1761.

Travers, L. H. (1977). Perception of high-density living in Hong Kong. In: *Proceedings of the Conference on Metropolitan Physical Environment*. USDA Forest Service general technical report NE 25. Syracuse, New York, 25–29 August, 1975. Upper Darby, PA: U.S. Department of Agriculture, Forest Service, Northeastern Forest Experiment Station: 408–414.

Tzoulas, K., Korpela, K., Venn, S., Yli-Pelkonen, V., Kazmierczak, A., Niemela, J. and James, P. (2007). Promoting ecosystem and human health in urban areas using Green Infrastructure: A literature review. *Landscape and Urban Planning*, 81(3): 167–178.

UNFPA (2009). *The State of World Population*. U.S.: United Nations Population Fund (UNFPA).

VDI (1997). *VDI-Standard: VDI 3787 Part 1 Environmental Meteorology – Climate and Air Pollution Maps for Cities and Regions*. Berlin: Beuth Verlag.

Walker, B. (2003). *Making Density Desirable*. Available at: http://www.forumforthefuture.org/greenfutures/articles/601476 (Accessed 8 October 2010).

Wang, U. and Ng, E. (2010). Parametric study on microclimate effects of different greening strategies in high density city. In: *Proceedings of The joint 3rd PALENC, 5th EPIC and 1st Cool Roofs Conference*. Rhodes Island, Greece, 29 September–1 October. Greece: Heliotopos Conference.

Weinreis, C., Letzel, M. O., Ng, E. and Katzschner, L. (2008). *LES studies on pedestrian level ventilation in Hong Kong*. In Special Reports of the Meteorological Institute, Albert-Ludwigs-University of Freiburg, 5th Japanese-German Meeting on Urban Climatology.

WMO (1999). *Towards a New Planning Process – A Guide to Reorienting Urban Planning towards Local Agenda 21*. World Meteorological Organization: European Sustainable Development and Health Series 3, WHO EUR/ICP/POLC 06 03 05 (C).

WMO (2003). *Manual on the Global Observing System. Vol. 1: Global Aspects*. Geneva: World Meteorological Organization.

Wong, K. S. (2009). *A Final Report on Building Design that Supports Sustainable Urban Living Space in HK*. Consultancy Agreement No. BA/01/2006, Jan 2009, Buildings Department HKSAR.

Wong, N. H., Lam, K. P. and Feriadi, H. (2000). The use of performance-based simulation tools for building design and evaluation – a Singapore perspective. *Building and Environment*, 35(8): 709–736.

Wong, N. H., Kardinal Jusuf, S., Aung La Win, A., Kyaw Thu, H., Syatia Negara, T. and Xuchao, W. (2007). Environmental study of the impact of greenery in an institutional campus in the tropics. *Building and Environment*, 42(8): 2949–2970.

Wood, R. (2007). *Dongtan Eco-city, Shanghai*. Available at: http://www.arup.com/_assets/_download/8CF-DEE1A-CC3E-EA1A-25FD80B2315B50FD.pdf (Accessed: 8 October 2010).

Yamashita, S., Sekine, K., Shoda, M., Yamashita, K. and Hara, Y. (1986). On relationships between heat island and sky view factor in the cities of Tama River basin, Japan. *Atmospheric Environment (1967)*, 20(4): 681–686.

Yan, Y. Y. (1997). An analysis of thermal stress of climate in Hong Kong. *Singapore Journal of Tropical Geography*, 18(2): 210–217.

Yan, Y. Y. (2000). The influence of weather on human mortality in Hong Kong. *Social Science & Medicine*, 50(3): 419–427.

Yip, K. M., Leung, Y. K. and Chang, W. L. (2006). Long term trend analyses of weather stress indices for human. *Hong Kong Observatory Reprint No. 627*. Available at: http://www.weather.gov.hk/publica/reprint/r627.pdf (Accessed 10 February 2014). (In Chinese).

Yip, K. M., Leung, Y. K. and Chang, W. L. (2007). Long-term trend in thermal index and its impact on mortality in Hong Kong. *Hong Kong Observatory Reprint No. 710*. Available at: http://www.hko.gov.hk/publica/reprint/r710.pdf (Accessed 10 February 2014).

Yoshie, R., Tanaka, H., Shirasawa, T. and Kobayashi, T. (2008). Experimental study on air ventilation in a built-up area with closely-packed high-rise buildings. *Journal of Environmental Engineering (Transaction of AIJ)*, 73(627): 661–667.

# Postscript

A postscript was not originally planned. However, after I read all the papers and edited this book, I believe there is a need to review the scene. In the preface I considered the IPCC AR5 Report and shared my view that the urban climate must now be firmly rooted in everything they are going to do in designing, planning, and making our cities. In particular, when we slowly, or, as in some parts of the world, rapidly, develop small towns into cities, we must not continue to make the same kind of urban climatic mistakes that we have been making. I concluded by calling on the need to bear in mind that there is an urban climatic threshold as to how far we can push and further develop our cities. At that point I left the future pretty well untouched.

However, now I believe it is time to talk about the future. We have talked about mitigation. We have talked about adaptation. These were pessimistic views. Let us now look at how we might chart a brighter future. The arrival of the internet and the e-ways of living in the city provide us with an opportunity to reflect. William Mitchell has speculated on the future of city living in his books, *City of Bits* (1996) and *E-topia* (1999). He prophesied a way to continue engaging in urban life without the need to be physically involved. Cities, unlike the 'good old days', are less important for providing spaces for things to be done, but more important as spaces to support things to be enjoyed. This introduces the need to further improve the environment of our cities – to enjoy rather than to tolerate.

For this to happen, the city must cater to its inhabitants' lifestyles. Jane Jacobs (1985) has discussed the need for economic and social diversity. Steane and Steemers (2004) and Kihato and Massoumi (2010) respectively have touched on environmental diversity. City inhabitants must be given the freedom to choose what to do and where to go. The high probability of city dwellers identifying, reaching, and thus enjoying the environment that they desire must therefore be the ethos of city planners.

As such, it is not only the physical environment, in terms of temperature, radiation, and so on, that we need to get right when drafting UCMaps. More importantly, it is the socio-physical urban environment, the probability of finding one's comfort, which may be more important. Future generations of UCMap may need to take this notion of the human dimension into account. Human bodies are not heat exchangers but perceptual thermal sensors. The thermal delight of our built environment is therefore something that may need to be researched further.

Imagine, one day your smartphone will be able to tell you how the urban environment around you feels. It can also tell you as a person, how to travel through or engage with the city in ways that you as a person would find a comfort and a delight. Imagine UCMaps as being there not only for planners and policymakers, but also for the community and for each one of us as individuals. Imagine UCMaps not so much as maps but more as poems and works of art.

I believe that future generations deserve something better than to spend their lives correcting the mistakes that we have made for them in the past. I believe they will have a better future as dignified individuals.

*Edward Ng, March 2014*

## References

Jacobs, J. (1985). *Cities and the Wealth of Nations*. New York: Vintage.

Kihato, C. W. and Massoumi, M. (eds.) (2010). *Urban Diversity: Space, Culture, and Inclusive Pluralism in Cities Worldwide*. Baltimore: Johns Hopkins University Press.

Mitchell, W. (1996). *City of Bits*. Boston: MIT Press.

Mitchell, W. (1999). *E-topia*. Boston: MIT Press.

Steane, M. A. and Steemers, K. (eds.) (2004). *Environmental Diversity in Architecture*. London: Routledge.

# Appendix 1: Chronology of world urban climatic map studies

| *Year* | | *Name* | *Country* |
|---|---|---|---|
| 1960s | (1963) | Knoch, K. (1963). *Die Landesklima-aufanhme.* | Germany |
| 1970s | (1978) | Hoffman, U. (1978). City climate of Stuttgart. In: Franke, E. (ed.), *City Climate: Data and Aspects for City Planning*. Trans. by Literature Research Company. FBW – A publication of Research, Building and Living, No. 18. | Germany |
| | (1978b) | Lüttig, G. W. (1978). Geoscientific maps of the environment as an essential tool in planning. *Geologie. en Mijnbouw*, 57(4): 527–532. | Germany |
| 1980s | (1982) | Sterten, A. K. (1982). A thematic mapping system and a description of local climatic conditions developed for urban planning purposes. *Energy and Buildings*, 4(2): 121–124. | Norway |
| | (1983) | Lindqvist, S., *et al.* (1983). Lokalklimatiska kartor for anvandning i kommunal oversiktlig planering. *Byggforskiningsradet*, 38. | Sweden |
| | (1984) | Schirmer, H. (1984). Climate and regional land-use planning. *Energy and Buildings*, 7(1): 35–53. | Germany |
| | (1985) | Stock, P. and Beckröge, W. (1985). *Klimaanalyse Stadt Essen*. Essen: Kommunalverband Ruhrgebiet. | Germany |
| | (1986) | Stock, P. *et al.* (1986). *Klimaanalyse Stadt Dortmund.* Planungshefte Ruhrgebiet, PO 18. Essen: Kommunalverband Ruhrgebiet. | Germany |
| | (1988) | Bründl, W. (1988). Climate function maps and urban planning. *Energy and Buildings*, 11(1–3): 123–127. | Germany |
| | (1988) | Beckröge, W. (1988). Climate as a factor of a planning project – demonstrated by the example of Dortmund Bornstrasse. *Energy and Buildings*, 11(1–3): 129–135. | Germany |
| | (1988) | Beckröge, W. *et al.* (1988). *Klimaanalyse Stadt Recklinghausen*. Essen: Kommunalverband Ruhrgebiet. | Germany |

| | | | |
|---|---|---|---|
| | (1988) | Katzschner, L. (1988). The Urban climate as a parameter for urban development. *Energy and Buildings*, 11(1): 137–147. | Germany |
| | (1988) | Mayer, H. (1988). Results from the research program 'Stadtklima Bayern' for urban planning. *Energy and Buildings*, 11(1–3): 115–121. | Germany |
| | (1989) | Lindqvist, S., and Mattsson, J. (1989). Topoclimatic maps for different planning levels – some Swedish examples. *Building Research and Practice*, 17(5): 299–304. | Sweden |
| 1990s | (1991) | Akasaka, H. (1991). A study on drawing climatic maps related to human thermal sensation. *Energy and Buildings*, 16(3–4): 1011–1023. | Japan |
| | (1991) | Paszynski, J. (1991). Mapping urban topoclimates. *Energy and Buildings*, 16(3–4): 1059–1062. | Poland |
| | (1991) | Lindqvist, S. (1991). *Local climatological maps for planning*. Gothenburg: Department of Physical Geography, University of Gothenburg. | Sweden |
| | (1992) | Nachbarschaftsverband Stuttgart (1992): Klimaatlas. Nachbarschaftsverband Stuttgart. | Germany |
| | (1992) | Baumüller, J. *et al.* (1992). *Climate Booklet for Urban Development*. Stuttgart: Ministry of Economy Baden-Württemberg (Wirtschaftsministerium), Environmental Protection Department (Amt für Umweltschutz). | Germany |
| | (1992) | Kiese, O. *et al.* (1992). Stadtklima Münster. Werkstattberichte zum Umweltschutz. *Umweltamt der Stadt Münster 1/1992*, 247 pages. | Germany |
| | (1992) | Matzarakis, A., and Mayer, H. (1992). Mapping of urban air paths for planning in Munich. Planning applications of urban and building climatology. *Wiss. Ber. Inst. Meteor. Klimaforsch. Univ. Karlsruhe*, 16: 13–22. | Germany |
| | (1992) | Mattig, U. (1992). Geoscientific maps for land-use planning: A review. *Lecture Notes in Earth Sciences*, 42: 49-81. | Germany |
| | (1992) | Swaid, H. (1992). Intelligent Urban Forms (IUF): A new climate-concerned, urban planning strategy. *Theoretical and Applied Climatology*, 46(2–3): 179–191. | Israel |
| | (1993) | Katzschner, L. (1993). *Urban Climatic Analysis Map for Kassel City*. | Germany |
| | (1994) | Lazar, R. *et al.* (1994). *Stadtklimaanalyse Graz*. Graz: Magistrat Graz, Stadtplanungsamt. | Austria |
| | (1995) | Parlow, E. *et al.* (1995). *Analysis of the Regional Climate of Basel/Switzerland*. | Switzerland |

| | | |
|---|---|---|
| (1996) | Matzarakis, A. and Mayer, H. (1996). Bioclimate maps of Greece for touristic aspects. Paper presented at the 14th International Congress of Biometeorology. | Germany |
| (1997) | VDI (1997). *VDI – Standard 3787, Part 1, Environmental Meteorology – Climate and Air Pollution Maps for Cities and Regions*. Berlin: Beuth Verlag. | Germany |
| (1997) | VDI (1997). *VDI – Standard 3787, Part 2, Environmental meteorology methods for the human biometeorological evaluation of climate and air quality for urban and regional planning at regional level, Part I: Climate*. Berlin: Beuth Verlag. | Germany |
| (1997) | Kuttler, W. (1997). Climate and air hygiene investigations for urban planning. *Acta Climatologica et Chorologica*, 31(A): 3–6. | Germany |
| (1998) | Synthetische klimaunktionskarte. (1998). *Klimaanalyse Stadt Schwelm*. Essen: Kommunalverband Ruhrgebiet. | Germany |
| (1998) | Baumüller, J. *et al.* (1998). 'Urban climate 21' – Climatological basics and design features for 'Stuttgart 21' on CD-ROM. *Report of Research Center for Urban Safety and Security, Kobe University*, Special Report Vol. 1: 42–52. | Germany |
| (1998) | Shimoda, Y. and Narumi, D. (1998). Climate analysis for urban planning in Osaka. *Report of Research Center for Urban Safety and Security, Kobe University*, Special Report Vol. 1: 95–99. | Japan |
| (1998) | Yoda, H. and Katayama, T. (1998). Climate analysis for urban planning in Fukuoka. *Report of Research Center for Urban Safety and Security, Kobe University*, Special Report Vol. 1: 63–78. | Japan |
| (1998) | Moriyama, M. and Takebayashi, H. (1998). Climate analysis for urban planning in Kobe. *Report of Research Center for Urban Safety and Security, Kobe University*, Special Report Vol. 1: 53–62. | Japan |
| (1998) | Yoshida, A. (1998). Climate analysis for urban planning in Okayama – Field investigation on thermal environments in Okayama. *Report of Research Center for Urban Safety and Security, Kobe University*, Special Report Vol. 1: 100–104. | Japan |
| (1999) | Klima- und immissionsokologische Funktionen Stadt Detamold, 1999. In Klimaanalyse 1999. Detamold, Germany: Stadt Detamold. | Germany |
| (1999) | Baumüller, J. and Reuter, U. (1999). *Demands and Requirements on a Climate Atlas for Urban Planning and Design*. Stuttgart: Office of Environmental Protection. | Germany |

| | | | |
|---|---|---|---|
| | (1999) | Helbig, A. *et al.* (1999). *Stadtklima und Luftreinhaltung*. 2nd edition. Berlin: Springer. | Germany |
| | (1999) | Lazar, R. and Podesser, A. (1999). An urban climate analysis of Graz and its significance for urban planning in the tributary valleys east of Graz (Austria). *Atmospheric Environment*, 33(24): 4195–4209. | Austria |
| | (1999) | Moriyama, M. and Takebayashi, H. (1999). Making method of 'Klimatope' map based on normalized vegetation index and one-dimensional heat budget model. *Journal of Wind Engineering and Industrial Aerodynamics*, 81(1–3): 211–220. | Japan |
| | (1999) | Scherer, D. *et al.* (1999). Improved concepts and methods in analysis and evaluation of the urban climate for optimizing urban planning process. *Atmospheric Environment*, 33(24–25): 4185–4193. | Switzerland |
| | (1999) | Taraxacum, E. V. (1999). *Klimabewertungskarte Kassel*. Kaofungen. | Germany |
| 2000s | (2000) | Architectural Institute of Japan (ed.) (2000). *Urban Environmental Climatic Atlas: Urban Development Utilizing Climate Information*. Tokyo: Architectural Institute of Japan. (In Japanese). | Japan |
| | (2000) | Ichinose, T. (2000). Climatic analysis for urban planning. Centre for Global Environmental Research. *NIES News*, 8–9. (In Japanese). | Japan |
| | (2001) | Fehrenbach, U. *et al.* (2001). Automated classification of planning objectives for the consideration of climate and air quality in urban and regional planning for the example of the region of Basel / Switzerland. *Atmospheric Environment*, 35(32): 5605–5615. | Switzerland |
| | (2001) | Nielinger, J. and Kost, W. J. (2001). *Klimaanalyse der Stadt Sindelfingen*. Stuttgart, IMA-Immisionen-Meteorologie-Akustik. | Germany |
| | (2001a) | Parlow, E. *et al.* (2001). Climatic analysis map for Grenchen and Umgebung, *CAMPAS, Klimaanalyse- und Planungshinweiskarten für den Kanton Solothurn*. Basel, Switzerland. | Switzerland |
| | (2001b) | Parlow, E. *et al.* (2001). Climatic analysis map for Olten and Umgebung, *CAMPAS, Klimaanalyse-und Planungshinweiskarten für den Kanton Solothurn*. Basel, Switzerland. | Switzerland |
| | (2002) | Steinicke, W. and Streifeneder, M. (2002). *Klimafunktionskarte für das Verbandsgebiet des Nachbarschaftsverbandes Heidelberg-Mannheim*. Mannheim: Nachbarschaftsverband Heidelberg-Mannheim. | Germany |

| | | |
|---|---|---|
| (2002) | Richards, K. (2002). Topoclimates and topoclimate mapping: What do the scientific abstracts tell us about research perspectives? Paper presented at the 14th Annual Colloquium of the Spatial Information Research Centre. | New Zealand |
| (2003) | SDUDB (2003). *Berlin Digital Environmental Atlas.* Berlin, Senate Department for Urban Development (SDUDB). | Germany |
| (2003) | Klimafunktionskarte und Planungshinweiskarte für Essen (2003). Essen: University of Essen. | Germany |
| (2003) | Erell, E. *et al.* (2003). Mapping the potential for climate-conscious design of buildings. *Building and Environment*, 38(2): 271–281. | Israel |
| (2003) | Katzschner, L. *et al.* (2003). A methodology for bioclimatic microscale mapping of open spaces. Paper presented at the Fifth International Conference on Urban Climate. | Germany |
| (2003) | Radosz, J. and Kaminski, A. (2003). Topoclimatic mapping on 1:50 000 scale. The map sheet of Bytom. Paper presented at the Fifth International Conference on Urban Climate. | Germany |
| (2003) | Röckle, R. *et al.* (2003). *Klimaanalyse Stadt Freiburg.* Freiburg: Stadtplanungsamt. | Germany |
| (2003) | Svensson, M. K. *et al.* (2003). A geographical information system model for creating bioclimatic maps – examples from a high, mid-latitude city. *International Journal of Biometeorology*, 47(2): 102–112. | Sweden |
| (2003) | Ward, I. C. (2003). The usefulness of climatic maps of built-up areas in determining drivers for the energy and environmental efficiency of buildings and external areas. *International Journal of Ventilation*, 2(3): 277–286. | UK |
| (2004) | Jittawikul, A. *et al.* (2004). Climatic maps for passive cooling methods utilization in Thailand. *Journal of Asian Architecture and Building Engineering*, 3(1): 109–114. | Japan |
| (2004) | Tanaka, T. and Morlyama, M. (2004). Application of GIS to make 'Urban Environmental Climate Map' for urban planning. Paper presented at the Fifth Conference on Urban Environment. | Japan |
| (2004) | Tanaka, T. *et al.* (2004). Urban environment climate map for community planning. Paper presented at the 4th Japanese–German Meeting on Urban Climatology. | Japan |
| (2004) | Wang, G. T. (2004). *Urban Climate, Environment and Urban Planning*. Beijing: Beijing Press. (In Chinese). | China |

| | | |
|---|---|---|
| (2004) | Moriyama, M. (2004). *Mitigation and Technique on Urban Heat Island*. Japan: Gakugei Syuppann Sya. (In Japaense) | Japan |
| (2005) | Charalampopoulos, I. and Chronopoulou-Sereli, A. (2005). Mapping the urban green area influence on local climate under windless light wind conditions: The case of western part of Athens, Greece. *Acta Climatologica et Chorologica*, 38–39, 25–31. | Greece |
| (2005a) | Moriyama, M. *et al.* (2005). Climate analysis for the mitigation of urban heat island in Kyoto city: No. 3 urban environmental climate map for the mitigation of urban heat island. Paper presented at the International Symposium on Sustainable Development of Asian City Environment. | Japan |
| (2005b) | Moriyama, M. *et al.* (2005). Urban environmental climate map for neighborhood planning. Paper presented at The 4th Japanese–German Meeting on Urban Climatology. | Japan |
| (2005) | Ustrnul, Z. and Czekierda, D. (2005). Application of GIS for the development of climatological air temperature maps: an example from Poland. *Meteorological Applications*, 12(1): 43–50. | Poland |
| (2005) | Matzarakis, A. et al. (2005). Urban climate analysis of Freiburg – An integral assessment approach. Paper presented at the 4th Japanese–German Meeting on Urban Climatology. | Germany |
| (2005) | Parlow, E. et al. (2005). Klima analysekarte, *Regionale Klliimaanalyse Südlliicher Oberrheiin (REKLIISO)*. Baden-Württemberg, Germany. | Switzerland |
| (2006) | Alcoforado, M. J. (2006). Planning procedures towards high climatic quality cities: Example referring to Lisbon. *Finisterra*, 41(82): 49–64. | Portugal |
| (2006a) | Alcoforado, M. J. *et al.* (2006). *Orientações climáticas para o ordenamento em Lisboa*. Lisbon: Centro de Estudos Geográficos da Universidade de Lisboa. | Portugal |
| (2006b) | Alcoforado, M. J. *et al.* (2006). *Report: Climatic Evaluation for Urban Planning in Lisbon*. Lisbon Universidade de Lisboa. | Portugal |
| (2006) | Baumüller, J. (2006). Implementation of climatic aspects in urban development: The example Stuttgart. Paper presented at the PGBC Symposium: Urban Climate + Urban Greenery. | Germany |
| (2006) | Katzschner, L. (2006). Urban climatology and urban planning. Paper presented at An Expert Forum on UCMap & CFD for Urban Wind Studies in Cities. | Germany |

| | | |
|---|---|---|
| (2006) | Ichinose, T. *et al.* (2006). Counteractions for urban heat island in regional autonomies: Activities in Councils of MOE, Japan. Paper presented at the 5th International Conference on Urban Climate. | Japan |
| (2006) | Narita, K.-I. (2006). Ventilation path and urban climate. *Wind Engineers, JAWE*, 31(2): 109–114. | Japan |
| (2006) | Sera, T. (2006). Japan's policy instruments on urban heat island measures by MLIT. Paper presented at the International Workshop on Countermeasures to Urban Heat Islands. | Japan |
| (2006) | Yamamoto, Y. (2006). Measures to mitigate urban heat islands. *Science & Technology Trends Quarterly Review*, 18(1): 65–83. | Japan |
| (2006) | Nery, J. *et al.* (2006). Thermal comfort studies in humid tropical city. Paper presented at the Sixth International Conference of Urban Climate. | Brazil |
| (2007) | Hsie, T. S. (2007). A combined computational method for determining natural ventilation potentials in the planning process. Paper presented at the PLEA conference 2007. | UK |
| (2007) | Ren, C., Ng, E. and Katzschner, L. (2007). An Investigation into Developing an Urban Climatic Map for High Density Living – Initial Study in Hong Kong. Paper presented at *The 2nd PALENC.* | Hong Kong |
| (2007) | Yamamoto, Y. (2007). Measures to mitigate urban heat islands. *Global Change and Sustainable Development*, 1(2): 18–46. | Japan |
| (2008) | Akashi, T. (2008). Creating 'wind paths' in the city to mitigate urban heat island effects – A case study in the central district of Tokyo. Paper presented at the CIB-W101 (Spatial Planning and Infrastructure Development) Annual Meeting 2008. | Japan |
| (2008) | Matzarakis, A. *et al.* (2008). Planungsrelevante Bewertung des Stadtklimas Urban Climate Map and Planning. *Umweltmeteorologie.* | Germany |
| (2008) | Moriyama, M. and Tanaka, T. (2008). Example of Osaka region: Urban environmental climate maps and plans for the future. Paper presented at the Workshop on Urban Planning and Climate Change. | Japan |
| (2008) | Reuter, U. (2008). Urban climate and planning in Stuttgart. Paper presented at the workshop on the application of UCMaps in urban planning. | Germany |
| (2008) | Röckle, R. (2008). Urban climate maps and planning. Paper presented at the conference on Thermal Comfort in Urban Planning and Architecture under Consideration of Global Climate Change. | Germany |

| | | |
|---|---|---|
| (2008) | Tanaka, T. *et al.* (2008). Urban environmental climate map for supporting urban planning related work in local government: Case study in city of Sakai. Paper presented at the 5th Japanese–German Meeting on Urban Climatology. | Japan |
| (2008) | Katzschner, L. and Mulder, J. (2008). Regional climatic mapping as a tool for sustainable development. *Journal of Environmental Management*, 87(2): 262–267. | Germany |
| (2009) | Smith, C. *et al.* (2009). A GIS-based decision support tool for urban climate risk analysis and exploration of adaptation options with respect to urban thermal environments. Paper presented at the 7th International Conference on Urban Climate. | UK |
| (2009) | Desplat, J. *et al.* (2009). EPICEA Project (2008–2010), multidisciplinary study of the impacts of climate change on the scale of Paris. Paper presented at the 7th International Conference on Urban Climate. | France |
| (2009) | ERDF (2009). *Urban Climatic Map for Arnhem, The Netherlands. Future Cities – Urban Networks to Face Climate Change*. Arnhem: The Municipality of Arnhem, The Netherlands, The European Regional Development Fund (ERDF). | Holland |
| 2009 | Tanaka, T. *et al.* (2009). Urban Environmental Climate Maps for supporting urban-planning related work of local governments in Japan: Case studies of Yokohama and Sakai. Paper presented at the Seventh International Conference on Urban Climate. | Japan |
| (2009) | Alcoforado, M. J. *et al.* (2009). Application of climatic guidelines to urban planning: The example of Lisbon (Portugal). *Landscape and Urban Planning*, 90(1–2): 56–65. | Portugal |
| (2009) | Tablada, A. *et al.* (2009). On natural ventilation and thermal comfort in compact urban environments – the old Havana case. *Building and Environment*, 44(9): 1943–1958. | Germany |
| (2009a) | Baumüller, J. *et al.* (2009). Climate atlas of a metropolitan region in Germany based on GIS. Paper presented at the Seventh International Conference on Urban Climate. | Germany |
| (2009b) | Baumüller, J. *et al.* (2009). Urban framework plan hillsides of Stuttgart. Paper presented at the Seventh International Conference on Urban Climate. | Germany |

| | | | |
|---|---|---|---|
| | (2009) | Katzschner, L. (2009). Manuel, nicht Kassandra: Frankfurt im Klimawandel. *THEMA DES TAGS*, D2. | Germany |
| | (2009) | Ng, E., Ren, C., Katzschner, L., *et al.* (2009). Urban climatic studies for the hot and humid tropical coastal city of Hong Kong. Paper presented at the Seventh International Conference on Urban Climate. | Hong Kong |
| | (2009) | Yoda, H. (2009). Climate Atlas in Fukuoka City. Paper presented at the Seventh International Conference on Urban Climate. | Japan |
| | (2009) | *Environmental aspects in spatial planning in Stuttgart 2009*. Stuttgart: The Office for Environmental Protection. | Germany |
| 2010s | (2011) | Houet, T. and Pigeon, G. (2011). Mapping urban climate zones and quantifying climate behaviors – An application on Toulouse urban area (France). *Environmental Pollution*, 159(8–9), 2180–2192. | France |
| | (2012) | Ng, E. (2012). Towards planning and practical understanding of the need for meteorological and climatic information in the design of high-density cities: A case-based study of Hong Kong. *International Journal of Climatology*, 32(4): 582–598. doi: 10.1002/joc.2292. | Hong Kong |
| | (2012) | Ren, C., Spit, T., Lenzholzer, S., Yim, H. L. S., Chen, L., Kupski, S. and Katzschner, L. (2012). Urban climate map system for Dutch spatial planning. *International Journal of Applied Earth Observation and Geoinformation*, 18: 207–221. doi: 10.1016/j.jag. 2012.01.026. | Netherlands |
| | (2013) | Ren, C., Lau, K.-l., Yiu, K.-P. and Ng, E. (2013). Application of urban climatic mapping in the urban planning of high-density cities: The case of Kaohsiung, Taiwan. *Cities*, 31: 1–16. doi: 10.1016/j. cities. 2012.12.005. | Taiwan |
| | (2013) | Acero, J. A., Arrizabalaga, J., Kupski, S. and Katzschner, L. (2013). Deriving an urban climate map in coastal areas with complex terrain in the Basque Country (Spain). *Urban Climate*, 4: 35–60. | Spain |

## Note

The second column of the table points to references in Chapter 2.

# Index

Note: page numbers in *italic* type refer to Figures; those in **bold** refer to Tables.